LANGUAGE INSTRUCTION

FOR STUDENTS WITH DISABILITIES
Fourth Edition

Edward A. Polloway
Lynchburg College

Lynda Miller
Independent Scholar

Tom E. C. Smith
University of Arkansas

LOVE PUBLISHING COMPANY®
Denver • London • Singapore

Published by Love Publishing Company
P.O. Box 22353
Denver, Colorado 80222
www.lovepublishing.com

Library of Congress Catalog Card Number 2010929834

Copyright © 2012 by Love Publishing Company
Printed in the United States of America
ISBN 978-0-89108-351-1

Contents

▌Part Two
Language Assessment and Intervention

6 **Language Assessment and Instruction for Adolescents   193**

7 **Reading Concepts and Assessment   249**

▊Part Three
Language Arts Instruction

8 **Reading Instruction   285**

9 **Handwriting Assessment and Instruction   335**

▌Tables

▌Figures

Preface

Language development and language competence are critical to the education of all children, particularly those with disabilities. The diverse fields within the language domain, including the areas of oral language, reading, and written language, remain the focus of ongoing innovations in research and programming. This fourth edition builds on the foundations of the earlier editions and has been revised to reflect current research across the specific domains covered within the language area. The book is intended to be used as a text for coursework in teacher education training programs, with particular emphasis on classes related to language acquisition, language arts instruction, curriculum and methods, and evidence-based practices.

The purpose of this book is to examine language and its components and to suggest instructional strategies for responding to language-related difficulties. Our primary target population comprises children and adolescents who have been identified in school settings as students with disabilities who have experienced problems within language domains.

This textbook is organized into three major parts, which present key concepts within the complex subject of language development and instruction for learners with special needs, with a strong focus on communication and language development across developmental levels. The first two chapters explore in depth language, speech, and communication and then analyze key developmental milestones related to communication, speech, and language development. In addition, extensive attention is given to considerations related to cultural and linguistic diversity. The second section of the book provides an extensive discussion of oral language assessment and intervention. These areas are often underplayed or not addressed at all in textbooks focused on special education. In this domain, extensive attention is given to language considerations for preschool, school-age, and adolescent students, with particular emphasis on the social–pragmatic aspects of language that underlie many of the problems experienced by students with disabilities. The third section of the book covers the areas that are traditionally referred to as language arts instruction. Two chapters address reading, three chapters address writing, and a final chapter provides special attention to language arts instruction for adolescent students with special needs. A note on pronoun use: for the purposes of clarity, each chapter alternates male and female pronouns for children and adults respectively.

▮Acknowledgments

We wish to thank those persons in our private and professional lives who have encouraged and supported our efforts in writing this book. While trying to be good teachers, we have found a need to be good learners as well. Therefore, we would like to acknowledge the students and colleagues whose knowledge, projects, and ideas contributed to our work on this book in one way or another. We particularly thank Allison Meade for her significant assistance with the preparation of this edition. The book has been enhanced tremendously by the contribution of Chapter 10 by Mary Beirne-Smith of the University of Alabama. We also acknowledge the special assistance of Amy Smith-Thomas in researching and updating portions of Chapter 8.

Finally, we remember the contributions of James E. Smith, Jr. Smitty was co-author of the first edition of the book and a close friend. His death left a significant personal void that has yet to be filled. In memory of his talents, knowledge, good will, humor, and commitment to friends and colleagues and especially to individuals with disabilities, we dedicate this book to Smitty.

EAP
LM
TECS

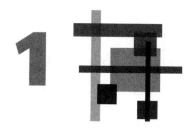

Introduction to Language, Speech, and Communication

A s global population increases and communicative interactions become faster, more frequent, and often briefer in duration, knowing the intricacies of how communication, language, and speech are intertwined becomes increasingly important. Because societies in developed and developing societies are rapidly evolving from manufacturing and delivering goods into a culture in which workers interact with each other—and with information—life and career successes depend more heavily on the ability to communicate effectively. The most often cited employability skills that employers expect of job-seekers are communication skills, including listening, speaking, and writing (Hansen & Hansen, 2009).

The National Communication Association (NCA; 2009a) takes the position that the skills needed to succeed in the work world can be cultivated in education during the elementary school years. The NCA's focus is on teaching students the communication skills they need to deal with problems such as bullying (including cyberbullying), negative peer pressure, and teasing, and to provide resources to teachers in topics such as leadership, media literacy, listening, conflict resolution, and public speaking (NCA, 2009b).

But what exactly *is* communication? How do humans communicate? What tools do they use to communicate? Answering these questions leads to an understanding of how children learn to speak, read, and write. This understanding serves as the foundation for designing and implementing intervention plans for students who need additional support and instruction.

▌Language, Speech, and Communication

Communication is typically viewed as the interchange of ideas, feelings, thoughts, experiences, and information. Humans communicate to share their understandings of the truth and to show how "thoughts are anchored to things and situations in the world" (Pinker, 2007, p. 3). Through linking words to emotions, scenarios, experiences, events, and processes, we communicate with our fellow humans how we feel, what we have seen and witnessed, and how we think things work.

We use a wide range of methods to communicate. For instance, we can communicate with each other through speech, Morse code, sign language, Braille, printed words, emails, text messages, tweets, flags, gestures, facial expressions, the pictures and videos we post on the internet, even the clothing we wear or how we style our hair. We sometimes communicate by not saying or signaling anything; we can convey messages through silence.

One of the most frequent ways we communicate is through language. **Language** can best be described as an arbitrary set of abstract symbols—and the rules that govern them—that we use to communicate. Language is a code, a set of conventions for representing our experiences, ideas, feelings, thoughts, and so on. Generally, the term *language* refers to the oral, printed, or electronic form (which is really a special type of printed form). An exception is sign language, which is conveyed through a conventionalized code based on hand, facial, and body gestures, movements, and spatial and temporal relationships.

You might have noticed that our definition of language includes the stipulation that the set of abstract symbols out of which language is constructed is **arbitrary**. This means that nothing about the inherent nature of an object, thought, process, event, or experience dictates how that object or thought is referred to in language. Arbitrariness means that nothing in the nature of an ocean indicates how we refer to it. It is called an ocean because someone, somewhere distant in time, called it an ocean perhaps for no good reason. This arbitrariness can puzzle young children and those whose language development is delayed or disordered.

The arbitrariness of language carries both great power and special challenges. On the one hand, because language is not tied in any inherent way to our world, we can use it to describe virtually anything. On the other hand, because it has no inherent ties to our world, some parts of it are not always easy to learn—which will become clearer in subsequent discussions of children's acquisition of the forms of language.

Another aspect of language that can present complications for children is that language operates on both literal and figurative levels. Words, phrases, and sentences can all carry both literal and figurative meanings, as in "pear, pare, pair," "blue in the face," or "visiting relatives can be a nuisance."

When we refer to **speech**, we refer to the oral sounds of the language code—the conventionally established combining of speech sounds into meaningful units of language. Thus, while speech is only one means of expression using language, most people understand *speech* to mean the same thing as *oral language*.

Our emphasis in this book will be on language—its various rules, processes, forms, usages, and contexts. Nevertheless, we will return often to the importance of communication and make the point several times that one of our primary objectives in designing language instruction is to assist students in being able to communicate effectively in situations that are important and relevant to their lives.

▌Literacy

It is hard to imagine anyone concerned with education today who has not encountered the term *literacy*. Writers and commentators in the popular media use the term almost with abandon, assuming that everyone knows what they mean. Literacy as a concept, however, has acquired multiple connotations, often stemming from the political intent of each writer or commentator.

The National Institute for Literacy, created in 1991, defines literacy as "an individual's ability to read, write, and speak … and compute and solve problems at levels of proficiency necessary to function on the job and in society (2009). This definition includes not only the abilities that children need to be proficient with language but also a variety of other competencies necessary for success in the world, including, among others:

- media literacy,
- information literacy, and
- computer literacy.

For our purposes in this text, we use the term **literacy** to refer to the set of competencies children develop with both oral and printed language (including electronic forms): listening, speaking, reading, and writing, regardless of the medium. Our definition includes the set of linguistic competencies that children must acquire to succeed in school, as well as in their lives outside school. Later, we will discuss the specific oral, print, and electronic language abilities comprising literacy, as well as the relationships among the oral, print, and electronic forms of language.

▌Models of Language

Humans have been interested in language for centuries. Over time, philosophers, mathematicians, and psychologists have weighed in with various theories about where language comes from and how it is learned. One scholar, Julian Jaynes (1976), suggested that, until almost 3000 years ago, although humans used language, they were unable to reflect on it and believed that it came from the gods. As yet unable to reflect on their own thinking and learning, ancient peoples were unable to "think" as we do today; instead, they experienced auditory hallucinations—voices from the gods, as heard in the *Old Testament* or in *The Iliad*—telling them what to do when they encountered novel or stressful circumstances (Jaynes, 1976).

Once humans developed retrospection, they became able to think about language and to formulate theories about how language is learned. Historically, the two most prevalent philosophical stances regarding language acquisition have been **rationalism** and **empiricism**.

Rationalism

In the rational view, the mind directs sensory experience through separating and organizing the information that reaches us through our sensory apparatus. The rationalist approach to language acquisition is that the child's mind is ready to learn language given the opportunity to do so. The child is seen as an active constructor of her reality, including language. One of the foremost modern-day rationalists, Noam Chomsky (1971), argued that the capacity for acquiring language—a sort of proto-grammar— is innate in humans and unfolds in relatively universal ways. More recently, social– constructivist, social interactionist, and pragmatics descriptions of language acquisition, discussed below, are direct descendants of the rationalist model.

Empiricism

Empiricism holds that the child is a blank slate, what the philosopher John Locke called the *tabula rasa*, on which experience is impressed. Experience and the environment play crucial roles in learning everything, including language. What children come to know reflects what exists in the real world—that which they can experience through the sensory mechanism. Language is acquired through the passive accumulation of bits of information that eventually form a collection of habits. Humans are viewed as passive reflections of external reality. The most recent empiricist model of language acquisition is the behaviorist approach, described most thoroughly by B. F. Skinner in the 1950s (Skinner, 1957).

The Nature–Nurture Continuum

Taken to their extremes, rationalism and empiricism delineate opposite ends of what is called the **nature–nurture continuum**. One perspective—rationalism—asserts that language arises solely because of the nature of the human brain. Specifically, this view maintains that the human brain is hardwired (organized) to learn language; we come already primed neurologically for language to develop. Children are seen as active constructors and shapers of their reality. This perspective relies largely on the belief that biological factors—how the brain is organized—primarily account for language acquisition.

The other view—empiricism—holds that language arises only as a result of the environment acting on the human; external forces are believed to shape the child's verbal behaviors into language. In this latter view, the child is seen as a passive reactor to external stimuli, and biological factors operate primarily in response to environmental processes (nurture).

A Compromise Approach: The Social Interactionist Model

As is usually the case when considering extreme ends of any continuum, a compromise position affords far greater power for explaining how language is acquired. Our approach here is that language development is a product of both nature and nurture. We believe that that, while children's brains are primed to learn the relationships between symbols and what they represent, they must have opportunities and practice with language to enable it to develop. We know that neither children who are deprived of social and linguistic stimulation nor children with specific forms of brain damage develop language abilities commensurate with their chronological ages.

The compromise model we use in this book is the **social interactionist model**. According to this view of language development, the interaction of genetic and biological abilities with environmental influences accounts for how and why language develops. This perspective is based on the idea that a child comes into the world with a brain ready to acquire language and that the interactions with people who are important to the child are crucial to the emergence and development of language abilities.

From the time they are born, children develop language as a natural consequence of their social and communicative interactions with important people in their lives. As children attempt to communicate and socialize (the nature aspect), their families or caregivers provide the language that is appropriate for these interactions (the nurture aspect). Each time the child produces a language form in the context of naturally occurring interactions with family or caregivers, the adults "up the ante." In response to the child's production of language, adults provide more complex forms, then the child produces the more complex form, and so on, in a cyclical manner. In this way, children learn more mature and sophisticated language forms until their language system and corresponding social skills approach and reach adult levels (Hulit & Howard, 2005).

The Building Blocks of Language

Until the 1980s, language was most often described in terms of comprehension and production. Most language professionals, however, now use Bloom and Lahey's model, which describes language in terms of three interrelated aspects, or modalities: form, content, and use (Bloom & Lahey, 1978). To the Bloom and Lahey model we add a fourth and a fifth modality: narrative discourse and nonverbal communication.

Language form refers to the structures of language—the rules governing sounds, meanings, words, and sentences. **Language content** encompasses the rules governing how meaning is derived from words and sentences, or our knowledge of vocabulary, objects, processes, ideas, events, and so on. **Language use** refers to the social functions of language—the rules governing how language is used in various communicative contexts. **Narrative** refers to the rules governing how conversations and stories are structured in terms of sequence, cause–effect relationships, and character motivations. **Nonverbal communication** refers to meanings conveyed outside of written or spoken words through gestures, facial expressions, glances, postures, movements, tone of voice, and body language.

Language Form

Language form incorporates three linguistic systems: phonology, morphology, and syntax. **Phonology** is the set of rules governing how we use sounds to make syllables and words. Every language contains a set number of sounds that are pronounceable, and languages differ in which sounds are deemed pronounceable. Pronounceable sounds, called **phonemes**, are the smallest linguistic units to carry meaning. Therefore, in any given language, some speech sound differences matter and some do not. In English, for instance, it does not matter if one pronounces the word *bite* with a puff of air on the *t* or without. In some languages, though, how one pronounces the *t* makes a difference in the meaning of words, and each different *t* is represented by a different phoneme.

Phonemes are typically represented by a notational system called the **International Phonetic Alphabet**. For instance, the word *luck* is represented phonetically as /lUk/, which, though it contains four letters, carries just three phonemes: /l/, /U/, and /k/. A more complex example is *change*, with five letters and six phonemes: /tSendZ/, and *mirror*, a six-letter word with four phonemes: /mIr'/.

English contains approximately 44 phonemes, which can be categorized into consonants and vowels, shown in Table 1.1, and voiced and voiceless consonants and nasal consonants, shown in Table 1.2.

Consonants may be further classified into three categories: place of articulation (Table 1.3), manner of articulation (Table 1.3), and voicing (Table 1.2).

Place of articulation refers to where in the mouth the articulatory contact or movement is made: lips, teeth, and alveolar ridge (i.e., just behind the upper teeth), and the hard and soft palate (i.e., rear portions of the top of the mouth). **Manner of articulation** describes how consonants are produced.

plosives or *stops*: small explosions that result from a stoppage of airflow out of the mouth, followed by a sudden release. The p in "pit" is a good example of a plosive.

fricatives: hissing sounds, such as the s in "silly," produced by forcing air through a narrow constriction in the mouth.

affricates: combinations of plosive and fricative qualities.

nasals: sounds resulting from the passage of air into the nose (e.g., the n sounds in "nonsense").

lateral: sounds that result from airflow being directed out of the mouth alongside the tongue (e.g., the two l sounds in "likely").

glides, or *semivowels*: sounds produced through movement rather than stoppage or constriction of the airflow (e.g., the y sound in "yes").

Vowels also are classified into three categories, shown in Table 1.4: height of tongue (high and low), location of primary resonance (front, mid, and back of mouth), and tongue tension (lax or tense). *High vowels* are those produced with the tongue

TABLE 1.1
Phonemes of the English Language

1. Consonants (25)		2. Vowels (19)	
/b/	ball	/æ/	cat
/tʃ/	church	/e/	cake
/d/	dog	/ɛ˞/	air
/f/	fox	/ɑr/	art
/g/	girl	/ɛ/	leg
/h/	home	/ɑ/	father
/dʒ/	judge	/i/	meal
/k/	cat	/ɪ/	fin
/l/	log	/ɑɪ/	ice
/m/	man	/ɔ/	dog
/n/	now	/o/	toad
/ŋ/	sing	/oɪ/	boy
/p/	pig	/ʊ/	book
/r/	rib	/u/	moon
/s/	sun	/ɔw/	cow
/t/	toy	/iu/	cube
/ʃ/	shin	/ʌ/	luck
/θ/	thin	/ɛ˞/	fur
/ð/	this	/ə/	sofa
/v/	vote		
/w/	wine		
/hw/	which		
/y/	yes		
/z/	zebra		
/ʒ/	measure		

held relatively close to the palate, resulting in a narrow oral resonating space. *Mid vowels* have wider resonating spaces because the tongue is held midway between the palate and the floor of the mouth. *Low vowels* have the most oral resonance, as the tongue almost rests on the floor of the mouth. *Back vowels* are those produced with rounded lips, whereas *front vowels* result from spread lips. *Mid vowels* fall midway between these two articulations.

Morphology is the set of rules governing how phonemes are combined into syllables and words to convey meaning, and **morphemes** are the smallest grammatical units that carry meaning. The word *sun* is an example of what is called a **free morpheme** because it can stand alone as a word. English (and other languages) also has **bound morphemes**, which are grammatical tags or markers, such as the plural -*s*, as in

TABLE 1.2
Voiced and Voiceless Consonant Pairs; Nasal Consonants

Voiced Consonants		Voiceless Consonants		Nasal Consonants	
/z/	zebra	/s/	sit	/m/	man
/b/	big	/p/	pig	/n/	now
/d/	dog	/t/	toy	/ŋ/	bang
/g/	girl	/k/	kick		
/dʒ/	judge	/tʃ/	church		
/v/	vine	/f/	fin		
/w/	why	/hw/	who		
/ʒ/	treasure	/ʃ/	ship		
/ð/	this	/θ/	thin		

suns and *dogs*. Other examples of bound morphemes include past tense markers, *-ed*, as in *fainted*; the present progressive tense marker, *-ing*, as in *running*, and *un-*, placed at the beginning of a word to indicate "not," as in *uninteresting*. Morphemes are used for functions such as indicating tense, person, and number in verbs, and for forming adjectives and adverbs from root words. The word "deinstitutionalization," for example, includes one free morpheme ("institution") and five bound morphemes.

Syntax is the study of the linguistic conventions for generating meaningful phrases and sentences. Syntax includes the rules governing word order, for example, and the rules operating when we wish to use the passive voice rather than the active voice in a sentence: *The dog was fed by the man* (passive voice), rather than, *The man fed the dog* (active voice). Syntactic rules underlie every phrase or sentence we utter, allowing us to make declarations, direct others to do something, ask questions, and form negatives, among others.

Language Content

Language content refers to the meaning level of language and often is called **semantics** or, as Pinker (2007) put it, the relations of words to reality. Semantics describes how people participate in a shared understanding of the truth and how their thoughts are "anchored to things and situations in the world" (p. 3), that is, their understanding of ideas, feelings, events, relationships, processes, and things. As a professional field of study, semantics investigates the various ways in which humans attribute meaning to their world and to their experiences in that world. Some scholars have argued that semantic ability is one reflection of what a person knows about the world; semantic knowledge is seen as a subset of cognitive knowledge (Pinker, 2005). When we assess children's vocabulary development, we are investigating one major component of their semantic abilities.

TABLE 1.3
Phoneme Place and Manner of Articulation

Place of Articulation

Lips		Teeth/Alveolar Ridge		Hard/Soft Palate	
/p/	pig	/t/	tin	/k/	cat
/b/	big	/d/	dog	/g/	goat
/f/	fin	/s/	sit	/ʃ/	ship
/v/	van	/z/	zebra	/ʒ/	azure
/w/	why	/θ/	thin	/tʃ/	church
/m/	man	/ð/	then	/dʒ/	judge
		/n/	now	/j/	yes
		/l/	log	/r/	rip
				/ŋ/	sing

Manner of Articulation

Plosives/Stops		Fricatives		Affricates	
/p/	pop	/f/	fish	/tʃ/	church
/b/	bob	/v/	vine	/dʒ/	judge
/d/	dog	/θ/	thin		
/t/	tin	/ð/	this		
/g/	goat	/s/	sing		
/k/	coat	/z/	zebra		
		/ʃ/	shine		
		/ʒ/	azure		

Nasals		Laterals		Glides/Semivowels	
/m/	man	/l/	lateral	/j/	yes
/n/	now			/r/	rock
/ŋ/	sing			/h/	hello
				/w/	where

Language Use

Language use refers to the conventions governing how language is used in various social contexts; it involves the rules a culture has developed for what people choose to say, to whom, how, and under which circumstances. The study of language use

TABLE 1.4
Vowels of English

	Front	Central	Back
High	i		u
	I		ʊ
Mid	e	ʌ, ə	o
	ɛ	ɚ, ɛ˞	
Low	æ		
	ɑ		ɔ

stems largely from a field of study called **pragmatics**, which developed into a major discipline in the middle 1970s and has had a profound impact on students of language development. Pragmatics is concerned primarily with the functions of language, especially the functions related to social contexts. This field is based on the idea that, when people speak, they are doing more than just uttering words organized by conventional rules of language. They are also using these words and linguistic constructions to get things done. They are performing what Austin (1962) called "speech acts."

In general, language use operates under what Bates (1976) described as a conversational code of conduct, including the following:

■ Coooperate with your conversational partner(s).
■ Tell the truth.
■ Offer only information assumed to be new and relevant to the listener.
■ Request only information you sincerely want to have.
■ Provide your listeners with just the right amount of background information so they will understand your point.
■ Be unambiguous.
■ Change your language to fit the current social situation.

In describing how language is used, Pinker (2007) described ordinary conversation as an ongoing "session of tête-à-tête diplomacy, in which the parties explore ways of saving face, offering an "out," and maintaining plausible deniability as they negotiate the mix of power, sex, intimacy, and fairness that makes up their relationships" (p. 23).

Often the diplomacy involves violating the code described by Bates (1976) in ways that have become conventionalized to carry separate meanings, as when we use politeness forms, which violate the truth principle. For instance, when someone asks us how we are and we reply, "Fine," even though we feel horrid, we are violating the truth principle in favor of the politeness required by the situation. Or when we use what Pinker (2005) calls a "sneak imperative" (p. 23)—for instance, asking a friend if he would be so good as to pass the guacamole—we are using language to accomplish two functions at once: We are conveying our request, and we are signaling an understanding of our relationship with the friend. Through such subtleties and nuances, we navigate our way through a variety of social relationships and still manage to get our messages across in ways that do not insult others or treat them as if they are subordinates whose only function is to do our bidding.

Narrative Ability

In the past three decades, language scholars have focused on a particularly important aspect of language development, **narrative ability**. For children in today's world, acquiring knowledge about and ability to produce narratives is crucial for academic success. Miller, Gillam, and Peña (2001) argue that children who enter school without well developed narrative abilities are at high risk for academic failure. They suggest that

> children who have little or no experience with narrative thinking fail to discover the critical links between spoken language and literacy (reading and writing). Attaining literacy is necessary for active participation in most cultural groups, and it is essential for the achievement of financial independence and success. (p. 1)

A **narrative** is usually described as a sequence of events tied together in a story. Narrative development is considered to be one of the major precursors to reading and writing and is fundamental to the ability to interact with the various other discourse genres that children encounter in school. In fact, Bruner (1990) has argued that narrative thinking is one of the two basic modes that humans use to formulate thought, the other being logical. Bruner indicated that the development of ability with narrative thinking is important not only to literacy but also as "an achievement of social practice that lends stability to the child's social life" (p. 68).

Although cultures vary in the ways they construct narratives, each contains some sort of **story grammar**. That is, stories usually contain some sort of **setting** (where and when) information, along with one or more **episodes**. Episodes themselves are composed of several components (Gillam & Bedore, 2000), which can be arranged in diverse ways according to culturally determined conventions:

- An **initiating event**, or something that motivates the main character (protagonist) to act
- **Attempts**, or the actions the protagonist takes in response to the initiating event
- A **consequence**, or the result of the actions

More complicated episodes may contain one or more additional components:

- An **internal response**, or how the protagonist feels about the initiating event
- A **plan**, or the characters' thoughts about what actions they can take
- **Reactions**, or the characters' thoughts and/or feelings about the consequences of their actions
- An **ending**, or a resolution or moral to the story

Cultural variation in storytelling can be described as following one of two predominant patterns: (a) topic centered or (b) topic associated. In general, cultures in which the most literate language forms tend to include little immediate context (think of a journal article or college lecture), stories tend to follow the topic-centered style (Gee, 1985). Stories that use this style follow a linear sequence described by Stein and Glenn (1982). A problem motivates a character to develop a plan and carry out an attempt to solve the problem. In these stories, the problem is always solved (one way or another), and the story contains some sort of evaluation of the resolution ("They lived happily ever after") or a moral ("Little girls should never talk with strangers").

Topic-associated stories are more often told in cultures in which language is situated and contextualized within a person's ongoing experiences. Stories emerge from shared conversations, and often the only people who are expected to tell stories are elders or people with high status (Paul, 2001). Topic-associated stories are anecdotal rather than linear, and the overall theme may never be stated explicitly (Kayser, 1993). People, places, and times may shift during the story, and the listener must infer relationships among them.

Nonverbal Language

Regardless of context, whenever we engage in conversation, we incorporate a set of nonverbal characteristics into our utterances, each of which carries information and meaning on its own. For instance, if someone says, "Bring me that hammer" in a calm voice at a conversational volume, holding out a hand to receive the hammer, you are likely to interpret the utterance as a request. But if the same person shouts, "Bring me that hammer!" while gesturing more broadly and with an angry facial expression, you most likely would interpret the utterance quite differently. Yet, the words and syntactic structures remain the same. What nonverbal signals do we use to make our different interpretations?

Nelson's classic description of the nonverbal aspects of language includes four modes: paralinguistics, proxemics, kinesics, and chronemics (Nelson, 1998). **Paralinguistics** refers to the aspects of language carried by the pitch and range of the voice, intonation pattern, vocal intensity, and how the various parts of the utterance are emphasized or stressed. In the example of the hammer, above, the second utterance most likely would be accompanied by a loud voice with raised vocal pitch and range, an intonation pattern typical of anger, and heightened emphasis on certain words.

Proxemics involves the conventions we use for establishing physical distance in our communications with various people over a diverse set of social contexts. Each cultural group has developed its own set of rules governing how close or far apart conversational partners can be, depending on their relationship; the environment; and the purpose of the conversation. For example, in most Western cultures, the physical distance between colleagues at work is significantly greater than that between friends conversing at their leisure over coffee.

Kinesics is the set of body and facial gestures, movements, and expressions that we use in communicating. Shrugging the shoulders often conveys a softening of whatever the utterance. Wrinkling the nose can indicate dislike or distaste, regardless of what is being said.

Chronemics refers to the timing factors that influence how we interpret our conversational partners' utterances. For example, a "pregnant pause" used by a listener after the speaker has said something weighty or difficult conveys a very different meaning than if a speaker says, "I'm not going to say anything for awhile." Chronemics also allow us to understand the differences across cultures in turntaking and simultaneous talking. In some cultural groups, several people talking simultaneously is considered normal, while in other groups, this same practice is viewed as rude.

▌Summary

People use language—both speech and writing—to communicate a variety of intentions to a wide range of communicative partners. Languages are composed of sets of rules governing how words are given meaning (semantics), which sounds and sound combinations can be used and which cannot (phonology), how sentences can be constructed (syntax), and how we are supposed to talk to each other in varying circumstances (pragmatics). In addition, languages consist of both literal and figurative levels, as well as multiple types of discourse, both spoken and written.

One aspect of language development that is crucial for academic success is the ability to engage in narrative thinking. Narrative ability is a precursor to the development of reading and writing and is believed to be fundamental in children's achievement with other forms of discourse—for instance, descriptive, explanatory, and argumentative or persuasive text.

Nonverbal language abilities play a role in communication as well. The use of body movements and gestures, facial expressions, eye movements and expressions, vocal characteristics (including silence), and physical positioning of the body in relation to conversational partners all carry specific meanings and must be learned to communicate successfully.

▌References

Austin, J. (1962). *How to do things with words*. London: Oxford University Press.

Bates, E. (1976). *Language and context: The acquisition of pragmatics*. New York: Academic Press.

Bloom, L., & Lahey, M. (1978). *Language development and language disorders*. New York: John Wiley & Sons.

Bruner, J. (1990). *Acts of meaning*. Cambridge, MA: Harvard University Press.

Chomsky, N. (1971). Language and the mind. In W. Leopold & A. Bar-Adon (Eds.), *Child language* (pp. 424–443). Englewood Cliffs, NJ: Prentice-Hall.

Gee, J. P. (1985). The narrativization of experience in the oral style. *Journal of Education, 167*, 9–35.

Gillam, R. G., & Bedore, L. M. (2000). Communication across the lifespan. In R. B. Gillam, T. P. Marquardt, & F. N. Martin (Eds.), *Communication sciences and disorders: From science to clinical practice* (pp. 25–61). Sudbury, MA: Jones and Bartlett.

Hansen, R., & Hansen, K. (2009). *What do employers really want? Top skills and values employers seek from job-seekers*. Retrieved from http://www.quintcareers.com/job_skills_values.html?False

Hulit, L. M. & Howard, M. R. (2005). *Born to talk: An introduction to speech and language development* (4th ed.). Boston: Allyn & Bacon.

Jaynes, J. (1976). *The Origin of consciousness in the breakdown of the bicameral mind*. Boston: Houghton Mifflin.

Kayser, A. (1993). Parent-implemented language intervention: An environmental system perspective. In A. Kaiser & D. Gray (Eds.), *Enhancing children's communication: Research foundations for intervention* (Vol. 2, pp. 63–84). Baltimore: Brookes.

Miller, L., Gillam, R. B., & Peña, E. C. (2001). *Dynamic assessment and intervention: Improving children's narrative skills*. Austin, TX: Pro-Ed.

National Communication Association (NCA). (2009a). *Communication skills training for elementary school students*. Retrieved from http://www.communicationcurrents.com/

National Communication Association (NCA). (2009b). *Kids communicating: For teachers*. Retrieved from http://www.kidscommunicating.org/page1/page1.html

National Institute for Literacy. (2009). *About the National Institute for Literacy*. Retrieved from http://www.nifl.gov/about/aboutus.html

Nelson, N. W. (1998). *Childhood language disorders in context: Infancy through adolescence* (2nd ed.). Boston: Allyn and Bacon.

Paul, R. (2001). *Language disorders from infancy through adolescence: Assessment and intervention* (2nd ed.). St. Louis, MO: Mosby.

Pinker, S. (2005). So how does the mind work? *Mind and Language, 20*(1), 1–24.

Pinker, S. (2007). *The stuff of thought: Language as a window into human nature*. New York: Penguin.

Skinner, B. F. (1957). *Verbal behavior*. New York: Appleton-Century-Crofts.

Stein, N. L., & Glenn, C. G. (1982). Children's concept of time: The development of a story schema. In W. Freeman (Ed.), *The developmental psychology of time* (pp. 255–282). New York: Academic Press.

2

Language Development from Infancy through Adolescence

For many years, the study of language development focused on the preschool years. Over time, as our knowledge increased about language acquisition from infancy through adolescence, we tended to describe language development in terms of preschool, school-age, and adolescent development. As we have extended our inquiry into more specific aspects of language development related to success in school, however, we realized the need to adopt a different approach.

Stages of Language Development

In this chapter and in Chapters 3–5, we will use the developmental model, based on landmark work by Roger Brown (1973), and described by Paul (2007):

- Communication in the prelinguistic period: up to the emergence of first words
- Emerging language: from first words to the first combining of words
- Developing language: from two-word utterances through the basic structures of language
- Language for learning (L4L): beyond the basics and into reading, writing, figurative language, and narrative and classroom discourse

■ Adolescent language development: into the abstract, including reading and writing various forms of expository discourse

Brown's (1973) most significant contribution to the study of language development has been his description of the stages most children move through, in a few short years, as they progress from signaling their intentions with nonspeech vocalizations and gestures to producing their first words, to understanding and producing most of the basic structures of language. He showed that, although the age at which preschool children acquire syntactic abilities varies, the variation in mean length of their utterances showed much less variability. Based on this finding, Brown used **Mean Length of Utterance** (MLU) as the best means of indexing syntactic development until MLU reaches approximately 5.0 (roughly the age at which most children enter school).

Mean length of utterance is computed by counting the total number of free morphemes and the total number of bound morphemes in each utterance of a language sample collected from the child. That total is then divided by the total number of utterances in the sample to yield the MLU. Table 2.1 shows how MLU increases as the child develops from roughly 12 months of age to almost 5 years of age.

To describe children's language development after age 5 or 6, we begin to incorporate information from all aspects of the child's languages system: semantics, syntax and morphology, phonology, pragmatics, and narrative abilities. The model of language development, infancy through adolescence, that we will refer to throughout our discussions of language development and language instruction is given in Table 2.2.

Communication in the Prelinguistic Period

The prelinguistic period of language development is usually considered to cover the time between birth and the emergence of the child's first real words. Communication

TABLE 2.1
Brown's Stages of Language Development

Stage I	Stage II	Stage III
MLU 1.0 to 2.0 morphemes	MLU 2.0 to 2.5	MLU 2.5 to 3.0
Typical age = 12–26 months	Typical age = 27–30 months	Tyical age = 31–34 months

Stage IV	Stage V	Stage V+
MLU 3.0 to 3.75	MLU 3.75 to 4.5	MLU > 4.75
Typical age = 35–40 months	Typical age = 41–46 months	Typical age > 47 months

Source: Adapted from *Born to Talk: An Introduction to Speech and Language Development* (4th ed.), by L. M. Hulit and M. R. Howard, 2011, Boston: Allyn & Bacon.

MLU = Mean Length of Utterance

TABLE 2.2

Stages of Language Development

Prelinguistic	Emerging Language	Developing Language
Typical developmental age: birth–12 months MLU: < 1.0 Expressive means: babbling, vocal intonation contours, jargon, gaze, facial expressions Communication: preintentional to intentional	Typical developmental age: 12–26 months MLU: 1.0–2.0 Expressive vocabulary: > 50 words and increasing rapidly Phonology: increasingly consistent phonetic forms Communication: increasingly linguistic Pragmatics: varied communicative intentions	Typical developmental age: 26–46 months MLU: 2.0–5.0 Expressive syntax: combining words into sentences; early negation, interrogatives, and imperatives; basic embedding Phonology: simplified adult forms Semantics: explosive vocabulary growth Communication: from sentences to stories Pragmatics: intentions expressed more often and over a wider range of function

Language for Learning	Adolescent Language/Later Language Development
Typical develomental age: 5–10 or 12 years MLU: 5+ Semantics: vocabulary development: wider and deeper; chunking meanings; from personal to shared meanings; elaborated definitions Syntax & morphology: passives, complex conjoining, embedding throughout sentences, noun and verb phrases, gerunds, adverbs from adjectives Phonology: gradual achievement of adult forms Pragmatics: conversational competence, conversational repairs, sophisticated indirect requests, increased presupposition skills Narrative development: embedded episodes in stories; increased ability with formal, literate discourse Metalinguistic awareness: increased ability to think, talk about, and analyze language and language components	Typical developmental age: 11+ MLU: no longer a valid indicator Semantics: understanding and using figurative language—idioms, similes, metaphors, adages, etc.; increased use of multiple meanings; vocabulary increases stem primarily from reading Syntax and morphology: increased sentence length, increasing use of subordinate and coordinate clauses, increased use of literate language style Phonology: Adult forms achieved Pragmatics: increased use of slang and in-group language; increased use of persuasion, negotiation, and establishing social dominance Discourse development and metalinguistic awareness: ability with class lectures and expository texts, increased production of expository and persuasive writing

during infancy is highly dependent on the actions and interpretations of the adults in the child's immediate world. For most children, having caring adults who talk to them, respond to them as if they are communicating, and construct conversations for them is just what is needed for the child to begin acquiring the basic forms and interactive behaviors that underlie language development.

When parents or caregivers talk to babies, they usually use a special form of language called "motherese." During the child's first 6 months, motherese tends not to emphasize words or meaning but, rather, to underscore pitch, rate, loudness, stress, rhythm, and intonation. They use a higher pitch than they use with other listeners, a much wider intonational range, and increased loudness and emphasis. In addition, parents tend to repeat their utterances and talk about things the infant can see or hear. Parents also look into their baby's eyes and smile frequently as they talk. When the infant makes any sort of vocalization, parents respond as if the baby has taken a conversational turn. Once babies reach approximately 6 months of age, parents change their conversational style somewhat and begin to use language that includes more information.

Perhaps the most important aspect of the parent–child interaction during infancy is the development of what Bruner calls **joint attention** and **joint referencing** (Bruner, 1975). The parent encourages joint attention by first looking at the baby's eyes and face while speaking, moving the baby when the baby looks elsewhere to regain the child's attention. Over time, the baby begins responding by looking at the parent's eyes whenever she speaks. Next, the parent brings an object into the conversation, perhaps a mobile or a toy. She makes sure the baby is looking at it while using motherese to talk about it. She may move the object so the baby has to turn to look at it, continuing to talk about it as she does so. Eventually, the baby begins to look at whatever object the parent brings into its focus, thus engaging in **mutual attending**.

Joint referencing develops out of joint attention. As the parent talks about the jointly attended-to object (e.g., a stuffed toy), she indicates what she is talking about by bouncing the toy or jiggling it—whatever it takes to call the baby's attention to the toy. As the baby grows, the parent begins telling him what these jointly attended-to things are called, indicating what she is talking about in the routine that she and the baby have developed. Most of the "conversation" takes place by the parent's both imitating the baby's cooing and gurgling and talking to the baby in motherese. Soon the baby begins gesturing toward the object, and the parent responds enthusiastically. Eventually, the two develop a routine of pointing at an object to indicate joint reference, and one of the most important pieces of the process of language acquisition has been established.

Babbling

Gradually the baby participates more and more in the "conversation" through body gestures, gurgling, smiling, and cooing, and, at around 6 months, through babbling. **True babbling** is usually described as the use of consonant–vowel (CV: C = consonant; V = vowel) syllables, such as "mamam" or "nanana" (Hulit & Howard, 2011). As children's babbling becomes more developed, their participation in conversations with their parents changes. Now the babies begin to imitate their parents, even though the babies clearly have no idea what they are saying. During this period, children engage in what is called **vocal play**, which includes grunts, squeals, growls, screams, and "raspberries" (Hulit & Howard, 2011).

Babies' babbling becomes more complicated as they grow, and between around 9 months and 18 months, the syllables produced during babbling change from simple CV syllables to CVC or VCV syllables, the most typical being "gug" or "ugu," sounds produced in the back of the mouth and easy for the baby's articulators to produce. Sometime during this period, children begin to attach intonation contours to babbling, sounding very much like the parents whose intonation patterns they have been listening to for months.

In the latter stages of babbling, it becomes clear to those around the baby that he has begun intending to communicate, and that he has begun initiating communicative interactions with those who are important to him. This intention to communicate is another part of the foundation of language, because it is from this intentionality that children develop their knowledge of pragmatics and the social-interactive language abilities they will need to succeed both in and out of school.

Communicating for a Purpose

Even before children are producing single words, they have become skilled at getting what they want from the adults in their lives: attention, juice, a toy, a ride in the car, a hug, comfort after a scare, and so on. As a result of all the conversations they have had with their parents, they have become ever more adept at joint referencing, now embellished by their own gestures, facial expressions, varied intonation contours, and vocal emphasis and pitch.

By now, parents begin recognizing that their children not only intend to communicate but also express several different **communicative intentions** (Roth & Spekman, 1984):

- Seeking attention, both for self and away from self
- Seeking conversational interaction
- Requesting objects, action, and information
- Greeting
- Giving (e.g., a toy to mom or dad)
- Protesting or rejecting
- Responding or acknowledging
- Informing

These communicative intentions reflect why children are communicating: They need to communicate to get things done, to make things happen, and to get what they want. As we shall see later in the chapter, communicative intentions continue to develop throughout childhood and well into adolescence.

Children's earliest forms of **negation** and **interrogative forms** emerge during this stage of development. At first, children indicate negation with a clear "No!"

Gradually, they begin putting *no* at the beginning of whatever they want to negate, for example, "No milk!" "No go." Early interrogatives are formed through the use of rising intonation, as in "Doggie?" or "Juice?"

Emerging Language

This stage of language development is known as Brown's Stage I, during which most children have an MLU between 1.0 and 2.0. Thus, this period of emerging language covers the time between the emergence of a child's first words and the child's production of first word combinations.

Semantics

Sometime between 12 and 18 months, most children begin using single-word utterances in their communication. Again, for most children, the first words name important people ("mama," "dada," "nanna"), or important objects (e.g., an approximation of the name of their favorite toy), or an important process (e.g., "ee" for *eat*, "bye bye" to indicate *let's go*).

When listening to children using words during this period, it is necessary to remember that what they mean may be quite different from what adults mean by the same word. For instance, children in this stage often use one word to refer to several objects or processes, as when a child uses *horse*, for instance, to mean anything with four legs. Similarly, children in the emerging language stage may use a word to refer to just one specific object or process and no other, say, using *dog* to mean only the family dog and not other dogs.

Gradually, though, children's vocabulary increases. By the end of the first year of life, children understand about 20 different words, and by the time they are 2 years of age, their vocabulary may reach 200 words (Gillam & Bedore, 2000). The words comprising children's lexicon at this stage serve a particular communicative purpose. The most common communicative purposes for which children use words during this developmental stage are (Bloom & Lahey, 1978):

- rejection (*no*),
- nonexistence or disappearance (*allgone*),
- cessation or prohibition of action (*stop*),
- recurrence (*more*),
- existence (*this*),
- action on objects (*kiss*),
- locative action (*up, fill, out*),
- attribution (*big*),
- naming, possession, commenting (*dog*),
- social interaction (*hi*).

According to Bloom and Lahey, the words serving these communicative purposes can be classified as either **relational** or **substantive** words. Relational words are not nouns and are used to signify relations between objects. Substantive words are nouns and are used to name people, pets, and toys, and objects the child operates on directly, such as preferred foods, labels for objects, and for social games and routines (Owens, 1998).

Syntax

Around 18 months of age, most children begin producing two-word phrases, signaling an intention to communicate about the relationships between ideas. Until the ability to generate two-word phrases emerges, children express these same semantic relationships through their single-word utterances. Hence, two-word phrases signal an ability to encode relationships in a more sophisticated and complex manner.

Almost universally, children's two-word phrases describe a relatively small number of semantic relationships between agents (the thing or person that initiates an action), actions (what happens), objects (things that are acted upon), and locations (places) (Gillam & Bedore, 2000). The following are the most typical two-word phrases that children produce:

Agent + Action	*Dog eat*
Agent + Location	*Dog chair*
Action + Location	*Go Nanna's*
Agent + Object	*Mommy hair*

During the emerging language stage, children come to realize that sentences must contain two kinds of information: a noun phrase and a verb phrase. In the earliest phases of this stage, some of their two-word utterances may not contain both a noun phrase and a verb phrase, as in *Mommy hair*. In this example, *Mommy hair* is a noun phrase and the verb phrase is understood: *This is* Mommy's hair. As children develop greater facility, they begin including both noun phrases and verb phrases in their utterances, resulting in utterances such as: *Dog chair* (The dog [noun phrase] is on the chair [verb phrase]).

Two important syntactic developments during this stage of language acquisition are the continued development of both negation and the interrogative form. Negation is most typically expressed by saying, "No," followed by whatever the child is negating, for instance, "No sleep" ("I don't want to go to bed yet"). The most typical interrogative form to appear at this stage is the application of a rising intonation contour onto the two-word utterance, as in, "More juice?" ("May I have some more juice?")

Phonology

Phonological development is a gradual process, extending over several years. During the emerging language stage of development, children's phonological abilities vary tremendously. Unable yet to use adult forms, they rely on **phonetically consistent forms** to produce words (Gillam & Bedore, 2000). What this means is that children may consistently use words that differ from the adult version but that the child's conversational partners recognize as having a particular meaning. For example,

Gillam and Bedore (2000) describe a child of their acquaintance who said /w√g bi/ (wugabee) to refer to a particular bear. At first, when his parents responded by referring to a different bear, the child shook his head, "no," and repeated /w√g bi/ until his parents realized what he meant. After that, he used the form consistently, and his parents knew precisely what he meant.

According to Gillam and Bedore (2000), the first set of phonemes acquired by most children by age 3 is: /m, b, n, w, d, p, h/. In terms of articulation, these phonemes represent the manner and place of articulation (see Table 1.3, in Chapter 1), most commonly represented in the child's babbling:

Manner of articulation = plosives (/p, b/), nasals (/m, n/), and glides (/h/);
Place of articulation = lips (/m, b, p/), contact between the tongue and the alveolar ridge (/d, n/, and air passing over the palate (/h/).

In choosing words, children tend to use not only their semantic knowledge but also the constraints on their phonological capacities. That is, they tend to choose words whose phonological characteristics are within their range of production ability rather than words beyond their ability. Thus, a child is much more likely to call a horse a horse than to refer to it as *thoroughbred*.

A characteristic of children in this stage of language development is that they typically simplify adult forms, using **phonological processes**. The most common in children between 2 and 3 years of age are (Gillam & Bedore, 2000):

- deleting what are known as "weak" (unaccented) syllables: *Saturday* becomes /sætɚde/,
- deleting final consonants: *ball* becomes /b<u>A</u>/, and
- velar fronting, which involves substituting front sounds such as /t/ and /d/ (velar stops) for back stops /k/ and /g/: /t√p/ *tup* for /k√p/ *cup*.

Pragmatics

During this developmental period, children's attempts to communicate more than double in frequency between 18 and 24 months (Paul, 2007). Chapman (2000) reports that 18-month-olds produce about five instances of intentional communication per minute, while 24-month-olds produce more than seven per minute. Also, the ratio of nonverbal-to-verbal communication changes drastically, with verbal communication becoming considerably more frequent than nonverbal communication. Clearly, children in this stage of development are communicating more often, and more often verbally. As a result, we can observe increasing sophistication in their communicative intentions and their abilities to take the listener into consideration during conversation.

Intentionality   As related in the preceding discussion of prelinguistic language development, children had begun signaling a variety of communicative intentions in their conversations. During the emerging language stage of development, the range of intentions that children express in their communication extends considerably, as shown in Table 2.3.

TABLE 2.3
Communicative Intentions at the Single-Word Stage

Intention	Definition	Examples
1. Naming	Common and proper nouns that label people, objects, events, and locations.	"dog," "party," "table"
2. Commenting	Words that describe physical attributes of objects, events, and people, including size, shape, and location; observable movements and actions of objects and people; and words that refer to attributes that are not immediately observable, such as possession and usual location. These words are not contingent on prior utterances.	"big," "here," "mine"
3. Requesting object		
a. present	Words that solicit an object that is present in the environment.	"gimme," "cookie" (accompanied by gesture and/or visual regard)
b. absent	Words that solicit an absent object.	"ball" (child pulls mother to another room)
4. Requesting action	Words that solicit an action be initiated or continued.	"up" (child wants to be picked up), "more"
5. Requestion information	Words that solicit information about an object, action, person, or location. Rising intonation is also included.	"shoe?" (meaning, "Is this a shoe?") "Wadæt?" ("What's that?")
6. Responding	Words that directly complement preceding utterances.	"crayon" (in response to "What's that?"), "yes" (in response to, "Do you want to go outside?")
7. Protesting/ Rejecting	Words that express objection to ongoing or impending action or event.	"no" (in response to being tickled), "yuk" (child pushes away unwanted food)
8. Attention seeking	Words that solicit attention to the child or to aspects of the environment.	"Mommy!" "Watch!"
9. Greetings	Words that express salutations and other conversationalized rituals.	"Hi," "Bye," "Nite-nite"

Source: From "Assessing the Pragmatic Abilities of Children: Part 1. Organizational Framework and Assessment Parameters," by F. Roth & N. Spekman. *Journal of Speech and Hearing Disorders, 49,* p. 4. Copyright 1984 by American Speech–Language–Hearing Association. Reprinted with permission.

In addition, children begin using more advanced communicative intentions called **discourse functions**. Rather than referring to objects or events, these discourse functions refer to previous speech acts, indicating that children are becoming aware of the social-interactive requirements of conversations. Paul (2007) lists discourse functions as the following:

- Requests for information, or the use of language to learn about the world. When this discourse function emerges, children may ask for the names of things, events, processes, and relationships. Later, they may use a *wh-* word, a rising intonation contour, or both.
- Acknowledgements, or letting the listener know that the previous utterance was received. The most common ways for children to signal this reception is to mimic the speaker's intonation pattern, imitate part of the utterance, or nod the head.
- Answers, or responding to someone's request for information with an appropriate reply.

Presuppositions A **presupposition** is an assumption the speaker makes about what the listener already knows in order to say just the right thing to make the communication work. For instance, you would provide different driving directions to someone you assume to live in your town than you would give to someone from out of town. In the earliest phase of emerging language, children most often assume that their listeners know everything they themselves know, and they speak accordingly. They provide no background information, they use linguistic shortcuts (*it, him, there*) without clues to their referents, they are unable to take the listener's perspective, and they are unable to respond to requests for more information or clarification. As a result, adults do most of the work of interpreting what children mean during this stage of development.

In the later parts of this stage, children become more adept at understanding that their listeners do *not* know everything they themselves know and in responding to requests for clarification. By the end of the emerging language stage, most children respond appropriately to *wh-* questions, they can provide some requested information, and they can clarify on request. But they still have difficulty understanding that their listeners do not share their own perspective, and they are unable to provide more than rudimentary background information for their listeners.

Turntaking Children in the prelinguistic stage of language development demonstrate an ability to take turns during conversations. Learning how to communicate arises from the give-and-take interactions between parent and baby, the joint attending and joint referencing that develops as a consequence of these early "conversations." During the emerging language phase, children develop a turntaking style that Hulit and Howard (2011) say resembles adult conversation. By the time they reach 18 months of age, most children demonstrate basic turntaking rules in their conversations

(Bloom, Rocissano, & Hood, 1976). Notice in the following conversation how the child responds to what the adult says:

A: *This is a <u>big truck</u>* (underline = emphasis).
C: *Uh, huh!* (moves truck across floor).
A: *Here it comes!*
C: *Fast.*
A: *I'd better move.*
C: *ook ow* (look out).

Though children in the emerging language stage clearly exhibit linguistic turntaking, their ability to take conversational turns over extended conversations is limited, as is their ability to share turns with more than one or two conversational partners.

Developing Language

This period of language development occurs between the ages of 27 months and 46 months in normally developing children. It includes Brown's Stages II through V and represents the tremendous language growth from the two-word utterance period through acquisition of the basic structures of language. Children in this phase of language development go from an MLU of 2.0 to an MLU of 4.5 morphemes, which means a significant growth spurt in understanding and use of all aspects of language. Almost all of the changes that children make in the developing language stage are elaborations of competencies that emerged in the previous stage of emerging language.

Semantics

Vocabulary development during this period is almost exponential. Gillam and Bedore (2000) report that, at age 2, children are able to say approximately 200 different words, and at age 4, they can say approximately 1,800 different words (2000). These same authors report that by age 4, most children probably understand as many as 3,000 to 4,000 different words. Not only are children using nouns and verbs, but now they add prepositions (e.g., *behind, in front of*), temporal words (e.g., *before, first*), adjectives (e.g., *big, little, purple*), and pronouns (e.g., *he, her, it*). And, as we shall see in the section on syntax, children in this period develop the ability to express complex-meaning relationships through the use of relatively simple syntax—for instance, *Jenny took the train to see her grandmother in Florida.*

During this stage of language development, children refine the meanings of their utterances through a variety of syntactic devices. Technically, many of the structures and devices that children learn during this period are considered to be morphemes, but, because they affect meaning, we include a brief discussion here.

During the developing language period, children begin using what are called **inflections** to change word meaning by adding a grammatical morpheme, as in *cats / cat's*. Children also begin inflecting verbs to indicate tense markers, for example, past or present, and they begin elaborating their understanding of the verb *to be*, which presents some interesting challenges because it can be used as either a main verb or **copula** (*She was angry*) or as an **auxiliary** verb (*She was running*).

Regular and **irregular** verb forms begin to emerge in children's language, though they may persist in regularizing irregulars for some time. For instance, to indicate past tense on the regular verb *walk* requires the addition of *-ed*, and the irregular verb *sing* undergoes an internal transformation to indicate past tense, *sang*. Often, children in this stage of language development say things such as, "I singed in class yesterday" or "I eated my breakfast." These regularizations indicate the normal process of children learning the more general—regular—rule, followed some time later with learning the less general—irregular—rule. Some normally developing children continue using regularized forms well into the school years. A fourth-grade student of ours, who had been reminded over the course of several months that "have tooken" should be "have taken" suddenly realized the rule and exclaimed one day, "Why didn't you tell me I can't say 'have tooken'?"

Another syntactic device that children learn during this period involves which words can and cannot be **contracted**. For instance, *He's hungry* is permissible, while *I's hungry* is not a permissible form in English.

Perhaps the most interesting aspect of semantic development during the developing language periods is how children acquire **pronouns**. In English, personal pronouns are considerably more complicated than nouns because different forms exist for use in various syntactic constructions, as shown in Table 2.4.

Because English personal pronouns convey information about gender (female, male, or neutral), position in the sentence (subjective, possessive, or objective), and number (singular or plural), they require some time to learn. Acquisition occurs in some order, though. Generally, children acquire subjective pronouns (*she, he*) before developing objective pronouns (*her, him*), although there are exceptions. Next, children usually acquire possessive pronouns (*her, their, his, our*), and then reflexive pronouns (*myself, yourself, herself*).

Early in the developing language phase, Brown's Stage II, children usually expand from the use of *I* and *it* to production of *my, mine, me,* and *you*, though they may not use these words appropriately (Hulit & Howard, 2011). In Brown's Stage III, children become more consistent in their use of *you, your, yours, she, he, we,* as well as the demonstrative pronouns *this, that, these,* and *those* (Hulit & Howard, 2005). By the time they enter Brown's Stage IV, children are more consistent in their use of *they, us, his, her, hers,* and *them* (Hulit & Howard, 2011). Finally, toward the end of this period, when they are in Brown's Stage V, children are using *its, our, ours, him, their, theirs, myself,* and *yourself* more consistently. Usage, however, may still vary, particularly in the more complex syntactic constructions. Most children do not completely master English personal pronouns until well into the L4L stage.

Syntax and Morphology

Syntax   Children's syntax changes dramatically during the developing language stage of development. At first, children usually are producing two-word utterances.

TABLE 2.4
English Personal Pronouns

	Singular			Plural		
	1st	2nd	3rd	1st	2nd	3rd
Subjective						
Female	she	you			you	
Male	he	you			you	
Neutral	I*		it, one	we*		they
Possessive						
Female	her, hers	your, yours			your	
Male	his	your, yours			your	
Neutral	my, mine*		its, one's	our*		their, theirs
Objective						
Female	her	you			you	
Male	him	you			you	
Neutral	me*		it, one	us*		them
Reflexives						
Female	herself	yourself			yourselves	
Male	himself	yourself			yourselves	
Neutral	myself*		itself, oneself	themselves*		themselves

*Self-referring pronouns are assumed to carry the gender of the person using them.

At the end of this stage, they may be using sentences that contain adjectives, prepositional phrases, and subordinate clauses (Miller, 2006). At the outset, children understand a sentence to have a noun phrase and a verb phrase, they form negatives by putting *no* or *not* at the beginning of the sentence, they produce *yes/no* interrogatives through rising intonation, and they can ask primitive *what, where,* and *why* questions (Hulit & Howard, 2011).

At the end of this stage, children are producing negative past tense forms of *to be* (*weren't, wasn't*), occasional past tense modals, (*wouldn't, couldn't*), asking *yes/no* questions through inverted word form ("Is he playing?"), using tag questions ("I'm playing now, okay?"), embedding relative clauses into the object position in sentences ("That's the one I want"), and conjoining clauses, usually with *and* (Hulit & Howard, 2011).

At the beginning of the developing language stage, children make their sentences more complex by adding modifiers or auxiliary verbs; near the end of this stage, they place phrases within clauses, and they combine two or more clauses into one (Hulit

& Howard, 2011). This combining, called **embedding**, represents an important syntactic leap because it allows children to express much more complicated relationships than they could express solely through added modifiers or auxiliaries.

Embedding takes two basic forms: embedding phrases within sentences and embedding clauses within clauses. Hulit and Howard (2011) delineated four types of phrases: **prepositional phrases**, **participial phrases**, **infinitive phrases**, and **gerunds**. Most children begin using prepositional phrases sometime during the developing language stage, usually by putting them at the end of their sentences. Participials (verbs functioning as adjectives, as in *running dog*) emerge somewhat later, as they require children to modify verbs to function as adjectives.

The earliest infinitive phrases that children use are those in which the subject of the phrase is the same as the subject of the sentence ("I want to go outside"). Later, children become able to use more complicated infinitives in which the subject of the sentence is different from the subject of the phrase ("I want my doll to go, too"). According to Paul (1981), gerunds (verbs ending in *-ing* functioning as nouns) emerge later than the other types of phrases, first showing up near the end of the developing language period stage. Those that do occur tend to be of the form, "Writing is hard."

Embedding clauses within clauses produces **complex sentences**, in contrast to **compound sentences**, which are produced by conjoining two clauses. Both types of sentences appear during the later part of this stage, though clauses joined with "and" appear somewhat earlier and continue to be favored by most children well into the school years. The complex sentences produced by children during this stage are the result of three types of embedded clauses: **object complement clauses, *wh-* question clauses**, and **relative clauses** (Brown, 1973).

Sentences with an object complement clause have an independent clause containing a verb followed by a noun phrase functioning as an object, as in, "I think he's okay." In this sentence, "he's okay" functions as the object of the verb *to think*, even though "he's okay" is a noun phrase.

Children in this stage also begin using sentences including a *wh-* clause functioning as a noun phrase, as in "I know where you went." As children begin using *wh-* clauses, they often invert the order to reflect the interrogatives they are acquiring at the same time ("Tell me where can I get one"). Usually, by the time children enter school, they have sorted out the word order required by *wh-* phrases, though this is not always the case, even in normally developing children.

Relative clauses emerge at the end of the developing language period. They are formed with *wh-* and *th-* words and modify the noun they follow in the sentence, as in "He's the one who came over" and "That's the one I saw." Because they are late to emerge, relative clauses continue to develop well after children enter school.

Morphology   According to Gillam and Bedore (2000), among the earliest morphemes that children use with any regularity are the plural marker *-s* (*The girls play*), the possessive marker *-s* (*The dog's bone*), and the progressive *-ing* (*The dog's eating*). Next to emerge are the third person singular morpheme *-s* (*The dog eats*) and the past tense marker *-ed* (*The boy jumped*). Later in this stage, children begin using both the copula and the "to be" verb forms, as in "Mommy *is* happy" (copula) and "The dog *is* eating" (auxiliary).

As children experiment with grammatical morphemes, they often generalize the rules they are acquiring, regardless of exceptions of usage. For instance, when children first begin using the plural morpheme *-s*, they use it everywhere, as in "childs" and "mouses." Only gradually do they narrow their usage to just those words requiring any morphemic rule. Another example of children's overextension of a morphemic rule is their use of the past tense marker *-ed*. As soon as the morpheme appears in their repertoire, they extend it to all the verb forms in their lexicon, resulting in words such as "eated" and "swimmed."

As with the past tense marker, though, children gradually narrow their application of the rule until it applies in the right places. In the meantime, as mentioned earlier, children are learning the exceptions to the rules, for instance, that irregular verbs require internal changes to express past tense (*swim* becomes *swam*) or certain nouns form plurals internally (*mouse* becomes *mice*). Part of this gradual morphemic specification occurs during the developing language stage, but some remains to be learned after children enter school.

Phonology

As pointed out earlier, the stage of developing language is one of rapid change. The child acquires most—though not all—of the phonological system during this time. Perhaps the most significant feature of children's phonological development is that, though most of the phonological system is acquired before children enter school, phonological development is not finished until an average of age 8.

Sometime between ages 3 and 5, children acquire the following phoneme set: / t, d, k, g, f, v, t<u>S</u> (ch), d<u>Z</u> (ju<u>dge</u>)/, and between 4 and 8 years of age, they acquire these phonemes: /<u>S</u> (sh), T (voiceless th), s, z, D (voiced th), l, r, <u>Z</u> (a<u>z</u>ure)/(Gillam & Bedore, 2000). These authors cautioned that, although this latter set of phonemes begins to appear during the developing language stage, children will often use these phonemes inconsistently over a long time before mastering them.

After age 3, the phonological process of simplification disappears as more complex phonological forms, such as consonant clusters, appear: /sp/ in *spin*, /str/ in *string*. For a time, the following new phonological processes emerge (Gillam & Bedore, 2000):

- Cluster reduction: two-consonant combinations are reduced to one: /ti/ for *tree* and three-consonant combinations are reduced to two: /stAIp/ for *stripe*.
- Substitution of a glide for a liquid: /twi/ for *tree*
- Epenthesis, or insertion of the *schwa*, as in /t wi/ for *tree*

Most of these processes disappear by the time children are 4 years old

Pragmatics

As children in the developing language stage begin producing more language, their abilities as conversational partners begin to grow and change in significant ways.

Early in this stage, children's **turntaking** abilities are relatively primitive, and they can maintain a topic for only one or two conversational turns. By the end of this period, however, they understand topic maintenance over a series of turns, especially if the topic is of interest to them.

Early in the period, children tend to interrupt their conversational partners, not allowing the speaker to complete his turn. Children seem to assume that any falling intonation pattern signals the end of an utterance and, therefore, a slot to talk. Later, children wait longer before they speak, but, because they are still sensitive to what they perceive as long pauses in the conversational flow, they tend to initiate their turn whenever they hear a pause longer than one second.

One of the earliest pragmatic developments in this stage is children's acquisition of knowledge about **conversational repair**. As you know from talking with young children, they often say things that do not provide enough information for others to understand what they mean. When asked for clarification, however, children in this stage of language development can respond by revising their utterance. At first the revisions may not actually clarify, but, as the children's skills increase, they become more adept at providing information that assists the listener who requests clarification.

In the previous discussion of emerging language, we pointed out children's lack of understanding of presuppositions, saying that children in that stage assumed adults knew just what they themselves knew, and so spoke accordingly. Early in the developing language stage, children become a bit more adept at providing sufficient background information, but only if prompted by an adult. Later in the period, children become better able to provide the information that listeners need if it is within their cognitive and linguistic abilities, and they become able to adjust their speech and language according to the age of their listener.

When children enter the developing language stage, one of their reasons for using language is to make requests. At this point, their requests are **direct requests**; when they say something, there is no question about what they mean. For instance, if a child wants more juice, he says, "I need more juice." Although including *need* indicates children's understanding that they are more likely to get what they want if they *need* it than if they merely *want* it, the request is still relatively direct. In learning how to make requests, children also are learning the politeness rules in their family. They may learn, for instance, that saying "please" at the beginning of the request works better than omitting "please."

Learning how to make **indirect requests** requires that children understand that words can mean more than one thing and that a sentence may not literally mean what it says. For instance, saying "I'm cold" might mean "Close the window," or saying "I'm thirsty" could mean "I want more juice." As children's understanding of nonliteral language increases, so does their ability to use indirect requests such as, "Could you close the door?" as a more polite way of saying, "Close the door."

Figurative Language

One of the most important aspects of children's language learning during this stage is their unfolding understanding that, because language is arbitrary, it can exist on several levels, ranging from the literal to the metaphoric. When language first emerges, children use it to get things done in the most direct and efficient way possible. As their abilities develop, they come to understand that how they use language can dramatically alter how and how efficiently things get done.

Early in this stage, children are virtually unable to understand that words can be separated from the things they represent. If a child has the same name as one of his parents, he either denies it as a possibility, ignores the person, or becomes agitated. Later, children come to accept that several different things in the world can have the same name. Later still, they discover that the same things can have several names, or synonyms, as in "couch," "sofa," or "divan." They become aware of homonyms (to, too, two) and double-meaning words (cold and warm).

Of particular interest is children's growing awareness of the metaphoric uses of language, particularly idiomatic expressions. By the end of this stage of language development, children have begun using the limited set of idioms used in their families, though at this stage they do not understand these as nonliteral.

Similarly, during this period, children begin developing an ability to understand and use various forms of humor, though not until they enter school do most children become adept with humor that relies on truly metaphoric language. For example, in this developing stage of language, children begin experimenting with knock-knock jokes. Their first attempts at humor may be to use a joke format without understanding how to make the content humorous. They may say something like, "Knock-knock." The listener responds, "Who's there?" And the child says his name, falling into gales of laughter at how "funny" the joke is.

The beginning of other forms of humor (e.g., riddles) may emerge at the end of this period, though children do not become adept with riddles until sometime during the next stage of development. During the latter phases of the developing language stage, children may experiment with the riddle format, though they cannot yet include humorous content. For instance, consider a conversation one of the authors (Miller) had with three children while having a snack on Halloween day. The participants were: Frannie, 2 years old, who watched and listened without saying anything; Christopher, almost 5; and Sam, age 7.

Sam to Miller:	"Do you know any Halloween jokes?"
Miller:	"Well, here's one that's pretty corny."
Christopher:	"What is it?"
Miller:	"Do you know why the skeleton didn't cross the road?"
Both boys:	"No, why?"
Miller:	"Because he didn't have the guts."

Both boys laughed and continued eating. When Miller asked Christopher why it was funny, he replied, "Because he couldn't run." When Sam was asked why it was funny, he said, rubbing his stomach, "He didn't have the courage," indicating that he was aware of the two meanings of the word "guts," even though he couldn't articulate this. Later, Miller asked the boys' parents (two separate families) if the boys had told them the joke. Both said they had. Sam's family reported that he had been able to accurately tell the joke, and Christopher's family reported that Christopher had asked, "Do you know why the skeleton didn't cross the road?" and the parents responded, "No, why?" Christopher said, "Because he fell down!" and laughed uproariously.

Narrative Development

Toward the end of the developing language stage, children begin telling stories containing fictional elements, and they begin constructing retellings of events they have experienced. Both processes require some knowledge of narrative, which begins to emerge during this period in language development. As pointed out earlier in this chapter, prior to the emergence of true narratives, children in the developing language stage produce what are called **protonarratives**, which take the form of loosely related utterances called **heaps** (Appleby, 1978). Heaps are typical of children early in the developing language stage, around 2 or 3 years of age. Later, at around age 3 1/2, children's protonarratives become somewhat more sophisticated and are composed of utterances centering on a central theme, character, or setting.

For most children, protonarratives give way, first, to a collection of utterances with a beginning, middle, and end, but no plot or cause–effect relationships. Next, children begin to produce **primitive narratives**, or stories containing a basic episode, by age 4 to 5. As Figure 2.1 shows, a basic episode consists of an initiating event (some problem that gets the action going), an attempt or action by a character to solve the problem, and a consequence, or resolution of the problem. Between ages 4 and 5, children begin to add to their basic episodes some information about the character's feelings or intentions, but the plot is still weak. Gradually, children add characters' thoughts or feelings about the actions they can take (a plan) and some thoughts or feelings about the consequences of their actions (reaction or ending). By the time children reach school age, most have begun true narratives, which we discuss next, involving the L4L period of development.

Earlier we described four types of narratives: recounts, eventcasts, accounts, and fictionalized narratives. During the developing language stage, children from middle-class homes are likely to use all four of these types of narratives, and by the time they enter school, they are usually proficient in each.

1. When their parents ask them what they did that day, they typically respond with a **recounting** of their day. Recounts always are in response to adult initiation.
2. Children use **eventcasts** to manipulate others' behavior. For example, a child who wants to go to his friend's house tomorrow might try to convince his parents by saying: "Tomorrow I'm going to Jonah's house, and we're going to play school until his little sister comes back from daycare. Then we'll play house with her and her mom will give us some cookies."
3. **Accounts** almost always begin with, "You know what?" and are initiated by children to tell others about their experiences, thoughts, or feelings.
4. Children use **fictionalized narratives** to describe events or processes that are based in reality, using a story form for the telling.

Once upon a time, _____ there was a _____.
(setting: time & place)   (main character/protagonist)

One day, _____. So s/he _____. Then
(initiating event)   (action)

_____.
(consequence)

The end.

FIGURE 2.1

Elements of a Basic Episode

Language for Learning

Though children in the previous stage of language development have made a tremendous leap in their understanding and use of language structure, content, and use, they have by no means finished the acquisition process, which continues well into adulthood. Paul (2007) calls this stage of language development the L4L period. For children in this period of development, language acquisition comes under the influence of their school experiences. Thus, their language development moves beyond the basics and into reading, writing, more sophisticated figurative language and the complexities of narrative and classroom discourse. This period of language acquisition encompasses the developmental ages of 5 through 10 or 11 years.

Most children entering school exhibit the following language characteristics (Hulit & Howard, 2011):

- Vocabulary consists of virtually all of the basic words of their language.
- The sound system is almost intact.
- Syntactic skills are fairly sophisticated. Children use declaratives easily, transforms declaratives into negatives and interrogatives, have some difficulty with passives, understand and use imperatives.
- Children have become fairly fluent conversationalists. They can use indirect requests, take turns appropriately, repair utterances on request, know the listener needs additional information.

Children from homes in which literacy practices are common come to school with additional language abilities. They know how stories work; they use stories in their own communications; they know the difference between print and nonprint; they have experience playing with language; they know how to use language to display their knowledge; and they know language consists of different, related forms such as speaking and reading, and reading and writing. In addition, these children arrive having experience with the tools and materials related to becoming literate with print. They know how to use books, computers, electronic devices, pens and pencils, paper, and magazines. They know that language can be used as a tool and that, if used properly, can be a powerful way to produce results. This knowledge becomes particularly important as children interact with the various forms of discourse associated with literacy, which we address in some depth in the upcoming discussion of pragmatic development.

The Relationship between Oral Language and Print

Of particular interest during this period of language development is the relationships among oral language, print, and children's progressions in learning to read. Hulit and Howard (2011) made a persuasive argument that oral language development stems from a stronger biological imperative than written language development. They state that, though every group of people throughout history has had a highly developed spoken language, some people have languages with no written form. Nonetheless, current American culture places a high premium on the ability to read and write, putting a certain amount of stress on children to learn these skills during the early school years.

How is oral language development related to learning to read and write? One thing we know is that the best predictor of who will become fluent readers is a home environment in which children are continually and regularly exposed to books and print (Wallach, 2007). Children who are read aloud to before they ever attempt to read for themselves are much more likely to become fluent readers than children who have not been read aloud to prior to entering school (Wells, 1986).

Reading aloud to children provides them with multiple opportunities to participate in filling in predictable parts and to retell their favorite stories from memory as they look at the book again and again. Through these experiences, children become aware that the print on the page is what carries the story, and they begin connecting what they are saying with what they are seeing (Hulit & Howard, 2011). Soon they begin recognizing words and letters, thereby taking an important step toward decoding print.

For most children in grades 1 and 2, when they read something new, they spend most of their attentional energy on decoding. They are engaged in learning the sound–letter correspondences and phonological syntheses that comprise decoding. These decoding processes, called **phonological awareness**, gradually become more natural for children. By the time they leave second grade, most are able to decode automatically enough that they can comprehend the content of what they are reading, and toward the end of fourth grade, most have become fluent enough to use reading as a means to learn.

Since the early 1970s, researchers in reading have become convinced that reading and writing are language-based skills that use visual input solely as an entryway into the language processing system (Catts & Kamhi, 1999). Research shows that visual-perceptual disorders play almost no role in reading disorders and that the primary deficits involved in reading disabilities are linguistic rather than visual (Tynan, 2008).

In addition, researchers have concluded that decoding a text utilizes the same cognitive systems that are used to decode oral language (Paul, 2007). What this means is that comprehending written texts depends on intact and well-developed oral language abilities in semantics, syntax, morphology, and pragmatics, as discussed next.

Semantic Development

Even though the most explosive vocabulary growth takes place during the previous stage of language development, children not only continue to add to their knowledge of new words in this stage—albeit a bit more slowly than before—but also learn how to use words they already know in new ways. Children develop proficiency in choosing among words to get just the right meaning for what they want to say, they can use the same word to mean different things, and they are able to differentiate among words with similar meanings. Many of these changes are related to children's growing competencies in reading, which brings new vocabulary into their experience.

Perhaps most important during this stage of development is children's development of the ability to classify words, at first into categories, then into hierarchical subcategories. A first category might include all the animal words the child knows; later, the category becomes differentiated to include subcategories (e.g., wild animals, tame animals, zoo animals, and those that live in water). Eventually, children develop more and more elaborate classification systems that continue throughout adulthood.

This process of categorizing and subcategorizing words based on their semantic relationships is called **chunking**, which assists children in remembering. Throughout this period of language development, children develop chunking strategies that allow them to sort words on the basis of the semantic roles they fill (Hulit & Howard, 2011).

During this period, children also develop semantic proficiency with shared definitions. Children in previous stages of language development tend to define words based on their own personal experiences with the objects labeled by words. For instance, a child growing up in a rural setting will have a very different conception of a cow than a child who grows up in an urban environment. As these children enter school, however, they encounter definitions of "cow" that transcend their own personal experiences and learn that words can be understood in a communally defined fashion.

Children's definitions of words progress in this period from the single-word definitions that are characteristic of children in the developing language stage to more elaborate definitions. In this stage, children begin to develop the ability to define words by providing details and explanations. This ability is aided by the child's growing proficiency in reading, which often provides the detail and explanation necessary to define words. This process of elaborating definitions continues throughout the lifespan.

Hulit and Howard (2011) discuss children's differentiation of nouns into subcategories during this period of language development. This process includes the following:

- **Common** nouns, or general classes of things, people, places, events, processes
- **Proper** nouns, or specific members of any given class
- **Concrete** nouns, or names of real things
- **Abstract** nouns, or names of ideas, concepts, thoughts
- **Collective** nouns, or names of groups of things
- **Count** nouns, or names of things that can be counted
- **Mass** nouns, or names of things that are conglomerates and cannot be counted

Not all of these differentiations occur at the same time. For instance, the distinction between mass and count nouns remains troublesome for some children throughout this period because each requires a different modifier: "too *few* carrots" is permissible, but "too *little* carrots" is not. And one can say "*many* sheep" but not "*many* milk."

Adverbs begin to appear, though some are easier than others for children at this stage. Hulit and Howard (2011) report that by the time children are in fourth grade, they understand the differences in the adverbs *definitely*, *probably*, and *possibly*. Children learn these adverbs at different times, with *definitely* being the first to appear in their sentences.

Fleshing Out the Pronouns   During this period, children complete their sorting of the English pronoun system (shown in Table 2.4). By the time children reach the end of this stage of development, they have successfully separated the subject pronouns from the object pronouns (Hulit & Howard, 2011):

Subject Pronouns	**Object Pronouns**
I, we, he, she, they	*me, us, him, her, them*

In addition, children will have mastered the reflexive pronouns (e.g., *myself, herself, himself, themselves*). During this period, children learn to recognize pronoun antecedents even when they appear in different sentences than the pronouns. For example, children can successfully interpret sentences such as these: "Joe's brother was badly hurt in an automobile accident. He [Joe] goes to see him [Joe's brother] every day" (Hulit & Howard, 2011, p. 236).

Figurative Language

Earlier we discussed children's emerging awareness that words can mean more than one thing and that different words can be used to describe the same thing. Although some children in the preceding stage of language development are able to recognize the nonliteral use of language, they are unable to use what is called **figurative language**. Children's knowledge of and ability to use figurative language develops primarily during the elementary school years, though it, too, continues to grow throughout the lifespan.

Figurative language includes metaphors, similes, idioms, adages, maxims, proverbs, and the like. In addition, many forms of humor rely on figurative expressions or double-meaning words, as in the example we gave earlier of the Halloween joke involving the skeleton that had no "guts."

A **metaphor** is a figure of speech involving an implied comparison between two dissimilar things. A **simile** is an explicit comparison. The metaphoric expression "He's a trip" implies a comparison between a person's characteristics and a roller-coaster ride or an unpredictable journey. "He's like a roller coaster" uses simile to compare the two directly.

Each cultural group has unique figurative expressions, known as **idioms,** that cannot be understood literally. Idioms present particular difficulty not only to young children but also to adults trying to learn a new language. Even adults within the same language group may encounter difficulty with idioms used in a different geographic region or by a different social group. Children at the beginning of the school-age years continue to use and understand language in a literal fashion. They may understand a few idioms used by their families, but they do not begin decoding the figurative meanings until somewhere around 7 or 8 years of age.

A few years ago, a popular cartoon strip showed a series of idioms used by an adult speaking to another adult while a young child sat listening. The cartoonist showed in thought balloons what the child was thinking, which, of course, was a literal rendering of the adult's story about a friend of theirs who had "hit the skids" and "gone down the tubes" because he had been "thrown out on his ear" by his boss, who thought he was "nothing but trouble." Adults found the strip very funny.

Proverbs, **adages**, and **maxims** are popular sayings thought to be wise renderings of truth. They usually contain relatively unusual syntax, unfamiliar words, or words used in an unfamiliar way (Hulit & Howard, 2011). Although some proverbs may be understandable to children in this period of development, most children do not become adept with them until they reach adolescence. They may be able to parrot what proverbs mean, particularly if they have been taught specific ones, but their understanding at this stage is not anchored in their own experience. For instance, on hearing, "a stitch in time saves nine," children in this stage typically do not understand its meaning as related to taking preventive care to reduce the need for more costly repair later.

Earlier we described children's attempts with **humor** and described the differences between two children, one a 5-year-old and the other a 7-year-old, when they heard and later retold a riddle. Recall that the 5-year-old was able to understand and manipulate the format of the riddle, but he was not able to say why it was funny or to retell it so he could retain the semantic relationships of the original joke. The 7-year-old, however, was able to tell why the joke was funny, and he later retold it almost verbatim to his parents.

The difference between the two boys illustrates the developmental change in children's humor during this period. When they enter this stage, they are manipulating the overall structure of various forms of humor. By the time most children are 7 or 8, they have become proficient enough with figurative language so they can combine it with humor formats to produce some funny jokes based mostly on phonological similarities between words, as in the following example:

"What do you get when you put a bunch of ducks into a box?"
"I don't know. What?"
"A box of quackers."

Somewhere after age 9, children hone their skills with jokes involving multiple meanings of words, as in this example from Hulit and Howard (2011): "What's big and white, has four wheels, and *flies*? A garbage truck!" (p. 230). Children continue to develop competence with humor throughout this period and well into the next—a topic to which we return when we discuss language development during adolescence.

Syntactic Development

During this stage of language development, children expand on the forms they have learned already, and they figure out some of the more difficult syntactic constructions.

Expanding Noun and Verb Phrases   During the school years, children use more elaborate noun and verb phrases, adding more adjectives and adverbs, including prepositional phrases and subordinate clauses. Children figure out the exceptions to rules for marking tense and plurality, and they begin to include the articles *a*, *an*, and *the*. They learn the rules for ordering adjectives (e.g., "big, white house," not "white, big house").

Figuring Out Passive Sentences Passive sentences remain difficult for children throughout this period, though by the end of it most children are using both **reversible passives** and **nonreversible passives**. Nonreversible passives are sentences in which meaning dictates that only one order is possible: "The doll was left by the child" is nonreversible because "The child was left by the doll" doesn't make sense. A reversible passive, in contrast, makes sense to say either way: "The child was hit by the ball" can just easily be said "The ball was hit by the child," though the meaning changes considerably. Early in this period, children are more likely to use reversible passives if they use them at all, though not until the end of this stage do children produce both forms consistently.

Learning Exceptions to the Rules As noted earlier, in acquiring language, children learn the most general rules first, followed later by exceptions to the rules. One particularly intriguing example that illustrates this process is described by Hulit and Howard (2005). They recounted the work of Carol Chomsky (1969), who studied children learning exceptions to the **principle of minimal distance**. This is a general rule governing which noun in a sentence serves as subject or subordinate clause, in which the preceding noun closest to the verb serves as the subject. For instance, in the sentence "The dog ate the bone," the noun "the dog" immediately precedes the verb "ate" and thus serves as the subject of the sentence. The principle becomes more complicated with certain verbs, especially when they are used as infinitives.

Chomsky (1969) showed that for three verbs—*ask*, *promise*, and *tell*— the principle of minimal distance can be violated. Children in this stage of language development have little difficulty finding the subject of the infinitive with *tell* because it usually adheres to the principle, as in the sentence, "Don told Carlos to hit the ball." "Carlos" is closer to the infinitive *to hit* than "Don" and serves as subject.

Children's mastery of sentences including infinitival forms of *promise* takes a bit longer, however, because it usually violates the principle. Consider the sentence, "Don promised Carlos to play ball." Though "Carlos" is closer to the infinitive, "Don" serves as the subject and thus violates the principle.

More difficult still is learning how to deal with *ask*, which sometimes adheres to the principle and sometimes violates the principle. In the sentence, "Don asked Carlos to play ball," "Carlos" is closer than "Don" to the infinitive, yet "Don" serves as the subject of the sentence, violating the principle. But in the sentence, "Don asked Carlos when to play ball," the principle does not work because the subject is "Don." It is not surprising that Chomsky (1969) found that children can correctly interpret *tell* and *promise* by age 9, but that they do not master *ask* until they are closer to age 10.

Embedding According to Hulit and Howard (2011), by the time children enter this stage of development, they are embedding infinitive phrases, object complements, and relative clauses that modify noun phrases in the object position but not in the subject position. Early work by Menyuk (1971) showed that at around age 7, children begin embedding in the subject position or in the middle of a sentence, sometimes appropriately deleting the relative pronoun. For example, a child at this age might say, "I have a book you'll like," or, "The boy who scored the point is her brother."

Children at this age, however, continue to base their understandings of embedded sentences on word order or semantic roles rather than their grammatical knowledge. Thus, when they hear a sentence such as, "The little kid the big kid hit went home," they might conclude the big kid went home. By the time they reach the end of this stage, though, they are much more able to rely on their grammatical knowledge of sentences to interpret potentially confusing embeddings.

Conjoining   Children enter their school years able to conjoin sentences using *and*, and most children acquire mastery over the other conjunctions during this stage of development. For instance, Menyuk (1969) studied children's acquisition of four types of conjunctions during this period:

1. Conditionals (e.g., *if*)
2. Causals (e.g., *because, therefore*)
3. Disjunctives (e.g., *but, or, therefore*)
4. Temporal (e.g., *before, after, when, then*)

In general, children acquire first those conjunctions that express relationships within their cognitive grasp (Menyuk, 1969). For instance, early in this period children can use causals that follow a logical order, such as cause preceding effect, as in, "The bus was late, *so* I was late." A bit later, as children learn about the concept of *contrast*, they begin using the disjunctive *but*, as in, "The bus was late, *but* I got home on time." As their cognitive understanding of conditionality develops, so, too, does their use of conjoining with the conditional *if*, as in, "I can go *if* I've finished my homework."

The conjunctions that express even more complicated relationships emerge somewhat later in this period, as, for instance, causals that do not follow a logical cause–effect order. In the sentence "I got locked out *because* I lost my key," the cause, losing the key, appears *after* the effect, getting locked out, making this construction more troublesome for children until they are nearer to age 10 or 11. Prior to mastering these "illogical" sequences, children's sentences may reflect their struggle to learn how to express these more complex relationships: "I lost my key *because* I got locked out."

Morphological Development

The three most significant morphological advances during this period of development are children's learning how to produce gerunds, how to produce the **agentive forms** of common verbs, and to produce the **adverb forms** of common adjectives by adding the bound morpheme *-ly* (Hulit & Howard, 2011).

Gerunds   During this stage, children learn how to make nouns from verbs by adding *-ing*, as in *paint > painting*.

Agentive Forms   By around age 7, children are adding the bound morpheme *-er* to verbs to identify the person performing the actions of the verb, as in *sing > singer*. Of course, the exceptions to this rule prove a bit difficult for a time, though by the end of this period, children no longer are adding *-er* to every verb to product agentives: *fish > fisher*, or *type > typer*.

Adverb Forms   By the time children are approximately age 7, they begin adding *-ly* to adjectives to produce adverbs, like, *careful > carefully*. Again, the exceptions develop a bit later but are virtually mastered by the end of this period. In between, children sometimes produce forms such as *fast > fastly*. In addition, some adverbs always function as adverbs and do not use the *-ly* form: *often, now, again* (Hulit & Howard, 2005), posing special cases for children to learn once they have acquired the basic "add *-ly*" rule.

Pragmatic Development

Regardless of the linguistic environment from which children arrive at school, they all face the same developmental hurdle of moving from using language as a primarily oral form to using language in the ways that our public school culture considers literate. At the same time, their oral conversational abilities continue to evolve. Children entering elementary school encounter types of discourse other than conversation and narrative. As children move farther toward the literate end of the continuum, they encounter various other forms of discourse, called **discourse genres**, each carrying its own set of stated and unstated usage rules.

Discourse is what Rogers (2004) called "ways of being in the world" (p. 5). From this perspective, discourse can be thought of as a sort of identity kit complete with the appropriate costume and instructions about how to talk, act, and write in ways that others will recognize. We are trained into discourses by enculturation into social practices, including what people say and how they say it.

It stands to reason that children's experiences with any particular discourse will render it familiar to them, as well as enhance their ability to engage successfully in it. Children whose families already use some of the types of discourse typical of the classroom are more likely to find school-based discourses familiar, customary, and unobtrusive. Children encountering these discourses for the first time, however, may find them confusing and difficult. The types of discourse most typical of the classroom, along with their characteristics, are discussed later in the chapter.

Conversational Competence   Most children enter school with some proficiency in oral language and conversation. Earlier, we discussed children's conversational competence and reported on several aspects, including their ability to take turns, maintain topics over turns, and provide adequate topic information for their listeners or repair utterances that do not contain enough information in the first place. What happens during the school years is that children become much better conversationalists on almost all fronts.

Children become more adept at sustaining topics, largely because they come to understand that older listeners sustain a topic longer if the topic is relevant or timely. They maintain a topic by adding more information rather than repeating what their conversational partner has said—the strategy children use in the preceding developing language stage. Children learn how to move in small increments from topic to topic so each shift is seen as related to what was talked about before. And by the time children reach the end of this period, they are able to discuss abstract topics (Hulit & Howard, 2011).

Children in this stage develop more finely tuned strategies for responding to a partner's request for clarification or repair. A younger child might provide a crude repair or give up, but children in this stage use the request itself as a guide for what to include in the repair. They use this request for repair or clarification to determine why and where the breakdown occurred and to respond accordingly (Hulit & Howard, 2011).

One of the more interesting aspects of pragmatic development during the school years is children's learning about understanding and using indirect requests. We already have pointed out that children in the developing language stage have begun the process of becoming indirect in their conversations, but their abilities are not well developed. During the school years, children's abilities increase dramatically. By the time children are around age 7, they are fairly proficient in producing indirect requests, and by the time they are 8, they understand the importance of politeness as a means of getting what they want (Hulit & Howard, 2011). After age 8, children's indirect requests are more finely tuned to specific listeners; that is, they modify their requests depending on their perceptions of what will work for each listener.

The Oral-to-Literate Shift   One of the most important language learning accomplishments that children achieve during their elementary school years is their shift from using language that is primarily oral to using language that is primarily literate, a concept described in detail by Westby (1991). Westby showed that literate language differs from oral language in terms of function, topic, and structure. Table 2.5 summarizes the major differences between the oral language children are using when they enter school and the literate language they encounter in the school environment.

At the beginning of this discussion about the language of learning, we pointed out that some home environments prepare children better than others for making this oral-to-literate shift. Children whose homes have already provided them with ongoing attention to language and exposure to print in its diverse forms are likely to be ready for interaction with literate language forms. In addition, children who are familiar with the linear, topic-centered narratives that are most predominant in schools bring an additional advantage.

TABLE 2.5
Differences between Oral and Literate Language

Function	Topic	Structure
Literate language style		
To regulate social interactions	Everyday objects and events	High-frequency words
To request objects and actions	Here and now	Repetitive, predictable, redundant
To communicate face-to-face with few people	Topics flow according to participants' desires	syntax and content
To share information about concrete events and objects	Meaning is contextually grounded	Pronouns, slang, jargon, shared meanings
		Cohesion based on intonation patterns
Oral language style		
To regulate thinking	Abstract or unfamiliar objects and events	Low-frequency words
To reflect and request information	There and then	Concise syntax and content
To communicate over time and distance	Discourse centers on a preselected topic	Specific, abstract vocabulary
To transmit information to large numbers of people	Meaning arises from inferences and from textually-defined information	Cohesion based on vocabulary and linguistic devices
To build abstract theories and discuss abstract ideas		

Source: Adapted from "Learning to Talk—Talking to Learn: Oral-Literate Language Differences," by C. Westby, in *Communication Skills and Classroom Success: Assessment and Therapy Methodologies for Language- and Learing-Disabled Children,* edited by C. S. Simon, 1991, Eau Claire, WI: Thinking Publications.

Another aspect of literate language that children must learn is the various **narrative genres**. Miller, Gillam, and Peña (2001) described six narrative genres that children are likely to encounter:

1. Structured play, in which a child or children play out a story of their own devising
2. Wordless books, which tell a story through visual images alone
3. Comic books, which provide a frame-by-frame unfolding of the story through both print and visual imagery, which supplies a nonprint layer of the story
4. Books on video or DVD, which provide one interpretation of the story through filmed sequences
5. Folk tales, which typically follow a traditional, linear order of story grammar elements
6. Trade books, in which all but the simplest contain multiple associated or embedded episodes

By the time children enter school, most will have had numerous experiences with these six genres. Developmentally, they offer a path from children's first attempts at oral storytelling to their increasing interactions with the literate language of schools.

Narrative Development

As children enter school, they begin telling stories that cannot yet be called true narratives because their stories do not yet include a complete episode. Thus, as children enter school, their stories typically contain a setting and a **basic episode,** which must include

■ an initiating event,
■ an attempt, and
■ a consequence.

True narratives emerge when children's stories contain a central theme, character, and plot and are considered to be complete by the adult standards of storytelling. The character is motivated to act, and events are sequenced logically.

At this point, children's narrative ability allows them to produce true narratives: setting and a **complete episode**, which includes the components of a basic episode plus (Miller et al., 2001)

■ an internal response—the character's feelings or intentions,
■ a plan—information about what the main character plans to do and why, and
■ a reaction or ending—information about the main character's reaction to the consequence.

The format for a complete episode is shown in Figure 2.2.

True narratives generally emerge in normally developing children sometime between 5 and 7 years of age.

Once upon a time, _____ there was a _____ . One
(setting: time & place)   (main character/protagonist)

day, _____ . (The main character) felt _____
(initiating event)   (internal response)

_____ , so s/he decided to _____
(plan)

_____ . S/he _____ . Finally, _____
(action)   (consequence)

_____ . This made (the main character) feel _____
(reaction/ending)

_____ .

The end.

Elements of a Complete Episode

The ability to produce true narratives, or stories with complete episodes, is viewed by Westby (1991) as a bridge between the oral language with which children are familiar and the literate language of schools, classrooms, and books. The ability to understand and produce topic-centered narratives has been shown to be an excellent predictor of school success (Bishop & Edmundson, 1987; Feagans & Applebaum, 1986; Kaderavek & Sulzby, 2000).

By the time most children reach the age of 7, their stories contain plots, albeit undeveloped ones. The plots that children prefer during this time center on clearly defined goals, as opposed to goals that are understated or unclear. For instance, most 7-year-olds would prefer telling (or hearing) a story about a child who goes looking for a treasure over a story about a child who watches birds sing in the backyard.

Sometime after 8 years of age, however, children begin to create stories with the following characteristics, which are more typical of adult narratives (Hulit & Howard, 2011):

- Clearly defined plots
- Problems that are clearly identified and resolved
- Details that are important but not superfluous
- Carefully established time and place settings
- Information about characters' feelings, thoughts, and motives

Learning New Discourse Forms

Classroom Discourse Developmentally, children usually enter school having some experience both with conversational discourse and with narratives, either spoken, written, or both. Once in school, they must quickly learn how to engage in the discourse of the classroom, some of which the teacher never verbalizes. This implicit discourse, which Cazden (1988) called the "hidden curriculum," follows what she characterized as the **Initiation-Response-Evaluation (IRE)** format: The teacher <u>I</u>nitiates a topic, a student <u>R</u>esponds, and then the teacher <u>E</u>valuates the student's response. For instance:

T: What is today's date?
S: February 4th
T: That's right. Good job.

As Paul (2007) points out, students who fail to adhere to the rules of this discourse are often perceived by teachers as rude or inconsiderate, and students to whom this discourse is unfamiliar often believe that their teachers are picking on them.

During the elementary school years, children progress from understanding and using classroom discourse to more abstract forms of discourse, including expository and argumentative or persuasive discourse.

Expository Discourse Expository discourse is, by definition, explanatory. Its primary purpose is to explain and/or describe something. Unlike narrative, however, expository discourse utilizes highly decontextualized language, as well as a structure that is quite different from the story grammar characteristic of narrative. As shown in Table 2.6, most expository discourse, whether oral or printed, follows the same format: a series of paragraphs, each containing a topic sentence that states the main purpose of each paragraph, followed by a set of facts or descriptions, and culminating in a sentence summarizing the paragraph.

More complicated expository texts are organized in sections composed of an introductory paragraph that serves as the topic paragraph for the section, a set of paragraphs supporting the main point (each adhering to the topic sentence-set of facts-summary arrangement), and culminating in a summary paragraph. The nested organizational scheme is somewhat more difficult for students to learn and typically emerges toward the end of the school-age period.

Argumentative or Persuasive Discourse Argumentative or persuasive discourse, as you can see in Table 2.6, uses even more abstract and complicated structures than expository text. Because of this, few students in the school-age years develop much proficiency with this form of discourse. Some, however, become moderately proficient in using oral forms of argument or persuasion, though their attempts usually contain only part of the format required for successful argument or persuasion (see Table 2.6).

The "Metas"

During the school-age period of language development, children become much more proficient with figurative language and the ability to reflect on and talk about language, referred to as **metalinguistic ability**. At the same time, they are developing competence in reflecting on and talking about how language is used, **metapragmatic ability**, and in reflecting on and talking about their own thinking and reasoning skills, **metacognitive ability**.

Metalinguistic Ability Elementary schooling presents a variety of metalinguistic challenges to students: defining words; identifying homonyms, antonyms, and synonyms; recognizing homophones and resulting semantic ambiguities; identifying syntactic and morphological elements in sentences; diagramming sentences; and matching sounds to letters.

Most children by age 8 have developed some competence in all of these metalinguistic skills. Developmentally, however, some children do not develop metalinguistic abilities until they are somewhat older, making the process of learning to read and write more difficult. For children who struggle with phonological awareness, or recognizing the sounds in words, the reading process can be agonizing and will require creative and plentiful attention from teachers.

Metapragmatic Ability We talked earlier about children's emerging competence as conversational partners. We discussed how, by the time children enter school, most will have developed some awareness of their listeners' perspective and prior knowledge so they can provide adequate information, either at first or when asked for clarification.

TABLE 2.6

Types and Characteristics of Classroom Discourse

Classroom Discourse: Lecture and Giving Directions	Classroom Narratives: Story-Based	Expository: Explanation and Description	Argumentative/Persuasive
Teacher chooses topic Teacher takes most of the turns Teacher determines: ■ whether student talks ■ when student talks ■ how long student talks ■ when student should relinquish a turn ■ if student's response is correct Follows IRE format: ■ Teacher initiates the topic ■ Student responds ■ Teacher evaluates student's response Language often decontextualized Requires metalinguistic skills	Follows a story grammar Contains settings, characters, and episodes Uses predictable language and form Uses highly contextualized language Sequence = plot-driven Information familiar to student	Decontextualized language: ■ states facts ■ states hypotheses ■ asks questions ■ draws conclusions ■ interprets ■ classifies ■ synthesizes ■ summarizes ■ hierarchic organization Paragraph format: ■ topic sentence stating main idea ■ clincher sentence summarizing main idea Abstract cause–effect Enumerative Comparison–contrast Sequence = logical Information new to student Requires metalinguistic skills	Takes others' perspectives and viewpoints Puts forward a fact or statement as proof or evidence Expresses disagreement Uses a set of statements so one follows logically as a conclusion from the others Formats (order can be reversed): 1. ■ a statement of fact ■ a set of supports for the fact Or ■ a set of supports for a fact ■ a statement of fact derived from the supports 2. ■ a statement of belief ■ a set of reasons that the belief is "true" Or ■ a set of reasons that a belief is "true" ■ a statement of belief Requires skill with the "metas"

Once they enter school, most children become even more adept at these **metapragmatic strategies**. For instance, somewhere between ages 5 and 8, most children will be able to recognize the different rules governing conversations in which the participants politely differ versus conversations in which the participants engage in an argument. As children become more competent with these metapragmatic strategies, they are better able to think about how to say things on reflection of, among others:

- varying social contexts,
- who has more authority in any given conversation,
- the degree of formality surrounding any given conversation,
- relative ages of the conversational participants,
- role of cultural differences among participants,
- one's own and others' conversational breakdowns,
- initiating and maintaining conversational turns,
- when and how to interrupt, and
- how to manage others' interruptions.

Another metapragmatic ability that emerges in this developmental period is that children begin decoding the rules governing classroom discourse, shown in Figure 2.3. Developing the ability to understand and engage in classroom discourse provides one of the key competencies necessary for success in the classroom. Children who develop this competency have the ability to attend to, process, and respond to the

---

Rule 1. Teachers mostly talk and students mostly listen—except when teachers grant permission to talk.

Rule 2. Teachers give cues about when to listen closely.

Rule 3. Teachers convey content about things and procedures about how to do things.

Rule 4. Teacher talk becomes more complex in the upper grades.

Rule 5. Teachers ask questions and expect specific responses.

Rule 6. Teachers give hints about what is correct and what is important to them.

Rule 7. Student talk is brief and to the point.

Rule 8. Students ask few questions and keep them short.

Rule 9. Students talk to teachers, not to other students.

Rule 10. Students make few spontaneous comments—and only about the process or content of the lesson.

Source: From "Formal Classroom Lessons: New Perspectives on a Familiar Discourse Event," by J. M. Sturm & N.W. Nelson, 1997, *Language Speech and Hearing Services in Schools, 28,* pp. 255–273. Copyright 1997 by American Speech–Language–Hearing Association. Reprinted with permission.

FIGURE 2.3

10 Rules Governing Classroom Discourse

various patterns of classroom discourse practiced by different teachers and in different classrooms (Nelson, 2009).

Metacognitive Ability   During the L4L stage of development, the demands of the classroom place increasing responsibility on children to reflect on and assess their own cognitive processes. This reflective process, called **metacognition**, has two major categories: **comprehension monitoring** and **organizational and learning strategies** (Paul, 2007).

Comprehension monitoring refers to children's emerging ability to recognize when they do and do not understand something (e.g., a teacher's instruction, a sentence in a book, a peer's oral story). Children between ages roughly 5 and 8 usually have the ability to recognize when they do not understand, and after age 8 they begin to develop strategies to remedy their lack of understanding. For instance, 5- to 8-year-olds, upon recognizing that they do not understand what the teacher has just said, may, for instance, simply sit passively; try to do *something*, even though it is unclear just what; vocalize that they do not understand; or ask a peer. After age 8, children begin to exhibit compensatory strategies: asking themselves what was just said; looking for contextual clues; reasoning what must be coming next from what has been going on; or looking to see if the teacher wrote the instruction on the board, a handout, or an overhead projection.

Organizational and learning strategies refer to the methods children use to organize themselves for learning. For instance, Wallach (2007) described how school-age children develop an **anticipatory** or **inferential set** when processing new information. That is, children in this period of development learn how to invoke what they already know about a topic in anticipation of learning something new about it, perhaps by asking themselves questions such as: "What do I already know about this?" or, "What do I need to ask to understand this?" Then they can make inferences from their prior knowledge to the new information, for example: "We're talking about Canada. I know Winnipeg is a city in Canada and it's cold there. Does that mean it's cold in Toronto, too?"

Writing

Prior to entering school, children exposed to what are called the materials and tools associated with print and its electronic cousins—such as paper, pencils, computers, electronic devices, books, magazines, lists, and notes—produce scribbles and marks that form the foundations of "real" writing. Once children learn the names of the letters, they try to replicate these letter forms. The first word that most children learn to write is their own name, followed by the names of the people in their family. On entering school, many children have already developed **graphophoneme awareness**, which means that they are associating letters of the alphabet and the sounds these letters most often represent (Hulit & Howard, 2011).

Once in school, children's writing usually develops through teacher-directed instruction. Regardless of the method used to teach writing, children's writing during this stage of development depends almost entirely on their oral language development, as well as on their burgeoning reading skills. In the beginning stages of learning to write, children's writing is dramatically *less* well-developed than their oral language abilities.

Until around fourth grade, the writing that most children produce is either in response to an assignment, or it is for the child's own amusement. Beginning somewhere around fourth grade, most children are asked to extend their writing abilities to write for other people. Fluent readers leaving elementary school produce writing that often is more complex than their oral language.

Adolescent Language/Advanced Language

For most students, adolescence marks the beginning of the transition between a childhood grounded in the family and an adulthood independent from the family. Adolescence is usually characterized by a reduction in reliance on the family, an increase in peer interaction, and a move toward nonschool contexts such as music, magazines, movies, and the internet. As expected, language development during adolescence builds on what children have already learned about language and its various forms, contexts, and styles. Paul (2007) believed that the language skills normal adolescents learn are:

- language for more socially intensive interactions,
- language at the literate end of the oral–literate continuum, and
- language abilities related to critical thinking.

Semantics

Not surprisingly, the vocabulary acquired by adolescents in school reflects the literate language forms they are encountering in their classrooms and, for some, their homes. According to Paul (2007), the most common include:

- advanced adverbial conjunct (e.g., *similarly, moreover, nonetheless, consequently*);
- adverbs of likelihood (e.g., *definitely, possibly*) and magnitude (e.g., *considerably*);
- precise and technical terms related to curriculum (e.g., *photon, coordinate, summative*);
- specific verb types, such as presuppositional (*regret*), metalinguistic (*predict, infer*), and metacognitive (*hypothesize, conclude*);
- multiple-meaning words (e.g., "Her *pitch* was perfect" cf. "The *pitch* of the roof was steep"; "He wanted to *palm* the coin" cf. "He wanted the *palm* plant");
- multiple-function words (e.g., *hard* stone, *hard* water, *hard* feelings)

In addition to enlarging their vocabularies, adolescents elaborate and expand on the meanings of words they already know (e.g., "She's a *cool* one," cf. "The air was *cool*"). They begin to understand the relationships among words related by derivation (*statistics, statistician*), meaning (antonyms, e.g., *reluctant*, cf. *eager*; synonyms, e.g., *couch,* cf. *sofa*); or sound (homonyms, e.g., *tier* cf. *tear*) (Paul, 2007).

During adolescence, students' word definitions mature considerably. Where they used simple, often one-word definitions before, now, according to Paul (2007), they increasingly provide what are called **Aristotelian** definitions: a superordinate term and a description with one or more characteristics. For instance, a *decree* is an administrative act (superordinate term) applying or interpreting aspects of law (description of characteristics).

Syntax

In adolescence, sentence growth occurs both within and between sentences. Adolescents produce longer sentences for specific purposes, such as narration, persuasion, or writing (Paul, 2007), and they use more (though not necessarily different types of) morphosyntactic markers—interrogatives, negatives, verb tense markers—than younger children (Reed, Griffith, & Rasmussen, 1998).

In addition to more coordinate and subordinate clauses, adolescents begin to produce low-frequency sentence structures characteristic of literate language (Paul, 2007). Wallach and Miller (1988) provide an example of how adolescents become adept at specifying noun or noun phrase referents for listeners or readers so they will understand the pronouns used later to refer to those nouns or noun phrases:

> It was late afternoon and Jane was getting ready to go to swim practice. *She* (refers to *Jane*) had reminded herself the night before to bring her new yellow swim suit to school so that she could wear *it* (refers to the swim suit) to practice. *She* (Jane) looked in her bag, but *she* (Jane) couldn't find *it* (the suit). *She* (Jane) looked all over the house, but *she* (Jane) still couldn't find *it* (the suit). Finally, *she* (Jane) threw *her* (Jane's) old red suit into *her* (Jane's) bag. *It* (the red suit) would have to do for today.

Pragmatics

By the time most children begin adolescence, they are skilled conversationalists who understand their listeners' needs, provide adequate background information for listeners, repair conversational breakdowns appropriately, and request clarification when they do not understand what someone is saying. They know how to initiate and maintain turns, how to interrupt appropriately (and sometimes inappropriately!), and how to yield turns according to the social context of the conversation. The most striking developments in pragmatics involve adolescents' increased abilities with figurative language and in negotiating the diverse discourses they encounter both in and out of school.

Figurative Language   Most teenagers are able to use some figurative language forms, such as puns and sarcasm (Paul, 2007). Adolescents' ability to comprehend metaphors improves considerably, as does their skill with similes and idioms:

Metaphor: "Her brain *is a supercomputer*."
Simile: "He's *like a dancer* on the court."
Idiom: "*It was raining cats and dogs*."

In addition to becoming skilled with metaphors, similes, and idioms, teenagers take great delight in using these to pester adults. Here is an example from author Miller's experience:

> A group of junior high school girls had developed a strongly expressed dislike for their music teacher, who, in their estimation, was clearly unfriendly, curt, and "snippy" in her communications with her students. If the teacher did not give precise instructions, the girls took advantage, for instance standing together unless the teacher had expressly forbidden them to do so. As a result, the teacher constantly reminded the girls to do *exactly* what she told them to do.
>
> Each time the teacher told them to do *exactly* what she said, the girls followed her instructions explicitly. If she told them to stand up straight, they exaggerated how they were standing. If she told them to sing more loudly, they practically shouted. And if she told them to sing more quietly, they whispered. And one day, exasperated, when she told them to "keep your eyes on the book," they each pretended to snap their eyes out of their heads and plop them in their books. Of course, the teacher was not amused, but the incident delighted the girls, who were heroines to their admiring classmates.

Adolescents derive great pleasure from playing with idioms and other humorous forms of language and also with the double meanings inherent in polite forms. Politeness generally follows a set of rules about relevance, brevity, reduction of ambiguity, and softening direct requests. When an unwitting adult uses a softened polite form, for instance, a typical teenage response is to take the statement literally, as in the following example (which also involves an idiom):

> A teenage girl was visiting family friends of her mother. The girl had been staying with the family for several days and had quickly deduced their forms of humor and the ways they enjoyed playing with language. She and the father had developed a warm linguistic bantering in which each tried to stump the other by using unusual words or making puns.
>
> Dinnertime was particularly lively, involving joke-telling, punning, and good-natured ribbing. One evening during dinner, as everyone was talking and eating, the father asked the girl to "Give me another handful of those potatoes, would you?" The girl quickly scooped up a mound of potatoes from the bowl and deposited it in his hand. Both laughed uproariously, and he reported later that, from that moment, he took the girl more seriously as an adult.

Slang, another form of figurative language, punctuates teenage language. In-group slang changes not only generationally but also with each new music group, music video, and internet chat room or Twitter conversation. Teenagers' capacity to apprehend how slang works and how to engage in it plays a major role in how peers perceive and accept them. Paul (2007) pointed out that, in adolescence, talk itself is the "major medium of social interaction" (p. 502). For teenagers, talking is a critical social tool. Friendships are negotiated through conversation, which serves as the medium for sharing intimacies and experiences (Raffaelli & Duckett, 1989). Being able to converse using the latest slang is, for adolescents, virtually a requirement for successful social participation.

School Discourses   By adolescence, most students will have had multiple experiences with classroom discourse as practiced by a variety of teachers and as manifested through diverse expository texts. In addition, teenagers will have practiced writing their own narratives and expository pieces. Once they enter middle school or junior high school, they encounter demands to both understand and produce more extensive forms of expository, argumentative, and persuasive discourse, all of which require heightened metacognitive, metapragmatic, and metalinguistic abilities (Paul, 2007).

The "Metas"

During adolescence, students' success in school depends to a large extent on their metacognitive, metalinguistic, and metapragmatic abilities. The structure of schooling for teenagers requires strength in **metacognition**, students' ability to reflect on their own understanding and comprehension of material, as well as their skill in developing and utilizing effective and efficient organizational and learning strategies. The nature of secondary education is built around students who are independent learners, responsible for their own success or failure. Of course, most schools also provide supports and scaffolds for students who are experiencing difficulties or failures, but, in the main, students whose metacognitive abilities are well developed are likely to negotiate the secondary school system successfully.

Teenagers develop a diverse set of verbal-reasoning and critical-thinking skills, largely as a consequence of their evolving cognitive abilities (Nippold, 1998). Among the abilities to emerge during adolescence are the following:

- Analogical or inductive reasoning, as in "Sweet is to sugar as sour is to lemon."
- Syllogistic or deductive reasoning, as in "A mecrin is larger than a therin. A therin is larger than a sorfet. Which is worth more—a sorfet, a therin, or a mecrin?"

To meet the demands of the curriculum during adolescence, teenagers must develop more sophisticated comprehension-monitoring strategies and strategies for organizing themselves for learning. For comprehension, this means that adolescents must be able to figure out which parts of any discourse they do not understand and be able to call on already-developed processes for getting the information they need in order to comprehend. As they practice comprehension monitoring, they typically create more sophisticated blueprints that increase efficiency and extend across discourses.

The organizational strategies that adolescents develop also capitalize on already existing schemes. To learn more difficult types of discourse, such as argumentative or persuasive texts, teenagers create more abstract processes, such as outlining logical hierarchies, devising a numerical system for organizing related topics and supporting information, color-coded highlighting to indicate each superordinate and its nested characteristics with a unique color, or creating visual diagrams that depict how ideas are related.

The very act of engaging in various types of discourse, both oral and print-based, carries significant metapragmatic requirements. Again, writing draws on a variety of metapragmatic processes: It involves knowing the purpose of one's writing; determining one's audience in order to know what and how much to say; choosing a discourse genre to match audience need as well as the goal, or purpose, of the piece; and deciding exactly how to construct one's sentences, again to match discourse type and audience need.

Metapragmatic abilities also play an important role in teenagers' social interactions and friendships. Metapragmatic skill underlies many of the conversations that teenagers have with each other, particularly their understanding of how and when to use slang, how to change the way they talk in different social contexts, understanding idiomatic expressions (or finding out what these expressions mean without seeming "stupid"), and how to use humor appropriately as a social currency.

These metapragmatic abilities become more and more necessary as adolescents navigate the curricular requirements of school. For instance, Paul (2007) identified the following curriculum demands typically encountered by teenagers:

- Dealing with multiple teaching and communication styles
- Meeting diverse sets of classroom rules
- Comprehending advanced, decontextualized types of discourse
- Increasing the amount of work produced
- Using "working memory" for reasoning and processing information
- Focusing for longer periods of time and more intensely
- Working independently in class and on homework
- Taking notes from spoken discourse
- Expressing through writing in various discourse types (narratives, essays, and exposition)
- Using higher order thinking (logical and critical) to evaluate information

A large part of school during adolescence hinges on students' metalinguistic knowledge: analyzing, reorganizing, synthesizing, and talking about both oral and printed language. Writing imposes an especially heavy metalinguistic load because it cannot be done without reflecting on and manipulating language. Metalinguistic processing is a given in secondary school; students who have poorly developed metalinguistic abilities suffer because they often do not understand what is required of them. Again, students whose metalinguistic abilities are well developed usually do succeed in the secondary curriculum.

The most typical metalinguistic abilities adolescents develop are:

- paraphrasing;
- summarizing;
- taking notes;
- defining words;
- recognizing syntactic, semantic, or morphological errors in oral or print form;
- recognizing and comprehending ambiguous sentences;
- understanding and using figurative language forms;
- using diverse literate styles in writing; and
- comprehending satire.

Like many other aspects of language, metalinguistic ability continues to develop throughout adolescence and into adulthood. It accounts for our abilities to attribute beauty to language, and to recognize its aesthetic qualities.

In addition, being metalinguistically capable affords us numerous opportunities for laughter. We are reminded of a story involving a young girl, probably 4 or 5 years old, her teenage sister, and their father. While the girls and their father were waiting in line at a delicatessen, they were conversing in Croatian. The man behind them in line, hearing them, remarked in English that he was unfamiliar with the language they were speaking. The girls' father told him that it was Croatian and proudly explained that his younger daughter could speak both English and Croatian, and that, like him and his wife, his older daughter could speak English, Croatian, and Russian. They talked a bit more about the advantages of being bilingual and trilingual. The man turned to the little girl and asked her if she was bilingual or trilingual. She told him she was bilingual. The man then asked her what people were who spoke only one language. But before she could respond, her older sister replied, "American."

Writing

If they are relatively fluent readers, by the time most students reach adolescence, reading and writing have become reciprocal processes. Because language is common to both, reading and writing are closely related for those who read fluently. Both require using language to compose meaning. Reading uses language to compose meaning *from* text, whereas writing uses language to compose meaning *into* text (Butler & Turbill, 1987, p. 11). Consequently, the more experience one has had with reading, the more that person knows about writing. Conversely, the more a person writes, the more that person will know about reading.

Language, therefore, is the common tool used in both reading and writing to construct meaning. Fluent readers build meaning not by sampling every detail (phonetic decoding) but, instead, by sampling only those bits of information that are necessary to derive meaning. Of course, the more unfamiliar the material, the more details we must sample to glean the necessary meaning. With more familiar content or type of discourse, we typically sample many fewer details in our quest to derive meaning.

Writing, in contrast, begins the other way around, with meaning. The writer's task is to render meaning(s) into language that best represents those ideas. To build the best representation, the writer must know who will be reading the material (i.e., who the audience is) to be able to match the type of discourse and literary style with that audience.

For fluent readers, adolescent writing usually demonstrates tremendous growth, most often in response to the school assignments given to teenagers. During adolescence, students become more proficient both technically with the mechanics of writing (syntax, vocabulary, spelling) and with different literary styles (Hulit & Howard, 2011). In addition, adolescents usually learn how to organize and develop their ideas in writing and to use writing to influence others (Nold, 1981).

Adolescents are required to produce various types of writing in school, identified by Scott and Erwin (1992):

- Personal experience narratives, such as when asked to describe the best thing they've ever done
- Story retelling, such as book reports
- Factual retelling, as when students are asked to summarize a passage of text
- Fiction or guided stories, for instance, in response to being asked to write a fairy tale or myth
- Expositions, as when asked to explain how to do something
- Descriptions, such as a description of a planet
- Reports, such as a recapitulation of something they experienced, such as a concert
- Persuasive pieces, such as an essay telling why their peers should vote for a particular candidate in an election
- Business letters
- Friendly letters

When producing these various types of writing, adolescents usually engage in three major processes: **planning**, **sentence generation**, and **revision** (Hayes & Flower, 1987). The planning process involves identifying the goal or purpose of the writing. Sentence generation entails selecting syntactic structures and vocabulary to match the selected discourse genre and target audience. During adolescence, students usually develop a set of sentence types and vocabularies from which to choose. Finally, revision includes reviewing and critiquing what has been written to refine or reorganize the piece, perhaps through several drafts. Not surprisingly, the best writers tend to lean heavily on the planning and revision processes.

▌Summary

Children's acquisition of language occurs in developmental stages. One of the early models was Roger Brown's Stages I–V, based on mean length of children's utterances from first word through approximately age 5. More recent models incorporate children's development past age 5 and include school-age children and adolescents.

At the beginning of the *prelinguistic period,* children's language consists primarily of babbling and, somewhat later, vocalizations accompanied by nonverbal body and facial gestures, signaling a limited range of communicative intentions. Children during this stage acquire the ability to mutually attend with an important adult, then to attend jointly with that adult to something of interest to them both, and later to jointly refer to an object outside of themselves.

The *emerging language stage* is characterized by the children stating their first words and increasing their range of communicative intent. By the end of this stage, their utterances have increased to two words and their vocabularies have increased substantially. Children are beginning to take turns during conversations, and the speech sounds they produce are usually consistent, though not yet adult-like.

During the *developing language* stage, children's utterances expand into complete sentences; by the end of this period, they are producing both compound and some basic complex sentences. Phonology continues to develop, though children at the end of this stage still do not produce the entire adult repertoire of acceptable sounds. Their vocabulary increases exponentially during this time.

For most children the developing language stage marks the beginning of the ability to use indirect requests and polite forms. They also become more adept at taking turns with others during conversations, though they still have some difficulty providing the right amount of information to unfamiliar partners. Narrative abilities progress so children understand basic story structure, and their own stories include setting, characters, or some sort of plot. Children in print-literate families show emergent literacy skills. For example, these children know how books and stories work, that print is speech written down, and that words can be broken down into smaller parts.

The *L4L* stage of development usually begins when children enter school. During this period, children acquire the ability to classify words into categories and subcategories, and they become able to use all aspects of the personal pronoun system. Their ability to understand and use figurative language, particularly idioms, flourishes, as do their skills with various types of humor. Syntactic structures become even more complicated, and their understanding and use of passive sentences increases substantially.

Children in the L4L stage develop increased proficiency with narrative genres and become able to tell stories that are complete in terms of setting, character information, plot development, and episode structure. In addition, they begin to access nonnarrative discourse genres, beginning with descriptive and explanatory text and moving to argumentative or persuasive text.

One of the most important developments during this period is the oral-to-literate shift, acquiring the ability to communicate not only in the here-and-now of everyday conversation but also to communicate across time and space through reading and writing and through ever more formal oral language genres. Accessing the literate forms of language requires the development of fluency with the "metas": metalinguistic, metapragmatic, and metacognitive ability.

Adolescent language development marks the transition from childhood and its emphasis on the here-and-now into an almost complete immersion, at least in the classroom, into literate forms of discourse, Of course, social communication continues to develop and grow. Reading and writing become much more important to continued language development, as both afford opportunities to access language forms and literary styles previously unencountered. Facility with figurative language continues to develop during this time, as does skill with the "metas."

▌References

Appleby, A. (1978). *The child's concept of a story: Ages 2 to 17.* Chicago: University of Chicago Press.

Bishop, D., & Edmundson, A. (1987). Is otitis media a major cause of specific developmental language disorders? *British Journal of Disorders of Communication, 21,* 321–338.

Bloom, L., & Lahey, M. (1978). *Language development and language disorders.* New York: John Wiley & Sons.

Bloom, L, Rocissano, L, & Hood, L. (1976). Adult–child discourse: Developmental interaction between information processing and linguistic knowledge. *Cognitive Psychology, 8,* 521–552.

Brown, R. A. (1973). *A first language: The early stages.* Cambridge, MA: Harvard University Press.

Bruner, J. (1975). The ontogenesis of speech acts. *Journal of Child Language, 2,* 1–19.

Butler, A., & Turbill, J. (1987). *Towards a reading–writing classroom.* Portsmouth, NH: Heinemann.

Catts, H., & Kamhi, A. (1999). *Language and reading disabilities.* Needham Heights, MA: Allyn & Bacon.

Cazden, C. (1988). *Classroom discourse: the language of teaching and learning.* Portsmouth, NH: Heinemann.

Chapman, R. (2000). Children's language learning: An interactionist perspective. *Journal of Child Psychology and Psychiatry, 41,* 33–54.

Chomsky, C. (1969). *The acquisition of syntax in children from 5 to 10.* Cambridge, MA: MIT Press.

Feagans, L., & Applebaum, M. (1986). Validation of language subtypes in learning disabled children. *Journal of Educational Psychology, 78,* 358–364.

Gillam, R. G., & Bedore, L. M. (2000). Communication across the lifespan. In R. B. Gillam, T. P. Marquardt, & F. N. Martin (Eds.), *Communication sciences and disorders: From science to clinical practice* (pp. 25–61). Sudbury, MA: Jones and Bartlett.

Hayes, J., & Flower, L. (1987). On the structure of the writing process. *Topics in Language Disorders, 7*(4), 19–30.

Hulit, L. M., & Howard, M. R. (2011). *Born to talk: An introduction to speech and language development* (5th ed.). Boston: Allyn & Bacon.

Kaderavek, J. N., & Sulzby, E. (2000). Narrative production by children with and without specific language impairment: Oral narratives and emergent readings. *Journal of Speech, Language, and Hearing Research, 43,* 34–49.

Menyuk, P. (1969). *Sentences children use.* Cambridge, MA: MIT Press.

Menyuk, P. (1971). *The acquisition and development of language.* Englewood Cliffs, NJ: Prentice-Hall.

Miller, L. (2006). *Introduction to communication sciences and disorders* (3rd ed.). Eau Claire, WI: Thinking Publications.

Miller, L., Gillam, R. B., & Peña, E. C. (2001). *Dynamic assessment and intervention: Improving children's narrative skills.* Austin, TX: Pro-Ed.

Nelson, N. W. (2009). *Language and literacy: Infancy through adolescence.* Boston: Allyn & Bacon.

Nippold, M. (1998). *Later language development: The school-age and adolescent years* (2nd ed.) Austin, TX: Pro-Ed.

Nold, E. (1981). Revising. In C. Frederiksen & J. Dominic (Eds.), *Writing: The nature, development, and teaching of written communication* (Vol. 2). Hillsdale, NJ: Erlbaum.

Owens, R. (1998). *Language development: An introduction* (4th ed.). New York: Macmillan.

Paul, R. (1981). Analyzing complex sentence development. In J. Miller (Ed.), *Assessing language production in children.* Baltimore: University Park Press.

Paul, R. (2007). *Language disorders from infancy through adolescence: Assessment and intervention* (3rd ed.). St. Louis: Mosby.

Raffaelli, M., & Duckett, E. (1989). We were just talking...": Conversations in early adolescence. *Journal of Youth and Adolescence, 18,* 567–581.

Reed, V., Griffith, F., & Rasmussen, A. (1998). The relative importance of selected communication skills for successful adolescent peer interactions. *Clinical Linguistics and Phonetics, 12,* 205–220.

Rogers, R. (2004). *An introduction to critical discourse in education.* Mahwah, NJ: Lawrence Erlbaum.

Roth, F., & Spekman, N. (1984). Assessing the pragmatic abilities of children: Part 1. Organizational framework and assessment parameters. *Journal of Speech and Hearing Disorders, 49,* 2–11.

Scott, C., & Erwin, D. (1992). Descriptive assessment of writing: Process and products. In W. Secord (Ed.), *Best practices in school speech–language pathology* (Vol. 2, pp. 60–73). San Antonio, TX: Psychological Corp., Harcourt Brace Jovanovich.

Sturm, J. M., & Nelson, N. W. (1997). Formal classroom lessons: New perspectives on a familiar discourse event. *Language Speech and Hearing Services in Schools, 28,* 255–273.

Tynan, W. D. (2008). *Learning disorder: Reading.* Retrieved from http://www.medscape.com/article/918143-overview

Wallach, G. P. (2007). *Language intervention for school-age students: Setting academic goals for academic success.* Philadelphia: Elsevier.

Wallach, G. P., & Miller, L. (1988). *Language intervention and academic success.* Boston: College-Hill.

Wallach, G. P. & Miller, L. (1998). *Language intervention and academic success.* Austin, TX: Pro-Ed.

Wells, G. (1986). *The meaning makers: Children learning language and using language to learn.* Portsmouth, NH: Heinemann.

Westby, C. (1991). Learning to talk—talking to learn: Oral–literate language differences. In C. S. Simon (Ed.), *Communication skills and classroom success: Assessment and therapy methodologies for language- and learning-disabled students* (pp. 181–218). Eau Claire, WI: Thinking Publications.

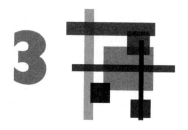

3

Cultural Diversity and Language Differences

The cultural and language makeup of American society varies significantly. Even classrooms that are considered relatively homogeneous likely have differences in race, gender, religion, ability level, dialect, ability and disability, social interactions, and other characteristics (Florence, 2010). Differences will inevitably be found any time and place where groups, including schools, are found. As a result, teachers must learn how to successfully provide educational opportunities for children from different cultural and linguistic backgrounds.

Language is a critical component in human exchange. One of the most significant differences between humans and other animal species, it is the foundation of our societies. Although learning language is a natural process and relatively easy, people with language differences have major problems in basic communication and academic, vocational, and social settings. Students from different cultural backgrounds frequently use different languages. Unfortunately, when students who do not speak English as their primary language enter schools in the United States, they must develop oral and written English language skills quickly or they will likely have major problems with academic tasks (Samson & Lesaux, 2009).

Culture can be defined in many ways. Basically, it refers to a group of individuals who share similar values, norms, and traditions. Culture represents the preferred ways in which groups understand and interact with each other (Chamberlain, 2005). Culture may also include different religious beliefs (Whittaker, Salend, & Elhoweris, 2009). Adding another level of complication, different cultures commonly have language differences. This means that beyond differences in dress, behavior, expectations, and religion, students from different cultural groups may have to deal with language differences.

Language is vital for communication. As a result, it is one of the most important tools that students have for learning and expressing their learning (Chamberlain, 2005). When students enroll in English-speaking schools without adequate English language skills, schools must address this disparity or deal with the likely failure of students. Language diversity in American schools continues to be a major challenge for educators.

▌Diversity in Society

The wide spectrum of racial, ethnic, and linguistic characteristics associated with students from different cultures reveals that the melting pot theory has not been realized. Actually, our society is getting more, not less, culturally diverse. U.S. society today can best be described as consisting of many different parts that make up the whole. Unlike classrooms in public schools in the 1950s, when most students were of the same race and socioeconomic background and spoke English as their primary language, classrooms today are composed of students representing a wide variety of languages, socioeconomic classes, and cultures. Indeed, diversity is increasing so quickly that, as Bogden (2000) noted, terms such as "minority" and "majority" will soon lose their relevance. Acceptance of such cultural diversity requires viewing individuals with different cultural backgrounds positively and viewing diversity among the population as positive for society.

The U.S. population encompasses individuals from many different cultural and linguistic backgrounds. Currently, approximately a fourth of the population consists of minority groups, and the U.S. Census Bureau (2009) projects that the number of individuals from culturally diverse backgrounds will increase over the next 40 years. Other projections from the report include the following:

- In 2042, minorities will account for more than 50% of the population.
- In 2050, minorities will account for 54% of the population.
- In 2023, minorities will account for more than half of all children.
- In 2050, 62% of children will be from minority groups.
- Between 2008 and 2050, the Hispanic population will triple, from 46.7 million to 132.8 million.
- Between 2008 and 2050, the Asian population will increase from 15.5 million to 40.6 million.

The projections indicate a growing diversity of the U.S. population. The Hispanic population is growing much more rapidly than any other group. Because many Hispanic individuals do not speak English as their primary language, cultural diversity and linguistic diversity will be an increasing issue for schools.

According to Langdon (1999), in the early 1990s more than 6 million Americans did not speak English well. Today, the number is significantly higher and will continue to grow substantially as the Hispanic population increases. Some individuals who do not speak English well are third- or fourth- and even later-generation Americans; others are first- or second-generation Americans. Among the nation's children, 4.5

million children did not speak English fluently in 2000–01 (Kindler, 2002). This number also will increase substantially as the Hispanic population increases.

Immigration continues to impact diversity in the United States. The number of immigrants coming into the United States has increased significantly since the 1960s. In 2007, the U.S. Census Bureau reported that more than 10% of the country's 302 million people were born in foreign countries (Foner, 2009). The number and diversity of new immigrants is dramatic. People moving into the United States represent many different language groups and dozens of nations. They come from modern industrialized nations including China, Japan, and Korea, as well as from rural and war-devastated nations such as Bosnia, Laos, and Cambodia. Some come from severely depressed rural regions of Mexico and Honduras, and others are fleeing civil wars in Central America.

Whereas a large number of new immigrants speak Spanish, increasing numbers speak Asian languages including Cambodian, Cantonese, Hmong, Japanese, Korean, Lao, Mandarin, Tagalog, Samoan, and Vietnamese, among others. Researchers have estimated that by the year 2020, nearly 50% of individuals living in the United States will be from African American, Asian, Latino, or some other non-European ethnic group (Woolfolk, 2008). European Americans will no longer be the definite majority. In 2006, in 54 of the nation's 100 largest school districts, minority students were the majority (Meyer & Rhoades, 2006). One fifth of all children in America's schools today are immigrants (Baghban, 2007).

As noted, with increased diversity come more students who do not speak English as their primary language. Between 1990 and 2005, the number of non–English language learners in the K–12 grades increased by 152%; more than 7.7 million students ages 5 to 17 in the school system speak a language other than English at home (National Clearinghouse for English Language Acquisition and Language Instruction Educational Programs, 2006).

Unlike the earlier trend toward assimilation, more recent immigrants tend to retain their traditional cultures and language. This chapter focuses on those groups that, at least in a generalized sense, demonstrate significant linguistic variance from the standard English of the majority culture. Although generalizing within or between minority groups can be difficult because of regional, cultural, and linguistic differences, research has shown that variances within groups often exceed variance between groups, indicating that minority cultural groups are often more alike than different.

The increasing cultural diversity found in educational settings can cause problems for teachers. Brown (2007), however, believes that these problems are not the result of the diversity of students but, rather, the way in which teachers and other educators have responded to this diversity. She notes that "a positive or negative response could affect the self-esteem and academic success of students from these varied racial, cultural, and linguistic backgrounds" (p. 57).

Unfortunately, teachers and other school personnel may hold onto myths surrounding students from diverse backgrounds. Some of these myths are (Manning & Baruth, 2004, p. 23):

■ all children of the same ethnic background have the same needs and intellectual abilities;

- all children who speak broken English or a dialect are intellectually deficient;
- all minorities are disadvantaged, lazy, and on welfare;
- all Asian American children are academically gifted; and
- all minorities are inferior.

Until educators realize that most of these myths are invalid for students from diverse backgrounds, teachers are unlikely to make substantial efforts in meeting the needs of this growing group of students.

Often, educators do not fully recognize and understand the nature of diversity in our schools. They must recognize this reality and make an effort to understand the cultures their students represent. Teachers can do several things to better understand different cultures, including (Manning & Baruth, 2004)

1. having reading materials related to cultural diversity,
2. obtaining information from various advocacy groups,
3. getting to know families of students from diverse backgrounds,
4. attending professional meetings where diversity is a focus, and
5. reading about diversity in materials designed for children.

Fortunately, over the past century, educators have begun to take a closer look at the needs and characteristics of students in their classes and have begun to realize that the population of our schools is growing ever more diverse. Unfortunately, though the number of students from racial and linguistically diverse backgrounds has increased dramatically, the number of teachers from minority backgrounds has increased much more slowly. The National Center for Education Statistics reported that between 1993 and 2004, the number of teachers from racial and ethnic minorities increased only from 13% to 17% (2007).

As noted earlier, the increasing number of students from diverse language and cultural backgrounds is predicted to continue. The U.S. Census Bureau predicts that by 2023, the majority of children in the United States will be from minority backgrounds. This prediction, in combination with the likelihood that children from the Hispanic population will increase substantially faster than children from other minority groups, means that schools must prepare for more students whose primary language is not English (National Center for Education Statistics, 2007).

■Disproportionality in Special Education

One of the challenges related to diversity and special education is the issue of disproportionality. Students identified as having disabilities and referred for special education services come from all backgrounds; however, certain demographic characteristics place students at a higher risk for identification as special education students (Skiba et al., 2008). For example, students from culturally and linguistically diverse backgrounds are frequently overrepresented in some disability categories (Oesterreich & Knight, 2008), and others may be underrepresented in other categories (Salend & Duhaney, 2005).

Although disproportionality has been discussed for more than three decades, it continues to be an area of concern for policy makers and educators (Samson & Lesaux, 2009). **Disproportionality**, which can result in overrepresentation or under-representation, is defined as "the representation of a group in a category that exceeds our expectations for that group, or differs substantially from the representation of others in that category" (Skiba et al., 2008, p. 266).

Overrepresentation is indicated when more students are placed in certain disability categories than would be expected, and underrepresentation means that fewer students than expected are placed in certain categories. An example of overrepresentation is the higher than expected number of students from some cultural backgrounds in the category of intellectual disabilities; underrepresentation is indicated when fewer students than expected from certain cultural groups are identified as gifted and talented (Salend & Duhaney, 2005).

Because no empirical evidence is available to explain why students from one cultural group are more prone than others to exhibiting disabilities or less likely than others to be classified as gifted, the general conclusion is that some special education programs exhibit disproportionality (Samson & Lesaux, 2009). Congress and professionals alike have recognized the problems with disproportionality. The 2008 reauthorization of IDEA requires that states investigate the problem and also review and revise policies to reduce the problem.

Skiba et al. (2008) conducted an extensive review of the literature aimed at determining the causes of disproportionality. They concluded that the numerous factors that cause and continue the disproportionate representation of culturally diverse groups in special education programs are complex and that the literature does not provide a basis for determining that only one factor causes such racial and cultural disparity.

The issue of overrepresentation is not new. It was first raised more than three decades ago by civil rights activists and was even referred to in Lloyd Dunn's classic article questioning the need for special education for students with mental retardation (MacMillan & Reschly, 1998). Salend and Duhaney (2005) identified several factors related to disproportionality, including

- biased standardized tests,
- misinterpretation of culturally based behaviors,
- inequitable school funding,
- minimizing family involvement, and
- failure of schools to evaluate their identification procedures.

The most likely variable that causes disproportionality is unfair assessment. This topic will be addressed later in the chapter.

Variables Affecting Special Education for Children from Minority Groups

Many different factors influence the provision of special education services for students from diverse cultural and linguistic backgrounds, include institutional racism; teachers' expectations for students; a disconnect between students' needs and curriculum; inappropriate pedagogy; lack of student, teacher, and parent involvement; and tracking. Table 3.1 points out each of these factors.

Despite these factors, IDEA requires that every child served in special education be provided with a free appropriate public education (FAPE). In addition, children who are not eligible for special education services under IDEA but who meet the eligibility requirements under Section 504 of the Rehabilitation Act of 1973 also must receive a free appropriate public education (Smith & Patton, 2007). Thus, school personnel must overcome whatever problems create barriers to the provision of FAPE for students served under IDEA and Section 504, including any problems associated with cultural and linguistic diversity.

TABLE 3.1
Description of Policies and Practices Affecting Educational Services for Minority Students

Policy/Practice	Description
Institutional Racism	Tacit acceptance of dominant white norms and privileges. Inherent racism based on history and tradition.
Expectations	Deeply held ideas about expected levels of achievement of different groups. Teachers and others simply expect less of minority students.
Curriculum	Significant mismatch between curriculum and the needs of many students. Textbooks also are not matched to the needs of students.
Pedagogy	Teachers teaching as they were taught, which often occurred in a very different cultural context than exists in today's public schools. Student-centered, empowering pedagogy is needed.
Tracking	An inequitable practice that persists in one form or another. Continues to be thought by many as the best way to teach students who have a variety of different skills.
Student, Teacher, Parent Involvement	Schools continuing to be run by professional educators and offering limited opportunities for parent and student involvement.

Source: From "Diversity: What Do Teachers Need to Know?" by S. Nieto, in *Foundations of Special Education* (pp. 191–199), edited by J. L. Paul, et al., 1997, Pacific Grove, CA: Brooks/Cole.

▋Cultural Models

When educating students from diverse backgrounds, educators have discussed and debated a variety of cultural models, including

1. the cultural deficit model,
2. the cultural mismatch model, and
3. the culturally different model.

By the late 20th century, it became obvious that linguistic diversity is the norm, not the exception. One only has realize that, currently, more than 6,000 languages are spoken in the world. Lewis (2009) actually described more than 6,900 languages. The top 10 languages are spoken by more than 96% of the world's population, and the remaining languages, altogether, are spoken by only 4% of the population.

Many Americans assume that English is the most widely spoken language in the world; however, the reality is that English is the third most frequently spoken language. An estimated 845 million people speak Mandarin Chinese, 539 million speak Spanish, and 328 million speak English (Lewis, 2009). With the wide range of cultures and racial groups represented in the United States, and with the obvious regional differences, language diversity should not be surprising. To the contrary, a lack of significant language diversity would be unusual.

The English language itself has substantial diversity. The form of English spoken in the United States is very different from versions used in other English-speaking countries, such as England, Scotland, and Australia. For example, few Americans would understand the statement, "I must get on the trunk line to my solicitor." Translated into the American form of English, this phrase means, "I must make a long distance call to my lawyer." This is only one of many phrases and language forms used in English-speaking countries that Americans would have difficulty understanding. The following list compares terms used in England and their meaning in the American form of English (Tiedt & Tiedt, 1986, p. 133):

English Form	**American Meaning**
biscuit	cookie
jelly	jello
tinned meat	canned meat
pud	dessert
tea	light meal, supper
boot	trunk of car
lorry	truck
lift	elevator
underground, tube	subway, metro
chemist	druggist, pharmacist
dustman	garbage collector

vest	undershirt
knickers	underpants
jumper	pullover sweater
fringe	bangs, hair

The United States is home to a minimum of 11 different regional dialects (Gollnick & Chinn, 2009). The America Dialect homepage describes eight linguistic regions in the United States:

1. Western
2. Upper Midwestern
3. Midland
4. Mountain Southern
5. Coastal Southern
6. Great Lakes
7. New York
8. New England

Examples of linguistic characteristics from some regions include the following:

New England: dropping Rs (e.g., *powa* for *power*)
Great Lakes: rotating short vowels (e.g., *talk* as *tuck*, *bit* as *bet*)
Upper Midwest: keeping long vowels (e.g., the long "o" in Minnesota)
Western: merging AU into O (e.g., *cot* for *caught*)

Ethnic, racial, and socioeconomic groups also speak varying English dialects. One of the best known dialects related to racial characteristics is black English, or African American English. Some schools have created controversy by using this form of English in instruction. Most linguists consider black English to be a legitimate form of communication that follows a specific rule system. Still, most majority group educators, and even some African American educators, view the use of black English negatively (Gollnick & Chinn, 2009).

A historical question that has often been posed is whether substantial linguistic variance constitutes a language defect, a cultural mismatch, or simply a language difference. The following discussion explores the different points of view on this issue.

The Cultural Deficit Position

Some educators assume that individuals who are culturally different are actually at a disadvantage because their behavior, customs, values, and language differ from the majority culture (Manning & Baruth, 2004). Advocates of the deficit viewpoint have asserted that the language of people from lower social classes represents a deficient code, not one that is just different from the majority culture. Popular during the 1950s,

1960s, and early 1970s, this viewpoint has been replaced primarily by the language difference position, or culturally different model. The deficit position is presented here to describe a hypothesis that was widely accepted at one time but no longer is considered appropriate.

The cultural deficit viewpoint was associated with the cultural deprivation theory, which assumed that various detrimental factors produced deprived homes and communities that fostered educational limitations (see Polloway & Patton, 1981). Within these environments at the bottom of the social class structure, several forces resulted in learning problems for children: lack of structure and organization in the home, authoritarian and inconsistent parenting practices, absence of strong achievement motivation, parent absenteeism, and practical problems associated with poverty. The language deficit viewpoint took this position one step farther: It implied strongly that language used in these environments actually caused and perpetuated many of the conditions just described.

Although this research is important to the deficit position, numerous reports from Bernstein (1961, 1964, 1970) were the most significant source of the deficit position. Bernstein's research focused on the language of working-class people in England and specifically on the concept of two forms of language: elaborated and restricted codes. Yet, Bernstein (1970) questioned the way his premises were applied to extremely poor children (particularly within the United States), stating, "The use (or abuse) of this distinction (between the codes) has been equated with linguistic deprivation, linguistic deficiency, or being nonverbal" (p. 26). Nevertheless, the hypotheses generated about these two codes became the basis for theories about children in American inner cities and, thus, warrant attention here.

The elaborated code is associated with a wide range of syntactical options available to the speaker. The verbal channel becomes the basic orientation of communications and affords the speaker the opportunity to explicitly state his or her intentions. The elaborated language pattern has greater flexibility in terms of vocabulary referring to abstract concepts (Bernstein, 1970).

A narrower range of syntactic and vocabulary possibilities characterizes the restricted code. It is more rigid in form and relies more on gestures, voice, and facial expressions. It is "we"-oriented, in contrast to the "I"-orientation of the elaborated form. As such, it represents an extensive collection of mutual experiences and expectations, such as those shared by prison inmates or adolescent gangs. In this sense, the code controls and transmits culture, but it may also result in stifling expression. Bernstein (1970) noted, "The use of a restricted code creates social solidarity at the cost of verbal elaboration of individual experience" (p. 32).

This point would be as valid for social groups adopting virtually programmed forms of communication, such as the stereotyped hip slang of the 1960s counterculture (e.g., "far out," "I'm hip," "dig it," "doing my own thing," "ripped off"), or even for husbands and wives. The most important implications, however, apply to developing children who must use this restricted code to receive and express aspects of their environment and mediate cognitive processes. Table 3.2 summarizes the characteristics of elaborated and restricted codes.

TABLE 3.2
Characteristics of Elaborated and Restricted Codes

Code	Characteristics
Elaborated	Associated with wide range of syntactic options
	Verbal channel is basic orientation to communication
	Great flexibility in using abstracts
	Oriented to "I"
Restricted	Narrower range of syntactic options
	More rigid in form
	Relies more on gestures, voice, and facial expressions
	Oriented to "we"
	Represents extensive collection of mutual experiences and expectations
	Contains much slang and stereotypic forms

Source: Adapted from "A Sociolinguistic Approach to Socialization: With Some Reference to Educability," by B. Bernstein, in *Language and Poverty,* edited by F. Williams, 1970, Chicago: Markham Publishing.

Specific aspects of the restricted code, drawn from the Bernstein hypotheses and related to the lower-class child, were noted by Ginsburg (1972, pp. 60–61):

1. Short, simple sentences, which are often incomplete and syntactically weak
2. Simple and repetitive use of conjunctions such as "so," "then," "and"
3. Few subordinate clauses
4. Limited and repetitive use of adjectives and adverbs
5. Statements that confuse reasons and conclusions, with the result being the production of categoric statements

The implications drawn for the language of inner-city children have often been of a stronger nature.

Since the late 1980s, the deficit orientation has lost popularity (Wallace & Goodman, 1989). Professionals who adopted this view may have developed some erroneous generalizations about children whose language was not standard English. One of the major invalid assumptions in this approach was that students who did not speak standard English had an automatic language deficiency (Ortiz, 1995). As U.S. society has moved toward integrating minority racial groups into schools, the workforce, and society in general, the notion has faded that a different linguistic system is inherently bad. Difference does not mean deficit (Turnbull, Wehmeyer, & Turnbull, 2006).

The Cultural Mismatch Model

Unlike the cultural deficit model, advocates of the cultural mismatch model do not assume that their cultural background is superior, only that there is a mismatch between expectations from the majority culture and the student's culture (Manning & Baruth, 2004). Using this model, educators believe that the best way to prepare individuals from diverse cultural groups for success in the majority culture is to close the gap between expectations of the majority culture and the reality of the student's culture. The belief is that the more similar a student from a diverse cultural group is to the majority culture, the better for the student.

This model, therefore, promotes an intervention approach aimed at helping students assimilate majority cultural values, behaviors, and language patterns as much as possible, thereby giving them more opportunities in majority cultural activities. Educators would use interventions similar to those in the difference position, discussed next.

The Difference Model (Culturally Different Model)

The culturally different model recognizes that there simply are differences between individuals from different cultures and that each culture has its own strengths and weaknesses. This position is similar in many ways to the mismatch position. While acknowledging these differences, proponents of this model still believe that "children and adolescents need to learn mainstream cultural values and knowledge" to maximize their success. (Manning & Baruth, 2004, p. 48). The language difference position differs significantly from the deficit orientation. Proponents of this position believe that all languages have the potential for communicating the full range of human experiences and for meeting all of the purposes of language.

Ortiz (1995) described a continuum of language skills in children who do not use standard English proficiently. Even though the continuum focuses primarily on language systems that are uniquely different from English, it underscores the idea that language systems may be different but not deficient. Black dialect, regional dialects, or competence in a language other than English are differences, not an absence of language functionality.

In discussions of the **difference position**, a primary area of concentration has been black dialect, also referred to as black English or Ebonics. **Ebonics** can be defined as a rule-based language system used predominantly by African Americans for communication purposes. It is considered to be a cultural dialect (Otto, 2010). Ebonics is probably the foremost dialectical variation of standard English studied since the mid-1970s. One reason for this interest is that African Americans constitute one of America's largest minority groups. Another reason is that many African Americans do not use the language forms that have been assumed to enable them to succeed in school. Most of these forms have traditionally been associated with the middle class.

Ebonics is also associated with a social class. Dialects associated with social classes, including Ebonics and Appalachian English, often result in stigmatizing behaviors. Frequently, individuals who are unable to speak proper English face social, educational, and even vocational discrimination (Gollnick & Chinn, 2009). Although many African Americans use Ebonics, it is used primarily by African Americans living in large urban centers, and it is observed most often in the language of children and teenagers. Certain aspects of the dialect are also found in the language of African Americans in other low socioeconomic areas, such as the rural Southeast. Significant variance, however, can be identified in the dialects spoken in the different geographical areas.

An essential element of the difference position is its use of the term "nonstandard" instead of "substandard" to refer to Ebonics and other variations of English. This perspective views all dialects as complete linguistic systems rather than as inferior and error-ridden deviations of standard English.

Ebonics and other nonstandard dialects have been the target of intense disagreements over the past two decades. Because some of these nonstandard dialects are typically used more frequently by individuals from certain racial, cultural, and socioeconomic groups, requiring all students to use standard English is seen by some as discriminatory. But some educators advocate teaching all students standard English because that is considered the appropriate language of the society (Gollnick & Chinn, 2009).

Nonstandard English not only negatively impacts students academically, but often there are biases against students who do not use proper standard English. There are assumptions that these students are less capable than students who do speak standard English. Unfortunately, when teachers and other educators make these assumptions, the results can be damaging to students. "Students may be treated as if they are less intelligent than they are, and they may respond in a self-fulfilling prophecy in which they function at a level lower than they are capable of reaching" (Gollnick & Chinn, 2009, p. 212). Educators must not let students' use of nonstandard English bias them in regard to students' ability levels.

▌Teaching Implications

Language is a powerful tool. Students must understand the language used in the classroom so they can learn (Chamberlain, 2005). Further, language can have a productive influence on subsequent adult adjustment (Bogden, 2000). Conversely, language snobbery can have significant negative effects in the classroom. Unless language bias is drastically reduced or eliminated, many linguistically different children may leave U.S. public schools unprepared to function successfully in the community, in part because of their general frustration and dissatisfaction.

Culturally Responsive Teachers and Classrooms

To be effective with students who represent broad cultural differences, teachers have to be culturally responsive. Culturally responsive teachers understand that students' cultures have an impact on their learning. Further, teachers must develop attitudes that enable them to appreciate students' cultural differences (Brown, 2007). Teachers who are culturally responsive have characteristics delineated in Table 3.3.

Culturally responsive teachers must have a thorough understanding of their own beliefs about different cultural groups. They must know what they think about their own culture, as well as the cultures represented by their students. To have an understanding

TABLE 3.3

Frameworks for Culturally Responsive Teachers

Framework	Culturally responsive teachers...
Ladson-Billings (2001) identified three propositions relevant to culturally responsive teachers.	1. Focus on individual students' academic achievement (e.g., clear goals, multiple forms of assessment). 2. Have attained cultural competence and help in developing students' cultural competence. 3. Develop a sense of sociopolitical consciousness.
Gay (2002) identified five essential elements of culturally responsive teaching.	1. Develop a cultural diversity knowledge base. 2. Design culturally relevant curricula. 3. Demonstrate cultural caring, and build a learning community (Harriott & Martin, 2004). 4. Establish cross-cultural communications (Harriott & Martin, 2004). 5. Establish congruity in classroom instruction.
Villegas and Lucas (2002) identified six characteristics that define culturally responsive teachers.	1. Are socioculturally conscious, that is, recognize that there are multiple ways of perceiving reality and that these ways are influenced by one's location in the social order. 2. Have affirming views of students from CLD backgrounds, seeing resources for learning in all students rather than viewing differences as problems to overcome. 3. See themselves as both responsible for and capable of bringing about educational change that will make schools responsive to all students. 4. Understand how learners construct knowledge and are capable of promoting learners' knowledge construction. 5. Know about the lives of their students. 6. Use their knowledge about students' lives to design instruction that builds on what they already know while stretching them beyond the familiar.
Wlodkowski and Ginsberg (1995) cited four motivational conditions that students and teachers continuously create.	1. Establish inclusion, creating learning atmospheres in which students and teachers feel respected by and connected to one another. 2. Develop attitude, creating a favorable disposition toward the learning experience through personal relevance and choice. 3. Enhance meaning, creating challenging, thoughtful learning experiences that include student perspectives and values. 4. Engender competence, creating an understanding that students are effective in learning something they value.

Note CLD = culturally and linguistically diverse.
Source: From "Educating All Students: Creating Culturally Responsive Teachers, Classrooms, and Schools," by M. R. Brown, 2007, *Intervention in School and Clinic, 43*(1), p. 59. Copyright 2007 by Sage Publications, Inc. Journals. Reprinted with permission.

of one's own culture and the culture of others, Cartledge and Kourea (2008) recommend that teachers self-reflect. Some questions that teachers could ask themselves in the process include the following:

1. What is the racial or gender breakdown of the students that I typically send from my class for disciplinary actions?
2. How often do I send the same students for disciplinary actions?
3. What messages am I communicating to the students who are the recipients of these actions?
4. What messages am I communicating to their classmates?
5. Is the behavior of my students getting better? How do I know? If it is not getting better, why not?
6. Do I dispense disciplinary referrals fairly on the basis of race and gender?
7. Are disciplinary actions therapeutic or simply punitive?
8. Do I distinguish culturally specific behaviors from behavioral inadequacies?
9. If students have substantial behavioral differences, have I taught them the skills they need to know?
10. Am I punishing students for my lack of skill in effective behavior management?
11. Do I punish students because of my lack of skill in effective instruction? (p. 355)

Because teachers are the classroom leaders, they must closely evaluate their personal attitudes and expectations of culturally different students. Effectiveness has to begin with tolerance toward, and acceptance of, culturally and linguistically different children.

Fair Assessment

When working with children whose predominant language is not English, one challenge that arises is to provide fair, accurate assessment. The disproportionality found in special education classrooms is largely a result of unfair assessment practices (Smith, Polloway, Patton, & Dowdy, 2008). Many norm-referenced standardized assessment instruments discriminate against individuals from minority cultural groups and lower socioeconomic environments (Chamberlain, 2005; Smith et al., 2008). A primary reason that students with English language difficulties are overrepresented in classes for students with disabilities is that general classroom teachers and educational diagnosticians often have difficulty differentiating underachievement related to disabilities and underachievement related to other factors, such as language (Chamberlain, 2005).

Many tests are simply not fair for students from minority cultures. These tests often reflect **content bias,** which includes items representing values different from students of minority cultures, and **construct bias**, in which the tests simply do not assess what they purport to assess. In addition, not enough tests are available in languages other than English (Chamberlain, 2005).

The traditional overrepresentation of minority groups in special education classes and the underrepresentation of the same groups in classes for gifted and talented students underscore the need for nondiscriminatory assessment procedures (Ford, Grantham, & Whiting, 2008). Substantial evidence indicates that these issues are being addressed (Smith et al., 2008). IDEA requires schools to use various methods to reduce discrimination in assessment, including:

- administering tests in the child's native language,
- using only tests that have been validated specifically for the purposes for which they are being used,
- conducting assessments using a multidisciplinary team, and
- using more than a single instrument to determine the existence of a handicapping condition.

Although these requirements do not guarantee nondiscrimination in assessment, they should help overcome the bias that often results in inappropriate labeling and placement of children from minority cultural groups in special education programs.

▍Instructional Approaches

Children from minority cultural backgrounds who have language problems because English is not their dominant language present a variety of challenges for teachers. Should teachers present all instruction in standard English and require students to learn the language as quickly as possible or fail? Should teachers be required to teach non-English-speaking students in their dominant language or dialect and hope that they eventually learn English incidentally? Or should teachers take advantage of the child's dominant language but maximize opportunities for helping the child acquire English for later success in school and in the community? These questions have been the subjects of debate for many years.

Many instructional approaches have been tried, ranging from almost total reliance on the culturally dominant language to heavy emphasis on maintaining the original language. Otto (2010) has described several major approaches, including English as a second language, bilingual education, submersion, and immersion programs. Each has unique characteristics, strengths, and weaknesses.

English as a Second Language Approach

English as a second language (ESL) programs rely totally on using English as the language of instruction and direct little attention to the student's native language. In this model, students' primary language is not a consideration and is not used in the instructional process. Teachers in ESL classrooms may not have knowledge or fluency in any language other than English. In these programs, students often receive daily, intensive English instruction for part of the day and instruction in English in their general education classes the remainder of the day (Otto, 2010). Many schools use ESL programs as the primary means for assimilating students into their classes (Manning & Baruth, 2003). Although this will likely help students assimilate into the English language quickly, it also can leave students with wide learning gaps that are difficult to overcome (Gollnick & Chinn, 2009).

Bilingual Education Approach

Bilingual education has been a major topic in U.S. public schools for many years (Lucido & McEachern, 2000). The major difference between ESL and bilingual approaches is how instruction is delivered. Bilingual education programs use both English and the student's native language during the instructional process (Gollnick & Chinn, 2009), whereas teachers using the ESL model provide instruction only in English.

Bilingualism can be defined as the ability to communicate in two languages, and teaching students using a bilingual approach takes advantage of both languages. The child's primary language and English are used in the instructional process (Otto, 2010). Individuals who are bilingual may not be equally competent in both languages, but they have the ability to understand and communicate with others using either language—a positive skill (Otto, 2010).

Bilingual education "reinforces the student's home language and culture and simultaneously teaches the ability to function in another language" (Manning & Baruth, 2004, p. 281). A great deal of research on bilingualism and bilingual education has led to the conclusion that children with bilingual skills have certain cognitive and sociocultural advantages over monolingual children (Lucido & McEachern, 2000). Children from minority cultures need to learn English to maximize their success in the dominant English-speaking society (Tiedt & Tiedt, 1986), but their learning of English language skills should not be at the expense of maintaining their initial language. From their study of the influence of bilingualism on English reading scores, Lucido and McEachern (2000) determined that "bilingual education actually enhances the potential academic success of students, in addition to giving them economic and social advantages" (p. 91). Bilingual educational programs do not seem to be detrimental to academic success, and they offer students from different language backgrounds the opportunity to maintain skills in their native languages.

Non-English-speaking children may suffer emotionally as well as academically if their native tongue is devalued and they do not receive the benefits of bilingual education. Emotionally, children can suffer a tremendous loss of self-esteem when they confront an educational process that is based on alien cultural and linguistic modes. With regard to the effect on academics, Brice and Roseberry-McKibbin (2001) noted, "The native or home language is the best medium for working with children and adds to the child's ability to communicate in the second language" (p. 11).

Indeed, the continued use of a child's nonmajority language may facilitate academic and cognitive development. The native language can also serve as a functional vehicle for acquiring memory and problem-solving skills, which in turn may help the child acquire English as a second language. The transition from teaching through the native language to teaching in English might come when the child is able to learn as well or better in a classroom taught in English. Bilingual education, therefore, can become a means of both preserving traditional cultures and helping children become functioning members of the English-oriented culture (Lucido & McEachern, 2000).

Submersion Programs

Submersion programs are used when schools do not have bilingual programs available for students. As a result, these students are placed in classrooms with English-speaking students without any supports. In these programs teachers may not have any language skills other than English and may not have received any preparation in teaching students who speak a language other than English (Otto, 2010). In this model, teachers expect students to develop the majority-culture language without the aid of their primary language. The model has been called a sink-or-swim model, in which students either become proficient in English or fall farther and farther behind because of limited English competence.

Although this model has been used extensively when teaching a second language to majority-culture students, it has resulted in significant controversy when used with minority-culture children in the United States. Submersion programs alone do not promote learning because, typically, the linguistic abilities of the teacher and other students far exceed the ability of the language-minority students (Otto, 2010).

Immersion Programs

Immersion programs take advantage of the student's primary language while the student learns English. In this model, students are placed in classes with other students who speak the same primary language. Teachers in immersion programs are fluent in both English and the students' native language. Teachers use the students' native language when teaching language arts but teach other subjects using English. There is no formal instruction in English (Otto, 2010).

Key elements of the model are that: (a) teachers are bilingual, (b) instructional activities are modified to involve the students' primary language, and (c) literacy in the primary language is encouraged and reinforced (Cummins, 1984). Minority students who are at risk for developing problems benefit much more from this model than from the models discussed previously; the level of support for these students is significantly greater.

There are numerous ways to teach students who are not proficient in English, and different schools use different models to teach this group of students. Chamberlain (2005) noted that "while there is no consensus in the country on the best way to educate students who are limited-English-proficient" (p. 196), bilingual programs are commonly offered during the early grades, and then students are transitioned into English-only classes in later grades.

▌Code Switching and Code Mixing

Regardless of the instructional model used, two processes may occur among students and teachers during bilingual education. The first, **code switching**, is common among young bilingual children as well as adults. Code switching is defined as "instances in which a speaker apparently consciously and deliberately uses two languages within the same sentence or from one sentence to another" (Otto, 2010, p. 405). It enables individuals to rely on their own language in specific situations.

A common misconception is that students who code-switch are not proficient in either language. Actually, students who use code switching abide by appropriate language rules in both languages. Students typically use code switching to emphasize something or to maintain their ethnicity (Otto, 2010). Because students who code-switch are using both languages properly, they should not be discouraged from the process.

The second process that is frequently found among individuals who use two languages is **code mixing**, or using more than one language system indiscriminately (Brice & Roseberry-McKibbin, 2001). Code mixing is described as "instances in which a speaker appears to be mixing two languages" (Otto, 2010, p. 405). Code mixing could be the result of students' parents using the native language at home, or it could be students' attempts to continue with a conversation even if the second language is not fully understood (Otto, 2010). Regardless of the method used, code switching and code mixing enable bilingual students to better understand English while maintaining the use of their native language.

▌Bilingual Education Materials

Although publishing companies are developing a variety of materials for teaching bilingual children, relatively few materials are available for students who also may have an intellectual or learning impairment. Because so few Spanish-language materials are available for teaching children with disabilities, attempts have been made to translate appropriate English materials into Spanish. Distortions sometimes result from direct translation, though.

Santos, Fowler, Corso, and Bruns (2000) recommended the following steps to assist in selecting appropriate materials for students with diverse cultural and linguistic backgrounds:

1. Consider the intended audience.
2. Check for congruence with the family's and community's values, beliefs, and practices and with current recommended practices.
3. Consider the effectiveness of the presentation.

4. Examine the graphics, illustrations, case studies, and photographs used.
5. Evaluate the translation of the material.

Guidelines and Teaching Strategies

It has long been recognized that teachers need to have more competence in cultural diversity and multicultural education. Unfortunately, although the intentions to improve this area of teacher preparation is obvious, factors such as limited experiences and apprehension of faculty have deterred success in this area (Trent, Kea, & Oh, 2008). A number of general guidelines and possible teaching strategies can be gleaned from the discussion in this chapter. Shore (2001) offered the following suggestions to help teachers meet the special classroom needs of language-different students:

1. *Assess needs*. Evaluate the English-language proficiency of new students who do not speak English as their native language. Continue with ongoing informal assessment even after the student has been in the class for several weeks.
2. *Empathize*. Help other students in the class understand how difficult it is for the student who is not a native English speaker. You might read a story to the class about a student who does not speak English and discuss problems that you could encounter if you go to a place where you do not understand all the people around you.
3. *Foster a sense of belonging*. Help the student feel welcome and a part of the class. This might require discussing with other students how they might make the student feel welcome, having the students ask the new student questions about his or her background, or having someone who can speak the new child's language serve as an interpreter for a few days.
4. *Assign a buddy*. One way to help the new student become assimilated into the new class is to assign a buddy. If several students are given the opportunity to serve as the new student's buddy, the new student will have a chance to meet more classmates.
5. *Use "sheltering" techniques*. Use language that is as simple as possible, speak more slowly, and use visual references.
6. *Teach key words*. Teach the student the most important words first, such as student, teacher, principal, bathroom.
7. *Read and reread books aloud*. Read to the student, or have another student, such as the student's buddy, read to him or her. Make sure that the materials being read are of high interest and that the content is understandable to the student.
8. *Provide opportunities for success*. Make sure that the student has some early successes, as nothing breeds success like success. For example, have the student read a story to the class in his or her native language.
9. *Keep track of progress in language learning*. Keep a portfolio or running record of the student's progress.

10. *Value bilingualism.* Encourage the student to maintain his or her native language while learning English. Provide opportunities for the student to read and write in the native language as well as English.
11. *Support the family's involvement.* Help parents feel involved with the school and their children's educational program. Make sure that parents understand school procedures so they will feel comfortable knowing when to be involved and when to leave issues to teachers.
12. *Foster an appreciation of cultural diversity.* Teach an entire unit or lesson on the child's original country or culture. This will help students understand the new student and give the new student a sense of pride. Provide samples of food, describe play activities, and include other activities that will help students understand one another better.

Multicultural Education

One of the major areas that educators must address is the growing number of students who do not speak English as their primary language. Regardless of whether the diversity involves language, traditions, behaviors, values, or other factors, schools must develop strategies to educate this growing number of students effectively.

One means of addressing the growing diversity of students is through **multicultural education**, which can be defined in many ways. Grant and Gillette (2006) define multicultural education as "the ways in which all aspects of schooling address the needs and talents of a diverse population to ensure equity for all. It is both a philosophy and a process. As a philosophical concept, it is rooted in the principles of democracy, social justice, equity, and the affirmation of human diversity. As a process, multicultural education undergoes modification to meet the needs and demands of a growing society" (p. 28). Gollnick and Chinn (2009) define multicultural education as

> an educational strategy in which students' cultural backgrounds are used to develop effective classroom instruction and school environments. It supports and extends the concepts of culture, diversity, equality, social justice, and democracy in the school setting. (p. 4)

Regardless of the definition, the intent of multicultural education is to provide educational opportunities that will improve the achievement and retention of these students.

In addition, the teacher must facilitate children's acceptance of diversity by positively discussing the differences and similarities between them and others. Teachers who discuss individual differences in a respectful manner send a positive message about those differences. This affirmative communication encourages acceptance of all students by other students. To avoid discussing differences or having a neutral position toward them can be almost as detrimental as making negative comments (Cristol & Gimbert, 2008).

To take advantage of differences of children in the classroom, the teacher should employ differentiation in classroom instruction. Differentiation aims to ensure that the content students learn, the methods by which they learn, and their ability to demonstrate that learning match their readiness level, interests, and favored method of learning (Tomlinson, 2004). By differentiating instruction for students, the teacher will build upon each child's unique characteristics to make learning more successful. Differences should not be seen as deficiencies in multicultural education (Gollnick & Chinn, 2006).

▌Dealing with Parents of Culturally Diverse Students

Children from culturally diverse backgrounds often have difficulties in school, which means that school personnel must at times interact with students' family members. Cultural differences that create problems for teachers who work with students can also negatively impact relationships with family members. Brandon (2007) lists numerous factors that can influence parental participation, including cultural and linguistic diversity, economics, family composition, parents' educational level, and school communication.

One factor that school personnel should consider relates to school–home communication. Educators should take proactive steps to improve school–home communication (Brandon, 2007). Table 3.4 provides some suggestions for improving this communication.

▌Summary

U.S. society encompasses a wide variety of individuals representing European, African American, Mexican American, Asian, South American, American Indian, and other cultures. The diversity, which has always been a characteristic of the United States, is increasing rather than diminishing. The "melting pot" theory has not come to fruition.

Students in U.S. schools speak a range of dialects of English. For years, professionals have debated whether substantial linguistic variance represents a language difference or a language deficit. Although the deficit theory was once widely accepted, the majority of professionals currently support the difference approach. In this view, the differences in languages are recognized but those differences are not considered deficits.

Along with the increase in immigration and cultural diversity has come an increase in students with varying degrees of bilingualism and accompanying teaching implications for students who have language problems related to cultural differences. The best way to provide instruction for the majority of bilingual children is

TABLE 3.4
School–Home Communication

Suggestion	Implementation
Establish a schoolwide communication system that serves as a consistent and predictable communication resource for parents.	■ Daily individual student report cards. ■ Weekly or biweekly phone calls or e-mails, depending on parents' access to a computer. ■ Monthly newsletters concerning school activities and happenings.
Develop a parent handbook that addresses questions commonly asked by parents.	■ Handbooks specific to each classroom or program. ■ School handbook that covers school policy, requirements, and the yearly calendar.
Provide parents with a calendar of parent conferences at the beginning of the year as well as an outline of a typical parent conference.	■ Include (a) purpose of the conference, (b) faculty/staff who will attend, (c) length of the typical conference (important for parents who take time off work), (d) suggested questions for parents to ask, and (e) items to bring.
Be polite.	■ Though this may seem like common sense, cultural groups may have different communication customs that should be followed. For example, African American family members should always be addressed formally (e.g., Mrs. Jones, Mr. Daniel, Dr. Smith) until an individual is asked to call them by a different name.
Be aware of the different methods through which people communicate.	■ Educators should reflect on their own beliefs as to how parents "should" communicate and evaluate whether or not these beliefs negatively affect their relationship with parents.
Explore the use of technology as a communiation tool.	■ The digital divide still exists, so it is important to explore parental access to technology prior to using it as a communication tool. However, e-mail, a school Web site, and online chats may facilitate communication with parents who have difficulty coming to school in person.

Source: From "African American Parents: Improving Connections with Their Child's Educational Environment," by R. R. Brandon, 2007, *Intervention in School and Clinic, 43*(2), p. 119. Copyright 2007 by Sage Publications, Inc. Journals. Reprinted with permission.

to take advantage of their native language while helping them develop their majority language.

References

Baghban, M. (2007) Immigration in childhood: Using picture books to cope. *Social Studies, 98* (2), 71–76.

Bernstein, B. (1961). Social class and linguistic development. In A. H. Halsey, J. Floud, & C. A. Anderson (Eds.), *Education, economy, and society* (pp. 24–38). New York: Free Press.

Bernstein, B. (1964). Elaborated and restricted codes: Their social origins and some consequences. *American Anthropologist, 66,* 6.

Bernstein, B. (1970). A sociolinguistic approach to socialization: With some reference to educability. In F. Williams (Ed.), *Language and poverty* (pp. 107–134). Chicago: Markham.

Bogden, W. K. (2000). Celebrating our diversity in the new millennium: An opportunity for success. *Teaching Exceptional Children, 32,* 4–5.

Brandon, R. R. (2007). African American parents: Improving connections with their child's educational environment. *Intervention in School and Clinic, 43,* 116–120.

Brice, A., & Roseberry-McKibbin, C. (2001). Choice of languages in instruction: One language or two? *Teaching Exceptional Children, 33,* 10–16.

Brown, M. R. (2007). Educating all students: Creating culturally responsive teachers, classrooms, and schools. *Intervention in School and Clinic, 43,* 57–62.

Cartledge, G., & Kourea, L. (2008). Culturally responsive classrooms for culturally diverse students with and at risk for disabilities. *Exceptional Children, 74,* 351–371.

Chamberlain, S. P. (2005). Recognizing and responding to cultural differences in the education of culturally and linguistically diverse learners. *Intervention in School and Clinic, 40,* 195–211.

Cristol, D., & Gimbert, B. (2008). Racial perceptions of young children: A review of literature post-1999. *Early Childhood Education Journal, 36,* 201–207.

Cummins, J. (1984). *Bilingualism and special education: Issues in assessment and pedagogy.* Clevedon, England: Multilingual Matters.

Florence, N. (2010). *Multiculturalism 101.* Boston: McGraw Hill.

Foner, N. (2009). The American melting pot is a rich stew. *Phi Kappa Phi Forum, 89*(2), 7.

Ford, D. Y., Grantham, T. C., & Whiting, G. W. (2008). Culturally and linguistically diverse students in gifted education: Recruitment and retention issues. *Exceptional Children, 74,* 289–306.

Gay, G. (2002). Preparing for culturally responsive teaching. *Journal of Teacher Education, 53,* 106–116.

Ginsburg, H. (1972). The myth of the deprived child. Englewood Cliffs, NJ: Prentice-Hall.

Gollnick, D. M., & Chinn, P. C. (2009). *Multicultural education in a pluralistic society.* Upper Saddle River, NJ: Merrill.

Grant, C. A., & Gillette, M. (2006). A candid talk to teacher edeucators about effectively preparing teachers who can teach everyone's children. *Journal of Teacher Education, 57,* 292–299.

Kindler, A. L. (2002). *Survey of states' limited English proficient students and available educational programs and services, 2000–2001 summary report.* Washington: U.S. Department of Education.

Ladson-Billings, G. (2001). *Crossing over to Canaan: The journey of new teachers in diverse classrooms.* San Francisco: Jossey-Bass.

Langdon, H. W. (1999) Foreign accent: Implications for delivery of speech and language services. *Topics in Language Disorders, 19,* 48–49.

Lewis, M. P. (Ed.), (2009). *Ethnologue: Languages of the world* (16th ed.). Dallas: SIL International.

Lucido, F., & McEachern, W. (2000). The influence of bilingualism on English reading scores. *Reading Improvement, 37*(2), 87–91.

MacMillan, D. L., & Reschly, D. J. (1998). Overrepresentation of minority students: The case for greater specificity or reconsideration of the variables examined. *Journal of Special Education, 32,* 15–24.

Manning, M. L., & Baruth, L. G. (2004). *Multicultural education of children and adolescents* (4th ed.). Boston: Allyn & Bacon.

Meyer, C., & Rhoades, E. K. (2006). Multiculturalism: Beyond food, festival, folklore, and fashion. *Kappa Delta Pi, 42*(2), 82–87.

National Center for Education Statistics. (2007). *2003–2004 Schools and Staffing Survey and 2004–2005 Teacher Follow-Up Study.* Washington, DC: National Center for Education Statistics

National Clearinghouse for English Language Acquisition and Language Instruction Educational Programs. (2006). *Elementary and secondary enrollment of ELL students in U.S.: 1989–90 to 2004–2005.* Retrieved from http://www.ncela.gwu.edu/expenyfaq/081eps.html

Nieto, S. (1997). Diversity: What do teachers need to know? in *Foundations of Special Education* (pp. 187–201), by J. L. Paul, et al. (Eds.). Pacific Grove, CA: Brooks/Cole.

Oesterreich, H. A., & Knight, M. G. (2008). Facilitating transitions to college for students with disabilities from culturally and linguistically diverse backgrounds. *Intervention in School and Clinic, 43,* 300–304.

Ortiz, A. A. (1995). Linguistically and culturally diverse students. In Podemski, R. S., Price, B. J., Marsh, G. E., & Smith, T. E. C. (1995). *Comprehensive administration of special education* (2nd ed., pp. 99, 129–154). Columbus, OH: Merrill.

Otto, B. (2010). *Language development in early childhood* (3rd ed.). Upper Saddle River, NJ: Merrill.

Polloway, E. A., & Patton, J. R. (1981). Psychological causes. In J. S. Payne & J. M. Patton (Eds.), *Introduction to mental retardation.* Columbus, OH: Charles E. Merrill.

Salend, S. J., & Duhaney, L. M. G. (2005). Understanding and addressing the disproportionate representation of students of color in special education. *Intervention in School and Clinic, 40,* 213–221.

Samson, J. F., & Lesaux, N. K. (2009). Language-minority learners in special education. *Journal of Learning Disabilities, 42,* 148–162.

Santos, R. M., Fowler, S. A., Corso, R. M., & Bruns, D. A. (2000). Acceptance, acknowledgment, and adaptability: Selecting culturally and linguistically appropriate early childhood materials. *Teaching Exceptional Children, 32,* 14–22.

Shore, K. (2001). Success for ESL students: 12 practical tips to help second-language learners. *Scholastic Instructor, 98*(5), 30–32.

Skiba, R. J., Simmons, A. B., Ritter, S., Gibb, A. C., Rausch, M. K., Cuadrado, J., & Chung, C. (2008). Achieving equity in special education: History, status, and current challenges. *Exceptional Children, 74,* 264–288.

Smith, T. E. C., & Patton, J. R. (2007). *Section 504 and Public Schools.* Austin, TX: Pro-Ed.

Smith, T. E. C., Polloway, E. A., Patton, J. R., & Dowdy, C. A. (2008). *Teaching students with special needs in inclusive settings* (5th ed.) Boston: Allyn & Bacon.

Tiedt, P. L., & Tiedt, I. M. (1986). *Multicultural teaching* (2nd ed.). Boston: Allyn & Bacon.

Tomlinson, C. A. (2004). *How to differentiate instruction in mixed-ability differented instruction.* Alexandria, VA Association for Supervision and Curriculum Development.

Trent, S. C., Kea, C. D., & Oh, K. (2008). Preparing preservice educators for cultural diversity: How far have we come? *Exceptional Children, 73,* 328–350.

Turnbull A. P., Wehmeyer, M. L., & Turnbull, R. (2006), *Exceptional lives: Special education in today's schools.* (5th ed.). Upper Saddle River, NJ: Prentice-Hall

U.S. Census Bureau (2009). *Current population reports.* Retrieved from http://www.census.gov

Villegas, A. M., & Lucas, T. (2002). Preparing culturally responsive teachers. *Journal of Teacher Education, 53,* 20–32.

Wallace, C., & Goodman, Y. (1989). Research currents: Language and literacy development of multilingual learners. *Language Arts, 66,* 542–550.

Whittaker, C. R., Salend, S., & Elhoweris, A. (2009). Religious diversity in schools: Addressing the issues. *Intervention in School and Clinic, 44,* 314–319.

Wlodkowski, R. J., & Ginsberg, M. B. (1995). A framework for culturally responsive teaching. *Educational Leadership, 53,* 17–21.

Woolfolk, A. E. (2008). *Educational psychology* (10th ed.). Boston: Allyn & Bacon.

Language Assessment and Instruction for Preschool Children

ypically developing children make the transition, during the preschool years, from nonverbal (the infant–toddler and prelinguistic stage) to verbal (the emerging language stage), and undergo a growth spurt in knowledge about the rules governing form, content, use, and narrative (the developing language stage). For students with disabilities, these developmental processes may be delayed. Also, children with disabilities—particularly children who are suspected of having various conditions associated with autism spectrum disorder—may differ substantially from their normally developing agemates. Some students enrolled in preschool may not show evidence of language development per se but, rather, display behaviors that are characteristic of infants or toddlers. For this reason, the discussion on assessment and instruction begins with a description of how best to address preschool children whose behaviors indicate that their communication development is at the infant–toddler and prelinguistic stage.

Assessing communication and language hinges on the purpose and goals of intervention and instruction. For preschoolers, the primary purpose in evaluating communication and language is to determine the child's developmental characteristics. The overall goal of intervention—instructional or otherwise—is to assist the student in moving to the next developmental stage. Therefore, instruction aims to assist the child in developing the necessary communicative and linguistic abilities. For preschoolers whose communication and/or language abilities are severely compromised, instruction will likely exclude academics and instead emphasize the social competencies required for negotiating the academic environment of the classroom.

▌Legislative Background

Beginning in 1986 with Public Law 99-457, the **Education of the Handicapped Act Amendments of 1986** (Part H), federal legislation has been enacted to help states establish early identification and intervention services for infants, toddlers, and their families. This legislation has been reauthorized several times, most recently in the Individuals with Disabilities Education Act (IDEA, PL 108-446) of 2004, which, like its predecessor, requires an **Individual Family Service Plan (IFSP)** for children from birth to age 3. The National Early Childhood Technical Assistance Center (2009) has compiled a list of state examples of model IFSP forms with guidance on developing the plans. For children over age 3, an **Individualized Education Plan (IEP)** is required, to include the child's family in the assessment and intervention processes. Model forms for the IEP can be found on the U.S. Department of Education (2009) website, idea.ed.gov.

The intent underlying IDEA is not only to maximize children's development but to support and assist the family as well. Thus, a crucial component of both assessment and intervention with preschool children is to incorporate the child's family to maximize the child's development, both with the help of professionals and at home.

▌Developmental Considerations for Preschool Children with Disabilities

To facilitate discussion, it is helpful to view assessment, intervention, and instruction in terms of severity of impairment. These processes take quite different forms depending on the extent to which the child's development is altered by the various conditions and situations that can affect development. Individual children, however, may not be so easily categorized. Therefore, this discussion should be viewed as a general guide rather than a hard-and-fast set of rules.

Assessment of communicative development in a preschool-age child whose development has been severely compromised usually focuses on whether the child has developed communicative intentions, how he expresses these intentions, and whether any language forms have emerged. Intervention and instruction for a child who is severely compromised emphasize establishing and developing communicative intent, as well as designing the best method by which the child can, if possible, communicate basic needs, desires, and thoughts either through gestural, visual, or linguistic means.

For a preschool-age student whose communication and language development are only moderately compromised, assessment is aimed at discovering which communicative intentions the child exhibits and whether the child understands or uses narrative language, how these intentions are expressed (language forms), and the content of what the child expresses (language content). Instruction would be designed to help the child develop more sophisticated social-interactive strategies (pragmatics), more elaborate linguistic forms (morphology, syntax, phonology), and more extensive vocabulary (content). The goal is to boost the child's language abilities enough to enter kindergarten successfully.

Assessment of preschool students whose communication and language are only mildly impaired targets each language system—form, content, or use, including narrative and nonverbal communication—to ascertain exactly where to pinpoint the instructional process. Because we know that mild language disorders often intensify the longer students are in school, instruction emphasizes the aspects of language development known to be correlated most highly with the linguistic demands they will face there. Special attention is given to narrative development and to phonological and metalinguistic awareness (see Chapter 2).

The most effective way to understand language development and design and execute an effective assessment plan, we believe, is to ascertain, as much as possible, the child's current developmental characteristics. These characteristics, in concert with what we know about the child's characteristics in other areas of development, form the basis for intervention and, for students who can benefit from it, for academic instruction.

▌Types of Assessment

Four primary types of assessment are used when evaluating the communication and language development of preschool children, regardless of whether they are in the infant–toddler and prelinguistic, emerging language, or developing language stages.

1. *Standardized tests* are used to learn how the child compares with same-age peers on some aspect of communication or language.
2. *Nonstandardized* approaches are used to sample a student's knowledge of specific aspects of language without comparison to peers.
3. *Interviews with parents and caregivers* are generally undertaken to learn how their child's communication and language development affects the child's everyday life. Types of interviews range from open-ended discussions to standardized or teacher-constructed questionnaires to behavior checklists and developmental scales. The interview process usually involves learning about the family's hopes, fears, and goals for the child, as well as their views on what they believe will be most helpful to the child's communication and language development.
4. *Observations of the child's play and routines* in familiar environments afford a view of how the child uses communication and language to get things done in his world. Observations generally show how well the child is functioning in his everyday life and which communicative or language abilities might be most useful to the child at any given time.

Standardized Testing

Standardized tests compare children's communication and language development to that of other children of the same chronological age. As a result, standardized instruments are called **norm-referenced** because measurements are taken from a large number of students and collected into statistical groupings based on chronological age. These statistical groupings are known as **norms** against which individual children are compared.

Thus, a standard score of 80 on a test instrument with a mean score of 100 and a standard deviation of 15 is considered significantly *below* average because it deviates significantly from the norm—the mean—for that chronological age. Similarly, a standard score of 122 on the same instrument would be considered significantly *above* average, as it deviates significantly from the mean for that chronological age.

Standardized tests are used to measure children's communication and language development because they exhibit these characteristics (Paul, 2006):

- Clear administration and scoring criteria
- Validity (they measure what they say they measure)
- Reliability (they measure the same thing each time and with different examiners)
- Standardization (they are based on a sample of students with specifically defined characteristics)
- Measures of central tendency and variability (the scores fall along a normal distribution, or Bell curve, allowing relatively accurate interpretation of scores that deviate from the mean)
- Standard error of measurement (the scores can be interpreted with a specific degree of confidence that they are, in fact, true)
- Norm-referenced scores (raw scores have been converted to standard scores, percentile ranks, stanines, or equivalent scores for ease of interpretation)

Standardized language tests yield information regarding a student's development relative to peers of similar chronological age. Obviously, knowing how a child's language development compares to peers of the same age provides data crucial to the diagnosis of communication and language disorders. By their nature, however, standardized tests are unable to describe how children use their language in contexts other than the testing situation. In addition, standardized tests often underestimate the language abilities of children for whom English is not their native language, a topic discussed in Chapter 3. Therefore, assessments of preschool children typically include interviews with parents and caregivers as well as observations of the child's play and daily routines in natural environments.

Nonstandardized Approaches

Nonstandardized approaches include criterion-referenced procedures, the use of developmental scales, and dynamic assessment. **Criterion-referenced** procedures provide a means to examine whether a child can attain a certain level of performance. These procedures are typically used to establish baseline communication or language function and to identify instructional targets by determining specifically what the child can and cannot do with communication and language. **Developmental scales** are used, usually in conjunction with interview or observation, to sample communication and language behaviors from a particular developmental period. In **dynamic assessment,** the child's ability to change a communicative or language behavior with structured help is observed, with a focus on the relevance of the behavior.

Interviews with Parents and Caregivers

Parents and caregivers represent rich sources of information about children's communication and language development, especially when the goal is "to look at the larger sociocultural context in which communication takes place and to look at how language is used to share knowledge and establish social order within a particular culture" (Paul, 2006, p. 185). When interviewing parents or caregivers, they must be enlisted as partners in assessing the child's developing communication and language abilities. The goal is to seek the family's perspective on the child's strengths and weaknesses and to determine their concerns and priorities for their child (Paul, 2006).

Interviewers can construct their own interview formats, they may choose existing developmental scales and behavior checklists, or they may use a combination of the two. Advantages of utilizing existing scales or checklists, particularly for beginners, is that these usually include clearly stated guides for administration, and they typically specify a developmental age. As a disadvantage, they may not target the communicative or language behavior that has been identified as problematic.

Observation of Children's Play and Routines in Familiar Environments

Observing how children play provides valuable information regarding their overall general development as well as their communication and language abilities. From children's viewpoints, having an adult watch them play may seem much less intrusive and strange than being asked by that same adult to respond to questions or directions. Furthermore, familiar surroundings and routines are more likely than unfamiliar settings and activities to produce representative language in children whose communication and language abilities may be compromised in some way.

Observations offer opportunities to discover the conditions that produce specific communication and language forms, usages, and content—knowledge that becomes critical in designing instruction that is likely to be successful for a given child. For instance, an observer may learn that a child produces significantly more vocalizations, conversational initiations, and conversational turns when he is interacting with an adult conversational partner using a set of play figures than when the conversational partner uses a picture book. Or an observer may discover that a different child produces a wider range of communicative intentions when he and the observer are walking around the building than when they are sitting together in an enclosed room.

The information gleaned from the observations in both of these examples can be embedded into the instructional plan for these students. For the first student, the teacher will likely be more successful in using toys rather than books. The second student will likely exhibit more targeted communication behaviors when physical movement is a part of the lesson than when he is asked to sit still.

Assessment of Preschool Children

Children enrolled in public school preschool programs generally range between 2 or 3 and almost 6 years of age. Some, particularly those with severely compromised language development, will have been identified through Child Find (mandated by IDEA) and may arrive from infant/toddler programs where they received services aimed at helping them in their overall development, including communication and language. Many children in these public school preschool programs, regardless of whether they received prior services, will not yet have entered the emerging language stage of development.

The purpose of assessing the communication and language abilities of preschool children is to determine their developmental characteristics so instruction can be designed to help them move forward through the developmental stages that are characteristic of preschool. For children whose communication is primarily prelinguistic, assessment will determine precisely which aspects of their communicative repertoire require bolstering so they can move into the emerging language phase.

Similarly, for children whose language abilities are characteristic of the emerging language stage of development, assessment pinpoints which linguistic processes require attention for the child to move into the developing language phase. Finally, assessing children whose language skills are in the developing language stage can show which of those abilities require emphasis and further development in preparation for entry into kindergarten.

Purpose of Assessment

The primary purpose of assessment for children in the prelinguistic period of language development—typical of infants or toddlers as described in Chapter 2—is to ascertain whether and how the child is communicating. Specifically, assessment is aimed at determining the following:

- Does the child attend to people and objects in the environment? If so, how?
- Does the child attend to novel events? If so, how?
- Does the child attend to faces? If so, how?
- Does the child orient his body toward people and objects or reach up to be held?
- Does the child vocalize? If so, what are the frequency and type of vocalizations?
- Does the child exhibit any intentions in communicating? If so, what forms does the child use to communicate intention, and what types of intentions (requesting, negating, "commenting")?
- Does the child babble? If so, does the child produce syllables?

- Does the child engage in mutual attending (described in Chapter 2)?
- Does the child engage in joint attending (described in Chapter 2)?
- Does the child engage in joint referencing (described in Chapter 2)?

For children whose language development has progressed beyond the prelinguistic stage and into the emerging language stage, the purposes of assessment become a bit more complex. Assessment shifts from whether and how the child is communicating to an emphasis on the range of communicative intentions the child expresses, the child's phonemic productions, which phonological processes are present, the pragmatic functions and discourse skills the child brings to bear, the semantic content the child displays, and the syntactic forms the child utilizes. Specifically, assessment is directed to the following aspects of communication and language (refer to Chapter 2 for a detailed description):

- Which communicative intentions does the child exhibit?
- How many words are in the child's receptive vocabulary (i.e., how many different words he understands)?
- How many words are in the child's expressive vocabulary (i.e., how many different words he uses)?
- Which words express relational processes?
- Which words express substantive processes?
- If the child is producing two-word phrases, which of the following types of semantic relationships are expressed:

Semantic relationship	Example
Agent + Action	*Dog eat*
Agent + Location	*Dog chair*
Action + Location	*Go Nanna's*
Agent + Object	*Mommy hair*
Noun Phrase + Verb Phrase	*Dog chair* ("The dog is on the chair")

- If the child is producing two-word phrases, is he expressing negation and interrogation? (e.g., "No sleep" ["I don't want to go to sleep"]; "More milk?" ["May I have more milk?"])
- Which phonemes is the child producing consistently?
- Which phonological processes are present in the child's speech?
- Which pragmatic functions (intentionality, presuppositions, turntaking) are present in the child's communicative interactions?
- Which aspects of stories does the child understand?
- Which aspects of stories does the child produce?

Assessing children whose language is characteristic of the developing language stage focuses on whether their language development is proceeding as expected for children who are ready to enter kindergarten. The assessment process for children in the developing language period addresses

- receptive and expressive vocabulary;
- pronoun usage;
- sentence compounding;
- phrase and sentence embedding;
- morphological marking;
- phoneme acquisition;
- turntaking, conversational repairs, and presuppositions;
- indirect requests and polite forms;
- figurative language and humor; and
- narrative development.

Standardized Testing and Nonstandardized Testing

Numerous instruments and tools are available for assessing infant development. Most include assessment of communication and language, whereas some assess only certain areas of development. Language disorders are the most common developmental problem occurring in the preschool period (Paul, 2006). Therefore, any infant or toddler who is at risk for a developmental order of any sort is considered to be at high risk for language deficits.

Tools for Prelinguistic Language   By far the majority of instruments available for children whose communication and language development is at the prelinguistic stage are nonstandardized scales and checklists. This is because children at this stage of development are unable to participate in standardized testing. However, a norm-referenced instrument, the *Test of Early Communication and Emerging Language* (TECEL) has been developed for infants and toddlers and for older individuals whose language development is just emerging (Huer & Miller, 2011). The TECEL is a norm-referenced test that utilizes both observation and interview to obtain the data necessary to score the test. Designed for children from birth to age 2, the TECEL assesses the individual's earliest communicative behaviors and emergent language skills.

According to Paul (2006), among the most commonly used assessment instruments for individuals whose language is in the prelinguistic stage are:

> *Assessment in Infancy: Ordinal Scales of Infant and Psychological Development* (Uzgiris, 1989)
> *Scales of Infant Mental Development–Revised* (Bayley, 1993)
> *Birth to Three Checklist of Language and Learning Behaviors* (BTC-3; Ammer, 1999)
> *Denver Developmental Screening Test–II* (DDST-II; Frankenburg et al., 1990);
> *Infant-Toddler Language Scale* (Rossetti, 1995)
> *Syracuse Dynamic Assessment for Birth to Three* (SDA; Ensher et al., 1997)
> *Vineland Adaptive Behavior Scales* (Sparrow, Cicchetti, & Balla, 2005)

Tools for Emerging Language   No standardized instrument exists to assess all aspects of children's emerging language abilities. Because most tools are directed to one or a few communication or language behaviors or competencies, more than one often have to be used to obtain comparative developmental data across the range of communicative and language abilities characteristic of the emerging language stage.

One of the more thorough and informative standardized instruments is the *Communication and Symbolic Behavior Scales* (Wetherby & Prizant, 2003). This instrument offers direct assessment through observation of videotaped interactions of parents and their child during both structured and unstructured activities such as reading a book, playing with toys for a variety of purposes, and playing a game that involves identifying body parts. The scales provide information about five areas of communication and language behaviors:

- Expressing a variety of communicative functions
- Using strategies for initiating, responding to, and repairing conversations
- Expressing intentions through gesture and/or vocal means
- Using facial expression and eye gaze appropriately during social interaction
- Using and understanding symbolic behavior, both with and outside language

Many of the communicative assessments listed for prelinguistic language assessment are also suitable for children in the emerging language stage. Some assess comprehension or production; others assess both. Several provide norm-referenced scores; others use scales or parent report to evaluate various aspects of communication and language development. Some of the most commonly used instruments are the following:

Expressive One-Word Picture Vocabulary Test–Revised (Gardner, 2000)
MacArthur Communication Development Inventory (Fenson et al., 1993)
Preschool Language Scale–3rd Edition (Zimmerman, Steiner, & Pond, 1992)
Receptive One-Word Picture Vocabulary Test–Revised (Brownell, 2000)
Reynell Developmental Language Scales III (Edwards et al., 1999)
Test of Early Language Development–3rd edition (Hresko, Reid, & Hammill, 1999).
Early Language Milestones (ELM Scale 2; Coplan, 1993)

Tools for Developing Language   Standardized instruments are used much more commonly with children whose language abilities are in the developing language stage. These tools fall into two broad categories: articulation assessment and language assessment. The latter is further divided into instruments that measure one aspect of linguistic competency and those that assess overall language capabilities. Regardless of what they measure, standardized measures sample a variety of behaviors within a given domain of language or communication to obtain valid comparisons across children. This means that, particularly with tests measuring overall language abilities, not many items will sample each specific aspect of language development. For this reason, the assessment battery typically includes one test of overall language ability and several tests of development in specific areas of language thought to be problematic.

Some of the most commonly used measures of *overall language* function in the developing language period are the following:

Clinical Evaluation of Language Fundamentals–Preschool, 2nd edition (CELF–Preschool 2; Semel, Wiig, & Secord, 2004)

Communication Abilities Diagnostic Test (CADeT; Johnston & Johnston, 1989)

Detroit Tests of Learning Aptitude–Primary–3 (Hammill & Bryant, 1991)

Evaluating Acquired Skills in Communication–Revised (EASIC–R; Riley, 1984)

Illinois Test of Psycholinguistic Abilities (Hammill, Mather, & Roberts, 2001)

Porch Index of Communicative Ability in Children (PICA; Porch, 1981)

Preschool Language Scale–3 (PLS–3; Zimmerman et al., 1992)

Sequenced Inventory of Communication Development–Revised (SICD–R; Hedrick, Prather, & Tobin, 1995)

Test of Early Language Development–3rd Edition (TELD–3; Hresko, Reid, & Hammill, 1999)

Test of Language Development–4:Primary (TOLD–4P; Newcomer & Hammill, 2008)

Utah Test of Language Development–3 (Mecham, 1989)

Woodcock Language Proficiency Battery–Revised, English and Spanish Form (Woodcock & Muñoz-Sandoval, 1991)

Assessment instruments for measuring *specific aspects* of language in the developing language stage include the following:

Assessing Semantic Skills Through Everyday Themes (ASSET; Barrett, Zachman, & Huisingh, 1988)

Assessment of Children's Language Comprehension (ACLC; Foster, Giddan, & Stark, 1983)

Boehm Test of Basic Concepts–Preschool (Boehm, 1986)

Carrow Elicited Language Inventory (CELLI; Carrow-Woolfolk, 1974)

Expressive One-Word Picture Vocabulary Test–Revised (EOWPVT; Gardner, 2000)

Expressive Vocabulary Test (Williams, 1997)

Miller–Yoder Language Comprehension Test (MY; Miller & Yoder, 1984)

Peabody Picture Vocabulary Test–4th edition (PPVT–IV; Dunn & Dunn, 2007)

Pragmatic Language Skills Inventory (Gilliam & Miller, 2005)

Receptive One-Word Picture Vocabulary Test (ROWPVT; Brownell, 2000)

Test for Auditory Comprehension of Language–3rd edition (TACL–3; Carrow-Woolfolk, 1999)

Test for Examining Expressive Morphology (TEEM; Shipley, Stone, & Sue, 1983)

Test of Pragmatic Skills (Revised; Shulman, 1986)

Test of Pragmatic Language–2 (TOPL2; Phelps-Terasaki & Phelps-Gunn, 2007)

Several nonstandardized instruments are available for assessing developing language abilities. Most are criterion-referenced, though some are developmental scales. Those used most commonly are the following:

> *Battelle Developmental Inventory* (BDI; Newborg, Stock, Wnek, Guidubaldi, & Svinicki (1988)
>
> *Coordinating Assessment and Programming for Preschoolers* (CAPP; Karnes & Johnson, 1991)
>
> *Grammatical Analysis of Elicited Language* (Moog & Geers, 1985)
>
> *Multilevel Informal Language Inventory* (MILI; Goldsworthy & Secord, 1982)
>
> *Preschool Language Scale–3* (PLS–3; Zimmerman et al., 1992) (Though this is a norm-referenced test, Paul [2006] suggests that it can be used as a criterion-referenced test for older children)
>
> *Vocabulary Comprehension Scale* (Bangs, 1975)
>
> *Wiig Criterion-Referenced Inventory of Language* (Wiig, 1990)

Interviews with Parents and Caregivers

In addition to standardized and nonstandardized assessment instruments, interviews with parents and caregivers often provide valuable information regarding the child's communication and language in everyday situations. Adults who are familiar with the child see the child in a variety of situations and can relate specifics about how the child's communication and language abilities vary from one situation to another. In addition, because they interact with the child regularly, they have an experiential perspective on the child's competence as a communication partner and language user.

Interviewing parents of preschool children varies somewhat depending on the child's developmental stage. Therefore, the design of the interview format, location, and process should reflect the purposes of assessment for each stage. Recall that the primary goals of assessing language in the prelinguistic stage are to determine whether the child is communicating and, if so, how the child is communicating. Thus, the objective is to discover the child's stage of communication and language development. Is the child's communication and language development typical of the prelinguistic period of development? Is it typical of the emerging language period of development? Or is it perhaps somewhere between the two? Our aim is to discover as much as possible so we can design an instructional plan with the best chance of helping the child move to the next developmental level.

Some of the assessment tools listed earlier incorporate interviews with parents or caregivers (e.g., the *Vineland Adaptive Behavior Scales*, 2nd Edition, [Sparrow et al., 2005]). As mentioned, utilizing existing interview instruments has the advantage of guiding a novice interviewer through the process. In addition, using an existing tool means that the interviewer need not build something from scratch, which can take valuable time.

Some assessment tools based on obtaining parents' reports about their child's communicative behaviors are the following:

MacArthur Communicative Development Inventories (Fenson et al., 1993)

Rossetti Infant and Toddler Language Scale (Rossetti, 1995)

Sequenced Inventory of Communication Development–Revised (SICD-R; Hedrick et al., 1995)

Test of Early Communication and Emerging Language (TECEL; Huer & Miller, 2010) (This test uses observation, interview, or a combination of both)

Utah Test of Language Development–3 (Mecham, 1989)

Constructing one's own interview, however, need not be an arduous task. Figure 4.1 contains a set of questions designed to elicit specific information about children's prelinguistic language development: children's intention(s) to communicate, their ability to engage in mutual attention with a significant adult, their ability to jointly refer to some external object or process, and the range of their communicative intentions. From the information gleaned using the questions in Figure 4.1, the interviewer can determine the child's communicative intentions, skill in participating in "conversations," ability to mutually attend, and competence with joint referencing. This information then will be combined with the other assessment data to develop instructional strategies, discussed later in the chapter.

When interviewing parents and caregivers of children in the emerging language stage, the primary goal is to learn which communicative intentions the child is producing, how these intentions are expressed, how the child is participating in conversations, which words he understands and uses, which types of two-word sentences he is producing, and how understandable his speech is. Figure 4.2 offers an interview format suitable for parents or caregivers of children in the emerging language stage.

Interviews with children in the developing language stage follow a similar format, though it is expanded to include information regarding the child's use of semantics, syntax, and pragmatics through linguistic means. Figure 4.3 is an interview format that can be used when interviewing parents or caregivers of children whose language development is within the developing language stage.

Observation of Children's Play and Routines in Natural Environments

To ascertain how children are using their language to get things done in their everyday world, diagnosticians and teachers rely on observations of children in their homes and at school. Two types of observation are typically used: passive and interactive. During *passive observation*, the observer visits the child in a setting familiar to the child, usually home, daycare, or school. The observer watches the child's interactions with peers and with adults, using an observational format or checklist to note pertinent communication and language behaviors. The interview questions in Figures 4.1 and 4.2 can be used to guide observational sessions.

In *interactive observation*, the observer communicates with the child during his play and interactions with others. Throughout the course of the interactions, the observer notes—physically and mentally—the child's communicative and language behaviors and also evaluates how easily the child learns something that the observer

The parent or caregiver is asked to describe the child's typical behaviors during communication. This offers a means for him or her to describe without being biased by a direct question. Because open-ended questions are sometimes insufficient to stimulate discussion, however, prompts can be used if necessary.

1. Describe how you talk to your child. Tell me what happens during your conversations with your child. (Prompts: What do you do to start a conversation with your child? Tell me how you take turns. Tell me what your child does when it's his or her turn to talk. How do you know what your child means or wants when he or she is talking?)

2. Tell me how you know your child is paying attention to what you're saying. (Prompts: Does your child look at your face? Hold eye gaze with you? Smile? Slow and quiet physically? Increase physical movement? Slow his or her breathing while you're talking?)

3. Tell me how you know your child is talking about the same thing you are. (Prompts: Does your child shift his or her eye gaze to the object or action you're talking about? Does your child shift his or her eye gaze to an external object or action when it's his or her turn to talk?)

4. List all the different things your child can tell you he or she wants or means. (Prompts: How do you know when your child wants to be held? To have your attention? To get more juice? To get a favorite toy? To say no? To request action or information? To greet someone? To ask you something? To inform you of something?)

5. Describe your child's use of gesture and body language when he or she communicates. (Prompts: Does your child orient his or her body toward you when you're having a conversation? Does your child reach toward your face and/or mouth when you're talking? Does your child point to indicate what is being referred to? Does your child increase physical activity during his or her turn?)

6. Describe your child's vocalizations during conversations. (Prompts: Does your child use the melody patterns typical of talking? Does your child use any recognizable syllables? Which ones? Does your child seem to be saying sentences, even though no words are recognizable?)

7. Describe how your child initiates a conversation. (Prompts: What does your child do to let you know that he or she wants to have a conversation? How often does he or she initiate conversation?)

FIGURE 4.1

Parent/Caregiver Interview Questions: Prelinguistic Communication

Because some of these items may require the parent or caregiver to observe the child over a period of time or to refer to baby books or videotapes of the child, the questions can be sent home prior to the actual interview.

1. List the words your child says.
2. List the words your child understands. (Prompts: Does your child understand a variety of types of words? Does your child understand names of familiar people? Which ones? Does your child understand "no"? Requests for information? Requests for clarification? Descriptions of events or actions?)
3. Describe how your child uses talking to get what he or she wants. (Prompts: Does your child use language to signal his or her intentions? Does your child take turns in conversations? What kinds of assumptions does your child make about his or her conversational partners? How does your child respond when someone doesn't understand what he or she is trying to convey?)
4. List any two-word sentences your child is producing.
5. Describe how your child expresses questions or negation. (Prompts: How does your child ask questions? How does your child refuse to do something or generally say no?)
6. Describe how easy it is to understand your child's speech. (Prompts: Which speech sounds seem to be missing in your child's speech? Are they consistently missing?)
7. Describe any words your child uses that aren't "real" words. (Prompts: Does your child use any made-up words to refer to something? Is his or her usage of these made-up words consistent? Does everyone in the family understand what these words mean? How does your child respond when someone does not understand?)
8. Describe how your child initiates conversation. (Prompts: What does your child do to let you know he or she wants to have a conversation? How often does your child initiate converstion?)

FIGURE 4.2

Parent/Caregiver Interview Questions: Emerging Language

teaches specifically. Peña and Davis (2000) call this process "interactive assessment" because it is based on the principles and procedures of dynamic assessment.

In interactive observation (and in dynamic assessment), the teacher notes a language process with which the child seems to be having difficulty and targets it for a short teaching sequence. The outcome of the observation/assessment is not a score. Rather, the process yields three types of information that can be used in instructional planning (Miller, Gillam, & Peña, 2001):

1. How the child approaches tasks, his error patterns, and self-monitoring abilities

1. Describe your child's vocabulary growth over the past year. (Prompts: How many words do you think your child understands? Uses? Is that number significantly higher than the number you would have given a year ago?).

2. Describe the different types of words your child uses—for instance, nouns, verbs, prepositions, pronouns, time words, action words, words describing processes ideas, adjectives, or adverbs.

3. Describe how your child changes words to indicate that things happened in the past, to indicate possession, or to indicate contractions. (Prompts: Does your child use past-tense words? If so, what are they? Does he or she use any words like "eated" or "swimmed?" If so, describe them.)

4. Describe your child's use of pronouns. (Prompts: Other than by name, how does your child refer to himself or herself? To familiar adults or pets?)

5. Describe some typical sentences your child says, word for word. (Prompts: Describe how your child asks questions. Describe how he or she refuses or says no. Does your child use any sentences with "and," "but," "or"?).

6. Describe any prepositional phrases your child uses.

7. Describe your child's speech. How understandable is it to you? To people unfamiliar with your child?

8. Describe your child as a conversational partner. (Prompts: How does your child initiate a conversation? End a conversation? Interrupt? What does your child do when someone doesn't understand what he or she is saying or asking? Describe your child's turntaking abilities. Does your child tell you everything you need to know in order to understand, or do you have to guess what he or she is telling you? When your child is talking with someone less familiar to him or her, does your child assume that person knows more than he or she does?)

9. Describe how your child asks for what he or she wants? (Prompts: Does your child ask directly for what he or she wants? Can your child ask indirectly [e.g., "I really need a cookie"]?)

10. Describe your child's understanding and use of polite forms. (Prompts: Does your child understand what you mean when you ask or tell him or her something in a polite fashion? Does your child use any polite forms? Which ones?)

11. Describe your child's understanding and use of words that have double meanings, such as warm, smooth, pear, and pair. (Prompts: Does your child understand words with double meanings? Does he or she use any in both meanings? Which ones?)

(continued)

FIGURE 4.3

Parent/Caregiver Interview Questions: Developing Language

12. Describe your child's understanding and use of humor and idioms. (Prompts: Which idioms does your child understand and/or use? What type of humor does your child enjoy most? Use?).

13. Describe your child's abilities to understand and tell stories. (Prompts: Does your child understand the components of stories: setting, characters, why characters do what they do, resolution? Does your child undersand stories with more than one episode? Do you consider your child to be a good story-teller? Explain. Does your child understand dialogue in stories? Does your child use dialogue in his or her stories?)

14. Describe how your child responds when asked to recount something he or she has done in the past. (Prompts: Does your child recount events in story form? As a list?)

15. Describe how your child spontaneously tells you (or familiar others) about his or her experiences, thoughts, or feelings. (Prompts: Does your child initiate telling you things? How? And how does your child organize the tellings?)

16. Describe how your child describes things that have already happened. (Prompts: Does your child describe these things as a story? In some other form?)

FIGURE 4.3 *(continued)*

2. The extent to which the child's responses are modifiable (Do the observer's interactions result in changes in the child's communication or language behavior?)
3. Teaching styles and strategies that work well to promote change

The teaching sequence is guided by helping the child understand the goal of the teaching, hypothesizing about how this learning is related to what the child already knows or has experienced, and developing strategies that will lead to success in the identified area of weakness (Miller et al., 2001). Following the teaching sequence, the observer notes how the child incorporated the new learning into his play and routines. Though this latter observation might take place at a different time or on a different day, ideally the setting remains the same. The observer may later choose to observe in a different familiar setting to discover whether the child has been able to incorporate the new learning into this context as well.

To make the most of observations, observers can construct a worksheet or checklist to organize their observations. Figures 4.4 through 4.6 are examples of worksheets to guide observation of communication and language behaviors of preschool children. Figure 4.4 addresses communication and language in the prelinguistic developmental period, Figure 4.5 gives a format for organizing observations of children in the emerging language period, and Figure 4.6 provides a worksheet for guiding observations of children in the developing language period.

Conversational Abilities

	Frequent	Sometimes	None	Examples
Mutually attends to "conversational" partner				
Takes turns during "conversations"				
Initiates "conversations"				
Jointly attends with partner to something exterior				
Engages in joint reference with partner				
Refers through gesture, posture, or facial expression				
Uses a variety of communicative intentions				
■ seeks attention for self				
■ seeks conversational interaction				
■ requests objects, action, information				
■ greets				
■ gives (e.g., toy, food)				
■ protests/rejects				
■ responds/acknowledges				
■ informs				
Vocalizes using intonational contours of sentences				

FIGURE 4.4

Observation Worksheet for Prelinguistic Language

Semantic Abilities

1. Uses words for the following communicative purposes:

■ rejection (*no*)
■ nonexistence or disappearance (*allgone*)
■ cessation or prohibition of action (*stop*)
■ recurrence (*more*)
■ existence (*this*)
■ action on objects (*kiss*)
■ locative action (*up, out*)
■ attribution (*big*)
■ naming, possession, commenting (*dog*)
■ social interaction (*Hi*)

2. Uses words of both these semantic types:

■ substantive (e.g., nouns that name things)
■ relational (e.g., words signifying relations between objects)

	Frequent	Sometimes	None	Examples
rejection				
nonexistence				
cessation				
recurrence				
existence				
action on objects				
locative action				
attribution				
naming				
social interaction				
substantive				
relational				

(continued)

FIGURE 4.5

Observation Worksheet for Emerging Language

Syntax

1. Uses these two-word phrase types:

	Frequent	Sometimes	None	Examples
Agent+ Action (e.g., *Dog eat*)				
Agent+ Location (e.g., *Dog chair*)				
Action+ Location (e.g., *Go Nanna's*)				
Agent+ Object (e.g., *Mommy hair*)				
Noun Phrase+ Verb Phrase (e.g., *Mommy go*)				

2. Negatives and Interrogatives

	Frequent	Sometimes	None	Examples
No + statement (e.g., *No sleep, No inside*)				
Rising intonation (e.g., *More juice?*)				

Phonology

1. Uses these phonemes:

	Frequent	Sometimes	None	Examples
m (e.g., *man*)				
b (e.g., *ball*)				
n (e.g., *no*)				
w (e.g., *walk*)				
d (e.g., *dog*)				
p (e.g., *pie*)				
h (e.g., *hair*)				

(continued)

FIGURE 4.5 *(continued)*

	Frequent	Sometimes	None	Examples
2. Uses these phonological processes:				
■ deletes "weak" (unaccented) syllables: *Saturday* becomes /sædeɪ/				
■ deletes final consonants: *ball* becomes /ba/,				
■ velar fronting (i.e., substitutes front sounds such as /t/ and /d/ for back stops /k/ and /g/ /tʊp/ *tup* for /kʊp/ *cup*)				

Pragmatics

	Frequent	Sometimes	None	Examples
1. Intentionality				
Attempts to communicate				
Verbal communication more frequent than nonverbal				
2. Discourse functions				
Requests information				
Acknowledges others' utterances				
Responds to requests for information				

(continued)

FIGURE 4.5 *(continued)*

	Frequent	Sometimes	None	Examples
3. Presuppositions				
Provides little background information				
Responds to -wh questions for information				
4. Turntaking				
Takes turns over a few turns				
Takes turns with one conversational partner				
Takes turns with one + partner				

FIGURE 4.5 (continued)

Semantics

1. Vocabulary (Note: Receptive vocabulary is typically much larger than expressive vocabulary)

   <u>Receptive</u>

   Recognizes pictured object by name

   Acquires new words easily

   Understands many more words than the child produces

   <u>Expressive</u>

   Acquires new words easily

   Easily retrieves names of things

   Names pictured objects

2. Word types expressed

   nouns and verbs

   prepositions (e.g., *behind, in front of*)

   adjectives (e.g., *big, little*)

   temporal words (e.g., *before, first*)

   pronouns (*he, her, it*)

Examples observed										

(continued)

FIGURE 4.6

Observation Worksheet for Developing Language

3. Uses personal pronouns:

I, me

my, mine

you, your, yours

he, she, it

his, hers, its

him, her, it

we, us

our, ours

they, them

their, theirs

Examples observed									

4. Uses inflectional markers and contractions:

past tense (-ed, -t)

plural (-s, -es, -z)

possessive (-s)

not (-n't)

am (-m)

is (-'s)

are (-re)

have (-'ve)

Examples observed									

(continued)

FIGURE 4.6 *(continued)*

Syntax and Morphology

1. Uses these sentence types:

   negative past tense (e.g., *weren't, wasn't*)

   yes/no questions with inverted word order

   (e.g., *"Is that a cat?"*)

   past tense modals (e.g., *wouldn't, couldn't*)

   tag questions (e.g., *I'm going now, okay?*)

Examples observed			

2. Uses embedded phrases:

   prepositional phrase at end of sentence

   (e.g., *"I want to go to the park."*)

   participial phrase (e.g., *running dog*)

   infinitive phrase as object of subject (e.g., *"I want to eat dinner"*)

   infinitive phrase as object of object (e.g., *"I want my sister to come"*)

   gerunds (e.g., *"Playing is fun"*)

   and compound sentences:

   using *and* (e.g., *"She came over and we played"*)

   using *but* (e.g., *"We went to the pool but we couldn't swim"*)

Examples observed					

(continued)

FIGURE 4.6 *(continued)*

3. Uses embedded clauses (in developmental order):

object complement clause

(e.g., I know *this is a dog*)

wh- question clause

(e.g., I know *what this is*)

relative clause

(e.g., That's the one *I saw*)

		Examples observed

4. Uses morphological markers (in developmental order):

plurals, possessives, & progressive *-ing*

(e.g., I see three cat*s*

Here's the cat'*s* toy

The cat's eat*ing*)

third person singular 's marker and past tense *-ed*

(e.g., The dog'*s* eating

The dogs jump*ed* the fence)

copula and auxiliary "to be" forms

(e.g., Daddy *is* hungry

The cat *is* running)

exceptions to rules: irregular verbs and tense markers

(e.g., mice, children, people, women, men, sheep, deer

swam, ran, ate, went, found, took)

					Examples observed

(continued)

FIGURE 4.6 *(continued)*

Phonology

1. Phoneme acquisition (set 1 before set 2)

__Set 1__

t (e.g., *toy*)

ŋ (e.g., *ring*)

k (e.g., *cat*)

g (e.g., *girl*)

f (e.g., *fur*)

v (e.g., *van*)

tʃ (ch) (e.g., *church*)

dʒ (dg) (e.g., *judge*)

__Set 2__

ʃ (sh) (e.g., *she*)

θ (voiceless th) (e.g., *thing*)

s (e.g., *sun*)

z (e.g., *zip*)

ð (voiced th) (e.g., *there*)

l (e.g., *light*)

r (e.g., *run*)

ʒ (e.g., *treasure*)

Examples observed						

Examples observed						

(continued)

FIGURE 4.6 *(continued)*

Phonological Processes
(most disappear by age 4.0)

	Examples observed
1. Cluster reduction:	
■ two-consonant combinations reduced to one (e.g., /ti/ for tree)	
■ three-consonant combinations reduced to two (e.g., /staip/ for stripe)	
2. Substitution of glide for liquid (e.g., /twi/ for tree)	
3. insertion of the schwa (e.g., /təwi/ for tree)	

Pragmatics

	Frequent	Sometimes	None	Examples
1. Turntaking				
Knows how to initiate conversations				
Sustains topic over several turns				
Allows partner to finish turn before interrupting				
Knows how to interrupt				
Knows when it's okay to interrupt				
Knows how to end conversations				
2. Presuppositions	Frequent	Sometimes	None	Examples
Gives listener right amount of background information				
Adjusts speech and language to listener's needs				

(continued)

FIGURE 4.6 *(continued)*

3. Conversational repair	Frequent	Sometimes	None	Examples
Can repair utterance on request for clarification				
Can repair and clarify on request for clarification				

4. Directness of requesting	Frequent	Sometimes	None	Examples
Uses direct requests (e.g., "I want more juice")				
States "urgent need" (e.g., "I <u>need</u> more juice")				
Incorporates some polite forms (e.g., "please")				
Uses indirect requests (e.g., "I'm thirsty")				

5. Figurative language	Frequent	Sometimes	None	Examples
Understands multiple-meaning words (e.g., to, two, too)				
Uses multiple-meaning words				
Understands different names for things (e.g., sofa, couch)				
Uses different names for things				
Understands familiar idioms				
Beginning to use humor (e.g., knock-knock jokes)				

(continued)

FIGURE 4.6 *(continued)*

Narrative Development

	Frequent	Sometimes	None	Examples
1. Recounts, eventcasts, and accounts				
Uses recounts in response to adults' initiation				
Uses eventcasts to manipulate adults' behavior				
Uses accounts to tell about experiences, thoughts, or feelings				
2. Story (narrative) structure	Frequent	Sometimes	None	Examples
Uses protonarratives centered on character, theme, or setting				
Tells stories with beginning, middle, and end				
Tells stories with initiating event, attempt, and consequence				
Tells stories with above + plan, reaction, or ending				
Tells complete narratives (all of the above)				

FIGURE 4.6 *(continued)*

Communication and Language Instruction

Among the mandates of IDEA, states must link students' IEPs with state learning standards. Although most states have developed learning standards for kindergarten through high school, few have designed learning standards for preschoolers. As one instance, the Illinois State Board of Education (2004) has developed a draft version of early learning standards for preschool children covering language arts, mathematics, science, social science, physical development and health, fine arts, foreign languages, and social/emotional development. Of particular interest here are the language arts and social/emotional development standards, the latter because pragmatic language development progresses in conjunction with social/emotional development. In the discussion of language instruction for children at the developing language stage, these standards and associated benchmarks become salient because they represent the knowledge and skills that preschool children must acquire to negotiate kindergarten and first grade successfully.

In addition to state learning standards, various professional groups devoted to the education of young children have formulated guidelines for teaching preschool children the skills and competencies that form the basis for learning to read and write. One such group, the National Association for the Education of Young Children (NAEYC), in association with the International Reading Association (IRA), has published a description of developmentally appropriate practices for teaching young children the abilities underlying the acquisition of reading and writing (Neuman, Copple, & Bredekamp, 2000).

In their position statement, NAEYC and IRA report that the single most important precursor to reading success is being read aloud to (Bus, Van Ijzendoorn, & Pellegrini, 1995) so the experience is meaningful and relevant to the child. For this to occur, children must feel emotionally secure (Bus & Van Ijzendoorn, 1995, Bus, Belsky, Van Ijzendoorn, & Crnic, 1997), and they must be active participants in the reading (Whitehurst et al., 1994).

Moreover, research has shown that when the adult asks questions that invite children to predict and analyze what is happening in the story, the children's vocabulary and story comprehension improve (Karweit & Wasik, 1996). The talk surrounding the story reading provides opportunities for children to engage in conversations with the adult about the pictures in the story, to tell the story again in their own words and describe their favorite parts, and to ask for multiple rereadings (Neuman, Copple, & Bredekamp, 2000). Snow and her colleagues (Snow, 1991; Snow, Tabors, Nicholson, & Kurland, 1995) believe that the conversation surrounding story reading is what helps children bridge the story to their own experiences, thus inducing children to move from what they see in front of them into what they can imagine.

In an earlier position statement, the IRA and NAEYC (1998) argued that the literacy goal for preschool children is to explore their environment in ways that build the foundations for learning to read and write. Specifically, they recommend that instruction should provide opportunities for children to (p. 53):

- enjoy listening to and discussing storybooks,
- understand that print carries a message,
- engage in reading and writing attempts,
- identify labels and signs in their environment,
- participate in rhyming games,
- identify some letters and make some letter–sound matches, and
- use known letters or approximations of letters to represent written language (especially meaningful words such as their name and phrases such as "I love you").

The statement further recommends that teachers focus on literacy development in preschool through (p. 59)

- sharing books with children, including Big Books, and model reading behaviors;
- talking about letters by name and sounds;
- establishing a literacy-rich environment;
- rereading favorite stories;
- engaging children in language games;
- promoting literacy-related play activities; and
- encouraging children to experiment with writing.

One of the most significant changes in children during elementary school is the shift from communicating primarily in the oral domain to communicating through a diverse array of literate language styles. Making that oral-to-literate shift hinges on acquisition of the oral language and communication abilities that are characteristic of the end of the developing language stage, which itself rests on the communicative and linguistic competencies acquired during the prelinguistic and emerging language stages. Learning to read, write, and spell requires the following language knowledge, called **metalinguistic awareness**, which most preschool children acquire by at the end of the developing language period:

- Recognizing that language can be talked about
- Understanding that words can be segmented into syllables and sounds
- Knowing that sounds can be represented by letters
- Recognizing that print contains valuable and relevant information
- Knowing that stories contain certain required elements
- Understanding that narratives progress in predictable ways, while nonnarratives are organized according to different organizational schemes
- Knowing that people use different language—both oral and written—for different purposes

Children who exhibit weaknesses in oral language development during the prelinguistic, emerging, and/or developing stages often display a variety of problems in learning to read, write, or spell, typically diagnosed as a **language-learning disability (LLD)**. Because most learning disabilities involve deficits in learning to read, write, or spell, these are believed to be a function of problems with the oral language abilities on which reading, writing, and spelling rest. Language-learning disability, first described in detail by Wallach and Butler (1984) and Wallach and Miller (1988), is considered to be the most common type of learning disability.

Language-learning disability is viewed as a more general type of language-based learning problem than dyslexia. **Dyslexia** usually is described as a deficit in single-word decoding, based on a problem in the phonological domain of oral language (Snowling, 1996). Paul (2006) argued that, in contrast to LLD, dyslexia typically carries a limited impact on comprehension. Language-learning disabilities, in contrast, involve problems with both single-word reading and comprehension. These deficits are believed to include not only the phonological system but the child's other language domains as well, including semantics, syntax, and pragmatics, particularly narrative abilities. In this view, then, language-learning disability constitutes one type of learning disability and dyslexia represents a specific type of language-learning disability.

These distinctions become important when planning and designing language instruction because, as mentioned earlier, children who are diagnosed as having LLD after they reach school usually have a history of delayed speech and language development during the preschool years, whereas most elementary school children diagnosed with dyslexia do not (Snowling, 1996). In addition, four major aspects of communication development have been shown to predict later language skills (McCathren, Yoder, & Warren, 1999):

1. Rate and complexity of babbling
2. Rate and range of expression of communicative intent
3. Level of comprehension
4. Rate and complexity of symbolic play

Therefore, language instruction for preschool children takes on added significance. It is aimed at helping children develop the oral language abilities necessary for them to function socially and in their everyday lives and also attempts to forestall the later emergence of a language-learning disability.

The long-term goal of language instruction for preschool children with disabilities is for them—if possible—to acquire the semantic, syntactic, phonological, and pragmatic abilities typical of the end of the developing language period. How quickly that long-term goal is realized depends on each child's developmental characteristics. A child whose communication and language abilities are characteristic of the emerging language stage most likely will reach the developing language stage sooner than a child whose communication and language skills are still in the prelinguistic period.

Once preschool children with any disability reach age 3, IDEA mandates that an IEP be developed to plan intervention services, including language instruction. The IEP must contain various sorts of information, shown in Table 4.1.

For preschool children whose language development is in the prelinguistic or emerging language stages, the IEP description of their present levels of performance

TABLE 4.1

What must be included in The IEP under IDEA 2004 34 CFR §§ 300.320-300.328(a)

1. Present levels of academic achievement and functional performance:

   A statement of the child's present level of educational performance, including:

   - how the child's disability affects his or her involvement and progress in the general curriculum;
   - for preschool children, as appropriate, how the disability affects the child's participation in appropriate activities.

2. Measurable annual goals, including academic and functional goals, including benchmarks and short-term goals:

   A statement related to:

   - meeting the child's needs—those resulting from the child's disability—to enable the child to be involved in and progress in the general curriculum; and
   - meeting each of the child's other educational needs that result from the child's disability.

3. Special education and related services, supplementary aids and services to be provided to the child, or on behalf of the child, and the program modifications or supports for school personnel:

   A statement showing what will be provided for the child to:

   - advance appropriately toward attaining the annual goals,
   - be involved and progress in the general curriculum and to participate in extracurricular and other nonacademic activities, and
   - be educated and participate with other children with disabilities and nondisabled children in extracurricular and other nonacademic activities.

4. An explanation of the extent, if any, to which the child will not participate with nondisabled children in the regular class and in extracurricular and other nonacademic activities.

usually focuses on how the disability affects their participation in appropriate activities, and the description of annual goals, including benchmarks or short-term objectives, emphasizes the abilities they need in order to be involved in and progress toward the goals of the preschool program. For children whose language falls within the developing language period, these descriptions are more likely to include reference to the learning standards adopted by each state. Therefore, the section on language instruction for children whose language is characteristic of the developing language period links the IEP to state learning standards (Miller & Hoffman, 2002).

For children in the prelinguistic and emerging language stages, our perspective is that, except for children with severe impairments, a developmental approach is the most effective way to address communication and language. This means that language instruction for most preschool children provides supports and teaching environments that help them progress through the developmental stages of language acquisition.

The following discussion describes how instruction might proceed for children at the prelinguistic stage and the emerging language stage. This is followed by a discussion of language instruction using state learning standards for children in the developing language stage. Finally, we will consider language instruction for preschool children for whom speech is severely or totally compromised.

Language Instruction for Preschool Children at the Prelinguistic Stage

The type of communication that best enhances children's language development is enriching and responsive (Clarke-Stewart, 1973). Children respond best when adults enter their attentional sphere, when the experience includes visual, tactile, and auditory information, and when the child is helped to explore novel (but safe) objects, events, and processes. Further, through rendering their communications responsive to and contingent on what the child is doing, adults bolster the child's communication and language development (Paul, 2006).

More specifically, instruction for preschool children whose communication and language abilities are in the prelinguistic stage (developmental level of 9 to 18 months) consists primarily of strategies for increasing the child's ability to

- vocalize,
- vocalize frequently and use different types of vocalizations,
- exhibit intentions in communicating,
- use different forms to communicate intention,
- exhibit several types of intentions (requesting, negating, "commenting"),
- engage in mutual attending,
- engage in joint attending, and
- engage in joint referencing.

For children who are just entering the prelinguistic period, language instruction models four types of interactive behaviors that are particularly effective in fostering children's communication: turntaking, imitation, joint attention, and anticipatory sets (Paul, 2006). Because the family is integral to the child's development and must be included in the child's IFSP, language instruction for preschoolers includes support and coaching for parents and caregivers, as well as direct instruction within the context of a preschool program.

Modeling each of the four communicative behaviors requires that those who are interacting with the child are attentive to the child's signals of readiness to engage in communicative interactions. Prelinguistic children indicate their readiness to communicate through a heightened state of alertness, gazing at the person with whom he wants to communicate and vocalizing comfort sounds (Paul, 2006). Because children produce these signs at different times and in different contexts, those providing language instruction must be ready to initiate communicative interaction during any of the activities in which children are involved.

Language instruction for preschool-age children, though it is definitely planned, must remain flexible and spontaneous. Typical preschool children are actively exploring their worlds. Most children with disabilities are just as are curious and want to discover how things work. Language instruction is most effective within the context of children's everyday lives, a part of which they spend in preschool programs. Therefore, the following discussions suggest instructional strategies and techniques suitable for children in a preschool setting.

Modeling Turntaking and Imitation

Adults' behaviors serve as powerful models for children, and communicative and linguistic behaviors are no exception. Babies learn their earliest communicative knowledge and behaviors from the adults in their families, including how to participate in conversations. In preschool programs serving children with disabilities, these adult models can be incorporated consciously into virtually every teacher–student interaction.

For children in the prelinguistic period of development, teachers' models of turntaking and imitation provide the following repeated examples of basic communicative interactions (Paul, 2006):

- Observing the child
- Using smiles and vocalizations to stimulate behavior from the child
- Waiting while the child expresses or performs some behavior such as vocalizing, moving limbs, or making faces
- Imitating whatever the child does
- Waiting for the child to do something else

In this process, the teacher waits for the child to do something, mimics it, waits for the child to do something else, mimics that, waits again, and so on. If the child is playing with blocks, for instance, the teacher can watch the child long enough to determine the child's intent and purpose with the blocks, then join the child. At first the teacher plays alongside the child, imitating the child's actions with the blocks and perhaps using one-word phrases to describe the child's actions.

When the child looks at the teacher, the teacher smiles and repeats the one-word phrase, then waits for the child to do or say something, which the teacher then mimics. Then the teacher waits for the child to make another move with the blocks, which she again imitates while verbalizing. Each time the child looks at the teacher, she smiles and verbalizes a positive response, such as, "Yes, that's right," or "Yes, I see you." Or the teacher can verbalize what the child just did, for example, saying "in" to indicate that the child has just put the block in the box, or "off" to reflect the child's removing the block from the table. Paul (2006) recommends vocalizing to the child and imitating his vocalizations as especially helpful in encouraging vocal development.

Modeling Joint Attention

In **joint attention**, as described in Chapter 2, the parent and the infant look at each other's faces while "conversing." To model joint attention, the adult must first identify the child's focus and share attention to whatever that focus is. For instance, if the child is looking at a stuffed animal, the adult looks at the toy, talks about it or gestures toward it, and then returns the child's gaze, perhaps smiling, or saying something like, "Yes, I see you, too." Once the child and the adult have shared attention in this manner, the adult introduces something new, perhaps a different toy, and comments on it while moving it in a different way. Again, when the child looks at the adult, the adult remarks on the child's gaze, perhaps saying, "I see you!"

Modeling Anticipatory Sets

Games such as "Peek-a-boo" and "Gonna getcha" foster joint attending and help the child establish what are called **anticipatory sets**. Paul (2006) described anticipatory sets as activities or games that have been repeated often enough that the child becomes familiar with the same sequence. Over time, the child begins to anticipate the entire sequence when a part of the sequence is presented. Anticipating in these predictable sequences is believed to provide the foundation for developing the scripts (or schemata) that help organize knowledge, as well as acquire the language used to encode this knowledge (Milosky, 1990).

Adults model anticipatory sets when they engage the child in predictable games and routines, use the same language to accompany each of these games or routines, and respond to the child's increasing efforts to participate. When the adult repeatedly reenacts the same routines, using the same words and phrases, the child develops an ability not only to anticipate the sequence but also to initiate it by spontaneously using an action in the routine as a request to play the game.

An example illustrates the process of modeling anticipatory sets: Mike, a 3½ year-old boy in the prelinguistic stage of language development, was enrolled in a preschool program for children with disabilities. Every day, the teacher took the children outside for a period of free play that included a routine in which each child requested piggyback rides from the teachers. Obviously, each child's request reflected his level of language development. Mike's request usually took the form of placing himself in front of a "free" adult and holding up his arms while looking backward over his shoulder at the adult. The adult would say, "Mike wants up," and swing him up onto her shoulder.

For several months this routine remained unchanged. One day, however, Mike placed himself in front of the teacher, whose attention at that moment shifted to another child walking through the play yard. As she started toward the other child, she did not see Mike in front of her with his arms raised until she walked into him. Suddenly Mike began saying, "Up! Up!" while waving his arms to gain her attention.

After that incident, Mike began saying, first, "Up," and soon after, "Want up," whenever he wanted his turn at a piggyback ride. In this case, his ongoing participation in the routine of requesting piggyback rides had prepared him to speak his request when he realized that his previous nonverbal strategy was insufficient for the situation.

Increasing Communicative Intentions

Communicating a variety of intentions underlies the ability to use the variety of semantic, syntactic, and morphological structures typical of the emerging language stage of development. One technique to foster the development of communicative intentions once children engage in joint attending and joint referencing is **communicative temptations** (Warren & Yoder, 1998). Communicative temptations involve structuring a situation in which the child is strongly motivated to communicate to the adult, followed by a quick and positive response from the adult. Examples of communicative temptations include the following:

- While engaging the child in play, stop and wait for the child to communicate either a desire to continue or directions about what to do next.
- During snack time, begin eating without offering the snack to the child.
- During play, turn attention away from the child.
- Present a closed bag of toys that requires adult help to open.
- In the middle of an interaction, stop and wait for the child to request a continuation.
- Put on an unusual piece of clothing.
- Put on a mask.
- Present the child with two masks and ask which he wants.
- Open a bubble jar and blow bubbles until the child indicates his desire to blow them.

Bookreading to Foster Language Development

Parents of typically developing children commonly begin reading books to their children when they are as young as 6 months of age (Elliott-Templeton, Van Kleeck, Richardson, & Imholz, 1992). Because these bookreading experiences have been shown to foster language development (Chomsky, 1972; Dickinson and Neuman, 2006; Snow, 1983; Whitehurst et al., 1988), they certainly are considered beneficial for children with disabilities as well. In addition, bookreading contributes to the development of children's comprehension of language, which becomes more important in the emerging language stage, discussed later in the chapter.

Picture books can be used to share joint attention, with the adult naming each picture and perhaps making one or two elaborative comments about each. Once the child is familiar with the book and the routine of looking at it with the adult, the adult can stop on any given page and wait for the child to initiate what is to happen next. For instance, once the child points to the picture, the adult names it for a period of time until the adult judges that it is time to begin requesting that the child name—or attempt to name—the picture.

Teaching continues in this manner, with the teacher establishing a series of routines in which the child's communicative response during the first routine is to share joint attention, in the next routine to point to the pictures, and in the final routine to name (or approximately name) most of the pictures. This same instructional process can be used with different picture books until the teacher judges that the child is developmentally ready for the more complex interaction involved with simple wordless storybooks.

The instructional process is the same for wordless storybooks as for picture books. The teacher establishes a routine for each book, perhaps beginning by telling the child that this book tells a story, and then telling, in short sentences, what is happening on each page. Once the child can predict the routine, the teacher begins asking the child to point to something the teacher is describing on each page. Once that routine is established, the teacher asks the child to name something that is happening on each page.

Language Instruction for Preschool Children at the Emerging Language Stage

Preschool children at the emerging language stage (a developmental level of 18–36 months) who receive language intervention make faster gains than those in normal development (McLean & Cripe, 1997). This means that language instruction during the emerging language stage takes on added significance for children with cognitive deficits; hearing impairments (whether associated with chronic middle ear disease or not); family history of speech, language, or learning problems; and/or social communication problems. Olswang, Rodriguez, and Timler (1998) identified a set of factors that predict the need for language intervention and instruction, including problems with

- language production: small vocabulary with few verbs, more transitive (*eat apple*) and general verbs (*make, do, go*), few intransitive (*sit, lie*) or **bitransitive** verbs (*take* the book to *the teacher*);
- language comprehension: significant problems with comprehension, gap between comprehension and production;
- phonology: few vocalizations prior to prelinguistic development, limited number of consonants, little variety during babbling, fewer than 50% of constants produced correctly, glottals and backs substituted for fronts, vowel errors, problems with syllable structure;
- imitation: few spontaneous imitations, imitation mostly in response to direct modeling and prompting.

More specifically, as described earlier, language instruction for preschool children at the emerging language stage focuses on the range of communicative intentions the child expresses, the child's phonemic productions, which phonological processes are present, the pragmatic functions and discourse skills the child brings to bear, the semantic content the child displays, and the syntactic forms the child utilizes.

Developing Symbolic Play

Attaching language instruction to children's play is based on research showing that, when early symbolic play behaviors are present in children with disabilities, language intervention is more likely to result in an increase in communication abilities (Yoder, Davies, Bishop, & Munson, 1995). Moreover, because children's cognitive skills develop at the same time as their language abilities, symbolic play offers a window into their communication and language development (Toth, Munson, Meltzoff, & Dawson, 2006). When symbolic behaviors emerge, the language skill normally associated with the behavior should be teachable at the same time. The absence of play skills at each stage suggests that the language ability characteristic of the same developmental stage is unlikely to emerge and instruction should focus on earlier emerging skills, particularly for children on the autism spectrum scale.

Further, knowing which play skills the child possesses reveals which activities, materials, and contexts will be most effective, relevant, and appropriate to support and encourage language learning (Paul, 2006). Finally, language instruction using play provides children with adult models of symbolic play, opportunities to imitate the models, and opportunities to develop receptive language abilities through hearing the teacher's language accompanying the play.

Symbolic play develops in stages (McCune, 1995; Nicolich, 1977):

1. Child expresses playful pretending (e.g., pretending to eat with a toy spoon, pretending to sleep), developmentally 18–24 months.
2. Child uses symbolism beyond self (e.g., feeds a toy bear, pretends to wash the table, moves toy car with appropriate noise), developmentally 24–36 months.
3. Child combines symbolic games (e.g., feeds pretend food to doll, then to self; holds toy phone to ear, pushes buttons, hands phone to teacher), developmentally 24–36 months.
4. Child uses hierarchical pretending showing planning (assembles utensils for making a "cake," measures pretend ingredients, puts pan in "oven," sets "timer"), developmentally 24–36 months.

Language instruction using symbolic play can address each of the various components of language development: semantics, phonology, syntax, and pragmatics.

Language instruction focused on *semantic* development through symbolic play has as its goal the acquisition of a receptive vocabulary between 200 words and 1,800 words, including both relational and substantive words. While engaged in symbolic play with children, the teacher's semantic emphasis can be on using a variety of different words to describe what is transpiring during the play, taking care to use both relational words and substantive words. **Relational words** are non-nouns that express the relationships between objects, whereas **substantive words** are nouns that label people, pets, toys, and objects the child operates on directly.

In addition, teachers should use words that serve the following communicative purposes (Bloom & Lahey, 1978):

- Rejection (*no*)
- Nonexistence or disappearance (*all gone*)
- Cessation or prohibition of action (*stop*)
- Recurrence (*more*)
- Existence (*this*)
- Action on objects (*kiss*)
- Locative action (*up, fill, out*)
- Attribution (*big*)
- Naming, possession, commenting (*dog*)
- Social interaction (*hi*).

To increase children's *syntactic skills* through symbolic play, teachers can model phrases for children, emphasizing the words that are most likely to appear in the children's own two-word utterances (emphasis underlined):

Agent + Action	e.g., "The <u>dog</u> is <u>eating</u>.
Agent + Location	e.g., "The <u>dog</u> is on the <u>chair</u>."
Action + Location	e.g., "Let's <u>go</u> to <u>Nanna's</u>."
Agent + Object	e.g., "That's <u>mommy's</u> <u>hair</u>."

Once children begin expressing two-word phrases, teachers can begin using phrases that include both a noun phrase and a verb phrase:

"The <u>dog</u> is <u>eating</u>."
"The <u>dog</u> is on the <u>chair</u>."
"The <u>horse</u> is <u>running</u>."
"The <u>cow</u> is <u>talking</u>."

Teachers can address children's production of interrogatives and negatives through symbolic play by providing opportunities for them to reject an action or object (negation) or to request an action or object (interrogative). For instance, while playing with farm animals, the teacher could have one of the animals do something that the child clearly does not want, which offers the child the chance to reject the action. If the child has grouped the animals by type, putting all the horses in one area, the cows in another, and the dogs in another, the clinician would move one of the horses into the cow area, giving the child an opening to reject the action by saying, for example, "No cow!"

To stimulate an interrogative during symbolic play requires a bit more strategy to set up the situation so that an interrogative is logical and appropriate. For instance, using the farm animal scenario above, the teacher could initiate a turntaking game in which teacher and child take turns putting the animals into various spots. During each of the child's turns, the teacher asks, "Which one do you want?" while gesturing to the pile of animals. When the child indicates which toy he wants, the teacher hands it over. During the teacher's turn to categorize the animals, she can wait for the child to ask which one he wants. If the child does not offer an interrogative, the teacher can model, saying, for instance, "Which one do I want? Hmm. Let's see," all the while looking at the child as a way to encourage him to participate by using an interrogative.

To encourage the development of *phonology*, and specifically the acquisition of the phonemes expected during the emerging language stage, symbolic play can be structured using materials and activities requiring words containing these phonemes /m, b, n, w, d, p, h/. As a consequence, throughout the play sessions, the teacher structures her utterances to contain words and phrases beginning and ending with these phonemes. When the child uses the most typical phonological processes—deleting unaccented syllables, deleting final consonants, and velar fronting—the teacher could model words and utterances containing the unmodified, adult version of the same syllables so the child has opportunities to listen to them without any pressure for production.

Symbolic play, because it entails a naturalistic, interactive process, presents multiple occasions for children to communicate over a wide range of communicative intentions and to develop *pragmatic skills*; moreover, it offers numerous opportunities for teachers to develop children's awareness of the social-interactive requirements of conversation, specifically communicative intentions and discourse functions.

Communicative Intentions and Discourse Functions The communicative intentions that teachers can model and that can be evoked through symbolic play include

- naming people, objects, experiences, events, and locations;
- commenting on the physical attributes of people, objects, and experiences (these include size, shape, color, and location; movements and actions of animals, objects, and people);
- requesting objects in the present environment and elsewhere;
- requesting the initiation or continuation of an action;
- requesting information or confirmation about objects, actions, people, or locations by using rising intonation;
- responding directly to preceding utterances;
- protesting or rejecting an ongoing or impending action or event;
- seeking attention to self or aspects of the current context;
- greeting through conversationalized rituals such as "hi," and "bye, bye."

Similarly, teachers can model the three most typical forms of discourse functions used by children during this period:

1. Requests for information—using language to find out about the world (e.g., asking for the names of things, events, proceses, and relationships)—this first appears through rising intonation, then a *wh-* word, then both

2. Acknowledgements to the conversational partner that the previous utterance has been received, typically through mimicking the speaker's intonation pattern, imitating part of the utterance, or nodding the head

3. Answers, or appropriate responses to a request for information from the conversational partner

Incorporating these intentions and discourse functions into play sessions with children is relatively easy and can be tracked with a checklist, such as the one shown in Figure 4.7. The checklist serves both to guide the teacher's language models during the play sessions and to document the child's production of the targeted pragmatic functions.

Presuppositions and Turntaking   Symbolic play can serve as a natural bridge for children during the emerging language stage. In the earliest part of this stage, children usually assume that their conversational partners know everything they themselves know, with the result that they provide little or no background information for their utterances, use linguistic shortcuts such as personal pronouns to refer to everything, and are unable to respond to requests for additional information or clarification.

One way the teacher can use symbolic play to support children's development of presuppositional abilities is to set up play scenarios during which she is not looking at what the child is doing. This requires the child to use more elaborate language to describe or explain what he is doing. If at first the child is unable to elaborate, the teacher can return her gaze to the child's actions and describe what is happening. Then, she again gazes elsewhere and asks the child to tell what is happening. Most children will respond by imitating at least a portion of what the teacher has just said. The teacher then responds by continuing the play actions.

Another possible scenario is for the teacher to model through the play how one character, perhaps a toy figure, tells another figure that has just joined the "game" what is happening. The "new" figure might ask questions to which the "old" figure can respond by giving more background information. After one or two question-and-answer turns, the teacher hands the old figure to the child and, speaking as the new figure, asks the same questions as the old figure for the child to respond to.

Turntaking skills can be supported in much the same way. Through play figures, the teacher can model how each can take turns conversing, using the semantic, phonological, and syntactic structures that have been selected as targets for this child. For instance, the teacher models two farm animals conversing about the wonderful grass in the field, the flowers they see, the creek from which they drink, and the food they expect to eat when they return to the barn.

The teacher could extend the turntaking over more than one turn, modeling for the child how the animals can talk in turn for two or three turns. Then the teacher might hand one of the animals to the child and repeat the opening comment from the other animal, thus offering the child an opportunity to mimic the turntaking the teacher just modeled. Over time, the teacher could include more than two animals to demonstrate how turntaking looks with more than two conversational partners.

Communicative Intentions	Frequent	Sometimes	None	Examples
Names people, objects, events, and locations				
Describes physical attributes:				
size, shape, and location				
movements and actions of objects and people				
references to attributes (possession and usual location)				
Requests objects in the present environment				
Requests objects outside the current environment				
Requests the initiation or continuation of an action				
Requests information about objects, actions, people, or locations				
Responds directly to preceding utterances				
Protests or rejects ongoing or impending action or event				
Seeks attention to self or aspects of the environment				
Greets through conversationalized rituals				

	Frequent	Sometimes	None	Examples
Asks for names of things, events, processes, and relationships:				
rising intonation, a wh- word, both				
Acknowledgments: mimics speaker's intonation pattern,				
imitates part of his or her utterance, or nods the head				
Appropriate responses to requests for information.				

FIGURE 4.7

Communicative Intentions and Discourse Functions Produced during Play

Language Instruction for Preschool Children at the Developing Language Stage

To reiterate—the primary goal of language instruction during the preschool period is to support children's development of the language abilities underlying success in school (i.e., the semantic, syntactic, phonological, and pragmatic abilities typical of the developing language period), as well as the early literacy skills typical in literate homes. For children whose language abilities are in the developing language stage, a fruitful approach to language instruction is to link their IEPs to existing state learning standards for preschool children.

Earlier we noted that individual states have begun to develop learning standards for preschool children and that, in most cases, the standards most salient to language instruction are those in language arts and in social/emotional development. For instance, Illinois' Early Learning Standards include five educational goals for Language Arts at the preschool level (Illinois State Board of Education, 2004, pp. 8–11):

1. Read with understanding and fluency.
2. Read and understand literature representative of various societies, eras, and ideas.
3. Write to communicate for a variety of purposes.
4. Listen and speak effectively in a variety of situations.
5. Use the language arts to acquire, assess, and communicate information.

Clearly, these goals for Language Arts are aligned directly with the state's learning standards for the elementary grades, and the framers of the draft standards understand that preschool children progress toward these goals in a developmental fashion. Accordingly, each goal is accompanied by two or three Learning Standards, and each in turn is linked to a set of Benchmarks reflecting the typical development of preschool children. For instance, two of the Learning Standards associated with the fourth goal are for children to listen effectively in formal and informal situations and to speak effectively using language appropriate to the situation and the audience. The benchmarks described for these standards are (Illinois State Board of Education, 2004, p. 11):

- listen with understanding, and respond to directions and conversations, and
- communicate needs, ideas, and thoughts.

Similarly, the learning standards associated with the fifth goal are for children to locate, organize, and use information from various sources to answer questions, solve problem, and communicate ideas. The benchmark described for these standards is to seek answers to questions through active exploration (Illinois State Board of Education, 2004, p. 11).

The easiest way to link the IEP with state learning standards is to use the learning standards as annual goals and to include the benchmarks from the learning standards as the IEP benchmarks as well (Miller & Hoffman, 2002). An example of a preschool child's IEP linked to learning standards is shown in Table 4.2. The communication rubric referred to in Sara's IEP is shown in Figure 4.8.

Instructional Products, Processes, and Contexts

A convenient way to organize language intervention and instruction is to focus on the communication and/or language *goals* established for the child, the instructional *methods* designed to help the child achieve the communication/language goals, and the instructional *settings* within which the instruction takes place.

Instructional Goals The instructional goals for enhancing the individual's communication and/or language can be established by linking them to state learning standards. As mentioned, few states at present have adopted learning standards for preschool children; however, the standards from states that use at least draft or published versions (e.g., Illinois, Ohio, and California) can be used until more states have adopted their own.

Again, the long-term goals driving the standards must be specified into benchmarks or short-term objectives that match the child's developmental needs. The benchmarks should lead cumulatively to the achievement of the overall, or annual, goals specified for each child (Paul, 2006). Using the example of Sara from Figure 4.8 and Table 4.2, the long-range, annual goal for her is:

> By June 3, 2011, Sara will visually/verbally signal awareness of the difference in language patterns used in her spoken communication contexts, especially at school, so as to progress toward meeting the Illinois Early Learning Standards Goal 4: Listen and speak effectively in formal and informal situations.

The benchmarks, or short-term objectives, are described on the communication rubric in Figure 4.8, which was constructed to show Sara's cumulative progress toward her annual goal, itself linked to Goal 4 of the Illinois State Learning Goals for Language Arts.

Thus, the general language goal specified in Sara's IEP is to speak and listen effectively in formal and informal situations, derived directly from the state learning standard document and applicable to a variety of children whose language is in the developing language stage.

The short-term objectives, or benchmarks, for Sara are more specific and unique to her specific linguistic and communicative needs. As shown on the communication rubric (Figure 4.8), language instruction for Sara has been designed to help her

- share information and increase conversational interactions with others;
- use effective voice and tone;
- constructively express her preferences, feelings, and needs; and
- use language to express her needs.

TABLE 4.2

IEP Linked to State Learning Standards

Individualized Education Program Description

What do we know about ___Sara___	What are we going to do to help ___Sara___ receive an appropriate education?	How will we know if we are succeeding?
Sara demonstrates limited awareness of differences in language patterns used in her spoken communication in the school context. Sara answers simple questions when asked by peers and adults; however, she doesn't request information or ask for clarification from others. She doesn't easily take turns in a conversation with her peers and does not attempt to repair her communication attempts when she's unsuccessful in communicating her ideas or needs. She is unsure whether the directions in class are suggestions for completing her work or are step-by-step instructions that must be followed.	Sara will receive classroom-based communication support 60 minutes per week in the preschool classroom, provided collaboratively by the speech and language pathologist and the preschool teacher. Sara will be provided with the following classroom supports: ■ Continual visual/verbal modelling and feedback regarding her communication attempts ■ Continual visual/verbal modeling and feedback regarding her requests for information and clarification ■ Continual visual/verbal modeling and feedback regarding her turntaking skills ■ Use of visual supports and verbal cues to increase her awareness and understanding of the flow of communication ■ Explicit descriptions of the expectations of classroom directions and work	By June 3, 2011, Sara will visually/verbally signal awareness of the differences in language patterns used in her spoken communication contexts, especially at school, so as to progress toward meeting the Illinois Early Learning Standards Goal 4: Listen and speak effectively in formal and informal situations. Progress will be measured using the communication rubric. ■ By Oct. 15, 2011, Sara will meet two of the four criteria in the "Getting There" category. ■ By Jan. 13, 2012, Sara will meet all four criteria in the "Getting There" category. ■ By April 1, 2012, Sara will meet two of the four criteria in the "Sometimes" category. ■ By June 3, 2012, Sara will meet all four criteria in the "Sometimes" category.
Included here would be Sara's present level of educational performance, her learning strengths, and how her disability affects her involvement in appropriate activities.	Included here would be information pertaining to Sara's special education services—personnel, frequency, duration, and location of services, as well as her accomodations, supplementary aids and services, transition services, extracurricular and other nonacademic activities or other services.	Included here would be Sara's goals and objectives, including evaluation procedures, objective criteria, and her expected dates for accomplishment. Sara's goals should lead to her being able to be involved in and progress in the general curriculum.

Communication Rubric

	Just Learning	Getting there	Sometimes
Shares information and increases conversational interactions with others.	I am beginning to learn how to take turns, stay on a topic, and end a conversation with others.	I am practicing using my conversational skills with other people by role playing, scripting, and social stories.	I can sometimes take turns, stay on a topic, and end a conversation with others.
Uses effective voice and tone.	Sometimes I forget to use my soft voice to talk.	I can use my soft voice when someone shows me how to show my strong feelings.	I can show strong feelings by using my soft voice without being reminded.
Constructively expresses preferences, feelings, and needs.	Sometimes I forget to use appropriate words and/or actions. Sometimes I call people names. Sometimes I push or hit people.	I have been using friendly and respectful words. I can use friendly body language when an adult reminds me.	I can use friendly and respectful words and body language. I can use words when I'm feeling uncomfortable or angry. I ask adults for help when I'm frustrated.
Uses language to express needs.	Sometimes I forget to use words to ask for what I need. Sometimes I use unfriendly words, actions, or tone of voice.	When an adult reminds me, I can use friendly words to ask for what I need.	I can figure out that I need something without asking an adult. I can use feeling words to say how I feel. I can let adults know what I need.

Source: From *Linking IEPs to Learning Standards* (p. 1), by L. Miller and L. Hoffman, 2001, Lockport, IL: Staff Development Center. Copyright 2001 by Lynda Miller. Reprinted with permission.

FIGURE 4.8
Communication Rubric used in Sara's IEP

Selecting specific benchmarks, or short-term objectives, is guided by a variety of factors. First, they must be developmentally in line with what the child needs to acquire next in the developing language stage. For Sara, these objectives were selected because they fall somewhere between her current level of communication and language functioning (as shown on her IEP in Table 4.2) and her potential level of performance, described by Vygotsky (1978) as the **Zone of Proximal Development**

(**ZPD**). Teaching within children's ZPD has been shown to be effective in leading the child to mastery, whereas choosing an instructional goal within the child's current knowledge base is considered to be a waste of instructional time (Lantolf & Poehner, 2004; Poehner & Lantolf, 2005). Those authors argue further that if children are using specific language forms with some degree of correctness, even if they are making errors, they are highly likely to achieve mastery without direct instruction.

A rough rule in determining a child's ZPD is to ascertain the percentage of correct productions of the targeted language form (Paul, 2006). If the child produces the targeted form around 80% of the time, Paul suggests that this indicates the child does not need direct instruction. But if the child produces the targeted form 40% of the time, he most likely would benefit from instruction, as this indicates that the form is within the child's ZPD. Productions at a rate significantly lower than 40%, however, usually signify a form that is beyond the child's current level of functioning and, thus, is a poor candidate for language instruction.

The benchmarks chosen for Sara can be used to illustrate using the ZPD to identify appropriate short-term objectives. During observations of Sara's communicative interactions with her peers, she was seen to display appropriate turntaking and staying on a topic approximately 41% of the time; her responses to adult requests for clarification of her previous statements, however, fell below 15%. Thus, turntaking and staying on a topic with a peer were selected as appropriate targets for language instruction, and responding to adult requests for clarification was determined to be outside her current ZPD and, therefore, inappropriate for direct instruction at the present time.

A second factor in selecting short-term objectives is the extent to which they are likely to improve the child's communicative effectiveness. Assessment of Sara's language skills had shown deficits not only in the pragmatic areas shown on her IEP but also in vocabulary (irregular verb forms, pronouns, and contractions) and syntax (complex sentences). The IEP team agreed, however that Sara would benefit more at present from focusing on the pragmatic aspects of her language development than emphasizing semantics or syntax, which would be addressed at least partially through specific curricular elements. For Sara to gain some communicative effectiveness with her peers seemed more important than for her to learn new vocabulary or syntactic structures.

A third factor in selecting benchmarks for children is how modifiable they are for each specific language product identified as requiring instruction. Miller et al. (2001) and Peña, Reséndez, and Gillam (2007) have described the concept of **modifiability** as a combination of the child's responsiveness during instruction (how the child responds to and uses new information), how much examiner effort is required to teach the child the new language form (both the quantity and the quality of the effort necessary to help the child change), and how well the child can transfer or generalize new language skills to new contexts.

Sara had demonstrated that she was able to use new language forms when she was unstressed, and she had been able to use appropriate linguistic means to express her wants and needs in more than one situation. Therefore, her teachers regarded her as at least somewhat modifiable to instruction regarding these skills.

A fourth factor guiding the selection of benchmarks is that certain language forms are more teachable than others because, according to Fey (1986), they are

- more easily demonstrated to the child or shown through pictures,
- taught through materials and activities that are easy to access and organize, and
- used frequently in naturally occurring situations in the child's everyday life.

For Sara, the language forms identified as benchmarks occurred almost every day in the preschool environment. Adults modeled for the children, and some of the other children demonstrated the very forms that Sara was trying to learn. In addition, the ongoing activities of the preschool program provided ample opportunities for Sara to engage in the conversational interactions that required her to use her newly emerging language forms.

A fifth principle directing selection of benchmarks stems from pioneering work by Slobin (1979), who showed that when children first begin using new language forms, they use them to serve "old" functions, or purposes already within their communicative systems. Conversely, when children begin using new functions, they use "old" forms that are already within their repertoire. This means that the selected benchmarks should require the child to do one of these two things, but not both at the same time. For instance, Sara's benchmarks emphasize the acquisition of new linguistic forms to express "old" functions already within her communicative means. She is not expected to produce new linguistic forms and new communicative functions at the same time.

Finally, selection of benchmarks should be guided by the child's phonological abilities (Fey, 1986; Schwartz & Leonard, 1982) because children are less likely to produce new words if the words contain phonological or syllabic elements that they are not already producing spontaneously (Schwartz & Leonard, 1982). This constraint is crucial in preschool children, whose language abilities are typically tender and tentative. Thus, even though certain vocabulary words may be appropriate targets for language instruction using the guidelines described above, the child's phonological capabilities may mitigate against using these words until they begin appearing in the child's spontaneous phonological repertoire. Once the words appear within the child's ZPD, these words are appropriate candidates for language instruction. For Sara, whose phonological abilities seemed to be developing at a normal pace, this principle did not apply.

Instructional Methods   Language instruction typically progresses from teacher directed to child centered, as shown in Table 4.3. Language instruction adhering to the approaches along the lefthand side tends to be more highly structured and less natural than the approaches described on the right. The intent of teacher-directed approaches is to provide stimuli that are clear to the students, to reduce extraneous activity and information, and to provide desirable reinforcement so the students will produce the language behavior.

TABLE 4.3
Continuum of Language Instruction

Teacher Directed	Combination	Child Centered
Drill: Based in behaviorist theory. Highly structured; teacher instructs student about what response is expected, provides a stimulus to be repeated (often with a prompt telling how to respond correctly) and provides a positive or negative reinforcement.	**Focused stimulation:** Teacher provides multiple models of a particular language form during play with the child; the child is not required to produce the targeted forms. Teacher provides nondirective feedback.	**Whole language:** Activities integrated around a theme, often from children's literature. Purpose is to promote general use of language for communicaton and problem solving.
Drill play: Same as drill except teacher provides a motivating event prior to the drill (e.g., she allows student to choose which a toy to play with after the drill is over).	**Milieu teaching:** Teaher uses imitation, prompting, cueing, and reinforcers during structured interactive activities. Activities provide natural opportunities for and consequences to communicative interaction.	**Indirect language stimulation:** Also called facilitative play. Teacher structures activities to elicit targeted language forms through what the student sees as play. Materials are chosen by the teacher; the student directs how the play evolves. Teacher interacts through
Modeling: Teacher provides a series of highly structured models. For example, teacher asks an assistant to describe what's happening in a series of pictures while child listens. After assistant provides 10–20 descriptions, teacher asks child to "talk like" the assistant to describe a similar set of pictures.	**Script teaching:** Teacher uses familiar routines, or "scripts," as activities, then violates the script to "challenge" the child to communicate to call attention to or repair the violation. In addition, a child can be asked to violate a script in order to produce a targeted language form.	■ self-talk: teacher describes own actions; ■ parallel talk: teacher provides self-talk for the child; ■ imitating the child's utterances; ■ expanding the child's language into a grammatically acceptable form; ■ recasting the child's sentences into a different type.

Paul (2006) indicated that in teacher-directed instruction, the teacher determines

- the materials to be used,
- how the student will interact with the materials,
- how the student will be reinforced,
- what constitutes an acceptable response, and
- the order of the activities.

Instructional approaches that are considered student centered (those along the right side) are considered more natural, less structured (though not necessarily less planned), and meaningful to children. In our experience, student-centered methods typically work better with students who refuse to engage in teacher-directed activities and with children who rarely initiate communication.

Approaches in the middle of the table combine characteristics from both the teacher-directed and the student-centered approaches. These approaches typically emphasize a small number of language goals; the teacher controls many of the activities and materials, though in a manner not necessarily noticeable to the student; and the teacher models and emphasizes specific linguistic forms during the instruction.

Crucial to the discussion of instructional processes is consideration of what teachers can do with their own communication and language when they are interacting with children who have disabilities. Paul (2006) offers a set of modifications that teachers can make to increase the likelihood that their students' language will improve:

- Reduce the rate of speech.
- Repeat utterances more than once.
- Highlight specific words and word order with exaggerated intonation and heightened vocal emphasis.
- Monitor linguistic complexity so the sentences are slightly longer than the student's, are well formed, and are semantically accessible to the student.
- Use pragmatically appropriate requests for linguistic production from the student (i.e., do not expect the student to use a complete sentence if the socially appropriate response is one or two words).

Instructional settings   Language instruction for preschoolers most often takes place in preschool programs, which vary widely in the way they are structured and conducted. Regardless of these differences, the teachers who design language instruction for preschool children have to consider how to structure the preschool experience for children so the targeted language forms can be learned and incorporated into their knowledge base.

Many children with disabilities will have been identified by a speech–anguage clinician as having a language disorder, and some of these same children will receive clinical services outside of the preschool program. A more prevalent approach, however, is for the speech–language clinician (referred to as the SLP, a holdover from an earlier title) to provide language intervention within the preschool program rather than to take children to a separate room or building for therapy sessions. The SLP acts as another teacher, albeit focusing specifically on language forms and structures identified as being disordered. Obviously, collaboration between the SLP and the preschool teacher is a prerequisite to the success of this sort of programming.

In preschool programs in which the SLP does not work within the classroom, the teacher can request suggestions from the SLP about activities, materials, and approaches that would be beneficial for specific students. In most cases, the SLP is happy to provide this sort of assistance. In addition, the SLP can keep teachers informed about an individual student's progress in language remediation. Conversely, teachers can assist the SLP by providing ongoing feedback about students' communication and language behaviors in the classroom.

Considered to be one of the most effective contexts for preschool, the language-based classroom is becoming more prevalent as teachers learn more about children's language development and as SLPs learn more about early childhood development and education. The most typical language-based classroom uses theme-based instruction in which units are planned around a central theme and incorporate typical preschool activities such as circle time, story time, center time, snack time, and outdoor play.

One of the most compelling arguments for a language-based classroom as the context for providing language instruction is that it offers ongoing experiences with the sorts of language and communication that constitute what is called **emergent literacy**, the gradual emergence of language learning about what stories are and how they work, what print is and what it looks like, what books are and how to interact with them, how sounds relate to letters and what letters look like, and what makes up reading and writing. Language-based preschool programs emphasize activities that encourage the development of emergent literacy through interaction with print on traffic signs, store logos, and food containers; drawing and scribbling (and providing the necessary materials); and "writing" stories and dictating shared class experiences (American Speech–Language–Hearing Association [ASHA], 2007). Table 4.4 gives examples of how emergent literacy activities can be included in a typical preschool program.

▌Children with Severely Compromised Speech

With children who are unable to develop sufficient ability to use oral speech to communicate and children with autism who need additional communication support, **alternative** and **augmentative communication (AAC)** modalities are used. These AAC systems are designed to assist children in communicating in their everyday lives, while at the same time helping them acquire the cognitive and symbolic behaviors that accompany further communication and language development. AAC systems range from low-tech communication boards utilizing eye-gaze encoding systems to high-tech computer-assisted speech.

The primary goal for individuals using AAC devices is the ability to engage in interactive communication. To help families decide which AAC device to choose, the ASHA (2009) offers guidelines for selecting the device that will provide the most effective interactive communication possible (ASHA, 2009). Factors to consider when designing instruction that uses AAC systems include

- which sort of symbol system to use,
- which sort of device to design,

TABLE 4.4

Emergent Literacy in the Preschool Classroom

	Book Knowledge	Story Knowledge	Print Knowledge	Sounds and Letters	Reading and Writing
Circle Time	Use a handmade picture book as the class calendar and another as a class roster.	Use narrative to describe everyday routines and shared class experiences.	Emphasize the letters in children's names, in labels, and in picture books.	Model letter sounds in children's names, in labels, and in picture books.	Have children take turns "reading" the calendar and class roster; they then "write" their names and labels for the picture books.
Story Time	Model how to handle books, turn pages, and read left to right and top to bottom.	Hghlight components of stories: setting, character, plot, and resolution. Ask questions about each.	Show children print on book covers and jackets and in book text.	Sound out rhymes, soundalikes, and endings of words. Model the sounds different letters make.	Have children "read" a story after you have read it. Ask them to "write" one or two words and illustrate the stories.
Play Time	Integrate various sorts of books into the play activities; have children make their own books.	Narrate children's play using story structures to emphasize initiating event, attempts to solve the "problem," and a resolution/ending.	Provide paper, pencils, crayons, or markers; attach labels to objects in the classroom; write names of things when talking about them.	Play with sounds, talk about talking and language, make up rhymes to accompany activities, make up nonsense words.	Encourage play that incorporates the use of print artifacts: pencils, pens, paper, computer keyboards, books, markers.

(continued)

TABLE 4.4 *(continued)*

	Book Knowledge	Story Knowledge	Print Knowledge	Sounds and Letters	Reading and Writing
Snack Time	Make a recipe book describing each week's snacks. Read to children during snack, emphasizing how books work.	Narrate snack time using story structures. Encourage children to tell how snack time works.	Label snack objects: food, utensils, plates, napkins, cups, table, refrigerator, etc. Make labels for whatever children talk about	Play with words that describe snack objects and activities. Emphasize sounds in the words; show what letters go with the sounds.	Have children take turns "printing" letters and labels for snack objects and activities.
Outdoor Play	Take photos of children playing outdoors; assemble them into a book format. Have children take turns "reading" each new book.	Narrate children's play using story structures. Encourage children's self-talk in narrative form.	Label play equipment, play areas, entrances, and exits. Point out any visible signs.	Point out individual letters in labels. Demonstrate the sounds the letters make.	Encourage children to "read" labels and signs. When back inside, have children "print" what they saw using models.

- ease of use for the child,
- ease of use for parents and teachers,
- social effectiveness of the system, and
- suitability for promoting language development.

Symbol Systems

The question of which symbol system to use rests on the child's ability to use his body for gestures, vocalizations, and body language (i.e., unaided systems) compared with his ability to interact with and manipulate a device or tool external to his body (i.e., aided systems). Unaided systems generally work best for preschool children who possess the motor skills to make the necessary gestures and movements.

The more a symbol resembles its referent, the more it is said to be iconic. Thus, symbol systems differ in the extent to which the symbols used resemble what they refer to, or their degree of **iconicity** (Paul, 2006). Examples of highly iconic symbols are the signs along roadways that inform travelers about road conditions and dangers. Figure 4.9 shows one such example.

Iconic symbols are easier to learn for young children, primarily because their cognitive abilities are not yet developed enough for them to understand more abstract symbols. For this reason, iconic symbol systems—for instance, Blissymbols—are typically used to introduce preschool children to symbolic referencing. An added advantage is that highly iconic systems are easier to understand for the child's conversational partners such as parents, teachers, and siblings.

Iconic systems are not always advantageous, however, especially because they inhibit the child's production of novel utterances. Precisely because they are iconic, symbolic systems are limited in their symbolic reach. They are easy to understand but severely limited in their ability to enhance the child's developing more symbolic, original language production. Consequently, although an iconic AAC system (e.g., a series of picture boards) may be designed to help preschool children enter the communication game, the ultimate goal is for children to utilize some sort of written system. Thus, as the child's cognitive development proceeds, iconic systems are replaced with more symbolic (and abstract) systems selected along a continuum from objects and photos, to line drawings and Blissymbols, to American Sign Language (ASL) and alphabetic writing.

AAC Devices

As noted, **AAC devices** range from low tech to computer-assisted speaking. Directed eye gaze, head pointing, finger pointing, and using a headstick or laser light to point are considered low tech; computers that produce synthesized speech are considered high tech. How the child interacts with the AAC device, however, need not be high tech even when the device itself is high tech. For example, computerized systems can be activated through a variety of means, ranging from eye movements to puffs

FIGURE 4.9

Example of Iconic Symbol

of air to finger pressure. Beukelman and Mirenda (1998) provide a comprehensive description of the range of AAC devices, along with discussion of the advantages and disadvantages of each.

Designing AAC devices for preschool children usually involves the entire IEP team and almost always proceeds in a trial-and-error fashion at first until the child interacts successfully with one over a period of time. Often, with young children, simpler devices work more effectively than sophisticated devices—flip books of pictures showing everyday objects, people, and activities and processes; a series of small communication boards with similar pictures; or laminated photos hung from a ring.

Ease of Use for Children, Families, and Teachers

As mentioned, iconic systems are usually the easiest for families and teachers unless they have had prior training in AAC systems. The most effective AAC systems are typically those developed in partnership among teachers, parents, and professionals who have extended knowledge of the children involved and their developmental needs.

Social Effectiveness of the System

Because communication is a social process, any communicative system must be socially effective. Oral languages have developed elaborate devices and rules for how conversations work. AAC systems must be able to tap into those same devices and rules so they can achieve their purpose—allowing the child to enter the communication game with a variety of conversational partners. Again, iconic systems are typically easy enough to use so almost any conversational partner can interact with the child, though, as pointed out, the range of what can be communicated through an iconic system is severely curtailed.

Promoting Language Development

Communication takes place between at least two people. If the child cannot interact with a conversational partner because that person cannot interact with the AAC the child is using, there is no communication and the AAC system has failed in one of its primary purposes. As discussed, iconic systems are usually easier for conversational partners to understand than more symbolic systems such as ASL.

By their nature, though, iconic systems are limited in promoting language development because they do not allow for the production of an unlimited number of utterances. The more symbolic the system, the greater is the range of expression. For this reason, when the child begins to exhibit symbolic play, symbolic AAC systems using synthesized speech are often introduced as a means of promoting phonological awareness (Foley, 1993) and increased vocal output and intelligibility of speech (Romski & Sevcik, 1996).

▌Summary

Preschool children typically develop language at an astonishing rate. Once they are beyond infancy and have acquired their first few words conveying a limited range of communicative purposes, they begin to produce two-word utterances with a rapidly expanding vocabulary and range of intentions. By the time they are 4 to 5 years old, their receptive vocabularies have increased almost tenfold, they have developed more subtle and nuanced communicative strategies for getting what they want, and their sentences are much more complex. By the time most of them enter kindergarten, they recognize some print, they know how books and stories work, and they can tell their own stories, albeit short and often without a point.

For children with disabilities, language assessment and intervention aim to assist in their developing the abilities they will need to negotiate school successfully. The purpose of assessing preschool children's language is to determine where they are along the language development scale; which structures, content, and functions will benefit most from instruction; and how language instruction can help families further their goals for their children.

Language instruction for preschool children emphasizes readiness for school, helping them learn, for instance, how to play with language, words, syllables, and letters; how to interact with books; how to understand and tell stories; and how to communicate what they want to listeners they do not know well.

Students with severely compromised speech are often introduced to AAC systems, ranging from low-tech systems relying on iconic symbols to high-tech systems utilizing computer-generated speech. For these students, a variety of interfaces is available and can be suited to the child's specific cognitive and motor abilities.

References

American Speech–Language–Hearing Association (ASHA). (2007). *Emergent literacy: Early reading and writing development.* Retrieved from http://www.asha.org/public/speech/emergent-literacy.htm

American Speech–Language–Hearing Association (ASHA). (2009). *Augmentative and alternative communication decisions.* Retrieved from http://www.asha.org/public/speech/disorders/CommunicationDecisions.htm

Ammer, J. (1999). *Birth to three checklist of language and learning behaviors.* Austin, TX: Pro-Ed.

Bangs, T. E. (1975). *Vocabulary comprehension scale.* Chicago: Riverside.

Barrett, M., Zachman, L., & Huisingh, R. (1988). *Assessing semantics skills through everyday themes.* East Moline, IL: LinguaSystems.

Bayley, N. (1993). *Bayley scales of infant mental development–Revised* (2nd ed.). New York: Psychological Corp.

Beukelman, D., & Mirenda, P. (1998). *Augmentative and alternative communication: Management of severe communication disorders in children and adults* (2nd ed.). Baltimore: Brookes.

Bloom, L., & Lahey, M. (1978). *Language development and language disorders.* New York: Wiley.

Boehm, A. E. (1986). *Boehm test of basic concepts–Preschool.* San Antonio, TX: Psychological Corp.

Boehm, A. E. (1986). *Boehm test of basic concepts–Revised.* San Antonio, TX: Psychological Corp.

Brownell, R. (2000). *Receptive one-word picture vocabulary test–2000 edition.* Novato, CA: Academic Therapy Publications.

Bus, A., Van Ijzendoorn, M., & Pellegrini, A. (1995). Joint book reading makes for success in learning to read: A meta-analysis on intergenerational transmission of literacy. *Review of Educational Research, 65,* 121.

Bus, A., Belsky, J., van Ijzendoorn, M. H., & Crnic, K. (1997). Attachment and book-reading patterns: A study of mothers, fathers, and their toddlers. *Early Childhood Research Quarterly, 12,* 8198.

Bus, A., & Van Ijzendoorn, M. (1995). Mothers reading to their 3-year-olds: The role of mother-child attachment security in becoming literate. *Reading Research Quarterly, 30,* 998–1015.

Carrow-Woolfolk, E. (1974). *Carrow elicited language inventory.* Chicago: Riverside.

Carrow-Woolfolk, E. (1999). *Test for auditory comprehension of language* (3rd ed.). Chicago: Riverside.

Chomsky, C. (1972). Stages in language development and reading exposure. *Harvard Educational Review, 42,* 1–3.

Clarke-Stewart, J. (1973). Interactions between mothers and their young children: Characteristics and consequences. *Monographs of the Society for Research on Child Development, 38* (6–7, serial no. 153).

Coplan, J. (1993). *Early language milestones* (ELM Scale 2). Austin, TX: Pro-Ed.

Dickinson, D. K., & Neuman, S. B. (2006). *Handbook of early literacy research* (Vol. 2). New York: Guilford.

Dunn, L., & Dunn, L. (2007). *Peabody picture vocabulary test* (4th ed). San Antonio, TX: PsychCorp.

Edwards, S., Fletcher, P., Garman, M., Hughes, A., Letts, C., & Sinka, I. (1999). *Reynell developmental language scales–III.* Windsor, UK: NFER-Nelson.

Elliot-Templeton, K., Van Kleeck, A., Richardson, A., & Imholz, E. (November, 1992). *A longitudinal study of mothers, babies, and books*. Paper presented at the American Speech-Language-Hearing Association National Convention, San Antonio, TX.

Ensher, G., Bobish, B., Garner, J., Michaels, T., Butler, S., Foertsch, R., & Cooper, F. (1997). *Syracuse dynamic assessment for birth to three*. Austin, TX: Pro-Ed.

Fenson, L., Dale, P., Reznick, S., Thal, D., Bates, E., Hartung, J., ... & Reilly, J. (1993). *MacArthur communicative development inventories*. San Diego: Singular.

Fey, M. (1986). *Language intervention with young children*. San Diego: College-Hill Press.

Foley, B. (1993). The development of literacy in individuals with severe congenital speech and motor impairments. *Topics in Language Disorders, 13,* 16–32.

Foster, R., Giddan, J., & Stark, J. (1983). *Assessment of children's language comprehension*. Palo Alto, CA: Consulting Psychologists Press.

Frankenburg, W., Dodds, J., Archer, P., Bresnick, B., Maschka, P., Edelman, N., & Shapiro, H. (1990). *Denver developmental screening test II*. Denver, CO: Denver Developmental Materials.

Gardner, M. (2000). *Expressive one-word picture vocabulary test–2000 edition*. Novato, CA: Academic Therapy Publications.

Gilliam, J., & Miller, L. (2005). *Pragmatic language skills inventory*. Austin, TX: Pro-Ed.

Goldsworthy, C., & Secord, W. (1982). *Multilevel informal language inventory*. San Antonio, TX: Psychological Corp.

Hammill, D., & Bryant, B. (1991). *The Detroit tests of learning aptitude–Primary–3*. Austin, TX: Pro-Ed.

Hammill, D., Mather, N., & Roberts, R. (2001). *Illinois test of psycholinguistic abilities–3*. Austin, TX: Pro-Ed.

Hedrick, D., Prather, E., & Tobin, A. (1995). *Sequenced inventory of communication development–Revised*. Austin, TX: Pro-Ed.

Hresko, W., Reid, K., & Hammill, D. (1999). *Test of early language development* (3rd ed.). Austin, TX: Pro-Ed.

Huer, M. B., & Miller, L. (2011). *Test of early communication and emerging language*. Austin, TX: Pro-Ed.

Illinois State Board of Education: Division of Early Childhood. (2004). *Illinois early learning standards*. Springfield, IL: Author.

Individuals with Disabilities Act. (2004). *Federal Register*/Vol. 71, No. 156/Monday, August 14, 2006/Rules and Regulations.

International Reading Association (IRA) & National Association for the Education of Young Children (NAEYC). (1998). Learning to read and write: Developmentally appropriate practices for young children. A joint position statement of the International Reading Association and the National Association for the Education of Young Children. *Young Children 53*(4), 30–46.

Johnston, E. B., & Johnston, A. V. (1989). *Communication abilities diagnostic abilities test*. Chicago: Riverside.

Karnes, M. B., & Johnson, L. J. (1991). *Coordinating assessment and programming for preschoolers (CAPP)*. Tucson, AZ: Communication Skill Builders.

Karweit, N., & Wasik, B. (1996). The effects of story reading programs on literacy and language development of disadvantaged pre-schoolers. *Journal of Education for Students Placed At-Risk, 4,* 319–348.

Lantolf, J. P., & Poehner, M. E. (2004). Dynamic assessment: Bringing the past into the future. *Journal of Applied Linguistics, 1,* 49–74.

McCathren, R., Yoder, R., & Warren, S. (1999). The relationship between prelinguistic vocalization and later expressive vocabulary in young children with developmental delay. *Journal of Speech, Language, and Hearing Research, 42,* 915–924.

McCune, L. (1995). A normative study of representational play at the transition to language. *Developmental Psychology, 31(2)*, 200–211.

McLean, L., & Cripe, J. (1997). The effectiveness of early intervention for children with communication disorders. In M. J. Guralnick. (Ed.), *The effectiveness of early intervention* (pp. 349–428). Baltimore: Brookes.

Mecham, M. (1989). *Utah test of language development–3*. Salt Lake City, UT: Communication Research Associates.

Miller, J. F., & Yoder, D. E. (1984). *Miller–Yoder language comprehension test*. Baltimore: University Park Press.

Miller, L., Gillam, R. B., & Peña, E.C. (2001). *Dynamic assessment and intervention: Improving children's narrative skills*. Austin, TX: Pro-Ed.

Miller, L., & Hoffman, L. (2001). *Linking IEPs to learning standards*. Lockport, IL: Staff Development Inservice.

Miller, L., & Hoffman, L. P. (2002). *Linking IEPs to learning standards: A step-by-step guide*. Austin, TX: Pro-Ed.

Milosky, L. (1990). The role of world knowledge in language comprehension and language intervention. *Topics in Language Disorders, 10(3)*, 1–13.

Moog, J. S., & Geers, A. E. (1985). *Grammatical analysis of elicited language*. St. Louis, MO: Central Institute for the Deaf.

National Early Childhood Technical Assistance Center. (2009). *State examples of IFSP plans and guidance*. Retrieved from http://www. nectac.org/topics/families/stateifsp.asp

Neuman, S. B., Copple, C., & Bredekamp, S. (2000). *Learning to read and write: Developmentally appropriate practices for young children*. Washington, DC: National Association for the Education of Young Children.

Newborg, J., Stock, J., Wnek, L., Guidubaldi, J., & Svinicki, J. (1988). *Battelle developmental inventory*. Chicago: Riverside.

Newcomer, P., & Hammill, D. (2008). *Test of language development–4 Primary*. Austin, TX: Pro-Ed.

Nicolich, L. (1977). Beyond sensorimotor intelligence: Assessment of symbolic maturity through analysis of pretend play. *Merrill-Palmer Quarterly, 23(2)*, 88–89.

Olswang, L., Rodriguez, B., & Timler, G. (1998). Recommending intervention for toddlers with specific language learning difficulties: We may not have all the answers, but we know a lot. *American Journal of Speech–Language Pathology, 7*, 23–32.

Paul, R. (2006). *Language disorders from infancy through adolescence: Assessment and intervention* (3rd ed.). St. Louis, MO: Mosby.

Peña, E. D., & Davis, B. L. (2000). Language disorders in infants, toddlers, and preschoolers. In R. B. Gillam, T. P. Marquardt, & F. N. Martin (Eds.), *Communication sciences and disorders: From science to clinical practice*. San Diego: Singular Thomson Learning.

Peña, E. D., Reséndez, M., & Gillam, R. B. (2007). The role of clinical judgements of modifiability in the diagnosis of language impairment. *International Journal of Speech–Language Pathology, 9* (4 December, 2007), 332–345.

Phelps-Terasaki, D., & Phelps-Gunn, T. (2007). *Test of pragmatic language 2*. Austin, TX: Pro-Ed.

Poehner, M. E., & Lantolf, J. P. (2005). Dynamic assessment in the language classroom. *Language Teaching Research, 9*, 233–265.

Porch, B. (1979). *Porch index of communicative ability in children*. Palo Alto, CA: Consulting Psychologists Press.

Riley, A. M. (1984). *Evaluating acquired skills in communication–revised (EASIC)*. San Antonio, TX: Communication Skill Builders.

Romski, M., & Sevcik, R. A. (1996). *Breaking the speech barrier: Language development through augmented means*. Baltimore: Brookes.

Rossetti, L. (1995). *The Rossetti infant and toddler language scale: A measure of communication and interaction.* East Moline, IL: LinguiSystems.

Schwartz, L., & Leonard, L. (1982). Do children pick and choose? Phonological selection and avoidance in early lexical acquistion. *Journal of Child Language, 9,* 319–336.

Semel, E., Wiig, E., & Secord, W. (2004). *Clinical Evaluation of Language Fundamentals–Preschool, 2nd edition (CELF–Preschool 2).* San Diego, CA: Harcourt Assessment.

Shipley, K. G., Stone, T. A., & Sue, M. B. (1983). *Test for examining expressive morphology.* Tucson, AZ: Communication Skill Builders.

Shulman, B. (1986). *Test of pragmatic skills (Rev).* Tucson, AZ: Communication Skill Builders.

Slobin, D. (1979). *Psycholinguistics* (2nd ed.). Glenview, IL: Scott, Foresman.

Snow, C. E. (1983). Literacy and language: Relationships during the preschool years. *Harvard Educational Review, 53,* 165–189.

Snow, C. E. (1991, Fall-Winter). The theoretical basis for relationships between language and literacy development. *Journal of Research in Childhood Education, 6,* 5–10.

Snow, C. E., Tabors, P. O., Nicholson, P., & Kurland, B. (1995). SHELL: Oral language and early literacy skills in kindergarten and first grade children. *Journal of Research in Childhood Education, 10,* 22–38.

Snowling, M. (1996). Developmental dyslexia. In M. Snowling & J. Stackhouse (Eds.), *Dyslexia, speech, and language: A practitioner's handbook* (pp. 1-11). London: Whurr.

Sparrow, S .S., Cicchetti, D. V., & Balla, D. A. (2005). *Vineland adaptive behavior scales II.* Circle Pines, MN: AGS.

Toth, K., Munson, J., Meltzoff, A. N., & Dawson, G. (2006). Early predictors of communication development in young children with autism spectrum disorder: Joint attention, imitation, and toy play. *Journal of Autism Developmental Disorders, 36,* 993–1005.

U.S. Department of Education. (2009). *Building the legacy: IDEA 2004.* Retrieved from http://idea.ed.gov/static/modelForms

Uzgiris, I. C. (1989). *Assessment in infancy: Ordinal scales of infant and psychological development* (5th ed.). Urbana: University of Illinois.

Vygotsky, L. (1978). *Mind in society: The development of higher psychological processes.* Cambridge, MA: Harvard University Press.

Wallach, G. P., & Butler, K. G. (1984). *Language learning disabilities in school-age children.* Baltimore: Williams & Wilkins.

Wallach, G. P., & Miller, L. (1988). *Language intervention and academic success* (pp. 136–145). Boston: College-Hill,

Warren, S., & Yoder, D. (1998). Facilitating the transition from preintentional to intentional communication. In A. Wetherby, S. Warren, & J. Reichle (Eds.), *Transitions in prelinguistic communication* (pp. 365–384). Baltimore: Brookes.

Wetherby, A., & Prizant, B. (2003). *Communication and symbolic behavior scales.* Baltimore: Brookes.

Whitehurst, G., Arnold, D., Epstein, J., Angell, A., Smith, M., & Fischel J. (1994). A picture book reading intervention in day care and home for children from low-income families. *Developmental Psychology, 30,* 679–689.

Whitehurst, G., Falco, F., Lonigan, C., Fischel, J., DeBaryshe, B., Valdez-Menchaea, M., & Caulfield, M. (1988). Accelerating language development through picture-book reading. *Developmental Psychology, 24,* 552–558.

Wiig, E. H. (1990). *Wiig criterion-referenced inventory of language.* San Antonio, TX: Psychological Corp.

Williams, K. T. (1997). *Expressive vocabulary test.* Circle Pines, MN: American Guidance Service.

Woodcock, R. W., & Muñoz, A. (1991). *Woodcock language proficiency battery–Revised, English and Spanish Form.* Itasca, IL: Riverside.

Yoder, P., Davies, B., Bishop, K., & Munson, L. (1995). Predicting children's response to prelinguistic communication intervention. *Journal of Early Intervention, 19(1)*, 74–84.

Zimmerman, I., Steiner, V., & Pond, R. (1992). *Preschool language scale–3*. San Antonio, TX: Psychological Corp.

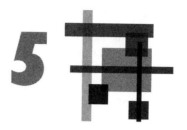

Language Assessment and Instruction for School-Age Children

School-age children with disabilities can have language abilities anywhere between the prelinguistic and the language for learning stages of development. Those with language characteristics of the prelinguistic stage or the emerging language stage are likely to have severe impairments, sometimes accompanied by other disabilities. Assessment and intervention for these children emphasize the functional communication and language skills necessary for them to participate in school as independently as possible. Short-term objectives focus on the language content, forms, and uses that will help them communicate more effectively in their everyday lives, both inside and outside of school.

The assessment goals and intervention procedures described in Chapter 4 are appropriate for school-age children whose communication and language abilities are in the prelinguistic or emerging language stages of development. The fundamental goal is to establish what Paul (2006) termed conventional forms of interacting so these children can communicate on at least a basic level. Once they develop language skills more typical of the developing language period, the emphasis shifts to school-related oral language skills and to emerging literacy.

School-age children whose language abilities are more typical of the developing language period are usually considered to have a language-learning disability (LLD), (described in Chapter 4). These children have acquired the basics of language—vocabulary, sentence structures, and pragmatic functions—but their language learning is usually delayed in comparison to their agemates. In addition, even after they have acquired the basics, they have difficulty with the aspects of language necessary for learning to read and write, especially phonological awareness; single-word, sentence, and paragraph comprehension; and narrative abilities. Consequently, language assessment and intervention for children with these language characteristics are directed more specifically to these latter language competencies. In this chapter we will learn about the assessment goals, procedures, and instruments and the intervention priorities, approaches, and practices that are best suited for school-age children in the developing language or language for learning phases.

▌Assessment Goals, Procedures, ▌and Instruments

Most, but not all, children entering school have participated in innumerable conversations with a variety of conversational partners: They have heard many stories, they have been read to by important adults in their lives, and they know that certain settings require shifts in how they use language. These children have learned most of the rules governing personal–social interactions in the cultural groups to which they belong, and they have learned the narrative discourse rules governing how books and stories work, what print is, and how letters represent sounds.

What they may not know is how to participate in classroom communication, how to use language outside of an ongoing social context (decontextualized language), and how to talk about language (metalinguistic ability). In addition, if they have a language-learning disability, their ability to manipulate language beyond the basic levels may be limited. Consequently, assessment for these children addresses four primary questions:

1. How can their language development be characterized in terms of semantics, syntax, phonology, and pragmatics?
2. How skilled are the children with narrative discourse?
3. What is their ability with nonnarrative discourse (using language in decontextualized situations)?
4. How competent are they at talking about language and communication?

Assessing Language Development

Before 1972, reading was believed to be a visual–perceptual skill independent of oral language abilities. In 1972, however, Kavanagh and Mattingly (1972) presented a convincing argument showing how reading develops from the foundation of oral language skills acquired by normally developing children. Catts and Kamhi (1999) argued that both reading and writing are language-based skills using a visual, rather than an auditory, entry into the language-processing system. Learning to communicate through oral language relies on auditory skills, whereas learning to read and write requires students to access visually based symbols. Consequently, while reading involves something more than just a well developed oral language system (discussed under the assessment of metalinguistic ability), learning to read is nearly impossible without the requisite oral language abilities (Tynan, 2008).

What are the oral language abilities underlying reading and writing? For the most part, they comprise the developmental abilities described in Chapter 2:

Semantics

- An understanding vocabulary of at least 3,000 to 4,000 words
- Use of inflections (grammatical morphemes) to change word meanings and to indicate verb tenses and auxiliaries
- Use of contractions
- Elaboration of personal pronouns

Syntax and Morphology, emergence of

- Negative past tense
- Past-tense modals
- Inverted word order and tag questions
- Embedded phrases
- Embedded clauses
- Regular and irregular verb forms

Phonology

- Acquisition of phoneme set characteristic of developing language (see Chapter 2)
- Disappearance of phonological processes (e.g., deleting "weak" or unaccented syllables, deleting final consonants, or velar fronting; see Chapter 2 for a more complete description).

Pragmatics

- Improved turntaking
- Emergence of conversational repairs
- Improved presuppositional knowledge
- Emergence of indirect requests
- Knowledge of how to use knowledge to display knowledge

Figurative language

- Emergence of understanding and use of synonyms, homonyms, and double-meaning words
- Emergence of use of idiomatic expressions
- Use of humor with metaphoric language

Narrative language

- Emergence of primitive narratives
- Knowledge of how books work

- Knowledge of how stories work
- Understanding that print is words written down

Metalinguistic awareness, can

- Talk about talking
- Talk about language
- Recognize sounds and syllables in words

Standardized Measures

School-age students' language development can be assessed in various ways. Most students with deficits in oral language undergo standardized testing as part of a state requirement regarding eligibility for special education services. Chapter 4 lists the most frequently used standardized measures for students in the developing language period. In addition, the following instruments are commonly used with school-age students:

> *Analysis of the Language of Learning* (Blodgett & Cooper, 1987)
> *Clinical Evaluation of Language Fundamentals–3* (Semel, Wiig, & Secord, 1998)
> *Communication Abilities Diagnostic Test* (Johnston & Johnston, 1990)
> *Detroit Test of Learning Aptitude–Primary 4* (Hammill & Bryant, 1999)
> *Peabody Picture Vocabulary Test–IV* (Dunn & Dunn, 2007)
> *Pragmatic Language Skills Inventory* (Gilliam & Miller, 2005)
> *Test for Auditory Comprehension of Language–3rd Edition* (Carrow-Woolfolk, 1999)
> *Test of Awareness of Language Segments* (Sawyer, 1987)
> *Test of Early Language Development–3rd Edition* (Hresko, Reid, & Hammill, 1999)
> *Test of Early Written Language–2* (Hresko, 1996)
> *Test of Language Development–Primary–Fourth Edition* (*TOLD-P4;* Newcomer & Hammill, 2008)
> *Test of Language Development–Intermediate–Fourth Edition* (*TOLD-I4;* Newcomer & Hammill, 2008)
> *Test of Pragmatic Language–Second Edition* (*TOPL-2;* Phelps-Terasaki & Phelps-Gunn, 2007)
> *Test of Problem Solving–Revised–Elementary* (Bowers, Barrett, Huisingh, Orman, & LoGiudice, 1994)
> *Test of Word Knowledge* (Wiig & Secord, 1992)
> *Test of Written Language–4* (*TOWL–4;* Hammill & Larsen, 2009)

Nonstandardized Measures

Because teachers observe their students every day in the classroom, an *observational checklist* offers an effective way to gather information about a student's language abilities. For instance, Catts's (1997) "Early Identification of Language-Based Reading

Disabilities: A Checklist" addresses speech sound awareness, word retrieval, verbal memory, speech production/perception, comprehension, expressive language, and what he calls "other important factors."

Applying Damico's (1985) work on children's pragmatic language abilities, Paul (2006) designed a checklist for use by classroom teachers. This checklist is particularly useful in that children with LLD are more likely to show difficulties in pragmatic language than in syntax and morphology. Another checklist, developed by Ripich and Spinelli (1985), uses an effectiveness rating scale to rate seven communication areas, including speech–language abilities:

1. Participation
2. Soliciting attention
3. Paying attention
4. Questioning
5. Appropriateness
6. Descriptive ability
7. Speech-language abilities.

Criterion-referenced measures and **behavioral observations** can yield valuable information about the language abilities of school-age students. Various procedures are available for assessing phonology, semantics, syntax and morphology, and pragmatics.

Phonology   Although students with LLD often sound intelligible in conversation, they also exhibit difficulties with phonologically demanding tasks—phonological processing—such as segmenting words into syllables and sounds, producing phonologically complex words or phrases, or pronouncing nonsense words. Several approaches can be used to assess students' phonological processing abilities.

In describing the importance of phonological awareness in learning to read, Chard and Dickson (1999) describe several activities for both assessing and teaching phonological processing skills on a continuum ranging from easiest to most difficult:

- Initial rhyming and rhyming songs
- Segmenting sentences
- Segmenting words into syllables and blending syllables into words
- Segmenting words into onsets and rimes (identifying the first sound in a word [the onset] and the first vowel sound in a word and any others that follow it in a syllable [the rime])
- Blending and segmenting individual phonemes

Students who are unable to do these tasks or struggle with them most likely are exhibiting phonological processing problems.

Dollaghan and Campbell (1998) devised a nonword-repetition task requiring students to repeat one-, two-, three-, and four-syllable nonsense words designed to be unfamiliar and unpredictable to students. Based on their research, students who score lower than 75% correct are at risk for LLD and in need of instruction.

Gilbertson and Bramlett (1998) designated three phonological awareness skills that predict high risk for reading difficulties:

1. Spelling nonsense words
2. From a set of four words, choosing the one that begins or ends with a different sound (e.g., pin, pipe, *nose*, pear)
3. Pronouncing a word made up of sounds spoken one or two seconds apart (e.g., /f - U̲ - n/)

Because it is highly correlated with reading ability, **rapid automatic naming (RAN)**, affords a view of students' higher level processing. Students are asked to name, as rapidly as they can, common objects that are presented to them in rapid sequence. Teachers can modify the RAN naming task by asking students to recite "overlearned" lists (e.g., months of the year, days of the week) as rapidly as possible. As is the case with Chard and Dickson's (1999) activities, students who are unable to do the task or who struggle with it are at risk for reading difficulties.

Semantics Children's receptive and expressive vocabularies are not the same, as pointed out earlier. Receptive vocabulary typically exceeds expressive vocabulary significantly, particularly once students begin encountering new words through reading. Students with LLD often have difficulty understanding terms that encode spatial ("diagonally down," "lateral") and temporal ("following," "consecutive") terms, as well as words that serve to tie together sentences, phrases, and words ("however," "nevertheless").

Teachers can assess their students' understanding of such instructional vocabulary informally by analyzing classroom instructions according to spatial, temporal, and cohesive words, and then observing students' attempts to understand and follow the instructions. For a more direct approach, the teacher can design a game in which the class is given a set of materials such as paper and several markers of different colors. Then the teacher instructs the class to draw various shapes in specific places on the paper, being sure to remember the directions for later comparison with students' efforts.

Often, students with LLD have difficulty understanding the vocabulary in their textbooks. Many textbooks include glossaries or vocabulary lists that the teacher can use to probe students' understanding. Spelling lists provide another means for assessing students' understanding of vocabulary. It should be noted that probing student understanding of vocabulary by asking students directly what a word means or to define a word may not work. Many students with LLD do not have the metalinguistic ability necessary to define words or to say what a word means. More fruitful approaches to probing students' vocabulary comprehension are to ask them to show examples of what a word means, to find a picture that depicts a word's meaning, or to show the meaning by demonstrating it with relevant materials.

Nonstandardized approaches to assessing students' expressive vocabulary usually involve lexical diversity and word retrieval. Lexical diversity increases with age, meaning that normally developing children use more new words each year between ages 5 and 11 (Watkins, Kelly, Harbers, & Hollis, 1995). Keeping informal tallies of students' use of new words during classroom activities provides an index into lexical diversity and information about possible targets for language instruction, described in the discussion of language instruction later in this chapter.

Students with LLD frequently display problems with word retrieval or word finding. As one indicator of a possible word-finding problem, a student's score on a receptive vocabulary measure is significantly higher than on an expressive vocabulary measure (Paul, 2006). Another indicator of word-finding problems is students' use of nonspecific words such as "thing," "whatchacallit," "deeleybob," or "thimajig." A third indicator is the student's struggling to find the right word to describe something, as when he says, "I need a … I need a … It's about this big, and it holds stuff together, and you have some on your desk … A paperclip!" Extensive writing about assessing word-finding difficulties and developing appropriate interventions for students exhibiting word-finding problems can be found in German (2000, 2001, 2002, 2005, 2008), German and Newman (2004, 2007), and Newman and German (2002, 2005).

Another aspect of expressive vocabulary that teachers can observe is a student's differentiation of nouns into subcategories:

- **Common nouns** (general classes of things, people, places, events, processes)
- **Proper nouns** (specific members of any given class)
- **Concrete nouns** (names of real things)
- **Abstract nouns** (names of ideas, concepts, thoughts)
- **Collective nouns** (names of groups of things)
- **Count nouns** (names of things that can be counted)
- **Mass** nouns (names of things that are conglomerates and cannot be counted)

Another aspect of expressive vocabulary knowledge is revealed by how students use personal pronouns and adverbs. By the end of the elementary school years, normally developing students have acquired the ability to use personal pronouns appropriately in almost all situations. In addition, they use a variety of different adverbs, and by the time they are ready to leave elementary school, their sentences typically include one or more adverbs.

Syntax and Morphology   Students are expected to understand and produce the syntactic and morphological forms typical of the language for learning stage of development. Students with LLD typically have problems elaborating noun and verb phrases, they usually do not include adjectives or adverbs, and their sentences ordinarily do not contain prepositional phrases and subordinate clauses. Teachers' observations of students' understanding and use of syntactic structures can attend to the appropriate use of (see Chapter 2 for a complete description)

- articles *(a, an,* and *the)*;
- exceptions to tense markers and plurals *(swam, geese)*;

- nonreversible passive sentences (*The picnic was cancelled by rain*);
- reversible passive sentences (*He was chased by Harry*);
- infinitive sentences (*I want to go to the movie*);
- embedded infinitive phrases, object complements, and relative clauses (e.g., *He's the one I saw at the mall*); and
- conjoining with conditionals, causals, disjunctives, and temporals (e.g., *If it rains, we can't go*).

Use of morphology can be observed by focusing on appropriate use of (again, see Chapter 2 for a more complete description)

- gerunds,
- agentive forms of common verbs, and
- adverb forms.

A third type of nonstandardized assessment is **dynamic assessment,** introduced in Chapter 4, which is based on Vygotsky's (1978) ideas about children's **zones of proximal development (ZPD).** ZPD is the distance between the level of functioning a child can exhibit independent of adult assistance, and the higher level at which she can function with assistance. Vygotsky was able to demonstrate that children could perform a previously difficult task successfully—and improve in academic achievement—if the teacher made minimal modifications based on what the teacher knew about the student's modifiability. Knowing the student's ZPD affords the teacher a view of the student's potential for learning (Miller, Gillam, & Peña, 2001).

Miller et al. (2001) and Peña, Iglesias, and Lidz (2001) described dynamic assessment as a test-teach-retest approach. The test phase begins by obtaining a baseline measure of the behavior of interest, in this case a language structure or function. Although the baseline measure can be either a formal assessment or an informal assessment, dynamic assessment usually uses informal measures.

Following the testing phase, the teacher provides one or two teaching sessions utilizing what the teacher learned about the student during the testing phase. The model used by both Miller et al. (2001) and Peña et al. (2001) follows a social constructivist teaching method called **mediated teaching,** which helps the student understand the goal of the session(s), why the language structure or function being worked on is important, how it is related to what the student already knows, and how to remember to use it in other settings.

Following the teaching phase, the teacher tests the student again on the same material to determine (Miller et al., 2001)

- how much change the student exhibited,
- how the student approached the tasks,
- the student's error patterns and self-monitoring abilities,
- how modifiable the student's responses were (i.e., did the teacher's interactions result in changes in the student's language or communication behavior?), and
- which teaching styles and strategies worked to promote change.

Assessing Narrative Discourse

Teachers have multiple opportunities to observe and assess their students' knowledge and use of narrative discourse. Two approaches that work well for assessing narratives are Appleby's stage model (1978) and Miller et al.'s component model (2001).

In Appleby's approach, the analysis centers on the types of narratives that students produce verbally. Developmentally, the first to appear is the **heap story**, produced by normally developing children between ages 2 and 3. In a heap story, the child provides labels and descriptions, with no central theme or organization from sentence to sentence. Sentences are most often simple declaratives.

For example, a student in the emerging language stage may tell a story similar to the following (these stories were told while looking at a wordless picture book, *Two Friends*, Miller, 1999b):

> They talking. The dog goes asleep. The cat leaves. The dog wakes up. Then he runs away. The dog talks to a dragon. Then he talks to an armadillo. He swims with the fishes. He sees the cat. Then they talked to each other.

The second type of story to appear in Appleby's model is the **sequence story**, produced by normally developing children at about age 3. In a sequence story, children label events around a central theme, character, or setting. These stories have no discernible plot, and events do not necessarily follow temporally or causally from each other. Here is an example of a sequence story from a student in the early developing language stage:

> Dog has boots. Here's a cat's tail. Dog and cat and here's water. Dog's laying there. Cat's sad. Then the cat's leaving. It's dark here. Here are stars. Dog's sitting up. Here's a bird and the dog is running. The dog's sitting by the dragon. Now he's sitting by the armadillo. He's swimming in the water. He's running out of the water. They're walking by the lizard.

The third type of story to appear is what Appleby (1978) calls the **primitive narrative**—stories with a core person, object, or event. Children at this stage, age 4 to 4½, tell stories containing what is called a *basic episode*. A basic episode consists of an initiating event (some problem that gets the action going), an attempt or action by a character to solve the problem, and a consequence, or resolution, of the problem. Here is an example of a primitive narrative containing a basic episode (using a wordless picture book, *Bird & His Ring*, Miller, 1999a):

> The bird saw the ring on the cactus. He taked the ring and gave it to the baby bird. Then he found his friend and took her to see it. But it was gone. The baby bird was crying. The big bird said, "Did you saw the ring?" The baby said no. So the big bird found the ring and showed it to the baby bird.

Stage 4, **chain narrative**, emerges around 4 to 5 years of age. Here, children show some notion of cause–effect, but the plot is still weak. Chain narratives may include some information about the character's feelings or intentions. In addition, the story contains a basic episode, as shown in the following story:

> The dog and cat are talking. The dog goes to sleep and the cat is sad. The cat leaves, but the dog doesn't wake up. He sleeps and sleeps. And then he wakes up and runs off. He finds a dragon and an armadillo. Now he's worried and he swims in the water. He sees the cat's tail! And they're talking to each other and the lizard goes by.

The last stage in Appleby's system is the **true narrative**, in which stories contain a central theme, character, and plot. The character is motivated to act, and events are sequenced logically. These stories include what is called a *complete* episode, consisting of an initiating event, an internal response (the character's feelings or intentions), an attempt, a plan (information about what the main character plans to do and why), and reaction or ending (information about the main character's reaction to the consequence) (Miller et al., 2001). True narratives emerge in normally developing children sometime between 5 and 7 years of age. Below is a story that is considered to be a true narrative (Miller et al., 2001):

> This is Gray. And that's Cottontail. One day Gray and Cottontail were standing in a field with fences. "Hello, Gray," said Cottontail. "Hello, Cottontail," said Gray. "What are you doing?' asked Cottontail. But by the time Cottontail had finished her question, Gray was dead asleep. Cottontail was sad. She sat. And she cried. She got so tired of waiting that she left. But Gray just kept on sleeping (and sleeping and sleeping).
>
> When he woke up, he felt like he had been knocked in the head. And he decided to go off and find his friend. But along the way he met a big green monster. He said, "Do you know where my friend Cottontail is?" And the big green monster said, "Ohaloheho." And Gray thought that meant, "No, I don't." Then along the way he met a purple armadillo. "Do you know where Cottontail is?" asked Gray to the purple armadillo. But the armadillo just hopped away. So Gray swam across the creek. And he swam. And he swam. And soon he saw sight of Cottontail's tail. And Cottontail said, "Gray, I'm glad you're back. I'm glad you found me. Let's go play some shape ball." So they went off happily ever after and played a good game of shape ball.

Miller et al. (2001) developed another perspective on narrative development. In this model, narrative ability is described developmentally in terms of three major aspects of narration: story components, story ideas and language, and episode elements and structure. Teachers can utilize this approach in their analysis of their students' oral stories. Later, when students begin producing written stories, this model can be a guide for students to develop complete episodes containing the story components and story ideas and language characteristic of mature writers. This approach is addressed more fully under the discussion of instruction.

Story Components

The first aspect of **story components** to emerge in children's narratives consists of setting: time and place. As children first try to tell stories, they include no *setting information*. Gradually they begin to include either time or place, and eventually, they provide both.

Next, children begin to include some *character information*. Again, at first they do not tell their listeners anything about the characters in their stories, but gradually they begin to include more and more details, eventually regaling their listeners with rich descriptions.

Third, though children's stories initially seem to be illogical and unrelated chronologically, they soon begin to include a *temporal order* to the events of their stories until they become adept at specifying the sequence of events. Last, children begin to include *causal information* in their stories. At first only some of the causal relationships are specified; however, children's stories eventually include well specified descriptions of the causal relationships driving the story.

Story Ideas and Language

Miller et al. (2001) argue that well-told stories contain ideas that are abstract and complicated, and at the same time they are so clearly told that listeners can understand them. Children who are just beginning to tell stories while looking at picture books tell literal stories referring directly to the pictures on the page. Later, they tell stories with ideas and parts interconnected well beyond the simple and concrete.

The first aspect of story ideas and language to emerge in children's stories is *complexity of ideas*. Early stories tend to be simple and concrete and gradually develop into more complex and abstract stories, transcending the literal story told in the images on the page. An example of a complex idea would be to make the story a parable or a satire.

Complexity of vocabulary develops next. Early stories use literal words that are basic and unelaborated, as when a child uses names of objects or events without adjectival or adverbial extension. Later in development, children's stories include figurative, nuanced vocabulary, including metaphors, similes, axioms, or maxims. Third, *grammatical complexity* ranges developmentally from the use of simple phrases or sentences, through the use of compound sentences, to the production of complex and compound–complex sentences. An example of this latter development was included in the story the description of Appleby's (1978) Stage 5 true narrative: "When he woke up, he felt like he had been knocked in the head."

Fourth, *knowledge of dialogue* ranges from the child's showing no evidence of knowledge about characters speaking to the elaborated use of dialogue. Again, a good example of well-developed knowledge of dialogue is shown above in the story from Appleby's (1978) Stage 5.

Finally, stories range in their *creativity*. Early stories are uninteresting—actually, boring—because they do not "hold together." In addition, they seem to have no high point, or turning point, that captures the listeners' interest. As children acquire the ability to tell true narratives, their stories become interesting enough that listeners are engrossed in the story. For most children, this happens between ages 5 and 7.

Episode Elements and Structure

Miller et al. (2001) proposed a developmental hierarchy showing how children's narratives develop. This scheme has six possible **episode elements** in stories (referred to previously):

1. Initiating event, or background information telling what propels the main character into action
2. Attempt, or information about the main character's attempt to achieve the goal—character's actions in response to the initiating event
3. Consequence, or information about the resolution of the initiating event
4. Internal response, or information about the main character's reactions to and/or feelings about the initiating event
5. Plan, or information about what the main character(s) intends to do and why
6. Reaction/ending, or information about the main character's reactions to the consequence—some kind of ending

In the Miller et al. (2001) model, children's episode structure develops in the following order:

1. No episodes provided
2. Incomplete episode (one or two episode elements)
3. Basic episode (initiating event, attempt, consequence)
4. Basic episode + one element
5. Basic episode + two elements
6. Complete episode (all episode elements present)
7. Multiple episode story

Assessing Nonnarrative Discourse Genres

When children enter school, they encounter **classroom discourse**, some for the first time. According to Nelson (2009), classroom discourse, or school talk, is significantly different from everyday conversation. In school talk, teachers control what is said, when people talk, and what they say. The teacher chooses the topic and expects students to comment on that topic—not others of their own choosing. Students who attempt to change the topic are discouraged or even rejected.

Turntaking in classroom discourse differs from everyday conversation in that the teacher decides which student will take a turn at any given time, how long the student will talk, when another student is to take a turn, and when the student is to relinquish her turn.

Cazden (1988) referred to what she called the "hidden curriculum," the unspoken set of rules about how students are expected to communicate and act. Because classroom discourse is mostly hidden, students with LLD often have difficulty negotiating it successfully. Often, their failure to recognize that they are not adhering to the set of rules governing classroom discourse results in their being perceived as rude, obstreperous, or unwilling to comply. Donahue's (1994) early research showed that students with LLD are more likely to be referred for evaluation for special education services because of their difficulties with classroom discourse than for academic failure.

The hidden curriculum adds an additional layer of expectation onto students. Not only are they expected to master the content curriculum (i.e., to know the right answers to the teacher's questions), but they are also expected to know how to communicate within the context of the classroom. This was pointed out more than two decades ago (see Westby, 1998) but is still rarely addressed in teacher education programs.

For many students with LLD, classroom discourse presents another difficulty because it occurs outside the context of the immediate environment within which everyday conversation occurs. It is decontextualized and requires language skills with which the students may not have had experience at home, particularly if they come from low-income families (Dickinson, Wolf, & Stotsky, 1993). Wallach (2007) pointed out that children in literate families are more likely than their peers from low-literate or nonliterate families to engage in the types of communicative interactions typical of school talk. In contrast, children in literate homes have had multiple opportunities to develop language suited to telling about their experiences; to retell something that has happened; to display their knowledge; and to explain or describe objects, events, or people. In addition, they develop an ability to talk about and play with language, discussed in the section on assessing metalinguistic ability.

In addition to classroom discourse, students entering school encounter four other nonnarrative types of discourse:

1. Descriptive
2. Poetry
3. Expository
4. Argumentative/persuasive

These types of discourse can be either oral or print-based, though students interact with them orally before they acquire the reading abilities necessary to access them in print. Making the oral-to-literate shift described in Chapter 4 depends on students' acquisition of the ability to negotiate these nonnarrative discourse genres successfully.

As mentioned, normally developing students from literate families usually begin producing *oral descriptions* before they begin school. Once they enter school, however, verbal descriptions become tied to academic content. This means that students are expected to understand and produce decontextualized descriptions related to subject matter rather than personal experience. Not surprisingly, most students with LLD have difficulty making this transition.

Most students who have been read or sung to will have heard many examples of *poetic language* by the time they begin school. Although poetry is not as important in today's curricula as it was even 20 years ago, some states include facility with poetry in their state learning standards. Consequently, students will have to be able to develop the skills to identify and understand the language structures and devices that comprise rhythm, meter, alliteration, and assonance. In addition, they will have to understand that the organizational structure of poetry, both rhymed and unrhymed, relies on the accumulation of stanzas, or units of the poem containing a fixed number of lines of verse.

Students with LLD frequently have difficulty with poetic language because they are unable to recognize the phonological aspects that render language poetic. Though they may be able to segment a poem into its stanzas (particularly visually), they may not hear rhyming sounds or the metric characteristics underlying poetry.

Students are usually exposed to *expository language*, or *expository text*, through print. Expository text is more abstract than descriptive language, either oral or printed, because it usually follows a hierarchical, multilevel organizational scheme. That is, to access expository text, students first must understand that the overall structure of the text is reflected in the top-level organizer: title, table of contents, index, and chapter titles. Second, students have to be able to utilize the organizational information available in the second-level organizer: boldface titles, subtitles, topic paragraphs, and topic sentences.

Facility with expository text becomes more important for children as they progress through the grades. In most states, kindergarten through second grade are devoted to teaching students the basics of how to read and write. Third grade marks a significant change in curriculum because the expectation is that students will be good enough readers so they can switch from learning to read to reading to learn. Reading to learn relies most heavily on expository textbooks to convey academic content, and by the end of fifth grade, students are expected to have the ability to write at least simple expository text.

For students with LLD, expository discourse may present difficulties because of its abstract, hierarchical nature. These students are likely to be unable to follow teachers' lectures in which they give directions or in which they present information about predictions, systems, models, generalizations, and conclusions (Nelson, 2009). Further, their difficulty in understanding expository text is likely to severely hamper their ability to gain access to the content in science, mathematics, and social studies. As a consequence, students with LLD may be denied one of the most important sources of information—the textbook.

Students encounter *argumentative/persuasive discourse* in oral, visual, and printed forms. In its oral form, persuasive discourse occurs most commonly as debate or critical commentary, in which the speaker attempts to persuade an audience about some point or belief. Persuasive discourse, both oral and print-based, often relies on formal arguments, organized in a logical, step-by-step fashion to induce the audience to accept the speaker's thesis. Sometimes persuasive speeches or texts utilize an emotional component in an attempt to induce the audience or reader to accept the thesis.

Examples of arguments based on emotional factors abound in print-based and visual forms of advertising.

Students' proficiency with argumentative text emerges later than their skill with expository text; most students will not gain skill with this type of discourse until after they leave elementary school. Print-based argumentative text requires a more complex understanding of the intended audience, the ability to view the entire argument at once, and to see the end of the argument before formulating the beginning of it–quite sophisticated cognitive proficiency for many students until they reach middle school and beyond. Chapter 6 addresses argumentative text in more detail.

Assessing the "Metas"

As described in Chapter 2, much language development during elementary school occurs in the realm of the "metas": metalinguistic, metacognitive, and metapragmatic abilities. These meta abilities become more important as students progress through the grades. Much of what transpires in the classroom hinges on students' awareness of language, thinking, and communicating as "things" that can be talked about, analyzed, and played with. Table 5.1 shows the three "metas" that students use the most.

Students whose phonological processing abilities are impaired are likely to have difficulty engaging in the sorts of metalinguistic activities shown in Table 5.1, as are students who have limited exposure to and experience in talking about talking, playing with language, and learning the permissible and nonpermissible forms of their language. Too, students who are late in developing phonological awareness are at risk for reading disabilities and may require intervention targeted specifically at the development of phonological awareness (described later in the chapter).

Pragmatics

Students identified as having pragmatic disorders typically have difficulty with metapragmatic tasks as well. Because they are struggling to learn the social-interactive rules for the discourse genres typical of school, they remain limited in their ability to reflect on the genres or the rules. Because of this limitation, these students might appear rude, disrespectful, or unwilling to learn. Their pragmatic abilities may have to be developed before they can begin to acquire the ability to reflect on the pragmatic aspects of language.

Most students develop the ability to reflect on their own thinking—metacognition—sometime during their elementary school years. Students with LLD often have difficulty developing these strategies on their own and may not know what to do even though they recognize that they have failed to understand something. They may sit passively, ask a peer for help, act out, or vocalize their dilemma. Instruction that develops their ability to think about and analyze their own thinking and learning processes often solves what may appear on the surface to be a problem with content.

TABLE 5.1

The Metas

Metalinguistic Ability

Recognition that language is something to be talked about, played with, and analyzed. Examples include

- defining words
- recognizing synonyms, antonyms, homonyms
- recognizing homophones and semantic ambiguities
- identifying syntactic and morphological elements in sentences
- choosing language forms and content for writing
- editing writing
- manipulating linguistic units (e.g., Pig Latin)
- using linguistic humor (e.g., riddles, puns)
- using figurative language
- exhibiting phonological awareness

Metacognitive Ability

Recognition that thinking is something to be talked about, analyzed, and modified. Examples include

- recognizing how one thinks and learns
- modifying one's learning process
- monitoring comprehension of various material
- making and describing inferences
- hypothesizing
- recognizing lack of understanding and finding an appropriate remedy
- using anticipatory sets to prepare for learning something new

Metapragmatic Ability

Recognition that the "rules" governing how language is used in different situations can be talked about and analyzed. Examples include

- violating the "tell the truth" principle in certain sanctioned situations
- understanding the unique characteristics of classroom discourse
- identifying the unspoken rules governing classroom discourse
- engaging in knowledge displays required in the classroom
- talking about different types of discourse (e.g., slang, school talk, church talk, home talk)
- talking about discourse rules
- using different discourse genres in writing

Language Instruction

Assessment and instruction were discussed in Chapter 4 within the context of IDEA 2004. One of the main points of that discussion was that IDEA mandates linking students' IEPs with state learning standards (see Table 4.2 and Figure 4.8). For school-age students, the linking process can serve as the foundation for designing language instruction. Miller and Hoffman (2002), for instance, have devised a step-by-step guide for linking learning standards to IEPs, giving examples that show how students' language needs can be addressed by helping the student meet standards. For individual students, the linking process begins with identifying existing state learning standards at the student's age or grade level and designing IEP annual goals and benchmarks that help the student progress toward the standard(s).

Some students with language problems do not qualify for special education services, usually because their difficulty is not severe enough to meet eligibility criteria. These students, however, may still require accommodations or modifications to the general curriculum even though they do not qualify for special education services. In these situations, instruction may be generated using what is known as a Section 504 plan.

In 1973, Congress passed Section 504 of the Rehabilitation Act, civil rights legislation specifying that agencies that receive federal money cannot discriminate against people on the basis of their disabilities. More specifically, Section 504 prohibits schools from excluding children with disabilities from the programs and activities offered to students without disabilities. Section 504 actually served as the precedent for PL 94-142, the Education for All Handicapped Children Act, which passed in 1975 and was reauthorized in 2004 as the Individuals with Disabilities Education Act (IDEA).

IDEA and Section 504 provide similar frameworks for designing instruction. Both require an evaluation of the student by people who are knowledgeable about the student, the placement procedures are similar under both laws, and both require a plan including goals and benchmarks (though 504 plans need not be written as IEPs) (Miller & Newbill, 2006). Both can be used effectively as a means of directing the planning, delivery, and evaluation of language instruction, particularly when they are linked directly to state learning standards.

As in Chapter 4, the discussion here considers three aspects of language intervention and instruction: (a) the communication and/or language goals established for the child, (b) the methods designed to help the child achieve the instructional goals, and (c) the settings within which the instruction takes place.

Language Goals

One of the goals of language instruction is to develop facility with the language structures, forms, and functions that appear during the language for learning period. Some students arrive at school with language abilities more typical of the developing language period, in which case the approaches discussed in Chapter 4 are appropriate.

Other students begin school having difficulties with some, though not all, of the language forms expected of the language for learning stage. Still others are older students whose language skills have been weak and are now more seriously affecting their abilities to learn and progress through the curriculum.

A second major goal of language instruction is to acquire a more literate language style through the oral-to-literate shift described previously. This shift enables students to use their oral language skills to support their own learning (what Paul [2006] termed "language for learning") and provides access to more literate types of print-based communication. Westby (1998) argued that narrative language plays a crucial role in students' acquisition of literate language because it serves as a bridge between conversational language, which is highly contextualized, and literate language, which is highly decontextualized.

Paul (2006) proposed two principles to guide language instruction focused on students' development of language structures: (a) Integrate oral and written language, and (b) focus on the "metas."

Integrating Oral and Written Language

By providing students with both oral and written opportunities to practice the forms and functions targeted for instruction, teachers can reinforce students' learning the relationships between speech and print as well as address the skills that students need for literacy socialization. Language targets can include the components of oral language development (semantics, phonology, syntax and morphology, and pragmatics), as well as narrative and nonnarrative forms of discourse.

An illustration shows how integrating oral and written language might look while emphasizing the components of oral language development. The state of Vermont (2008) has learning standards for communication in five categories—reading, writing, listening, expression, and information technology—in which proficiency differs by grade level. Thus, for a second-grade student with difficulties in pragmatics and phonological awareness, the annual goals, based directly on the relevant standards from all five categories of communication, are shown in Table 5.2.

Within the framework of the goals shown in Table 5.2, instruction can incorporate activities that emphasize whichever semantic, syntactic, phonological, and morphological structures the assessment has shown to require instruction. For instance, the teacher can select reading material that includes specific vocabulary words, perhaps abstract words, to emphasize semantic comprehension in print, while asking the student to incorporate the same words into oral descriptions or storytelling activities. Or the student might be asked to identify target words in the book she has just read.

To focus on phonological awareness, the student can be asked to identify whether words are "long" or "short," which sounds the words begin and end with, and how many syllables are included in each word. To highlight English writing conventions, the teacher can ask the student to identify the words that begin printed sentences and to explain what clue can be used to make the identification. Similarly, students can be asked to tell how they know where the end of a written sentence is. Then, when

TABLE 5.2
Sample of Annual Goals Linked to Learning Standards

Learning Standard/Goal	Evidence	Benchmark 1
Reading:		
Student will use a variety of strategies to help her read.	Student will identify sounds, syllables, and letter patterns.	By October 1, student will identify: the initial sounds in single-syllable words, the number of syllables in three-syllable words, and will recognize the letters representing five speech sounds.
Student will read for meaning, demonstrating initial understanding and personal response.	Student will make connections between text and personal experience.	By October 1, student will read two books and describe a personal experience that is similar to the story in each.
Writing Conventions:		
Student's independent writing exhibits command of appropriate English conventions.	Student will exhibit understanding of word order and punctuation (capitalization and period).	By October 1, student will write four-word sentences, using a capital at the beginning and a period at the end.

Note: This sample is for a second-grade student with difficulties in pragmatics and phonological awareness.

the students are writing, the teacher can remind them to use the same clues for remembering how to begin and end written sentences.

Narrative language offers multiple opportunities for students to integrate oral and written language. One of the learning standard/goal statements for the student annual goal shown Table 5.2 can be used to illustrate how this might take place. The standard states: "Student will read for meaning, demonstrating initial understanding and personal response." As a way to weave oral and written language together, the following progression could be used. The student

- listens to a familiar story, draws a picture that tells the same story, and retells the story in her own words;
- listens to an unfamiliar story, draws a picture telling the same story, and retells the story in her own words;
- listens to an unfamiliar story, draws a picture telling the same story, retells the story in her own words, and writes one or more labels for parts of the picture;
- listens to a story, draws a picture telling the same story, retells the story in her own words, and writes one or two words from the story somewhere in the drawing;
- listens to a story, retells it in her own words, and lists three words from the story;
- listens to a story, retells it, and writes a word telling the beginning of the story, a word from the middle, and a word from the end;
- listens to a story, retells it, and writes a sentence telling the beginning of the story, a word telling the beginning, and a word telling the end;
- listens to a story, retells it to herself, and writes a sentence telling the beginning, a sentence telling the middle, and a sentence telling the end;
- listens to a story, retells it to herself, writes one sentence each for the beginning, middle, and end of the story (leaving space between each sentence), and lists two or three things that go with each sentence;
- listens to a story, retells it to herself, writes one sentence for the beginning, middle, and end of the story (leaving space between the sentences), and writes one or two sentences telling what goes with the beginning, two or three sentences telling what goes with the middle, and two or three sentences telling what goes with the end;
- listens to a story, retells it to herself, writes two or three sentences telling what happens at the beginning of the story, two or three that tell what happened in the middle, and two or three telling what happened at the end.

After the student has finished the above progression, she is ready to use the integration of oral and printed language to focus on the salient aspects of narrative discourse as described in the earlier section on assessment: story components, story ideas and language, and episode elements. As noted, Miller et al. (2001) described these three aspects of narrative discourse in developmental order. Selecting which of the three *aspects* to begin with should be based on the teacher's judgment about which would benefit the student most in the classroom. After making that choice, the *subcomponents* should be taught in order, beginning with whichever one the student demonstrates beginning knowledge.

Again, using the information from Table 5.2 and assuming that the teacher has elected to begin with the story components, the student might follow a progression in which she

- listens to a familiar story, draws a picture of the setting for the story, and tells where or when the story takes place;
- listens to a story, draws a picture of the setting, and tells where and when it takes place;
- listens to a story, draws a picture of the setting, tells where and when it takes place, and writes on the drawing one word telling where (e.g., "forest," "desert") and one telling when (e.g., "once," "Tuesday");
- listens to a story, draws a picture of the setting, tells where and when it takes place, and writes a sentence telling where or when the story takes place;
- listens to a story, draws a picture of the setting, tells where and when it takes place, and writes one sentence telling where the story takes place and one telling when;
- listens to a story, draws a picture of one or more characters from the story, and tells something about one character (e.g., name, attributes, thoughts, feelings);
- listens to a story, draws a picture of all (or several) of the characters from the story, and tells something about each;
- listens to a story, draws a picture of all (or several) of the characters from the story, tells something about each, and writes one word describing each (e.g., "big," "furry," "blue," "dog");
- listens to a story, draws a picture of all (or several) of the characters from the story, tells something about each character, and writes one sentence describing each character;
- listens to a story, draws a picture of one event from early in the story and one event from later in the story, and describes orally what each picture depicts;
- listens to a story, describes orally one thing that happened early in the story and one thing that happened later in the story, and writes one word describing each event (e.g., "feast," "sleeps," "swims");
- listens to a story, describes orally three events that happen, one early, one in the middle, and one later in the story, and writes one sentence describing each event;
- listens to a story and describes why the main characters did what they did;
- listens to a story, describes why the main characters did what they did, and writes two or three words describing why the main characters acted as they did;
- listens to a story, describes why the main characters did what they did, and writes one sentence telling why the main characters did what they did.
- listens to a story and describes the setting, character(s), the order of events, and why the characters did what they did;

- listens to a story, describes the setting, character(s), the order of events, and why the characters did what they did, and writes one word to signify each of the four story components;
- listens to a story, describes the setting, character(s), the order of events, and why the characters did what they did, and writes one sentence describing each of the story components.

Table 5.3 shows the same type of progression that can be used to help students integrate oral and written language while focusing on story ideas and language and for episode structure.

TABLE 5.3
Integrating Oral and Written Language Story Ideas and Language and Episode Structure

Story Ideas and Language

Complexity of Ideas

The student:

- Listens to a story, orally retells the story in a literal fashion.
- Listens to a story, retells it literally, and draws a picture of something from the story that was not actually told or shown.
- Listens to a story and retells it while incorporating something that was not actually told or shown.
- Listens to a story, retells it while incorporating something that was not told or shown, and writes three or four words describing the "untold" or "unshown" parts.
- Listens to a story and writes one or two sentences describing the "untold" or "unshown" parts.

Complexity of Vocabulary

The student:

- Listens to a story and retells it using two or more adjectives or adverbs.
- Listens to a story, retells it with two or more adjectives or adverbs, and writes the adjectives and adverbs down.
- Listens to a story, retells it with at least one figurative word or phrase or an idiomatic phrase (e.g., "The cat was <u>cold</u> to him at first," "The dog was <u>up and running</u>," "He felt <u>like he was asleep</u>.")
- Listens to the same story and writes down the figurative words from his or her previous retelling.
- Writes one sentence for each of the figurative words used in her or his previous retelling.

Grammatical Complexity

The student:

- Listens to a story and retells it using one adjective phrase and one prepositional phrase.
- Listens to a story and retells it using two compound sentences.
- Listens to a story and retells it using one adjective phrase, one prepositional phrase, and two compound sentences.

(continued)

TABLE 5.3 *(continued)*

- Listens to a story, retells it with phrases and compound sentences, and writes one of the phrases.
- Listens to a story, retells it with two types of compound sentences, and writes one of them.
- Listens to a story, retells it with at least one complex sentence, and writes it.

Knowledge of Dialogue

The student:

- Listens to a story and retells it using simple dialogue.
- Listens to a story and retells it using at least two examples of dialogue.
- Listens to a story and retells it using dialogue embedded in a sentence (e.g., "He said, 'Have you seen my friend?'").
- Listens to a story, retells it using dialogue, and writes down one example of dialogue.
- Listens to a story, retells it using dialogue, and writes down several examples of dialogue.

Creativity

The student:

- Listens to a story and retells it without adult support.
- Listens to a story and retells it with teacher helping find the exciting part(s).
- Listens to a story, retells the exciting part, and writes it in one or two sentences.
- Listens to a story, retells it, including the exciting part, and writes five sentences retelling the story with the exciting parts.

Episode Structure and Elements

Basic Episode

The student:

- Listens to a story, tells the initiating event (what propelled the main character into action), and draws a picture depicting it.
- Listens to a story, tells what the attempt is (what the character did in response to the initiating event), and draws a picture depicting it.
- Listens to a story, tells what the consequence is (how was the initiating event resolved), and draws a picture depicting it.
- Listens to a story, tells the initiating event, the attempt, and the consequence.
- Listens to a story, tells the initiating event, attempt, and consequence, and writes one word describing each.
- Listens to a story, tells the initiating event, attempt, and consequence, and writes one sentence describing each.

Complete Episode

After successfully engaging in the above steps to write about a basic episode, the student:

- Listens to a story and tells the internal response (the main character's reactions to and/or feelings about the initiating event).
- Listens to a story and tells the plan (what the main character planned to do after the initiating event and/or the internal response).
- Listens to a story and tells the reaction/ending (the main character's reactions to the consequence).
- Listens to a story, tells the internal response, plan, and ending, and writes one word describing each.
- Listens to a story, tells the internal response, plan, and ending, and writes one sentence describing each.

Nelson (2009) recommended giving students multiple opportunities to write expository text, beginning with lists as soon as they can write. She argued that expository writing serves as a way to organize students' thinking. Again, using the example from Table 5.2, the student can progress through increasing levels of difficulty linking oral and print output. As the student succeeds at each level, she moves to the next level of difficulty in the following progression in which she orally

- first describes an activity of interest (e.g., participating in a rollerblading tournament), orally summarize the description, and list in writing the main points of the tournament;
- describes a different activity or event, orally summarizes it, and writes a list of the main points of the activity, including one example for each;
- describes and summarizes a different event or activity, followed by listing in writing the main points and writing a complete sentence, providing an example for each main point;
- summarizes a different activity or event, lists in writing the main points and examples for each, and writes an introductory paragraph describing it;
- orally summarizes a different activity or event, writes an introductory paragraph describing it, writes a topic sentence for each main point, and lists examples for each;
- orally summarizes a different activity or event, writes an introductory paragraph, writes a topic sentence for each main point, and writes a sentence describing one example for each.
- orally summarizes a different activity or event, writes an introductory paragraph, writes a topic sentence for each main point, writes a sentence describing one example for each, and writes a concluding sentence.

Focus on the Metas

One of the most useful skills that students learn in elementary school is to reflect on and talk about communication, language, and thinking (Miller, 2006). Paul (2006) urged teachers to plan activities that engage students on both the concrete and the meta levels. To do this, she suggested that teachers use modeling and practice with particular forms and functions of language to show students how they work (discussed in Chapter 4), directing students' attention to the concrete level of using language to communicate. On the more abstract meta level, students are encouraged to talk about the language forms they are using, how and why they are using those forms, and which other language forms might be used for the same purposes.

A particularly effective way to bring students' awareness to the metas is to have them perform different pieces from the literature (e.g., *Miss Nelson Is Missing* [Allard & Marshall, 1977] or *The Lorax* [Geisel, 1971]), preparing for the final performance by rehearsing over a period of days or weeks. The rehearsal process serves as the instructional context during which students can try out different voices for their characters. This calls their attention to which voice works best and why and how changing the voice changes the character's intention and believability.

Rehearsal can also be used to direct students' attention to why the author of the piece chose the words he did and what they think he had in mind in having characters say what they do. Students can be asked to tell what they believe the characters think, and what clues they use to reach their conclusions. Figure 5.1 shows how *Miss Nelson Is Missing* (Allard & Marshall, 1977) can be adapted for use with a group of students.

Rehearsing the performance of pieces of literature also affords students opportunities to hear about and speak different types of discourse, to try out different ways of initiating a topic, maintaining a topic, taking turns, and yielding the floor to other speakers. Without the demands of generating spontaneous language, by rehearsing lines, students can focus on how to talk about talking, language, and thinking.

Narrative Discourse

Previous discussions have emphasized the importance of narrative discourse and the role that narrative plays in students' acquiring the more literate forms of language typical of textbooks and teacher language, especially the lecture and persuasive formats. Previously, we learned how narrative language can be used to integrate oral and written language, thus providing students with multiple opportunities to practice narrative abilities.

Miller et al. (2001) designed an approach for teaching students more directly about narrative discourse, based on the principles of dynamic assessment (described in Chapter 4) and mediated teaching. In this model, students are first given a wordless picture book, *Two Friends* (Miller, 1999b). The teacher tells the student that the book tells a story, that it has no words, and that the student is to look at all the pages and then tell the teacher the story the pictures tell. The teacher writes down the student's story, and, using a set of guidelines for analyzing the story, determines which aspects of the story are missing or underdeveloped. Using the developmental criteria specified in the model, the teacher selects two aspects of the story that are developmentally appropriate for the student and conducts two teaching sessions on those aspects. During the teaching sessions, the teacher uses a mediated teaching procedure to help the student understand what is being worked on, why it is important, how it relates to her own experience, and how to remember to put it into her stories.

Following the second teaching session, the student is given another wordless book, *Bird & His Ring* (Miller, 1999a), and is asked to tell the story that these pictures tell. The teacher compares the student's second story to the first story to see which aspects of the teaching sequence seemed to help the student the most. Using this information, the teacher then designs a set of activities highlighting the story aspects that the student is most likely to develop next.

In their approach, Miller et al. (2001) described a set of classroom activities that teachers can use with a variety of narrative genres, including trade books, puppets and play figures, books on video, and comic books. Although Miller et al.'s procedure was designed for use with individual students, it can be easily modified for either small group or classroom activities.

Narrator:	The kids in Room 207 are misbehaving again.
Lucy:	(Covering her eyes) Charlie is throwing a spitball!
Charlie:	(Satisfied) It's sticking to the ceiling—yay!
Lucy:	(Amazed) David is making a paper plane.
David:	Ha—look at it fly!
Narrator:	They are the worst-behaved class in the whole school.
Miss Nelson:	(Sweetly) Now settle down.
David:	(Whispers loudly) Do we have to?
Jenny:	(Laughs) Look at Lucy; her hair is standing on end!
Lucy:	That's because Charlie is pulling it—stop it!
	(Charlie, Jenny, and David laugh)
Narrator:	They are even rude during story hour.
Larry:	Look, I can stand on my head!
Miss Nelson:	Larry, sit down, please. David, will you please pick up those airplanes? Jenny, leave Lucy's hair alone. Children, please! Open your reading books to page 10.
Jenny:	I want to draw <u>now</u>. Please, Miss Nelson, let's draw. (She shows her doodlilng to Larry)
Narrator:	(Shaking head) They always refuse to do their lessons.
Miss Nelson:	Something will have to be done.
Narrator:	The next morning ... Miss Nelson didn't come to school.
Larry:	Wow! Now we can <u>really</u> act up!
Charlie:	Look at this extra super plane!
Lucy:	It is pretty cool. Look, I can throw it, too!
Jenny:	Way to go, Lucy!
David:	Today, let's just be terrible!
Miss Swamp:	(Hisses) Not so fast!
Narrator:	A woman in an ugly black dress stood at the front of the room.
Miss Swamp:	I'm your new teacher, Miss Viola Swamp.
Narrator:	She raps the desk with her ruler.
Larry & Charlie:	Where is Miss Nelson?
Miss Swamp:	Never mind that! Open those arithmetic books!
Lucy:	(Looks at Jenny) But I want to draw!
Miss Swamp:	Keep your mouths shut! Sit perfectly still! And if you misbehave, you'll be sorry!
Kids:	Gee, this is no fun!
Narrator:	The kids did as they were told. They could see that Miss Swamp was a real witch. Right away she put them to work. The kids in Room 207 had never worked so hard!

Source: From *Language Intervention Through Performance of Literature,* by L. Miller, 1989, American Speech–Language–Hearing Association Annual Meeting, St. Louis. Copyright 1989 Lynda Miller. Reprinted with permission.

FIGURE 5.1

Focus on the Metas—Excerpt from an Adaptation of *Miss Nelson is Missing*

Nonnarrative Discourses

Nelson (2009) recommended beginning to teach students about nonnarrative (expository) discourses by having them discriminate between narrative and nonnarrative discourse structures. To recognize that the two genres are different requires the student to have at least a beginning understanding of what comprises narrative discourse. Once students understand that the two discourses differ, they can undertake the process of identifying what makes nonnarrative different from narrative. Nelson (1998) summarized the most salient characteristics of nonnarrative types of discourse into the schema shown in Figure 5.2.

Teachers can use these graphic schemas as visual organizers for students to use to recognize the organizational structure of different types of expository text and to organize their own oral or written reports. Teachers select from among the structures schematized in Figure 5.2 to highlight one at a time, perhaps having students find examples of the "list" schema in their textbooks and then having them make notes using the list schema in preparation for an oral report. Finally, students can be asked to use the list schema to organize their writing of a report. Once students demonstrate proficiency with one type of nonnarrative discourse, they can begin to work on another, following the same protocol described above.

Students also can gain insight into nonnarrative discourse by learning to recognize key words that characterize different kinds of expository text. Westby (1991) described the key words characteristic of six types of expository text: description, collection/enumeration, sequence/procedure, comparison/contrast, cause/effect explanation, and problem/solution. For instance, Westby identified the following key words as characteristic of descriptive text: *is called, can be defined as, is, can be interpreted as, is explained as, refers to, is a procedure for, is someone who, means* (p. 12).

Teachers can develop activities in which students discover the key words of different types of text, which greatly increases their facility to access expository text. For instance, the teacher can prepare the following materials for students:

- A sheet with three different types of expository text (e.g., an example of descriptive text, an example of a cause/effect explanation, and an example of comparison/contrast)
- A set of three keys, one for each of the above types of expository text, shown in Table 5.4. Students are instructed to use their key sheets to
  - □ circle the key words from the descriptive text in red, the cause/effect text in blue, and the comparison/contrast in green;
  - □ write the type of expository text next to each of the three examples, using the corresponding ink color matching the key words;
  - □ use one or more of the "How It's Set Up" phrases from each text type to write a sentence that could fit into each of the three text types.

Mathematics: A Special Case of Expository Discourse

The language of mathematics constitutes a special case of expository, or nonnarrative, discourse (Nelson, 2009). Most mathematics instruction in the early grades takes the

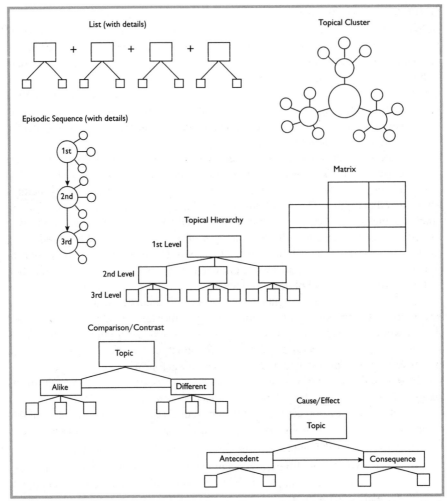

Source: From *Childhood Language Disorders in Context: Infancy through Adolescence* (2nd edition, p. 419) by N.W. Nelson, 1998, Boston: Allyn & Bacon. Copyright 1998 Pearson Education, Inc. Reprinted with permission.

FIGURE 5.2

Nonnarrative Discourse Types

form of teacher direction-giving—telling students how a given mathematical operation works. In addition, teachers give students mathematical symbols, which they are expected to be able to "read." These activities require students to remember the teacher's directions in the proper sequence and be able to use the symbols as guides to the sequence of steps that must be taken to solve the problem successfully. The most successful students then use self-talk to guide themselves through the process.

TABLE 5.4
Keys for Expository Text Types

	Descriptive	Cause-Effect	Comparison/Contrast
What It Does	Tells what things are	Gives reasons why something happened	Shows how things are alike and different
Key Words	is called, is defined as, is, can be interpreted as, is explained as, refers to, is a procedure for, means	because, since, reasons, then, therefore, for this reasons, results, effects, consequently, so, in order to, thus, depends on, influences, is a function of, produces, leads to, affects, hence	different, same, alike, similar, although, however, on the other hand, contrasted with, compared to, rather than, but, yet, still, instead of
How It's Set Up	Define... Describe... List the features of... What is...? Who is...?	Explain ... Explain the cause(s) of ... Explain the effect(s) of ... Predict what will happen ... Why did ... happen? How did ... happen? What are the causes (reasons for, effects, results, etc.) of ...?	Compare and contrast ... and ... How are ... and ... alike and different?

Source: From Steps to Developing and Achieving Language-based Curriculum in the Classroom (p. 12), by C. E. Westby, 1991. (Rockville, MD: American Speech-Language-Hearing Association. Copyright 1991 by American Speech-Language-Hearing Association. Reprinted with permission.

Not surprisingly, students with LLD have difficulty learning the language of math. They fail to remember the correct order from the teacher's directions, use less self-talk, and confuse the symbols. Most complete fewer problems than their peers, and when they encounter story problems, their difficulties intensify.

Story problems require students to re-present the problem in two stages: first before the mathematical operation(s) is applied, and then after the application, to see what has changed. Students with LLD often fail to understand the language of the first stage, ensuring that they either apply the wrong operation or will solve the problem incorrectly.

Nelson (2009) recommended teaching students with LLD deliberate, specific, and accurate self-talk strategies to guide themselves through computation problems. For story problems, she recommends analyzing the discourse structure and then sketching the structure graphically. She developed a set of worksheets with a box for the graphic sketch at the top of the page, a reminder to use self-talk below that, and blank work space at the bottom of the sheet for the student to write the computations.

Methods for Language Instruction

Chapter 4 presented the methods for language instruction as existing along a continuum, shown in Table 4.3, ranging from teacher directed at one end to student directed at the other. Teachers are probably most familiar with teacher-directed approaches, which involve the teacher, perhaps in collaboration with the speech–language clinician, to help the student learn specific language forms or structures. A variety of materials is available for teacher-directed instruction in phonological processing, semantic and syntactic development, morphological development, and pragmatics. A sampler of materials is shown in Table 5.5.

Another approach to language instruction is **scaffolding,** which falls somewhere in the middle of the continuum from teacher-directed to student-centered language instruction (refer to Table 4.3 in Chapter 4). Scaffolding is the process by which adults mediate specific experiences, such as using particular language forms or functions, to help students become more competent with those forms or functions.

The mediated teaching approach described by Miller et al. (2001) utilizes scaffolding through the process of mediated teaching. Mediated teaching can be an effective way to teach specific language structures and functions to school-age students. In the Miller et al. (2001) model, mediated teaching is based on a set of learning principles and follows a specified sequence.

As described earlier, dynamic assessment and mediated teaching comprise the process of using a test-teach-retest approach to determine how much a student can change in a specific language or communication behavior with teacher support, how modifiable the student's language or communication behavior is, what sorts of errors the student makes, what the student's self-monitoring behaviors are, and which teaching styles and strategies work best to promote change in the student's communication, language or both (Miller et al., 2001).

TABLE 5.5

Sampler of Materials for Teaching Language to School-Age Students

Phonological Processing	Vocabulary	Syntax & Morphology	Pragmatics
Word Scramble (Johnson, 2001)	100 Everyday Words to Read, Write, and Understand: A Guide for Teaching the Instant Usage of High Frequency Words (Mannix, 1998)	HELP for Grammar (Lazzari, 1997)	That's Life: Social Language (McConnell & LoGiudice, 1998)
Take Home: Phonological Awareness (Robertson & Salter, 2001)		Syntax It Is! : Reproducible Stories and Posters for Language Skills (Atkins, 1996)	Pragmatic Activities for Language Intervention: Semantics, Syntax, and Emerging Literacy (Paul, 1999, 2006)
Phonological Awareness Training for Reading (Torgeson & Bryant, 2001)	Workbook for Synonyms, Homonyms, and Antonyms (Rea-Rosenberger, 1997)	Syntaxercises™: Language Games for Syntax Practice (Housel, Polson, & Herron, 1996)	Exploring Pragmatic Language: Games for Practice (Bernarding, 1996)
The Lindamood® Phoneme Sequencing Program for Reading, Spelling, and Speech (Lindamood & Lindamood, 2001)	Language Quicktionary (Richardson, Hoerchler, & Hollis, 1996)		Scripting Junior (Miller, 2004)
Sounds of Our Language Audiotape (Greene, 1998)	Curriculum Vocabulary (Lacapa, 2001)		Social Star: Peer Interaction Skills (Gajewski, Hirn, & Mayo, 1994)
Working Out with Phonological Awareness (Schreiber et al., 2000)	Understanding Math Story Problems (McGlothlin, 1995)		

In the Miller et al. (2001) model of mediated teaching, the teaching sessions follow a specific sequence of teaching strategies, five of which are required and two are optional, depending on the student's responses and level of understanding.

First, the teacher shows the student the materials she will be using for the session and tells her what she will be working on, or the goal of the session (the *Intention to Teach* strategy). The telling can consist of various sorts of instruction. For instance, at the beginning of a session designed to have a student include information about the causes of events in stories, the teacher might say, "Today we're going to talk about why things happen in stories. When people tell you a story, you understand it better when they tell you *why* things happen. They use words like *because, and so*, and *the reason....*" To ensure the student's understanding, the teacher might tell the student two short stories, one with causal words and one without, and then ask her which made more sense.

Second, once the teacher is certain that the student understands the Intention to Teach strategy, he presents the *Meaning* strategy to explain why the task or goal is important (Miller et al., 2001). To explain why using causal words in stories is important, the teacher might say, "If you want people to understand your stories, it helps to tell them *why* things happen the way they do" (p. 58). To support the student's understanding of the Meaning strategy, the teacher might have her act out the story she is working with and freeze the action each time she comes to a point where she could use a causal word.

Third, the teacher presents one or more *Examples* to highlight what they are working on. For instance, the teacher could say to the student, "Let's look at the book again and see if we can explain why [whatever the precipitating event was]." The teacher helps the student describe why the character did what he did, perhaps by showing her several pictures or sentences that explain the cause of the events. The teacher supports the student's attempts to structure a logical reason that the events unfolded the way they did, perhaps by again having her act out a pertinent scene and then using a causal word to describe what was happening.

Fourth, if the student was able to add the causal information without too much help, the teacher presents the *Hypothesizing/Transcendence* strategy, asking the student why the characters did various things in the story. The point is to help the student understand that using causal words and phrases helps listeners understand the story. To help the student hypothesize beyond the current setting, the teacher can ask the student if she knows of another story in which the author told why the characters were doing certain things. If she is unable to think of one, the teacher can present a familiar story and help her discover the causative elements.

Fifth, if the student needed extra support understanding the Examples strategy, the teacher can skip Hypothesizing/Transcendence and, instead, present the *Self-Evaluation* strategy. The teacher might say, "We've been talking about telling why the characters did what they did. Why is that important?" To help the student understand, the teacher might remind the student of the facial expressions and body gestures showing how the characters felt and, therefore, why they might have done what they did.

Sixth, the teacher presents the *Planning* strategy by asking the student, "The next time you tell a story, what are you going to remember to put in it?"

Last, to help the student develop a way to remember to use the language structure outside the present context, the teacher presents the *Transfer* strategy. He might say, "We've been talking about why characters do what they do, the reasons they act like they do in stories. The next time you tell a story, how are you going to remember to explain why things happen the way they do?"

Throughout mediated teaching sessions, teachers can track students' responses to discover how much change they were capable of with appropriate teacher support, and which of the support strategies–Intention to Teach, Meaning, Example, Hypothesizing/Transcendence, Self-Evaluation, Planning, or Transfer–worked best for each student. The interaction between teacher and student—described in terms of student responsivity and teaching effort—also provides information that will be useful in planning further instructional programs and activities. For instance, if a student was highly responsive during the mediated teaching sessions, the targeted language structure of function may have been too easy for that student. But if the student was not responsive, the target may have been too hard.

Similarly, if the teacher were to expend only minimal teaching effort during the mediated teaching sessions, the targeted language may have been too easy for the student, Or if the teacher expended a lot of teaching effort, the target may have been too difficult. In either case, the teacher will want to refine the selection of language targets so, during mediated teaching, the student is at least somewhat responsive and the amount of teaching effort required is in the moderate range. For a more thorough discussion of the relationships between teaching effort and student responsivity, see Miller et al. (2001, pp. 42ff).

Two further examples of scaffolding are Wallach's (1989) narrative development approach and Westby's (1999) book report sequence. To reduce the amount of stress that students with LLD frequently experience when they are assigned to write a book report, Wallach (1989) developed a list of books that the student might use independently—on their own "bookshelf"—rather than choosing a book from the class library. Wallach's list is arranged in developmental order using Appleby's model so the teacher can help students select books according to their individual level of development in narrative and reading. As students' narrative understanding and comprehension improve, they can select books from the next higher level of narrative development.

Westby's (1999) approach to the book report writing difficulties shown by most students with LLD was to develop a set of seven formats, arranged in developmental order from easiest to most difficult. At each respective level, students are asked to do the following:

Level 1: Write the title and author of the book on a piece of paper and draw a picture of your favorite part of the story.

Level 2: Write the title and author of the book, list the major characters, tell the first thing that happens in the story, and tell how the story ends.

Level 3: Write the title and author of the book, list the major characters, tell three things, in sequence, that happened in the story, and retell the story with pictures.

Level 4: Write the title and author of the book, tell why a character did something in the story, relate three things, in sequence, that happened in the story, and retell the story, using pictures.

Level 5: Write the title and author of the book, tell how one of the characters in the story feels, tell how you know the character felt that way, and retell the story, using pictures;

Level 6: Write the title and author of the book, tell how one of the characters in the story felt, tell why the character felt that way, and retell the story in your own words.

Level 7: Write the title and author of the book, tell what the problem is in the story, tell how the characters solved the problem, and retell the story in your own words.

One of the most prominent student-directed types of language instruction used for elementary school students is **whole language**. Whole language uses children's literature to introduce students to reading and emphasizes the communicative functions served by written language. In addition, whole language instruction integrates oral and written language across the curriculum, which is an advantage for most classroom teachers. Often, whole language instruction occurs in the context of theme-based units. For example, a web-based unit for K–5 developed by Chapman and Herring (2001) uses the theme of oceans and underwater life. Language instruction can be woven across various content areas, including Literature/English, History, Social Studies, Math, Health/Science, and Arts.

Using Chapman and Herring's unit, the teacher could modify existing activities only slightly to emphasize specific language structures or functions or discourse structure and functions. For instance, Chapman and Herring describe a Literature/English activity that involves reading *Monster Beach* by Paraskevas (1995). The class then picks a dangerous sea creature (real or imagined), and the students write about a narrow escape from this creature. This writing activity could be modified requiring individual students to include specific linguistic features. For instance, a student working on developing more complex vocabulary could be required to use one or more similes in his account, and a student working on including causal relations in narratives could be required to tell why the main character (most likely the student, writing in first person) did what she did to escape.

Another Literature/English activity described by Chapman and Herring (2001) begins by the teacher reading *Sea Gifts* (Shannon, 2000) aloud to the class. Then the teacher and students discuss and list some of the treasures found by the man who trades with the sea (anemones, a blue glass bubble from a fishing net, an empty shell). The students list what he did with these objects (put them on his shelf, saved wood to mend his home, carved wood). Finally, the students choose one phrase from each list and uses these to write original Sea Gifts poems. Again, they could be instructed to incorporate into their poems specific linguistic structures, such as a complex sentence, dialogue, or a description of a person or sea creature.

Chapman and Herring (2001) described a History/Social Studies activity that can be structured for students' language needs. The teacher instructs students to find out more about an ocean-related occupation, perhaps by doing an internet search or reading a book from the library. Students then report their findings to the class or write a short report titled "A Week in the Life of a _____." Based on their language needs, the students could be assigned either an oral or a written report. In either case, the teacher can specify the structure to be used to emphasize the students' targeted language structures or functions.

For instance, a student working on writing descriptive text could be instructed to incorporate into his written report five or six examples of key words from Table 5.4. The student could also be instructed to follow the "How It's Set Up" format for descriptive text shown in Table 5.4, making sure to describe the occupation she chose to research, list the features of that occupation, and answer the questions: "What is a(n) [occupation]?" and "Who are [occupation]?"

The whole language approach to reading instruction is discussed further in Chapter 8.

Settings for Language Instruction

Although language instruction for students in elementary school can be found along the same continuum, most teacher-designed language instruction will take place in the context of the classroom. In some schools, teachers provide language instruction in collaboration or consultation with the speech–language clinician (SLP). In other schools, specific classrooms are designed to be language-based, with teachers and SLPs team-teaching with a focus on instruction that supports students' learning more advanced language forms, structures, and usages.

When SLPs provide consultation only for classroom teachers, their goal is to increase the likelihood of a student's success in the classroom. To that end, SLPs typically visit the classroom; evaluate classroom procedures, materials, and textbooks in terms of language and communication demands; and may evaluate specific students' communication and language abilities. Usually, the SLP will ask teachers about individual students' communication and language difficulties and how the SLP can best aid the teacher in helping the students succeed. Based on this information, the SLP will suggest possible ways to modify instruction to help students with LLD understand and produce higher quality language.

Most SLPs are willing to collaborate with teachers to make the suggested modifications. For instance, if one of the suggestions is for the teacher to provide contextual cues so students will have more information about what is to be discussed, the SLP might devise an overhead transparency outline for each of several topics; construct charts, pictures, or diagrams that visualize the components of specific topics; or provide a list of questions for the teacher to use in reviewing the major points for student to focus on for each topic (Lasky, 1991).

Collaboration with SLPs takes a variety of forms. One of the most rewarding is for the teacher and SLP to team-teach specific lessons or units to provide the support that students with LLD need to be able achieve greater success in the classroom. For classroom collaboration to work effectively, the SLP should have some familiarity with the curriculum, classroom content, and classroom procedures. Collaborative teaching between teachers and SLPs can take a variety of forms, ranging from one person teaching while the other observes, to each person taking a "station" at which each teaches a different part of the lesson to half the class and later switching students, to both sharing the same set of students but teaching different subject matter.

When teachers and SLPs develop lesson plans together, the SLP can take the lead initially because of his more detailed knowledge and expertise in language development and disorders. The teacher and the SLP, however, must take responsibility for joint planning to ensure that the resulting lesson will work effectively for the whole class and that it will be woven into the other activities and themes in the classroom (Paul, 2006). In many cases, once the lesson has been presented, the SLP suggests using small-group instruction as a way to divide the class so the students with LLD (and some without) are in his group while students without special needs are in the teacher's group. Clouss's (2009) short description of her initial experiences working with classroom teachers shows how the process looks to the SLP.

Web-Based Instruction

With the development of the internet, web-based instruction has become more widely used in providing instruction. Many teachers host web pages, which they use for student instruction as well as for linking with other teachers. Teacher- and state-sponsored networks in South Carolina, Indiana, and Vermont, among others, support teachers in developing their own web pages for instructional use. One Alabama district, Mountain Brook Schools (2009), sponsors a website from which teachers have access to multiple technologies to support their instruction, including the following:

- Moodle—software that allows educators to create an online version of their courses, which students can access as a virtual classroom.
- MBS Portal.
- Voice Thread—a multimedia collaborative tool. Threads may consist of pictures, documents, and/or videos. Students can navigate pages from anywhere at any time and leave comments in several ways: voice (with a microphone or telephone), text, audio file, or video (via a webcam). A Voice Thread can be shared with other students (from Mountain Brook or from around the world), parents, and experts for them to record comments, too. Using Voice Thread, students can write on the screen with a digital pen while commenting, use multiple identities via commenting avatars, and pick which comments they wish to be shown to others.

Case Western Reserve University (2009) has developed a website tutorial for teachers, called "The Internet and the Classroom Teacher: Preparing an Instructional Lesson Using the Resources of the Internet." This can be used as a template for teachers who wish to use the internet to develop instructional lessons with a language focus. The recommended procedure is as follows:

1. Design the goals of the lesson.
2. Conduct the research.
3. Write specific learning objectives and lesson content.
4. Design a student workbook.
5. Deliver the lesson.
6. Evaluate student learning.
7. Conduct follow-up activities.

Internet4Classrooms (2009) has provided a list of web design resources specifically for teachers. Among the resources are links to general web page help, including color for web pages and school web page templates, web page hosting and assistance, graphics for web pages, HTML information and tutorials, and Javascript information and tutorials.

Kuster (2009) has compiled a listing of websites where teachers can find materials suitable for language instruction. Her list includes interactive sites, sites offering reproducibles, clip art, storybooks, newspapers and magazines, clinical materials and ideas, freeware/shareware sites, and computer-assisted treatment resources.

The "For Teachers" page on the LD Online website (2009a) offers a collection of information for teachers and special educators regarding students with learning disabilities, including specific instructional strategies for teaching language and reading, learning strategies, mathematics, and writing. This site provides links to information about using technology in the classroom, designing accommodations, working with adolescents, behavior and social skills, working with parents, and special education requirements. Links are also provided to a variety of resources, including organizations and websites, state resources, and books (LD Online, 2009b).

▌School-Age Children with ▌Severe Impairments

School-age children with severe impairments—among them, students diagnosed with autism—may exhibit communication and language development that is more typical of the emerging language or developing language stages. The primary goal for these students is to help them achieve as much independence as possible in daily living and vocational settings. The emphasis for these students is to develop a functional repertoire of communication and language skills. To this end, language instruction may be aimed at matching students' communication and language development to the requirements of their everyday lives, including the social demands of recreation, work, and domestic life.

This is not to say that students with moderate to severe language impairments should be excluded from exposure to literacy. To the contrary, developing even a beginning ability to read and write will help them fill out job applications; read signs and newspaper advertisements; write letters inquiring about housing or jobs; and organize their domestic lives by copying recipes, making shopping and to-do lists, paying bills, and keeping records (Paul, 2006).

Ideally, language instruction for students with moderate to severe disabilities should take place in the context of community living, vocational training, or functional life skills courses. For example, in a unit on eating out at a restaurant, students could be taught the vocabulary they are likely to encounter, perhaps by studying a variety of menus from local restaurants. Once students achieve confidence and skill in reading menus, they might test their knowledge by going with their teacher on an outing to a nearby restaurant.

Writing can be taught in a unit on shopping and meal planning, for example. Students could make shopping lists and plan menus for a class party. The unit could include an excursion to the grocery store, where the student-generated shopping lists would be used to purchase the food and supplies for the party. In preparing for the party, the students would use their menu plans to guide food preparation, table setting, and place card arrangements.

Several published programs are available for teaching functional language and communication to students with moderate to severe impairments. Two of those used most commonly are

- *Functional Curriculum for Elementary, Middle, and Secondary Age Students with Special Needs* (2nd edition) (Wehman & Kregel, 2004), and
- *Life Skill Curriculum: A Multidisciplinary Unit* (Weber, 2001).

Some school-age students with severe impairments do best with an alternative and/or augmentative communication (AAC) system. Chapter 4 included factors that must be considered when deciding to use an AAC system. For students whose language abilities are within the language for learning stage, AAC devices using some form of printed words are recommended. Print-based devices offer students more opportunities to develop the literacy skills they need to communicate through print—which means that they can communicate with a wider range of conversational partners than would be the case if they were to use non-print-based systems.

AAC devices utilizing voice output (usually computers that "speak," or synthesize, what the student selects to communicate) may help students who use them to match auditory images (spoken words and sentences) to their intended meanings and to improve phonological awareness. Paul (2006) reviewed a series of studies showing that voice output AAC devices benefited children's literacy development. Other researchers have found that voice output AAC devices facilitate both speech and language growth in children (Foley & Staples, 2003; Romski & Sevcik, 1996).

One drawback to voice output AAC systems is that they do not offer opportunities for students to develop skill in writing. Also, the written language of students who do not speak may exhibit syntactic and morphological omissions (Kelford-Smith, Thurston, Light, Parnes, & O'Keefe, 1989). Students who are most successful using

AAC systems and who develop the reading and writing skills associated with literacy are those whose communication and language instruction utilizes the AAC device (or devices, as the choice of systems changes as the child develops) to support the student's language development and academic achievement.

Teachers can provide support and accommodations to help students using AAC devices acquire literacy skills. Smith, Patton, Polloway, and Dowdy (2007) offered recommendations for teachers to follow with students using AAC devices. Among them are the following:

- Provide opportunities for students to play.
- Encourage students to talk with their teachers and peers.
- Encourage conversational skills through story reading.
- Use music and play games.
- Use storytelling and process writing.

Tufte and Maro (1999) developed a procedure that teachers can use to build literature-based communication boards or overlays for other AAC devices for stories, songs, and vocabulary. The teacher first selects a story, using a repetitive-phrase book or a book of interest to the student. Next, the teacher sequences the story onto the AAC device so the student can access it by pushing sequential keys. Scanning devices are set to "step scan" so each time the switch is activated, the cursor advances to the next line.

A more recent development in computer software design offers another way for an AAC system to assist students with LLD. **Speech recognition software**, originally adapted for computer security purposes, has been adapted for use by students who have difficulties with composing and writing. Gardner (2008) argued that students using speech recognition software can experience significant gains in their writing productivity, content, and ideas. In addition, Raskind and Higgins (1999) found that using speech recognition technology improved the reading and spelling performance of students with learning disabilities. Though this technology is in its beginning phase of development for use with students who have LLD, it should be explored as an option for any student who has difficulty producing written language.

Various assistive technologies are currently used with students with LLD, including multimedia software, computer-based study strategies, technology integrated into the standard curriculum, videos, reading software, and software-supported math instruction. The website hosted by LD Online (2009b) provides more detailed discussions of each of these technologies. The site includes links to online technology resources and useful publications and an up-to-the-minute listing of hardware and software products for people with all types of learning disabilities.

▮Summary

During the elementary school years, typically developing children refine most of the rules of syntax and morphology; their vocabularies increase considerably, particularly as they begin to encounter new words through reading; and they become adept at conversational interactions. Their awareness of the phonological aspects of language serves as a foundation for becoming able to decode print, and they develop facility with various forms of discourse, both narrative and nonnarrative. Most students make the oral-to-literate shift as they gain experience with more formal language styles, both oral and print-based.

By the time they are ready to leave elementary school, most students are using reading as a primary means to learn new information. In addition, their writing ability has developed enough for them to produce narratives with complete and/or embedded episodes. They can think and talk about communication, language, and speech, and they are aware of themselves as language users.

For students with language disabilities, the aim of assessment and instruction is to help them develop phonological awareness (i.e., the skills they need to understand the relationships between speech sounds and print, particularly letters and syllables); facility with narrative and nonnarrative discourse; and the ability to reflect on language and communication as things that can be talked about, analyzed, and synthesized. In many schools, the speech–language clinician (SLP) is available to consult and/or collaborate with classroom teachers to design specific programs for students with language disabilities.

For students with severe impairments, AAC systems offer the best means for providing language instruction. These systems range from basic communication boards to sophisticated speech recognition devices that can be used by students who struggle with composition and writing.

References

Allard, H., & Marshall, J. (1977). *Miss Nelson is missing*. Boston: Houghton Mifflin.

Appleby, A. (1978). *The child's concept of a story: Ages 2 to 17*. Chicago: University of Chicago Press.

Atkins, P. L. (1996). *Syntax it is! : Reproducible stories and posters for language skills*. Austin, TX: Pro-Ed.

Bernarding, M. B. (1996). *Exploring pragmatic language: Games for practice*. Austin, TX: Pro-Ed.

Blodgett, E., & Cooper, E. (1987). *Analysis of the language of learning: The practical test of metalinguistics*. East Moline, IL: LinguiSystems.

Bowers, L., Barrett, M., Huisingh, R., Orman, J., & LoGiudice, C. (1994). *Test of problem solving–Revised–Elementary*. East Moline, IL: LinguiSystems.

Carrow-Woolfolk, E. (1999). *Test for Auditory Comprehension of Language* (3rd ed.). Chicago: Riverside.

Case Western Reserve University. (2001). *The internet and the classroom teacher preparing an instructional lesson using the resources of the internet*. Retrieved from http://www.cwru.edu/affil/cni/review/tomei.html?nw_view=1252086214&

Catts, H. (1997). The early identification of language-based reading disabilities. *Language, Speech, and Hearing Services in Schools, 28*, 88–89.

Catts, H., & Kamhi, A. (1999). *Language and reading disabilities*. Needham Heights, MA: Allyn & Bacon.

Cazden, C. (1988). *Classroom discourse: The language of teaching and learning*. Portsmouth, NH: Heinemann.

Chapman, L., & Herring, D. (2001). *Oceans and undersea life*. Retrieved from http://www.lib sci.sc.edu/miller/Ocean.htm

Chard, D. J., & Dickson, S. V. (1999). *Phonological awareness: Instructional and assessment guidelines*. Retrieved from http://www.ldonline.org/article/Phonological_Awareness:_In structional_and_Assessment_Guidelines

Clouss, W. (2009). *SLP's, literacy, and inclusion*. Retrieved from http://www.wy-os.net/speech/slp.htm

Dickinson, D., Wolf, M., & Stotsky, S. (1993). Words move: The interwoven development of oral and written language. In J. B. Gleason (Ed.), *The development of language* (3rd ed.). (pp. 369–420). New York: Macmillan.

Dollaghan, C., & Campbell, T. (1998). Nonword repetition and child language impairment. *Journal of Speech, Language, and Hearing Research, 41,* 1136–1146.

Donahue, M. (1994). Differences in classroom discourse styles of students with learning disabilities. In D. Ripich & N. Creaghead (Eds.), *School discourse problems* (2nd ed., pp. 229–362). San Diego: Singular.

Dunn, L., & Dunn, L. (2007). *Peabody picture vocabulary test* (3rd ed.). San Antonio, TX: Pearson.

Foley, B., & Staples, A. H. (2003). Developing augmentative and alternative communication (AAC) and literacy interventions in a supported employment setting. *Topics in Language Disorders, 23*(4), 325–343.

Gajewski, N., Hirn, P., & Mayo, P. (1994). *Social Star: Peer Interaction Skills*. Eau Claire, WI: Thinking Publications.

Gardner, T. J. (2008). Speech recognition for students with disabilities in writing. *Physical Disabilities: Education and Related Services, 26*(2), pp. 43–53

Geisel, T. S. (1971). *The Lorax*. New York: Random House.

German, D. J. (2000). *Test of word finding* (2nd ed.). Austin, TX: Pro-Ed.

German, D. J. (2001). *It's on the tip of my tongue, Word-finding strategies to remember those names and words you often forget*. DeKalb, IL: Janelle Publications.

German, D. J. (2002). A phonologically based strategy to improve word-finding abilities in children, *Communication Disorders Quarterly, 23*(4), 179–192.

German, D. J. (2005). *Word-finding intervention program* (2nd ed.). Austin, TX: Pro-Ed.

German, D. J. (2008). Formulate a second hypothesis: Word-finding based oral reading errors. Featured article in *Newsletter of the Illinois Speech–Language–Hearing Association (ISHA), 33*(2), 10–12.

German, D. J., & Newman, R. S. (2004). The impact of lexical factors on children's word-finding errors. *Journal of Speech, Language, and Hearing Research, 47*(3), 624–636.

German, D. J., & Newman, R. S. (2007). Oral reading skills of children with oral language (word finding difficulties). *Reading Psychology, 28*(5), 397–442.

Gilbertson, M., & Bramlett, R. (1998. Phonological awareness screening to identify at-risk readers: Implications for practitioners. *Language, Speech, and Hearing Services in Schools, 29,* 109–116.

Gilliam, J., & Miller, L. (2005). *Pragmatic language skills inventory*. Austin, TX: Pro-Ed.

Greene, J. F. (1998). *Sounds of our language* [audiotape]. Longmont, CO: Sopris West.

Hammill, D., & Bryant, B. (1999). *The Detroit tests of learning aptitude–Primary 4*. Austin, TX: Pro-Ed.

Hammill, D., & Larsen, S. (2009). *Test of written language–3*. Austin, TX: Pro-Ed.

Housel, S., Polson, D., & Herron, N. (1996). *Syntaxercises™: Language games for syntax practice*. Austin, TX: Pro-Ed.

Hresko, W. (1996). *Test of early written language–2*. Austin, TX: Pro-Ed.

Hresko, W., Reid, K., & Hammill, D. (1999). *Test of Early Language Development* (3rd ed.). Austin, TX: Pro-Ed.

Individuals with Disabilities Act of 2004, 20 USC 33 ¤. (2004). 1400 et seq.

Internet4Classrooms. (2009). *Helping teachers use the internet effectively*. Retrieved from http://www.internet4classrooms.com/web.htm

Johnson, P. F. (2001). *Word scramble: A phonological awareness and word-building game*. East Moline, IL: LinguiSystems.

Johnston, E. B., & Johnston, A.V. (1990). *Communication abilities diagnostic abilities test*. Chicago: Riverside.

Kavanagh, J., & Mattingly, I. (1972). *Language by ear and by eye*. Cambridge, MA: MIT Press.

Kelford-Smith, A., Thurston, S., Light, J., Parnes, P., & O'Keefe, B. (1989). The form and use of written communication produced by physically disabled individuals using microcomputers. *Augmentative and Alternative Communications, 5,* 115–124.

Kuster, J. M. (2009). *Speech & hearing therapy: Net connections for communication disorders and sciences: An internet guide*. Retrieved from http://www.telosnet.com/ov/v_speech.html #Net%20Connections%20for%20Communication%20Disorders%20and%20Sciences

Lacapa, K. (2001). *Curriculum vocabulary*. East Moline, IL: LinguiSystems.

Lasky, E. (1991). Comprehending and processing of information in clinic and classroom. In C. S. Simon (Ed.), *Communication skills and classroom success* (pp. 113–134). San Diego: College-Hill Press.

Lazzari, A. M. (1997). *HELP for grammar*. East Moline, IL: LinguiSystems.

LD Online (2009a). *Educators*. Retrieved from http://www.ldonline.org/educators

LD Online. (2009b). *Technology: Teaching with technology*. Retrieved from http://www.ldon line.org/ld_indepth/technology/technology.html#classroom_applications

Lindamood, P. & Lindamood, P. (2001). *The Lindamood phoneme sequenging program for reading, spelling, and speech* (3rd ed.). Austin, TX: Pro-Ed.

Mannix, D. (1998). *100 Everyday words to read, write, and understand: A guide for teaching the instant usage of High frequency words*. Austin, TX: Pro-Ed.

McConnell, N. & LoGiudice, C. (1998). *That's life: Social language*. East Moline, IL: LinguiSystems.

McGlothlin, M. (1995). *Understanding math story problems*. Austin, TX: Pro-Ed.

Miller, L. (1989). *Language intervention through performance of literature*. Paper presented at the American Speech–Language–Hearing Association Annual Meeting, St. Louis.

Miller, L. (1999a). *Bird & his ring*. Austin, TX: Neon Rose Productions.

Miller, L. (1999b). *Two friends*. Austin, TX: Neon Rose Productions.

Miller, L. (2004). *Scripting Junior*. Eau Claire, WI: Thinking Publications.

Miller, L. (2006). *Introduction to communication sciences and disorders* (3rd ed.). Eau Claire, WI: Thinking Publications.

Miller, L., Gillam, R. B., & Peña, E. C. (2001). *Dynamic assessment and intervention: Improving children's narrative skills*. Austin, TX: Pro-Ed.

Miller, L., & Hoffman, L. P. (2002). *Linking IEPs to Learning standards: A step-by-step guide*. Austin, TX: Pro-Ed.

Miller, L., & Newbill, C. (2006). *Section 504 in the classroom: How to design and implement accommodation plans* (2nd ed.). Austin, TX: Pro-Ed.

Mountain Brook Schools. (2009). *Technologies*. Retrieved from http://www.mtnbrook.k12.al. us/cms/Technologies/69.html

Nelson, N. W. (1998). *Childhood language disorders in context: Infancy through adolescence* (2nd ed). Boston: Allyn & Bacon.

Nelson, N. W. (2009). *Language and literacy: Infancy through adolescence*. Boston: Allyn & Bacon.

Newcomer, P., & Hammill, D. (2008). *Test of language development–4 Primary*. Austin, TX: Pro-Ed.

Newcomer, P., & Hammill, D. (2008). *Test of language development–4: Intermediate.* Austin, TX: Pro-Ed.

Newman, R. S., & German, D. J. (2002). Effects of lexical factors on lexical access among typical language-learning children and children with word-finding difficulties. *Language and Speech, 43*(3), 285–317.

Newman, R. S., & German, D. J. (2005). Life span effects of lexical factors on oral naming. *Language and Speech, 48*(2), 123–156.

Paraskevas, B. (1995). *Monster beach.* San Diego: Harcourt Brace.

Paul, R. (1999). *Pragmatic activities for language intervention: Semantics, syntax, and emerging literacy.* Austin, TX: Pro-Ed.

Paul, R. (2006). *Language disorders from infancy through adolescence: Assessment and intervention* (3rd ed.). St. Louis: Mosby.

Peña, E., Iglesias, A., & Lidz, C. S. (2001). Reducing test bias through dynamic assessment of children's word learning abilities. *American Journal of Speech-Language Pathology*, Vol. 10, 138–154.

Phelps-Terasaki, D., & Phelps-Gunn, T. (2007). *Test of pragmatic language–2.* Austin, TX: Pro-Ed.

Raskind, M. H., & Higgins, E. L. (1999). Speaking to read: The effects of continuous vs. discrete speech recognition systems on the reading and spelling of children with learning disabilities. *Journal of Special Education Technology eJournal, 15*(1), Winter 2000. Retrieved from http://jset.unlv.edu/15.1/higgins/first.html

Rea-Rosenberger, S. (1997). *Workbook for synonyms, homonyms, and antonyms.* Austin, TX: Pro-Ed.

Rehabilitation Act of 1973. (1973). 29 U.S.C. §701 *et seq.*

Richardson, D., Hoerchler, S., & Hollis, J. P. (1999). *Language quicktionary.* East Moline, IL: LinguiSystems.

Ripich, D., & Spinelli, F. (1985). *School discourse problems.* San Diego: College-Hill Press.

Robertson, C. & Salter, W. (2001). *Take home: Phonological awareness.* East Moline, IL: LinguiSystems.

Romski, M., & Sevcik, R. A. (1996). *Breaking the speech barrier: Language development through augmented means.* Baltimore: Brookes.

Sawyer, D. (1987). *Test of awareness of language segments.* Austin, TX: Pro-Ed.

Schreiber, L., Sterling-Orth, A., Thurs, S. A., & McKinley, N. L. (2000). *Working out with phonological awareness.* Eau Claire, WI: Thinking Publications .

Semel, E., Wiig, E., & Secord, W. (1998). *Clinical evaluation of language fundamentals–III.* San Antonio, TX: Psychological Corp.

Shannon, G. (& Azarian, M., illustrator). (2000). *Sea gifts.* Boston: Godine.

Smith, T. E. C., Patton, J. R., Polloway, E. A., & Dowdy, C. A. (2007). *Teaching students with special needs in inclusive settings.* Boston: Allyn & Bacon.

Torgeson, J. K. & Bryant, B. R. (2001). *Phonological awareness training for reading.* Austin, TX: Pro-Ed.

Tufte, L., & Maro, J. (1999). *Creating literature based communication boards.* Retrieved from http://www.aacintervention.com/litboards.htm

Tynan, W. D. (2008). *Learning disorder: Reading.* Retrieved from http://www.medscape.com/article/918143-overview.

Vermont Department of Education. (2008). *Vermont's framework of standards and learning opportunities.* Retrieved from http://education.vermont.gov/new/html/pubs/framework.html

Vygotsky, L. (1978). *Mind in society: The development of higher psychological processes.* Cambridge, MA: Harvard University Press.

Wallach, G. P. (1989). *Children's reading and writing disorders: The role of the speech–language pathologist* (ASHA Teleconference Tape Series). Rockville, MD: American Speech–Language–Hearing Association.

Wallach, G.P. (2007). *Language intervention for school-age students: Setting academic goals for academic success.* Philadelphia: Elsevier.

Watkins, R., Kelly, D., Harbers, H., & Hollis, W. (1995). Measuring children's lexical diversity: Differentiating typical and impaired language learners. *Journal of Speech and Hearing Research, 38,* 476–489.

Weber, W. (2001). *Life skill curriculum: A multidisciplinary unit.* Retrieved from http://teachers.k12.sd.us/ ww008/functional_life_skills_unit.htm

Wehman, P., & Kregel, J. (2004). *Functional curriculum for elementary, middle, and secondary age students with special needs* (2nd ed.). Austin, TX: Pro-Ed.

Westby, C. (1991). *Steps to developing and achieving language-based curriculum in the classsroom.* Rockville, MD: American Speech–Language–Hearing Association.

Westby, C. (1998). Communicative refinement in school age and adolescence. In W. Hayes & B. Shulman (Eds.), *Communication development: Foundations, processes, and clinical applications* (pp. 311–360). Baltimore: Williams & Wilkins.

Westby, C. (1999). Assessing and facilitating text comprehension problems. In H. Catts & A. Kamhi (Eds.), *Language and reading disabilities* (pp. 154–223). Boston: Allyn & Bacon.

Wiig., E. H., & Secord, W. W. (1989). *Test of language competence* (expanded ed.). San Antonio, TX: Psychological Corp.

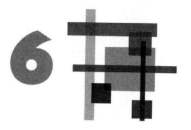

Language Assessment and Instruction for Adolescents

Adolescent students with language disabilities will have been identified as having a language-learning disability (LLD) during elementary school, for the most part, and will have received prior instruction specific to their language needs. Although their basic language skills may be intact, many of these students will require additional assistance in developing some of the higher order language competencies to be able to negotiate middle school and high school successfully. The reading and writing demands of the secondary curriculum increase considerably, placing stress on weak language systems. Students encounter new types of discourse with which they must gain familiarity, and they must develop more sophisticated skills with the types of discourse they have met already. The unique social demands of adolescence, particularly for students with autism, can strain slow or lean pragmatic abilities.

Middle school presents an experience different from elementary school. Students are now dealing with multiple teachers, each with a unique teaching style and classroom rules. The amount of required work increases significantly, and students must rely on prior knowledge and skills to complete assignments. Class sessions may be lengthier, which means that students must sustain attention over longer periods of time. The various test formats require students to demonstrate their knowledge through means including written essay, description, narrative, explanation, and persuasion. Information becomes more decontextualized and abstract, and new symbol systems are used (particularly in math) to encode content.

In adolescence, the metas—metacognition, metalinguistic knowledge, and metapragmatics—become more important. Students are expected to take more control over their own learning, and they are required to recognize and reflect on their own thought processes and learning. They are expected to use logical and critical thinking to evaluate information and to write in different discourse styles, including the electronic styles essential in adolescent social networks such as texting, posting on internet social network sites, and playing online computer games.

Teachers begin requiring students to take responsibility for knowing when they do not know something, knowing how to get assistance when necessary, working independently, and knowing how to utilize a variety of resources to complete assignments. Students with special needs often have difficulty with these expectations and requirements, and they can benefit from instruction on how to study, learn, and use language productively.

This chapter and Chapter 12 both address language disabilities in adolescents. Like Chapters 4 and 5, this chapter uses the language development model described in Chapters 1 and 2 to discuss methods for assessing and providing instruction for language disabilities. Chapter 12 describes the nature of adolescence and the impact of language disabilities on adolescents' lives. Although these chapters overlap somewhat, together they provide a comprehensive view of the impact of language disorders on adolescents and illustrate how different perspectives on language disabilities can lead to similar instructional approaches.

■Assessment Goals, Procedures, ■and Instruments

Upon entering secondary school, students with disabilities, especially those with language-learning disabilities (LLD) often need to learn the language skills at the literate end of the oral-to-literate continuum, the critical thinking skills characteristic of the metas (see Chapter 5), the discourse abilities required to comprehend and interact with the curriculum, and the pragmatic language skills necessary to function in their peer group. Consequently, assessment for these students asks three primary questions:

1. How adept are the students with using the social discourse necessary to fit in with peers and to succeed in the classroom?
2. How can their language development be characterized in terms of literate language forms, including the various discourse genres characteristic of secondary school?
3. How skilled are they with metalinguistic, metacognitive, and metapragmatic abilities?

Students with severe impairments will require a more intensive, differentiated approach to both assessment and instruction. These needs will be discussed in the final section of this chapter.

Standardized Measures

Standardized instruments designed to measure advanced language abilities often fail to identify students whose basic oral language is minimally adequate but who are having difficulty with the extended discourse contexts of the secondary curriculum. In addition, standardized measures of advanced language rarely yield information that can lead directly to instructional planning. Nevertheless, such measures can be used to sample students' abilities across the multiple dimensions of language (oral language, written expression, and comprehension of language forms in reading and writing) to identify which dimensions of language disorder require instruction (Nelson, 2009). The most commonly used are the following:

Clinical Evaluation of Language Fundamentals–3 (Semel, Wiig, & Secord, 1989)—assesses students' abilities with grammatical production

Test of Adolescent Language–4 (Hammill, Brown, Larsen, & Wiederholt, 2007)—assesses across syntactic forms in listening, speaking, reading, and writing grammar

Test of Language Competence–Expanded (Secord & Wiig, 1993)—assesses students' understanding of structural ambiguities, figurative language, and the ability to draw inferences

Test of Language Development–Intermediate–4 (Hammill & Newcomer, 2008)—assesses abilities related to spontaneous discourse production

Test of Word Knowledge (Wiig & Secord, 1992)—assesses students' knowledge of definitions, synonyms, antonyms, metalinguistics, and figurative language

Utah Test of Language Development–4 (Mecham, 2003)—measures a variety of expressive language skills

Written language assumes greater importance for students in secondary school than previously. They are expected to produce longer, more elaborated language, and to use this language in a variety of discourse genres, not just narrative. Not surprisingly, students with LLD often have difficulty with written discourse (Wallach, 2007). These students produce shorter samples with more errors and of lower quality than their typically developing peers (Scott, 1999). In addition, their writing is less informative, rarely takes into account the audience for which it is intended, and reflects little understanding of the structural constraints of the different expository genres.

Norm-referenced instruments that have been developed to assess written language include the following:

Picture Story Language Test (Myklebust, 1965)—a diagnostic test of written expressive language

Test of Written Language–4 (Hammill & Larsen, 2009)—measures students' written structural elements

Writing Process Test (Warden & Hutchinson, 1992)—a direct measure of a student's ability to plan, write, and revise an original composition

In addition, the following diagnostic instruments designed for adolescents include sections that measure written language abilities:

> *Test of Adolescent and Adult Language–4* (Hammill et al., 2007)
> *Woodcock-Johnson Psychoeducational Battery–III* (Woodcock, McGrew, & Mather, 2001)

Nonstandardized Assessment

The aspects of language that are most crucial to success in secondary school are semantics, syntax and morphology, and pragmatics, particularly as the curriculum becomes more literate and less oral. In addition, metacognition, metalinguistics, and metapragmatics gain importance as students are expected to take more responsibility for themselves as learners and thinkers and as the social world becomes more ascendant in their experience.

Semantics

Nippold (2007) identified six types of literate vocabulary, or the **literate lexicon**, that emerges in typically developing students during adolescence:

1. Advanced adverbial conjuncts (*similarly, moreover, consequently, in contrast, rather, nonetheless*)
2. Adverbs of likelihood (*definitely, possibly*) and magnitude (*extremely, considerably*)
3. Verbs with components related to presupposition (*regret*), metalinguistic reference (*imply, predict, infer*), and metacognitive reference (*observe, hypothesize*)
4. Technical and precise terms (*pollination, demagoguery, cosine, ordinate*)
5. Multiple-function words (*sweet juice, sweet thought, sweet paint job*)
6. Multiple-meaning words (*harbor a fugitive, boat harbor; boat tender, tender finger*)

Nippold (2007) pointed out that students' vocabulary abilities must also expand to include the ability to use Aristotelian definitions, which include a superordinate term and a description with one or more characteristics. For instance, an Aristotelian definition of *pear* includes a superordinate ("a pear is an edible fruit") with descriptions of characteristics ("that grows on trees and that contains seeds inside skin-covered flesh"). Nippold et al. (1999) found that by the time typically achieving students reach 12th grade, they produce an average of six Aristotelian definitions out of 16 total definitions, whereas 6th graders produce only one or two out of 16. These researchers developed a scoring rubric that can be used to assess students' abilities to define words selected by the teacher from student texts or homework assignments. The teacher asks the student to provide definitions for each word, then scores the responses according to the rubric:

2 points: for definitions that include an appropriate superordinate term and a description containing one or more characteristics (e.g., "A lever is a rigid

bar used to exert a pressure or sustain a weight at one point of its length by the application of a force at a second and turning at a third on a ful- crum" [*Merriam-Webster*, 2009]).

1 point: for definitions that contain an appropriate superordinate but do not de- scribe the word accurately (i.e., "A lever is a simple machine consisting of a rod attached by one end to a fixed point"), or for definitions that pro- vide one or more accurate characteristics but a missing or inaccurate su- perordinate term (i.e., "A lever is when you use a plank over a railing to lift something on one end by pushing on the other").

0 points: when the student attempts a response but does not provide an accurate su- perordinate term or accurate descriptions, or when the student does not respond.

In a study by Nippold and Haq (1996), typically developing students in 6th grade re- ceive at least one point for more than half of the words presented; students in 9th grade received at least one point for more than 75% of the words presented; and stu- dents in 12th grade received 2 points for more than half the words presented.

The secondary curriculum introduces students to two special classes of verbs (Nippold, 2007):

1. Verbs used to interpret spoken and written language and to talk about cog- nitive and logical processes
2. Verbs used to convey specific presuppositional information

The first class includes metacognitive verbs such as *remember, infer, hypothesize, in- terpret,* and *assume,* and metalinguistic verbs such as *imply, argue, predict,* and *con- firm.* The second set includes both **factitives,** or verbs that presuppose the truth of what follows (e.g., "We *acknowledge* receipt of your letter"), and **nonfactitives,** or verbs that presuppose uncertainty about what follows (e.g., "I *imagine* that's true"). Factitive verbs include *acknowledge, know, forget,* and *regret*; and nonfactitives include *think, believe, figure, guess,* and *suppose.* Because these verb types continue to develop throughout adolescence in typically developing students, students with LLD may have difficulty with them, particularly in writing.

Vocabulary development in adolescence extends beyond simple word meanings and definitions. Students also need to become competent with how words are related through derivations and etymology and through sound (e.g., homonyms such as *pear, pair, pare*) and meaning (e.g., antonyms and synonyms) (Nippold, 1998). Students must be able to consider that words may have multiple meanings, and, particularly in their writing, they have to be able to use different words to convey the same thing to avoid using the same words again and again (Paul, 2006).

In addition, students must be able to compare and contrast words so they can judge which will be most effective in any given context, especially in writing. Paul (2006) argued that spelling and pronunciation become more important in secondary school, as does the ability to use context to ascertain which word is being used in case of ambiguity (e.g., "I *led* my teammates in the drill" cf. "I *lead* my teammates in the drill" or "I *read* every night before I go to sleep" cf. "I *read* last night before I went to sleep").

The secondary curriculum requires that students develop considerable ability to understand and use **figurative language**, especially in their reading and writing. The most common figurative language forms that students develop are similes (e.g., "The train was *like* a giant dragon, curving its way around a bend"), metaphors (e.g., "He was *the king of his neighborhood*"), idioms (e.g., "It was *raining cats and dogs*"), and proverbs (e.g., "*Let sleeping dogs lie*"). An easy way to assess students' knowledge of figurative language is to excerpt examples from students' textbooks and homework assignments, present them to students in an appropriate context, and ask them to provide interpretation (Scott, 1999). In determining criteria to use in judging student responses, Nippold's (1998) general sequence of acquisition for figurative language can act as a guide:

- Terms or phrases referring to concrete objects, events, and processes emerge earlier than those referring to abstract objects, events, and processes (e.g., "A bird in the hand is worth two in the bush" develops earlier than "Hope springs eternal").
- Familiar sayings develop earlier than unfamiliar ones (e.g., "The first step is the hardest" develops earlier than "One falsehood spoils a thousand truths").

Syntax and Morphology

Secondary students' syntactic and morphological skills also expand toward the literate. Typically developing students in secondary school are able to recognize and comprehend virtually all types of sentences. The length of oral sentences increases, particularly when used for narration and persuasion, and the length of sentences in written samples increases regardless of type of discourse. Subordinate and coordinate clauses appear more often, as do low-frequency syntactic structures typical of a literate language style. **Morphosyntactic markers** such as tense, number, gender, mood, and case, also increase in frequency (Reed, Griffith, & Rasmussen, 1998), particularly when students are producing persuasive writing (Nippold, 2000).

One of the best ways to assess secondary students' syntax and morphology is to use narratives, because student-generated narratives are likely to contain language at the literate end of the continuum (Paul, 2006). In addition, obtaining narrative samples from students provides a sample that can be analyzed for other aspects of advanced language, including cohesion, episode structure, literate vocabulary, and figurative language. Chapter 5 includes two assessment procedures to analyze narrative samples: Appleby's (1978) stage model, and Miller, Gillam, and Peña's (2001) dynamic assessment model using wordless picture books.

As a way to elicit an oral narrative sample with adolescents, Weiss, Temperly, Stierwalt, and Robin (1993) reported using cartoon strips with the words covered or erased. Written samples can be obtained in the same manner, or by adapting Miller et al.'s (2001) approach so students produce their stories in writing. Using the same materials and procedures for both the oral and the written samples has an added advantage: The teacher can compare the two samples to determine where instruction is most likely to be needed and to be effective (Paul, 2006).

Analysis of students' oral and written language samples can address three aspects of syntactic development. The first is **T-unit length**, the number of different main clauses (main clause + attending subordinate clauses) and coordinate clauses in the sample. T-unit length continues to increase throughout adolescence, showing greater increases in writing than in speaking (Loban, 1976). For typically-developing students in 6th and 7th grades, T-unit length in oral samples was greater than in written samples; for students in 8th grade, it was roughly equal; and for 10th grade, written samples showed greater T-unit length than oral samples. Scott (1999) reported that T-unit length did not differentiate students with LLD from typically developing students, but teachers must recognize that the goal for all students is to increase the complexity and sophistication of their written language.

The second aspect of syntactic development is **clause density**, the average number of main and subordinate clauses in the sample. Also called the **subordination index**, clause density as a way to elicit an oral narrative sample from typically developing adolescents follows roughly the same sequence of development as T-unit length. In early adolescence, clause density is higher in spoken language than written language samples, whereas by mid to late adolescence, clause density in written samples is similar to or somewhat higher than in spoken samples. Although clause density provides one window into syntactic development during adolescence, it does not change dramatically (Paul, 2006). In addition, clause density varies by context and audience (Scott & Stokes, 1995), which means that teachers should be careful to use a sampling context that will elicit language at the literate end of the continuum.

Paul (2006) provided a rough rule of thumb to use in interpreting clause density: The subordination index (obtained by summing the number of clauses for each T-unit and dividing by the number of T-units) should be at least 1.3 in both spoken and written samples, and the index in written samples should be at least equal to the index in spoken samples. If a student's subordination index is close to 1.0, or if the index in spoken samples exceeds that in written samples, instruction should focus on developing the student's proficiency with subordinate clauses.

The third aspect of syntactic development consists of high-level structures, or the presence of low-frequency syntactic structures that mark an advanced literate style (e.g., nouns generated from verbs, as in *adaptation*), noun phrase elaboration ("Her calculated, strategic approach to the game"), verb phrase elaboration ("We *had been* walking for hours"), adverbials ("It happened *awfully* fast"), complex sentence types ("The girl *who's the best student in our algebra class* is our school's tennis champion") (Nippold, 1998).

The appearance of high-level syntactic structures also depends on context. Eckert (1990) reported that these structures appear only in relatively formal situations. Scott and Stokes (1995) propose using narrative sampling as a way to increase the probability that students will include these syntactic forms. They instruct students to tell the story of a movie they have seen recently and to tell it the way it would sound if the teacher were to read about it in a magazine. For written samples, they instruct students to write it as if they were writing a book or magazine article about the movie.

Because these high-level syntactic forms appear with relatively low frequency, Paul (2006) reminded teachers that they are looking only to see whether students include examples of a few in any given sample. If they do, and if T-unit length and the subordination index seem to be on schedule, the teacher can conclude the student has some proficiency with literate language. If the student's samples do not include any high-level syntactic forms, and if T-unit length and the subordination index are not on schedule, instruction should be directed to developing the range of syntactic forms measured by these indices. However, if the samples contain no examples of high-level syntactic structures, but T-unit length and clause density are developing as expected, more careful sampling should be done to determine whether the student is able to use any of the more literate syntactic forms.

Pragmatics

During adolescence, students develop new pragmatic abilities that allow them to understand and use figurative language such as metaphors, similes, proverbs, and idioms, as discussed earlier (Nippold, 2007). Facility with figurative language becomes a crucial prerequisite for peer group acceptance through understanding and using slang and in-group language, both in face-to-face conversations and in virtual conversations carried out through texting, posting to social network sites, and playing online games. All of these media are critical for social interaction during adolescence, during which friendship is negotiated by "just talking," whether through virtual or nonvirtual means.

Adolescents use language to establish social dominance through persuasion and negotiation, often couched in the "in" language of the day, and they use language for the sake of communication alone. Students whose pragmatic development is slow, or "wobbly," as Nelson (2009) called it, might be denied acceptance in their peer group on the basis of their language skills alone.

Two areas of pragmatic development that undergo significant and obvious changes during adolescence are conversational competence and facility with discourse genres.

Conversational Competence   Often, the conversational abilities of students with LLD seem more characteristic of younger, normally developing children. Students with LLD seem unable to fine-tune their language to show empathy, for instance, or to negotiate the interpersonal nuances required for affiliation with peers. The three aspects of conversational competence that are most critical for successful interaction are topic maintenance, repair strategies, and proficiency in asking relevant questions during conversations (Brinton & Fujiki, 1994).

A more comprehensive assessment procedure, developed by Larson and McKinley (1995), looked at both linguistic and pragmatic features, specifically communicative functions and conversational rules. Their procedure uses an unstructured conversation between the student and an adult, and it yields information about the student's abilities in both listening and speaking. Speaking skills are assessed in the following areas (Larson & McKinley, 1995):

- Linguistic features
- Paralinguistic features (e.g., inflection, juncture, rate, fluency, and intelligibility)
- Communicative functions
- Discourse management
- Rules for cooperative conversation
- Nonverbal behaviors

During adolescence, students develop proficiency in using language to negotiate, particularly to persuade others; to present their viewpoint; and to resolve conflicts. This aspect of conversational competence has a large effect on self-esteem and popularity, and it presages students' adjustment as they move from adolescence into adulthood (Paul, 2006). Not surprisingly, students with LLD typically have difficulties in using negotiation strategies.

Two procedures that are often used to assess students' negotiation abilities are role playing and hypothetical situations. Role playing offers a means for teachers to ascertain how (and whether) students alter their language when they are given different contexts in which to play roles. For example, the teacher presents a situation requiring the student to ask her parent to use the family car, and judges whether the student uses pragmatic devices such as indirect requests or hints ("Dana [the student's friend] needs a ride home right after school"), polite forms ("I was wondering if I could use the car for a little while tonight"), or slang ("I could sure use some wheels tonight!").

McDonald and Turkstra (1998) developed a set of scenarios of hypothetical situations, each describing a potential conflict, to assess students' abilities with negotiation. Teachers can use the scenarios to stimulate students to tell, for each situation, what the main character (protagonist) should say and ask students to describe the conflict, tell why they chose the language they chose, and say how they would feel if they were in that situation. Teachers can analyze students' responses by looking at the extent to which they can talk about the long-term consequences of the protagonist's actions and judging whether the students were able to find a solution that could preserve the characters' relationship through compromise and mutual agreement (Paul, 2006). The less mature responses describe a solution that benefits only one of the characters, show less awareness of how the characters felt or what they thought, and utilize a short-term rather than a long-term solution.

Developing the pragmatic flexibility to be able to use slang is often difficult for students with LLD. The pragmatic rules governing slang are esoteric; that is, outsiders (particularly adults, though an outsider is any naïve listener) have difficulty understanding it (Paul, 2006). Also, these rules change rapidly: The same words can take on different meanings in just a matter of hours. Speakers must be able to figure out which pragmatic convention governs the use of each term, and they must be linguistically flexible enough to adapt to shifting forms and usages.

Nelson and Rosenbaum (1972) developed a procedure to assess slang vernacular, in which the teacher asks students—both with LLD and typically developing—to list all the slang words they know for a topic (for example, sports, popularity, music, or clothes). The responses of the students with LLD are compared to those of their typically developing peers to determine whether the two types of responses are different. If they are, the teacher can infer that the students with LLD are having difficulty with in-group language, and instruction can be designed to help them, perhaps by employing a metapragmatic approach.

Discourse Genres   Chapter 5 discussed the various discourse genres that students encounter, particularly in the upper elementary school years. Though the same genres are present in the secondary curriculum, several changes are apparent. **Classroom discourse** in the secondary environment utilizes more formal literate formats (e.g., lecture) than those used in the elementary setting. At the secondary level, more emphasis is placed on students' abilities to produce the different genres in writing; narrative discourse becomes more abstract, complex, and elaborate; and **expository** (descriptive and explanatory) and persuasive (argumentative) forms assume more importance, both receptively (e.g., textbooks, reference texts) and expressively (e.g., essays, various report formats) (Paul, 2006).

Work, Cline, Ehren, Keiser, & Wujel, (1993) devised a sample interview format that teachers can use to assess students' facility with classroom discourse. This format can easily be modified into an observational checklist.

- How well does the student do at following classroom directions?
- How well does the student do in answering questions in class?
- How well does the student listen?
- How well does the student understand lectures?
- How well does the student understand classroom conversations?
- What problems does the student have in class?
- Which aspects of the curriculum present the greatest challenge or stumbling block for the student?

Even though most teachers want desirable classroom behaviors, many classroom behavior problems reflect students' inability to understand and engage successfully in classroom discourse (Simon, 1998). To assess students' knowledge about classroom discourse, teachers can use the following to evaluate how well students are doing with classroom discourse or, alternatively, they can ask students to rate themselves on their ability to:

- follow directions,
- show respect to fellow students and to teachers,
- work cooperatively with fellow students,
- appear to be interested in class,
- take notes,

- successfully skim texts and reference sources for information,
- participate in class discussions, and
- give oral reports.

One of the most crucial aspects of students' success in the secondary setting is the ability to listen critically in the classroom, primarily because students spend the majority of their classroom time listening, and the listening they are expected to do requires them to go beyond a literal understanding of the material being presented (Paul, 2006). Larson and McKinley (1995) suggested that critical listening includes the ability to differentiate fact from fiction; to recognize when a speaker's communicative intent is to persuade; and to identify when speakers use false reasoning, bias, or propaganda.

Those authors developed a system for analyzing listening skills that involves evaluating listening on the literal level and listening on the critical, or metalistening, level. To evaluate literal listening skills, they utilize a dynamic assessment approach, in which the teacher presents a videotape of a classroom lecture and asks the student to describe the main idea and several relevant details related to the main idea. Then the teacher asks the student to view a videotape of a second lecture, this time with an accompanying handout listing the major topics covered in the lecture. By comparing the student's responses to the unsupported videotape (without the handout) to the supported videotape (with the handout), the teacher can determine whether supporting materials are beneficial to the student.

If the supporting materials do not seem to benefit the student, assessment should shift to the semantic, syntactic, and morphological elements underlying the content in an effort to pinpoint exactly where the student's language abilities become deficient. If, however, the dynamic assessment shows that supporting materials do seem to help the student, the teacher can begin to develop various sorts of supplementary handouts to accompany lecture material. These handouts might take different forms, at first including only the overall main point and one or two details for a given lecture. As the student gains skill, the handouts become more complicated, perhaps showing not only the overall main point and two or three supporting details but also the topic sentence of each section of the lecture, accompanied by two or three points supporting each. In this way, the teacher can lead the student to a deeper understanding of the literal information being presented.

Larson and McKinley's (1995) approach to assessing students' critical listening abilities involves the teacher having the student view a videotape of a television commercial or part of a political speech, followed by asking the student to draw an inference about the speaker's communicative intent (e.g., to sell, persuade, convince). The teacher can delve further into the student's critical listening skills by asking the student to identify whether the text (or videotape) contained fact, opinion, propaganda, or a combination and to judge how effective or convincing the message was and why.

For students who have difficulty with the critical listening task, teachers can direct instruction to helping students identify the characteristics of argumentative or persuasive text and the most typical types of language (or visual elements, as in television commercials or magazine ads) used in persuasive texts. In addition, teachers can chart students' progress in learning critical listening skills by using Brickson's (2001) or IRA/NCTE's (2007) rubrics for assessing students' ability to evaluate persuasive text.

The **narrative abilities** most critical for secondary students are those involving the ability to understand characters' motivations, plans, and feelings; the inferences that can be drawn to summarize the story; and the ability to provide listeners and readers with sufficient cohesive marking in stories to show that they understand how the various elements and components are tied together (Scott, 2004).

Providing listeners and readers with information about characters' motivations, plans, and feelings lets the listener or reader know what motivates the story. To assess students' abilities to provide this sort of information, the teacher can ask—either informally or through a written assignment—probing questions such as the following:

- What happened to make (main character) decide to do what she did? In other words, what was the problem that started things moving in the story?
- How did (main character) plan to "solve" the problem?
- What did (main character) actually do to "solve" the problem?
- Who else in the story knows what (main character's) plan is?
- What do those characters think about (main character's) plan?
- Does (main character's) plan work? In other words, does (main character) solve the problem?
- How does (main character) feel at the end of the story? Why do you think she feels this way?
- How do other characters feel at the end? Why do you think they feel this way? Do you think they feel the same as they did before they knew (main character's) plan? If not, why not?

If students are unable to respond appropriately to these questions, the teacher can direct instruction to helping students identify the difference between the characters' intentions and their actions, if any. From there, instruction can emphasize developing facility with describing characters' feelings and how those feelings relate to what happens in the story.

Assessing students' skills in drawing inferences, or "reading between the lines," can be done easily by reading a selected piece of narrative aloud to the student, stopping at a critical juncture and asking the student to guess what will happen next. If the student is unable to guess, the teacher can add support by asking the student if he has ever been in a similar situation and, if so, what he did then (Miller et al., 2001). Or the teacher can ask the student what he would do if he were in the same situation as the protagonist in the selection being read. Paul (2006) suggested reading aloud to the student a description of a character in a story, then asking the student what else he might know about the character based on the description, using a series of specific questions derived directly from the selection not yet described explicitly.

By the end of the elementary school years, most children are able to retell relatively complete and complicated narratives. Retelling involves reporting and recounting the events and episodes in the original narrative with no attempt to compress or unify the content. Summarizing, by contrast, is a higher order ability dependent on the earlier acquisition of skills in basic listening and reading comprehension at the literal level of meaning. Summarizing involves integrating and distilling the story, described by Johnson (1983) as having five abilities:

1. Understanding the individual propositions, ideas, and events in the story
2. Understanding how the propositions are related to each other
3. Identifying the story grammar components that serve to organize the story
4. Selecting the most salient information to include in the summary
5. Distilling that information into a version that is concise and cohesive

Teachers can assess students' summarizing abilities directly by asking them to provide summaries of short stories, chapters, or movies. Paul (2006) suggested evaluating the adequacy of students' summaries by judging whether they include a reasonably close facsimile of the sequence of events in the story, the most central elements of the story (and not minor details), and a concise and coherent summary that relates the gist of the story.

An important aspect of summarizing narratives is to use what are called **cohesive markers**—pronouns, conjunctions, conjunctive adverbs (e.g., *on the other hand, moreover*), **ellipses** (e.g., eliminating redundancies through omission), and the definite article *the* (Paul, 2006). Cohesive markers cue the listener or reader to look outside the immediate sentence to complete its meaning, as in, for instance, "The bird saw a beautiful ring. *He* decided he'd take it back to his nest" or, "At first he thought he'd leave it there. *Still*, it was beautiful, and he wanted to show it to Baby Bird."

Another type of cohesive marker, **connectives**, represent one of the most significant ways by which students can link propositions within their stories, whether oral or written. Connectives are considered to be a form of high-level syntax (Nippold & Undlin, 1992) because they include both conjunctions (linking propositions within sentences) and conjuncts (linking propositions across sentences). **Conjunctions** include both coordinating conjunctions (e.g., *and, or, neither, nor*) and subordinating conjunctions (e.g., *for, so, because, while, whether, what, as, until*). **Conjuncts** include both concordant (e.g., *similarly, therefore, furthermore, moreover*) and discordant (*yet, instead, nevertheless, rather, conversely*) forms.

Scott (1988) suggested that, for adolescents, a minimum of five different connectives would be present in a writing sample of 30 to 50 T-units. If the teacher finds that connective use is relatively sparse in a student's writing sample, she can assess more directly by asking students to make up a sentence containing each of various connectives. Alternatively, the teacher could produce one set of cards containing sentences and another set containing connectives. Then students are asked to use the cards to construct a complex sentence—that makes sense—using one of the connectives from the other card set. Nippold and Undlin (1992) developed an assessment procedure in which the teacher gives the student a sentence and a connective and asks the student to devise a second sentence so the whole makes sense. If students have difficulty with these assessment procedures, the teacher would assess their comprehension of the connectives, as well as their understanding of the syntactic structures necessary to complete each procedure.

Nation (2008) identified a sophisticated set of cohesive devices that good writers use to aid in understanding and to link all the pieces into a coherent whole:

1. *Lexical cohesion* includes repetition, synonyms, near synonyms, and superordinates to refer to the same item in a passage, as in, "Our *Maria* is an amazing athlete. *She* plays soccer and basketball, and *she* rides her own horse in jumping contests. *Her* mom says that, even though *Maria* is her '*baby*,' *she's* a very accomplished young *lady*."
2. *Reference* is used through pronouns and special verb forms such as *do* or *can*, as in, "Africanized killer bees may swarm and sting without provocation. If they *do*, the best thing to do is to seek treatment immediately" or, "Magpies are opportunistic. If they *can*, they will place their eggs in other birds' nests."
3. *Substitution* is the use of a synonym for a mutual referent, as in, "Hurricane Katrina caused widespread and costly damage. *Its* effects were devastating."
4. *Ellipsis* refers to leaving something unsaid because an earlier part of the passage contains the information necessary for understanding, as in, "Magpies are opportunistic but less than crows" (less *opportunistic* than crows).
5. *Comparison* is the use of specific words such as *same, similar, identical, different, other, more, less* to compare two or more ideas, objects, events, experiences, or processes, as in, "This egg is *smaller* than a robin's egg."
6. *Conjunctions* relate sentences or parts of sentences to each other by showing how what is to follow is connected to what has come before, as in, "The climate in the desert is hot and dry. *However*, the nights are usually cool."

In addition to stories, narrative discourse takes other forms with which secondary students are expected to gain facility, particularly by producing written samples. The most common types of narrative discourse are

- novel,
- comic book,
- folk tale,
- myth,
- tall tale,
- personal essay,
- autobiographical narrative, and
- oral history.

The secondary school curriculum contains a high percentage of **expository texts**, in both oral and written form. As mentioned earlier, oral forms include lecture, oral reports, laboratory reports, and research reports; printed forms include essay, description, narrative, letter, explanation, and argument/persuasion. Students are expected to comprehend and produce both oral and printed forms. The common types of expository discourse are

- description,
- list,
- explanation,
- argument/persuasion,
- historical essay,
- biography,
- reports (e.g., book report, science report),
- lecture, and
- letter.

Nonstandardized approaches to assessment of students' comprehension and production of oral expository discourse can be part of the ongoing curriculum. When assessing students' oral expository discourse ability, the aim is to discover whether one type presents more difficulty or whether all types seem to present the same challenge. It should be noted that students' understanding and production of oral and written persuasive and argumentative texts develops later than other expository forms of discourse.

When presented with various expository forms, the teacher can take special note of a student's comprehension, observing, for example, whether lectures present more or less difficulty than book reports. To assess a student's ability to produce oral expository discourse, again, the teacher can note whether one expository form is easier for the student to produce. Accordingly, instruction can begin by helping the student analyze both the structure and the communicative intent of that form, and it can be extended by having the student discover how the other expository forms are related, or, in the case of persuasive text, how it is different in both structure and intent. The Online Writing Lab (OWL, 2007) offers a wide variety of resources for teaching expository text.

Like the assessment of students' ability with oral expository discourse, nonstandardized assessment of students' facility with the written forms of expository discourse can be part of the existing curriculum. In evaluating samples of students' writing, Hayes and Flower (1987) reported that of the three stages of writing—planning, sentence generation, and revision—students with LLD spent less time in the planning and revision stages than did their normally achieving peers. Because of these differences, Scott and Erwin (1992) proposed that teachers direct attention to the process of writing as well as to the actual written products or samples (see Chapter 11). Paul (2006) recommended the "Think-Aloud Protocol," in which the teacher asks students to verbalize aloud what they are thinking about the writing throughout a writing exercise. Its goals are threefold:

1. Discovering whether the student identifies the goal or purpose of the writing, which dictates the choice of discourse genre; although both may be part of an assignment, the teacher will want to check to see whether the student is

able to recognize the goal and choose the appropriate genre
2. Ascertaining whether the student considers his potential audience and writes accordingly
3. Finding out whether the student is able to revise and refine his thinking through the writing process

When assessing the student's written product, teachers can follow Scott and Erwin's (1992) model, which contains five elements:

1. Fluency = the degree to which the sample is long enough and elaborated enough to convey the intended information to the intended audience
2. Lexical maturity = the number of words with more than seven letters in a given sample, which correlates highly with scores on achievement tests (Paul, 2006); *and/or* the presence of literate vocabulary words; *and/or* the presence of low-frequency words that provide "spark" to the writing (Scott & Erwin, 1992)
3. Sentential syntax = T-unit length; subordination index (clause density); presence of higher level, low-frequency syntactic structures
4. Grammatical and mechanical errors = misuse of tense; subject–verb disagreement; unmarked plurals, possessives, or other inflections; use of nonstandard forms (e.g., *I seen, He don't*, when they are not dialectal variants); poor legibility; errors in spelling, punctuation, and capitalization; run-on paragraphs
5. Text-level analysis = overall quality and effectiveness of the writing; includes assessment of content, organization, macrostructure, cohesion, transitions, extent of accomplishing intended purpose, and provision of adequate information (Paul, 2006)

Rubrics can be useful tools in evaluating students' expository writing. Paul's (2006) comprehensive six-point rubric for expository writing includes five areas of analysis:

1. Organization (text structure)
2. Content/theme (coherence)
3. Written language (syntax, cohesion strategies, and vocabulary)
4. Written conventions (mechanics)
5. Sense of audience

The Alaska Department of Education (2009) has published another rubric for evaluating students' facility with expository text; the rubric matches their performance benchmarks and is suitable for students in grades 3, 6, 8, and high school. Hosford Middle School (2009), in Portland, Oregon, uses rubrics for several writing genres, including expository.

Another nonstandardized assessment procedure that can be used to evaluate students' expository writing is **portfolio assessment**, in which the teacher collects samples of the student's writing over the course of, for example, one unit. The portfolio could include written samples (notes, drafts at various stages of completion, teacher feedback), as well as various nonprint materials (photos, illustrations, tape recordings, reference materials, computer disks). Because students are actively involved in selecting what is included in their portfolio, the assessment process can be used as a way not only to provide instruction about expository text but also to encourage students to use self-evaluation strategies as part of the assessment.

Portfolio assessment can include both product and process. Hosford Middle School's (2009) rubric for assessing student portfolios awards points for three categories:

1. Overall set-up including organization and presentation
2. Presentation of individual sections
3. Evaluation including the development of quality in the student's work, effort demonstrated throughout the portfolio, the student's own personal reflections about the portfolio, and peer reviews of specific materials in the portfolio

The Meta Level

The importance of metacognitive, metapragmatic, and metalinguistic skills is discussed in other chapters and in the introduction to this chapter. For secondary students, these abilities take on added significance. Writing draws on students' metalinguistic knowledge when they:

- edit their own or others' work,
- paraphrase or summarize a story or piece of expository text,
- choose the most effective vocabulary words, and
- select appropriate syntactic and morphological structures.

The teacher can assess students' metalinguistic abilities by observing them as they plan and write drafts and as they edit their own and others' writing. Having the student talk through why he is choosing or selecting particular words or syntactic and morphological forms can reveal the degree to which he is using a metalinguistic strategy. Attending to how the student proceeds through the editing process will show the teacher whether he is having difficulty. If so, Paul (2006) recommended using a dynamic assessment by highlighting errors in a writing sample and seeing whether the student is then able to make the corrections. If not, the teacher may want to first highlight a writing sample, then make one or two template corrections (e.g., showing how to use a synonym), and asking the student to make two or three other corrections of the same type. The teacher then can assist the student in proceeding systematically through the sample, focusing on a specific type of correction on each go-round.

To assist students with paraphrasing, Paul (2006) suggested asking them to read from a classroom text or a piece of literature—first at the sentence level and progressing to longer units—and then restating their meaning. The teacher can help students by asking questions such as, "Can it mean anything else?" or, "How else could you say this?" Once students develop some proficiency with sentences and paragraphs, the teacher can ask them to summarize or paraphrase longer units, perhaps a page or a section, then later a short story or essay.

Students' metapragmatic abilities take on added significance as they are expected to modify the way in which they converse in a variety of interactive contexts. They are expected to figure out and abide by the conversational rules—and their common violations—governing different situations. For instance, though most normally achieving students quickly ascertain the most effective way to talk and converse in different classrooms, students with LLD often have difficulty making those shifts.

In Chapter 2 we mentioned the importance of students developing an understanding of the unspoken rules for participating in formal classroom discussions (Sturm & Nelson, 1997). In general, the rules indicate that teachers do most of the talking, they indicate (sometimes indirectly) how and when students are to respond, and they determine the content of what is talked about. Not surprisingly, individual teachers have different ways of structuring classroom discourse.

Creaghead (1992) generated a set of questions that teachers can use to assess students' awareness of the classroom rules required by individual teachers:

- How do you know when to be quiet in (name of teacher)'s class?
- How do you know when it is okay to talk in (name of teacher)'s class?
- How do you know when you can ask questions in (name of teacher)'s class?
- In (name of teacher)'s class, how do you know what kind of answer you are supposed to give (short or elaborated)?
- In (name of teacher)'s class, how do you know whether it's okay to ask another student for help?
- In (name of teacher)'s class, is it important to use correct grammar and spelling in your writing?

Critical listening was discussed earlier in this chapter, but it can also be viewed as an aspect of *metacognition*, the ability to think about and reflect on one's cognitive processes. It is reflected in how people plan, organize, revise, and reassess in various learning situations. Nelson (2009) included, as metacognitive strategies, the students' abilities to talk and write about what they know, what they need to know, and what they need to do to remember new information. One useful approach to assessing students' metacognitive abilities is based on Gardner's (2006) idea that people are smart in several different ways, known as **multiple intelligences (MI)**:

- *Linguistic*: understanding and using language and its various forms
- *Spatial:* including how things look in the physical and representational worlds and in art
- *Quantitative*: including how things can be grouped and nested
- *Logical:* including how things are organized
- *Musical*: including how sound is arranged harmonically and melodiously
- *Intrapersonal:* including how we think about and take care of ourselves

- *Interpersonal:* including how we think about and care for others
- *Physical:* including how we use our bodies to know and solve problems
- *Naturalist:* including how we understand and interact with the natural world

Using Gardner's MI model, Miller and Miller (1998) developed an assessment instrument, *The Quick Smart Profile* (QSP), which teachers can use to help students discover how they think, learn, organize, and remember. The QSP is a 64-item, multiple-response questionnaire for students 11 years and older. It was developed to show how students pay attention most naturally in everyday situations. The results yield a profile of a rank ordering of these attentional patterns, which the teacher can use to guide instructional planning.

In an online workshop, thirteen.org (2004) provides a clear overview of MI, its benefits in the classroom, and ways to incorporate it into instruction. The workshop includes:

- an interactive self-inventory for teachers and students, as well as demonstrations of how a number of schools are using MI;
- explorations of how teachers can use MI to structure subject matter, identify opportunities for students to demonstrate understanding of subject matter, and lead students to understand how knowing their own intelligences profile helps shape their education;
- an implementation section with exercises demonstrating how to use MI to structure learning centers, simulations, and presentations; and
- a step-by-step MI lesson plan guide.

Comprehension monitoring is the process students use, while learning something new, to keep track of what is missing, what they understand and what they do not, and what they need to do to fill in what is missing or what they do not know. Because a large part of students' learning in secondary school takes place within a lecture format, it is important to assess their ability to monitor comprehension during lectures. Paul (2006) recommended using audiotapes of teacher lectures that have been altered so crucial pieces of information are missing.

First the teacher plays an unaltered tape to determine whether the student is comprehending the material. If so, the teacher then plays the altered tape to discover whether the student can identify that something is missing. The teacher notes how the student signals the missing information so the signal can serve as the basis for developing the necessary instruction.

If the student fails to indicate that information is missing, Paul (2006) suggested using dynamic assessment by telling the student to stop the tape if he wants to hear anything or has missed something. If the cueing helps, the teacher can use the MI approach to determine which of the intelligences are most natural for the student and design strategies based in that intelligence for the student to try. For instance, if the student's most natural intelligences are spatial and physical, the teacher could provide the student with strategies such as those shown in Figure 6.1.

Providing instruction for comprehension monitoring will be discussed later in

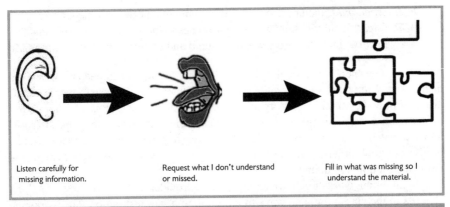

FIGURE 6.1

Sample Learning Strategies: Spatial and Physical

this chapter.

Purpose of Language Instruction

Language instruction for students with disabilities is usually executed for one of the following purposes (Paul, 2006):

- To eliminate or cure an impairment
- To change the impairment
- To change how the student responds to the impairment by providing compensatory strategies

For preschool students, language instruction usually aims at eliminating the impairment, whereas for elementary school students, the purpose is more likely to emphasize ameliorating the impairment. Once students reach adolescence, the purpose often shifts to providing compensatory learning strategies—academic, functional, or both—along with strategies for helping students manage and improve their own learning abilities.

For students to be most successful with the compensatory learning strategies approach, they must function within the average range of intelligence and have language skills at least comparable to a fourth-grade level (Larson & McKinley, 1995). To reflect on their own learning, they must be capable of metalinguistic, metapragmatic, and metacognitive thinking. Some students without these capacities, however, have been able to succeed with a compensatory learning approach. Teachers will have to decide on a student-by-student basis.

Students functioning at lower cognitive levels are more likely to benefit from instruction aimed at improving their basic language skills. For these students, teachers can use the approaches described for students in the language for learning stage, described in Chapter 5. Language instruction for secondary students with severe disabilities will be discussed at the end of this chapter.

When considering the academic and functional language needs of adolescents with LLD, teachers should consider that approximately one third of adolescents with learning disabilities enroll in a postsecondary school within 5 years of graduating from high school (Aune & Friehe, 1996). The students who do go on to postsecondary education will obviously benefit from instruction in the language skills necessary for success in the academic world, and both they and their peers who do not continue their education will be well served by instruction that also includes instruction on functional language skills.

The secondary curriculum functions primarily at the literate end of the oral-to-literate continuum. As discussed, students encounter a variety of forms of discourse, both oral and print, that are characteristic of literacy. They are expected to engage appropriately in the culture of various classrooms, which means quickly apprehending individual teachers' rules for classroom discourse, their expectations about participating in that discourse, and their requirements for producing oral and written text following the structure and format of a variety of discourse genres. Students must be able to use their language skills to learn new ideas, processes, and information, and they must be able to reflect on and modify their own ideas, language, and interactions.

Semantics

Students' vocabulary knowledge must expand to incorporate words relevant to the *literate lexicon*. Literate vocabulary development becomes critical for students' continuing academic success. Using existing curricula, teachers can help students increase their knowledge of and facility with literate words in several ways.

Ellis (2002) developed a set of approaches for teaching vocabulary based on elaboration. One recommendation is to teach new vocabulary in the context of a meaningful subject-matter lesson rather than as an isolated activity. The teacher encourages students to use the selected vocabulary words themselves in their discussions and writings about the subject matter, and the teacher provides multiple contexts and multiple opportunities for students to use the selected words. The guidelines teachers can use to select which words students should learn include the following:

- Teach fewer words in greater depth, and avoid teaching words that are highlighted somehow in the text or teacher's guide.
- Teach words that are integral to the unit or theme being studied, and avoid teaching words that are unrelated to the unit or theme.
- Teach words that encode key concepts or ideas, and avoid assigning large quantities of words.

■ Teach terms that will be used repeatedly throughout the grading period, and avoid assigning words that students will rarely or never encounter again in class.

A second elaboration technique described by Ellis (2002) involves helping students learn to paraphrase definitions to identify the key concept encoded by the word, followed by helping students distinguish critical features of the new word. Paraphrasing word definitions shows that definitions consist of two parts—the overall concept and specific parts of the definition that clarify the overall concept. Paraphrasing word definitions is analogous to paraphrasing the overall idea of a paragraph (its gist) and identifying the important details in the paragraph.

A third elaboration technique discussed by Ellis (2002) is to connect student's background knowledge—what they already know—to the new term. Integral to this approach is for students to explain the connection; for instance, "They can identify how the term is related to previous subject-matter they have learned, they can identify something from their personal life experiences the term reminds them of, they can create metaphors or similes for the term, or they can say how the term relates to understanding or solving some form of real-life problem" (Elaboration technique #3, paragraph 1).

Fourth, Ellis (2002) described an elaboration in which the teacher asks students to identify examples and applications of the new word, followed by nonexamples and nonapplications. Students are advised to look at different contexts to see how they could apply (or not apply) the new term.

Fifth, Ellis (2002) strongly recommended providing multiple formats within which students can practice elaborating on new terms. These might include opportunities to

■ talk about the terms, their definitions, their applications, examples of where they might be used, and how they are related to what students already know;
■ opportunities to act out or role-play meanings;
■ creating mnemonic pictures to portray the new meanings; and
■ creating stories that capture the new meanings.

The Family Learning Association (2009) offers a six-step vocabulary development program on its Kids Can Learn website. Though it was designed for parents, teachers can use it to help students learn vocabulary that is part of the literate lexicon. The steps involve:

1. reading and using context to see if the word is defined in the surrounding text; the teacher encourages students to keep a list of new words they encounter as they read and to help them figure out new meanings from surrounding sentences and words;
2. searching for synonyms and antonyms, first by listing familiar ones, then by looking for new examples;
3. looking for related words by searching for commonalities and similar roots, focusing on prefixes and suffixes to see how they change the meaning of

the root word;

4. using word maps—laying out associated words—to show definitions by clarifying four important relationships: (a) class, (b) example, (c) attribute, and (d) related concepts;
5. showing how English has borrowed words from other languages; and
6. using the dictionary when none of the above steps provides satisfactory information.

The Department of Secondary Education in the Denver Public Schools includes a Literacy Support Team (2009), whose website includes tips for teachers on how to help students to expand their literate vocabulary. The tips, each contributed by an individual teacher, are similar to Ellis's (2002) elaboration techniques, though the following ones also include reading aloud to students daily, as well as a set of resources that teachers can download:

- A sample word definition map (graphic organizer)
- A Venn diagram template for showing how words are similar in meaning
- A set of questions that teachers can use to show students how words are connected
- A "word wall," which shows and explains how words can be displayed on the walls of the classroom so students have access to them
- A set of examples of prefixes and roots
- A sample content-area reading lesson composed of activities to support student learning before, during, and after a reading assignment
- A "vocabugame" based on texts the students are currently reading

Several approaches to semantics stem from a metalinguistic process, among them, Crais's (1990) root word strategy, in which the teacher introduces a root word from a text or piece of literature related to what the students are studying. She then helps students identify possible inflectional endings (*-ing, -s, -ed*) and derivational suffixes (*-ly, -tion, -less*) and prefixes (*in-, un-, dis-*) that change the meaning or part of speech of the root word. Students are encouraged to find their own examples of inflections or derivations and to describe how these devices can be used as clues to the meaning of a word. Students are to focus on the relationships between words and to use what they already know when they encounter a new word (Ellis, 2002).

Another metalinguistic approach to semantics is to teach students how to use context to figure out the meanings of new words. Sternberg and Powell (1983) developed a set of context-based strategies in which the students are taught a range of cues they can use based on the following types of information:

- Temporal
- Spatial
- Descriptive state or function
- Causal
- Class membership

1. The teacher writes the following on the board or an overhead:

   Anna looked at the faifel's eyes. Even in the failing light, they were the color of the ocean in a storm. As she watched, it turned and glithered toward the tree by the well. Then it stopped, turned, and deebered at her, as if to say goodbye.

2. The teacher writes these cues on the board/overhead:

   Temporal =
   Spatial =
   Descriptive state or function =
   Class membership =
   Grammatical category =

3. The teacher helps the students fill in the blanks:

   Temporal = "in the failing light"
   Spatial = "toward the tree by the well"
   Descriptive state or function = failing
   Class membership
        faifel = has eyes, similar to Anna ... mammal?
        glithered = same as "stop" and "turn"
        deebered = same as "stop" and "turn"
   Grammatical category
        faifel = 's ending, comes after "the," which means it's probably a noun
        glithered = -ed ending, parallel to "turned," which means it's probably a
            verb
        deebered = -ed ending, parallel to "turned," which means it's probably a
            verb

4. The teacher asks students to find an unfamiliar word in one of their textbooks of literature books and to use as many cues as possible to figure out what it means.

5. Students check their guesses by using a dictionary to look up the word.

6. The teacher leads a discussion about the importance of using contextual strategies.

FIGURE 6.2

Using Context to Decipher Meaning

- Grammatical category
- Equivalence

The teacher provides a passage containing nonsense words and helps the students to decipher the cues. Figure 6.2 provides an illustration.

A third metalinguistic approach to semantics is German's (2005) reflective pausing method, in which students are taught to use "pause time" to retrieve word meanings. To reduce the frequency of inaccurate responses students make when they are having word retrieval problems, she recommended teaching students the following set of self-cuing strategies to use whenever they have difficulty retrieving a word:

- Graphemic cuing: remembering what the word looks like in written form
- Gesture cuing: an iconic movement related to the meaning of the word (e.g., holding an imaginary telephone to the ear to retrieve *telephone*
- Associative cuing: using a word related in meaning or associated with it to cue the target word (e.g., *writing* to cue *pencil*)
- Visual cuing: imagining what the actual referent looks like (e.g., picturing a telephone to cue *telephone*)

Figurative language plays a critical role in the secondary curriculum. Students are expected to understand and use similes, idioms, metaphors, allegories, irony, sarcasm, and proverbs, among other figurative language. Because reading is the main avenue by which most students encounter figurative language, students with LLD may not have as much experience with it as their typically developing peers. Paul (2006) advocated that teachers expose their students to figurative language by reading aloud to them, selecting poetry and literature where figurative language appears. To see how one teacher teaches about figurative language, see Martin's (2009) website, which includes free PowerPoint presentations on figurative language, including simile, metaphor, alliteration, onomatopoeia, personification, hyperbole, idioms, and clichés.

Ted Nellen, an English teacher, hosts the Cyber English website (Nellen, 2001a), on which you will find descriptions of and links to how he and a large number of other teachers are teaching language arts, including figurative language. His page devoted to literary terms includes links to descriptions and discussions of more than 80 literary terms, many of them figurative language concepts (Nellen, 2001b).

Another website, AskERIC.com (Ford, 2009), offers lesson plans for teaching figurative language, among them one for junior high school students, on recognizing euphemisms. The lesson plan includes objectives and a set of activities and procedures to help students recognize what a euphemism is and to give examples of offensive words and euphemisms for each.

Teague (2009) has developed a unit on creative writing that includes emphasis on figurative language. The unit comprises three lessons: one on creativity and poetry, one on creativity and collaboration, and one on text and design. Students read a variety of texts, including picture books, and investigate the power of poetry through its breaking of the rules of standard language. They also create text utilizing a particular authorial style, point of view, visual images, and specific types of figurative language (e.g., alliteration). The unit can be used as a template for teaching other types of figurative language, including assonance, metaphor, idioms, and similes.

Because humor is another vehicle for figurative language, teachers can use jokes and puns as a way to teach figurative language. The teacher can institute a weekly (or more often) humor time during which students can talk about jokes and puns they have heard and collected. The teacher can help students develop their own jokes by helping them recognize the ambiguity underlying humor and the most typical formats within which jokes and puns are told.

Hamersky (1995) developed a program using cartoons to teach students figurative language and humor. The program consists of eight units, each addressing one element characteristic of figurative language and/or humor. An example is the unit on ambiguity, in which students learn to identify the underlying meanings in sentences such as, "Visiting relatives can be unpleasant." Hamersky (1995) recommended teaching students to paraphrase the statement so they can recognize that more than one paraphrase is possible. For each unit, she includes cartoons illustrating its concept, along with discussion points that teachers can use with their students.

Syntax and Morphology

Not only must secondary students acquire a literate vocabulary, but they also must develop syntactic and morphological abilities at the literate end of the oral–literate continuum. Sentences regarded as literate typically contain one or more conjunctions, phrases, and clauses, ranging in complexity from sentences conjoined with *and* or *but* to sentences containing relative clauses, passive voice, subjunctive mood (cf. indicative), and/or tense markers indicating possible or continuing time: "He might have been the one the bed fell on, were he to have been present at the party."

The secondary curriculum offers students numerous opportunities to read literate sentences, which can serve as models for their own speaking and writing. Gerber (1993) recommended a procedure for using content or themes the students are studying as a springboard for the teacher to develop a set of exercises showing students how to combine sentences into more and more complex renderings. The teacher provides sets of related sentences to students and asks them to combine them using a syntactic device such as a relative clause. Teachers can add other syntactic devices to the procedure so students have practice in changing simple sentences into more complex and literate forms. Table 6.1 shows some examples.

Gerber (1993) suggested another way of helping students develop more syntactic flexibility. They were provided with phrases and clauses on separate cards, then encouraged to write as many different combinations as they could. For instance, students could be given the following phrases and clauses:

- eating ice cream
- at the movie theater
- when we went to the movie
- we saw some friends
- with some friends from another school

For students whose reading skills make it difficult for them to comprehend grade-level textbooks or literature, Paul (2006) recommends having peers or parents read

TABLE 6.1

Examples of Reworking Sentences into Literate Form

Simple Sentences	Syntactic Device	Literate Form
Everyone was afraid to say anything. They heard noises. The noises seemed to be getting louder.	Relative clause	Even when they heard noises that seemed to be getting louder, everyone was afraid to say anything.
The senators dropped the rider from the bill.	Passive voice	The rider was dropped from the bill by the senators.
If it rains, we can't go on the picnic.	Subjunctive mood	If it were to rain, we wouldn't be able to go on the picnic.
We studied until late last night.	Perfect aspect + auxiliary	We might have been studying late last night.
Several breeds of dog are used for hunting birds. Spaniels, labrador retrievers and golden retrievers are often used.	Elaboration	Several breeds of dog, such as spaniels, labrador retrievers, and golden retrievers, are often used for hunting birds.
We'll study first. Then we'll go eat something.	Adverbial clause	After we study, we'll go eat something.
It was tough to ride my bike in the sand.	Subject noun clause	Riding my bike in the sand was very tough.
It was hard to ride my bike in the sand.	Object noun clause	The hard part was riding my bike in the sand.
I'll go to the concert if my parents will let me. If not, I'll go to the movie.	Adverbial connective	If my parents will let me, I'll go to the concert. Otherwise, I'll go to the movie.
First, plants need adequate light and food. Then they can grow.	Temporal clause	Before plants can grow, they need adequate light and food

them aloud. Alternatively, students can listen to the material on tapes obtained from libraries or produced by parents and friends. Another way for students to hear literate language is to watch teacher- or librarian-recommended movies or videos with sophisticated scripts that use literate language forms. Teachers could use movie scripts as guides in developing activities that focus students' attention on literate language forms. For instance, the dialogue in *To Kill a Mockingbird* includes various syntactic devices.

If students' metalinguistic and metacognitive abilities are sufficiently developed, the teacher can utilize self-cueing in the context of editing syntax and morphology. To assist students in editing their work, teachers might begin by having them edit others' work before attempting to edit their own. Scott (1999) found that when students begin by editing others' work, they do better editing their own. The teacher encourages students to write several drafts, each time using a set of questions to refine what they have written. Typical questions might include the following:

"Is it clear?"
"Are the ideas connected?"
"Is the style appropriate for the audience?"
"Does it sound mature?"

Once students develop some skill in editing their peers' work, they can turn to their own, following the same procedure of writing several drafts, asking the self-cueing questions when reviewing each draft.

Pragmatics

Conversational competence takes on greater importance as students strive to fit in with their peers, participate in social peer groups, and move toward more independence from parents. To be successful, students have to develop skills in negotiating, persuading, making appropriate assumptions about conversational partners, and using the appropriate tone and style of speaking in different social contexts (Paul, 2006).

To teach students oral persuasion skills, teachers could use, for instance, Zimbalist and Driggs's (2001a) lesson plan "Can scientists discover a limit to discovery?" This lesson takes students through the process of evaluating opposing sides to a debate, analyzing excerpts from a debate, and evaluating different methods of persuasion. Zimbalist (1998) designed a science lesson in which students examine how the media present ideas of "ideal" health through a series of activities, many of which ask students to identify the subtle and not-so-subtle ways in which the media use persuasion to convey a message.

Hoskins (1996) developed a program to teach students communication strategies for both conversational and classroom discourse. Her approach can be used in either one-on-one or group settings to teach students about conversational moves by:

■ introducing a topic,
■ maintaining a topic,
■ extending a topic,

- changing a topic,
- requesting clarification,
- introducing a topic in an elaborated form, or
- responding to requests for clarification.

The lessons in Hoskins' (1996) program provide teachers with the specific objective related to each conversational move; the materials necessary to teach each move, how to introduce each move and the purpose of the lesson, ideas on how to set up and maintain a conversation that will facilitate each specific conversational move, and how to provide students with feedback about their use of each move.

Gallagher (1991) described a peer modeling approach to help students improve their conversational competence within the context of cooperative learning groups. Students are paired with normally achieving peers in activities in which the normally achieving peer models a particular conversational device. For instance, Cantlon (1991) used an interviewing activity in which normally achieving peers were instructed to interview their partner, asking questions about his name, family, music, sports, hobbies, and the like. The interviewers are instructed to ask at least three questions and to write notes about their partner's answers.

Upon a signal from the teacher, the students switch roles, and the student with LLD goes through the same procedure. Once the teacher is satisfied that the interviews are complete, the students are asked assemble and the teacher leads them in a discussion of what they have learned about each other from their interviews.

To help students with **classroom discourse**, Silliman and Wilkinson (1991) used a method they call "dialogic mentoring," in which teachers provide verbal cues or alternative choices to help students solve a problem or answer a question. In dialogic mentoring, the teacher gives students models of adequate scaffolding (i.e., self-cues or alternative verbal choices). The purpose of providing models of scaffolding is for students to learn to use the same process for themselves.

Brown and Palinscar (1987) developed a dialogic mentoring procedure based on helping students develop skills in

- predicting, in which students examine what they already know about the selected topic, develop a purpose for their reading or listening, and express what they expect to learn from the explanation or description;
- question generating, in which students ask questions they think the teacher might ask;
- summarizing, in which the students paraphrase what has been read or heard; and
- clarifying, in which the students identify what they did not understand or what is still not clear.

To teach these four steps, the teacher first leads the students in examining their prior knowledge on a selected topic (e.g., a math problem). Next the teacher models a set of steps that solve the problem, verbally highlighting when she moves to the next step (e.g., saying "The first step is…," "The second step is…," "The last step is….") Following the elucidation of steps, the teacher leads the students to generate questions about the procedure. For instance, she might ask, "What do you need to do first?" "What happens next?" "What's the last thing you need to do?" Then the teacher chooses students, one at a time, to follow the same steps in solving a similar problem and eliciting questions from their classmates. After each student has had a chance to try out the procedure, the teacher leads them in summarizing what they learned and in clarifying what they did not know or what remains unclear.

Graphic organizers often help students with LLD manage classroom discourse rules. To help students understand the rules of classroom discourse, Norris and Hoffman (1993) asked them to first list the rules for each class, then describe the similarities and differences in the rules they follow in different classes. Paul (2006) recommended having students use a script-analysis procedure in their effort to list the rules for different classes. In script analysis, the teacher asks students to tell everything they know about a selected activity (e.g., listening to a book report), then arranges their comments into list form. Once they are satisfied that they have a complete list, the teacher asks them to brainstorm what they would do if something unusual were to happen (e.g., "What would you do if there were a fire drill while you were listening to a book report?"). Next, the teacher encourages the students to identify the cues she offers when students are giving oral book reports. For instance, she might ask, "What does Ms. A. do when you're not looking at the presenter?"

To help students become more aware of how the teacher gives cues during a given routine, she has them role-play the script of listening to a book report, playing the roles of both student and teacher. Following each role play, the teacher leads the students in discussing what was clear, what they did not understand, and how they might change what they are looking for during the next role play.

Finally, the teacher leads the students in a discussion of what they can do to remind themselves to follow the script. For students who are having difficulty with certain parts of the script, she might have them write cue cards listing the steps in the listening-to-a-book-report routine. Alternatively, the teacher might list the steps of the script on a wall chart so the students can refer to it when needed.

Narrative discourse skills continue to develop throughout secondary school, particularly as students are exposed to more sophisticated narratives in reading literature, drama, and poetry. Students are expected to produce oral and written stories that are well plotted and that include multiple embedded episodes (Sutton-Smith, 1986).

As discussed earlier, the best way to develop narrative ability is to read good stories. The American Library Association's website http://www.ala/org provides an annotated list of books that appeal to adolescents, on the "Quick Picks for Reluctant Young Adult Readers" page: http://www.ala.org/yalsa/booklists/quickpicks/

Page and Stewart (1985) suggested that teachers scramble parts of stories their students are expected to read for the students to resequence. The teacher can provide pictures or illustrations to help the students figure out which sequence makes the best sense. Care must be taken when using pictures to use images that accurately depict the events described in the story. In addition, the images must show a clearly delineated sequence that matches that of the story.

Another approach to teaching narrative discourse was developed by Stewart (1985), who recommended providing students with story frames that they complete to specify story topic(s), main character(s), motivating problem(s), initial attempts at solving the problem(s), subsequent attempts, and resolution of the problem. These fill-in tasks might include statements such as these:

1. This story is about_____.
2. What happened to get things going in this story was_____.
3. The main character responded to the problem by_____.
4. The problem was solved when_____.

After using the frames successfully over a period of time, students can begin eliminating them one by one until they are able to describe and summarize the story without cuing.

Students with LLD also can benefit from listening to audiotaped books, available from the library. As another option, some audio books can be downloaded to an iPod or iPhone (Apple, 2009).

The New York Times Online (2001) website has compiled an archive of lesson plans, many of which teach students about writing narrative discourse. One example is a lesson plan developed by Zimbalist and Driggs (2001b), in which students use photographs from the newspaper to write first-person descriptive narratives. The lesson plan includes a set of questions for students to answer while observing the photographs. They then use their responses to the questions to develop their descriptive narratives. The lesson plan is designed to address academic learning standards and provides links to state standards, as well as to a compendium of standards and benchmarks for K–12 education developed by Mid-Continent Research for Education and Learning (2001). If teachers do not have access to the exact materials described in the lesson plan, they can easily modify it, using materials available to them.

Chapter 5 referred to literature-based performance as a method for instructing students about narrative discourse. This process is similar for secondary students. The teacher selects a piece of literature, preferably a poem or short story. The students are involved in rewriting the script so it is suitable for them to perform. The teacher can guide the students in learning about what constitutes a narrative problem, character development, narrative voice, plot development, embedding episodes, and resolution of the problem.

As part of the script-writing process, the teacher asks the students to answer questions about each aspect of the story. The following are some typical questions:

- What happens to begin the story? (i.e., what is the narrative problem?)
- Why does the protagonist do what he or she does?
- What is the protagonist's plan?
- How does the protagonist's plan turn out?
- How does the protagonist feel about what happens?

- How do other characters feel about what happens?
- What does the narrator say?
- Who is the narrator talking to?

Once the script has been written, the students begin rehearsing its performance. The rehearsal process can be used to direct students' attention to the same questions that were used during the writing process. They can compare their responses as performers to their responses as writers to see whether either context influences them in some way that is different from the other. Throughout the rehearsal process, the

---

Story Components

This story takes place _____ and _____.
                                (where)   *(when)*

The main characer _____.
                                (describe what he or she looked like, said, did, thought, felt)

Events in the story happened in this order _____.
                                          (first, next, then, and then, last)

Events in this story happened because _____.

Story Ideas and Language

The literal events that occured in this story were _____.

Some things that happened that weren't described in words are _____.

Some things this story could mean that weren't described in words are _____

_____.

Some words that were used that mean more than one thing are _____.

Some examples of figurative words (simile, metaphor, irony, satiric) used in this

  story are _____.

Some examples of grammatically complex sentences used in this story are _____

_____.
                          (compound, complex, compound/complex)

An example of dialogue I particularly liked and why: _____.

Here's what made this story interesting: _____.

_____.

(continued)

FIGURE 6.3

Narrative Outlines of Stories

Episode Structure

Here's what happened to start the story (the problem): _____.

Here's what the main character did in response to the problem: _____.

Here's how the main character felt about the problem: _____.

Here's what the main character intended to do (and why) about the problem:

_____.

Here's how the problem was solved: _____.

Here's how the main characer reacted to the solution: _____.

If there was another episode in this story, what happened to start it? _____.

How did the main character of this episode respond to this problem? _____.

How did the main character feel about this problem? _____.

What did the main character intend to do (and why) about this problem? _____.

How was this problem solved? _____.

If there was more than one episode, how were the episodes related to each
  other? _____.

How did the overall story end? _____.

How did the main character(s) feel about how the problems were solved? _____.

FIGURE 6.3 *(continued)*

teacher can encourage students to rewrite selected portions of the script as they gain insights into how their performance might be enhanced by such changes.

Explicit instruction about story grammars represents a more metacognitive approach to teaching narrative. Stewart (1985) devised a method in which the teacher gives students simplified outlines of story grammar elements (setting, problem, response, and outcome) as a way to help them organize stories. Using Miller et al.'s (2001) description of narrative discourse, teachers can help students learn not only about story grammar (which Miller et al. term "episode structure"), but also story components and story ideas and language. Figure 6.3 shows sample question guides for episode elements and structure (story grammar), story components, and story ideas and language.

B. L. Miller (1988) developed an instructional technique for teaching narratives, using model narratives incorporating various aspects of narratives (i.e., setting, problem, action, outcome, and ending). When first introduced to the model narratives, students were asked to use color-coded markers to identify aspects of the story. Miller used models in which one key narrative aspect (e.g., outcome) was missing so students had to identify not only which aspects were present but also which ones might be lacking. Once her students became familiar with this approach, Miller taught them to use it with their own stories, as well as those written by their peers.

Graves and Montague (1991) suggested using a story grammar checklist to help students organize their understanding of how stories work. The teacher can devise a checklist that serves as a story guide for students to use to record each aspect of a story and check off the pertinent story grammar elements, consisting of

- setting (when, where, who),
- problem,
- internal response,
- plan or attempt,
- response, and
- consequence or resolution.

For narratives to work, they must contain cohesive markers that guide the listener or reader in understanding how events are related. Although most elementary school students develop some ability to manipulate cohesive markers to tie their stories together, secondary students are expected to understand and produce stories with more sophisticated cohesive devices.

A metacognitive approach to teaching cohesive markers can be used to help students identify them in the curricular and literary material they are reading. For instance, the teacher might select a passage from a story the students are currently reading and mark several types of cohesion found there:

- *Lexical* (e.g., "The *field* stretched over the hills and into the distance beyond the barn. As the sun slowly descended, the *green* appeared to be lit from within")
- *Pronoun* (e.g., "*Ray* looked at the dog's face, wondering how *he* would know when it was ready to bite")
- *Ellipsis* (e.g., "The *dogs* looked friendly. There were *several of them*, all wagging their tails")
- *Definite article* (e.g., "*The* dog was big, though it didn't look like it could run fast")
- *Conjunction* (e.g., "We left *after* the other kids did")
- Conjunctive adverb (e.g., "The museum is the most expensive one ever built in this city. *However*, it's worth it because it's so beautiful")
- Conjunct (e.g., "The clock's hands seemed to be flying. *Yet* it also seemed as if no time had passed")

For each example, students are asked how the markers guide readers' understanding of what is happening in a story. Paul (2006) described an activity in which students write a group story and each student is asked to provide one of the devices they have been studying. Once students develop some facility with describing how cohesive devices work, they can be asked to use an example of a cohesive marker in their next oral or written narrative. Over a period of several assignments, the teacher can require that specific cohesive markers be produced one at a time until the students have used one or more of each type successfully. This same procedure can be used to teach students about cohesion in nonnarrative discourse.

With the exception of literature texts, most books that students encounter in secondary school contain expository discourse (descriptive, explanatory, persuasive/argumentative, letter, and biographical). All 50 states have developed learning standards, benchmarks, or both for students that include reference to the ability to understand, analyze, evaluate, and produce various forms of expository discourse. For example, the North Carolina Department of Public Instruction (2001), in its description of the 8th grade English language arts curriculum, refers to students developing facility with various forms of narrative and expository discourse, with special attention to argumentative and persuasive texts. California's (2010) learning standards for grades 9 and 10 refer to students' ability to critique expository text through evaluating the credibility of the author's claim or argument. The standards also require students to be able to produce various types of discourse, including argumentative, persuasive, and analytical essays, as well as research reports.

The different types of expository discourse can be taught in terms of the **macrostructure,** or overall text structure that serves to organize their content. Wallach and Miller (1988) indicated that the most typical macrostructure for expository text consists of

- title of the book or article,
- chapter headings or first-level article headings,
- first-level chapter headings or second-level article headings, and
- second-level chapter headings or third-level article headings.

Using this macrostructure, the teacher can develop an outline or checklist for students to follow, both for comprehending and for writing the various types of expository discourse. Wallach and Miller described an expository text organizer that students can use to learn about this generic macrostructure.

In analyzing different expository discourse types, Westby (1998) identified a set of expository devices to help students learn how expository text works. Paul (2006) provided comprehension cues corresponding to each of these six expository devices. These cues can be used to help students visualize the way each device is organized and structured. Figure 5.2 in Chapter 5 provides a visual scheme showing organizational structures for nonnarrative discourse, and Figure 6.4 here shows sample worksheets for various expository devices.

Teaching students to understand how persuasive discourse functions can be done utilizing a variety of media. Perhaps the most obvious (and most far reaching) is visual advertising, which is readily available. One askERIC lesson plan developed by Duffy (2009) uses magazine ads to show students how visual advertising works through persuasive techniques such as catchy words, testimonials, bandwagon, pos-

Cause–Effect

Questions to ask yourself:
1. What is being explained or argued?
2. What reasons are given to explain why something happens or exists?
3. What conclusions are drawn?

Key words:
because, since, so, reasons, in order to, therefore, consequently, hence, thus, leads to, produces

For text that is explanatory:
One-sentence summary of the effect (what is the author's conclusion?):

One-sentence summary of the cause (what is the author explaining?):

For text that is argumentative or persuasive:
One-sentence summary of the effect (what is the author's argument or point?):

One-sentence summary of the cause (why does the author believe her or his argument to be true?):

Descriptive

Questions to ask yourself:
1. What is being described?

Key words:
is called, is defined as, refers to, means, is, is a person who

One-sentence summary of the thing being described and its description:

Compare and Contrast

Questions to ask yourself:
1. What is being compared?
2. What is it being contrasted with?
3. How is it like what it is being compared to?
4. How is it different from what it is being compared to?

Key words:
same or different, however, yet, rather than

(continued)

FIGURE 6.4

Examples of Worksheets to Teach Expository Devices

One-sentence summary of the theme:

One-sentence comparison with the idea, concept, event, experience it is being compared to:

One-sentence contrast with the idea, concept, event, experience it is being contrasted to:

Sequence

Questions to ask yourself:
1. What is the topic?
2. Is it something that happened?
3. Is it how to make or do something?

Key words:
first, then, next, last, following, after, before, eventually

For something that happened
One-sentence summary of what happened:

For how to make or do something
One-sentence summary of how to make or do it:

Enumerative

Questions to ask yourself:
1. What is being listed and described?

Key words:
an example, for instance, an illustration, such as

One-sentence summary of what is being listed and described:

Problem/Solution

Questions to ask yourself:
1. What is the problem?
2. What are the proposed solutions?

Key words:
the problem is, a solution is

One-sentence summary of the problem and proposed solution(s):

FIGURE 6.4 *(continued)*

itive appeal, negative appeal, product character, product slogan, product comparison, and repetition. These visual persuasion techniques are analogous to those used in writing argumentative discourse and can be lead-ins to reading and writing persuasive text.

Simon (1991) produced a program that teaches students to understand argumentative discourse. First, the teacher helps students differentiate emotional and logical arguments. Through an examination of advertising in various media, students identify examples of both emotional and logical appeals. Another aspect of Simon's program involves students reading letters to the editor of their local or school newspaper. The objective is to identify the point (premise) and conclusion of each letter. The teacher then helps the students develop a syllogism from the letter's argument. For example:

> Early morning classes are beneficial to high school students only if it can be shown that their grades do not slide. This year's evidence shows that grades in early morning classes are lower than grades in classes held later in the day. Therefore, early morning classes are not beneficial to high school students.

The teacher then helps the students develop a counter argument by constructing a different syllogism and translating it into a letter to the editor.

To help students develop skill in writing expository discourse, teachers can teach students to use **rubrics**, or sets of benchmarks differentiating levels of performance in producing expository writing. Paul's (2006) developmental rubric, described earlier in this chapter, can be used in this regard. The rubric uses scores ranging from a low of 1 (developmentally at the beginning) to a high of 6 (developmentally sophisticated). Each scoring level addresses five aspects of expository writing:

1. How the text is organized and structured
2. How coherent it is (i.e., what is the content and how is it developed)
3. The developmental level of syntax, vocabulary, and cohesion strategies used
4. Extent to which writing mechanics are followed
5. Sense of audience

Several commercial websites offer materials, lessons, and activities designed to help students learn how to produce different types of expository text. For example, the Paradigm Online Writing Assistant http://www.powa.org/ offers free online instruction in organizing, revising, and editing various sorts of expository discourse, including informal, exploratory, and argumentative essays, and documenting sources. Teachers can use the site as a resource for activities and in-depth information about each type of expository discourse. If students can work independently, it also can be used as a self-study tutorial.

The New York Times Online (2010) lesson plan archive includes several lessons addressing expository discourse. For instance, one lesson plan, developed by Shulten and Harrod (2000), shows students how to identify controversial topics on which they have strong opinions. Then, using Shulten and Harrod's script, the students write their own persuasive opinion pieces modeled after a featured article they read. Like the lesson plans described above for narrative discourse, this one provides links to the K–12 learning standards developed by the Mid-Continent Research for Education and Learning (2001) and to individual state learning standards sites.

Students with LLD often have problems with three phases of writing expository discourse: (a) generating ideas, (b) generating and organizing sentences into coherent wholes, and (c) editing their work. Writers typically generate ideas from a variety of sources, including their own personal experiences and the knowledge they have acquired through reading. They may have difficulty generating ideas for writing for two reasons. First, encoding experience with language may pose challenges for these students. Second, they often do not read as well or as much as their typically developing peers. Consequently, they may not have acquired a sufficient knowledge base from which to draw, or they may not be able to access the knowledge base they have acquired.

Several strategies developed by teachers and researchers who work with students who have LLD rely on metalinguistic, metacognitive, and metapragmatic abilities, which will also be addressed separately later in this chapter and in Chapter 11. To use the approaches described here, teachers must be certain that their students are able to reflect on their own thinking, learning, and writing processes and that they are able to take the perspective of their proposed reading audiences.

To help students in the planning stage, Graham and Harris (1999) recommended a three-step strategy:

1. The student *thinks* who the audience is:
   a. Who will read this?
   b. What do I know about this topic?
   c. What do I want to say about it?

2. The student *plans* what to say:
   a. What are some different things I can say?
   b. How are some different ways to say these things?
   c. How can I organize what I'll say?

3. The student *writes* the piece, then *adds to* it by asking the same questions again.

A similar approach was proposed by Gerber (1993), who suggested providing students with the following list of questions to ask themselves when they are planning a composition:

- What do I know about this topic?
- How do I feel about this topic?
- What experience do I have with this topic? How has this experience influenced what I believe about this topic?

■ What could I explain, describe, argue, or prove about this topic?

■ What do my classmates already know about this topic?

■ What do I want them to know about it?

A second challenge for students with LLD is to generate the actual sentences and organize them into a coherent composition. One approach is for teachers to give copies of the visual organizers (shown in Figure 6.3) to the students to remind them of the characteristic devices used in the various types of expository discourse.

Another approach is to develop a set of prompt cards that students can refer to while using the various expository discourse strategies in their writing. Wong, Butler, Ficzere, & Kuperis (1996) suggested that teachers ask students to incorporate three types of phrases, along with examples of each, into their expository writing: introductory, explanatory, and concluding phrases. Figure 6.5 provides sample prompt card templates for the six types of expository devices described earlier.

The third phase of writing successful expository text involves editing, which also poses difficulties for students with LLD. During editing, attention shifts from the process of writing during the planning and sentence-generation phases to the product itself, with its attendant mechanical and grammatical requirements. Paul (2006) urged teachers to separate the writing process from the product phase so the students will feel less inhibited about errors and more inclined to generate ideas spontaneously. Once the attention shifts to the product, however, it becomes necessary to edit and revise for organization, clarity, and mechanics (Paul, 2006).

A first step that teachers can take to help students learn about editing is to have them read their compositions aloud. This shifts the emphasis onto how the piece holds together and makes sense as the author (and perhaps classmates) listen to the words. Wiig (1984) recommended that students edit in "passes," or read-throughs focusing on different aspects. During the first read-through, students focus on one aspect of the mechanics: spelling, grammar, punctuation, capitalization, or how paragraphs are organized. If, for instance, the first pass is to look at spelling, the teacher helps students develop strategies for checking spelling, perhaps using computer-based spell checks, reading the composition from the end to the beginning, or trading papers with a peer for careful proofreading.

Graham and Harris (1999) advised teachers to help students with LLD understand that correcting errors is not the sole function of editing. Rather, these authors say that revising is an essential aspect of writing because its purpose is to improve the overall quality of the product. To help students learn how to revise, Graham and Harris suggested a series of self- and peer-prompts to make their compositions clearer and more understandable to the intended audience:

1. Self-prompts

   a. Read my composition.

   b. Find the main idea and decide if it is clear.

   c. Add two sentences to make it clearer.

Cause–Effect

Introductory phrases

"This paper explains ...," "I will explain why ...," "_____ is caused by ...."

Explanatory phrases

"The reasons for ...," "For this reason ...," "As a result ...," "In order to ...."

Concluding phrases

"To sum up ...," "In conclusion, the explanation for _____ is _____;" "As I have shown, the cause of _____ is _____."

Descriptive

Introductory phrases

"This paper describes ...," "I will describe ...," "_____ is described as ...."

Explanatory phrases

"_____ is called ...," "_____ is defined as ...," "_____ refers to ...," "_____means ...."

Concluding phrases

"To sum up ...," "In conclusion, the description of _____ is _____;" "As I have shown, the description of _____ is _____."

Compare and Contrast

Introductory phrases

"This paper compares _____ with _____," "This paper compares _____ and _____."

Explanatory phrases

"_____ and _____are the same in these ways ...."
"_____ and _____ are different in these ways ...."

Concluding phrases

"To sum up, _____ and _____ can be compared in these ways ...," "In conclusion, _____ and _____ can be contrasted in these ways ...."

(continued)

FIGURE 6.5

Sample Prompt Cards for Six Types of Expository Discourse Structure

Sequence

Introductory phrases

"The topic of this paper is …," "I will tell how _____happened," "I will tell how to make_____"

Explanatory phrases

"First …," "Second …," "Next …," "Finally …." "Before you do _____, you need to do _____."

Concluding phrases

"To sum up …," "In conclusion, the way _____ happened is _____;" "As I have shown, the way to make _____ is to _____."

Enumerative

Introductory phrases

"This paper lists and describes …," "I will list describe …," "_____ is listed and described as …."

Explanatory phrases

"For instance …," "An illustration of _____ is …."

Concluding phrases

"To sum up …," "In conclusion, the list of _____ includes _____," "As I have shown, the list of _____ is _____."

Problem/Solution

Introductory phrases

"The problem discussed in this paper is _____,"
"The solution offered in this paper is _____."

Explanatory phrases

"_____ is a problem that can be controlled by _____."

Concluding phrases

"To sum up, _____ can be solved by _____."
             (problem)   (solution)

FIGURE 6.5 *(continued)*

d. Scan each sentence of the composition to see if it makes sense—whether it is connected to the rest of the composition, I can add anything else, or it has any errors to correct.

e. Make noted changes (either on my paper or in the computer).

f. Reread my composition and make any final changes.

g. Recopy or print out the final, revised version of my composition.

2. Peer prompts (I act as a consultant with a classmate)

a. Listen to my classmate read his composition.

b. Read along as my classmate reads his composition.

c. Tell what my classmate's composition was about.

d. Tell what I liked best about my classmate's composition.

e. Reread my classmate's paper and note whether everything is clear and whether any details can be added.

f. Discuss my revision suggestions with my classmate;

3. Peer prompts (a classmate acts as a consultant to me)

a. Read my paper to my classmate.

b. Listen as he tells me what he thinks my paper was about.

c. Listen as he tells me what he liked best about my paper.

d. Listen to my classmate's suggestions for revisions.

e. Revise my composition, incorporating my classmate's suggestions.

f. Exchange papers and check for mechanical errors in capitalization, spelling, and punctuation.

g. Recopy or print out the final, revised version of my composition.

Teachers can also encourage students to use rubrics to evaluate and critique their own writing. For instance, the Secondary School Educators website About.com Secondary Education (2009) posts rubrics, some developed for students and some for teachers, for evaluating compare and contrast, expository, debate, and persuasive essays. The rubric for expository essays contains five categories—focus, organization, conventions, understanding, and support—each of which is scored on a 6-point scale. Along with the sample rubrics, this website provides a tutorial on writing rubrics for any assignment, not just writing.

Another set of rubrics was developed by C. Miller (2009) to evaluate writing, using language that appeals to eighth-grade students. Miller has developed rubrics for personal expression, informing, and persuasion, designed for students and utilizing a 4-point scale.

The Meta Level

Much of the language processing required of secondary students involves the metas. Earlier in this chapter we learned about approaches to language instruction that utilize students' metalinguistic, metacognitive, and metapragmatic skills. Some students with LLD require additional, explicit instruction in comprehension monitoring and metacognitive strategies for acquiring and retaining information as it is presented in the secondary curriculum—through reading texts and listening to lectures.

One approach that teachers can use to teach comprehension monitoring is the curriculum in practical intelligence developed by Sternberg, Okagi, and Jackson (1990) to help students learn three self-monitoring processes that contribute significantly to school success:

1. Managing oneself, which includes knowing one's learning style(s) and intelligences and ways to improve as a learner
2. Managing tasks, including how to solve general and specific, situation-related problems
3. Cooperating with others, including communication and fitting in

From the curriculum, the teacher can select those aspects pertinent to a given student's needs. For instance, for a student needing instruction in managing himself, the teacher could teach the student about

- kinds of intelligence and learning styles,
- how test scores are and are not related to one's intelligences and learning styles,
- how to collect his thoughts and set goals, and
- how to accept responsibility for his own learning.

For a student who needs help with managing tasks, the teacher can teach the student how to view problems by

- discovering whether there is a problem,
- defining the strategies the student is using currently,
- developing a process to help him solve problems,
- planning ways to prevent problems, and
- breaking habits.

For a student who could benefit from learning how to cooperate with others, the teacher might teach the student about

- communicating in class discussions,
- knowing what to say in different situations,
- fine-tuning his conversations,
- putting himself in another's place, and
- solving communication problems.

To help students develop comprehension-monitoring skills when listening to classroom lectures, Knapczyk (1991) developed a program utilizing taped lectures from the regular curriculum. Designed to be used in a small group or an individual setting, the students listen to the tape, which is stopped periodically. Each time it stops, the students are required to ask a question that is relevant to what is being discussed on the tape. The teacher helps the students structure their questions so they understand

- the main idea,
- examples that illustrate or support the main idea,
- when it is appropriate during the lecture to ask questions, and
- how to ask questions that will aid their understanding.

To help students learn to monitor their own comprehension of written material, one of the most successful approaches has been the SQ3R (Schumaker et al., 1982), described in detail in Chapter 12.

Most instruction related to metacognition emphasizes teaching strategies and tactics for gleaning information from lectures and texts and for recalling information on tests. Bowen, Hawkins, and King (1997) took a different approach, based on MI, that centers on helping students discover how they naturally pay attention and learn. They developed a set of teaching units to be integrated into existing curriculum. Their experience in working with students with disabilities was that teaching them how they think and learn increased their motivation and ability to set realistic learning goals for themselves. In addition, these authors found that students who are highly motivated believe that their learning is under their control; that they can usually solve their own learning problems, given appropriate resources and instructional support; and that, if something adverse happens, they can control how they behave.

Bowen et al.'s (1997) approach, designed around Bloom's taxonomy of educational objectives and using MI as the vehicle, involves the teacher's leading students through seven steps:

1. Knowledge, or recognizing and recalling information
2. Comprehension, or translating and summarizing (paraphrasing)
3. Application, or interpreting through generalizing, defining, and making connections between facts
4. Applying knowledge, or solving problems through identifying them and the skills necessary for their solution
5. Analyzing, or assessing all parts of a problem to see how they are alike and dissimilar (seeing patterns)
6. Synthesizing, or solving a problem by using original, creative thinking
7. Evaluating, or comparing and discriminating between ideas

One of the units in the Bowen et al. (1997) program teaches students what a learning strategy is and how they can use their understanding of MI to develop strategies for learning. Using the MI concept, those authors developed teacher resource sheets showing academic strategies for language arts, science, math, social sciences, fine art, and geography. Students are taught general learning strategies, as well as some tailored to general communication, getting into focus and attending, staying organized, and solving problems.

Teachers who wish to use speech-recognition technology to help adolescents with writing can refer to the discussion in Chapter 5. The techniques, activities, and resources described there can be used with secondary students.

Multimedia projects can also be used to help students with writing. These media include CDs and DVDs, digital cameras, iPods, video cameras, photographs, keyboards, writing, illustrations, drawings, and computers. Collaborating around a theme—for instance, an adventure story—students with learning disabilities and their typically developing classmates can plan, design, and produce a multimedia project. Finished projects can then be made available on the class website or on DVD for classmates and their teachers to view. LD Online (1999) offers a detailed description of using multimedia with students with learning disabilities.

■Secondary Students with ■Severe Impairments

Because most secondary students with severe disabilities will have been identified before entering school, little additional standardized testing will be required for diagnostic purposes. Observational or criterion-referenced assessments, however, can be used to determine what sorts of language instruction will best meet these students' needs. For some—for example, students identified as having mild or moderate autism—the assessment will emphasize academic language, and the teacher can refer to the assessment procedures and instruments described in earlier sections of this chapter.

Functional Language Skills

The emphasis for most students with severe impairments is on their functional communication skills. For these students, language assessment centers on the language skills they need for success in vocational and/or independent-living programs. Most of these students will already have IDEA-mandated Individualized Transition Plans (ITPs), which address

- the student's progress toward graduation from high school,
- his postsecondary education or training needs,
- support required for community living, and
- plans for helping the student succeed in employment and daily living.

The ITP will include information regarding the student's specific needs in each area, and language assessment will be designed to evaluate which language skills the student needs in order to succeed in each.

Paul (2006) recommended that teachers assess the discourse environments and rules the student currently deals with daily, as well as those the student will be expected to face in the near future. In addition, she advised that teachers should target these students' literacy skills even if they have few reading or writing skills. The purpose of these assessments is to determine what sort of language instruction will benefit them most in their day-to-day living, and the primary goal of instruction is to foster independence in vocational, domestic, and recreational settings.

Improved conversational skills lead to greater acceptance—of great value to adolescents who will be making the transition from a school environment into a larger community context. One time-honored approach to instructing students in conversational discourse uses peer modeling of greeting, elaborating greetings, making requests, and offering objects (Gaylord-Ross, Haring, Breen, & Pitts Conway, 1984). Another approach utilizes structured situations in which peers model particular conversational behaviors such as appropriate topic initiation and maintenance or using open-ended questions and follow-ups to keep a conversation moving (Bryan, 1986).

Another instructional program, developed by Kilman and Negri-Schoultz (1987) for high-functioning students with autism, can be easily modified for students with other types of disabilities. The goal of the program, which is structured around a social club for students with disabilities, is for the students to develop conversational abilities through discussion groups. Each discussion group is planned around a preselected topic, such as social isolation, academic stress, and how to meet peers. The teacher models conversational strategies (e.g., appropriate greetings, how to start and continue a conversation, how to ask appropriate questions to keep a conversation going), and the students discuss their experiences while practicing the conversational strategies.

For adolescents with severe disabilities, instruction in conversational discourse can include teaching two skills Lord (1988) identified as particularly important to adolescents: communicative rituals and how to identify appropriate conversational topics. Conversational rituals can be taught as scripts of conversational patterns, especially those associated with greetings (e.g., "Hi, how are you?" "Fine, thanks, how are you?"), introductions, separating, requesting, negating, and questioning. The teacher can help students learn to identify conversational topics by instructing them in listening for a while before attempting to enter a conversation, using a question to verify what they think the topic is (e.g., "Are you talking about the prom?"), and using a question to initiate a topic (e.g., "Do you want to talk about my new computer game?").

Teachers can help students by helping them develop the communication skills necessary for self-advocacy. Paul (2006) recommended that teachers provide students with instruction and practice in talking with friends, neighbors, and potential (or current) employers about their disability. The goal is for students to be able to explain the impact that their disability has on their lives and to ask for what they need so they can participate in the community. West et al. (1999) suggested having students role play various situations to practice such skills as

- setting up a class schedule,
- moving out of the home,

- asking for accommodations needed for a course,
- meeting with a rehabilitation counselor or a social service caseworker,
- meeting with a medical provider,
- working with a personal-care attendant,
- interviewing for a job, and
- making choices in an IEP meeting.

In addition to improving social communication skills, secondary students have to gain facility with the language demands they will face outside the school environment. Teachers can guide students by providing opportunities to practice reading online and hard copy job applications, newspaper and magazine ads, work agreements, menus, and topics of interest. Students can practice writing by filling out sample forms, copying recipes, paying sample (or real) bills, keeping sample (or real) household records, and filing records. When developing sample materials, teachers should take care to ensure these are age-appropriate and relevant to students' experiences.

For students who have developed sufficient metalinguistic ability, Sturomski (1996) developed a script that students can use for functioning in independent living situations. The teacher helps the student develop a plan to follow the steps in the script:

1. Define what the problem is.
2. Brainstorm several possible ways to solve the problem.
3. Evaluate each of the possibilities.
4. Choose the best one.
5. Set a goal.
6. Figure out the steps you have to take to reach the goal.
7. Begin the steps toward the goal, keeping a record of your progress.
8. Evaluate the outcome: Did you reach your goal? If so, are you satisfied? If not, why didn't you? What could you have done differently to reach your goal?
9. If you did reach your goal, reward yourself for your achievement.

Alternative and Augmentative Communication (AAC)

The goals of language instruction for students using AAC devices are the same as those for other students with severe disabilities: to develop appropriate social and interpersonal communication skills and to develop flexibility in conveying and comprehending meaning in a variety of language modalities (Damico & Damico, 1993).

Most adolescents using AAC systems will enter secondary school with a device. Because the communicative, linguistic, and social contexts differ significantly from those in elementary school, the ITP team should ask these questions:

- Is the current system adequate for the student's present communication needs?
- Is the current system adequate for the student's cognitive abilities?

- Is the current system capable of expanding as the student's cognitive and communicative abilities develop?
- Is the current system suitable for nonacademic environments?
- Will the student be able to maintain his current AAC system in vocational, recreational, domestic, and academic environments?
- If not, how will the maintenance occur?

The teacher has two primary roles in responding to these questions. The first is to determine the communication and language abilities the student needs for successful classroom and academic performance. The second is to assess the effectiveness of the AAC device in the student's development of the communication skills needed to complete academic and vocational courses and to interact with classmates.

The American Speech–Language–Hearing Association (ASHA) (2009) developed a guide for users of AAC devices that explains the sorts of systems available, the best system for a variety of different communication situations, the professionals who help select and/or develop an AAC system, the rights of people seeking professional assistance in selecting and using AAC devices, and a glossary of AAC terms. In addition to providing information about AAC devices and the professionals most likely to work with students using them, the guide includes a list of questions teachers can use to evaluate current or proposed systems. The questions can also be reproduced for students and their families.

Various resources are available for teachers to use in evaluating the effectiveness of the AAC device. The school speech–language clinician (SLP) will likely be a part

---

Email Correspondence

Introductory phrase

"Hi, my name is_____ and I'm writing to _____."
(purpose)

Key phrases

"In my experience ...," "Something that happened to me was ...," "I found that ...," "I believe that ...." "Here's an idea I have: ...."

Concluding phrases

"To sum up ...," "It all adds up to ...," "All of these things lead me to conclude ...," "In sum ...."

Topic maintenance

"I'd like to hear from anyone who ...," "Has anyone else had that experience?" "Is this an idea anyone else finds interesting?" "Does anyone have any other information that I might be able to use?"

FIGURE 6.6

Sample Prompt Card to Guide Email Correspondence

of the IEP and ITP teams and can serve as an in-classroom consultant. The SLP will be able to collaborate with teachers in developing a checklist or questionnaire regarding the effectiveness of the AAC system. The teacher can also take advantage of numerous resources available on the internet. A good place to begin is the website of Augmentative.inc, http://www.augcominc.com/links.html for a list of a set of links to organizations devoted to AAC, AAC device vendors, and AAC-related product vendors. The site also offers links to online articles of interest to teachers on topics relating to AAC.

Teachers might consider helping their students access an online users listserv such as the Augmentative Communication On Line Users Group (ACOLUG), hosted by the University Affiliated Program at Temple University (2009). This listserv was created so people using augmentative communication could exchange their experiences and information with others. The listserv uses email, which allows people using AAC devices to communicate easily. The teacher can use listserv as a means to enhance students' writing skills. For instance, the teacher can develop a prompt card similar to the one shown in Figure 6.6 to guide students' email correspondence.

▊Summary

Students entering secondary school encounter an environment that is considerably changed from the one they left in elementary school. Language assessment and intervention shift to social discourse, the literate forms of both narrative and expository discourse, and the metas: metacognition, metalingusitics, and metapragmatics.

In secondary school, social demands increase substantially, placing added stress on the communication abilities of students with LLD. Social discourse takes on added importance, and adeptness with language is the defining characteristic of fitting in with peers. Classroom discourse changes as well. Students are expected to listen, take notes, and extract meaning and significance from lectures, and they are expected to make oral presentations using language forms that are typical of the literate end of the oral–literate continuum.

Perhaps the biggest challenge for students with LLD is the more complex narrative discourse, along with the greater importance of expository forms of discourse, both oral and written. The literature that students encounter may contain more than one protagonist with competing points of view, the plot may be complicated and complex, there may be multiple embedded episodes, and vocabulary and syntax may be unfamiliar.

Other than texts used in classes focused on literature, most texts secondary students are exposed to are some form of expository discourse. Teachers expect their students to comprehend and produce text that lists, describes, explains, persuades, and informs. Because each utilizes a different organizational structure and structural devices, students must be able to use metalinguistic, metacognitive, and metapragmatic strategies.

Students with severe disabilities will need instruction in the functional language necessary for making transitions into work, recreation, and independent living. Students with severe disabilities who are using AAC systems must receive a careful assessment of the utility and effectiveness of their device in contexts other than the academic world.

References

About.com: Secondary Education. (2009). Retrieved from http://7-12educators.about.com/cs/rubrics/

Alaska Department of Education. (2009). *Alaska comprehensive system of student assessment.* Retrieved from http://www.eed.state.ak.us/tls/assessment/sba/AK6ptInstructionalrubric 2004.pdf

American Speech–Language–Hearing Association (ASHA). (2009). *Augmentative and alternative communication (AAC).* Retrieved from http://www.asha.org/public/speech/disorders/AAC.htm

Apple. (2009). *Audiobooks.* Retrieved from http://www.apple.com/itunes/whatson/audiobooks.html

Appleby, A. (1978). *The Child's Concept of a Story: Ages 2 to 17.* Chicago: University of Chicago Press.

Aune, B., & Friehe, M. (1996). Transition to postsecondary education: Institutional and individual issues. *Topics in Language Disorders, 16,* 1–22.

Bowen, J., Hawkins, M., & King, C. (1997). *Square pegs: Building success in school and life through MI.* Tucson, AZ: Zephyr Press.

Brickson, S. (2001). Genocide: Are you indifferent to it? A WebQuest for 8th grade (Language Arts, Social Studies). Retrieved from http://projects.edtech.sandi.net/ofarrell/genocide webquest/

Brinton, B., & Fujiki, M. (1994). Ways to teach conversation. In J. Duchan, L. Hewitt, & R. Sonnenmeier (Eds.), *Pragmatics: From theory to practice* (pp. 59–71). Englewood Cliffs, NJ: Prentice-Hall.

Brown, A., & Palinscar, A. (1987). Reciprocal teaching of comprehension strategies. In J. Day & J. Borkowski (Eds.), *Intelligence and exceptionality; New directions for theory, assessment, and instructional practice* (pp. 81–132). Norwood, NJ: Ablex.

Bryan, T. (1986). A review of studies on learning-disabled children's communicative competence. In R. L. Schiefelbusch (Ed.), *Language competence: Assessment and intervention* (pp. 227–259). Austin, TX: Pro-Ed.

California Department of Education. (2010). *Grades nine and ten: English language arts content standards.* Retrieved from http://www.cde.ca.gov/be/st/ss/documents/elacontents tnds.pdf

Cantlon, T. (1991). *The first four weeks of cooperative learning.* Portland, OR: Prestige.

Crais, E. (1990). World knowledge to word knowledge. *Topics in Language Disorders, 10*(3), 45–62.

Creaghead, N. (1992). Mutual empowerment through collaboration: A new script for an old problem. In W. A. Secord (Ed.), *Best practices in school speech–language pathology* (Vol. 2, pp. 109–116). San Antonio, TX: Psychological Corp.

Damico, J., & Damico, S. (1993). Language and social skills from a diversity perspective: considerations for the speech–language pathologist. *Language, Speech, and Hearing Services in Schools, 24*(4), 236–243.

Duffy, R. K. (2009). Magazine ads and you, the teenager. *AskERIC Lesson Plans.* Retrieved from http://ericir.syr.edu/Virtual/Lessons/Health/Consumer_Health/COH0003.html

Eckert, P. (1990). Cooperative competition in adolescent "girl talk." *Discourse Processes, 13*, 91–122.

Ellis, E. S. (2002). The clarifying routine: elaborating vocabulary instruction. *LD Online Newsletter.* Retrieved from http://www.ldonline.org/ld_indepth/teaching_techniques/ellis_clarifying.html

Family Learning Association. (2009). *Building vocabulary for success.* Retrieved from http://www.kidscanlearn.com/parental/partalk/vocabulary.html

Ford, M. (2009). Euphemisms. *AskERIC lesson plans.* Retrieved from http://askeric.org/cgi-bin/printlessons.cgi/Virtual/Lessons/Language_Arts/Vocabulary/VOC0003.html

Gallagher, T. (1991). Language and social skills: Implications for assessment and intervention with school-age children. In T. M. Gallagher (Ed), *Pragmatics of language: Clinical practice issues* (pp. 11–41). San Diego: Singular.

Gardner, H. (2006). *Multiple intelligences: New horizons.* New York: Basic Books.

Gaylord-Ross, R., Haring, T., Breen, C., & PittsConway, V. (1984). The training and generalization of social interaction skills with autistic youth. *Journal of Applied Behavior Analysis, 17*, 229–247.

Gerber, S. (1993). *Language-related learning disabilities: Their nature and treatment.* Baltimore: Brookes.

German, D. (2005) *Word finding intervention program* (2nd ed.) (WFIP-2). Austin, TX: Pro-Ed.

Graham, S., & Harris, K. (1999). Assessment and intervention in overcoming writing difficulties: An illustration from the self-regulated strategy development model. *Language Speech and Hearing Services in Schools, 30*, 255–264.

Graves, A., & Montague, M. (1991). Using story-grammar cueing to improve the writing of students with learning disabilities. *Learning Disabilities Research and Practice, 6*, 246–250.

Hamersky, J. (1995). *Cartoon cut-ups: Teaching figurative language and humor.* Eau Claire, WI: Thinking Publications.

Hammill, D. D., Brown, V. L., Larsen, S. C., & Wiederholt, J. L. (2007). *Test of adolescent and adult language–4.* Austin, TX: Pro-Ed.

Hammill, D. D., & Larsen, S. C. (2009). *Test of written language–4.* Austin, TX: Pro-Ed.

Hammill, D. D., & Newcomer, P. (2008). *Test of language development–intermediate–4.* Austin, TX: Pro-Ed.

Hayes, J., & Flower, L. (1987). On the structure of the writing process. *Topics in Language Disorders, 7*(4), 19–30.

Hosford Middle School. (2009). *Documents employed in all classes.* Retrieved from http://users.rcn.com/jcala/rubrics.html#writing

Hoskins, B. (1996). *Conversations: A framework for language intervention.* Eau Claire, WI: Thinking Publications.

IRA/NCTE (2007). *Rubric for evaluating persuasive texts.* Retrieved from http://www.readwritethink.org/lesson_images/lesson1040/rubric.pdf

Johnson, N. (1983). What do you do when you can't tell the whole story? The development of summarization skills. In K. E. Nelson (Ed.), *Children's language* (Vol. 4, pp. 315–381). Hillsdale, NJ: Erlbaum.

Kilman, B., & Negri-Schoultz, N. (1987). Developing educational programs for working with students with Kanner's autism. In D. J. Cohen & A. M. Donnellan (Eds.), *Handbook of autism and pervasive developmental disorders* (pp. 440–451). New York: Wiley.

Knapczyk, D. (1991). Effects of modeling in promoting generalization of student question asking and question answering. *Learning Disabilities Research and Practice, 6,* 75–82.

Larson, V. L., & McKinley, N. (1995). *Language disorders in older students.* Eau Claire, WI: Thinking Publications.

LD Online. (1999). *Multimedia and more: Help for students with learning disabilities.* Retrieved from http://www.ldonline.org/article/Multimedia_and_More:_Help_for_Students _with_Learning_Disabilities

LD Online. (2001). *LD in depth: Technology.* Retrieved from http://www.ldonline.org/ld_in depth/technology/technology.html#general

Literacy Support Team. (2009). *Secondary literacy.* Retrieved from http://www.denver.k12.co. us/departments/secondary/tip.htm

Loban, W. (1976). *Language development: Kindergarten through grade twelve.* Urbana, IL: National Council of Teachers of English.

Lord, C. (1988). Enhancing communication in adolescents with autism. *Topics in Language Disorders, 9*(1), 72–81.

Martin, P. (2009). *Figurative language.* Retrieved from http://languagearts.pppst.com/figura tive.html

McDonald, S., & Turkstra, L. (1998). Adolescents with traumatic brain injury: Assessing pragmatic function. *Clinical Linguistics and Phonetics, 12,* 237–248.

Mecham, M. J. (2003). *Utah test of language development–4.* Austin, TX: Pro-Ed.

Merriam-Webster (2009). Retrieved from http://www.merriam-webster.com/dictionary/lever

Mid-Continent Research for Education and Learning (2001). *K–12 Standards.* Retrieved from http://www.mcrel.org/standards-benchmarks/

Miller, B. L. (1988). *Effects of intervention on the ability of students with hearing impairments to write personal narrative stories.* Unpublished master's thesis, Western Michigan University, Kalamazoo.

Miller, C. (2009). *"Kid language" writing rubrics.* Retrieved from http://www.intercom.net/ local/school/sdms/mspap/kidwrit.html

Miller, L., Gillam, R. B., & Peña, E. C. (2001). *Dynamic assessment and intervention: Improving children's narrative skills.* Austin, TX: Pro-Ed.

Miller, L., & Miller, L. C. (1998). *The quick smart profile.* Austin, TX: Smart Alternatives, Inc.

Myklebust, H. (1965). *Development and disorders of written language* (Vol. 1). *Picture story language test.* New York: Grune and Stratton.

Nation, I. S. P. (2008). *Teaching ESL/EFL reading and writing.* New York: Routledge.

Nellen, T. (2001a). *Cyberg English: An internet project.* Retrieved from http://www.tnellen. com/cybereng/

Nellen, T. (2001b). *Literary terms.* Retrieved from http://www.tnellen.com/cybereng/lit_terms/

Nelsen, E., & Rosenbaum, E. (1972). Language patterns within the youth subculture: Development of slang vocabulary. *Merrill-Palmer Quarterly, 18,* 273–285.

Nelson, N. W. (2009). *Language and literacy: Infancy through adolescence.* Boston: Allyn & Bacon.

New York Times Lesson Plan Archive. (2009). Retrieved from http://www.nytimes.com/learn ing/teachers/lessons/archive.html

Nippold, M. (1998). *Later language development: The school-age and adolescent years.* Austin, TX: Pro-Ed.

Nippold, M. (2000). Language development during the adolescent years: Aspects of pragmatics, syntax, and semantics. *Topics in Language Disorders, 20(2),* 15–28.

Nippold, M. (2007). *Later language development: School-age children, adolescents, and young adults.* Austin, TX: Pro-Ed.

Nippold, M., & Haq, F. (1996). Proverb comprehension in youth: The role of concreteness and familiarity. *Journal of Speech and Hearing Research, 39,* 166–176.

Nippold, M., Hegel, S., Sohlberg, M., & Schwarz, I. (1999). Defining abstract entities: Development in pre-adolescents, adolescents, and young adults. *Journal of Speech, Language, and Hearing Research, 42,* 473–481.

Nippold, M., & Undlin, R. (1992). Use and understanding of adverbial conjuncts: A developmental study of adolescents and young adults. *Journal of Speech and Hearing Research, 35,* 18–118.

Norris, J., & Hoffman, P. (1993). *Whole language intervention for school-age children.* San Diego: Singular.

North Carolina Department of Public Instruction. (2001). *English language arts curriculum.* Retrieved from http://www.ncpublicschools.org/curriculum/languagearts/scos/ 2004/ 25grade8

Online Writing Lab. (2007). *The expository essay.* Retrieved from http://owl.english.purdue. edu/owl/resource/685/02#resourcenav

Page, L., & Stewart, S. R. (1985). Story grammar skills in school-age children. *Topics in Language Disorders, 5*(2), 16–30.

Paul, R. (2006). *Language disorders from infancy through adolescence: Assessment and intervention* (3rd ed.). St. Louis: Mosby.

Reed, V., Griffith, F., & Rasmussen, A. (1998). Morphosyntactic structures in the spoken language of older children and adolescents. *Clinical Linguistics and Phonetics, 12,* 205–220.

Schumaker, J., Deshler, D., Alley, G., Warner, M., Clark, F., & Nolan, S. (1982). Error monitoring: A learning strategy for improving adolescent academic performance. In W. M. Cruickshank & J. W. Lerner (Eds.), *Best of ACLD* (Vol. 3). Syracuse, NY: Syracuse University Press.

Scott, C. (1988). Spoken and written syntax. In M. Nippold (Ed.), *Later language development* (pp. 49–96). Boston: College-Hill Press.

Scott, C. (1999). Learning to write. In H. Catts and A. Kamhi (Eds.), *Language and reading disabilities* (pp. 224–258), Boston: Allyn & Bacon.

Scott, C. (2004). Learning to write. In H. Catts & A. Kamhi (Eds.), *Language and reading disabilities* (2nd ed.). Boston: Allyn & Bacon.

Scott, C., & Erwin, D. (1992). Descriptive assessment of writing: Process and products. In W. Secord (Ed.), *Best practices in school speech–language pathology* (Vol. 2, pp. 60–73). San Antonio, TX: Psychological Corp.

Scott, C., & Stokes, S. (1995). Measures of syntax in school-age children and adolescents. *Language, Speech, and Hearing Services in Schools, 26,* 309–317.

Secord, W., & Wiig, E. (1993). *Test of language competence–expanded.* San Antonio, TX: Psychological Corp.

Semel, E., Wiig, E. H., & Secord, W. (1998). San Antonio, TX: Psychological Corp.

Shulten, K., & Harrod, D. B. (2001). Making the personal political: Writing opinion pieces about meaningful issues to kids. *New York Times Online.* Retrieved from http://www.ny times.com/learning/teachers/lessons/20000414friday.html

Silliman, E., & Wilkinson, L. C. (1991). *Communication for learning: Classroom observation and collaboration.* Gaithersburg, MD: Aspen.

Simon, C. (1991). Teaching logical thinking and discussion skills. In C. S. Simon (Ed.), *Communication skills and classroom success* (pp. 219–241). San Diego: College-Hill.

Simon, C. (1998). When big kids don't learn: Contextual modifications and intervention strategies for age 8–18 at-risk students. *Clinical Linguistics and Phonetics, 12,* 249–280.

Sternberg, R., & Powell, J. (1983). Comprehending verbal comprehension. *American Psychologist, 38,* 8788–893.

Sternberg, R. J., Okagaki, L., & Jackson, A. S. (1990). Practical intelligence for success in school. *Educational Leadership, 48*(1), 35–39.

Stewart, S. R. (1985). Development of written language proficiency: Methods for teaching text structure. In C. Simon (Ed.), *Communication skills and classroom success: Therapy methodologies for language-learning disabled students* (pp. 341–361). San Diego: College-Hill.

Sturm, J. M., & Nelson, N. W. (1997). Formal classroom lessons: New perspectives on a familiar discourse event. *Language Speech and Hearing Services in Schools, 28,* 255–273.

Sturmonski, N. (1996). The transition of individuals with learning disabilities into the work setting. *Topics in Language Disorders, 16,* 37–51.

Sutton-Smith, B. (1986). The development of fictional narrative performances. *Topics in Language Disorders, 7*(1), 1–10.

Teague, J. (2009). *Creativity and the Middle School Writer.* Retrieved from http://hti.math.uh.edu/curriculum/units/2000/02/00.02.05.php

Temple University Institute on Disabilities. (2009). Augmentative communication on-line users' group (ACOLUG). Retrieved from http://disabilities.temple.edu/programs/aac/acolug/

thirteen.org (2004). *Workshop: Tapping into multiple intelligences.* Retrieved from http://www.thirteen.org/edonline/concept2class/mi/index.html

Wallach, G. P. (2007). *Language intervention for school age students: Setting goals for academic success.* Philadelphia: Elsevier.

Wallach, G. P., & Miller, L. (1988). *Language intervention and academic success.* Boston: College-Hill.

Warden, M., & Hutchinson, T. (1992). *The writing process test.* Chicago: Riverside.

Weiss, A., Temperly, T., Stierwalt, J., & Robin, D. (1993, November). *Use of cartoons to elicit narrative language samples from children and adolescents with severe TBI.* Paper presented at American Speech–Language–Hearing Association Annual Conference.

West, L. L., Corbey, S., Boyer-Stephens, A., Jones, B., Miller R. J., & Sarkees-Wircenski, M. (1999). *Transition and self-advocacy.* Retrieved from http://www.ldonline.org/ld_indepth/transition/transition_self_advocacy.html

Westby, C. (1998). Communication refinement in school age and adolescence. In W. Haynes & B. Shulman (Eds.), *Communication development: Foundations, processes and clinical applications* (pp. 311–360). Baltimore: Williams and Wilkins.

Wiig, E. (1984). Language disabilities in adolescence: A question of cognitive strategies. *Topics in Language Disorders, 4*(2), 41–58.

Wiig, E., & Secord, W. (1992). *Test of word knowledge.* San Antonio, TX: Psychological Corp.

Wong, B., Butler, D., Ficzere, S., & Kuperis, S. (1996). Teaching low achievers and students with learning disabilities to plan, write, and revise opinion essays. *Journal of Learning Disabilities, 29,* 197–212.

Woodcock, R., McGrew, K. S., & Mather, N. (2001). *Woodcock-Johnson psycho-educational battery–III.* Allen, TX: DLM Teaching Resources.

Work, R., Cline, J., Ehren, B., Keiser, D., & Wujek, C. (1993). Adolescent language programs. *Language, Speech, and Hearing Services in Schools, 24,* 45–53.

Zimbalist, A. (1998). Bigger than life, but not necessarily better: Evaluating images of health in American science. Retrieved from http://www.nytimes.com/learning/teachers/lessons/19981222tuesday.html

Zimbalist, A., & Driggs, L. (2001a). Can scientists discover a limit to discovery? *Daily Lesson Plan.* Retrieved from http://www.nytimes.com/learning/teachers/lessons/19981110tuesday.html

Zimbalist, A., & Driggs, L. (2001b). Photographic memories: Creating stories from photographs: A photojournalism exercise. *Daily Lesson Plan.* Retrieved from http://www.nytimes.com/learning/teachers/lessons/19990402friday.html

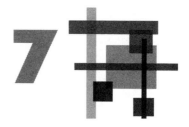

Reading Concepts and Assessment

Reading is the most common area of difficulty for children and adolescents. For many students identified as having disabilities, reading is the first problem area identified by classroom teachers, leading to referral and frequently to the delivery of specialized programs. For students who are more seriously impaired, reading may obstruct independent functioning. Reading difficulties are rarely isolated; they may affect other academic skills, as well as personal, social, and behavioral adjustment. Although reading is discussed in this chapter and in Chapter 8 as a discrete subject area, it should not be perceived as isolated from other language, academic, and life-skills domains.

Students who progress at a slower rate in spite of reading interventions have been referred to by a variety of terms, including difficult to remediate, treatment resisters, nonresponders, and lower responders (Vaughn et al., 2009). A number of special considerations are noteworthy regarding students with reading difficulties.

A key consideration in reading is the achievement gap between students in general and students with disabilities. This gap typically increases during school years and has been referred to as the **Matthew effect**, with reference to the biblical verse from Matthew 25:29, "For everyone who has will be given more and he will have abundance. Whoever does not have, that what he has will be taken from him." Stanovich (1986) further explained that

> one mechanism leading to Matthew effects is the facilitation of further learning by a previously existing knowledge base that is rich and elaborated.... The very children who are reading well and who have good vocabulary for reading more, learn more word meanings, and hence

read better. On the other hand, those who experience reading difficulties will often develop a failure set about reading, have diminished
motivation for success, and will have compounding difficulties over time,
thus increasing the potential gap related to their reading ability. (p. 381)

Figure 7.1 depicts a model of Matthew effects in reading in example B.

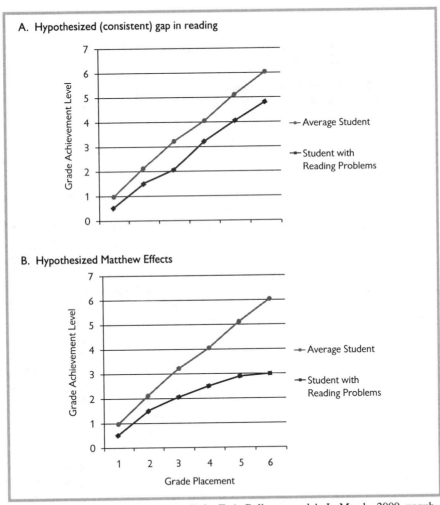

A. Hypothesized (consistent) gap in reading

B. Hypothesized Matthew Effects

Source: From *Models in Education* (p. 1), by E. A. Polloway and A. L. Meade, 2009, unpublished manuscript, Lynchburg College, Lynchburg, VA. Copyright 2009 by E. A. Polloway
and A. L. Meade. Reprinted with permission.

FIGURE 7.1
A Model for Matthew Effects in Reading

To illustrate the above point, Shaywitz (2003) noted that students who are poor readers read only 8,000 words per year, compared to the 1.8 million words read per year by good readers. Bradford, Alberto, Houchins, Shippen, and Flores (2006) indicated that students who have limited opportunities to access reading texts continue to fall farther behind their classmates, "resulting in an increasingly widening performance gap as they progress through school. Thus, reading holds cognitive consequences that limit one's quality of life" (pp. 333–334).

Swanson (2008) reported on 21 observation studies of students with learning disabilities in classrooms and noted four key areas of concern:

1. The students spent limited time engaged in instruction in key areas of reading (e.g., phonics, fluency, comprehension).
2. The grouping structures that were used were often inappropriate and frequently did not include small-group instruction.
3. Comprehension instruction was not only limited but also focused primarily on literal-type questions.
4. Students were not engaged in actual reading of textual material for a sufficient timeframe to make a difference in terms of, for example, fluency.

A particular problem is with reading achievement at the secondary school level. The Alliance for Excellent Education (2005) summarized its work on instructional initiatives in reading for adolescent learners by stating that

> students are less motivated to read in later grades.... The lack of incentive and engagement also explains why even skilled readers and writers often do not progress in reading and academic achievement in middle and high schools. The proportion of students who were not engaged or motivated by their school experiences grows at every grade level and reaches epidemic proportions in high school. (p. 3)

Hock et al. (2009) conducted a comprehensive analysis of the reading skills of adolescent learners in urban schools and concluded that

> in all component areas of reading, struggling readers were found to score statistically lower than their proficient reader counterparts.... While the areas of greatest deficit were fluency and comprehension, many poor readers also demonstrated significant deficits at the word level (order to act, decoding, word recognition, and rate). (p. 34)

Englert et al. (2009) spoke to the difficulties of reading (and writing), particularly in specific subjects and noted that the challenges of content-area curriculum relate to:

■ dense conceptual and technical vocabulary,
■ students' limited background knowledge regarding academic concepts,

- unfamiliar text structures that may include in chapters a hybrid of structures,
- subject area teachers not seeing themselves as reading instructors, and
- literacy tasks required without explicit instruction.

Because reading is one of the keys to school success or failure, it has been researched more thoroughly than any other instructional domain in education. In addition, more assessment instruments and curricular materials have been developed in the area of reading than in any other language domain. To accommodate the significant amount of information available to the practitioner, we are addressing the topic of reading in two chapters. This chapter addresses the concept of reading and reading problems, the development of reading, approaches to assessing reading, and general principles for developing a reading program. Chapter 8 proposes strategies for reading instruction.

▌Reading Challenges

Reading requires students to break down linguistic codes and translate them into meaningful thought as the basis for appropriate response. To achieve true reading, the learner is confronted with numerous tasks. Figure 7.2 provides a schematic of key component areas.

Mathes and Torgesen (1998) identified three major challenges related to successful reading. First, students need to understand and use the alphabetic principle (i.e., written words represent spoken words; words are made of letters; and letters correspond to specific sounds) (see Figure 7.3). A total of 26 letters, or graphemes, are used to map the 44 sounds, or phonemes. Second, students need to transfer spoken language comprehension skills to reading and learn new strategies for comprehending. Third, they need to develop the motivation to read and develop an appreciation of the rewards of successful reading.

When evaluating the reading ability of students with disabilities, teachers must be aware that reading problems can originate in a variety of areas, including

1. prerequisite knowledge and skills for written language decoding,
2. visual skills that enable discrimination of letters and words,
3. phonological skills that allow segmentation and blending of sounds into words,
4. memory necessary for retaining images of specific words and their meanings and the meaning of passages or stories, and
5. specific cognitive abilities related to the ability to comprehend what is read.

Given the intricate nature of reading, and the tremendous inter- and intra-individual differences among students, few easy answers are forthcoming for reading assessment and instruction. When considering not only an individual's skills but also how she attempts to analyze words and comprehend passages, the complexity of the task of reading instruction becomes even more apparent.

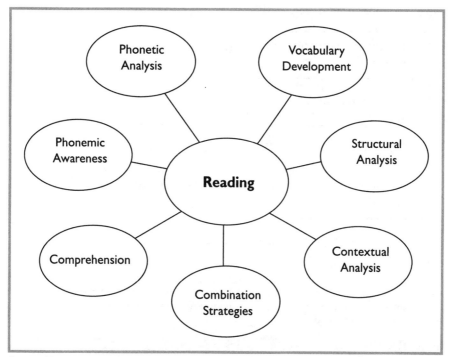

Source: From *Models in Education* (p. 2), by E. A. Polloway and A. L. Meade, 2009, unpublished manuscript, Lynchburg College, Lynchburg, VA. Copyright 2009 by E. A. Polloway and A. L. Meade. Reprinted with permission.

FIGURE 7.2
Key Reading Components

▌Development of Reading

In reality, reading is a progression of abilities and skills that change continually throughout a student's academic career. The progression moves from an effort to learn to read (recognizing letters and words, learning sound–symbol correspondence) to eventually reading to learn (using reading skills as an instrument to acquire content knowledge and skills) (Chall & Snow, 1988). In addition to learning the specific skills involved at each stage of reading development, the teacher must consider how the student, at these various stages, learns to read. In the following discussion, we embed information on specific skills within these stages of reading, acknowledging that these skills are by no means limited to that stage (e.g., comprehension is factor across all stages).

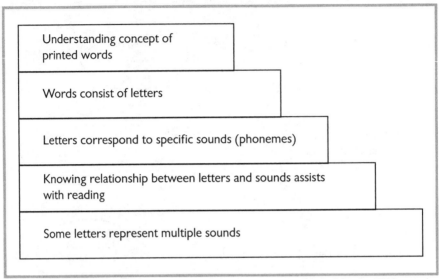

Understanding concept of printed words

Words consist of letters

Letters correspond to specific sounds (phonemes)

Knowing relationship between letters and sounds assists with reading

Some letters represent multiple sounds

Source: From *Models in Education* (p. 3), by E. A. Polloway and A. L. Meade, 2009, unpublished manuscript, Lynchburg College, Lynchburg, VA. Copyright 2009 by E. A. Polloway and A. L. Meade. Reprinted with permission.

FIGURE 7.3
Elements of the Alphabetic Principle

Early Reading

The concept of early reading reflects a stage of emergent literacy and includes all reading-related opportunities prior to, and at the initiation of, formal instruction. Determining a child's readiness to read has been based on a variety of criteria, ranging from specific chronological age (5 or 6 years), to the child's developmental level, to the instructor's readiness to teach the child to read.

Regardless of the definition of readiness to read, to best help children in this stage, teachers should focus on the skills that relate most closely to the act of reading and should evaluate readiness for further instruction on advanced skills on the basis of the children having acquired those skills. Knowledge of letter names and sound–symbol correspondences are critical predictors of later success in reading. In addition, fluency in oral language and an interest in books and other printed matter project a child's ability to succeed in formal reading instruction.

Coyne, Kame'enui, and Simmons (2001) stressed that initial reading instruction should be built on a foundation of three "big ideas." These include phonemic awareness, alphabetic understanding (the link between speech sounds and printed words), and automaticity with the phonological/alphabetic code.

The following summarizes some key early reading skills. This list is intended as an illustration rather than as a comprehensive classroom checklist.

A. Visual discrimination

1. Identifies likenesses and differences in pictures
2. Recognizes various shapes
3. Recognizes sizes of objects
4. Notices specific details in pictures
5. Recognizes primary colors
6. Demonstrates left-to-right directionality by following a line of print
7. Identifies likenesses and differences in letters
8. Identifies number of words in a printed phrase or sentence
9. Identifies likenesses and differences in words
10. Recognizes own name in manuscript form

B. Phonological awareness

1. Locates the source of sounds
2. Discriminates among sounds in the environment
3. Reproduces sounds heard
4. Identifies words that are dissimilar as same or different
5. Reproduces words that are heard
6. Identifies initial sounds as same or different
7. Identifies words with minimal differences as the same or different
8. Identifies final sounds as same or different
9. Identifies simple one-syllable words that rhyme
10. Produces general rhyming words when given a one-syllable stimulus

C. Alphabet recognition

1. Matches letter forms that are similar
2. Identifies letter forms that are dissimilar
3. Selects letters named from an array of choices
4. Identifies individual letters when flashed visually
5. Recognizes the difference between uppercase and lowercase letters
6. Matches uppercase letters with the lowercase counterparts

D. Linguistic considerations

1. Uses substantial and varied oral vocabulary in verbal expression
2. Demonstrates listening skills at age-appropriate levels
3. Demonstrates understanding of letters and words as symbols for oral language
4. Follows directions presented orally
5. Demonstrates auditory attention span at the level appropriate for instruction
6. Recalls and relates simple stories
7. Can sequence past events in logical fashion
8. Predicts outcomes of simple stories or picture sequences
9. Comprehends meaning of common vocabulary words used in early reading programs, and illustrates comprehension by using the words in context

10. Can evaluate subjective variables about stories in terms of characters, emotions displayed, and reality versus fantasy

An important area of research on early reading has been related to the role of phonological and phonemic awareness. Table 7.1 provides benchmarks. Phonological awareness includes the following emphases (Polloway, Patton, & Serna, 2008):

- Discriminating between words and between sounds
- Identifying sounds within words
- Manipulating the sounds that are within words
- Identifying specific phonemes
- Isolating sounds (such as in the initial, medial, and final positions)

Troia (2004) described **phonemic awareness** as

> representing the deepest level of phonological awareness that is most crucial to success in reading and spelling. It facilitates the process by which many beginning readers identify printed words, converting single

TABLE 7.1
Benchmarks of Typical Development in Phonological Awareness

Grade Level	Average Child's Ability
Beginning kindergarten	Can tell whether two words rhyme
	Can generate a rhyme for a simple word (e.g., cat or dot) or can be easily taught to do these tasks
End of kindergarten	Can isolate and pronounce the beginning sound in a word (e.g., /n/ in nose or /f/ in fudge)
	Can blend the sounds in two phoneme words (e.g., boy /b/–/oi/) or me (/m/–/e/)
Midway through first grade	Can isolate and pronounce all the sounds in two- and three-phoneme words
	Can blend the sounds in four-phoneme words containing initial consonant blends
End of first grade	Can isolate and pronounce the sounds in four-phoneme words containing initial blends
	Can blend the sounds in four- and five-phoneme words containing initial and final blends

Source: From *A Basic Guide to Understanding, Assessing, and Teaching Phonological Awareness* (p. 7), by J. Torgesen and P. G. Mathes, 2000, Austin, TX: Pro-Ed. Copyright 2000 by Pro-Ed. Reprinted with permission.

letters and letter strings into their corresponding phonemes and then re-assembling the sounds to pronounce the written word. (p. 1)

Elements of phonemic awareness include syllable awareness, segmentation related to the first sound in a word, onset-rime awareness, onset–rime blending, onset–rime segmentation, blending individual sounds, and segmentation of individual sounds (Bursuck & Damer, 2007).

Burnette (1995) noted the following:

Many children with learning disabilities have deficiencies in their ability to process phonological information. Thus, they do not readily learn how to relate letters of the alphabet to the sounds of language. For all students, the processes of phonological awareness (i.e., the ability to identify and manipulate the sounds of language), including phonemic awareness, must be explicitly taught. (p. 1)

According to Torgesen and Mathes (2000), phonological awareness in general (and a phonemic awareness in particular) is important for three reasons:

1. *Helps children understand the alphabetic principle.* Without at least a beginning level of phonological awareness, children have no way of understanding how the words from their oral language are represented in print. Unless they understand that words have sound segments at the level of the phoneme, they cannot take advantage of an alphabetic script . . . [and will not] understand the rationale for learning individual letter sounds, and the common strategy of sounding out words in beginning reading will not make sense to them.

2. *Helps children notice the regular ways that letters represent sounds in words.* . . . This ability to notice the match between the letters and sounds in words has two potential benefits to children learning to read. First, it reinforces knowledge of individual letter-sound correspondences, and second, it helps in forming strong memories of whole words so they can be accurately recognized when they are encountered in print again.

3. *Makes it possible to generate possibilities for words in context that are only partially sounded out.* Consider a first-grade child who encounters . . . "John's father put his bicycle in the car" and cannot recognize [bicycle]. . . . A relatively early level of phonological awareness supports the ability to search one's mental dictionary for words that begin with similar sounds. Thus, if the child knows the sound represented by the letter "b," he or she can mentally search for words that begin with that sound and fit the context. (p. 4)

Although the majority of research on phonological awareness has been conducted with students with learning disabilities and those at risk for having reading disabilities, it has also been confirmed as important to the reading success of individuals with intellectual disabilities (Saunders & DeFulio, 2007).

Acquisition of Initial Reading Skills

After acquiring many early reading skills, the student can begin what traditionally was defined as "formal reading instruction." For children who have early reading problems, instruction should be directed to helping the child develop a sight vocabulary and acquire basic word analysis skills. Attention to vocabulary and skills acquisition must be augmented by helping children acquire an understanding of reading as the process of gathering meaning from the printed page. The key message from the research on reading problems is that

> from the earliest stages of reading acquisition, children destined to become poor readers have a more difficult time learning to easily recognize words by sight, and when they come to a word they cannot recognize, they are not able to productively use phonetic cues to help decipher it. (Torgesen, 2000, p. 57)

To acquire a **sight vocabulary,** a child must learn words that are used frequently in reading materials and often are phonetically irregular. The Dolch 220-word list, developed in the 1920s, has been the most common source for a listing of high-frequency words. Figure 7.4 presents a revision of the Dolch list. In addition, reading at this stage includes what will become a consistent focus on developing a strong vocabulary in terms of word meanings as well as word recognition.

Word analysis skills refer to the reader's ability to analyze words not easily identified on sight. Three skills that can benefit a reader in this regard are phonetic, structural, and contextual analysis. During the initial stage of reading, a main instructional focus is on phonetic analysis. The remainder of this section describes this area of emphasis.

With **phonetic analysis,** the reader uses sound–symbol correspondences to decode unknown words. The successful reader learns to internalize specific phonetic generalizations, apply them to new words, and then blend the sounds of the phonemes represented by the various graphemes.

The two most common forms of phonetic analysis are (a) analytic phonics and (b) synthetic phonics. Based on the work of the National Reading Panel (NRP), Pullen and Lloyd (2007), defined analytic phonics as "teaching students to analyze letter-sound relations in previously learned words to avoid pronouncing sounds in isolation." They defined synthetic phonics as "teaching students explicitly to convert letters into sounds (phonemes) and then blended sounds to form words" (p. 2).

The National Reading Panel (2000) reported that phonetic analysis programs using systematic phonics instruction make more significant contributions to achievement than do unsystematic phonics instruction or programs that provide no such instruction. The instruction is most effective with children in kindergarten and first

Rank	Word	Rank	Word	Rank	Word	Rank	Word	Rank	Word
1	the	45	when	89	many	133	know	177	don't
2	of	46	who	90	before	134	while	178	does
3	and	47	will	91	must	135	last	179	got
4	to	48	more	92	through	136	might	180	united
5	a	49	no	93	back	137	us	181	left
6	in	50	if	94	years	138	great	182	number
7	that	51	out	95	where	139	old	183	course
8	is	52	so	96	much	140	year	184	war
9	was	53	said	97	your	141	off	185	until
10	he	54	what	98	may	142	come	186	always
11	for	55	up	99	well	143	since	187	away
12	it	56	its	100	down	144	against	188	something
13	with	57	about	101	should	145	go	189	fact
14	as	58	into	102	because	146	came	190	through
15	his	59	than	103	each	147	right	191	water
16	on	60	them	104	just	148	used	192	less
17	be	61	can	105	those	149	take	193	public
18	at	62	only	106	people	150	three	194	put
19	by	63	other	107	Mr.	151	states	195	thing
20	I	64	new	108	how	152	himself	196	almost
21	this	65	some	109	too	153	few	197	hand
22	had	66	could	110	little	154	house	198	enough
23	not	67	time	111	state	155	use	199	far
24	are	68	these	112	good	156	during	200	took
25	but	69	two	113	very	157	without	201	head
26	from	70	may	114	make	158	again	202	yet
27	or	71	then	115	would*	159	place	203	government
28	have	72	do	116	still	160	American	204	system
29	an	73	first	117	own	161	around	205	better
30	they	74	any	118	see	162	however	206	set
31	which	75	my	119	men	163	home	207	told
32	one	76	now	120	work	164	small	208	nothing
33	you	77	such	121	long	165	found	209	night
34	were	78	like	122	get	166	Mrs.	210	end
35	her	79	our	123	here	167	thought	211	why
36	all	80	over	124	between	168	went	212	called
37	she	81	man	125	both	169	say	213	didn't
38	there	82	me	126	life	170	part	214	eyes
39	would*	83	even	127	being	171	once	215	find
40	their	84	most	128	under	172	general	216	going
41	we	85	made	129	never	173	high	217	look
42	him	86	after	130	day	174	upon	218	asked
43	been	87	also	131	same	175	school	219	later
44	has	88	did	132	another	176	every	220	knew

*The word "would" mistakenly appeared twice in the original list.

Source: From "The Dolch List Reexamined," by D. D. Johnson, 1971, *Reading Teacher, 24,* pp. 455–456. Copyright 1971 by Dale D. Johnson and the International Reading Association. Reprinted with permission.

FIGURE 7.4

Basic Sight Vocabulary List

grade, providing basic foundational knowledge. Phonetic analysis instruction ultimately has a positive impact on comprehension as well as decoding.

Although phonetic analysis usually begins during the initial stage of reading, children acquire many specific skills at a later developmental level. For ease of discussion, however, the following is an illustrative list of fundamental phonetic analysis skills; the sequence with which these skills are acquired will vary based on the way that a given program presents the skills.

1. Recognize single initial consonants (e.g., *t, d, b, p*)
2. Recognize short vowel sounds (e.g., *a, e, i*)
3. Recognize variant consonant sounds (e.g., hard and soft *c*, hard and soft *g*)
4. Recognize single final consonant sounds
5. Identify consonant-vowel-consonant (cvc) trigrams (e.g., *fat, bat, bit, tug*)
6. Recognize long vowel sounds and patterns (e.g., *ee* in *seen*, *a-e* in *bake*, *ai* in *pain*)
7. Identify a variety of simple three- and four-letter words (e.g., *ate, bite, pine, bone*)
8. Recognize initial and final consonant blends (e.g., *bl-, br-, st-, tr-; -nd, -id, -ft, -st*)
9. Recognize initial and final consonant digraphs (e.g., *sh-, th-, ch-, sh-; -sh, -th, -ng*)
10. Recognize vowel diphthongs and controlled vowels (e.g., *ou, oi, oy, ar, ir*)
11. Recognize silent consonants (e.g., *k* in *knight*, *g* in *gnome*)
12. Apply basic generalizations to all one-syllable (regular) words, demonstrating knowledge of open and closed syllables (e.g., *go* and *got*, respectively)

Figure 7.5 presents a list of the most regular sound–letter relationships. Mastery of both common and regular phonetic generalizations opens up a new world of words to the reader. For a child with reading disabilities, these represent a bridge to subsequent developmental stages.

Broad Skill Acquisition

After students reach approximately the second-grade reading level, they are able to learn new words and process messages more quickly. Chall's (1983) description of reading development at this stage as "confirmation, fluency, ungluing from print" provides a flavor of this period. When they achieve rapid reading and a broader base of skills, students have reached a level of automatic decoding (Snider, 1989).

Achieving automaticity is critical to the development of **fluency** in reading. Fluency bridges the gap between word recognition and comprehension as students not only read more automatically in terms of speed and accuracy but also with expression.

Structural analysis, a word analysis tool that focuses on word form, basically requires students to learn the parts of a word that serve as meaning or pronunciation units. Identifying morphemes within words is an essential task in structural analysis, because it makes the unit easier to recognize and understand. Structural analysis subsumes a variety of skills, including the following:

1. Identify common suffixes or inflectional endings for verbs (e.g., *-ing, -ed, -s, -es*)

a	as in fat	g	as in goat	v	
m		l		e	
t		h		u-e	as in use
s		u		p	
i	as in sit	c	as in cat	w	"woo" as in well
f		b		j	
a-e	as in cake	n		i-e	as in pipe
d		k		y	"yee" as in yuk
r		o-e	as in pole	z	
ch	as in chip	ou	as in cloud	kn	as in know
ea	beat	oy	toy	oa	boat
ee	need	ph	phone	oi	boil
er	fern	qu	quick	ai	maid
ay	hay	sh	shop	ar	car
igh	high	th	thank	au	haul
ew	shrewd	ir	first	aw	lawn

Source: From "Thirty Years of NICHD Research: What We Now Know about How Children Learn to Read," by the Center for the Future of Teaching and Learning, 1996, *Effective School Practices, 15*(3), p. 40. Copyright 1996 by the Association for Direct Instruction. Reprinted with permission.

FIGURE 7.5

The 48 Most Regular Sound–Letter Relationships

2. Identify common plural forms for nouns (e.g., *-s, -es, -ies*)
3. Identify common suffixes that indicate comparatives or superlatives (e.g., -er, -est) or specific actions or states of being (e.g., *-ful, -ness, -tion*) (See Table 7.2 for further examples)
4. Identify common prefix forms (e.g., *re-, dis-, mis-, pre-*) (see Table 7.2)
5. Find and identify root words when combined with affixes
6. Recognize and demonstrate understanding of logical compound words (e.g., *baseball, fireplace, cowbell, shoelace*) (see Figure 7.6 for further examples)
7. Recognize and demonstrate understanding of more obscure or illogical compound words (e.g., *butterfly, breakfast*)

TABLE 7.2
Common Suffixes and Prefixes

Suffix	Meaning	Examples
-able	capable of being	trainable, breakable
-ance	state of being	attendance, guidance
-ant	one who	servant, informant
-ent	being, one who	excellent, dependent
-er	relating to, like	painter, baker
-ful	full of	careful, wonderful
-fy	to make	purify, simplify
-ish	like	childish, yellowish
-ist	one who	terrorist, machinist
-ive	relating to	attractive, excessive
-less	unable to, without	harmless, homeless
-ly	in a way	slowly, simply
-ment	state of being	judgment, payment
-ness	state of being	goodness, weakness
-ous	full of	joyous, dangerous
-tion	act, state of being	action, election
-ward	turning to	eastward, homeward

Prefix	Meaning	Examples
anti-	against	antiwar, antifreeze
co-	with, together with	coworker, coeducation
de-	down, from, away	deflate, detour
dis-	opposite	dislike, discontinue
en-	in, into, make	enforce, endanger
ex-	former, from	ex-president, express
im-	not, in	imperfect, impress
in-	not, into	insane, inland
inter-	between	interstate, interview
ir-	not, into	irregular, irresponsible
mis-	wrong	mistake, misplace
non-	not	nonsmoker, nonsense
pre-	before	prefix, preview
pro-	for, in front of	pro-American, pronoun
re-	back, again	repay, review
semi-	half, partly	semicircle, semisweet
sub-	under, less than	subway, substandard
super-	over, above	supernatural, superhighway
trans-	beyond, across	transplant, transcontinental
un-	not	unhappy, unlock

8. Recognize pronoun-verb contracted forms or words and substitute the equivalents (e.g., *I'll, he's, I've, they've*) (Figure 7.7 gives a partial listing)
9. Recognize negative contracted forms of words and substitute the equivalents (e.g., didn't, won't, can't, haven't)
10. Identify the number of syllables in a spoken word
11. Divide and decode unknown words into syllables, using phonetic and related structural analysis generalizations

inside	bookcase	something	wherever	snowball
outside	workbook	sometime	become	cowboy
indoors	cookbook	somewhere	maybe	cowgirl
outdoors	handbag	anyone	weekday	raincoat
upstairs	necktie	anywhere	without	rainbow
downstairs	dustpan	anytime	within	railroad
doorbell	popcorn	anybody	forgot	mailman
bedroom	rowboat	anything	himself	mailbox
bathroom	sailboat	nobody	herself	milkman
hallway	somewhat	everyone	myself	sunshine
downtown	sometimes	everywhere	yourself	sunset
homework	somehow	everything	themselves	windmill
notebook	someone	everybody	basketball	weekend
classroom	somebody	whenever	football	

Source: From: *Campbell County (VA) Reading Skills Sequence,* edited by C. H. Polloway, undated. Rustburg, VA: unpublished manuscript. Copyright by C. H. Polloway. Reprinted with permission.

FIGURE 7.6
Partial Listing of Compound Words

Contextual analysis bridges word recognition and comprehension. The reader uses syntactic and semantic cues to anticipate words that are likely to appear in a given phrase, sentence, or story. Used with other word analysis skills, it promotes a smooth, effective reading style by minimizing interference with the process of understanding. For beginning readers, contextual analysis may mean using picture cues that visualize the action in a sentence or short story. At more advanced levels, it is

I've	doesn't	they're
we've	can't	we're
you've	hasn't	you've
they've	hadn't	I'm
I'll	didn't	
they'll	wouldn't	it's
we'll	couldn't	who's
you'll	shouldn't	that's
he'll	weren't	he's
she'll	isn't	she's
	aren't	let's
I'd	don't	here's
we'd	haven't	there's
you'd	hasn't	what's
they'd	wasn't	
he'd	won't	
she'd	mustn't	

Source: From: *Campbell County (VA) Reading Skills Sequence,* edited by C. H. Polloway, undated. Rustburg, VA: unpublished manuscript. Copyright by C. H. Polloway. Reprinted with permission.

FIGURE 7.7
Commonly Used Contractions

based primarily on context cues in the semantic and syntactic features of a written passage. Although the use of context cues can enhance the reading of mature readers, Stanovich and Stanovich (1995) encouraged caution emphasizing it with less skilled readers, who achieve more success from relying on sound cues (i.e., phonetic analysis) than from using the more conceptually challenging task of contextual analysis.

Contextual analysis skills develop in the following progression:

1. Complete an unfinished oral sentence meaningfully
2. Supply a meaningful missing word in a sentence when given a picture cue
3. Provide a meaningful missing word in a sentence when given an initial consonant cue
4. Supply a meaningful missing word in a sentence
5. Arrange scrambled words into a meaningful sentence
6. Decode an unknown word in a sentence using phonics skills in conjunction with context cues
7. Select the correct dictionary definition of a word with multiple meanings based on the context in which the word is used in a sentence
8. Define an unknown word from the context of a sentence or paragraph

Advanced Reading

By about the fourth-grade level, students increasingly read voluntarily and for pleasure. At this stage, students stop "learning to read" and shift to "reading to learn" (Snider, 1989); hence, Chall (1983, p. 20) referred to this period as "reading for learning the new." If a child has a history of reading problems, reading instruction likely will include attention to the continued development of word analysis skills. The most significant concern, however, will be for comprehension—that is, true reading, or the reception of language-based information from visual symbols.

Students at this stage face new challenges in their reading, and this period is associated with a slump in the reading developmental patterns of many students. Chall and Snow (1988) pointed out that the reading materials for students at this age are more abstract and complex, and vocabulary is more specialized. They suggested that unless the texts selected are "user-friendly" (clearly structured, coherent, and appropriate for the audience), they will give rise to problems beyond superficial readability concerns (as measured by formulas).

During the advanced reading stage, **comprehension** clearly becomes the emphasis of educational efforts. Three key elements that influence reading comprehension are (a) student variables (prior knowledge, background, skill level, motivation), (b) the content actually to be read (vocabulary level, content, concepts), and (c) the reading process to be followed (setting purpose, expectations, rate of reading).

Idol (1997, p. 112) defined three types of comprehension:

1. *Text-explicit*: text-dependent, in that the answer is stated explicitly in the text (i.e., passage or picture).

2. *Text-implicit*: implied within the text (or pictures); this type of information is based upon two or more nonexplicitly connected details of the passage or picture.
3. *Script implicit*: requires integration of prior knowledge about the subject being read with one or more details from the passage or picture.

The higher level skill of reading comprehension has led to analyses of key contributors to successful comprehension. One model holds that reading comprehension can be evaluated as a function of decoding × listening comprehension, given that these two skills make a significant contribution to the variability of readers in text comprehension (see Georgiou, Das, & Hayward, 2009, for an analysis).

The following are specific comprehension skills important in reading development. Many of these skills, of course, are also important in earlier phases of reading development.

1. Identify specific details after oral and silent reading of a passage
2. Recognize and synthesize the central idea of a given passage
3. Relate the sequence of events within a story
4. Demonstrate the ability to draw conclusions and inferences and predict outcomes based on the information implicit in a passage
5. Follow written directions of increasing complexity
6. Apply multiple meanings to words
7. Recognize absurdities in printed material
8. Ascertain cause-and-effect relationships within passages
9. Compare and contrast specific features within or between passages and stories
10. Distinguish among personal biases, fiction, and factual information
11. Interpret or analyze the underlying themes of material read
12. Create fresh insights or new ideas based on what has been read

The specific aspects of comprehension are virtually boundless, ranging from simple factual recall of explicitly stated information to the interpretive skills involved in literary criticism. Nevertheless, aspects of comprehension can be defined and approached instructionally (Gersten & Carnine, 1988). This is significant, because the importance of comprehension, particularly in this stage, cannot be overstated.

Refined Contextual Reading and Life Applications

During this stage, students are encouraged to read independently. The emphasis is on further developing comprehension as well as increasing the rate of reading, enhancing the student's ability to read for a variety of purposes, and helping the student develop more mature study skills. The interrelationship between reading and various content areas (e.g., mathematics, government, science, and history), which builds throughout the school experience, reaches its peak during this stage.

When a student masters the skills that develop at this stage, she will be able to do the following:

1. Adjust the reading rate to correspond to purpose (e.g., scanning, skimming, slow rereading)
2. Study the material through selective "passes" through content
3. Sustain sufficient attention to specific reading tasks to accomplish the purpose
4. Use maps, charts, graphs, and diagrams to enhance comprehension
5. Use a book's table of contents and index
6. Interpret dictionary word presentations in terms of derivations, syllabication, accents, and parts of speech
7. Use encyclopedias and other reference books for suitable purposes
8. Identify and use various sections of newspapers
9. Demonstrate the ability to use library facilities
10. Write an accurate summary of the material read
11. Organize the main ideas and supporting details into an outline form after reading a passage or story
12. Compare and contrast major points from textual material

∎Reading Assessment

Assessment of a student's reading abilities guides instructional planning and delivery. Because no other curricular area can boast the number and variety of assessment tools that have been developed for reading, teachers can draw on a wealth of sources to plan instructional programs. The complexity of the reading process renders any single measure of reading limited in providing a comprehensive view of an individual's skill. Any judgments derived from assessment activities require continuous, systematic, and ongoing revision as teaching progresses.

A primary concern in assessment is the ongoing use of performance data as teachers monitor students' progress and make determinations about their specific instructional needs. Complementing these data with information about strengths and interests will provide a strong foundation for instructional planning (NJCLD, 2008). Fuchs and Fuchs (2005) noted that

> professional pedagogy demands ongoing monitoring of student progress ... respective of instructional program, so that non-responders can be identified promptly for more tailored attention.

Further, the National Joint Committee on Learning Disabilities (2008)) noted that assessment should be

> designed to gather multiple sources of qualitative and quantitative information, including measures that reflect student background knowledge, readability of textbooks used in different subject areas, classroom

expectations, information about the use of literacy skills outside the
school setting, and the need for in the level of ability to use assistive
technology. (p. 214)

[Further, the information should be] integrated so that data interpretation results in a clear profile of the student's strengths and weaknesses, describes the literacy needs of the student, and provide specific
recommendations that are tied to instruction, learning/behavioral supports, and transition planning. (p. 42)

Before instruction can begin, teachers have to determine their students' approx-
imate levels of reading and identify their specific reading strengths and weaknesses.
With knowledge of their students' reading levels, teachers have a "ballpark" figure
with which to make preliminary decisions about grouping, scheduling, and selecting
educational materials. Awareness of reading levels is especially important for teachers
who are about to begin work with a new class or who need a general score to serve
as a measure for pre/post evaluation. Although practitioners often use the term "reading level" with some confidence, different tests may produce widely variant measures
for an individual child.

After establishing a general sense of reading levels, teachers have to assess the
specific needs of each child so they can devise teaching strategies. Formal tests can
be used to determine the level of reading, whereas informal approaches are typically
more useful for assessing individual strengths and weaknesses.

Formal Tests

Formal, or standardized, tests are most often used to provide quantitative information
comparing the performance of a student to others in the norm group (determined, for
example, by age, grade, and gender). Scores are usually reported in the form of test
quotients, percentiles, and age or grade equivalents. These tests are especially useful
early in an assessment procedure when little is known of a student's abilities, for these
tests can identify not only reading level but also problem areas in which information
assessment can begin. The ability to compare a student to her age and grade peers is
also helpful in making eligibility and placement decisions and fulfilling related administrative mandates. In addition, formal instruments

- provide a capsule picture of a student's overall levels of functioning;
- require no time for teacher construction;
- are objective and have validity and reliability information available;
- give direction to teachers, who may be unsure of informal assessment strategies;
- may be available in different forms, allowing for reliable evaluations of
progress in a test-teach-test sequence; and
- meet certain legal requirements that may govern eligibility for special education purposes.

Formal instruments may also have some distinct limitations and disadvantages, including the propensity for teachers to misuse or overgeneralize their results. Many of these potential disadvantages reflect test abuse rather than use per se. In addition, formal instruments

- provide results that may lack direct relevance for instructional decisions,
- report results that may be influenced by day-to-day fluctuations and thus may be distorted,
- call for rigid administration procedures that may cloud the tester's ability to gain insight into the learners' problems,
- require large time commitments for training and/or administration, and
- may be invalid if used with students who are not represented within the standardization sample.

The numerous formal instruments that assess reading abilities can be divided into two groups: (a) survey (general evaluative) instruments and (b) diagnostic instruments. Survey tests serve mainly to establish estimated levels of performance. Because the tests are used to screen new students and to make global, long-term evaluations of their progress, they have value mainly when they are used for initial referrals and annual reviews. Diagnostic tests provide teachers with general information, such as how well students do with material at different grade levels, but their primary purpose is to supply relevant information for planning educational programs. Diagnostic tests offer a more comprehensive analysis of specific abilities and disabilities than do survey tests, and thus they yield more precise data for determining how a child attempts to read. The two groups are not dichotomous, and many of the tests can serve dual purposes. Several examples are described next.

Wide Range Achievement Test (WRAT-4; Wilkinson & Robertson, 2006)

The WRAT-4, a survey achievement test widely used by educators, provides an estimate of a child's spelling, word recognition, and arithmetic skills. The spelling subtest begins with a series of marks for nonreaders to copy. The child is then asked to spell her name and an additional set of words. The reading subtest targets letter and word recognition, requiring the examinee to name and match letters and to read a list of 100 words. The test does not assess reading comprehension.

Woodcock Reading Mastery Test—Revised—Normative Update (WRMT-RNU; Woodcock, 1998)

The WRMT-RNU provides six subtests (Salvia & Ysseldyke, 2001). The subtests, which are appropriate for individuals from kindergarten through adulthood, include letter and word identification, word attack, word comprehension, passage comprehension, and a measure of reading readiness. The letter identification subtest begins with Roman letters and moves on to cursive and more elaborate types of letters. The word attack subtest can be paired with the word identification subtest to analyze phonetic difficulties. The word comprehension subtest is actually a test of word analogies: It requires the test taker to provide a word that matches the relationship demonstrated by the stimulus words. The passage comprehension subtest uses a cloze procedure with phrases and pictures at the lower levels and more complex passages at higher levels.

Gray Oral Reading Test (4th edition; GORT-4; Wiederholt & Bryant, 2001)

The Gray Oral is a classic test of reading skills that has been revised and renormed twice. It consists of reading passages ranging from preprimer through college levels of difficulty. The test is administered individually and can be used to measure oral reading fluency and to identify specific oral reading difficulties. Comprehension is measured by questions accompanying each passage. Relatively easy to administer, the Gray Oral serves as a transitional evaluation tool because it can be used as both a survey test and a diagnostic test. As the name indicates, the test does not have a silent reading component.

Test of Phonological Awareness (2nd edition; Plus; TOPA-2+; Torgesen & Bryant, 2004)

The TOPA is intended to measure young children's awareness of individual sounds in specific words. The test assumes that children who are not sensitive to the phonological structure of words will have more difficulty learning to read than children who are sensitive to phonological structure. The kindergarten version of the TOPA is intended to screen for kindergarten children who can benefit from phonological awareness activities as a basis for reading instruction. An early elementary version of the test is intended to assess difficulties in reading that may be present in first and second graders.

Lindamood Auditory Conceptualization Test (3rd edition LAC-3; Lindamood & Lindamood, 2004)

The LAC Test is not a formal instrument but rather is a criterion-referenced assessment instrument. The test measures the individual's ability to discriminate one speech sound or phoneme from another and to segment the spoken word into its component phonemic units. Its intent is to identify students who will be at risk for reading and spelling as a result of poor phoneme-grapheme correspondence ability. Its primary intent is to measure the ability to distinguish and manipulate sounds as a basis for success in reading and spelling.

Informal Assessment

Informal tools and teacher evaluation of the results can provide information on how a child approaches a reading task, her specific reading strengths and weaknesses, other intra-individual variables, and interaction between the reader and the text. Thus, informal assessment can assist the teacher in determining how a student learns to read. Informal assessment is fundamental to daily, ongoing assessment.

The major advantage of informal assessment should be the direct application of results to teaching programs. By incorporating informal assessment tools into the teaching program and monitoring student responses daily, teachers can achieve reliable measurements that can reveal specific patterns of fluctuation in performance. The purpose of assessing comprehension is to

> help us make informed decisions regarding the level of materials our students can handle. But knowing what they can read is only the first step. We also need to know how they read so we can build on strong strategies and introduce new ones. Assessment thus both alerts us to the ways in which our students are capable comprehenders and strategy users, and helps us to see their instructional needs. (Blachowicz & Ogle, 2001, p. 62)

Other advantages of informal assessment include the following:

- Instruments can be readministered frequently, easily, and quickly.
- Information gathered will often be directly relevant to instruction.
- The validity of criterion-referenced measures can be established relatively easily.
- The instruments can be used to further explore weak areas revealed through diagnostic tests.
- The process of informal assessment is inexpensive in comparison to formal procedures.
- Assessment is integrated with instruction, minimizing the amount of time spent away from teaching.

Limitations or disadvantages of informal tools may include the following:

- The instruments can be highly specific and thus limited in scope.
- Developing the tests requires substantial teacher time and effort.
- Subjectivity is often present in the choice and presentation of items and in scoring.
- Lack of awareness of the reading skills hierarchy can result in a distorted diagnosis and misguided instruction.
- An orientation to isolated skills may take precedence over general considerations.

Several informal assessment approaches that may help teachers collect data with direct relevance to reading instruction are described next.

Informal Reading Inventory (IRI)

IRIs represent a prototypical model for informal assessment that uses a series of graded reading paragraphs to generate specific diagnostic information. The inventories generally consist of 50- to 200-word passages from outdated basal readers. Although they are nonstandardized tools, IRIs are typically developed systematically following a set construction pattern. They can be used to determine reading competence levels and to highlight specific skill deficiencies and trends.

Inventories for word recognition are typically compiled from the vocabularies used in diverse instructional materials. Administration of the test continues with increasingly more difficult words on the lists until the student misses 25% of the words. Commonly, 20–30 words are included within a grade list (Polloway et al., 2008).

Figure 7.8 presents a sample IRI score sheet based on a passage from an outdated basal series. Notations on the score sheet indicate the source of the oral reading passage (book/level/page), the number of words it contains, an error deduction multiplier to use in computing the overall percent of errors, the passage itself, comprehension questions, and a scoring summary section. A system for designating

---

Come With Me (Primer Level)

Source: page 92   Passage Length: 55 words   Error Multiplier: 1.82

Oral Reading Passage

"Here, Nancy," said Mother. "This money is for the paper. The paper boy will stop for it." Nancy put the money in her book. "I will sit here," she said. "I have a new book to read. The paper boy can see me here." Mother went down the street to the store.

Type	Comprehension Questions
detail	1. Why did Mother give some money to Nancy? (to pay for the paper)
vocabulary	2. What is a paper boy? (boy who delivers papers)
main idea	3. Why couldn't Mother pay the paper boy herself? (she was going down the street to the store)
detail	4. Where did Nancy put the money? (in her book)
inference	5. What makes you think Nancy and her family like to read? (they get the paper, and Nancy has a new book to read)

Oral Recording	# of Errors	Types of Questions	Correct/Total
Omissions	_____	Main Idea	_____
Substitutions	_____	Vocabulary	_____
Inversions	_____	Inference	_____
Miscalling	_____	Detail	_____
Teacher Assistance	_____		
		Total	_____
Total	_____		

Source: Adapted from *Informal Reading Inventory,* undated, by the McGuffey Reading Center, unpublished manuscript, University of Virginia, Charlottesville, VA.

FIGURE 7.8

Sample IRI Score Sheet

specific errors is provided in Figure 7.9. Similar passages can be selected for other grade levels and for silent reading exercises as well. After using this tool, the teacher can determine error trends as related to sequence of skills and reading level, as discussed next.

Four reading levels are commonly computed from an IRI and suggest general considerations that can subsequently guide the selection of appropriate reading materials. With the following discussion, the percentage figures reflect, respectively, appropriate levels of accuracy (from Karlin, 1991) for word recognition, literal comprehension, inferential comprehension, and vocabulary.

1. The *independent level* indicates fluent reading, accurate recall, and thus high comprehension. This level represents the difficulty level of materials that would be appropriate for student-directed free-reading periods. (99%+, 90–100%, 90–100%, 100%)

2. The *instructional level* implies that passages present some difficulty but that students can be taught to handle them and will profit from reading information at this level. (90–95%, 80–90%, 70–80%, 90%)

3. The *frustration level* represents the reading level at which fluency breaks down, the child becomes dismayed by the difficulty of the task, and comprehension suffers dramatically. (<90%, <70%, <60%, <80%)

---

1. <u>Mispronunciations:</u> Write the child's pronunciation above the word.
   brought
   (e.g., They bought the bread at the store.)

2. <u>Assistance:</u> Write the letter A above each word pronounced for the child after allowing 5 seconds to elapse.
   A
   (e.g., Hawkeye performed the delicate operation.)

3. <u>Omissions:</u> Circle each word or portion of word that the student omits.
   (e.g., After the race, the runner was winded.)

4. <u>Letter or Word Inversions:</u> Use the traditional typographical mark to indicate this type of error.
   (e.g., The ball seemed to fly forever—it was a homerun!)

5. <u>Self-correction:</u> Write the letter C above the word if the student corrects an error on his or her own.
   C
   arose
   (e.g., They were late, but they arrived just in time to ride the train.)

6. <u>Insertions:</u> Use a caret to indicate additions inserted by the reader.
   old
   (e.g., She was afraid to go into the ᴧhaunted house.)

7. <u>Hesitations and Repetitions:</u> Though not errors, these can be noted by a check mark and a wavy line, respectively.
   ✓
   (e.g., The dog scratched and itched until they put on his flea collar.)

FIGURE 7.9

Oral Reading Scoring Systems

4. The *capacity level* indicates the comprehension to expect from each student. It is based on the student's responses to material presented orally, and thus is viewed more accurately as a listening comprehension measure. Therefore, it provides a somewhat crude guide in the assessment of reading disability as compared to measures of oral receptive skills. (n/a, 80–90%, 70–80%, 90%)

Curriculum-Based Assessment

Curriculum-based assessment (CBA), or curriculum-based measurement (CBM), is a systematic approach to evaluation based on the use of tools that are typically constructed informally and are tied to the actual curriculum as the criterion standard. CBA provides a measure of a student's specific skills as well as information relative to overall skill competency levels. The instrument's direct connection to the curriculum, of course, greatly facilitates the formulation of goals and objectives in reading (and other areas).

Because CBA encourages reliance on methods keyed to the curriculum and direct, frequently collected measures and is to be administered by classroom teachers, it is also more ecologically valid than norm-referenced testing (Fuchs & Fuchs, 1986). Curriculum-based measures can be developed through systematic analysis of the reading curriculum, selection of specific items, and construction of assessment formats (e.g., questions, cloze activities, worksheets).

Using Assessment Data

With the variety of tools and techniques available for evaluating reading, the skilled teacher can develop detailed profiles of the difficulties that students face. Naturally, evaluative judgments should emerge from a series of observations rather than from a single test administration. The underlying purpose is to identify a reader's specific problems, hypothesize reasons for the difficulties, and then derive implications that can guide instructional planning.

Among the possible problems that may be detected with assessment are poor attention to words, word details, or sentences; poor recognition of high-frequency words; inability to apply phonetic analysis skills for which competence has been demonstrated in drill exercises; failure to use contextual analysis as indicated by comparable (or superior) levels of accuracy for words presented in isolation versus those encountered in context; overattention to word analysis that may interfere with meaning cues and comprehension; and significant deviations between recall in oral reading and recall in silent reading.

Figure 7.10 presents a useful form for summarizing these kinds of diagnostic data. Again, however, assessment must not simply result in reducing the interactive reading process to the reader's isolated skills but, rather, should place these data within the context of the reading act.

Selected Teaching Strategies

Numerous instructional strategies can be used to support an effective reading program, the following of which are some of the most important. This discussion serves as a transition to Chapter 8.

A. Objective:

Given a visually presented list of unknown polysyllabic words in context, the child will correctly pronounce the unknown words with 90% accuracy by employing syllabication as a word analysis skill.

B. Prerequisite skills:

1. Possession of basic sight vocabulary (e.g. Dolch lists)
2. Ability to produce sounds of consonants, consonant blends, and consonant digraphs
3. Ability to produce sounds of long, short, and variant vowels (*r*-controlled and dipthongs)
4. Ability to predict vowel sounds in open and closed syllables

C. Component skills:

1. Given a list of orally presented polysyllabic words, the child will orally identify with 100% accuracy the number of syllables each word contains.
2. Given a list of orally presented polysyllabic words, the child will orally divide the words into syllables with 100% accuracy.
3. Given a visually presented list of unknown polysyllabic words, the child will determine the number of syllables each word contains with 100% accuracy by counting the vowels that will be heard.
4. Given a list of visually presented unknown two-syllable words containing the *vc/cv* pattern, the child will correctly divide and phonetically pronounce each word with 90% accuracy.
5. Given a list of visually presented unknown three- and four-syllable words containing only the *vc/cv* pattern, the child will correctly divide and phonetically pronounce each word with 90% accuracy.
6. Given a list of visually presented unknown two-syllable words containing the *v/cv* pattern, the child will correctly divide and phonetically pronounce each word with 90% accuracy.
7. Given a list of visually presented unknown three- or four-syllable words containing only the *v/cv* pattern, the child will correctly divide and phonetically pronounce each word with 90% accuracy.
8. Given a list of visually presented unknown polysyllabic words containing the *vc/cv* pattern and the *v/cv* pattern, the child will correctly divide and phonetically pronounce each word with 90% accuracy.
9. Given a list of visually presented unknown polysyllabic words containing the *vcccv* or the *vccccv* pattern, the child will correctly divide and phonetically pronounce each word with 90% accuracy.
10. Given a list of visually presented unknown words ending with -le, the child will correctly divide and phonetically pronounce each word with 90% accuracy.
11. Given a list of visually presented unknown polysyllabic words, the child will correctly divide and phonetically pronounce each word with 90% accuracy.
12. Given a visually presented passage containing unknown polysyllabic words in context, the child will correctly pronounce the unknown words with 90% accuracy.

FIGURE 7.10

Task Analysis of Syllabication

Direct Instruction of Critical Skills

A key instructional strategy for teaching reading skills, and particularly decoding skills, is **direct instruction.** This is a systematic, explicit approach to teaching that is aimed at clear outcomes. The teacher is directly responsible for the instructional activities, but active student engagement is essential.

Instruction begins by gaining students' attention, followed by precise sequencing of content. Teachers monitor students' responses and provide corrective feedback. Most important, direct instruction has to be intensive and explicit. By requiring higher rates of appropriate responses and by carefully matching instruction to student ability and skill level, teachers are able to provide instruction consistent with student needs.

Learning Stages

In developing an instructional strategy, the first concern is to consider the stage of learning indicated by the instructional objective to be taught. The stages of learning are acquisition, proficiency, generalization, and maintenance. Each stage dictates specific demands for supervision, feedback, and reinforcement from the teacher. Careful attention to effective procedures should result in instruction that is systematic and explicit.

Acquisition Learning   First, the child is exposed to previously unlearned material. For acquisition learning to take place, several key elements must be present:

1. The teacher must take an active role by modeling or demonstrating the appropriate skill. Techniques might include, for example, the teacher reciting a reading or rhyming words from word families.
2. The instruction must be repetitive and, when appropriate, varied. The most effective way to teach a new vocabulary word, for example, is to present it frequently in a variety of modes and relate it to natural settings. Tying it to its natural usage provides a context for the word and associates the word with its meaning.
3. Acquisition learning requires feedback and continuous reinforcement. Children will grasp a new skill or concept faster when practice is followed by feedback.

Proficiency Learning   At the proficiency stage, the student has learned the skill and now must develop mastery. At this point, the student becomes adept at exhibiting the newly acquired skill and may demonstrate this mastery through increases in rate or accuracy. To maximize both teaching efficiency and learner independence, the shift from acquisition learning to proficiency learning should be timed carefully, based on the teacher's verification that initial learning has taken place (e.g., through observation of the student's correct verbal responses to teacher questions).

At the proficiency stage, the teacher's role is based more on providing opportunities for independent drill and practice. To determine when students are ready for proficiency activities, the teacher can test them with supervised drills; those who succeed in the drills are ready for independent practice. For example, after initial instruction on consonant blends, the teacher can closely observe how a student locates and pronounces the blends in a series of words. If the student completes this task accurately, the teacher can give the student specific practice assignments.

Independent completion of tasks is the key to successful fluency learning. Activities that can be used at the proficiency stage of learning include peer tutoring, board work, group projects, work in individual seatwork folders, instructional games, interest centers, programmed materials, short compositions on current topics of interest, working with partners, silent reading assignments, tutoring other students, drill-and-practice software programs, and workbook assignments.

Generalization Learning   The transfer of skills and concepts to other situations is termed **generalization**. Teachers often overlook the critical nature of this stage of learning, basing their evaluation of students primarily on classroom responses. Only when previous skills are applied to new settings, however, can a program be considered truly effective. Providing for generalization is the option to a "train and hope" philosophy (Stokes & Baer, 1977).

To assure generalization, teachers should train for generalization across settings, persons, time, skills and domains, and reinforcers. Generalization across settings is facilitated by using various situations and conditions for learning. For example, if a child has been practicing specific words in one resource setting, the teacher should make sure that she uses those words and reinforces them in various classroom writing assignments.

Generalization across persons is important, because different people impose different conditions on the learner. One way to facilitate this type of generalization is to include parents in the reading program (e.g., through reading with their children at home).

Generalization over time can be assessed through ongoing evaluation of response maintenance over designated intervals and involves students' developing the ability to use a learned skill throughout the day. To facilitate this type of generalization, reading instruction, for instance, can occasionally be scheduled for different times of the day, simulating real-life situations.

A key concern is for the generalization of skills and strategies in reading. The NJCLD (2008) noted that

> it is often necessary to re-teach skills and strategies and to provide guided practice in their functional application of higher and higher levels of complexity. For struggling learners, particularly those with learning disabilities, it is not sufficient to simply teach learning strategies; continued support for the use and generalization of strategies is required for real change to occur. (p. 215)

Generalization across skills and domains involves applying skills both within and across domains of language. Therefore, opportunities to integrate speaking, reading, and writing help to emphasize the interrelationships among language skills.

Maintenance Learning The ability to retain what has been learned over time, termed **maintenance**, takes learners from acquisition/proficiency to the establishment of a fact, concept, or skill in their response repertoires. The maintenance stage may best be viewed as a combination of remembering and refining learned material.

The maintenance stage has elements of both proficiency and generalization in that it stresses the need for continued mastery of a skill so it can be used or applied in the future.

Recommendations for Teachers

Following are considerations related to effective instructional programs.

Emphasize Success

A blend of challenge and success is productive for most learners. If students have failed in the past, teachers should emphasize success by choosing activities that are well within the students' abilities, by beginning instruction with success experiences, and by concluding individual lessons with a review of skills that the child has learned. Children are motivated if they are successful. Techniques such as graphing can illustrate skills acquisition and serve as a consistent reminder of progress for the student.

Provide Incentive

Various tools can be used to provide incentive to students who are not motivated to read or who find reading uninteresting or perhaps even repulsive. Some students respond to social recognition for achievement in the form of praise, achievement certificates, or notes to parents. Other students benefit from more extrinsically oriented reinforcement.

Encourage Cooperation

Cooperative learning involves the four elements of positive interdependence, individual accountability, skills and collaboration, and problem solving together. For example, students can be invited to help set short-term goals for themselves and to select the instructional activities to meet those goals. In addition, special education professionals can collaborate with other teachers, sharing responsibility for instruction.

Peer-mediated strategies are an important component of reading instruction. A good example is the peer-assisted learning strategies approach (Fuchs and Fuchs, 2005). This evidence-based approach matches a student with a same-age peer and typically includes a higher and lower performer within the class. The higher performing student reads first for each of the instructional activities to model the goal performance.

Avoid Substitutive Programs

The field of learning disabilities has historically produced many reading-related instructional approaches oriented to processes that are purported to be related to reading achievement. Support for these programs has not been impressive, though. Perceptual training programs, for example, take time away from the direct teaching of reading skills. Research validates the adage, "The best way for students to learn to read is to teach them to read."

Shift from Oral to Silent Reading

Oral reading is a significant component in a total reading program. It is necessary particularly in the early stages of reading instruction, because it gives the teacher insight into the beginning reader's knowledge of sight words and decoding skills. In reading instruction for most children, oral reading is used for three major purposes: diagnosis, conveying directions or instruction, and personal pleasure. For learners with special needs, oral reading has the additional purposes of vocabulary practice, memory reinforcement, rereading for better comprehension, and group participation.

Although initial reading and skills development work is best accomplished through oral reading, because it allows the teacher to monitor the skills of beginning readers, teachers should keep in mind that this emphasis is a vehicle toward reading, not a long-term goal. As children progress beyond this initial stage, the emphasis must shift to silent reading, which enhances both reading rate and comprehension and helps students develop self-monitoring abilities. Once this shift has occurred, oral reading can be used primarily for diagnostic purposes or to reinforce specific skills or concepts.

Provide Sufficient Time

Time is a critical variable in reading instruction, as it is in instruction in all other curricular areas. Academic engaged time is critical to success in learning in any area and particularly significant in reading. Given that not all of the time available in the school day actually involves engagement, the teacher must maximize the amount of time available for students to be engaged in the process of reading. Mastropieri and Scruggs (2000) recommended that teachers streamline the process of transitions, minimize the frequency of inappropriate vocalizations and inappropriate social behavior, assign work of appropriate difficulty, maintain proximity to students, and provide appropriate reinforcement.

Use Effective Grouping Strategies

Effective grouping strategies constitute a critical element of reading instructional programs. Of particular concern is the apparent trend toward whole-class grouping in reading instruction. Reporting on several studies, Schumm, Moody, and Vaughn (2000) indicated that the majority of general education teachers use "whole class, mixed ability instruction as their primary grouping pattern" and that students with learning disabilities made little academic progress over time and their attitudes about reading did not improve (pp. 477–478).

From their earlier review of research in this area, Elbaum, Vaughn, Hughes, and Moody (1999) reached the following conclusion:

> Many teachers consider whole-class instruction to be the preferred approach to reading instruction in both special and general education settings. Although some teachers report that they implement small-group instruction or student pairing occasionally, observations in their classrooms over a year-long period indicate that this rarely occurs. (p. 411)

Use Scaffolding

The concept of scaffolding is derived from the field of construction but has been used for education effectively. **Scaffolding** refers to the specific interactions between teachers and students that facilitate learning.

> In providing temporary assistance to children as they strive to accomplish a task just out of their [range of] competency, adults are said to be providing a scaffold, much like that used by builders in erecting a building. [Scaffolding] connotes a custom-made support for the "construction" of new skills, a support that can be easily disassembled when no longer needed. It also connotes a structure that allows for the accomplishment of some goal that would otherwise be either unattainable or quite cumbersome to complete. (Stone, 1998, p. 344)

In education, scaffolding is a temporary support system to help students reach independence with minimal errors (Humphrey, 2006). In scaffolding instruction, one strategy that teachers use is to think aloud or talk through the steps to reach a specific conclusion. As the students begin to understand the process, they gradually take over this talking-through procedure, and the teacher acts only as a coach, providing prompts when needed.

Continue Instruction at Secondary Level

The NJCLD (2008) identified the increased academic demands on students in middle and high school as follows:

> greater complexity of tasks; steadily increasing amounts of information; need for comprehension of complex linguistic forms and abstract concepts; high stakes testing and graduation requirements; ... increased focus on specific content with tightly scheduled timeslots; ... increased reliance on print (including a shift from narrative texts to emphasis on informational content/expository text structures and domain-specific vocabulary); increased expectations for greater output within shorter amounts of time requiring rapid and accurate retrieval of information and consolidation of learning into long-term memory; increased

demands from digital (versus traditional) literary proficiency; increased
need for self-advocacy and individual responsibility. (p. 213)

Given these challenges, continued instruction in reading is essential for secondary
school educators.

Promote Home–School Cooperation

Developing good working relationships with parents can enhance reading instruction
in the classroom. Homework has been demonstrated to have a positive effect on
achievement and reading proficiency, especially for adolescents (e.g., Cooper, 1989).
For younger students, homework can help to develop good "habit-formation" in terms
of reading practices, study skills, and the building of positive attitudes (Epstein, Polloway, Foley, & Patton, 1993).

Jayanthi, Bursuck, Epstein, and Polloway (1997) identified a series of strategies
that have been found to be effective in encouraging parental involvement in students'
homework performance. As summarized by Smith, Polloway, Patton, and Dowdy
(2008), these strategies include the following:

- Provide parents with periodic reports on their child's homework performance.
- At the beginning of the year, give parents information regarding assignments,
  homework adaptations available in the classroom, and policies related to
  missed assignments and extra-credit homework.
- Communicate with other teachers to avoid overloading students with homework and discouraging them from completing it at home.
- Help students meet homework deadlines (e.g., periodically remind students
  of assignment due dates; assign homework in small units; write assignments
  on the board).

Teachers should carefully consider programs that involve parents in assisting their
children at home. To promote positive attitudes toward achievement, parents should
establish a designated study area and set study time, provide encouragement, and establish rewards for their child's homework completion. In addition, parents should
be encouraged to read regularly to their children and to have their children read to
them as well.

▌Summary

Reading is the most common area of difficulty for students in general and students
with disabilities in particular. Reading competency is necessary in a variety of academic tasks and life skill demands. Reading involves a series of skills and abilities
that children acquire in a developmental progression. Understanding those skills and
this progression is essential to effective instruction.

Numerous assessment tools are available within the reading domain. Formal tests can provide both survey and diagnostic information. Informal measures offer more specific information that assists in designing instructional programs. In building a reading program, teachers must take into account a number of principles that affect assessment and instructional practices.

■References

Alliance for Excellent Education (2005). Reading Next: A vision for action and research in middle and high school literacy. Retrieved from http://www..atacess.org/respo\ources/atk 12/default.html

Blachowicz, C., & Ogle, D. (2001). *Reading comprehension: Strategies for independent learners*. (ERIC Document Reproduction Service No. ED479063). Reston, VA: ERIC Clearinghouse on Disabilities and Gifted Education.

Bradford, S., Alberto, P., Houchins, D. E., Shippen, M. E., & Flores, M. (2006). Using systematic instruction to teach decoding skills to middle school students with moderate intellectual disabilities. *Education & Training in Developmental Disabilities, 41*, 333–343.

Burnette, J. (1995). *Beginning reading and phonological awareness for students with learning disabilities* (ERIC Digest #E540, Report No. EDO-EC-95-3). (ERIC Document Reproduction Service No. ED 392 197)

Bursuck, W., & Damer, M. (2007). *Reading instruction for students who are at risk or have disabilities*. Boston: Allyn & Bacon.

Center for the Future of Teaching and Learning. (1996). Thirty years of NICHD research: What we now know about how children learn to read. *Effective School Practices, 15*(3), 40.

Chall, J. (1983). *Stages of reading development*. New York: McGraw-Hill.

Chall, J. J., & Snow, C. E. (1988). Influences on reading in low-income children. *Education Digest, 54*, 53–56.

Cooper, H. M. (1989). *Homework*. White Plains, NY: Longman.

Coyne, M., Kame'enui, E., & Simmons, D. (2001, May). Prevention and intervention in beginning reading: Two complex systems. *Learning Disabilities Research & Practice (Blackwell Publishing Limited), 16*, 62.

Elbaum, B., Vaughn, S., Hughes, M., & Moody, S. W. (1999). Grouping practices and reading outcomes for students with disabilities. *Exceptional Children, 65*, 399–415.

Englert, C., Mariage, T., Okolo, C., Shankland, R., Moxley, K., Courtad, C., et al. (2009). The learning-to-learn strategies of adolescent students with disabilities: Highlighting, note taking, planning, and writing expository texts. *Assessment for Effective Intervention, 34*, 147–161.

Epstein, M. H., Polloway, E. A., Foley, R. M., & Patton, J. R. (1993). Homework: A comparison of the teachers' and parents' perceptions of the problems experienced by students identified as behaviorally disordered, learning disabled, and non-disabled. *Remedial and Special Education, 14*(5), 40–50.

Fuchs, L. S., & Fuchs, D. (1986). Effects of systematic formative evaluation: A meta-analysis. *Exceptional Children, 53*, 199–208.

Fuchs, L. S., & Fuchs, D. (2005). Peer-assisted learning strategies: Promoting word recognition, fluency, and comprehension in young children." *Journal of Special Education, 39*, 34–44.

Georgiou, G., Das, J., & Hayward, D. (2009). Revisiting the simple view of reading in a group of children with poor reading comprehension. *Journal of Learning Disabilities, 42*, 76–84.

Gersten, R., & Carnine, D. (1988). Direct instruction in reading comprehension. In E. L. Meyen, G. A. Vergason, & R. J. Whelan (Eds.), *Effective instructional strategies for exceptional children* (pp. 65–79). Denver: Love.

Hock, M., Brasseur, I., Deshler, D., Catts, H., Marquis, J., Mark, C., et al. (2009). What is the reading component skill profile of adolescent struggling readers in urban schools? *Learning Disability Quarterly, 32,* 21–38.

Humphrey, E. (2006). *Scaffolding.* Unpublished manuscript, Lynchburg College, Lynchburg VA.

Idol, L. (1997). *Reading success: A specialized literacy program for learners with challenging reading needs.* Austin, TX: Pro-Ed.

Jayanthi, M., Bursuck, W., Epstein, M., & Polloway, E. A. (1997). Strategies for successful homework. *Teaching Exceptional Children, 30*(1), 4–7.

Johnson, D. D. (1971). The Dolch list reexamined. *Reading Teacher, 24,* 455–456.

Karlin, R. (1991). *Teaching elementary reading.* New York: Harcourt, Brace, Jovanovich.

Lindamood, P., & Lindamood, P. (2004). *Lindamood Auditory Conceptualization Test* (3rd ed.). Austin, TX: Pro-Ed.

Marzano, R. J., Hagerty, P. J., Valencia, S. W., & DiStefano, P. P. (1987). *Reading diagnosis and intervention: Theory into practice.* Englewood Cliffs, NJ: Prentice Hall.

Mastropieri, M. A., & Scruggs, T. E. (2000). *The inclusive classroom: Strategies for effective instruction.* Columbus, OH: Prentice Hall/Merrill.

Mathes, P., & Torgesen J. (1998). All children can learn to read: Critical care for the prevention of reading failure. *Peabody Journal of Education, 73,* 317–340.

McGuffey Reading Center. (n.d.). *Informal reading inventory.* Unpublished manuscript, University of Virginia, Charlottesville.

National Institute of Child Health and Human Development. (2000). *Report of the National Reading Panel. Teaching children to read: An evidence-based assessment of the scientific research literature on reading and its implications for reading instruction* (NIH Publication No. 00-4769). Washington, DC: U.S. Government Printing Office.

National Joint Committee on Learning Disabilities (NJCLD). (2008). *Adolescent literacy and older students with learning disabilities.* Retrieved from www.ldonline.org/njcld

National Reading Panel (NRP). (2000). *Report of the National Reading Panel: Teaching children to read.* Washington, DC: National Institute of Child Health and Human Development.

Polloway, C. H. (Ed.). *Campbell County (VA) Reading Skills Sequence* (n.d.). Unpublished manuscript, Rustburg, VA.

Polloway, E. A., & Meade, A. L. (2009). *Models in Education.* Unpublished manuscript, Lynchburg College, Lynchburg, VA.

Polloway, E. A., Patton, J. R., & Serna, L. (2008). *Strategies for teaching learners with special needs* (9th ed.). Columbus, OH: Pearson.

Pullen, P. C., & Lloyd, J. W. (2007). A focus on phonics. *Current Practice Alerts, 14,* 1–4.

Salvia, J., & Ysseldyke, J. E. (2001). *Assessment* (8th ed.). Boston: Houghton Mifflin.

Saunders, K., & DeFulio, A. (2007). Phonological awareness and rapid naming predict word attack and word identification in adults with mild mental retardation. *American Journal on Mental Retardation, 112,* 155–166.

Schumm, J. S., Moody, S. W., & Vaughn, S. (2000). Grouping for reading instruction: Does one size fit all? *Journal of Learning Disabilities, 33,* 477–488.

Shaywitz, S. (2003). *Overcoming dyslexia: A new and complete science-based program for reading problems at any level.* New York: Knopf.

Smith, T. E. C., Polloway, E. A., Patton, J. R., & Dowdy, C. A. (2008). *Teaching students with special needs in inclusive settings* (4th ed.). Boston: Allyn & Bacon.

Snider, V. E. (1989). Reading comprehension performance of adolescents with learning disabilities. *Learning Disability Quarterly, 12,* 87–96.

Stanovich, K. (1986). Matthew effects in reading: Some consequences of individual differences in the acquisition of literacy. *Reading Research Quarterly, 21,* 360–407.

Stanovich, K. E., & Stanovich, P. J. (1995). How research might inform the debate about early reading acquisition. *Journal of Research in Reading, 18,* 87–105.

Stokes, F., & Baer, D. M. (1977). An implicit technology of generalization. *Journal of Applied Behavior Analysis, 10,* 349–367.

Stone, C. A. (1998). The metaphor of scaffolding: Its utility for the field of learning disabilities. *Journal of Learning Disabilities, 31,* 344–364.

Swanson, E. (2008). Observing reading instruction for students with learning disabilities: A Synthesis. *Learning Disability Quarterly, 31,* 115–133.

Torgesen, J. (2000). Individual differences in response to early interventions in reading: The lingering problem of treatment resisters. *Learning Disabilities Research and Practice, 15,* 55–64.

Torgesen, J., & Bryant, B. (2004). *Test of Phonological Awareness–PLUS* (2nd ed). Austin, TX: Pro-Ed.

Torgesen, J. K., & Mathes, P. G. (2000). *A basic guide to understanding, assessing, and teaching phonological awareness.* Austin, TX: Pro-Ed.

Troia, G. A. (2004). A focus on phonological awareness acquisition and intervention. *Current Practice Alerts, 10.*

Vaughn, S., Wanzek, J., Murray, C., Scammaca, N., Linan-Thompson, S., & Woodruff, T. L. (2009). Response to early reading intervention: Examining higher and lower responders. *Exceptional Children, 75,* 165–183.

Wiederholt, J., & Bryant, B. (2001). *Gray oral reading tests* (4th ed.). Austin, TX: Pro-Ed.

Wilkinson, G. S., & Robertson, G. J. (2006). *Wide range achievement test* (4th ed.). Lutz, FL: Psychological Assessment Resources.

Woodcock, R. W. (1998). *Woodcock Reading Mastery Test–Revised (Normative Update).* Circle Pines, MN: American Guidance Service.

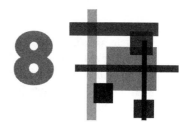

Reading Instruction

Practice and empirical data have shown certain reading instruction techniques to be effective for teaching learners with special needs. This chapter presents word recognition strategies, reading comprehension strategies, and commercial reading programs.

As highlighted in Chapter 7, beginning reading instruction should be founded on three big ideas that govern instruction: phonemic awareness, alphabetic understanding (i.e., the linkage between speech sounds and print), and automaticity with the phonological/alphabetical code (Coyne, Kameenui, & Simmons, 2001). These considerations, of course, must be complemented with rich, meaningful literary experiences that promote vocabulary development and comprehension. These emphases provide a basis for considering approaches to reading instruction.

Reading instructional approaches have traditionally been classified as "bottom-up" or "top-down" in orientation. The former are skills-oriented approaches characterized by attention to reading letters, then words, sentences, and paragraphs; they include what are referred to as **decoding** approaches. The latter, often termed **holistic** approaches, emphasize the meaning of what is read and thus focus on the way the reader comprehends the printed word.

Pressley and Fingeret (2005) noted that young students who have difficulties in reading benefit most significantly from instruction in decoding during the primary grades. Those with higher ability often benefit more from instruction directed to developing meaning through reading comprehension.

Moats (2003) identified the following as research-validated approaches to teaching reading:

- The direct teaching of both decoding and comprehension skills
- Instruction in phonemic awareness

- Systematic and explicit instruction in decoding skills
- Exposure to multiple and varied texts
- Instruction on word meanings, structure, and origins
- Comprehension strategies that promote prediction, summarizing, clarification, and questioning

Given the challenges faced by learners with special needs, balanced programs (including decoding and comprehension emphases, as well as teacher- and student-directed instructional experiences) are needed. Successful, comprehensive reading instructional programs for children and adolescents with learning disabilities reflect a combination of direct instruction by teachers and strategy instruction that enhances the ability of students to work independently (Swanson, 1999).

The development of reading instructional programs too often has been the focus solely of elementary schools. Continued attention is needed in middle and secondary schools, however, especially for students with special needs, as noted in Chapter 7.

> Given that many students will need instruction in all reading components (word identification, fluency, comprehension, vocabulary), but at different levels of intensity, secondary schools must develop ways to provide an array of instructional alternatives that address students with reading needs, especially for students with learning disabilities. (Hock et al., 2009, p. 35)

This chapter discusses curriculum and methodology in the areas of phonemic awareness and word recognition, including phonetic analysis, vocabulary, fluency, and comprehension. Table 8.1 provides an overview of the essential areas of reading instruction. The study of reading is so vast that all teachers must continue to be learners themselves. The goal of this chapter is to provide a foundation for this ongoing learning process.

▌Phonemic Awareness

Phonological awareness is the awareness of the phonological structure of language and encompasses the key area of **phonemic awareness**, which concerns the awareness of the speech sounds in words. Research has consistently indicated a significant relationship between reading acquisition and phonemic awareness and has supported the contention that individuals become better readers if they understand the relationship between phonemic correspondences and the reading process.

Phonemic awareness includes concern for discriminating between sounds and between words, identifying certain sounds within words, manipulating the sounds in words, identifying phonemes (e.g., *ax* = *a/k/s*, *bake* = *b/a/k*, *thing* = *th/i/ng*), and isolating sounds in words, such as sounds in the initial, medial, and final positions

TABLE 8.1
Overview of Key Areas of Reading Instruction

Essential Component	Importance	Instructional Considerations
Phonemic awareness	■ Improves children's word reading and reading comprehension. ■ Helps children learn to spell.	Most effective when ■ children are taught to manipulate phonemes by using the letters of the alphabet. ■ instruction focuses on only one or two rather than several types of phoneme manipulation.
Phonetic analysis (Phonics)	■ Leads to an understanding of the alphabetic principle—the systematic and predictable relationships between written letters and spoken sounds.	Effective when ■ it is systematic; the plan of instruction includes a carefully selected set of letter–sound relationships that are organized into a logical sequence. ■ it is explicit; the programs provide teachers with precise directions for the teaching of these relationships. ■ it provide ample opportunities for children to apply what they are learning about letters and sounds to the reading of words, sentences, and stories.
Fluency	■ Frees students to understand what they read.	Can be developed ■ by modeling fluent reading. ■ by having students engage in repeated oral reading.
Vocabulary	■ Beginning readers use their oral vocabulary to make sense of the words they see in print. ■ Readers must know what most of the words mean before they can understand what they are reading.	Can be developed ■ indirectly, when students engage daily in oral language, listen to adults read to them, and read extensively on their own. ■ directly, when students are explicitly taught both individual words and word learning strategies.
Text Comprehension	■ Comprehension is the reason for reading.	Effective when strategies are taught ■ through explicit instruction. ■ through cooperative learning. ■ by helping readers use strategies flexibly and in combination.

Source: Adapted from *Put Reading First: The Research Behind Building Blocks for Teaching Children to Read,* by B. B. Armbruster, F. Lehr, and J. Osborn, 2003. Jessup, MD: National Institute for Literacy.

(Polloway, Patton, & Serna, 2008). From a comprehensive review of studies on phonemic awareness, the National Reading Panel (NRP, 2000) concluded the following:

- Instruction in phonemic awareness is effective in enhancing the ability of children to attend to and manipulate speech sounds in words.
- Instruction in the manipulation of the sounds of language subsequently assists students in learning how to read.
- The value of phonemic awareness instruction is more significant for word reading than for comprehension.
- Instruction is most effective when it is directed to the manipulation of phonemes using letters (as opposed to only the manipulation of speech sounds).
- Phonemic awareness is a means, not an end. Consequently, including letters in instruction is important so the phonemic skills can be transferred to reading and writing tasks.
- Providing early instruction in phonemic awareness is not a guarantee of later success in literacy.

From its review of the research, the NRP (2000) noted:

> The most reasonable conclusion ... is that adding well-designed [phonemic awareness] instruction to a beginning reading program or a remedial reading program is very likely to yield significant dividends in the acquisition of reading and writing skills. Whether the benefits are lasting will likely depend on the comprehensiveness and effectiveness of the entire literacy program that is taught. (pp. 2–7).

Torgesen and Mathes (2000, pp. 45–48) provided the following general recommendations for instruction in phonological awareness:

1. Instruction should begin with easier tasks and move toward more difficult tasks. . . . Many programs begin with general listening activities designed to help children attend to sequences of individual sounds, and then move to activities that help children become aware of individual words in sentences, and then syllables in words. . . . It may be easiest for children to move next to activities that involve comparing words on the basis of first, last, and middle sounds. . . . Once children have some beginning proficiency with sound comparison tasks, they can be moved to training activities that involve segmenting beginning sounds and blending of onset–rhyme patterns (i.e., *c-at, d-og*). The final series of tasks should be those that involve completely segmenting the sounds in simple words, or blending all the sounds, or manipulating the sounds in words (e.g., "What word do we have if we say cat but don't say the /k/ sound?").
2. Instruction should be a regular part of the curriculum . . . [and activities] should take place for 15 to 20 minutes every day throughout the entire

kindergarten year. . . . For children who require more intensive instruction, small-group or individual tutoring should be provided daily.

3. Teachers should expect that children will respond at widely varying rates to instruction in phonological awareness.

4. Instruction should involve both analytic and synthetic activities. Analytic activities require children to identify individual sounds within whole words (e.g., "Tell me some words that begin with the same sound as dog"). . . . In contrast, synthetic activities involve blending together separately presented phonemes (e.g., "What word do these sounds make: /f/a/t/?").

5. Because the first goal of instruction is to help children notice the individual sounds in words, teachers should speak slowly and carefully and should pronounce individual sounds correctly.

To illustrate the types of activities that can promote phonological awareness, Figure 8.1 provides a sequence of activities ranging from less complex to more complex.

In his review of research, Troia (2004) confirmed the effectiveness of training in phonemic awareness. He offered a caution, though: Some students will have difficulty

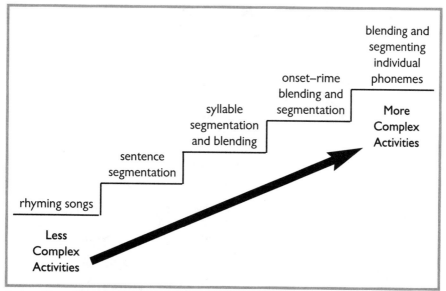

Source: From "Phonological Awareness: Instructional and Assessment Guidelines," by D. J. Chard and S. V. Dickson, 1999, *Intervention in School and Clinic, 34,* p. 262. Copyright 1999 by Sage Publications, Inc. Journals. Reprinted with permission.

FIGURE 8.1

Continuum of Complexity of Phonological Awareness Activities transferring specific phonological skills, such as segmentation and blending, if phonemic awareness instruction is not followed by intensive instruction in phonetic analysis.

▌Word Recognition

When presented with a passage to read, a child must respond to two demands: (a) identifying the specific words presented and (b) understanding what he has read. The former includes word recognition and analysis, and the latter is concerned with reading comprehension. Methods for teaching four critical elements of word recognition and analysis are discussed next, followed by a discussion of comprehension and its development. By emphasizing both concerns, teachers should be able to build an effective program without stifling student interest.

Figure 8.2 provides a schematic regarding word recognition considerations. The word-recognition approaches discussed here are sight word identification, phonetic analysis, structural analysis, and contextual analysis. The former is associated with

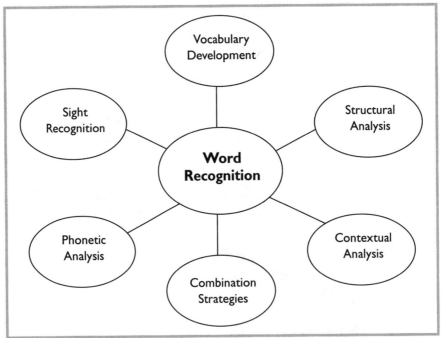

Source: From *Models in Education* (p. 4), by E. A. Polloway and A. L. Meade, 2009, unpublished manuscript, Lynchburg College, Lynchburg, VA. Copyright 2009 by E. A. Polloway and A. L. Meade. Reprinted with permission.

FIGURE 8.2

Word Recognition Emphases

immediate word identification, and the latter three can be termed word attack or analysis strategies.

Sight Word Identification

Sight word identification strategies assist children in identifying given words without having to analyze their components. The word list presented in Chapter 7 (Figure 7.4) includes prime examples of high-frequency words that should be recognized on sight, although lists of this nature do not convey an absolute sequence for presenting new words. The ultimate goal for mature readers is to recognize virtually all words quickly on sight.

The goal of sight vocabulary building is automatic recognition, or **automaticity,** the immediate identification of words, to maintain the flow of reading. To achieve automaticity, readers must have words firmly in their memories, ready for rapid recall. Therefore, the basis of sight word instruction is to provide children with repeated exposures to a variety of words. Depending on the learner, teachers should think in terms of 20 or more exposures before a student locks a word into his memory store. Obviously, the student's ability, relevance of the word, and extrinsic motivation involved will affect the number of exposures needed.

Jitendra, Edwards, Sacks, and Jacobson (2004) identified the following research-based strategies that promote the recognition and recall of sight words:

- Direct instruction
- The development of semantic maps (see subsequent discussion of reading comprehension)
- Constant time delay (for example, a constant time delay of 0 seconds would involve saying the word and providing the meaning immediately, whereas a delay of 5 seconds would give students that much time to produce the word and the meaning before assistance is provided)
- Computer-assisted instruction
- Mnemonics strategies
- Activity-based instruction (such as in science, in which hands-on experimentation is used to bring vocabulary to life)

Teachers should draw upon various instructional activities to achieve this frequency of exposures. The following approaches represent some tools for building a strong sight vocabulary. Although they include some activities based on teaching words in isolation (e.g., timed drills), these efforts should be complemented by strategies that teach words in context (e.g., repeated readings).

Word Banks

Sight word building can be oriented toward the use of word banks—either as an outgrowth of a language experience approach (see discussion later in this chapter) or as a technique in its own right. With this system, each word is written on a separate index card and filed in a plastic box as a new, an instructional, or a mastery word. The words can be used for a variety of exercises, including flashcard activities; timed drills that require a child to recognize a specified number of words per minute; and meaning activities in which the child writes definitions, uses the words in sentences, or constructs short stories. The teacher should evaluate student progress regularly when word cards are used to ensure that learning is being transferred to reading in context.

Fernald Approach

Grace Fernald's multisensory method utilizes the visual, auditory, kinesthetic, and tactile (VAKT) modalities to teach reading. Although the Fernald approach is discussed here as a sight word technique, it has functions far beyond this limited sphere. The text containing the program was published in 1943 and updated by Lorna Idol in 1988.

Fernald (1943) discussed the four stages of her method. Initially, each student selects the words to learn. These words become the basis for story writing and thus can be used for comprehension as well. The following are the four stages in this approach.

1. *Tracing*. The student traces each new word with his index finger, saying each part of the word during the process. This step is repeated until the child can write the word from memory. After the word is written, the teacher ensures that the child can identify the word by having him read it. In addition, the child must demonstrate use of the word in context.
2. *Writing without tracing*. The student looks at each word, says it several times, then writes it from memory. Teachers should use index cards to file the words during this stage.
3. *Recognition of words in print*. The student at this level should be able to retain words by merely looking at them and saying them aloud several times. Although putting the words on cards is less important during this stage, writing can be used for words that present difficulty.
4. *Transfer to word analysis*. In the final stage, the student transfers word recognition skills to the analysis of new words. Phonetic analysis is not taught as such, but students are encouraged to analyze unknown words by comparing them to words they already know and noting resemblances.

The Fernald method is an intensive instructional program with a decidedly clinical orientation and clearly specified steps to be taken in reading instruction. Teachers, however, may want to vary the steps to meet classroom realities or the needs of individual children.

Edmark Program

Edmark is a reading program aimed at building a sight word vocabulary. Its systematic procedures have been shown to be effective for individuals who have significant reading problems, including those with intellectual disabilities. It is discussed with commercial reading approaches later in the chapter.

Building a Functional Reading Vocabulary

A goal in teaching reading to students with disabilities is to help them develop a functional vocabulary so they are able to read for survival. This objective is based on students' need to develop a protection vocabulary (e.g., *cold, hot, men, women*) that facilitates daily living and provides a basis for successful independent functioning. For individuals with severe reading disabilities, survival reading frequently serves as the primary focus of instruction. For students with high-incidence (and less severe) disabilities, it is simply one of many important instructional objectives.

Particularly for individuals with significant disabilities and for some students with autism spectrum disorders, the ability to function independently is influenced significantly by the survival words and phrases the individual knows. Although a dominant role for survival words in basic reading curricula is not being advocated, these words should be a critical part of reading programs for students with significant reading disabilities.

Tables 8.2 and 8.3 present functional lists of survival words and phrases that were developed based on a survey of teachers working with adolescents with learning problems. In the survey, the teachers were asked to rate from 1 (limited value) to 5 (essential) the importance of each word and phrase in developing daily living skills.

From vocabulary such as that in these two tables, teachers can select the terms of greatest relevance to individual students in terms of their background, abilities, community, and future life goals. Because it would be unreasonable for a student to learn all survival words—and unwieldy for the instructor to teach all of them—a practical approach is to first teach the words and phrases that are most functional. Logically, the most relevant words to the students will be the easiest for them to learn and retain because of their meaningful value and potential for use.

Protection words, or survival words, should be taught as sight words because students need to recognize these words when they appear in their daily life. In essence, teaching survival words can be justified for those with severe disabilities if they can learn to respond differentially to the words taught (e.g., by entering the correct room marked MEN or WOMEN). In addition, the words being taught must be determined to be functional in the students' current or future environment. The approaches discussed in the remainder of this section have been effective in teaching survival words and can be adapted for use with other sight words.

The emphasis in this chapter on the recognition of words on sight should not obscure the importance of developing vocabulary in the sense of word meanings. Teachers should incorporate vocabulary-building activities as appropriate into sight word instruction as well as into comprehension instruction. Vocabulary (i.e., word meaning) development is discussed later in the chapter.

TABLE 8.2
50 Most Essential Survival Vocabulary Words

Word	N*	$\overline{X}$†	Word	N*	$\overline{X}$†
1. Poison	52	4.90	26. Ambulance	54	4.02
2. Danger	53	4.87	27. Girls	54	4.00
3. Police	52	4.79	28. Open	53	3.98
4. Emergency	54	4.70	29. Out	53	3.98
5. Stop	53	4.66	30. Combustible	54	3.94
6. Hot	53	4.53	31. Closed	54	3.90
7. Walk	53	4.49	32. Condemned	54	3.90
8. Caution	54	4.46	33. Up	53	3.89
9. Exit	53	4.40	34. Blasting	54	3.87
10. Men	54	4.39	35. Gentlemen	52	3.86
11. Women	53	4.32	36. Pull	53	3.73
12. Warning	53	4.32	37. Down	53	3.72
13. Entrance	53	4.30	38. Detour	53	3.71
14. Help	54	4.26	39. Gasoline	54	3.70
15. Off	52	4.23	40. Inflammable	53	3.70
16. On	53	4.21	41. In	54	3.68
17. Explosives	52	4.21	42. Push	53	3.68
18. Flammable	53	4.21	43. Nurse	52	3.58
19. Doctor	54	4.15	44. Information	54	3.57
20. Go	53	4.13	45. Lifeguard	52	3.52
21. Telephone	53	4.11	46. Listen	54	3.52
22. Boys	54	4.11	47. Private	53	3.51
23. Contaminated	54	4.09	48. Quiet	53	3.51
24. Ladies	53	4.06	49. Look	53	3.49
25. Dynamite	52	4.04	50. Wanted	54	3.46

*The number of participants varies due to omissions or errors by raters.
†Maximum rating of item was 5; minimum was 1.

Source: From "Validation of a Survival Vocabulary List," by C. H. Polloway and E. A. Polloway, 1981, *Academic Therapy, 16,* p. 446. Copyright 1981 by Sage Publications, Inc. Journals. Reprinted with permission.

Phonetic Analysis

Many readers who have disabilities cannot automatically recognize words on sight. For them, word analysis skills are essential for "cracking the code" and reading the words. **Phonetic analysis**, or **phonics**, requires the individual to determine sound–symbol correspondences and then blend the sounds together.

Phonics instruction is critical for many learners with exceptional needs. These students may have difficulty recognizing whole words and need a systematic approach for attending to details. Phonics generalizations, or rules about how letters and letter combinations represent sounds, thus act as verbal mediators that students with

TABLE 8.3
50 Most Essential Survival Vocabulary Phrases

Phrase	N	$\overline{X}$	Phrase	N	$\overline{X}$
1. Don't walk	53	4.70	26. Wrong way	53	3.96
2. Fire escape	54	4.68	27. No fires	54	3.96
3. Fire extinguisher	54	4.59	28. No swimming	53	3.92
4. Do not enter	53	4.51	29. Watch your step	52	3.92
5. First aid	54	4.46	30. Watch for children	54	3.91
6. Deep water	50	4.38	31. No diving	54	3.91
7. External use only	53	4.38	32. Stop for pedestrians	54	3.89
8. High voltage	54	4.35	33. Post office	52	3.85
9. No trespassing	52	4.35	34. Slippery when wet	53	3.85
10. Railroad crossing	52	4.35	35. Help wanted	54	3.85
11. Rest rooms	52	4.35	36. Slow down	53	3.81
12. Do not touch	52	4.33	37. Smoking prohibited	54	3.80
13. Do not use near			38. No admittance	54	3.78
open flame	53	4.24	39. Proceed at your		
14. Do not inhale fumes	53	4.24	own risk	53	3.77
15. One way	53	4.24	40. Step down	52	3.77
16. Do not cross	53	4.17	41. No parking	52	3.75
17. Do not use near heat	53	4.11	42. Keep closed	54	3.74
18. Keep out	53	4.09	43. No turns	53	3.73
19. Keep off	54	4.07	44. Beware of dog	54	3.72
20. Exit only	53	4.07	45. School zone	53	3.72
21. No right turn	52	4.04	46. Dangerous curve	53	3.71
22. Keep away	52	4.00	47. Hospital zone	54	3.70
23. Thin ice	53	3.98	48. Out of order	53	3.66
24. Bus stop	54	3.98	49. No smoking	53	3.66
25. No passing	52	3.98	50. Go slow	52	3.65

Source: From "Validation of a Survival Vocabulary List," by C. H. Polloway and E. A. Polloway, 1981, *Academic Therapy, 16,* p. 447. Copyright 1981 by Sage Publications, Inc. Journals. Reprinted with permission.

disabilities do not spontaneously produce but that they can be taught to apply. The memory demands for a few phonics rules may be significant, but they are relatively minor compared to those required for sight recognition. Although Francis's (1958) classic estimate that 85% of all English words are regular may seem generous, many words confronting the child have a common phonetic basis.

After evaluating the research literature on phonics instruction, the NRP (2000) reached the following conclusions:

∎ Programs that involve the use of systematic phonics instruction make larger contributions to reading achievement than do alternative programs that provide no such instruction or unsystematic phonics instruction.

- Systematic phonics instruction can be effective through a variety of delivery modes including tutorial approaches, small-group instruction, and class instruction.
- Phonics instruction is most effective when taught to younger children (i.e., grades K–1). It should begin with basic foundational knowledge that includes instruction on letters and phonemic awareness.
- Systematic phonics instruction results in significant improvement in the reading performance of young children who are at risk for developing further problems and also for readers with disabilities (i.e., students with average intellectual levels but poor reading skills). In general, however, low-achieving readers, as defined in the studies, make less progress.
- Rather than interfering with students' ability to read and comprehend textual material, systematic phonics instruction has a positive effect on their growth in this area.

The Panel followed its summary of findings on phonics instruction with several cautions.

> Phonics teaching is a means to an end. . . . [Students] need to be able to blend sounds together to decode words, and they need to break spoken words into their constituent sounds to write words. [However,] programs that focus too much on the teaching of letter-sounds relationships and not enough on putting them to use are unlikely to be very effective. . . . Educators must keep the end in mind and insure that children understand the purpose of learning letter-sounds and are able to apply their skills in their daily reading and writing activities. (pp. 2–96).

Building on this research base, Bursuck and Damer (2007) noted that systematic phonetic analysis programs are ones that help teachers explicitly teach students to relate sounds and letters, to blend sounds into words, and to break words into sounds. In so doing, they also help the students understand the relationships between sounds and letters; promote the application of phonics skills as they are reading words and sentences; and stress alphabetic knowledge, phonemic awareness, vocabulary development, and text reading.

Teaching phonics skills has often been associated with instructional programs for elementary-aged students. An emphasis on the explicit and systematic teaching of word reading skills, however, can also influence the achievement of adolescents positively, reinforcing the value of continued emphasis on instruction in basic skills in middle and secondary schools (Joseph & Schisler, 2009).

Joseph and Seery (2004) reviewed research on phonetic analysis instruction and reported that individuals with mild/moderate intellectual disabilities also

> have capabilities to grasp and generalize phonetic analysis skills from one context to another. . . . Teachers might want to consider incorporating explicit teaching of sound–symbol correspondences as well as

prerequisite skills like phonemic awareness, in their literacy program. (p. 93)

Further attention continues to be needed regarding the effectiveness of phonics instruction for students with more significant disabilities, including those with autism.

Phonetic analysis must be balanced with other instructional approaches. To use phonics instruction effectively, teachers should do the following:

1. Teach phonics as a way to learn to read, not as reading per se.
2. Begin phonics instruction after the child has acquired a small sight vocabulary of about 50 words, so the child is familiar with common sounds.
3. Provide structured opportunities for the child to apply the skills learned, and ensure the transition to reading in context. Phonics instruction should not involve isolated skill development.
4. Be certain that comprehension instruction is not neglected while phonics is being taught.
5. Avoid emphasis on the teaching of high-frequency, irregular words through phonetic analysis.
6. Teach those generalizations that will be most useful for students.

With reference to the last point, teachers should be aware of the extent to which various rules are functional. Some rules that have low usefulness are still functional when restricted to a given instructional vocabulary. For example, the common rule, "When two vowels go walking, the first one does the talking" has less than 50% utility, yet students can be given a controlled vocabulary that lets them appropriately apply this generalization. At a later point, teachers can introduce strategies for handling exceptions. Table 8.4 summarizes utility values for some common generalizations.

Teaching Phonics Skills

Phonetic analysis instruction can include both analytic and synthetic approaches, as shown in Table 8.5. Analytic phonics involves the child breaking down and analyzing known words into their component phonemes (e.g., bat → /b/ /a/ /t/); it is most often just a beginning approach. In synthetic phonics, the learner blends known sounds into new words (e.g., */b/ /a/ /t/ → bat).*

Analytic Phonics

- Reading vocabulary developed from speaking vocabulary
- Learning sounds from existing reading vocabulary
- Sight vocabulary as one prerequisite to phonetic analysis
- Analyzing known words
- Teaching segmentation of known words to individual sounds (e.g., r / i / d / e)

TABLE 8.4
Utility of Common Phonic Generalizations

Generalization	No. of Words Conforming	No. of Exceptions	Percent of Utility
1. When there are two vowels side by side, the long sound of the first one is heard and the second is usually silent.	309 (bead)	377 (chief)	45
2. When a vowel is in the middle of a one-syllable word, the vowel is short.	408	249	62
Middle letter	191 (dress)	84 (scold)	69
One of the middle two letters in a word of four letters	191 (rest)	135 (told)	59
One vowel within a word of more than four letters	26 (splash)	30 (fight)	46
3. If the only vowel letter is at the end of a word, the letter usually stands for a long sound.	23 (he)	8 (to)	74
4. When there are two vowels, one of which is final e, the first vowel is long and the e is silent.	180 (bone)	108 (done)	63
5. The r gives the preceding vowel a sound that is neither long nor short.	484 (horn)	134 (wire)	78
6. The first vowel is usually long and the second silent in the digraphs *ai, ea, oa,* and *ui*.	179	92	66
ai	43 (nail)	24 (said)	64
ea	101 (bead)	51 (head)	66
oa	34 (boat)	1 (cupboard)	97
ui	1 (suit)	16 (build)	6
7. Words having double e usually have the long e sound.	85 (seem)	2 (been)	98
8. When words end with silent e, the preceding *a* or *i* is long.	164 (cake)	108 (have)	60
9. When the letter *i* is followed by the letters *gh*, the *gh* is silent and the *i* is long.	22 (high)	9 (neighbor)	71
10. When y is the final letter in a word, it usually has a vowel sound.	169 (dry)	32 (tray)	84
11. When y is used as a vowel in words, it sometimes has the sound of long *i*.	29 (fly)	170 (funny)	15
12. When c and h are next to each other, they make only one sound.	103 (peach)	0	100
13. When c is followed by e or i, the sound of s is likely to be heard.	66 (cent)	3 (ocean)	96
14. When the letter c is followed by o or a, the sound of k is likely to be heard.	143 (camp)	0	100
15. The letter g often has the sound similar to that of j in jump when it precedes the letter *i* or e.	49 (engine)	28 (give)	64

Source: Adapted from "The Utility of Phonic Generalizations in the Primary Grades," by T. Clymer, 1963, *Reading Teacher, 16,* pp. 223–225. Copyright 1963 by Theodore Clymer and the International Reading Association. Reprinted with permission.

Synthetic Phonics

- Starting with sounds that are easier to learn (e.g., continuous consonants - /s/ as in *sun*)
- Teaching common vowels (e.g., short and long *a*)
- Teaching sound blending to build words
- Synthesizing words from known sounds
- Using onset-time to build words
- Teaching advanced consonant and vowel sounds

When all phonics generalizations are taught, phonics instruction places great demands on the student. Therefore, a sequential program emphasizing the most critical elements is essential. Children with reading problems usually need help synthesizing this information into a workable system of word analysis skills and need repeated opportunities to practice these rules with unknown words. A common instructional sequence includes the following steps:

1. Teaching initial and final consonant sounds
2. Teaching consonant digraph sounds (e.g., *ch, sh, th*)
3. Teaching short vowel sounds (*vc, cvc* stems)
4. Teaching consonant blends (e.g., *bl, st, tr*)
5. Teaching long vowel sounds (final *e*, double vowel patterns)
6. Teaching r-influenced vowels
7. Teaching diphthongs and other vowel sounds (e.g., *aw, ou, ow, eu, ew, oi*)

A method for teaching phonics as it applies to one-syllable words is discussed in the following paragraphs. Later in this chapter, in the section on syllabication, a similar strategy is applied to polysyllabic words.

As teachers begin instruction on analyzing one-syllable words, consonant sounds should be taught first because they are easier than vowels for students to learn. Consonants are associated most consistently with only one sound, they often begin words, and they relate well to context (Heilman, Blair, & Rupley, 1986). Teachers should begin this instruction by ensuring that students can discriminate between the initial consonant sound being taught and different consonant sounds that begin words. In introducing *b*, for example, the child should be able to tell that *butter* and *ball* start with the same sound but that *butter* and *fish* begin with different sounds. Consonant sounds are best taught with associated key words and pictures.

When a student masters an individual consonant sound, he will be able to

1. identify the symbol from a spoken word (What is the letter that names the first sound you hear in buttonhole?);
2. produce the sound when decoding an unknown printed word (If *at* is pronounced "at," what does it become when *b* is added at the beginning, as on this card?); and
3. use the sound to spell an unknown word (e.g., *bax, bap*).

Individual consonants and digraphs should be introduced one at a time and then reviewed along with all the sounds taught previously. Later, teachers can introduce blends along with instruction on short vowels, providing instructional drills that encourage the transition from single consonants to blends (e.g., *r* + *at*, followed by *b* + *rat*).

Before moving to vowel sounds, students should have mastered consonant sounds in the initial and final positions and should be able to blend teacher-pronounced sounds into words (e.g., *c* + *at, sn* + *ail*). Teachers should also determine students' sight vocabulary, especially if the students are older. With this information, the teacher can provide drill words that are unknown to the students and require them to practice the skills being taught.

A sequential presentation for vowels, such as the following, is particularly useful:

1. As with consonant sounds, give the child auditory experiences that demand discrimination between similar vowel sounds. This phase is critical because a student must be able to hear how a sound is different and unique before he can reproduce it in a new word or identify it in a word to be spelled. Teachers might use the words *igloo* and *ice cream* to teach short and long *i*, for example, and then ask students to categorize *i* words by vowel sounds. Children should first learn to discriminate between words with *i* in the initial position. When they have mastered this skill, they can move on to words with *i* in the medial position.

2. Teach students to blend a vowel sound to final consonants and consonant blends and to spell these stems. With short *i*, the child would learn to pronounce and spell stems such as *ick, id*, and *ist*.

3. Teach students to blend initial consonant sounds to these stems. Using short *i* as an example, the child would be asked again to pronounce *ick* and then *t* + *ick* or to pronounce *int* and then *h* + *int*.

4. Present words containing the vowel sound being taught, and have the student rehearse the following procedure:

   a. Find the vowel.
   b. Cover all the letters that come before it.
   c. Pronounce the vowel stem.
   d. Add the initial consonant or blend.
   e. Pronounce the whole word.

5. When the child can analyze words that in isolation contain the sound in question, provide guided opportunities that allow the child to use the new sound to decode unknown words in the context of a sentence.

After a child masters an individual phonic element, he must integrate it with previously learned sounds. For example, after learning short *a* and short *i*, and before going on to short *o*, the child must be able to discriminate, pronounce, and spell words containing short *a* and short *i*. Although most students have relatively little difficulty learning single phonic elements in isolation, they may have problems when faced with an assortment of words requiring them to integrate new elements with previously learned information.

These procedures for teaching vowel sounds also can be used to teach the two long-vowel patterns (*cvvc, cvcv*), *r*-controlled vowels (e.g., *-ar, -ir*), and the most common diphthong patterns. In this way, students can learn the most important generalizations for these sounds.

For variant sounds and exceptions to the rules, teachers can rely on the context to supply meaning, freeing phonics from rigid sound–symbol correspondences. If, for example, a child were to decode the word "bread" according to the basic double vowel rule, he would pronounce it "breed." But a child who does not know this word and encounters it in the sentence, "There is a loaf of bread on the table," may skip past the word to the end of the sentence and possibly pronounce the word correctly because he knows its meaning. Contextual analysis is discussed further later in this chapter.

Structural Analysis

Structural analysis enables readers to see the forms of words and their subparts. Generally, this word recognition strategy requires a morphemic analysis of words—a focus on **morphemes**, or meaning units. Students should learn to find the morphemes within words to facilitate both word recognition and word comprehension. One key structural analysis skill, **syllabication,** does not use morphologic, or meaning-based, cues.

Attention to structural analysis can improve word recognition ability and both word and passage comprehension skills. As with phonetic and contextual analysis (discussed later in this chapter), teachers might initially use drill activities but must then have students apply these skills in actual reading opportunities.

Compound Words

To orient a child to recognize compound words, teachers should design various activities that highlight the two components of these words. Particularly beneficial exercises include the following:

- Matching drills using two lists of words with pairs that can be combined
- Adapting cloze procedures in which one half of each compound word is left blank (e.g., "When the winter winds blow, we huddle around the —place").
- Having students label ridiculous pictures that represent compound words (e.g., a stick of flying butter for butterfly)
- Providing a list of invented words or colloquialisms to be defined (e.g., slam-dunk, skyhook)

Affixes

Teachers can help students develop an orientation toward root words, prefixes, and suffixes by devising exercises that highlight common forms and indicate how they affect word meanings. In addition to the discussion in Chapter 7, Table 8.5 provides a summary of key affixes to teach. Some appropriate activities are

- color-coding the affix being taught;
- using word wheels that have root words in the center and prefixes surrounding them, or suffixes in the center and root words surrounding them; and
- speed listing words that begin with a given prefix (e.g., *un-*: undress, untie, uncover, undo).

Contractions

Many of the activities described for compound words and affixes can be adapted for teaching contractions, the third structural analysis skill with a morphological basis. With contractions, students have to know which forms are equivalencies for specific words.

Syllabication

One of the most practical structural analysis skills is **syllabication.** Many students face a dilemma when they confront polysyllabic words that do not seem to respond to basic phonetic rules. A structured program teaching syllabication can provide a decoding method for generalizing previously learned rules to new, longer words.

TABLE 8.5
Using Affixes: Common Forms

Affix	Meaning	Example
un–	not	unhappy, unlock
re–	back, again	repay, review
in–	not, into	insane, inland
dis–	opposite	dislike, discontinue
en–	in, into, make	enforce, endanger
non–	not	nonsmoker, nonsense
over–	excessive	overcharge, overwork
mis–	wrong	mistake, misplace
–en	made of, consisting of	golden, wooden
–er	relating to, like	painter, baker
–ish	like	childish, yellowish
–ly	in a way	slowly, simply
–ize	to act in a certain way	alphabetize, minimize
–ist	one who	terrorist, machininist
–ism	a principle, belief, or movement	conservatism, feminism

Source: From *Models in Education* (p. 10), by E.A. Polloway and Meade, 2009, unpublished manuscript, Lynchburg College, Lynchburg, VA. Copyright by E. A. Polloway and A. L. Meade. Reprinted with permission.

Instruction in syllabication should follow a system that blends a variety of word analysis tools into an instructional sequence for attacking polysyllabic words. One approach is described as follows. This syllabication system has only two key rules (described later in this section) and eliminates the need to teach variations and exceptions. Using the system, a child first decodes irregular words as if they followed the rules of the system, then relies on context clues to clarify slight pronunciation distortions.

For example, students who have been taught to syllabicate using this system would divide the unknown word *between* as "bet/ween." Then, when they pronounce the word accordingly, they would hear a slight distortion, which would become readily recognizable when they place the word in the context of a sentence. Because the reader does not have to make exact sound–symbol correspondences, many syllabication rules and their inconsistencies can be discarded.

This program is aimed at readers who already have the prerequisites for basic sight vocabulary, know the sounds of consonants; blends; long, short, and variant vowels; diphthongs; and digraphs, and who are able to predict vowel sounds in open and closed syllables. Once the skills are developed, the student is ready to learn the system's two basic rules of syllabication:

Rule 1: When a word has the pattern of vowel, two consonants, and vowel, divide between the consonants (*vc/cv*).

Rule 2: When a word has the pattern of a vowel, consonant, and vowel, divide between the first vowel and the consonant (*v/cv*).

These rules are divided into 11 steps, taught one at a time. The student learns each step using known words and then practices using unknown words out of context. Surnames can be used for the practice words so that pronunciation distortions are not critical to meaning and are not readily apparent to the student. When students have mastered this principle, they move on to decoding unknown words from reading materials, using context to correct distortion. The steps are outlined in Figure 8.3.

Teachers should devote one instructional period to presenting the concept for each step and having students practice. Additional periods should be used for repetition and overlearning to produce mastery. Step 11 should be continued until the teacher feels confident of the student's ability to use syllabication independently. This system is based on the application of various word analysis skills to words of two or more syllables. As such, it can help children cross a major word recognition hurdle encountered at approximately the third- or fourth-grade reading level.

Contextual Analysis

Contextual analysis can help bridge the gap between the graphic emphasis of phonetic and structural analysis and the underlying meaning of the sentence. Its value is in providing semantic and syntactic cues that facilitate identification of words that might be more difficult to recognize in isolation. In this regard, contextual analysis is a skill that students need to develop. In addition to complementing the use of other word analysis strategies, it has ties to comprehension because the better one comprehends

1. Identify how many syllables are heard in a known word; students will be able to divide a known word orally.
   - Teacher orally explains the concept and demonstrates with known words.
   - Student is given known words to divide orally.

   Sample word list: tomato sunshine toe cucumber peanut

2. Recognize that a word has as many syllables as vowels heard.
   - Teacher writes and says known words, and student tells how many syllables are heard and how many vowels are seen and heard in each word.
   - The procedure is continued until student draws the conclusion that the number of vowels heard in a word equals the number of syllables.

   Sample word list: tomato sunshine toe cucumber peanut

3. Determine how many syllables an unknown word has.
   - Review silent e rule and the rule stipulating that when two vowels come together, one sound results.
   - Teacher writes an unknown word; student determines which vowels will be silent and predicts the number of syllables.

   Sample word list: domino barbecue stagnate

4. Syllabicate words that follow the vc/cv pattern (Rule 1).
   - Teacher writes and student divides two-syllable known words that fit the pattern.
   - Student practices dividing and pronouncing two-syllable vc/cv words.
   - Teacher demonstrates the process of dividing longer known words:
     - ☐ Determine number of syllables.
     - ☐ To establish first division, start with first vowel and look for vc/cv pattern, then divide.
     - ☐ To establish second division, start with second vowel and look for vc/cv pattern, then divide.
     - ☐ Continue procedure until all syllables are determined.
     - ☐ Pronounce word.
   - Student practices dividing and pronouncing unknown words that contain vc/cv pattern.

   Sample word list:
   - Teaching words: rabbit bitter pepper mixture
   - Practice words: Volpone Venneer Bellew Aspic

5. Syllabicate words contain the v/cv pattern (Rule 2).
   - Follow instructions for Step 4, substituting v/cv pattern.

   Sample word list:
   - Teaching words: labor favor basic demand
   - Practice words: Cahill Zuzo Theimer Tatum

(continued)

FIGURE 8.3

Syllabication Instructional Program

6. Syllabicate words that contain both vc/cv and v/cv patterns.
   - Teacher writes and student divides known words that contain both patterns.
   - Student practices dividing and pronouncing unknown words that contain both patterns.

   Sample word list:
   - Teaching words: envelope cucumber remainder resulting
   - Practice words: Provenzano Tedesco Dannewitz Oberlin

7. Syllabicate words that have a vcccv or vccccv pattern.
   - Teacher writes and student divides known words that containing vcccv or vccccv patterns until student recognizes that the division is based on consonant blends and digraphs.
   - Student practices dividing and pronouncing unknown words containing vcccv or vccccv pattern.

   Sample word list:
   - Teaching words: concrete pitcher contract merchant abstract
   - Practice words: Omohundro Annentrout Marshall Ostrander

8. Syllabicate words that end with –le.
   - Teacher writes and student divides known words ending with –le until student generalizes that when preceded by l, final e is silent but produces a syllable that contains –le and the preceding consonant.
   - Student practices dividing and pronouncing unknown words containing the –le ending.

   Sample word list:
   - Teaching words: candle rattle dribble staple
   - Practice words: Whipple Biddle Noble Radle

9. Recognize that y in the medial or final position is a vowel and must be treated as such.
   - Teacher tells student that y will be a vowel in the medial or final position.
   - Teacher writes and student divides known words containing y in both positions.
   - Student practices dividing and pronouncing unknown words that contain y in the medial or final position.

   Sample word list:
   - Teaching words: funny my cranky style
   - Practice words: Snydor Murtry Tyson Gentry

10. Divide and pronounce unknown words containing any of the patterns taught.
    - Student practices dividing and pronouncing unknown words containing all the patterns taught.

    Sample word list: Hirshoren Shirly Ruckle Espenshade

11. Syllabicate and pronounce unknown words in context.
    - Student silently reads material on instructional level.
    - After reading is completed, teacher checks student's accuracy in decoding unknown words in context.

FIGURE 8.3 *(continued)*

what is being read, the better he can use context. It also encourages hypothesis testing because the student is learning how to make predictions.

To help students use contextual analysis, teachers must help them understand that only a few possible words can fill a place in a sentence. Specifically, this includes teaching children to expect the types of words that may come up in a sentence, to anticipate specific unknown words, and to attack an unknown word based on its position in the sentence and on the known words that surround it. The successful use of context cues, however, presumes that the reader can either recognize or sound out every word in the sentence. Phonetic and structural cues can complement contextual analysis.

The **cloze procedure** is a common contextual analysis skill-building activity. In this method, approximately every fifth word is removed from reading passages at the student's instructional level, and students are required to complete the sentences by filling in the blanks. Figure 8.4 presents a sample cloze procedure exercise based on fourth-grade reading material. An alternative approach to this form of the cloze procedure would be to select words to remove from a passage according to the role they play in the structure or meaning of a sentence. The following steps can be used to construct a cloze exercise:

1. Select a reading passage of approximately 250–300 words from a story at the student's instructional level.

A significant moment in history occurred in 2008 with _____ election of Barack Obama, _____ African-American citizen, as _____ of the United States. _____ a nation that had _____ the slavery of African-American _____ for several hundred years _____ that had subsequently enacted _____, particularly in the South, _____ restricted basic human rights, _____ election was truly a _____ historical event for the _____ States.

Mr. Obama, whose mother _____ American and father Kenyan by _____ , had served in the _____ States Senate representing the _____ of Illinois prior his _____ for the presidency. During _____ campaign for the presidency, _____ ran on a platform _____ hope and change. With _____ vice presidential candidate, Joe Biden _____ Delaware, Mr. Obama and _____ Democratic Party were successful _____ winning the November 2008 _____ , running against the Republican _____ slate of Sen. John McCain _____ Arizona and Gov. Sarah Palin _____ Alaska.

FIGURE 8.4

Cloze Procedure

2. Do not alter the initial sentence. Beginning with the second sentence, delete every fifth word until reaching a total of 50 deletions.
3. Replace each of these deleted words with a blank.
4. Add one more complete sentence after the sentence containing the last deletion.

For students in elementary school, listening vocabulary and comprehension may be more advanced than their decoding skills, and thus their ability to use context may be relatively effective. Many elementary school students can use structural and meaning cues to anticipate forthcoming words in sentences and make guesses about words that they might not be able to recognize on sight. Difficulties in the use of context, however, become more pronounced at the middle school level. As Greene (1998) noted:

> New content-area vocabulary words do not preexist in [middle school students'] listening vocabularies. They can guess "wagon." But they can't guess "circumnavigation" or "chlorophyll" based on context. . . . These words are not in their listening vocabularies.
>
> When all of the words readers never learned to decode in grades one to four are added to all the textbook vocabulary words that don't preexist in readers' listening vocabularies, the percentage of unknown words teeters over the brink; the text now contains so many unknown words that there's no way to get the sense of the sentence. (p. 76)

Thus, the task for teachers is to encourage the use of context primarily when it enhances comprehension of text (e.g., by providing clues to the meaning of new words) and for figuring out the occasional word, but not to overemphasize it as a primary strategy used by the student.

The Center for the Future of Teaching and Learning (1996) posited that an overemphasis on prediction from context can have a negative effect on reading and delay successful reading acquisition. They indicated that it is incorrect to assume that predicting forthcoming words in sentences is a relatively easy activity and one that results in a high level of accuracy. The Center summarized the challenge for children as follows:

> Much research has evaluated the effectiveness of prediction [i.e., contextual analysis] as a strategy for word recognition. Though prediction is valuable in comprehension for predicting the next event or predicting an outcome, the research indicates that it is not useful in word recognition. (p. 41)

Combining Word Recognition Strategies

Once a student acquires syllabication skills, the teacher can implement a program using multiple word recognition strategies to promote an efficient reading style that minimizes interruptions in the flow of the passage. Steps that may be involved in such an approach are as follows:

1. Determine whether the word is important to meaning. If pronunciation does not seem crucial to overall meaning (e.g., a proper noun or a foreign phrase), read past the word unless it recurs regularly.
2. If the word is important to meaning, rapidly survey initial phonetic elements to help predict the word.
3. Identify major structural features of the word (e.g., roots, affixes) that may suggest cues as to meaning or pronunciation.
4. Break the word into syllables, and use phonetic analysis to facilitate pronunciation.
5. Utilize context clues to figure out which word(s) would fit the meaning and syntax of the sentence (useful for occasional unknown words).
6. Use a dictionary or seek help from a teacher or aide to determine the word's pronunciation or meaning if it affects the meaning of the passage.

Teachers can help students remember these steps by teaching them a word identification strategy such as that suggested by Polloway et al. (2008). Figure 8.5 outlines steps in this strategy.

Another strategy is entitled DISSECT (Discover the context, Isolate the prefix, Separate the suffix, Say the stem, Examine the stem, Check with someone, Try the dictionary; see Bremer, Clapper, & Deshler, 2002; Lenz & Hughes, 1990). Bryant et al. (2000) researched this strategy for students with reading disabilities, low-achieving students, and average-achieving students at the middle school level. The researchers found that although the students collectively made progress in the use of DISSECT,

---

- **C**onsonant: Focus on the consonant in the initial position.

- **R**apid: Rapidly focus on initial consonant and vowel sounds, and check prefixes and suffixes while reviewing whole words.

- **U**nimportant: Skip over unimportant words that do not require precise pronunciation (e.g., names).

- **S**yllabicate: Apply syllabication strategies if the word is essential.

- **C**ontext: Use the context to determine vocabulary and meaning.

- **H**elp: Seek help (e.g., from teacher, peer, dictionary).

Source: Adapted from *Strategies for Teaching Learners With Special Needs* (9th ed., p. 192), by E. A. Polloway, J. R. Patton, and L. Serna, 2008, Columbus, OH: Pearson.

FIGURE 8.5

CRUSCH Word Identification Strategy

those with reading disabilities had difficulty reaching mastery. Bryant et al. suggested that it works best when the word being read is already within the student's listening vocabulary. More intensive instruction was deemed necessary to ensure learning as well as to enhance transfer to other classes in which the students were enrolled.

▌Vocabulary

A key area of reading instruction is the development of a strong vocabulary (i.e., word meanings). The NRP (2000) reviewed the existing research on vocabulary instruction and drew the following conclusions:

- Computer vocabulary instruction shows positive learning gains over traditional methods.
- Vocabulary instruction leads to gains in comprehension.
- Vocabulary can be learned incidentally in the context of storybook reading or from listening to the reading of others.
- Preinstruction of vocabulary words prior to reading can facilitate both vocabulary acquisition and comprehension.
- The restructuring of text materials or procedures facilitates vocabulary acquisition and comprehension (for example, substituting easy for hard words). (pp. 4-4)

Polloway et al. (2008) further summarized research on vocabulary development by noting the following:

- Vocabulary acquisition is influenced positively by the time spent engaged in reading.
- Vocabulary knowledge serves as a foundation to successful comprehension.
- Receptive vocabulary usage tends to be easier than expressive vocabulary usage.
- Approximately 300 new words can be learned annually as a result of direct instruction on vocabulary with approximately 8–10 per week.
- Instruction should focus on teaching words that are important, useful, and difficult for students.

Bryant, Ugel, Thompson, and Hamff (1999) identified a series of research-based approaches to enhancing vocabulary development. These include

- teaching specialized and technical vocabulary prior to the lesson,
- presenting new vocabulary in semantically related groups,
- providing multiple exposures to words across context,
- providing instruction on a limited number of new words in each lesson and relating words to the content area text,
- having students link new vocabulary with their background knowledge by describing what they already know about the topic,

- having students make up sentences using new vocabulary,
- having students identify word relations (e.g., synonyms, anonyms) and dictionary definitions in combination with using words in context, and
- having students develop word lists or banks. (p. 298)

A strategy for developing vocabulary, based on a graphic organizer, is presented in Figure 8.6. The concept of graphic organizers, which are particularly useful for developing reading comprehension, is discussed later in the chapter.

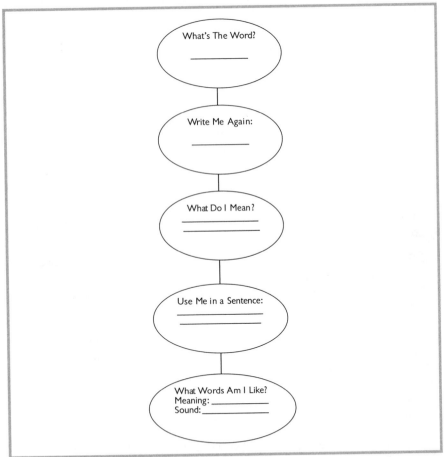

Source: From *Models in Education* (p. 5), by E. A. Polloway & A. L. Meade, 2009, unpublished manuscript, Lynchburg College, Lynchburg, VA. Copyright 2009 by E. A. Polloway and A. L. Meade. Reprinted with permission.

FIGURE 8.6
Vocabulary Development

▌Fluency

Another key concern is to develop fluency in reading. It serves as an appropriate bridge between word recognition and comprehension because as students are able to read sentences and passages more fluently, they are subsequently better able to follow the text meaning. **Fluency** can be defined as "the ability to read text accurately, quickly, and with expression. All three of its elements—accuracy, speed, and expression—are essential if students are to understand what they read" (Bursuck & Damer, 2007, p. 169).

Effective strategies for promoting fluency include the use of repeated readings, unison reading (in which the teacher and student read a text together), paired reading in which a more mature person reads with a less skilled reader, and, of course, the usual opportunities to engage in reading both orally and silently. Kubina and Hughes (2007) noted that "many students, even when they become accurate decoders, do not automatically become fluent readers and must be taught to do so by providing meaningful practice through repeated exposure to text" (p. 1).

Repeated Readings

An important fluency approach, which also can support both the development of decoding skills and comprehension, is a repeated reading or multiple oral reading (MOR) approach. MOR is based on the assumption that limiting the number of possible responses results in an increased probability of accuracy. The greater the problems the child has with word recognition, the greater the need for vocabulary redundancy. Moyer (1982) outlined the following steps for MOR:

1. Choose materials at a level that results in limited difficulty in word recognition.
2. Have the child read the passage at a comfortable pace.
3. Have the child reread the passage three or four times, increasing the speed with each reading.
4. Use passages of approximately three or four paragraphs on average; vary according to the student's needs.

Figure 8.7 provides a list of steps for implementing repeated reading strategies that complements the procedures already noted.

From their review of research, Mastropieri and Scruggs (1997) concluded that reading the same passage three or four times had a positive effect on both fluency and passage comprehension. The authors cautioned, however, that additional readings would yield diminishing returns and that repeated readings of a given text may have positive effects on the reading of other texts only to the extent that words overlap significantly. Mastropieri, Leinart, and Scruggs (1999) concluded that "fluency can be improved when students with reading difficulties are provided with specific instructions, including repeated readings, guidance, and procedures for monitoring their reading performance" (p. 280).

Repeated Reading Directions for the Teacher

1. Explain to students how practice helps reading.
2. Select appropriate reading rate goals for each student.
3. Select reading selections at appropriate reading levels for each student.
4. Determine how to calculate the reading rates by using precounted passages or by using a designated amount of minutes each time.
5. Teach students how to calculate, record, and interpret reading rates.

Repeated Reading Directions for the Learner

1. Choose a story that interests you from the list provided by your teacher.
2. Practice reading the story by yourself or with your teacher or friend for 10 minutes. (Alternatively, read the story or selection three times.)
3. Ask for help in pronouncing words when you need it.
4. After practicing the story, read it as fast as you can while using the stopwatch to time yourself.
5. Record your progress on your graph.
6. Compare your performance with the reading rate given to you by your teacher.

Source: From "Strategies to Increase Reading Fluency," by M. A. Mastropieri, A. Leinart, and T. E. Scruggs, 1999, *Intervention in School and Clinic, 34,* p. 280. Copyright 1999 by Sage Publications, Inc. Journals. Reprinted with permission.

FIGURE 8.7
Steps for Implementing Repeated Reading Strategies

From its review of the research on reading and reading instruction, the NRP (2000) concluded that the use of repeated oral reading procedures positively affects students' reading in terms of word recognition, fluency, and comprehension. The NRP noted:

> In the early stage of reading instruction, the beginning reader may be accurate in word recognition but the process is likely to be slow and effortful. With increased practice and repeated exposure to the words in the texts that the student reads, word recognition continues to be accurate [and improvements are] evident in the speed and ease of word recognition as well. Continued reading practice helps make the word recognition process increasingly automatic. (p. 3–8)

Pressley and Fingeret (2005) reviewed research on multiple readings subsequent to NRP's 2000 report. They indicated that repeated readings were effective in enhancing reading fluency. Further, they noted that teacher guidance was the most critical component and that students evidenced more significant gains in both fluency and comprehension when teachers were guiding their reading than when the students were reading passages on their own.

Although repeated readings have been recognized for decades as an appropriate approach to promote reading achievement and, in particular, fluency, it should be used with caution. In a review of evidence-based practices with students with learning disabilities, Chard, Ketterlin-Geller, Baker, Doabler, and Apichatabutra (2009) reported that repeated reading did not meet the exacting criteria to be a qualified "as an evidence-based or promising practice for students with or at risk for learning disabilities" (p. 276). Other reviews found positive effects from repeated reading when combined with explicit instruction in word skills or fluency (e.g., Joseph & Schisler, 2009), so teachers will want to assess the value of this approach to promote fluency and also to enhance practice in word recognition and ultimately link to comprehension.

▌Comprehension

Comprehension is clearly the focus of reading. As a consequence, many approaches are available to enable those who teach children with reading problems to develop effective instructional strategies. In their review of reading comprehension strategies, Mastropieri and Scruggs (1997) defined **comprehension** as "a process of constructing meaning from written texts, based on a complex coordination of a number of interrelated sources of information" (p. 197). As they noted, comprehension is arguably the most critical academic skill taught in school.

Specific levels of comprehension include the following (see also Figure 8.8):

1. Literal: the stated points of a passage
2. Inferential: the implied as well as direct meanings of a passage
3. Critical: judgments and evaluations that hinge largely on the reader's interpretations

The National Joint Committee on Learning Disabilities (NJCLD, 2008) noted that students with learning disabilities experienced difficulty with one or more of the following skill areas:

> literal understanding of what is read; ability to identify specific aspects of the text that reflect overall meaning; extension of the ideas in the text by making simple inferences; drawing conclusions based on the text. (p. 211)

As part of its comprehensive assessment of research on reading and reading instruction, the NRP (2000, pp. 4–6) reviewed 203 text comprehension studies and

---

Sample questions after reading *Goldilocks and the Three Bears*

1. Literal: What did the author say? Choose Two.
   - Goldilocks did not like porridge.
   - Goldilocks broke the wee bear's chair.
   - Goldilocks found the middle-sized bed just right.
   - The bears came home and frightened her.

2. Inferential: What did the author mean? Choose Two.
   - The wee bear had more in common with Goldilocks than Papa & Mama did.
   - Goldilocks was a vandal.
   - Goldilocks was a very curious little girl.
   - The bears were not friendly.

3. Critical: How can we use the meanings? Choose Two.
   - A bear's home is his castle.
   - Trespassing is forbidden.
   - Girls should stay out of strange bedrooms.
   - Locking your door may save your porridge.
   - Children's curiosity often gets them into trouble.

FIGURE 8.8

Levels of Comprehension

---

concluded that eight kinds of instruction appeared to be most effective and promising for classroom instruction in the area of reading comprehension:

1. Comprehension monitoring: Readers learn how to be conscious of their understanding of the material during reading and learn procedures to deal with problems in understanding as they arise.
2. Cooperative learning: Readers work together to learn reading strategies.
3. Graphic and semantic organizers: Readers learn to graphically represent the meanings of the material and the relationships of the ideas.
4. Story structure: Readers learn to ask and answer who, what, where, when, and why questions about the plot and map out the timeline, characters, and events in stories.
5. Question answering: Readers answer questions posed by the teacher and are given feedback on the correctness of their answers.
6. Question generation: Readers ask what, when, where, why, what will happen, how, and who questions.
7. Summarization: Readers attempt to identify and write the main idea that integrates the other meanings of the text into a coherent whole.
8. Multiple-strategy teaching: Readers use several of these procedures and interact with the teacher over the text.

Holistic Programs

Reid and Kuykendall (1996) summarized key concepts associated with holistic approaches as follows:

- Language, including speaking, listening, reading, and writing, develops interdependently as well as in a social context.
- Students learn to write by engaging in the writing process.
- Students are involved in daily writing activities that focus on real-life situations and experiences.
- Teachers serve as mediators during the whole language process, providing support but not overly interfering with the learning process.
- Students become involved in writing connected to their own lives.
- Students should be immersed in an environment that is filled with language materials and activities, including high-interest reading materials and print that they have helped produce.
- Students must be encouraged and motivated to share their experiences derived through literature.

Specific activities consistent with holistic approaches may include the following, as summarized by Polloway et al. (2008):

- Discussions of short stories led by the teacher
- Sharing of literacy experiences derived by students by reading books and stories
- Specific silent reading periods after which students write their reactions to the material read and share their reactions with other students and the teacher
- Group story writing (e.g., the language experience approach, discussed in the next section of this chapter)
- Individual student writing exercises, after which students share their work and engage in collaborative revisions
- Use of reading and writing to develop themes within specific content areas of the curriculum

The **language experience approach (LEA)** is based on the child's own oral language, which the student and the teacher develop into stories for reading. LEA has the advantages of being a relevant approach, with built-in motivation, that adopts a holistic philosophy by integrating speaking, listening, reading, and writing. Capitalizing on LEA's motivational benefits, the teacher can use the technique to present specific sight words to the child by embedding them within the child's stories and by providing a helpful context to assist the child in developing vocabulary and understanding meaning.

Tompkins (2005) outlined these stages for using the LEA:

1. Provide an experience to serve as the stimulus for writing.
2. Talk about the experience prior to writing.

3. Record the dictation from students on writing paper or in small booklets.
4. Read the text after the teacher has read it aloud while pointing to individual words.
5. Have the students then join in reading the new text.

The use of dictated stories can add an element of incentive and variation for teaching word recognition and building vocabulary, in addition to building comprehension.

Although holistic programs have been touted as appropriate for students with special needs, they typically do not offer the kind of systematic and explicit skills-based instruction that is necessary to acquire critical decoding skills. Consequently, such programs are best used to provide a literacy balance to comprehensive reading programs.

Teacher-Directed Questioning Strategies

Most programs (including basal readers) designed to develop comprehension skills rely, at least initially, on opportunities for students to read passages under the teacher's direction. These approaches provide questioning strategies that orient students to the reading task and support their efforts.

The directed reading/thinking activity (DRTA) approach is a common teacher-directed approach. Using this method, teachers help students develop reading expectations before the students read a passage. Specific questions and discussion give students a purpose before starting to read and a means of anticipating events that may occur in the passage. This orientation to task prepares students for what will be read and enables them to comprehend and recall key features.

The steps employed in DRTA vary according to the students, the specific skills being taught, and the overall lesson goals the teacher establishes. Basically, however, the method entails the following procedure.

1. Teachers orient students to the story and stimulate their interest and enthusiasm by discussing aspects of the story to be read. The title, pictures, and first sentence are good places to begin.
2. Teachers tell students what method of reading to use. The students should understand the purpose for reading so they know whether to skim quickly or to read carefully for details. In addition, specific questions can be asked to help set the purpose for the passage, although teachers should be careful not to make the questions so self-limiting that they impede comprehension. Teachers can provide cues to possible problem words in these questions. For example, they might say: "Read the first paragraph to find out why the boy had to go to the hospital." Depending on the students' ability level, teachers may direct silent reading for a sentence, a paragraph, a page, or a full story.
3. Once the reading assignment is complete, the students answer and discuss questions about the passage. Topics related to the purpose of the assignment can be explored, and questions tapping skills at various comprehension levels should be among those asked.

4. Silent rereading for specific objectives or oral reading as reinforcement can be included in the lesson.

Teacher questioning strategies are critical for helping children develop specific comprehension skills. Because students' comprehension needs vary widely, the questions should be designed to achieve appropriate results. Frequently, the vast majority of teachers' questions are literal, requesting factual recall and recognition. Questions of that nature, however, may strengthen some abilities to the exclusion of other skills.

Student-Directed Strategies

A key component of instruction in general, and reading comprehension in particular, is the incorporation of student-centered strategies for learning. Students are taught to develop their own "inner voice" as instructional responsibility moves from teacher-directed to self-directed learning. It forms the basis for self-regulation and learning strategy training. To be successful, students must become active learners, which means that they are goal-directed, are problem-solvers, are reflective, accept responsibility for their work, are aware of their thinking and related thinking strategies, and are able to adapt to variant task demands.

Reading comprehension strategies are "among the most thoroughly researched interventions in special education" (Brigham, Berkley, Simpkins, & Brigham, 2007, p. 3). Comprehension strategies include the process of students asking themselves questions and answering those questions about textual material prior to, during, and following the reading process (Brigham et al., 2007). Consistent with effective practices in strategy instruction in general, student use of specific comprehension strategies must follow an intensive instructional sequence in which teachers model the strategy, students practice it with teacher guidance, and then students learn to use it independently.

Klingner, Vaughn, Arguelles, Hughes, and Leftwich (2004) pointed out two reasons that students need strategies to understand expository text in particular:

1. This type of writing is common in general education classes and creates significant demands to read and to learn from textual material.
2. Areas in which expository text would be most common, such as science and social studies, may also be class periods in which supported instruction provided by special education professionals may not be present.

Given these concerns, an essential aspect of instruction must be to assist students in the development and use of strategies to comprehend independently. Instruction in strategies for comprehension is critical because it enables students to monitor their comprehension while they are learning new words and learning new concepts that are presented within textual material (Vaughn & Edmonds, 2006). Pressley and Fingeret (2005) recommended that teachers focus on a small number of comprehension strategies, clearly explain them to students, and model them until the students are able to select and use these strategies on their own.

Comprehension Monitoring

To learn to read, children must actively participate in the learning process, taking responsibility for their own learning and engaging in metacognition as they think about what they are reading. **Comprehension monitoring,** or self-questioning, promotes the development of metacognitive skills, leading to improvement in comprehension. Initially, Wong (1979) promoted comprehension monitoring for use with readers having learning disabilities and developed metacomprehension or comprehension monitoring strategies.

Whereas successful readers learn to monitor how well they understand the text they are reading while they are reading, students with disabilities often find this a challenge. Discussing this problem, Gersten and Baker (1999) indicated

> Typically, students with learning disabilities must learn several self-monitoring techniques. . . . Students who are taught a number of strategies to use as they read, such as asking themselves questions as they read and summarizing what they read, generally experience more improvements in comprehension than students who were taught a single, specific comprehension skill. It is essential for students to learn "repair strategies" to use when they find themselves not understanding the text they are reading. (p. 4)

Several features characteristic of self-monitoring strategies that promote enhanced reading comprehension are (Mastropieri & Scruggs, 1997, p. 205):

- clear, explicit instruction in a strategy associated with enhancing reading comprehension,
- detailed self-monitoring procedures that require students to mark off steps on a card as they proceed,
- informing students about the purpose of the strategy instruction, and
- attributing success to controllable factors (e.g., reminding students that their use of a strategy will be beneficial to them and will influence their success).

The central element of comprehension monitoring is students' use of questions. Bryant et al. (1999) identified the following series of potential questions for students to ask before, during, and after reading:

Before:

1. What is my purpose for reading?
2. What do I already know about this topic?
3. What do I think I will learn about this topic?
4. What are my predictions?

During:

1. Does what I am reading make sense?
2. Is this what I expected?

3. Should I revise my predictions or suspend judgment until later?
4. How are the important points related to one another?
5. What parts are similar or different?
6. What can I do to increase my understanding? Should I read on, reread, or stop and use a fix-up strategy?

After:

1. What were the most important points?
2. Which sections supported these points?
3. What is my opinion? How do I feel? Do I agree or disagree?
4. What new information did I learn?
5. Should I reread for better understanding? Are there other strategies that I should use? (p. 301)

Englert et al. (2009) developed the *Reads-It* approach to engage students in reading and understanding expository text. This approach helps students connect main ideas and details and also apply strategies to keep them actively engaged during the reading process.

Jitendra, Hoppes, and Xin (2000) studied the effectiveness of a main-idea strategy and a self-monitoring instructional procedure with middle school students who have high-incidence disabilities. The intervention included the use of a prompt card to cue the main idea (see Figure 8.9) complemented by a self-monitoring strategy. Students placed a check mark on a self-monitoring card if they read the paragraph, used the main idea prompt card to recall the particular step, applied the strategy to identify the main idea, and selected (or wrote) the main idea.

Other Student-Centered Strategies

In addition to the student-centered strategies discussed above, there are several other important examples of tactics that can enhance the ability of students to take responsibility for their own comprehension of what they read. Three examples are discussed below.

RAP RAP is a strategy developed by the Kansas Institute for Research on Learning Disabilities to enhance reading comprehension. With this strategy, students are instructed to **R**ead a paragraph, **A**sk themselves what the main idea was, and then **P**ut the response into their own words. Successful use of RAP facilitates students' paragraph-by-paragraph reading of text with a self-monitoring strategy available to continue to think about what is being read.

The Survey-Question-Read-Recite-Review (SQ3R) The SQ3R technique was intended as a student-directed strategy when it was originally developed by Robinson (1946). It can be modified for various teaching or learning situations. The five steps in SQ3R are survey, question, read, recite, and review. The survey step introduces a story by focusing on pictures, the title, and the first sentence. Then questions orient the student to each paragraph or series of paragraphs. Next, students read each

FINDING THE MAIN IDEA

Does the paragraph tell:

What or who the
Subject is?   Action is?
(Single or Group)   (Category)

Why – something happened?

Where – something is or happened?

When – something happened?

How – something looks or is done?

Note: Some paragraphs may contain a sentence or two that don't tell about the main idea!

Source: From "Enhancing Main Idea Comprehension for Students With Learning Problems: The Role of a Summarization Strategy and Self-Monitoring Instruction," by A. K. Jitendra, M. K. Hopps, and Y. P. Xin, 2000, *Journal of Special Education, 34,* p. 130. Copyright 2000 by Sage Publications, Inc. Journals. Reprinted by permission.

FIGURE 8.9
Prompt Card for Main Idea

section to find answers to the questions and attempt to recite the responses without referring back to the text. After students complete the story, they review it by answering direct questions and reading selected sections aloud.

Collaborative Reading   A number of peer-mediated strategies can enhance comprehension. One such approach, developed by Vaughn and Klingner (1999), encourages the use of collaborative strategic reading to enhance the comprehension skills of students with disabilities. The authors identified four specific strategies that encompass this approach: Preview, Click and Clunk, Get the Gist, and Wrap-Up. Procedures for using these four approaches are summarized in Figure 8.10.

A good example of peer mediation is the peer assisted learning strategies approach (PALS), which matches a student with a same-age peer and typically includes a higher and lower performer within the class (Fuchs & Fuchs, 2005). The roles of the tutors are reciprocal, but the program has a student who is higher performing read first for each of the instructional activities, to model the goal performance.

Peer-mediated reading programs can be beneficial for both tutors and tutees. Mastropieri et al. (2001) reported, for example, that middle school students with

Preview

We preview before reading. Previewing has two steps:

- Brainstorming. Think about what you already know about the topic.
- Predicting. Find clues in the title, subheadings, or pictures about what you will learn. Skim the text for keywords that might give you hints.

Click and Clunk

We find clicks and clunks while we are reading. When we understand what we read, everything "clicks" along smoothly. But when we don't understand, "clunk," we stop. When we get a clunk, we use the following fix-up strategies to figure out what the clunk means:

- Reread the sentence with the clunk and the sentences before or after the clunk, looking for clues.
- Reread the sentence without the word. Think about what would make sense.
- Look for a prefix or suffix in the word.
- Break the word apart and look for smaller words.
- Use a picture.
- Ask for help.

Get the Gist

We get the gist after reading each paragraph or section of a passage. To get the gist means to summarize or restate the most important idea. Do not include the supporting details. State the gist in your own words using the following cues:

- Decide who or what the paragraph is mostly about (the topic).
- Name the most important idea about the topic.

Wrap-Up

We wrap up after finishing the day's reading assignment. Wrap-Up includes:

- Asking (teacher-like) questions about the passage.
- Reviewing by thinking about what was important that you learned from the day's reading assignment.

Source: Strategies for Teaching Students with Learning and Behavior Problems (p. 214, Figure 5.16), by C. S. Bos and S. Vaughn, 1998, Boston: Allyn & Bacon. Copyright 1998 by Pearson Education. Reprinted with permission.

FIGURE 8.10

Steps in Collaborative Strategic Reading

disabilities enjoyed a reciprocal tutoring approach with their peers, wanted to expand its usage, and achieved more significant gains in comprehension than did students participating in a more traditional instructional approach.

Graphic Organizers

Graphic organizers (GO) include a variety of strategies that provide a visual model for students to understand text and concepts and see relationships. Graphic organizers have been supported consistently in research. For example, Ae-Hwa Kim, Vaughn, Wanzek, & Shangjin Wei (2004, p. 116) reported that "semantic organizers, cognitive maps with and without mnemonics, and framed outlines promote comprehension. These visual systems enhance reading comprehension by helping them organize the verbal information and thereby improving their recall."

Englert et al. (2009) noted the value of graphic organizers (both teacher developed and student generated) as related to text structure in particular:

> The ability to recognize the text structure and to construct the conceptual relationships among ideas is a critical skill that is not mastered by numerous students. Many students are passive learners who lack the skills for processing and organizing textual information. . . . Instructionally, this suggests that teachers must be diligent in providing explanations and graphical models that help students connect the superordinate and subordinate concepts of the curriculum.
>
> The use of graphical organizers is an effective learning tool that can be used to advance students' expository comprehension and composition performance . . . but there is one instructional caveat. Teachers must not only present graphic organizers; they must teach students to design and construct their own organizers as a basis for planning, comprehending, interpreting, and composing expository texts.
>
> Students need to become strategic and flexible in recognizing and arranging the expository information to address the different learning purposes and goals associated with the different text structures (e.g., cause–effect, problem–solution, compare–contrast, explanation, chronological sequence). Otherwise students will remain dependent on teachers for content guidance (p. 159).

An important graphic technique for reading as well as for studying content material is **semantic mapping.** Essentially, student use their prior knowledge of a topic to assist in developing a diagram of what is to be read. This procedure can focus on the introduction of words with unknown meaning as well as the association between key themes or concepts within the passage being read. The steps in a semantic mapping process are as follows:

1. The teacher presents students with either a stimulus word or a specific core question central to a selection to be read.
2. The students generate words related to the stimulus word or predict answers to the question, and the teacher lists the words or answers on the board.
3. Students, with the teacher's assistance, group related words or answers and draw connecting lines between the groups to form a semantic map.

4. After reading the selection, the students and teacher discuss the categories in the map and rearrange or add to the map.

Rooney (1988) developed a systematic procedure for efficient studying that derives from the concepts of graphic organizers. Referred to as "wheels for reading," it uses the wheel as the basis for organizing and keeping track of main ideas and details. Figure 8.11 illustrates a graphic organizer as a wheel.

Three other useful GOs are provided in Table 8.6 and Figures 8.12 and 8.13. These provide examples of using graphic organizers as story maps and for summarizing what was read, respectively.

Misquitta (2009) offered four models of expository text structures. These visual representations can provide graphic organizers for students reading guidance in the comprehension of these respective forms of text (see Figure 8.13).

■Students with Significant Disabilities

Although some of the various strategies presented in this chapter also have merit for students with more significant disabilities and for students with autism spectrum disorders (ASD), clearly these students warrant special attention in designing effective programs. An overview of special considerations is provided in Figure 8.14.

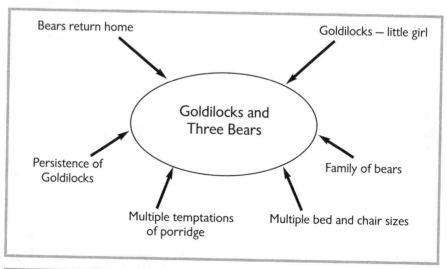

FIGURE 8.11

Wheels for Reading

TABLE 8.6
Using a Story Map: Snow White

Questions	Examples
Who are the characters?	■ Snow White ■ Seven Dwarfs ■ Wicked Queen ■ Prince Charming ■ Magic Mirror
Where does it take place?	A faraway land
When does it begin?	Once Upon A Time
What is the problem?	Snow White is in an enchanted sleep due to a poison apple.
What is the goal?	To awaken Snow White with true love's kiss
What are the events?	■ Magic Mirror reveals Snow White is the fairest in the land. ■ Wicked Queen tries to have Snow White killed. ■ Snow White escapes and meets Dwarfs. ■ Snow White eats poison apple. ■ Prince Charming kisses Snow White.
What is the final result?	The Prince and Snow White live happily ever after.

Source: From *Models in Education* (p. 6), by E. A. Polloway, and A. L. Meade, 2009, unpublished manuscript, Lynchburg College, Lynchburg, VA. Copyright by E. A. Polloway and A. L. Meade. Reprinted with permission.

▌Commercial Reading Programs

A variety of curricular materials can serve as either core or supplemental programs in the development of reading skills. We will review a sample of reading materials that have been used successfully with learners who have special needs.

Lindamood Phoneme Sequencing Program for Reading, Spelling, and Speech (Lindamood & Lindamood, 1998)

This program promotes the development of phonemic awareness by teaching learners to identify and sequence individual sounds in order within words, thereby promoting

---

Summarizing

What do I know after reading?

■ _____

■ _____

■ _____

What questions/answers do I have for my buddy (partner)?

■ _____

■ _____

■ _____

How can I summarize what I read in one paragraph?

_____

_____

_____

_____

_____

Source: From *Models in Education* (p. 7), by E. A. Polloway and A. L. Meade, 2009, unpublished manuscript, Lynchburg College, Lynchburg, VA. Copyright by E. A. Polloway and A. L. Meade. Reprinted with permission.

FIGURE 8.12
Summarizing: A Graphic Organizer Strategy

competence in reading, spelling, and speech. The key element is learning consonant and vowel sounds through feedback following articulation of the sounds. The program includes a training manual, a research booklet, videotapes, photographs of correct mouth formation for phoneme pronunciation, and a variety of instructional materials. A comprehensive research review by Truch (1998) confirmed the effectiveness of the Lindamood program within the context of an analysis of the role of phonological processing in reading and spelling.

Phonological Awareness Training for Reading (Torgesen & Bryant, 1994)

This program was designed to increase phonological awareness in kindergarten children at risk for failure and in first- and second-grade children who have begun to

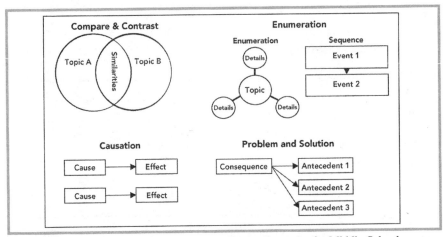

Source: From "Unraveling Expository Texts: Effective Strategies for Middle-School Students with LD," by R. Misquitta, March 2009, *LD Forum,* p. 2. Copyright 2009 by CLD. Reprinted with permission.

FIGURE 8.13

Expository Test Structures

- Determine realistic literacy goals based on past progress of student and time remaining in school.
- Assess importance of literary skills in context of other key school and life skills.
- Teach core functional vocabulary including survival words and coincidentally teach word meanings.
- Develop a sight vocabulary of common words (consider the Edmark Program).
- Determine whether success can be achieved with the teaching of phonetic analysis skills and proceed if so.
- Use constant time delay to promote sight word recognition.
- Tie initial reading to the use of picture cues.
- Use a picture exchange communication system (PECS) to promote communication in general as well as literacy.
- Select reading material that is relevant and interesting to students, such as those with Asperger syndrome.
- Teach sight words in general, and survival words in particular, in the context where they are actually to be used (e.g., community settings) to assist with learning and generalization.
- Use errorless discrimination strategies in which students identify words from a cluster of visually unlike words that gradually become more familiar.
- Use graphic organizers to promote conceptual development and comprehension.

FIGURE 8.14

Selected Considerations for Teaching Reading to Students with Significant Disabilities, Including Autism Spectrum Disorder

experience difficulty in learning to read. The approximately 12-week-long program teaches sensitivity to the phonological structures of words and includes a training manual, picture word cards, rhyming picture cards, and a variety of other instructional materials. In their review of the program, Wanzek, Dickson, Bursuck, and White (2000) reported that it addressed the key curricular principles necessary for effective use with at-risk learners.

Edmark Reading Program (Edmark Associates, 2002)

Edmark teaches basic reading skills through stories and activities and is available in a software version. Level 1 was designed to teach a 150-word sight vocabulary derived from the Dolch list and primary books to students with retardation. Its target population could include nonreaders who have mild through severe retardation, as well as students with learning disabilities. Prerequisites for the program include basic receptive vocabulary, verbal skills (i.e., can repeat the words), and an ability to make gestural or verbal responses. Specific emphases as stated in the program include word endings (-s, -ed, -ing), capitalization and punctuation, left-to-right reading/tracking, visual memory of words (sets of letters), thinking and discrimination skills, combined sentences for meaningful stories, development of independence, and reading practice. Level 2 of the program teaches 200 additional sight words, also derived from the Dolch list and primary books. The Level 2 material includes adolescent characters in the stories (see Figure 8.15).

Gillingham–Stillman Remedial Reading Manual (Gillingham & Stillman, 1970)

This program was developed in the 1940s to teach reading, writing, and spelling to children with specific learning disabilities in these areas. Based on the language research of Samuel Orton, the program demonstrates the symbolic nature of printed language and identifies the relationships of sounds to words. The method for teaching reading and spelling is basically phonetic in nature, with multisensory emphases reflected in exercises involving the visual, auditory, and kinesthetic channels.

Phonetic spelling regularities are taught first, and then the words are practiced through reading, writing, and spelling drills. Rules for phonetic spelling of exceptions, syllabications, plurals, and affixes then are taught.

Practicing handwriting to correct reversals is an important aspect of the program. The manual includes word cards for drill and stories. Although the program requires teacher training and a clinical setting for its successful implementation, the manual itself contains helpful teaching guides that instructors can modify. The reader may wish to consult Bhat, Rapport, and Griffin (2000) for an informative discussion of legal perspectives related to parental concerns over a child's academic progress and parents' preference for more intensive, clinical approaches such as the Gillingham-Skillman approach.

Level 1:

- Sequenced, highly repetitive sight-word approach
  - ☐ Students reading below first grade level
  - ☐ 150 sight words as well as simple endings (-s, -ed, -ing)
  - ☐ Sight words correlated with Dolch word list

- Goal: Bring students to first grade reading level
- Lessons presented 1 to 1 (individually with aide or teacher)
- Each lesson takes 5–10 minutes
- Each lesson builds on prior lessons, taught in same manner
- Students point to word in isolation, then point to word paired with 3 different words, then read word

Additional Materials:

- Supplemental Stories
- Direction Cards
- Picture/Phrase Cards

Level 2:

- Introduces 200 words, including compounds
- Lessons: same pattern as Level 1
- Stories longer, direction cards harder, picture/phrase lessons longer sentences
- Goal: Students reach reading level of 2.0–3.0

Source: Adapted from *Edmark Reading Program Presentation*, by V. Casto, 2004 unpublished manuscript, Lynchburg College.

FIGURE 8.15

Edmark Reading Program

Reading Mastery Program (Engelmann, 2003)

The Reading Mastery Program evolved from the reading program of the Direct Instructional System for Teaching Arithmetic and Reading (DISTAR), designed as a 3-year teaching program for preschool and primary-grade children. Reading Mastery is a phonetically-based program that emphasizes auditory and sound-blending skills. A phonetic alphabet of 40 symbols is taught in a highly sequential manner before letter names are introduced. In each daily lesson, the teacher reads the material to a small group of students and asks individuals to respond orally when given certain designated symbols. Each child's behavior and responses are carefully monitored during this exercise.

The program also contains reading materials using the special symbols, as well as seatwork activities including word analysis and comprehension drills. A sight vocabulary covers phonetically irregular words, and teachers can assess skill development throughout the program using the tests provided. Other materials in this series are teacher's guides, lesson plans, reading books, workbooks, spelling books, take-home readers, and cassettes with sound pronunciations.

SRA Corrective Reading Program (CRP; Engelmann, 1999)

CRP was designed for 4th- to 12th-grade children with poor decoding skills. Decoding skills are improved by a combination of drills, repetitious reading of phonetic and sight vocabulary words, and reinforcement of the behavioral system. A comprehension program is also available.

The decoding program within the CRP has been the most widely used and researched component of the program. It teaches a carefully sequenced hierarchy of continuous skills; allows for monitoring of progress through criterion-referenced tests; includes lessons of about 45 minutes, in which pupils give group and individual oral responses as well as individual written responses; and incorporates reinforcement of pupil improvement through positive verbal feedback and by earning points. Placement into one of the three levels of the reading program is determined by performance on an assessment measure.

Level A is essentially for the nonreader; it deals with basic skills such as sound blending, rhyming, sounding-out, and word and sentence reading. Level B covers critical letter and word discrimination, letter combinations, story reading, and questions. Level C is designed for students who are ready to decode a wide variety of words and sentence constructions, such as those they will encounter in varied reading materials. It emphasizes advanced word-attack skills, affixes, vocabulary, story-reading with comprehension questions, and outside reading applications.

Corrective Reading is among the few programs that have demonstrated effectiveness with older students who have reading difficulties. Studies that have supported the program's effectiveness with older students were conducted by Lloyd, Cullinan, Heins, and Epstein (1980) and by Polloway, Epstein, Polloway, Patton, and Ball (1986). In the former study, Lloyd et al. reported that fourth-, fifth-, and sixth-graders with learning disabilities who took part in the program significantly enhanced their scores on measures of reading and language skills. Polloway et al. reported positive results with middle school and high school students identified as having learning disabilities or mild retardation. Joseph and Schisler's (2009) review of the literature also confirmed the efficacy of the CRP with adolescent learners.

Basal Readers

A significant percentage of teachers choose basal readers from the variety of core programs available. These series have both distinct advantages and disadvantages. On the positive side, they contain inherent structure and sequence, controlled vocabulary, a wide variety of teaching activities, and preparation for the teacher. On the negative side, they cannot match pacing to the needs of each individual child, they overemphasize certain skills to the exclusion of others, and they tend to encourage a large-group instructional orientation. For the inexperienced teacher, however, basal readers may represent an appropriate place to begin developing a responsive reading program.

▌Summary

Reading instruction can be based on a variety of models of learning how to read. Some approaches emphasize a decoding orientation, and others adopt a top-down approach that emphasizes the importance of meaning in reading.

A foundation for effective reading it is in the area of phonemic awareness. Developing skills in this area provides a foundation for decoding skills. Four key word recognition strategies are offered to assist the reader. *Sight word instruction* emphasizes the development of automaticity as students learn to recognize an ever-increasing number of words immediately upon sight. *Phonetic analysis* provides a vehicle for teaching students to learn to use sound–symbol correspondences in analyzing unknown words. *Structural analysis* provides the reader with the ability to analyze words by considering affixes, contractions, compound words, and syllables. *Contextual analysis* bridges the gap between the analysis of words and the meaning of a passage and thus provides students with a syntactic and semantic cuing system. The development of a strong vocabulary, in terms of word meaning and fluency, is also critical to effective reading

Comprehension is the essential goal in all reading instruction. Teachers can enhance students' comprehension by selecting instructional activities that include a variety of teacher- and student-directed strategies. A variety of commercial programs are available to promote successful reading.

▌References

Ae-Hwa Kim, B., Vaughn, S., Wanzek, J., & Shangjin Wei, J. (2004). Graphic organizers and their effects on the reading comprehension of students with LD: A synthesis of research. *Journal of Learning Disabilities, 37*, 105–118.

Armbruster, B. B., Lehr, F., & Osborn, J., (2003). *Put reading first: The research building blocks for teaching children to read. Kindergarten through grade 3*. Jessup, MO: National Institute for Literacy.

Bamman, H., & Whitehead, R. (1968). *With American heroes*. Westchester, IL: Benefic Press.

Bhat, P., Rapport, M. J. K., & Griffin, C. C. (2000). A legal perspective in the use of specific reading methods for students with learning disabilities. *Learning Disability Quarterly, 23*, 283–297.

Bos, C. S., & Vaughn, S. (1998). *Strategies for teaching students with learning and behavior problems*. Boston: Allyn & Bacon.

Bremer, C., Clapper, A., & Deshler, D. (2002). *Improving word identification skills using strategic instruction model (SIM) strategies. Research to practice brief.* (ERIC Document Reproduction Service No. ED475506)

Brigham, F. J., Berkley, S., Simpkins, P., & Brigham, M. S. P. (2007). A focus on reading comprehension strategy instruction. *Current Practice Alerts, Winter 2007*(12), pp. 1–4.

Bryant, D. P., Ugel, N., Thompson, S., & Hamff, A. (1999). Instructional strategies for content area reading instruction. *Intervention in School and Clinic, 34,* 293–302.

Bryant, D. P., Vaughn, S., Linan-Thompson, S., Ugel, N., Hamff, A., & Hougen, M. (2000). Reading outcomes for students with and without reading disabilities in general education middle school content area classes. *Learning Disabilities Quarterly, 23,* 238–252.

Bursuck, W., & Damer, M. (2007). *Reading instruction for students who are at risk or have disabilities*. Boston: Allyn & Bacon.

Casto, V. (2004). *Edmark reading program*. Unpublished manuscript, Lynchburg College, VA.

Center for the Future of Teaching and Learning. (1996). Thirty years of NICHD research: What we now know about how children learn to read. *Effective School Practices, 15*(3), 33–46.

Chard, D., Ketterlin-Geller, L., Baker, S., Doabler, C., & Apichatabutra, C. (2009). Repeated reading interventions for students with learning disabilities. Status of the evidence. *Exceptional Children, 75,* 263–281.

Chard, D. J., & Dickson, S. B. (1999). Phonological awareness: Instructional and assessment guidelines. *Intervention in School and Clinic, 34,* 261–270.

Clymer, T. (1963). The utility of phonic generalizations in the primary grades. *Reading Teacher, 16,* 252–258.

Coyne, M. D., Kameenui, E. J., & Simmons, D. C. (2001). Prevention and intervention in beginning reading: Two complex systems. *Learning Disabilities Research and Practice, 16*(2), 62–73.

Edmark Associates. (2002). *Edmark reading program*. Seattle: Riverdeep Interactive Learning.

Engelmann, S. (1999). *SRA Corrective reading program*. Chicago: Science Research Associates.

Engelmann, S. (2003). *Reading mastery program*. Chicago: Science Research Associates.

Englert, C., Mariage, T., Okolo, C., Shankland, R., Moxley, K., Courtad, C., et al. (2009). The learning-to-learn strategies of adolescent students with disabilities: Highlighting, note taking, planning, and writing expository texts. *Assessment for Effective Intervention, 34,* 147–161.

Fernald, G. M. (1943). *Remedial techniques in basic school subjects*. New York: McGraw-Hill.

Fernald, G. M. (1988). *Remedial techniques in basic school subjects* (L. Idol, Ed.). Austin, TX: Pro-Ed.

Francis, W. N. (1958). *The structure of American English*. New York: Ronald Press.

Fuchs, L. S., & Fuchs, D. (2005). Peer-assisted learning strategies: Promoting word recognition, fluency, and comprehension in young children." *Journal of Special Education, 39,* 34–44.

Gersten, R., & Baker, C. (1999). Reading comprehension instruction for students with learning disabilities: A research synthesis. In *Keys to successful learning: A national summit on research in learning disabilities* (pp. 4–6). Washington, DC: National Center for Learning Disabilities.

Gillingham, A., & Stillman, B. (1970). *Remedial teaching for children with specific difficulty in reading, spelling, and penmanship*. Cambridge, MA: Educators Publishing Service.

Greene, J. E. (1998). Another chance: Help for older students with limited literacy. *American Educator, 22*(1–2), 74–79.

Heilman, A., Blair, R., & Rupley, W. (1986). *Principles and practices of teaching reading.* Columbus, OH: Merrill.

Hock, M., Brasseur, I., Deshler, D., Catts, H., Marquis, J., Mark, C., et al. (2009). What is the reading component skill profile of adolescent struggling readers in urban schools? *Learning Disability Quarterly, 32*(1), 21–38.

Jitendra, A., Edwards, L., Sacks, G., & Jacobson, L. (2004). What research says about vocabulary instruction for students with learning disabilities. *Exceptional Children, 70,* 299–322.

Jitendra, A. K., Hoppes, M. L., & Xin, Y. P. (2000). Enhancing main idea comprehension for students with learning problems: The role of a summarization strategy and self-monitoring instruction. *Journal of Special Education, 34,* 127–139.

Joseph, L., & Schisler, R. (2009). Should adolescents go back to the basics? A review of teaching word reading skills to middle and high school students. *Remedial & Special Education, 30,* 131–147.

Joseph, L., & Seery, M. (2004). Where is the phonics? *Remedial and Special Education, 25,* 88–94.

Klingner, J., Vaughn, S., Arguelles, M., Hughes, M., & Leftwich, S. (2004). Collaborative strategic reading: Real-world lessons from classroom teachers. *Remedial and Special Education, 25,* 291–302.

Kubina, R. M., & Hughes, C. A. (2007). Reading fluency. *Current Practices Alert, Fall 2007*(15), pp. 1–4.

Lenz, B. K., & Hughes, C. A. (1990). A word identification strategy for adolescents with learning disabilities. *Journal of Learning Disabilities, 23,* 149–158, 163–164.

Lindamood, C., & Lindamood, P. (1998). *The Lindamood phoneme sequencing program for reading, spelling, and speech.* Austin, TX: Pro-Ed.

Lloyd, J. W., Cullinan, D., Heins, E., & Epstein, M. H. (1980). Direct instruction: Effects on oral and written comprehension. *Learning Disability Quarterly, 4,* 70–76.

Mastropieri, M. A., Leinart, A., & Scruggs, T. E. (1999). Strategies to increase reading fluency. *Intervention in School and Clinic, 34,* 278–283, 292.

Mastropieri, M. A., & Scruggs, T. E. (1997). Best practices in promoting reading comprehension in students with learning disabilities. *Remedial and Special Education, 18,* 197–213.

Mastropieri, M. A., Scruggs, T., Mohler, L., Beranek, M., Spencer, V., Boon, R. T., & Talbott, E. (2001). Can middle school students with serious reading difficulties help each other and learn anything? *Learning Disabilities Research and Practice, 16,* 18–28.

Misquitta, R. (2009, March). Unraveling expository texts: Effective strategies for middle-school students with LD. *LD Forum,* 1–3.

Moats, L. C. (2003). Why have teachers been left unprepared to teach reading? *Phi Delta Kappan, 84,* 679–681.

Moyer, S. B. (1982). Repeated reading. *Journal of Learning Disabilities, 15,* 619–624.

National Joint Committee on Learning Disabilities (NJCLD). (2008). *Adolescent literacy and older students with learning disabilities.* Retrieved from www.ldonline.org/njcld

National Reading Panel (NRP). (2000). *Report of the National Reading Panel. Teaching children to read: An evidence-based assessment of the scientific research literature on reading and its implications for reading instruction* (NIH Publication No. 00-4769). Washington, DC: U.S. Government Printing Office.

Polloway, C. H., & Polloway, E. A.(1981). Validation of a survival vocabulary list, *Academic Therapy, 16,* pp. 443–448.

Polloway, E. A., Epstein, M. H., Polloway, C. H., Patton, J. R., & Ball, D. (1986). Corrective reading program. An analysis of effectiveness with learning disabled and mentally retarded children. *Remedial and Special Education, 7*(4), 41–47.

Polloway, E. A., & Meade, A. L. (2009). *Models in Education* Unpublished manuscript, Lynchburg College, Lynchburg, VA.

Polloway, E. A., Patton, J. R., & Serna, L. (2008). *Strategies for teaching special needs* (9th ed.). Columbus, OH: Pearson.

Pressley, M., & Fingeret, L. (2005). What we have learned since the National Reading Panel: Visions of a next version of Reading First. Retrieved from www.msularc.org/sympo sium2005/pressley_paper.pdf

Reid, D. K., & Kuykendall, M. (1996). Literacy: A tale of different belief systems. In D. K. Reid, W., P. Hresko, & H. L. Swanson (Eds.), *Cognitive approaches to learning disabilities* (3rd ed., pp. 497–544). Austin, TX: Pro-Ed.

Robinson, H. (1946). *Why pupils fail in reading.* Chicago: University Chicago Press.

Rooney, K. (1988). *Independent strategies for efficient study.* Richmond, VA: J. R. Enterprises.

Swanson, H. L. (1999). Reading research for students with learning disabilities: A meta-analysis of reading outcomes. *Journal of Learning Disabilities, 32,* 504–532.

Tompkins, G. E. (2005). *Language arts patterns of practice* (6th ed.). Columbus, OH: Merrill/Prentice Hall.

Torgeson, J., & Bryant, B. (1994). *Phonological awareness training for reading.* Austin, TX: Pro-Ed.

Torgeson, J. K., & Matthes, P. G. (2000). *A basic guide to understanding, assessing and teaching phonological awareness.* Austin, TX: Pro-Ed.

Troia, G. A. (2004). A focus on phonological awareness acquisition and intervention. *Current Practice Alerts, Summer 2004*(9), pp. 1–4.

Truch, S. (1998). *Phonological processing, reading and the Lindamood Phoneme Sequencing Program: A review of related research.* Austin, TX: Pro-Ed.

Vaughn, S., & Edmonds, M. (2006). Reading comprehension for older readers. *Intervention in School & Clinic, 41,* 131–137.

Vaughn, S., & Klingner, J. K. (1999). Teaching reading comprehension through collaborative strategic reading. *Intervention in School and Clinic, 34,* 284–292.

Wanzek, J., Dickson, S., Bursuck, W. D., & White, J. M. (2000). Teaching phonological awareness to students at risk for reading failure: An analysis of four instructional programs. *Learning Disabilities Research and Practice, 15,* 226–238.

Wong, B. Y. L. (1979). The role of theory in learning disabilities research. Part II: A selective review of current theories of learning and reading disabilities. *Journal of Learning Disabilities, 12,* 649–658.

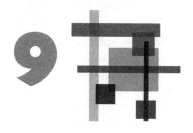

Handwriting Assessment and Instruction

P rior to the advent of personal computers, smart phones, and other technological devices, individuals communicated in writing using typewriters and handwriting. There was no such thing as instant communicating, such as is available today. Text messaging, twittering, and other new technologies have impacted, and will undoubtedly continue to impact, how communication between individuals occurs. Despite this increased use of technology, a primary mode of communication in U.S. society continues to be written language using handwriting (Smith, Polloway, Patton, & Dowdy, 2008). Handwriting remains a critical skill.

Handwriting can be defined as "a complex motor act drawing on multiple sensory systems (visual and kinesthetic), motor systems (motor planning and sequencing, motor control, and motor execution), and muscle systems (proximal, near the writing instrument, and distal, far removed from the writing instrument)" (Berninger et al., 2006, p. 6). More simply, it could be described as "the formation of alphabetic symbols on paper" (Tompkins, 2002, p. 569). Although individuals may prefer to use more sophisticated technologies, the best of compositions, notes, and correspondence may be ineffective unless they are handwritten. Without the ability to communicate through legible handwriting, individuals are at a major disadvantage. And, as noted later in the chapter, poor handwriting can have a negative impact on other skill areas as well.

At one time in the history of education in the United States, handwriting instruction received a great deal of attention (Berninger et al., 2006). Currently, however, handwriting has a low priority status in many schools, especially considering the emphasis on other aspects of literacy—reading in particular (Medwell & Wray, 2007). Vaughn and Bos (2009) have described handwriting as "the most poorly taught subject in elementary curriculum" (p. 391). Among several reasons for this, some professional educators and researchers believe that handwriting is no longer an important skill to teach to elementary school students (Luftig, 1989). They contend that everyone eventually will be using computers and other technological devices that could make handwriting unimportant.

Although the advances in technology have clearly impacted on the everyday use of handwriting for some people, competencies in this skill are definitely needed. Think how often during a given day individuals write something—a phone number, an address, a name, a to-do list, a grocery list, or some other essential piece of information. Without the ability to communicate through handwriting, individuals would be unable to make notes, take down information quickly, and communicate with others in writing when technological devices are unavailable. Even in the era of laptop computers, palm pilots, smart phones, and other technological devices, and the growing use of texting and twittering, the ability to use handwriting effectively can make the difference between effective and ineffective communication.

Simply being able to take notes is not sufficient. How often have people made notes only to realize later that they could not read their own writing or determine exactly what they meant? Notes and written communications must be legible and understandable. In addition to difficulties with their own written communication, think what others must deal with when they try to read their writing!

Handwriting is used most often in school settings. Teachers typically depend on students' handwriting to evaluate their learning (Mlyniec, 2001). For students to be successful in academic work, they must be able to use handwriting skills in note-taking, copying information from the board, and completing written work in a legible, understandable form. Students themselves understand the importance of handwriting. In a study by Kos and Maslowski (2001), 53% of second graders rated handwriting as a skill that students need to become better writers. Even with the rapid expansion of technology, the need for handwriting skills is unlikely to diminish significantly in the foreseeable future.

Research shows that handwriting skills may be linked directly to overall academic achievement (Cahill, 2009). In this way, handwriting is to composing what fluency is to reading. If students spend too much time and effort decoding words, they may have difficulty with comprehension. Likewise, if students spend too much time on the mechanics of writing, they may not express their ideas and thoughts efficiently.

After reviewing research on the impact of handwriting on other academic areas, Cahill (2009) concluded that handwriting skills may be linked to spelling skills, improved reading skills, and composition skills. These conclusions strongly support a renewed interest in teaching handwriting to students who have deficiencies in this area. Other research has shown handwriting related to working memory. When students must rely on large amounts working memory to perform tasks such as handwriting, less working memory is available for higher cognitive needs (Medwell &

Wray, 2007). Thus, students need to develop a level of automaticity in their writing to free up working memory space. Medwell and Wray (2007) noted that

> handwriting, and in particular the automaticity of letter production, appears to facilitate higher-order composing processes by freeing up working memory to deal with the complex tasks of planning, organizing, revising, and regulating the production of text. (p. 14)

Writing "is as important to literacy as is reading" (Berninger et al., 2006, p. 27). Without adequate writing skills, students are more likely to develop behavior problems, drop out of school, not receive passing grades, and even commit suicide (Berninger et al., 2006).

Teachers expect most of their students to complete academic assignments using handwriting. Students whose handwriting is illegible are at a significant disadvantage in school: Their handwriting deficiencies can diminish their chances for success across all subject areas. Teachers develop impressions about students based on a number of factors, one of which is the legibility of their handwriting. Handwriting must be taught for another reason as well. Graham, Harris, and Fink (2000) found that students' overemphasis on the mechanics of handwriting may impact the entire writing process negatively. For all of these reasons, handwriting is an essential skill for young children that must be taught in school (Tompkins, 2002).

When students exit from school, they still need adequate handwriting skills. One postschool setting in which handwriting can play a major role is the workplace, where individuals without adequate handwriting skills may have a major disadvantage. Therefore, handwriting can be integral in the transition from high school to adulthood and vocational success. Potential employers want their employees to be able to write legibly. Completing a job application requires good handwriting skills. Even if handwriting is totally unrelated to the specific demands of a given job, the ability to complete a job application with neat, legible handwriting makes an impression on the employer (Polloway, Patton, & Serna, 2008).

Adults also need legible handwriting to write personal letters, fill out mail orders, complete forms such as those for income tax, and provide information for the schools their children attend (Hagin, 1983). Although handwriting may seem to be much less essential than it was before the age of computer technology, competence in this basic skill remains vital for children and adults.

▌Trends

Even though continued fluency in handwriting is needed, emphasis on handwriting instruction has declined significantly during the past several years, for several reasons. Some technological advances have resulted in educators' questioning the need to teach handwriting (Polloway et al., 2008). In addition, the emphasis on the process of writing has often left instruction in handwriting as a secondary focus, with little or no attention to it (Combs, 2003). The contention that handwriting is less important than it was in the past and the fact that some teachers may not understand how to teach handwriting (Manning, 1986) have had a detrimental impact on students' handwriting skills. The effects include illegibility, slowness, tension, and fatigue (Furner, 1983). Although numerous programs are available to prevent problems in other academic areas, such as reading, limited efforts have been made to prevent handwriting difficulties (Graham et al., 2000).

The most recent trends in elementary curriculum development do show renewed attention to handwriting instruction (Phelps & Stempel, 1989). Teachers are increasingly accepting that "handwriting is a basic skill that needs to be systematically taught so that children can learn to use written language to communicate their knowledge and express their ideas" (Bertin & Perlman, 2000, p. 1).

Further, teachers are realizing that the speed and fluency with which students are able to utilize handwriting can have a major impact on their academic success (Mlyniec, 2001). Indeed, studies have shown a relationship between handwriting skills and the overall writing process (Graham et al., 2000). The first sign that a student might have difficulty developing composing skills is the inability to produce letters legibly and automatically (Berninger et al., 2006).

All students with normal gross- and fine-motor skills are capable of learning to write legibly; the only missing ingredient is effective instruction (Manning, 1986). For students without adequate gross- and fine-motor skills, specific instruction addressing these problems may be warranted.

Because the importance of handwriting is being realized once again, many students are beginning to receive appropriate instruction. Most students in elementary schools learn to use handwriting to express themselves and to complete necessary forms without a great deal of difficulty. Some students, however, have major problems with their handwriting. As could be expected, many of the students with problems in handwriting also receive special education services (Reis, 1989). Many students, especially those with disabilities, experience handwriting problems when it is not taught properly (Polloway et al., 2008). Therefore, teachers working with students who have disabilities should be aware of the handwriting process, common handwriting deficiencies, approaches to assess handwriting problems, and strategies for implementing remedial programs focused on handwriting deficiencies. Combs (2002) described the purposes of handwriting instruction:

- To provide instruction in patterns of formation that will allow handwriting to become fluid and eventually unconscious, and
- To help children see the purpose of legibility as a vehicle to clear communication. (p. 221)

Handwriting skills can be taught in isolation or in context. When handwriting skills are taught in isolation, teachers provide instruction in the specific steps involved in making letters and combining letters into words and sentences. These mechanical skills can be taught using commercial materials or can be teacher-made activities. During the past several years, teaching handwriting skills in context with other language skills has become popular. Known as the **whole language approach**, this model fosters language arts skills by having students write their own compositions. This is an effective means of teaching handwriting to many students, but many other students benefit from being taught specific skills related to the mechanics of writing. This chapter takes the latter approach.

▌The Nature of Handwriting

The mechanics of expression become more complex as children move from using oral language to expressing themselves in writing. Handwriting is not a simple process: It involves integrating and coordinating visual, motor, and memory skills. It is so complex that it is amazing that so many young children learn to express themselves in writing as easily as they do.

Visual acuity, visual perception, and visual and sequential memory all enable the writer to see letters and words. Without the ability to see the forms constructed, individuals would not be able to perceive similarities and differences among them or remember what they saw. Motor skills require controlled movement to write, and the combination of visual and motor skills makes the task even more difficult. If you try to write a sentence efficiently and legibly with your nondominant hand or with your eyes closed, the importance of motor and visual coordination becomes quickly apparent.

Unlike speech or gestures, handwriting is a perceptual–motor skill that requires the individual to perceive a letter form and then translate the perceived form into a written symbol using motor skills. At the same time, the writer integrates previous perceptual images through memory and new visual images, including the current working surface and the markings that have been made already. Similar perceptual–motor acts are required to play games such as golf, baseball, ping-pong, and tennis. Integrating visual and motor abilities is a complex process that reaches its height in the demand of fine-motor activities such as writing.

Another characteristic that separates handwriting from speech or gestures is the amount of time required to produce an end product. Despite the time demands of writing, the permanence of written materials makes good handwriting even more critical. Because written language is relatively permanent, it is scrutinized more frequently and closely than other language forms. Speed, accuracy, and neatness are important in handwriting. Slow and sloppy handwriting causes students to spend more time completing assignments, which makes the process tedious and may increase their dissatisfaction with school assignments and perhaps with school itself. From teachers' standpoint, a student's handwriting may affect his attitude toward the student positively or negatively and influence grading.

The development of handwriting skills begins before children enter school and engage in formal instruction and takes two basic forms—continuous curvy lines or a series of circles or straight lines, or both. Ferreiro and Teberosky (1982) grouped these early efforts into the following five levels. Within each of these levels, children experiment and "write" as part of their literacy development.

Level I   Children use separate graphic characters that look alike but that the children consider different.

Level II   Graphic forms are more defined, and conventional letters have more similarities. There is a fixed number of forms.

Level III   Children assign a sound value to each of the forms; each form equates to a syllable.

Level IV   Children abandon the notion that each form equates to a sound, and they utilize more analysis of each form.

Level V   The code is broken, and children realize that each form equates to a sound.

This early development of "writing" displays children's desires and willingness to learn written communication skills. It gives children practice in fine-motor activities and also motivates them to learn how to communicate in writing.

▌Sequence of Skills

The sequence of skills in handwriting begins with a variety of prewriting exercises and ends with the proper use of punctuation in written expression. In general, the following sequence of skills must be developed to achieve an acceptable level of handwriting:

1. Grasping and using crayons and paintbrushes
2. Grasping and holding a pencil
3. Moving the pencil in random patterns
4. Reproducing patterns, such as line and wave patterns, letters, numbers, and words
5. Copying letters and words
6. Writing letters and words in manuscript
7. Developing flowing movements required for cursive writing
8. Copying cursive letters and words
9. Writing cursive letters and words
10. Writing sentences and paragraphs

Figure 9.1 delineates several steps that are accomplished in the sequence of children's handwriting development, and Figure 9.2 depicts some examples of handwriting at different grade levels. Although the sequence of skills seems to be simple and brief, most students take several years to become competent in all of these areas.

Although children develop writing skills at different rates, they typically follow a certain pattern in this development. Generally speaking, in kindergarten and first grade, students learn basic prewriting skills including proper posture, proper pencil grip, and how to recognize and form uppercase and lowercase manuscript letters

1. Handwriting Before First Grade

   Teachers teach basic handwriting skills during kindergarten.
   - Children learn how to hold a pencil.
   - Children learn to recognize and form upper- and lowercase letters.
   - Children learn to write their names and other common words.

2. Handwriting in the Primary Grades

   Primary-grade students develop legible manuscript handwriting.
   - Children learn to form upper- and lowercase manuscript letters and space between letters.
   - Children often use "fat" beginner pencils even though research does not support this practice.
   - Children use wide, lined paper with a dotted midline to guide them in forming lowercase letters.

3. Transition to Cursive Handwriting

   Teachers teach students to both read and write cursive handwriting because it is a new writing system.
   - Children are introduced to cursive handwriting in second or third grade.
   - Children learn to read cursive writing.
   - Children learn to form upper- and lowercase letters and to join letters.
   - Children continue to use manuscript writing during the transition, especially for writing related to theme cycles.

4. Handwriting in the Middle and Upper Grades
   - Teachers expect children to use both manuscript and cursive handwriting in daily writing activities.
   - Children have learned both manuscript and cursive handwriting forms.
   - Children develop their own trademark styles.
   - Children vary the legibility and neatness of their handwriting for private and public writing.

Source: From *Language Arts: Content and Teaching Strategies* (5th ed., p. 579), by G. E. Tompkins, 2002, Columbus, OH: Merrill.

FIGURE 9.1

Steps in Handwriting Development

(Meese, 2001). In the second grade, students refine their manuscript writing and may begin to form some cursive letters. Although some students still use manuscript letters in the fourth grade, by the end of that grade, most students rely totally on cursive writing. Beyond the fourth grade, the emphasis typically is on written expression, not on the mechanics of handwriting, but individual students may continue to need assistance with handwriting, particularly those with a history of learning or motor difficulties.

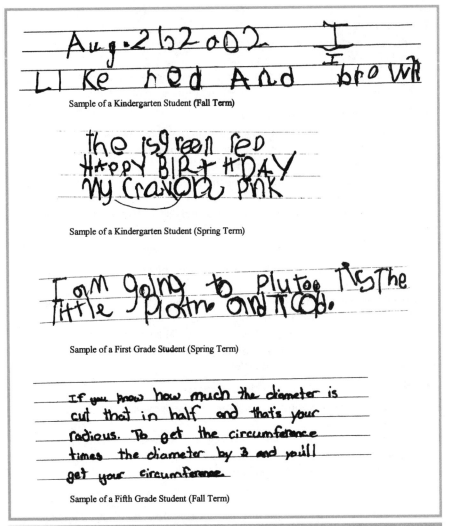

Sample of a Kindergarten Student (**Fall Term**)

Sample of a Kindergarten Student (Spring Term)

Sample of a First Grade Student (Spring Term)

Sample of a Fifth Grade Student (Fall Term)

FIGURE 9.2

Sample Handwriting

▌Assessment of Handwriting

As with any skill, before developing intervention plans, it is essential to assess specific skills that the student has or does not have. Because writing problems are fairly common, comprehensive assessment of handwriting skills is a necessary component of educational planning and intervention. Unfortunately, assessment of handwriting skills has not received a great deal of attention. There are hundreds of formal, standardized assessment instruments for reading, math, written expression, spelling, and general information, but the number of formal tests for assessing handwriting is extremely limited. Teachers' observations and informal assessment procedures are used most often to determine an individual student's handwriting skills (Polloway et al., 2008).

Assessing handwriting skills varies a great deal from teacher to teacher, from writing program to writing program, and from one formal assessment device to another. Even so, a commonality can be found among assessment methods in the types of errors determined. These include errors in letter formation, spacing, slant, line quality, letter size and alignment, and writing rate (Smith, Dowdy, & Finn, 1993). Another similarity is that all of the assessment methods start with students producing writing samples (Combs, 2003). Most handwriting assessments are informal, but a number of formal assessment instruments are available. Both types of assessments can provide valuable information for teachers who are developing intervention programs.

Formal Assessment

The number of formal assessments for handwriting is limited, especially compared to the number of norm-referenced instruments for reading, math, and written expression. Some of the formal handwriting scales are the following (Pierangelo and Giuliani, 1998):

> *Denver Handwriting Analysis* (Anderson, n.d.)
> *Picture Story Language Test* (Myklebust, n.d.)
> *Test of Early Written Language–2* (Hresko, n.d.)
> *Test of Written Language–2* (Hammill & Larsen, 1988)
> *Test of Written Language–3* (Hammill & Larsen, n.d.)
> *Written Language Assessment* (Grill & Kirwin, n.d.)
> *Zaner-Bloser Evaluation Scale* (Zaner-Bloser, 1984)
> *Test of Legible Handwriting* (Larsen & Hammill, 1989)
> Scales by Bezzi (1962) and Freeman (1959)

In addition to these instruments with a focus on handwriting, some general achievement tests include sections to measure handwriting skills.

For the most part, formal, commercial assessment instruments are limited in scope. Only a small sample of handwriting is obtained to determine whether a student can write and whether her written productions are adequate (Smith et al., 1993). Without extensive handwriting sampling, an individual student's strengths and weaknesses cannot be determined accurately. In addition, many of the tests that determine handwriting skills also measure other academic areas. Limited attention to handwriting skills in tests that measure many skills could result in a poor handwriting sample.

General Limitations

Handwriting scales have been available since the early 1900s. These scales were the first attempt to systematically measure handwriting skills and take measurement error into consideration. Primarily, handwriting scales require students to write letters or words, either by copying them or from memory. The evaluator then attempts to match the student's writing to a set of graded samples that are normally arranged in a hierarchical format (Graham, 1986).

Although formal handwriting scales provide a controlled method of assessing handwriting skills, this type of assessment has some inherent problems. First, scales do not include a broad enough sample of handwriting performances to cover the full repertoire of skills (Graham, 1986). Second, only a few graded samples are provided for comparison purposes. For example, the Test of Written Language–2 (TOWL-2) includes just 10 graded samples, ranging from illegible (0) to highly legible (10) (Hammill & Larsen, 1988).

In addition, most of the available handwriting scales do not report reliability, do not provide teachers with actual proficiency ratings, and do not help teachers individualize instruction or monitor the effectiveness of interventions (Graham, 1986). Therefore, though they may provide a general evaluation of a student's handwriting skills, they do not assist teachers in developing appropriate intervention strategies to improve students' handwriting.

Another negative characteristic of handwriting scales is their lack of differentiation between the handwriting of males and females (Graham, 1986). Such differentiation in the evaluation of handwriting samples could add validity to the measures, because many studies suggest that, for whatever reason, girls have better handwriting than boys (Wood, Webster, Gullickson, & Walker, 1987).

Regardless of these weaknesses, handwriting scales can provide a great deal of valuable information for teachers who work with students who have handwriting deficiencies. Teachers can use the scales as a screening mechanism to determine which students need additional handwriting assessment and interventions. They can also use the assessment information obtained from the scales to develop and refine their informal assessments related to handwriting (Graham, 1986).

Specific Scales

Only a few handwriting scales are available on the market. For the most part, these instruments can be administered in a short time and give teachers a general measure of the student's handwriting skills. Pierangelo and Giuliani (1998) summarized some of the most currently used formal handwriting assessments. Table 9.1 describes six of these scales. In addition to these scales, some schools use the *Test of Handwriting Skills* (Gardner, 1998), which has recently been revised. This instrument, which is normed on students ages 5 to 11 years, can be administered individually or in small groups and assesses skills in manuscript and cursive writing (Taylor, 2009).

Informal Assessments

As noted, formal, norm-referenced tests for assessing handwriting abilities are limited, and those that are available do not provide detailed information that can be used to develop and implement intervention programs. As a result, teachers should use

TABLE 9.1

Summary of Handwriting Assessment Scales

Test	Age Appropriateness	Administration Time	Areas Assessed	Scores	Strengths/Weaknesses
Denver Handwriting Analysis	8–13	20–60 minutes	Near point copying Writing the alphabet Far point copying Manuscript–cursive transition Dictation	Subskill analysis Performance analysis Raw scores	Strengths: Focuses only on handwriting Can be given to groups Provides detailed information on handwriting Weaknesses: None reported in literature
Picture Story Language Test	7–17	20–30 minutes	Productivity scale Syntax scale Abstract–concrete scale	Age equivalents Percentile ranks Stanines	Strengths: Easy to administer Wide range of areas assessed Weaknesses: No longer widely used Scoring of writing sample is subjective and lengthy Norms are dated
Test of Early Written Language–2	3–7	10–30 minutes	Basic writing Contextual writing	Standard scores Normal curve equivalents Age equivalents Percentile ranks	Strengths: Newer test Useful in assessing and planning activities Weaknesses: Scales similar to IQs Additional validity needed

(continued)

TABLE 9.1 (*continued*)

Test	Grade	Time	Areas Assessed	Scores	Strengths/Weaknesses

Test of Written Language–2	2–12	40–60 minutes	Vocabulary
			Spelling
			Style
			Logical sentences
			Sentence combining
			Thematic maturity
			Contextual vocabulary
			Syntactic maturity
			Contextual spelling
			Contextual style
				Percentile ranks
				Standard scores
					Strengths:
					  Wide range of areas assessed
					  Includes writing sample
					  Useful to determine additional assessments
					Weaknesses:
					  Reading and writing skills required
					  Scoring time-consuming
					  Tester must be very familiar with test

Test of Written Language–3	2–12	40–60 minutes	Vocabulary
			Spelling
			Style
			Logical sentences
			Sentence combining
			Contextual conventions
			Contextual language
			Story construction
				Discrepancy analysis
				Grade equivalents
					Strengths:
					  Easy items helpful to poor writers
					  Not gender or race biased
					  Reliability/validity strengthened
					Weaknesses:
					  Reading/writing required

Written Language Assessment	8–18 and older	1 hour	General writing ability
			Productivity
			Word complexity
			Readability
				Analytic techniques
				Written Language Quotient
					Strengths:
					  Can be administered by classroom teacher
					  Uses real writing tasks
					  Three types of samples obtained
					Weaknesses:
					  None reported

Source: From *Special Educator's Complete Guide to 109 Diagnostic Tests* (pp. 96–99), by R. Pierangelo and G. Giuliani, 1998, New York: Center for Applied Research in Education

informal measures to ascertain specific strengths and weaknesses related to handwriting and to devise intervention strategies. The best way to implement informal assessment measures is to do so with student work products developed in the natural setting—classrooms (Taylor, 2009).

One method is to determine which specific skills, within a series of skills, a student has mastered. Then teachers can develop interventions at the problem point. The following is a hierarchy of handwriting skills:

1. Grasping the pencil. Proper pencil grip, according to Mendoze, Holt, and Jackson (1978), requires (a) holding the pencil with the thumb, index finger, and middle finger, approximately 1 inch above the pencil point; (b) resting the pencil on the near side of the middle finger; (c) placing the thumb on the other side of the pencil, opposite the middle finger; (d) resting the index finger on the top surface of the pencil; and (e) resting the remaining portion of the pencil in the round space between the second joint of the thumb and the index finger.
2. Holding the pencil at the proper slant
3. Making random marks
4. Making free-form (controlled) marks
5. Imitating line and wave patterns and variant strokes
6. Reproducing nonmeaningful patterns
7. Reproducing meaningful patterns appropriate for manuscript or cursive writing
8. Copying letters
9. Writing letters
10. Copying words
11. Writing words
12. Copying sentences
13. Writing sentences

In a classic study by Newland (1932), a team of 24 reviewers assessed the handwriting of more than 2,300 students. The most common forms of illegibilities were found in the letters *a, e, f*, and *t*. The study also revealed that teachers tend to be most concerned about letter formation, spacing, and legibility (Otto, McMenemy, & Smith, 1973).

Among the several aspects of letter formation that may cause problems for students are

■ difficulty forming letters at approximately a 45–90-degree angle to the horizontal line upon which they are written;
■ difficulty keeping straight lines straight; and
■ difficulty forming curved or circle portions of letters correctly.

When learning cursive writing, students sometimes have difficulty forming letters at approximately a 45–90-degree angle to the horizontal line upon which they are written, creating the correct slant and curve, and producing letters of the proper size.

Some students need to practice keeping lowercase letters proportionally smaller than uppercase letters.

Spacing requires leaving the correct amount of space between individual letters and words. Spacing can be assessed fairly objectively. Legibility creates a more difficult assessment problem.

Legibility is not a simple characteristic of handwriting. It has many elements, including size, shape of letters, formation of letters, slant, alignment, neatness, and spacing (Wood et al., 1987). Two concerns regarding the assessment of legibility relate to the criteria used in the assessments and the accuracy of judgment (Stowitschek & Stowitschek, 1979). Traditionally, legibility scales have been used to evaluate writing legibility. These scales require subjective judgment to determine how legible the student's writing is. After reviewing legibility scales, Graham (1986) noted several disadvantages of these measures:

1. The scales do not contain sufficient samples of handwriting to cover the possible writing skills of any one group of children.
2. The scales are only moderately reliable.
3. The utility of the scales has not been demonstrated.
4. Most important, the scales do not provide teachers with adequate evaluation information or information for individualizing instruction.

Despite these problems, legibility scales can provide beneficial information to teachers, including information about where to target interventions.

Although many of the traditional legibility scales have not been validated effectively, trained teachers and evaluators can still use them to determine students' general writing legibility. As Otto et al. (1973) indicated, once individuals are trained to use legibility scales, they are able to generally assess legibility without using any scale.

Otto and his colleagues evaluated children's handwriting under three different conditions using materials familiar to the students that contained all the letters of the alphabet. For example, using sample sentences (e.g., "The quick brown fox jumped over the lazy dog"), teachers instructed pupils to write the sentences in (a) their "best" handwriting, (b) their "usual" handwriting, and (c) their "fastest" handwriting. Students were given 5 minutes for their first two efforts. The procedure enabled teachers to evaluate whether a student could produce fluent and legible handwriting under the optimal condition and also in normal and accelerated conditions.

Teacher-made checklists enable teachers to evaluate writing while maintaining a record for later evaluations and comparisons. Hammill and Bartel (1990) suggested that checklists allow teachers to evaluate specific handwriting skills, such as letter formation. Figure 9.3 provides an example of a checklist that can help in evaluating letter formation.

Regardless of whether teachers use formal assessment scales or informal methods such as those described here, the purpose of the assessment is to determine what specific interventions should be used. As long as teachers have gained a good understanding of where to implement remediation strategies, assessment can be considered successful.

	Wrong	Right
1. a like o	$\mathscr{o}$	$\mathscr{a}$
2. a like u	$\mathscr{u}$	$\mathscr{a}$
3. a like ci	$\mathscr{ci}$	$\mathscr{a}$
4. b like li	$\mathscr{li}$	$\mathscr{b}$
5. d like cl	$\mathscr{cl}$	$\mathscr{d}$
6. e closed	$\mathscr{e}$	$\mathscr{e}$
7. h like li	$\mathscr{li}$	$\mathscr{h}$
8. i like e with no dot	$\mathscr{e}$	$\mathscr{i}$
9. m like w	$\mathscr{w}$	$\mathscr{m}$
10. n like u	$\mathscr{u}$	$\mathscr{n}$
11. o like a	$\mathscr{a}$	$\mathscr{o}$
12. r like i	$\mathscr{i}$	$\mathscr{r}$
13. r like n	$\mathscr{n}$	$\mathscr{r}$
14. t like l	$\mathscr{t}$	$\mathscr{t}$
15. t with cross above	$\mathscr{\bar{t}}$	$\mathscr{t}$

Source: From *Teaching Students with Learning and Behavior Problems* (5th ed., p. 270), by D. D. Hammill and N. R. Bartel, 1990, Boston: Allyn & Bacon. Copyright 1990 by Allyn & Bacon. Reprinted with permission.

FIGURE 9.3

Sample Checklist for Evaluating Letter Formation

▌Remediating and Teaching Handwriting Skills

The accountability movement that accompanied the No Child Left Behind Act resulted in significant efforts to improve students' reading and math skills. Unfortunately, the other "R," writing, has received little attention. It is not clear how most teachers even approach teaching handwriting (Bridge & Hiebert, 1985). Handwriting instruction is unpopular with many teachers. As noted previously, however, handwriting can cause difficulties for some students, so teachers must address handwriting deficiencies to facilitate the success of these students (Mlyniec, 2001).

The amount of time that teachers spend on handwriting activities varies considerably from school to school and from grade to grade. With the emphasis on reading, many teachers spend little to no time on handwriting practice. Bridge and Hiebert (1985) observed six classrooms in two schools to determine the nature and quantity of handwriting activities. Their observations indicated that the writing tasks used most often were practicing individual letter forms and words, filling in words in blank spaces, copying sentences, and making a list of spelling words. The authors concluded that "children spend very little time in writing activities and that most of this time is spent in transcription activities that involve verbatim copying of other writers' texts" (p. 169).

The time that teachers spend on handwriting instruction often involves commercial teaching programs. Meese (2001) described some of the popularly used programs, including *Better Handwriting for You*, the *D'Nealian Handwriting Program* (Thurber, 1993), *The Cursive Writing Program*, the *Palmer Method*, *SRA Lunchbox Handwriting*, the *Tactile-Kinesthetic Writing Program*, and *Zaner-Bloser Handwriting* (Hackney & Lucas, 1993). These are described in Table 9.2.

Little evidence supports one teacher program over the others. Wood et al. (1987) collected data on handwriting from 89 elementary schools, which yielded more than 3,000 individual handwriting samples. All of the schools in the survey used the Palmer, the Zaner-Bloser, or the D'Nealian handwriting program. The researchers found that "comparable legibility resulted after receiving instruction in the three commercial handwriting programs" (p. 28).

In a review of the literature comparing the Zaner-Bloser program and the D'Nealian program, Cahill (2009) found that "researchers disagree on which program facilitates a smoother transition to cursive" (p. 225). Therefore, the specific commercial program used in handwriting instruction may not have a major impact on students' handwriting skills. What may be more important is how teachers implement their program, regardless of which program they use.

It really does not matter whether teachers use a specific program or their own instructional methods for teaching handwriting skills. The key is that teachers understand the importance of such instruction and keep several instructional principles in mind. First, teachers should teach handwriting skills and encourage practice in handwriting during functional activities. "Students may be more apt to write for an extended period of time if they are interested, find value in the activity, and are not worried about receiving grades" (Cahill, 2009, p. 227). Other instructional principles related to handwriting are the following (Vaughn & Bos, 2009):

- Teach handwriting explicitly, including letter formation.
- Provide modeling and feedback to ensure correct letter formation. It may be necessary to guide the stroke of the pencil by providing manual assistance.

TABLE 9.2
Popular Handwriting Programs

Handwriting without Tears (Olsen, 1994)

Program that uses a set of pre-k through cursive writing lessons that focus on having fun. The curriculum encourages active involvement in the writing process and incorporates a comprehensive approach that includes posture, grip, and paper positioning. www.hwtears.com/whyitworks/research. Retrieved 11/3/10

Handwriting Help for Kids (Marnell, n.d.)

Uses a "letter story" for each manuscript letter that uses both visual and auditory learning. Students using this program learn where to start, form, and end letters. Stars are used as the starting point for all letters. www.pages.drexel.edu retrieved 11/16/10

Loops and Other Groups (Benbow, n.d.)

Cursive writing program. Letters are introduced according to the lead-in stroke of each letter. Students are encouraged to experience the "feel" of the letter strokes. www.otideas.com retrieved 11/16/10

First Strokes Multi-Sensory Handwriting Program

This program includes a print and cursive version. It focuses on large gross-motor learning beginning with grip. The program includes a handwriting assessment and classroom handwriting modifications. www.firststrokeshandwriting.com retrieved 11/2/10

Big Strokes for Little Folks (Rubell. n.d.)

This program helps students learn proper letter and number formation; letters and numbers are groups based on similar characteristics. Targets children ages 5 – 9 and includes objectives, teaching guide, and worksheets. www.therapro.com Retrieved 11/2/10

D'Nealian Handwriting Program (Thurber, 1993)

This program is a transitional program from print to cursive. Letter used share characteristics with manuscript and cursive letter.

Zaner-Bloser Handwriting (Hackney & Lucas, 1993)

This program includes basal workbooks and assessment scales for grades K through 8. Dot-to-dot forms are available to help students learn initial letter formation.

- Initially focus on the motor pattern, and then increasingly on legibility.
- Teach handwriting frequently, several times a week.
- In addition to separate mini-lessons on handwriting and letter formation, provide short handwriting lessons in the context of the students' writing assignments.
- Have the students overlearn handwriting skills in isolation, then apply the skills in context, and periodically check the students' work.
- Ask students to evaluate their own handwriting and, when appropriate, the handwriting of others.

■ As the teacher, provide a model of handwriting for the students to follow.
■ In the beginning stages of letter formation, integrate letter writing with letter naming, letter sounds, or spelling words.
■ After students acquire proficiency in letter formation, provide opportunities for them to improve fluency through speed and accuracy of letter writing. (p. 394)

Handwriting and the Whole Language Curriculum

One means of teaching handwriting skills that gained popularity during the 1980s in some schools is the whole language curriculum. This holistic approach was intended to help students understand the relationships among reading, writing, spelling, and comprehension, allowing teachers to provide handwriting instruction in the context of other language arts skills.

Teachers who used the whole language model to teach writing did not teach the mechanics of handwriting as an isolated skill. Rather, they taught handwriting skills in the context of students' compositions. In the whole language classroom, students received encouragement and reinforcement for writing. As a result, their writing skills generally improved, including skills related to the mechanics of writing (Zemelman & Daniels, 1988).

During the past few years, use of the whole language approach has declined in many elementary schools. As a result, many of the skills that had been taught as part of the whole language approach (e.g., reading, writing, handwriting, and spelling) are now taught as specific skills. Since the decline in using the whole language model, explicit instruction in handwriting skills has come to the forefront.

Manuscript versus Cursive Writing

There is no one, best method for teaching students to write. Rather, teachers use a variety of methods and, as noted, sometimes exclude the teaching of writing altogether in favor of other areas of literacy. One question that has been pervasive in handwriting instruction for decades is whether to teach manuscript or cursive writing first. Various researchers have attempted to determine whether one approach is superior to the other, but the matter continues to be debated. Currently, most students learn both styles. Manuscript writing is typically taught first, usually beginning in kindergarten or first grade, and instruction in cursive writing begins in the second or third grade (Meese, 2001). Although the issue is debated for all learners, it is more critical for children with disabilities because learning two different styles and systems takes more time.

The traditional method of teaching manuscript began in the early 1900s, when Edward Johnson developed a simple manuscript alphabet for beginning writers. By the 1920s and 1930s, teaching manuscript first was the generally accepted method (Hagin, 1983). Traditional arguments for starting instruction with cursive or manuscript writing hinge on the alleged advantages of one form over the other. Advantages include the following (Hagin, 1983):

1. It is regarded as being easier to learn because the letter forms are simpler.
2. It resembles the print in books, so the child does not have to accommodate two graphic styles.
3. Beginning writing in manuscript is more legible than cursive.
4. It is required through life in applications and documents.
5. It promotes the independence of letters within words in teaching spelling. (p. 267)

Currently, most elementary school teachers start with manuscript instruction Since the late 1980s, a few educators have advocated for teaching cursive first. Individuals recommending this approach note that cursive "is continuous and connected, makes it more difficult to reverse letters, teaches student to perceive whole words, and is easier to write" (Vaughn & Bos, 2009, p. 392). An additional reason for teaching cursive first is that it avoids the later transition from manuscript to cursive, which is often difficult for many children. Table 9.3 lists reasons for teaching manuscript or cursive first. Although the debate continues, the preponderance of evidence supports teaching manuscript first in early elementary grades, then transitioning to cursive in the second or third grade (Vaughn & Bos, 2009).

TABLE 9.3
Manuscript versus Cursive

Manuscript	Cursive
1. It more closely resembles print and facilitates learning to read.	1. Many students want to learn to write cursive.
2. It is easier for young children to learn.	2. Many students write cursive faster.
3. Manuscript is more legible than cursive.	3. Many adults object to students using manuscript beyond the primary grades.
4. Many students write manuscript at the same rate as cursive and this rate can be significantly influenced through direct instruction.	
5. It is better for students with learning disabilities to learn one writing process well than to attempt to learn two.	

Source: From *Strategies for teaching students with learning and behavior problems*, p. 392. by S. Vaughn & C. S. Bos, 2009, Upper Saddle River, NJ: Prentice Hall. Copyright 2009 by Pearson Education. Reprinted with permission.

▌Alternatives to Manuscript and Cursive

As the debate continues, several alternatives to manual and cursive approaches have been developed.

D'Nealian Handwriting Program

The D'Nealian Handwriting Program (Thurber & Jordan, 1978), which continues to be one a popular commercial handwriting program (Wood et al., 1987), ties the manuscript letterforms closely to the cursive letterforms by having the student produce each manuscript letter by making a continuous stroke without lifting the pencil. The purpose of this approach is to "reduce teaching/learning time by initially establishing the letter formations, rhythm, size, slant, and spacing that will be used for cursive writing" (Polloway et al., 2008, p. 234).

This system facilitates the transition to cursive because all printed letters except *f, r, a, v,* and *z* can become their cursive counterparts simply by adding "joining" strokes. Thurber (1975) claimed that this system is a viable alternative to what he referred to as the illogical way children are typically taught to write—using the circles and sticks of manuscript print. Figure 9.4 depicts the D'Nealian Handwriting alphabet.

Mixed Script Approach

Another alternative model is the "mixed" script approach developed by Mullins, Joseph, Turner, Zawadski, and Saltzman (1972). This approach combines parts of manuscript and cursive with the need to transition from manuscript to cursive. Figure 9.5 provides a sample of the script and the guidelines for writing it. The script combines many advantages of both cursive and manuscript forms, including (a) making letters (especially uppercase) relatively similar to the printed word; (b) avoiding the difficult flourishes and loops of cursive; (c) achieving rhythm by linking lowercase letters; (d) being able to keep the pen on the paper, emphasizing directionality; and (e) possibly eliminating reversals. Although this form has not been used widely in the classroom, samples of adult handwriting anecdotally show that many people commonly use some modification of the mixed script.

Slanted Approach

The slanted approach to writing instruction is another alternative to manuscript and cursive. This method, which is considered a transition between manuscript and cursive, uses slanted letter that are unconnected. Proponents suggest that slanted letters are easier to write than cursive letters, but similar enough that students do not have to learn two different alphabets. Research suggests, however, that when comparing

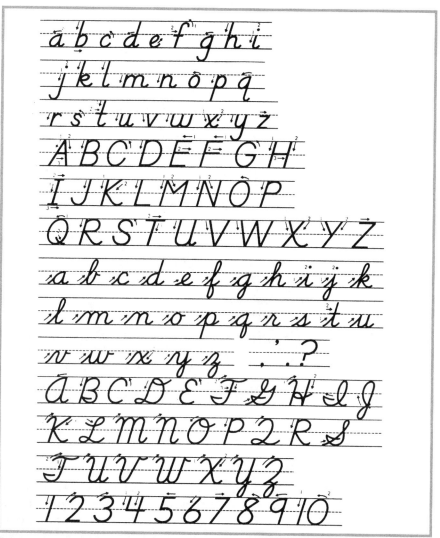

FIGURE 9.4

D'Nealian® Alphabet and Numerals

the slanted approach to the manuscript approach, students tend to do better with the manuscript model. The manuscript approach has been found to be easier to read and write for children and easier to teach and integrate (*Six questions*, 2009).

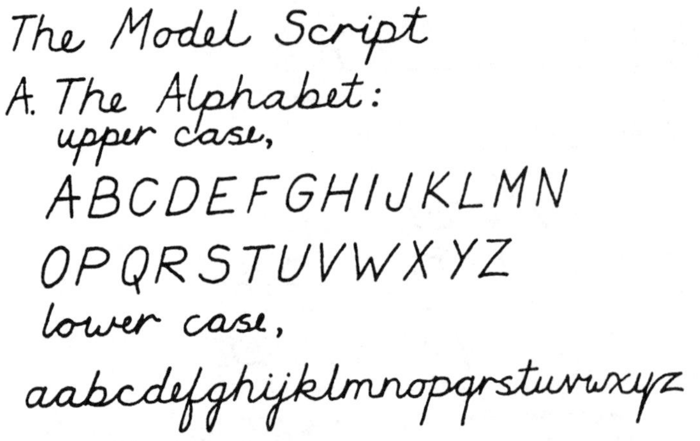

The Model Script

A. The Alphabet:
  upper case,

ABCDEFGHIJKLMN
OPQRSTUVWXYZ

  lower case,

  aabcdefghijklmnopqrstuvwxyz

B. *Guidelines for writing:*
  1. *Start words with a downstroke (an exception is the lower case "e").*
  2. *Keep pen on paper until word is completed (an exception is a word beginning with a capital letter).*
  3. *Give writing a slight slant.*
  4. *Leave space between words.*
  5. *Start at the left of the paper.*

Source: From "A Handwriting Model for Children with Learning Disabilities," by J. Mullins, F. Joseph, C. Turner, R. Zawadski, and L. Saltzman, 1972, *Journal of Learning Disabilities, 5,* p. 309. Copyright 1972 by Sage Publications, Inc. Journals. Reprinted with permission.

FIGURE 9.5

Model Script

Typing/Keyboarding

Typing, or keyboarding, another alternative to cursive and manuscript handwriting instruction, has become popular as a result of the personal computer explosion. Advocates for this approach say that students can learn to "write" more efficiently using a computer keyboard. For example, upper elementary students may be able to type as many as 20–25 words per minute, compared to handwriting only 10–15 words per minute (National Business Education Association, 1997). This approach may be particularly beneficial for students with learning disabilities or physical impairments who have problems with fine-motor coordination and control.

Additional advantages that accrue from developing typing or keyboarding skills include improved legibility as well as inherent motivational advantages. Vacc (1987) studied the differences between correspondence written by adolescents with disabilities using handwriting and correspondence written by the same students using word processors. The results indicated that students who used the computer spent more time on their letters, made more changes, and wrote longer letters than those who used handwriting. Research has also shown a strong relationship between handwriting speed and typing speed (Cahill, 2009), suggesting another reason to teach handwriting skills even for students who will likely use computers later.

Keyboarding skills are as important for students who use computers for writing as handwriting is for students who write manually (Cahill, 2009). As such, several methods have been developed to teach keyboarding skills to young children (e.g., Typing Keys and Typing Our Language). In addition, numerous computer programs are available for teaching typing skills to children (e.g., Kids on Keys).

Regardless of whether the teacher prefers to teach manuscript, cursive, or alternative handwriting methods, several other factors should be considered when determining which approach to utilize. These include the student's readiness, visual–motor skills, age, physical abilities, and previous writing history. Sometimes these variables play a significant role in which writing method teachers employ.

▊Instructional Activities

Handwriting is necessary to provide students with the skills to be successful in school and after they finish school. As has been pointed out, many educators do not understand the need to instruct students in handwriting, and others simply do not have the time to teach handwriting because of the heavy emphasis on literacy, math, and science. Often, teachers who do include instruction in handwriting rely on commercial materials in their handwriting programs.

Although there is no one best method for teaching children how to write (Smith et al., 1993), some general guidelines are applicable. These are germane to instruction in this area, whether the teacher uses a commercial program or teacher-made activities.

Readiness Skills

Various skills are prerequisite for students to learn to write successfully, regardless of whether manuscript, cursive, or an alternative writing method is taught first. These skills generally emerge in prekindergarten and kindergarten. Two primary objectives at this stage are (a) developing handedness (the preferred hand for writing) and (b) developing visual–motor integration skills. Activities that can assist students in these two areas include manipulating objects, tracing objects in sand, using scissors for cutting paper, and crayon and fingerpainting (Polloway et al., 2008).

Several skills that students should develop prior to formal handwriting instruction are

1. concepts of left to right, forward and backward, and start and stop;
2. movement along a guided line;
3. movement in a groove;
4. movement with resistance;
5. movement without a solid guide;

6. making figures without a guide;
7. making figures without a pattern; and
8. proper pencil grip.

In developing these writing readiness skills, students achieve two basic prewriting goals: (a) enhanced coordination of visual and motor movements and (b) development of handedness. Achieving the former goal leads directly into refinement of fine-motor skills. Achieving the latter helps teachers emphasize the correct hand for writing.

Because visual–motor skills are the building blocks of good handwriting, readiness activities should be directed to these skills. Among the numerous activities that can effectively foster eye–hand coordination are the following (Cook, Klein, & Tessier, 2008):

Cutting	Painting
Coloring	Paper folding
Drawing	Copying design
Sewing	Outlining with stencils or templates
Puzzle building	Copying
Bead stringing	Pasting
Lacing	Building block towers
Geoboards	Stacking
Tracing	

Initial tracing and coloring activities, for instance, should consist of giving students simple pictures of people, animals, houses, or vehicles and having them trace the outlines of these figures on tracing paper. After students learn to trace objects, they can develop finer motor skills by coloring in the pictures. During this period, teachers should also introduce specific geometric shapes such as triangles, rectangles, and circles.

Cutting activities should follow the same process, with students starting on large articles and gradually moving to smaller ones. Children might begin by drawing and cutting large seasonal symbols (valentines, leaves, snowmen) for display, then moving to more refined tasks as their skills improve. More challenging tasks include cutting pictures from magazines for collages and making small snowflakes.

Manipulative activities can further develop coordination. Teachers should have students pick up small objects, make objects from play dough, and use nuts and bolts. Playing with jacks, Lincoln Logs, Tinkertoys, and Pick-Up Sticks can also help to refine manipulative skills.

Beginning to Write

After readiness skills have been developed, students can begin actual writing exercises. This instruction usually begins in kindergarten (Tompkins, 2002). Proper posture for writing and proper pencil grip are both important during this phase of learning how to write (Meese, 2001). Proper pencil grip must be taught before children develop bad habits. Teachers can help students to develop the proper grip by having them hold the pencil 1 inch from the pencil point using their thumb and first two fingers. To make this easier, teachers might use felt-tip markers, primary pencils, or pencils wrapped with tape. The Hoyle Gripper, a three-sided plastic holder that comfortably forms the child's fingers into the correct position for gripping, is another effective option. Although more current research does not support these sorts of aids to improve students' grips or initial handwriting (Tompkins, 2002), some primary teachers have found them to be useful.

After attending to pencil grip and posture, teachers should work on integrating the child's visual–motor abilities into prerequisite writing skills. Activities that facilitate this integration might follow this progression:

1. Encourage free scribbling so children get the feel of the pencil and build a foundation for later strokes.
2. Provide directionality exercises to teach students the basic left-to-right orientation necessary for writing. Using templates and writing stencils, help students develop these skills.
3. Help students develop the basic strokes necessary for writing by having them make circles, straight lines, curved lines, and diagonal lines.
4. Provide a logical progression of assistance by modeling procedures, using physical prompts, giving nonverbal cues, providing forms to copy, and, finally, having students write items from memory.
5. Provide purposeful chalkboard exercises for young students as a transition to writing.

Numerous supports can facilitate the development of handwriting skills (Cahill, 2009). Table 9.4 lists a series of questions and suggestions related to the support of handwriting development. Educators should review this list to determine whether students have adequate support for developing this skill.

Keller (2001) described the Handwriting Club, using sensory integration strategies to improve handwriting. The club, designed for third and fourth graders with handwriting deficits and problems in social skills, provided an opportunity for students to use a social club as the basis for improving handwriting instruction. Figure 9.6 shows the typical handwriting club activities. Through the use of the club, Keller (2001) noted major improvement in students' handwriting skills as well as their level of social interactions.

Manuscript Writing

After students acquire prewriting skills and the proper pencil grip, educators who teach manuscript writing before cursive must teach or remediate manuscript writing skills. As noted earlier, this type of instruction typically begins in the latter part of kindergarten or in first grade. Although no specific set of letters should be used in the beginning phase of handwriting instruction, uppercase and lowercase letters composed of simple sticks and circles are usually the focus of initial instruction. Letters made

TABLE 9.4
Questions to Consider and Suggestions to Support Handwriting Development

Questions to Consider	Suggestions to Support Handwriting
Does the student have enough space on his or her desk to complete the writing task?	Remove clutter from desks and tabletops. Children with poor posture might need space to lean or rest their elbows while writing.
Can the student place both feet squarely on the floor and still rest his or her elbows on the desk for support?	Be sure that when students sit, their ankles, knees, and hips are bent at 90° angles and they can comfortably rest their elbows on their desks. Chairs and desks that are too tall require students to expend extra energy while writing. If students are unable to comfortably rest their feet on the floor, ask the building engineer to adjust their desk and chair heights or provide students with a short stool or a stack of books to rest their feet on. These adjustments will increase students' postural stability, which will allow them to exercise greater distal control and use their writing instruments more proficiently.
Does the student switch hands or complain that his or her hand hurts during long writing tasks?	Students who have established hand dominance and continue to switch hands or complain of fatigue while writing may have decreased hand strength. Provide writing tools with a greater diameter and opportunities to develop hand muscles through activities such as cutting, playing with clay, and using manipulatives.
Does the student use excessive force when writing as evidenced by thick marks that leave deep indentations on the paper?	Excessive force when writing may indicate decreased hand strength or difficulty processing sensory information. Provide writing tools with a greater diameter and let students experiment with placing their writing papers on top of different textures, such as bubble wrap, sandpaper, and cardboard. For example, students who press too hard while writing on top of bubble wrap will rip their papers. This will cue them to reduce the force they use on their writing instruments. The other textured materials will provide them with varied sensory feedback. This may help to build muscle memory and increase automatic letter writing.
Does the student use a mature pencil grip?	Some students hold their pencils incorrectly or develop inefficient habits. If students are still learning to hold writing utensils, instruct them how to hold their pencils correctly and see whether a pencil gripper helps them to maintain this position. If students already have an established pencil grip, consult with an occupational therapist to determine whether the grip is efficient and will promote writing speed.

(continued)

TABLE 9.4 *(continued)*

Does the student consistently rest his or her head on the desk, rub his or her eyes, squint or close one eye when reading or writing?	Students who demonstrate any of these characteristics may have difficulty with vision. Refer these students to the school nurse for a vision screening. Remind students who have glasses to wear them as prescribed.
Does the student appear distracted by the amount of visual information presented on a worksheet?	Reduce the amount of visual stimulation by removing unnecessary pictures, using large fonts, reducing the amount of information on a single page, and providing well-defined spaces or lines for answers.

Source: From "Where Does Handwriting Fit In? Strategies to Support Academic Achievement," by S. M. Cahill, 2009, *Intervention in School and Clinic, 44*, p. 226. Copyright 2009 by Sage Publications, Inc. Journals. Reprinted with permission.

1. **Gross Motor Warm-up Activities (5 minutes)**
   Do jumping jacks
   Do crab walk
   Perform push ups on floor
   Chair push-ups
   ■ Seated student places hands on either side of chair next to thighs
   ■ Straightens arms and lifts bottom off the chair
   Balance on one leg with eyes closed
   Walk toe-to-heel on a masking tape line on the floor

2. **Fine Motor Warm-up Activities (5–10 minutes)**
   Rub hands together
   Squeeze tennis balls
   Rub hands in circles on the carpet
   Play with Wikki Stix
   Build with small Lego blocks
   String small beads
   Roll clay between fingers
   "Walk" fingers up and down the pencil

3. **Letter Introduction (2–3 minutes)**
   The teacher models writing the letter on the board and describes the steps
   The students imitate by writing in the air using large arm movements and repeating steps aloud
   The students then continue to say the steps while writing on the table with pointer finger

4. **Guided Practice Activities (10 minutes)**
   Write on board (white or chalk) while wearing wrist weights
   Write on another student's back and have him or her guess the letter
   Write with:

Color Change Markers	Scented markers
Magna Doodle™	Battery-operated pens
Paint	Chalk on sidewalk
Finger paint, pudding or shaving cream	

   Write in:

Clay tray	Salt, rice, or sand tray

5. **Semi-independent Practice (5–10 minutes)**
   Students write in their handwriting books with teachers monitoring

6. **Independent Practice**
   Homework
   Additional activities: Writing for a purpose (i.e., make holiday cards or write thank you notes)

Source: From "Handwriting Club," by M. Keller, 2001, *Intervention in School and Clinic, 37.* Copyright 2001 by Sage Publications, Inc. Journals. Reprinted with permission.

FIGURE 9.6

Typical Club Session Format and Sample Activities

solely from vertical and horizontal lines, such as *E, F, H, L, T,* are easier to teach than letters requiring curved lines, such as *b, f,* and *p* (Meese, 2001). Polloway et al. (2008) suggested grouping letters by their shapes. Figures 9.7 and 9.8 show how letters can be grouped using shapes.

Teachers who use commercial teaching programs for handwriting instruction may have to modify the materials or develop individualized programs when working with children who have disabilities. In manuscript writing, the student's first task is to master straight lines, curves, and circles. When working with students who have disabilities, the teacher should introduce these strokes to the student gradually and systematically, using a progression designed especially for the individual student's needs. In the absence of a preferred sequence based on empirical data, the teacher can develop an instructional program that asks students to follow these steps and guidelines:

1. Be legible; speed is not as important.
2. Trace letters or words with the index finger and then with a writing instrument.
3. Trace letters on the chalkboard; ensure proper direction and sequence.
4. Connect dot letters.
5. Make letters in the air.
6. Complete letter fragments.
7. Copy letters from a written copy.
8. Write letters from memory (without copy).
9. Combine letters to form simple words.
10. Copy words from a written copy.
11. Trace words on the chalkboard and on paper.
12. Write words from dictation (without copy).
13. Write experience stories.

Although there is no one best way to teach manuscript writing, teachers must use the chosen approach consistently (Polloway et al., 2008). Once students have learned the basic skills of manuscript writing, instruction in cursive writing should begin.

o a d g q / b p / c e /
t l i k / r n m h / v w
x y / f j / u / z / s

Source: From *Strategies for Teaching Learners with Special Needs* (p. 232), by E. A. Polloway, J. R. Patton, L. Serna, 2008, Upper Saddle River, NJ: Prentice Hall. Copyright 2008 by Pearson Education. Reprinted with permission.

FIGURE 9.7

A Sequential Grouping of Lowercase Manuscript Letters According to Common Features

```
LHTEFI/JU/
PRBDK/AMN
VWXYZ/S/
OQCG
```

Source: From *Strategies for Teaching Learners with Special Needs* (p. 232), by E. A. Polloway, J. R. Patton, L. Serna, 2008, Upper Saddle River, NJ: Prentice Hall. Copyright 2008 by Pearson Education. Reprinted with permission.

FIGURE 9.8

A Sequential Grouping of Uppercase Manuscript Letters According to Common Features

Cursive Writing

Most children are eager to move from manuscript to cursive writing. They view cursive writing as the way "big kids" and adults write, and they want to develop the skills for this type of writing as soon as possible (Mlyniec, 2001). As noted, the transition from manuscript to cursive usually begins in second or third grade, although some students begin to learn cursive in first grade after they have mastered manuscript writing.

Instruction in traditional cursive letterforms or alternative cursive-like scripts can be based on many of the techniques noted previously in this chapter. Because cursive letters are more complex and require more skill to produce, however, teachers may have to provide additional opportunities for children to practice what they have learned and to copy both uppercase and lowercase letters.

Cursive letters can be grouped into categories for instruction, enabling teachers to focus first on letters that present the fewest problems for students. Applying these criteria, instructors would start by teaching looped letters (e.g., *e* and *l*), humped letters (e.g., *n* and *m*), or members of the *c* or "two o'clock" family (e.g., *c, a*, and *d*) (Meese, 2001). In this way, students have an opportunity to enjoy successful experiences as they begin to acquire these skills. Polloway et al. (2008) show how letters can be grouped according to common features. Figures 9.9 and 9.10 show these groupings.

In teaching cursive writing, teachers should have students follow these steps and guidelines:

1. Be legible; speed is not as important as legibility.
2. Practice rhythm writing; trace and copy increasingly difficult rhythmic patterns.
3. Trace cursive letters on paper and on the chalkboard.
4. Write letters from copy and dictation.

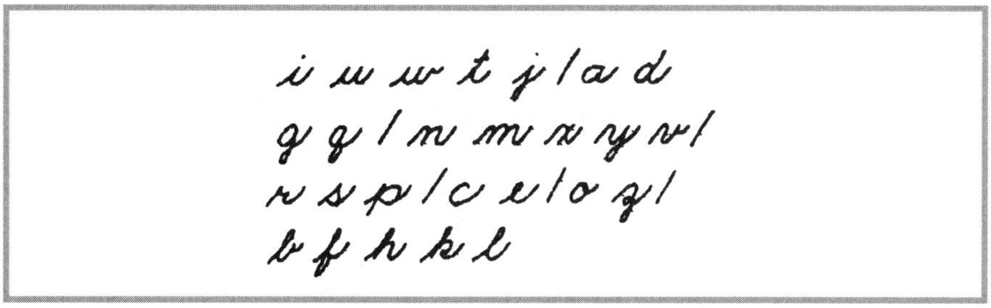

Source: From *Strategies for Teaching Learners with Special Needs,* by E. A. Polloway, J. R. Patton, L. Serna, 2008, Upper Saddle River, NJ: Prentice Hall. Copyright 2008 by Pearson Education. Reprinted with permission.

FIGURE 9.9

A Sequential Grouping of Lowercase Cursive Letters According to Common Features

5. Connect cursive letters to form words.
6. Trace words.
7. Connect dots to form written words.
8. Write words from copy and dictation.
9. Write experience stories.

Once students have acquired the basic handwriting skills necessary to communicate effectively, practice in penmanship is important, as it improves legibility and rate—two factors associated with effective handwriting. Mlyniec (2001) suggested the following for parents overseeing children's penmanship practice at home:

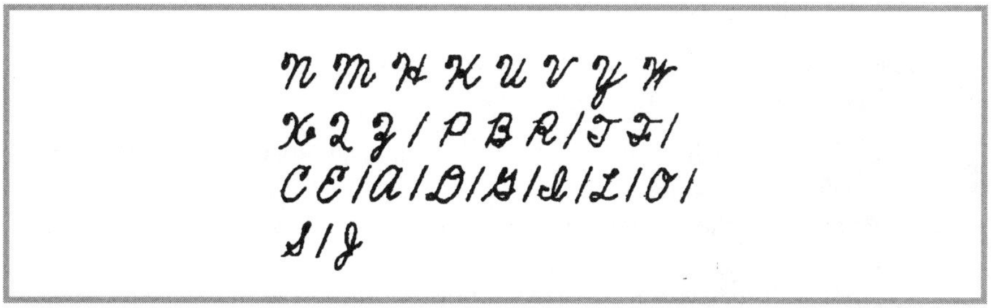

Source: From *Strategies for Teaching Learners with Special Needs,* by E. A. Polloway, J. R. Patton, L. Serna, 2008, Upper Saddle River, NJ: Prentice Hall. Copyright 2008 by Pearson Education. Reprinted with permission.

FIGURE 9.10

A Sequential Grouping of Uppercase Cursive Letters According to Common Features

1. Borrow or buy teaching materials similar to the ones used in the child's school.
2. Keep practice time short, say 5 minutes per day.
3. Demonstrate how to form letters and connections between letters.
4. Check pencil grip.
5. Use pencil grips if the child does not hold the pencil properly.

In addition to these general guidelines, teachers should devise transitional activities to help move students from manuscript to cursive writing, directing special attention to (a) joining or connecting letters, (b) letter slant, (c) dotted or crossed letters, and (d) positioning the paper.

Many teachers prefer commercial programs, and others develop their own instructional program. In either case, the handwriting instruction should be formalized as a standard part of the school day in the elementary grades. Teachers have to remember that there is no one best way to teach handwriting. Flexibility and adapting instruction to meet the needs of individual students constitute the best approach.

Handwriting Programs

Although no one approach to teaching handwriting has been found to be superior, all effective instructional programs have some common characteristics (Wood et al., 1987):

1. Students should learn to verbalize rules about letter formation. This enables them to solidify their visual image of letters and reinforces the letter formation rules.
2. Students should receive opportunities for self-evaluation and multiple forms of feedback.
3. Students should be given a lot of practice in copying letters, as this seems to be more effective than tracing letters.

Einhorn (2001) recommended the following guidelines regardless of the methods used to teach handwriting skills:

1. Combine modalities. Utilize both visual and auditory modalities during instructional activities.
2. Bring it together. Combine letter names, sounds, and physical descriptions of letters.
3. Guide self-assessment. Teach children to critique their own handwriting.
4. Provide media other than pencil and paper. Use fingerpaints, sand, rice, and other media during handwriting activities.
5. Have children write for a purpose. Make sure that handwriting is put to real-life uses.
6. Introduce letters according to similarity of formation. Combine letters that have similar shapes and formations for instructional purposes.

Practice in handwriting is essential for all students, and especially for those requiring remediation, who understand the importance of practicing their handwriting (Kos & Maslowski, 2001). They can practice through various handwriting activities in the classroom and at home. Mlyniec (2001) offered the following suggestions for parents to encourage handwriting practice at home:

- Keep a variety of eye-catching stationery, colorful pens, and fine-tipped markers easily available.
- Slip notes in your child's lunchbox or under her pillow, and encourage her to write back.
- Have a family letter-writing time.
- Make a scrapbook and have your child write the captions.
- Encourage your child to make his own greeting cards and wish lists.
- Give your child a special notepad to take on outings. Encourage her to jot down her impressions to share with you.
- Let your child write down activities on the family calendar. (p. 170)

Remedial Programs

Remediation is required for some students who are having difficulty with handwriting. Just as the number of programs available for teaching handwriting is limited, so are approaches to remediating handwriting skills. Therefore, teachers must individualize handwriting remediation based on the student's strengths and weaknesses. Hagin (1983) offered the following guidelines to teachers implementing handwriting remediation programs for students with disabilities:

1. The style of writing must be appropriate for the child's level of motor control.
2. Handwriting should be taught as a process involving body image, spatial orientation, awareness of kinesthetic feedback, and sequencing, not as just a visual or motor activity.
3. Children must be given opportunities for visualizing letterforms.
4. Verbal cues from the teacher, slowly faded out, will assist students in learning handwriting skills.
5. Handwriting instruction should be direct and individualized.
6. Children must be taught to monitor their own handwriting.
7. Sufficient practice must be available for overlearning.
8. Handwriting must be viewed as a highly complex task.

Hagin (1983) developed a remedial writing program, Write Right—or Left, based on the premise that "handwriting is a complex visual-motor-body image-kinesthetic-verbal skill that must be automatic to be effective" (p. 268). The program incorporates the guidelines just enumerated.

Left-Handedness

Left-handed writers have special needs and, therefore, may present special instructional challenges. Approximately 10% of the U.S. population is left-handed, which means that most classrooms will have two or three left-handed students (Tompkins, 2002). Because left-handedness conflicts with the process of writing English from left to right, many young left-handed children have been urged or, in some cases, virtually forced to write with the right hand. As a result of this teaching error, legions of adolescents and adults cannot write legibly with either hand. Current thinking opposes forcing children to write with the right hand when their natural preference is left-handedness (Hammill & Bartel, 1990; Lerner, 1988).

Left-handed writers encounter some unique challenges that teachers should address. The problems do not simply result from handwriting for left-handers being the reverse of handwriting for right-handers. The primary difference between right-handed and left-handed students is their physical orientation to writing. As Tompkins (2002) explained, "Right-handed students pull their arms toward their bodies as they write, whereas left-handed students push away. As left-handed students write, they move their left hand across what they have just written, often covering it" (p. 582).

To deal with these issues, left-handed writers can make several major adjustments to facilitate their handwriting. For example, they can position the writing paper differently. Another simple adjustment is to have students grip their pencil or pen farther from the tip than right-handed writers. This, plus maintaining the same grip that right-handed writers use and not writing with the hand in a hooked position, can improve these students' handwriting (Polloway et al., 2008).

As additional suggestions, hard-lead pencils should be used to avoid smudging by the hand as it moves across the page, and left-handed desks should be used when possible. Left-handed peer models who write well should be enlisted to assist other left-handed writers.

Even though left-handed individuals account for only about 10% of the U.S. population, society and the school should make modifications for these individuals. This is even more important for left-handed students with disabilities. Teachers who instruct left-handed students can obtain further suggestions and assistance from materials designed especially for this group, such as the workbook available from Educational Publishing Company.

∎Summary

School-age children have to use handwriting regularly to respond to their teachers' requests, and students respond to tests and other assignments using handwriting. For adults, handwriting is required to function in many job settings as well as in a variety of social and personal situations. Without an effective means of written expression, individuals are at a major disadvantage.

Handwriting is a complex skill that requires hand–eye coordination, fine-motor coordination, and visual perception. Deficits in any of these areas can result in problems.

Formal and informal ways to assess handwriting include informal assessments, which focus primarily on student work products developed in natural settings, and formal assessments, comprised mostly of commercially prepared handwriting assessments. Some of the commercial programs include the *Denver Handwriting Analysis, Test of Early Written Language, Test of Written Language,* and *Zaner-Bloser Evaluation Scale.*

Among the most popular commercial programs are *Better Handwriting for You, D'Nealian Handwriting Program,* and *Zaner-Bloser Handwriting,* and teachers can develop their own as well. Debate continues as to whether it is best to teach manuscript or cursive writing first. It was concluded that one method may work better than the other for some students, but neither method always works for all students. Specific activities that teachers can use to teach handwriting include using direct instruction to teach letter and word formation, providing modeling and feedback to students, teaching handwriting skills regularly, providing good handwriting as a model, providing opportunities for practicing handwriting, and encouraging students to use handwriting to express themselves as frequently as possible.

■|References

Anderson, P. L. (n.d.). *Denver handwriting analysis.* Novato, CA: Academic Therapy Publications.

Berninger, V. W., Rutberg, J. E., Abbott, R. D., Garcia, N., Anderson-Youngstrom, M., Books, A., & Fulton, C. (2006). Tier 1 and tier 2 early intervention for handwriting and composing. *Journal of School Psychology, 44,* 3–30.

Bertin, L. A. & Perlman, B. K. (2000). After your students write: What's next? *Teaching Exceptional Children, 20,* 4–9.

Bezzi, R. (1962). A standardized manuscript scale for grades 1, 2, and 3. *Journal of Educational Research, 55,* 339–340.

Bridge, C. A., & Hiebert, E. H. (1985). A comparison of classroom writing practices, teachers' perceptions of their writing instruction, and textbook recommendations on writing practices. *Elementary School Journal, 86,* 155–172.

Cahill, S. M. (2009). Where does handwriting fit in? *Intervention in School and Clinic, 44,* 223–228.

Combs, M. (2002). *Readers and writers in the primary grades* (2nd ed.). Upper Saddle River, NJ: Pearson Education.

Combs, M. (2003). *Readers and writers in the middle grades.* (2nd ed.) Upper Saddle River, NJ: Merrill.

Cook, R. E., Klein, M. D., & Tessier, A. (2008). *Adapting early childhood curricula for children with special needs.* Upper Saddle Creek, NJ: Pearson.

Einhorn, K. (2001). Handwriting success for all. *Scholastic Instructor, 98,* 35–39.

Ferreiro, E., & Teberosky, A. (1982). *Literacy before schooling.* London: Heinemann Educational Books.

Freeman, B. A. (1959). A new handwriting scale. *Elementary School Journal, 59,* 218–221.

Furner, B. A. (1983). Developing handwriting ability: A perceptual learning process. *Topics in Learning and Learning Disabilities, 3,* 41–54.

Gardner, M. (1998). *THS: Test of Handwriting Skills.* Hydesville, CA: Psychological and Educational Publications.

Graham, S. (1986). A review of handwriting scales and factors that contribute to variability in handwriting scores. *Journal of School Psychology, 24,* 63–71.

Graham, S., Harris, K. R., & Fink, B. (2000). Is handwriting causally related to learning to write? Treatment of handwriting problems in beginning writers. *Journal of Educational Psychology, 92,* 620–633.

Grill, J. J., & Kirwin, M. M. (n.d.). *Written language assessment.* Novato, CA: Academic Therapy Publications.

Hackney, C., & Lucas, V. (1993). *Zaner-Bloser handwriting: A way to self expression.* Columbus, OH: Zaner-Bloser.

Hagin, R. A. (1983). Write right—or left: A practical approach to handwriting. *Journal of Learning Disabilities, 16,* 266–271.

Hammill, D. D., & Bartel, N. R. (1990). *Teaching students with learning and behavior problems* (5th ed.). Boston: Allyn & Bacon.

Hammill, D. D., & Larsen, S. (1988). *Test of written language–2.* Austin, TX: Pro-Ed.

Hammill, D. D., & Larsen, S. C. (n. d.). *Test of written language–3.* Austin, TX: Pro-Ed.

Hresko, W. P. (n.d.). *Test of early written language–2.* Austin, TX: Pro-Ed.

Johnson, D. J., & Myklebust, H. R. (1967). *Learning disabilities: Educational principles and practices.* New York: Grune & Stratton.

Keller, M. (2001). Handwriting club: Using sensory integration strategies to improve handwriting. *Intervention in School and Clinic, 37,* 9–12.

Kos, R., & Maslowski, C. (2001). Second graders' perceptions of what is important in writing. *Elementary School Journal, 101,* 567–586.

Larsen, S., & Hammill, D. D. (1989). Test of Legible Handwriting. Austin, TX: Pro-Ed.

Lerner, J. (1988). *Learning disabilities* (5th ed.). Boston: Allyn & Bacon.

Luftig, R. L. (1989). *Assessment of learners with special needs.* Boston: Allyn & Bacon.

Manning, M. L. (1986). Responding to renewed emphasis on handwriting. *Clearing House, 59,* 211–213.

Medwell, J., & Wray, D. (2007). Handwriting: What do we know and what do we need to know? *Literacy, 41,* 10–15.

Meese, R. L. (2001). *Teaching learners with mild disabilities* (2nd ed.). Belmont, CA: Wadsworth/Thomson Learning.

Mendoze, M. A., Holt, W. J., & Jackson, D. A. (1978). Circles and tape: An easy teacher-implemented way to teach fundamental writing skills. *Teaching Exceptional Children, 10,* 48–50.

Mlyniec, V. (2001). Handwriting help. *Parents, 76,* 169–170.

Mullins, J., Joseph, F., Turner, C., Zawadski, R., & Saltzman, L. (1972). A handwriting model for children with learning disabilities. *Journal of Learning Disabilities, 5,* 306–311.

Myklebust, H. R. (n.d.). *The picture story language test.* San Antonio, TX: Psychological Corp.

National Business Education Association. (1997). *Elementary/middle school keyboarding strategies guide.* Reston, VA: Author.

Newland, T. E. (1932). An analytical study of the development of illegibilities in handwriting from the lower grades to adulthood. *Journal of Educational Research, 26,* 249–258.

Otto, W., McMenemy, R. A., & Smith, R. J. (1973). *Corrective and remedial teaching.* Boston: Houghton Mifflin.

Phelps, J., & Stempel, L. (1989). Help for handwriting: Procedures at Texas Scottish Rite Hospital. *Education, 109,* 388–389.

Pierangelo, R., & Giuliani, G. (1998). *Special educator's complete guide to 109 diagnostic tests.* New York: Center for Applied Research in Education.

Polloway, E. A., Patton, J. R., & Serna, L. (2008). *Strategies for teaching learners with special needs* (9th ed). Columbus, OH: Merrill.

Reis, E. M. (1989). Activities for improving the handwriting of learning disabled students. *Clearing House, 62,* 217–219.

Six questions educators should ask before choosing a handwriting program. (1997). Columbus, OH: Zaner-Bloser.

Smith, T. E. C., Dowdy, C. A., & Finn, D. (1993). *Teaching students with mild disabilities*. Ft. Worth, TX: Harcourt Brace.

Smith, T. E. C., Polloway, E. A., Patton, J. R., & Dowdy, C. A. (2008). *Teaching students with special needs in inclusive settings* (4th ed.). Boston: Allyn & Bacon.

Stowitschek, C. E., & Stowitschek, J. J. (1979). Student help in evaluating handwriting performance. *Journal of Learning Disabilities, 12,* 203–206.

Taylor, R. L. (2009). *Assessment of exceptional students* (8th ed.) Upper Saddle River, NJ: Pearson.

Thurber, D. N. (1975). *D'Nealian manuscript: A continuous stroke print*. Glenview, IL: Scott Foresman. (ERIC Document Reproduction Service No. ED 169 533)

Thurber, D. (1987). *D'Nealian manuscript*. Glenview, IL: Scott Foresman.

Thurber, D. N. (1993). *D'Nealian handwriting*. Glenview, IL: Scott Foresman.

Thurber, D. N., & Jordan, D. R. (1978). *D'Nealian handwriting*. Glenview, IL: Scott Foresman.

Tompkins, G. E. (2002). *Language arts: Content and teaching strategies* (5th ed). Columbus, OH: Merrill.

Vacc, N. N. (1987). Word processor versus handwriting: A comparative study of writing samples produced by mildly mentally handicapped students. *Exceptional Children, 54,* 156–165.

Vaughn, S., & Bos, C. S. (2009). *Strategies for teaching students with learning and behavior problems* (7th ed.). Upper Saddle River, NJ: Pearson.

Wood, R. W., Webster, L., Gullickson, A., & Walker, J. (1987). Comparing handwriting legibility with three teaching methods for sex and grade difference. *Reading Improvement, 24,* 24–30.

Zaner-Bloser. (1984). *Zaner-Bloser evaluation scale*. Columbus, OH: Author.

Zemelman, S., & Daniels, H. (1988). *A community of writers*. Portsmouth, NH: Heinemann.

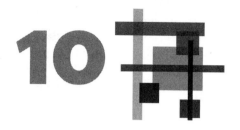

Spelling Assessment and Instruction

Mary Beirne-Smith

Spelling is a complex act that involves attending to several levels of word structure: sounds, syllables, word parts, and specific letters that represent each of them (Moats, 1995). Society considers proficiency in spelling to be a sign of an educated person (Graham, Harris, & Fink-Chorzempa, 2002; Jennings, 1997; Moats, 2006; Tompkins, 1998). Proficient spelling is a courtesy to the reader and aids in communication (Zutell, 2000). Proficient spelling is also important because misspelled words can change the meaning of the text, misspellings are a distraction to the reader (Jennings, 1997) and may discredit the author, and a misspelled message may imply a careless attitude and careless thinking.

Because spelling requires proficiency in word knowledge, most good spellers are accurate and fluent readers. Students with mild learning disabilities often have difficulty with reading, and, consequently, many of these students have trouble learning to spell. Their difficulties in spelling are often developmental in nature and seem to be related to a lack of understanding of the basic orthographic properties of the English language.

English Orthography

Stubbs (1980) defined **English orthography** as a fundamentally alphabetic system in which speech sounds (phonemic units) are represented by letters or letter combinations (**graphemes**). In a perfect system, each phoneme would be represented by one grapheme and each grapheme would have only one sound. The English language, in this sense, is not perfect. It consists of 26 letters, variant and invariant sounds, silent letters, 300 different letter combinations for 17 vowel sounds, and words of foreign origin (Allred, 1977). Moreover, for the 26 letters of the alphabet, 44 phonemes are used in speech and more than 500 spellings represent those phonemes (Tompkins, 1998).

These apparent irregularities in the English language have led some to question the predictability of sound–symbol associations and the advisability of teaching *rule-based approaches* to spelling. Proponents of *word study approaches* to spelling argue that our written language is hardly a transcription of speech sounds. Horn (1960), for example, noted that children often have difficulty learning word analysis skills, that most sounds have numerous spellings, that misspelled words are frequently phonetically correct, and that intensive instruction in phonics is not superior to methods that do not teach phonic skills.

In contrast, proponents of *phonetic approaches* to spelling argue that although the sound–symbol association aspect of spelling is important, it is not the only factor that must be considered in determining the regularity of the English orthographic system. Other phonological factors, as well as morphological, semantic, syntactic, and frequency-of-use factors, are equally important. In a study of 17,000 words frequently used in children's writing, early researchers Hanna, Hanna, Hodges, and Rudorf (1966) found that when phonological factors such as syllabic stress, position in syllables, and internal constraints were taken into account, phoneme–grapheme associations were consistent 80% of the time. Kessler (2003) opined that English spelling is hardly irregular when considering that the English spelling system has been shaped by conservatism (once a spelling is adapted, it tends to stick), unadapted spelling of loan words (English borrows words form other languages and retains the original spelling), and representation of nonphonemic information (in many sets of English words, the spelling reveals more about the meanings than the pronunciation alone could). Moats (2006) set forth five principles that govern the regularity of English spelling:

1. Words' language of origin and history of use can explain their spelling.
2. Words' meaning and part of speech can determine their spelling.
3. Speech sounds are spelled with single letters and/or combinations up to four letters.
4. The spelling of a given sound can vary according to its position within a word.
5. The spellings of some sounds are governed by established conventions of letter sequences and patterns. (p. 3)

In practice, the two approaches to spelling—rule-based and word study—are not necessarily mutually exclusive. Even though phonemic awareness is fundamental to spelling, it alone does not seem to be sufficient for spelling proficiency. Blachman (1994), Hodson (1994), and Moats and Tolman (2008), for example, found that phonological awareness abilities were good predictors of later ability to spell and that all children use phonological processes in their development.

Smiley and Goldstein (1998) reported that most children with disabilities are able to distinguish phonological segments and have learned possible spellings for those segments. Difficulty, however, arises when word segments have more options for spellings. Smiley and Goldstein concluded that students need to learn strong visual memory strategies to help them with words and word segments. When words conform to phonetic generalizations or when word patterns are readily apparent, a rule-based approach to spelling instruction is both sensible and productive. However, because spelling is not totally rule-driven, word study approaches (Bear, Invernizzi, Templeton, & Johnson, 2004) also have an appropriate place in the instructional program.

▌Differences in Spellers

Although few efforts have been made to determine the prevalence of spelling disorders, most experts believe that these disorders are widespread. Individuals who have difficulty in spelling tend to fall into two general categories: (a) those who demonstrate isolated deficits in specific spelling skills and (b) those who exhibit a general pattern of academic and language-learning disabilities (LLD).

Knowledge of the order that is inherent in the English orthographic system is one factor that distinguishes good spellers from poor spellers (Moats, 1995, 2006; Morris, Blanton, Blanton, Nowacek, & Perney, 1995). Proficient spellers, although frequently unable to articulate the reasons for their ability to spell, typically depend on sensitivity to patterns of letters, have visual ability to distinguish when words look correct, and have strong phonemic awareness and knowledge of spelling patterns (Moats & Tolman, 2008; Norton, 1997). For them, spelling is both an associative and a conceptual task: They remember specific words and the principles of written language representation (Moats, 1995).

When faced with unknown or unfamiliar words, proficient spellers access, devise, or apply strategies to determine the correct spelling of the word. They use their knowledge of phonemic and morphemic rules to spell the word phonetically, generate several alternative spellings of the word, and then use revisualization to determine the correct spelling, or they consult an outside source such as the teacher, a peer, or the dictionary (Harris & Graham, 1998; Jennings, 1997).

Less fluent spellers, in contrast, seem to lack the skills essential to producing correctly spelled words. Students with spelling difficulties are not similar to students who progress normally in how they learn. Teachers have reported that students with spelling problems experience word confusion and failure with recall, and they have unexpected problems remembering certain words (Moats, 1995).

Professionals who work with children and adolescents with difficulties in spelling have noted that spelling problems are often chronic and are usually difficult to remedy. In a review of longitudinal studies of spelling abilities of children who have specific language disabilities, Moats (1995) wrote, "Students with specific language disabilities make very limited progress in spelling achievement up to adulthood" (p. 55). Among the many factors that can jeopardize the ability of a student to learn to spell are: inadequate or inappropriate instruction, including lack of teacher content and pedagogy knowledge; poor selection of materials; overdependence on commercial materials (especially basal spelling series); failure to differentiate instruction; failure to use evidence-based instructional techniques; and inadequate allocation of instructional time. Success for students with specific deficits in spelling skills depends to a large extent on accurate diagnosis of the problem and implementation of an appropriate instructional program.

Disorders in spelling related to general academic or language-based learning problems can be more difficult to remediate than problems related to specific skill deficits (Moats, 1995). Because spelling is an act of communication and is primarily a written language skill, it cannot be considered apart from the total literacy curriculum (Conrad, 2008; Norton, 1997). Difficulties in language-related areas, such as articulation or mispronunciation, vocabulary development, handwriting, and reading, can interact with one another and with general problems in learning such as lack of motivation, difficulty in understanding and following directions, and lack of attention to task, which makes identification and remediation of spelling disorders problematic.

For these reasons, some educators advocate a word study approach to spelling instruction. A word study approach to spelling is designed to increase students' knowledge of the order inherent in English orthography (Williams, Phillips-Birdsong, Hufnagel, Hungler, & Lundstrom, 2009).

Research comparing spelling skills in students who achieve at expected levels and students with mild learning disabilities has contributed to our knowledge of how spelling develops and how to assess and remedy spelling problems. This research is discussed next.

▌Development of Spelling Skills

Research on initial spelling attempts indicates that children develop spelling skills in much the same way as they acquire language: hierarchically and sequentially. Children's strategies for spelling words develop in a broadly predictable sequence (Bear & Templeton, 1998; Gentry, 2000; Norton, 1997; Templeton & Morris, 1999), with closer approximations of the correct spelling of words reflecting the child's increasing linguistic awareness and knowledge of orthography.

These initial attempts at spelling, termed **invented spellings,** occur in children in a prephonetic stage or in the phonetic stage, in which consonant or vowel sounds closest to the letter name they represent serve as the written word. In competent spellers, spelling attempts progress to the point at which the speller spontaneously categorizes, compares, and contrasts words at a preconscious level of perception referred to as **spelling by analogy,** and applies knowledge of the redundancies in words to learning to spell new words (Bailet, 1991; Templeton & Morris, 1999). According to Bear and Templeton (1998), this phonological awareness develops throughout the lifetime and seems to be related more to experience with the written word than to experience with spoken language. Experience with the written word alone, however, does not ensure that the child will mature into a competent speller.

The progression in developing spelling skills requires increasingly complex cognitive knowledge. As children's linguistic awareness and knowledge of orthography increase, qualitative changes in spelling that result from their experiences with written language become apparent, and systematic and predictable changes in spelling patterns (i.e., error types) occur. Simply stated, as uncertainty about orthography is reduced, better quality spellings are observed.

Gentry (1982, 1997, 2000) provided a five-stage system for identifying developmental spelling errors:

1. *Precommunicative spelling*: Spellers randomly string together letters of the alphabet without regard to letter–sound correspondence (e.g., OPSOP = eagle; RTAT = eighty).
2. *Semiphonetic spelling*: Letters represent sound, but only some of the letters are represented (e.g., E = eagle; A = eighty).
3. *Phonetic spelling*: Words are spelled like they sound. The speller represents all of the phonemes in a word, although the spelling may be unconventional (e.g., EGL = eagle; ATE = eighty).
4. *Transitional spelling*: A visual memory of spelling patterns is apparent. Spellings exhibit conventions of English orthography, such as vowels in every syllable, e-marker and vowel digraph patterns, correctly spelled inflectional endings, and frequent English letter sequences (e.g., EGUL = eagle; EIGHTEE = eighty).
5. Words are spelled correctly.

Bear and Templeton (1998) developed a modified classification system for spelling development. Similar to Gentry's model in the first three stages, the model's last three stages differ from the last two stages of Gentry's model. Bear and Templeton's classification system is as follows:

1. Precommunicative spelling
2. Semiphonetic spelling
3. Phonetic spelling
4. Within-word pattern: ability to spell long-vowel patterns and complex single syllable words
5. Syllable juncture: ability to spell most two- and three-syllable words correctly, including words with common prefixes and suffixes; development of understanding of syllable combinations; and ability to spell lower frequency vowel patterns correctly
6. Derivational constancy: ability to spell most words correctly, make the meaning connections among words that share bases and roots, choose more varied words in writing, and show better understanding of meaning through vocabulary choices

Whether the final three stages presented by Bear and Templeton are actually stages is the subject of some controversy (Gentry, 2000).

Results of the studies on the development of spelling skills indicate that children with learning disabilities who have difficulty learning to spell pass through the same developmental stages as their peers who achieve at expected levels, but they do so at a slower rate (McNaughton, Hughes, & Clark, 1994; Templeton & Morris, 1999). In some instances, students with spelling problems have been found to possess the orthographic knowledge needed to reduce response uncertainty, but they fail to use it. Templeton and Morris (1999) recommended that, regardless of the students' age or grade level, spelling instruction should be at the appropriate level of development.

From the evidence on development of spelling skills, Hodges (1981) reached the following conclusions:

1. Children make few, if any, random errors in spelling, and by observing and analyzing spelling errors, teachers can determine the child's scheme for spelling words.
2. Efficient spellers possess visual, morphophonemic, phonetic, and semantic information that they use to spell unknown words.
3. Learning to spell is constrained by the cognitive and linguistic factors inherent in the acquisition of language.
4. Learning to spell involves developing an understanding of the total framework of the orthographic properties of the English language. Therefore, children do not necessarily move sequentially from one aspect of orthography to another—that is, from sounds and letters to syllables and words.

Like others who have studied spelling development, Hodges recognized the unresolved issues regarding spelling instruction. Despite these concerns, however, most authorities agree that the most recent perspectives on how spelling develops in children have substantially altered the ways in which we view the assessment and remediation of spelling problems.

▌Assessment

Once the nature of the orthographic system and the general development of spelling skills are understood, the teacher's next task is to devise a system of assessment that accurately documents and monitors students' progress in the school curriculum and informs the teacher's instruction in meaningful ways. To assess a student's spelling skills, the teacher can select a number of formal and informal procedures.

Formal Assessment

The rationale for using formal tests to assess spelling skills depends on the purposes for which the test results will be used. In most educational settings, formal tests are used for administrative, identification, and placement purposes, or to detect or document a school performance problem. Formal tests provide a basis for pre- and post-testing because they represent an unbiased measure of progress. They may also be used to compare proficiency in reading to proficiency in spelling to ascertain the scope and relative importance of the student's spelling skills. In these instances, formal tests are quite useful.

Using formal tests for educational planning, however, is quite another matter. Because the assessment of spelling skills seems relatively straightforward, teachers are often tempted to make decisions about instruction based on the number of correct and incorrect responses. The practice of administering formal tests solely to obtain test scores must be viewed with caution. At best, test scores only inform the teacher of the student's standing relative to the norm group. Test scores provide little more than an estimated level of difficulty for choosing instructional programs and materials. More useful information can be obtained if the teacher analyzes the student's errors and performance to identify the source of the problem.

Teachers must also be aware that the manner in which a spelling task is presented can affect a student's performance on a test. Some tests require students to write the spelling word from dictation; others require students to find the correctly spelled word in a series of words. Tasks of recall and tasks of recognition require different skills, and the implications for instruction, therefore, differ.

With these cautions in mind, teachers can choose from a variety of formal instruments that assess spelling skills. Several broad-range achievement tests contain subtests with limited attention to this area. Those that employ a traditional dictation format include

- the *Wide Range Achievement Test* (4th edition; Wilkinson and Robertson, 2006),
- the *Test of Written Spelling* (4th edition; TWS-4; Larsen, Hammill, & Moats, 1999), and
- the *Kaufman Test of Educational Achievement* (2nd edition; Kaufman & Kaufman, 2004).

Others, such as the *Peabody Individual Achievement Test–Revised/Normative Update* (Markwardt, 1998), require the student to recognize the correctly spelled word from a choice of words. The *Woodcock-Johnson III Tests of Achievement* (Woodcock, McGrew, & Mather, 2001) test both spelling recognition and recall on its Dictation and Proofing subtests.

Teachers who are skilled in assessment might analyze individual responses on broad-range tests of achievement to locate the source of the student's problem. Because the skills measured by these tests are limited by the number of items that test each skill, however, the tests do not provide a comprehensive assessment of the student's skill in spelling and, thus, are of limited value in instructional planning.

The Test of Written Spelling (4th edition; TWS–4; Larsen et al., 1999) provides a more comprehensive measure of spelling skills. The TWS–4 reflects the authors' theories that mastery of a certain number of spelling rules is necessary for independence in spelling and that words that do not conform to standard generalizations must be learned by rote memorization. The test is designed for students ages 6 years 0 months to 18 years 11 months and may be administered as either an individual test or a group test. It uses a standard dictation format and consists of two tests of equivalent lists of 50 words each. Words for the lists were selected because they occur frequently in six commonly used basal spelling series. The TWS–4 requires 15 minutes to administer (more time is required for group administrations) and yields raw scores, percentile ranks, standard scores, spelling ages, and grade equivalents for each test, as well as a total test score.

The TWS–4 has high reliability in the areas of content sampling, time sampling, and scorer differences; however, the manual fails to report concurrent validity and whether students with disabilities were included in the standardization sample. (The authors reported that the sample is consistent with the 1990 census data.) Despite these concerns, the TWS–4 is a useful tool for assessing spelling skills.

Informal Assessment

Informal assessment of spelling skills entails gathering student spelling data from a wide variety of sources. Typically, spelling samples can be collected from dictated tests, free writing and compositions, responses to written questions in other content areas, and varied independent work assignments.

Informal assessment has a number of advantages over formal assessment. By using a variety of sources, teachers have the opportunity to evaluate the student's ability to transfer skills, analyze trends both within and between content areas, avoid false positives resulting from limited samples, and avoid false negatives created by a limited range of opportunities for spelling to be evaluated. Further, because informal assessment is often curriculum-based, it provides teachers with a way to monitor student progress and differentiate instruction to meet the collective and individual needs of all students in the classroom. Progress monitoring, particularly curriculum-based assessment, is effective in informing teachers of individual student performance relative to other students in the class and guiding the level and intensity of teachers' instruction (Roehrig, Duggar, Moats, Glover, & Mincey, 2008). The information that is gathered can be translated readily into teaching strategies that meet the instructional needs of all students in the classroom. Finally, testing can be accomplished in a relatively short time, so informal assessment is practical to use as a continuous measure of progress.

Error Analysis

Before realizing the full value of informal assessment, the teacher must understand error analysis. **Error analysis** is a technique used to investigate the types of problems the student experiences, to discern trends in errors, and to determine the reasons for the problem. The procedure can be applied to any sample of student spelling.

Error analysis is based on the premises that students' production of words represents their best attempts at spelling and that spelling errors tend to be nonrandom and consistent. Most of the students' errors in spelling are consistent across dictated word lists (Moats, 1995), and these tend to be errors of omission and substitution or errors in vowels in mid-syllables when word segments have more options for spellings (Smiley & Goldstein, 1998). Spache (1940) listed common spelling errors, which still hold true today:

1. Omission of a silent letter (e.g., *wether* for *weather, reman* for *remain, fin* for *fine*)
2. Omission of a sounded letter (e.g., *requst* for *request, plasure* for *pleasure, personl* for *personal, juge* for *judge*)
3. Omission of a doubled letter (e.g., *suden* for *sudden, adress* for *address, sed* for *seed*)
4. Doubling of a letter (e.g., *untill* for *until, frriend* for *friend, deegree* for *degree*)
5. Addition of a single letter (e.g., *darck* for *dark, nineth* for *ninth, refere* for *refer*)
6. Transposition or partial reversal of letters (e.g., *was* for *saw, nickle* for *nickel, bron* for *born*)
7. Phonetic substitution for a vowel (e.g., *prisin* for *prison, injoy* for *enjoy*)
8. Phonetic substitution for a consonant (e.g., *prizon* for *prison, sekond* for *second, vakation* for vacation)
9. Phonetic substitution for a syllable (e.g., *purchest* for *purchased, financhel* for *financial, naborhood* for *neighborhood, stopt* for *stopped*)
10. Phonetic substitution for a word (e.g., *weary* for *very, colonial* for *colonel*)
11. Nonphonetic substitution for a vowel (e.g., *rad* for *red, reword* for *reward*)
12. Nonphonetic substitution for a consonant (e.g., *watching* for *washing, inportance* for *importance*)

Other authors (Mercer & Mercer, 2005; Vaughn and Bos, 2009) have identified common errors in spelling such as mispronunciation or evidence of dialect usage and failure to use common rules for spelling (e.g., changing *y* to *i* before adding a suffix that begins with a vowel or placing *i* before *e* except after *c*).

Error analysis is a relatively simple procedure that can help the teacher determine where a student is within the developmental stages of spelling (Moats, 1995). The teacher gathers a representative sample of the student's spelling performance and analyzes the student's errors. As Moats (1995) and Smiley and Goldstein (1998) pointed out, however, the problem inherent in using error analysis alone is that many errors have several plausible explanations and teachers cannot always determine at which stage of spelling development the student falls.

Beirne-Smith and Riley (2008) recommended that teachers use observations and clinical interviews to gain additional assessment information. These authors suggested that teachers make notes of the student's speed of response and the strategies that students employ during spelling (e.g., sounding out words). Beirne-Smith and Riley further suggested that during clinical interviews teachers ask questions such as the following:

1. How did you approach spelling this word?
2. Does this word look like any other word that you know how to spell?
3. Can you sound out this word? What letter(s) make the sounds that you say when you sound out this word?
4. (For multisyllabic words) What part of this word did you find difficult to spell?
5. Can you think of any spelling rule that will help you spell this word? (or this part of the word?)
6. What spelling strategies did you use when you spelled this word? (p. 6)

After obtaining a sample of the student's work, the teacher can decide which type of analysis to apply and can analyze the words by error type and error tendency using an error analysis chart such as the one shown in Figure 10.1. As indicated, spelling errors can be analyzed as errors in whole words, syllables, sound clusters, or letter sequences. Analysis of whole words yields information only on the number of correct and incorrect responses. Although this approach is generally adequate with students who do not have difficulties in spelling, it is insufficient for planning an instructional program for a student with a significant spelling disorder.

For the student with significant problems in spelling, the teacher has to look more closely at errors in individual words. For example, the teacher may count and record the number of correct syllables or sound clusters in the student's spelling attempt. In this approach, the student who spelled *sensible* as *sensable* would score 2 of 3 possible correct responses for syllables correct; the student who spelled *truck* as *trk* would score 1 of 3 possible correct responses for sound clusters correct.

When the problem is persistent, counting the number of correct letter sequences provides the best instructional information. In this procedure, the student is awarded a point for each correct letter pair and for beginning and ending the word correctly. Carets are used to mark correct letter sequences and correct beginning and ending letters. The following is an example of this procedure:

	^ ^ ^ ^ ^ ^ ^ ^ ^ ^	
Spelling 1	p h o t o g r a p h	11 correct
	^ ^ ^ ^ ^ ^ ^	
Spelling 2	p h o t g r p h	7 correct
	^ ^ ^ ^ ^	
Spelling 3	f o t o g r a f	5 correct

Teachers who apply error analysis procedures to spelling assessment data are a step closer to designing an effective remedial spelling program. It should be noted, however, that Moats (1995) and Smiley and Goldstein (1998) identified an inherent

		Regular	Predictable	Irregular	Comments
	Rules/Patterning				
Type	Consonants				
	Vowels				
	Order				
	Substitution				
Tendency	Insertion				
	Omission				

Student _____ Date _____

Material/Level _____

Word List (/)   Paragraph (/)   Other _____

TYPE OF ANALYSIS
   Scoring: Word (/)   Syllables (/)   Clusters (/)   Letters ( )

PART OF WORD ERRED

Beginning Time _____   Ending Time _____   Number minutes _____

Corrects _____   Errors _____

Source: Adapted from "Consistency of Learning Disabled Students," by V. DeMaster, C. Crossland, and T. S. Hasselbring, 1986, *Learning Disability Quarterly, 9,* pp. 89–96; and *A Microcomputer-based System for the Analysis of Student Spelling Errors,* by T. S. Hasselbring and S. Owens, 1981, Nashville, TN: Peabody College of Vanderbilt.

FIGURE 10.1
Spelling Error Analysis Chart

problem in using error analysis: Many errors have several plausible explanations. Thus, teachers cannot always be certain at which stage of developmental spelling a student falls.

Criterion-Referenced Tests

Unlike norm-referenced tests, which compare a student's performance to that of age- or grade-level peers, **criterion-referenced tests (CRTs)** are designed to compare the student's spelling performance to a specified level of mastery or achievement. The purposes of criterion-referenced tests are (a) to determine which skills the student has or has not mastered at a pre-set level of performance (e.g., 80%) and (b) to provide an objective measure of student progress on tasks of progressive levels of difficulty. Teachers can select from available published CRTs, or they can construct their own informal spelling inventories.

Published CRTs

The *Brigance Comprehensive Inventory of Basic Skills–Revised* (Brigance, 1999) is one published CRT. The *Brigance* includes tests for elementary and secondary students. The elementary inventory consists of a grade placement test that assesses skill in initial consonants, initial blends, initial diagraphs, and affixes. The secondary inventory assesses the same skills and includes tests of number words, days of the week, and months of the year.

Informal Spelling Inventories

Teachers often find it desirable to construct their own assessments of students' spelling skills. Teacher-constructed informal spelling inventories may be designed around specific skills or may be curriculum based. In specific skill assessment, test items are designed to evaluate specific aspects of spelling. The test might be constructed to measure a single spelling skill (e.g., the spelling of words with short vowel sounds) or a combination of skills (e.g., the spelling of words with long and short vowel sounds and vowel diphthongs). After generating a list of rule exemplar words and administering the test, the teacher uses error analysis to determine which rules should be taught.

Progress Monitoring

In curriculum-based assessment, test items evaluate the skills required by the school's curriculum or the skills described in the objectives in a student's individualized educational program (IEP). Curriculum-based assessments may be designed by selecting a representative sample of words from the basal spelling series used by the school or from IEP objectives related to survival, high-utility, basic, or content-area vocabulary words. Mann and Suiter (1974) recommended that for the basal series test, the teacher should randomly select 20 words from each grade level, begin testing two grade levels below the student's actual grade placement, and end testing at the level at which the student makes seven errors.

Most often, the purpose of assessing spelling skills is to facilitate the planning and implementation of an appropriate instructional program. Used individually, both formal and informal assessment procedures contribute to the teacher's knowledge of the student's present level of performance. In combination, the two procedures allow the teacher to identify specific areas of strengths and weaknesses more accurately. When error analysis is added to assessment procedures, the teacher has a powerful tool for formulating an instructional program that is effective in meeting the student's unique learning needs. In short, the best approach to assessment combines a variety of techniques for evaluating the student's skill in spelling and provides useful information for instructional decision making.

Instructional Approaches

The complex nature of the English orthographic system and of associated LLDs frequently interferes with the acquisition of spelling skills by students who have mild learning disabilities. The importance of spelling in the education of these students often is not fully appreciated. Nevertheless, competency in spelling is essential to the student's ability to function in other areas of the literacy curriculum. Competent spellers are less distracted by determining the correctness of the written word and more able to concentrate on other elements of written expression such as clarity, sequencing, and expressiveness.

Fluency in spelling allows the speller to progress in related academic areas and to more ably communicate meaningful ideas to the reader. Better communication results in improved interpersonal relationships and higher self-esteem. As adults, spellers who are not conspicuous by their errors are freer to pursue a broad range of education and employment options.

Purpose of Spelling Instruction

The purpose of spelling instruction for students with disabilities is to produce spellers who are competitive with individuals who do not demonstrate significant difficulties in spelling. To meet this aim, instructional programs must be effective and have clearly stated objectives. Vaughn and Bos (2009) recommended the following principles for teaching spelling to students with learning difficulties:

- Teach in small units.
- Teach spelling patterns.
- Provide sufficient practice and feedback.
- Select appropriate words.
- Teach spelling using direct instruction.
- Use appropriate instructional language.
- Maintain previously learned words.
- Motivate students to spell correctly.
- Include dictionary training.

In a review of the literature on spelling instruction for students with learning disabilities, McNaughton et al. (1994) found seven common practices that have proven to be effective:

1. Limit the number of new vocabulary items introduced each day.
2. Provide opportunities for self-directed and peer-assisted instruction.
3. Direct students to name letters aloud as they practice phonemic analysis.

4. Include instruction in morphemic analysis.
5. Provide immediate error imitation and correction.
6. Use motivating reinforcers.
7. Implement periodic retesting and review.

Graham (1985) noted that effective spelling programs are comprehensive, student oriented, varied, direct, individualized, and based on a solid foundation of empirical research. Hodges (1981) recommended that, to be effective, spelling instructional programs should

- be incorporated into the general study of language to provide students with the opportunity to apply their knowledge of spelling and to examine the relationship between written and spoken language,
- employ a variety of materials and methods to accommodate differences in learning styles and rates,
- include regular writing activities that foster natural curiosity and encourage students to apply their increasing orthographic knowledge, and
- include multiple opportunities for students to assess their attempts at spelling so they can learn from their mistakes.

Various instructional approaches have been developed to help students acquire spelling skills and ultimately develop an extensive written vocabulary. Some of these methods are better than others, but no single method has yet been determined to be the best way to teach spelling to students with difficulties in this area (Graham, 1999). Teachers should carefully consider assessment information for the individual student when making goal-setting and programming decisions and be flexible when selecting the most appropriate strategy. In many instances, the needs of a single student are best met by combining several instructional techniques in the total spelling program.

Traditional Approaches

Most educators are familiar with the traditional patterns of spelling instruction in U.S. schools. Instruction in spelling is conducted during a brief, isolated period in the daily school schedule. Typically, spelling instruction lasts from 1 to 30 minutes during the school day (McNaughton et al., 1994). Commercial spelling texts provide the basis for the program, and students progress through a series of daily activities designed to teach the spelling of linguistically similar words. A typical weekly schedule of spelling activities might be:

Monday:	Introduce new words.
Tuesday:	Have students write each word three times.
Wednesday:	Have students write each word in a sentence.
Thursday:	Have students take a practice test.
Friday:	Have students take a final test.

The continuing use of this routine in U.S. classrooms suggests that teachers perceive it to be an effective way to teach students to spell. Indeed, many students who are exposed to this type of instruction succeed in learning to spell. For students with difficulties in spelling, however, a simple pattern of this sort has not proven effective.

Unadapted, the whole group instructional approaches common to commercial spelling texts are unsuccessful in meeting the needs of students with spelling disorders. Frequently, spelling series texts fail to provide for individualized instruction, sufficient opportunities for word study, adequate practice, or guidance in the development of strategy instruction (Schlagal & Schlagal, 1992). Often, these series contain a large selection of inappropriate or ineffective activities, some of which actually may inhibit the student's ability to learn to spell (Cohen, 1969). Certainly, commercial spelling texts encourage teachers to view spelling as a product, not a process, and discourage the integration of skills related to spelling in the larger language arts curriculum.

Because commercial spelling texts are readily available in schools, teachers are often reluctant to abandon them as an instructional option. Teachers who select these materials as the foundation for their instructional program should carefully consider how they can be adapted to meet their students' needs. Many of the procedures described in the remainder of this chapter can easily be adapted for use with commercial spelling programs.

Remedial Approaches

Remedial approaches to spelling provide ways for the teacher to supplement traditional spelling programs or to offer viable instructional alternatives for students who have difficulty in learning to spell. These approaches emphasize individualization, a systematic method of word study, distributed repetitive practice, and performance feedback. Graham and Voth (1990) recommended the following curriculum modifications for implementing remedial spelling programs:

1. Instruction should be limited (at least initially) to high-frequency words and misspelled words from the student's own writing.
2. Words should be organized into small units (6–12 words) that emphasize a common structural element.
3. Distributed practice should be provided by introducing several words on successive days.
4. New and previously introduced words should be tested at the beginning and end of the daily spelling period; periodic maintenance checks should be conducted.
5. During daily tests, students should be encouraged to predict whether they will spell and to check that they did spell words correctly. Students should correct the test with teacher supervision.
6. Students should use a systematic study procedure to study words missed on the daily pretest.

7. Students should practice missed words on succeeding days, using games and other interesting activities to improve fluency and accuracy.
8. The teacher should work to establish a strong link between instruction in spelling and the students' writing. Written products should be examined to determine whether learned spellings are being generalized.
9. Students should be taught strategies or provided with resources to help them with their spelling while writing.

The remedial approaches described next are appropriate for individuals of all ages and for students with a variety of spelling problems. Teachers should select the approach that best fits their personal beliefs about teaching, their teaching style, and the individual needs of their students. When a combination of approaches is indicated, the teacher should ensure that the approaches selected are compatible: One method should enhance the effect of the other method(s). Finally, the teacher should make an effort to determine which procedures are most efficient for the student.

Multisensory Approaches

Multisensory approaches to spelling involve the visual, auditory, and motor modalities. These approaches are based on the understanding that, to spell a word, students must be able to demonstrate auditory and visual discrimination of the sounds and letters in the word and possess the motor control necessary to write the word.

Although the efficacy of multisensory approaches is supported primarily by anecdotal reports, the techniques are useful in providing students with a systematic method of word study and repetitive practice. Figure 10.2 indicates several word study techniques that employ multisensory approaches to spelling.

Linguistic Approaches

Linguistic approaches to spelling emphasize the regularity of sound–symbol associations in the English language and their graphic representations in orthography. The instructional methodologies accent rules governing the phonological, morphological, and syntactic features of words. Words are selected for instruction on the basis of their appropriateness for teaching phonics generalizations, structural analysis, or linguistic patterns (Bear & Templeton, 1998; Smiley & Goldstein, 1998; Templeton & Morris, 1999).

As mentioned previously, some controversy surrounds the advisability of teaching spelling generalizations, particularly to students with disabilities. Some students with mild disabilities have difficulty in learning any rules, some may succeed in learning and applying only a few rules, and others will learn a rule but be unable to apply it in their written language. Because many words in the English language illustrate "productive relationships" (Hodges, 1966, p. 332) between sounds and symbols, however, instruction in rules can be an important mediating influence in spelling.

Students with mild learning disabilities can profit from rule-based instruction in spelling if the teacher guides the development of useful conventions by presenting a

Fitzgerald Method (Fitzgerald, 1951)

1. Look at the word carefully.
2. Say the word.
3. With eyes closed, visualize the word.
4. Cover the word and then write it.
5. Check the spelling.
6. If the word is misspelled, repeat steps 1–5.

Horn Method 1 (E. Horn, 1919)

1. Look at the word and say it to yourself.
2. Close your eyes and visualize the word.
3. Check to see if you were right. (If not, begin at step 1.)
4. Cover the word and write it.
5. Check to see if you were right. (If not, begin at step 1.)
6. Repeat steps 4 and 5 two more times.

Horn Method 2 (E. Horn, 1954)

1. Pronounce each word carefully.
2. Look carefully at each part of the word as you pronounce it.
3. Say the letters in sequence.
4. Attempt to recall how the word looks, then spell the word.
5. Check this attempt to recall.
6. Write the word.
7. Check this spelling attempt.
8. Repeat the above steps if necessary.

Visual-Vocal Method (Westerman, 1971)

1. Say word.
2. Spell word orally.
3. Say word again.

4. Spell word from memory four times correctly.

Gilstrap Method (Gilstrap, 1962)

1. Look at the word and say it softly. If it has more than one part, say it again, part by part, looking at each part as you say it.
2. Look at the letters and say each one. If the word has more than one part, say the letters part by part.
3. Write the word without looking at the book.

Fernald Method Modified

1. Make a model of the word with a crayon, grease pencil, or felt-tip pen, saying the word as you write it.
2. Check the accuracy of the model.
3. Trace over the model with your index finger, saying the word at the same time.
4. Repeat step 3 five times.
5. Copy the word three times correctly.
6. Copy the word three times from memory correctly.

Cover-and-Write Method

1. Look at word. Say it.
2. Write word two times.
3. Cover and write one time.
4. Check work.
5. Write word two times
6. Cover and write one time.
7. Check work.
8. Write word three times.
9. Cover and write one time.
10. Check work.

Source: From "Spelling Research and Practice: A Unified Approach," by S. Graham and L. Miller, 1979, *Focus on Exceptional Children, 12*(2), p. 11. Copyright 1979 Love Publishing Company. Reprinted with permission.

FIGURE 10.2

Word Study Techniques

limited number of important and functional rules. Although dated, the suggestions that Brueckner and Bond (1955) provided for teaching spelling rules still generally apply:

1. Select a rule to be taught. Teach a single rule at a time.
2. Secure a list of words exemplifying the rule. Develop the rule through the study of words it covers.
3. Lead the pupils to discover the underlying generalization by discussing with them the characteristics for the words in the list. If possible, have the pupils actually formulate the rule. Help them to sharpen and clarify it.
4. Have the pupils use and apply the rule immediately.
5. If necessary, show how the rule, in some cases, does not apply, but stress its positive values.
6. Review the rule systematically on succeeding days. Emphasize its use, and do not require pupils to memorize a formalized statement. (p. 374)

Teachers must bear in mind, however, that students with mild learning disabilities frequently have difficulty with discovery approaches to learning. For these students, direct teacher instruction is more likely to be successful than the inductive approach (Graham, 1999).

Students need knowledge of some rules about the contexts in which conventional phoneme–grapheme correspondences are used (Willson, Rupley, Rodriguez, & Mergen, 1999). Although they acknowledged that not all rules are useful, Howell, Fox, and Morehead (1993) designated the following high-utility rules as applicable more than half the time:

1. Double the letters f, l, s, or z in most one-syllable words when preceded by a short vowel. *Examples*: cliff, sniff, bluff, whiff, cuff, puff, fell, tell, swell, ball, spill, fill, spell, brass, press, cross, miss, fuss, pass, buzz, fizz, jazz. *Exceptions*: bus and gas.
2. The silent e at the end of a word makes a short vowel long. *Examples*: pin and pine, dim and dime, hat and hate, mat and mate, rat and rate, cub and cube, plan and plane, cap and cape, at and ate, mad and made, mop and mope, kit and kite, rod and rode, hid and hide, rip and ripe, fad and fade, cut and cute, tub and tube, can and cane, hop and hope, not and note, and fin and fine.
3. When you hear k after a short vowel, spell it ck; when you hear k after a long vowel or consonant, spell it k. *Examples*: neck, dusk, flank, track, hunk, slack, stuck, deck, rink, milk, check, tuck, task, fleck, lack, coke, make, rock, knock, stink. Use c at the end of polysyllabic words when you hear ik. *Examples*: attic, plastic, metric, cosmic, classic, Atlantic, optic, frantic.
4. When you hear j after a short vowel, you usually spell it dge. After a long vowel or consonant, you use ge. *Examples*: age, gadget, lodge, huge, strange, cage, nudge, stage, page, bridge, change, hinge, edge.

5. When you hear ch after a short vowel, use tch. When you hear ch after a long vowel or consonant, you use ch. Ch is always used at the beginning of a word. *Examples*: chop, bench, batch, pinch, church, witch, blotch, pitch, porch, crutch, lunch, sketch, fetch, patch. Exceptions: rich, which, much, such, sandwich.

6. When you have a one-syllable word with a consonant at the end that is preceded by a short vowel and you add a suffix that begins with one vowel, double the consonant before the suffix. If any one of these conditions is not met, don't double. *Examples*: ship and shipper, ship and shipping, hot and hottest, slop and sloppy, mad and madder, rob and robber, star and starry, fat and fatter, fog and foggy, wit and witness, grin and grinning, mad and madly, cold and colder, farm and farming, dust and dusty, rant and ranted, boat and boating, weed and weeding, blot and blotter, grim and grimmest, rest and restless, flat and flatly, slim and slimmer, feed and feeding, and win and winning.

7. A word ending in a silent e drops the e before a suffix beginning with a vowel but does not change before an ending beginning with a consonant. *Examples*: hope and hoping, dive and diving, write and writing, tune and tuneful, shine and shiny, time and timer, hope and hopeless, take and taking, sore and soreness, flame and flaming, fame and famous, care and caring, hide and hiding, hope and hoped, lone and lonely, use and useful, sure and surely, close and closely, make and making, life and lifeless, like and likeness, shade and shady, noise and noiseless, and tire and tiresome.

8. Double the consonant when adding a suffix after a short vowel. (Do not double the consonant after a long vowel.) *Examples*: capped, caper, capping, moping, mopping, mapped, filling, filed, filing, filled, taping, tapping, taped, tapped, tapper, hopped, hoped, hopping, hoping.

9. In words ending in y preceded by a consonant, the y changes to i before any ending except -ing or -ist. In words ending in y preceded by a vowel, keep the y. *Examples*: cry and crying, rely and reliance, pray and prayer, worry and worrying, joy and joyful, enjoy and enjoyment, say and saying, sleepy and sleepiness, glory and glorious, delay and delayed, merry and merriest, study and studying, lonely and loneliness, pay and payable, carry and carried, stray and strayed, fly and flier, supply and supplied, healthy and healthier, spy and spying, funny and funniest, tiny and tiniest, injury and injurious.

10. When adding ble, dle, fle to a word, consider the initial vowel sound. A long vowel or consonant preceding the ending simply requires ble, dle, fle. A short vowel continues to need all the help it can get. *Examples*: buckle, freckle, puddle, ruffle, stable, rifle, stifle, staple.

11. Most nouns form the plural by adding -s to the singular, but nouns ending in s, x, sh, and ch form the plural by adding -es. A noun ending in y preceded by a consonant forms the plural by changing the y to i and adding -es. *Examples*: cats, dogs, kisses, boxes, fishes, churches, and candies.

12. An apostrophe is used to show the omission of a letter or letters in a contraction. The possessive of a singular noun is formed by adding an apostrophe

and s. The possessive of a plural noun ending in s is formed by adding an apostrophe. *Examples*: cannot and can't, will not and won't, I had and I'd, I will and I'll, had not and hadn't, Jim's car, the dog's bone, the groups' scores. (p. 312)

Word Study Approaches

Word study approaches consider spelling as a conceptual process rather than a rote memorization process. Unlike linguistic approaches, which employ a skill-sequence or bottom-up approach to learning, word study approaches favor a top-down or holistic approach to spelling instruction. Word study approaches to learning reject, in theory at least, the rule-based techniques that define linguistic approaches to spelling instruction. The focus in word study approaches is on immersing the student in written language experiences that facilitate discoveries about the way words are represented in print.

In a word study approach, students are encouraged to experiment with spelling in keeping with their stage of spelling development. The teacher acts as a nonjudgmental evaluator whose purpose is to facilitate the refinement of spelling skills. For example, teachers select spelling words that contain certain spelling patterns. Students engage in spelling activities such as sorting words by predetermined patterns, constructing word walls, or developing word study notebooks. Orthographic principles are introduced only when the student demonstrates a need to learn a specific rule. Norris (1989) set forth five principles for applying word study approaches to spelling instruction:

1. Language learning begins with contextual language. By contextualizing spelling instruction, children simultaneously discover properties of word structure while attaching meaning and use to the process of spelling.
2. Writing is a communication process in which experience is shared. Rather than being viewed as a task to complete for purposes of demonstrating mastery, spelling is viewed as a means of sharing meaning with an interested listener/reader.
3. Instruction begins with the child's level of spelling knowledge. Spelling progresses through predictable stages as children acquire increasing experience with and knowledge of written language.
4. Instruction is discovery-based. The teacher's impact is designed to facilitate refinement rather than to demand correctness and accuracy.
5. The goal of instruction is to facilitate a developmental change in the strategies a child uses to represent words rather than in the child's mastery of the correct words. (pp. 99–101)

Implementing a word study approach requires different instructional techniques from those that teachers typically use in spelling instruction. Teachers who choose word study approaches must be organized, creative, and, to a certain extent, intuitive in determining when and in what areas to introduce instruction related to the ortho-graphic properties of language. The advantage of word study approaches is that students have greater opportunity to use knowledge about spelling in context. A potential disadvantage is that students with disabilities frequently have difficulty generalizing the skills and concepts they learn. Because word study approaches introduce skills only when the need arises, these students may fail to learn spelling principles that teach the relationships between words.

Bruck, Treiman, Caravolas, Genesee, and Cassar (1998) compared two groups of third graders who had either all word study instruction in spelling or all phonics-based instruction during their years in elementary school. The findings indicated that children in word study programs did not spell at a level appropriate for their age or their reading ability. Their word and nonword spelling scores were significantly lower than those of students using phonics-based programs. Word study students differed in their knowledge of conventional phoneme–grapheme correspondences and lacked knowledge about the contexts in which various correspondences are used.

Researchers have concluded that students need explicit strategy instruction in conjunction with a word study approach to assist them in developing appropriate spelling skills (Bruck et al., 1998; Butyniec-Thomas & Woloshyn, 1997). Templeton and Morris (1999) summarized the findings about word study approaches to spelling instruction by stating:

> For most students, an inductive, exploratory approach [to spelling] is appropriate; for severely struggling spellers who are working at an appropriate developmental level, a more deductive, systematic, and direct approach is preferred. (p. 5)

Word Lists

Teachers of students with mild learning disabilities often elect to teach spelling from word lists. Depending on the student's individual needs, the teacher may decide to use high-frequency word lists such as Horn's (1960) "Words Most Commonly Used in Writing;" various functional word lists such as survival words and phrases; spelling demons, as adapted in part from Otto, McMenemy, and Smith (1973) and listed in Figure 10.3; or lists compiled by the teacher from content area texts or mistakes in the student's own writing.

Graham, Harris, and Loynachan (1994) developed the "Spelling for Writing List," consisting of 335 words that are considered high-frequency writing words by the end of third grade (see Figure 10.4). When determining which words were more important to learn to spell, these authors used three principles to guide the broad applicability and relevance:

1. Words commonly used in writing are the best source for spelling words.
2. Lists should be generated from all types of students' writings.
3. Spelling vocabulary words should be derived from children from all stations of life.

apostrophe	desperate	Mississippi	they're
Arkansas	dessert	Missouri	thought
arrangement	forty	nickel	threw
attendance	greasy	ninety	through
believe	Halloween	occasionally	vacuum
breathe	Hawaii	principal	Wednesday
choose	Illinois	principle	you're
chose	interest	receive	your
clothing	knowledgeable	separate	yours
commitment	loose	straight	
deceive	lose	their *that you are*	
desert	Massachusetts	there	

FIGURE 10.3

Demons in Spelling

Graham et al. (1994) recommended that the word list be used with children identified as poor spellers. They suggested the following:

- Use the list initially as a source for spelling words.
- Group words in the list by common phonic and orthographic principles, and teach them as word families.
- Use the list to confirm that high-frequency writing words are not being inadvertently overlooked.

Word lists can be categorized as fixed lists or flow lists. With *fixed lists*, a new set of words is assigned each week. The student engages in a series of activities designed to teach the spelling of the words on the list, and a test is given at the end of the week. Follow-up on missed words is usually not provided, and words on a new list may bear little or no resemblance to words on the previous list. With *flow lists*, the number of words initially presented is limited. Once the student masters a word, it is dropped from the list and a new word is added. An advantage to flow lists is that students do not waste valuable time practicing words they know. Most authorities agree that flow lists are more beneficial than fixed lists in teaching spelling to students with mild learning disabilities, especially when routine review of previously mastered words is included in the teaching procedure.

Cognitive Approaches

Cognitive approaches to spelling instruction are based on research on the developmental model of the acquisition of spelling skills. According to this perspective,

Grade 1 Word List

a	day*	into*	play*
all	did	is	ran
am*	do	its*	red
and*	dog*	let	ride
at	for*	like*	run
ball	fun*	look	see
be	get*	man	she
bed	go	may	so
big	good*	me*	stop
book	got*	my*	the*
box	had*	no*	this
boy*	he*	not	to*
but	her*	of	two*
came*	him*	oh	up
can*	his*	old	us
car	home*	on*	was*
cat	I*	one*	we*
come*	it	out*	will*
dad	in*	you*	yes

Grade 2 Word List

about*	door	help	mother*	school*	time*
after	down*	here*	much	sea	today*
an*	each	hit	must	ship	told
any	eat	hope*	myself*	show*	too*
are*	end	horse	name*	sleep	took
as	fast	house*	new*	small	tree
ask	father*	how*	next	snow	try
away	feet	just*	nice*	some*	used
baby*	fell*	keep	night	soon*	very*
back	find	kid	now*	start	walk
bad	fire	know*	off*	stay	want*
been*	first*	land	only	still	way

(continued)

Source: From "The Spelling for Writing list," by S. Graham, K. R. Harris, & C. Loynachan, 1994, *Journal of Learning Disabilities, 27,* pp. 213–214. Copyright 1994. Reprinted with permission.

FIGURE 10.4
Spelling for Writing List

Grade 2 Word List *(continued)*

before*	fish	last	open	store*	week
being	five	left	or*	story	well*
best	food	little*	other	take	went*
black	four	live	our*	talk	were*
boat	from*	long	outside*	tell	what
both	funny	looking	over	than*	when*
brother*	game	lot	park	that	while*
buy*	gave	love	playing	them*	while*
by	girl	mad	put	then*	who
call	give	made*	read	there*	why
candy	going*	make*	room	they*	wish
city	happy	many*	said*	thing	with*
coming*	hard	men	same	think*	work
could	has*	more	saw*	three	your
doing	have*	most		say	

Grade 3 Word List

again*	ever	I'll*	own	team
air	every*	I'm*	party*	that's*
almost	everyone*	it's*	people*	their*
also	everything*	kind	person	these*
always*	eye	knew*	place	thought*
another*	face	lady	ready	trip
anything*	family*	later	real	trying
around*	few	let's*	right*	turn
because*	found*	life	running*	walking
better	friend*	lunch	says	wasn't
can't*	front	maybe*	should	watch
catch	getting*	might*	sister	water
children*	great	money*	someone*	where*
class	hair	morning*	something*	which
didn't*	half	Mr.*	sometime*	won
dinner	having*	Mrs.*	stopped*	world*
does	head	Ms.	summer*	would*
don't*	heard*	never	talking	year
earth	hour	nothing	teacher*	you're
even	hurt*	once*		

FIGURE 10.4 *(continued)*

spelling is a complex, high-order cognitive skill. Children develop spelling skills in a series of predictable stages related to their specific knowledge of the orthographic properties of language and their general problem-solving skills. Students with disabilities who have difficulty learning to spell pass through the same stages as their peers who achieve at expected levels, but at a slower rate. These students may possess but fail to use the orthographic problem-solving behaviors necessary to produce correctly spelled words; their difficulties in spelling often result from their inefficient organization and retrieval of orthographic information (Gerber, 1984; Gerber & Hall, 1989; Wong, 1986).

According to Wong (1986), effective spelling instruction addresses the phonological or linguistic structure of language called domain-specific knowledge and teaches learning strategies for spelling, such as self-questioning or self-monitoring. Wong provided the following self-questioning strategy:

1. Do I know the word?
2. How many syllables do I hear in the word (write down the number)?
3. I'll spell out the word.
4. Do I have the right number of syllables down?
5. If yes, is there any part of the word I'm not sure of spelling? I'll underline that part and try spelling the word again.
6. Now does it look right to me? If it does, I'll leave it alone. If it still doesn't look right, I'll underline the part I'm not sure of the spelling and try again. (If the word I spelled does not have the right number of syllables, let me hear the word in my head again and find the missing syllable. Then I'll go back to steps 5 and 6.)
7. When I finish spelling, I'll tell myself I'm a good worker. I've tried hard at spelling. (p. 172)

Specific Instructional Strategies

In addition to the more general approaches for spelling instruction already discussed, teachers should investigate a host of specific strategies to ensure a flexible and responsive educational program. Here are some instructional considerations that might prove useful in building such a plan.

Corrected-Test Method

In their review of research on spelling, Harris and Graham (1998) reported that the corrected-test technique resulted in the greatest spelling improvement. Under the teacher's direction, students correct specific spelling errors immediately after being tested. The authors noted that this procedure enables students to observe which words are particularly difficult, to identify the part of the word creating the difficulty, and to correct the error under supervision.

Study–Test Versus Test-Study-Test

In the test-study-test procedure, a pretest is administered to the student, who then studies only the words he misspelled. A posttest is administered at the end of the unit of study to determine the student's level of mastery. Progress is charted, and words missed on the posttest are added to the word study list for the following week.

The study–test procedure differs from the test-study-test procedure in that a pretest is not given. The pretest is omitted to avoid frustration arising from poor performance and, as a consequence, development of a failure set toward certain words. Petty (1966) and Stevens, Hartman, and Lucas (1982), however, determined that the test–study–test method was superior to the study–test method.

Instructional Cues

Teacher prompting or cuing of instructional stimuli can facilitate the correct spelling of individual words. The purpose of this technique is to simplify the student's task in producing correct responses and thus reduce or eliminate errors.

To implement a cuing response, the teacher must first identify the student's specific spelling difficulties. For example, specific vowel sounds, certain serial positions in words, or nonphonetic elements may prove troublesome for the student. Color coding can be used to cue certain letters or combinations of letters. For older students who might be offended by the primary-grade implications of the color-coding approach, underlining the trouble spots often works.

Configuration, or outlining the shapes of words, may also be useful in helping a student to learn difficult-to-spell words. In configuration, the teacher blocks the shapes of words and the student selects the word that fits each configurational pattern. The teacher should be aware that configuration loses its utility when words have similar configurational patterns (e.g., look, hook, book). Also, to our knowledge, configuration as a method for teaching spelling has no empirical support.

Mnemonic Devices

Mnemonic devices have been found useful in teaching students memory tasks in reading. They are also useful when lists of information must be learned in content areas. The task of learning a series of mnemonic devices, however, can place as much strain on the student's memory as the memory task itself. Therefore, teachers are advised to limit the use of mnemonic devices in spelling to those the student can associate with previous learning and can easily remember. Examples of spelling mnemonics are illustrated in Figure 10.5.

Motivational Techniques

Because the task of learning to spell is difficult for many students with mild learning disabilities, teachers should be aware of activities and teaching techniques that increase motivation. Games, peer tutoring, and computer and other media activities can offer

> "i before e except after c,
>
> except in *neighbor and weigh,* when ei sounds like a"
>
> *Meant* is the past tense of *mean*
>
> **Coarse** things are **hard.**
>
> You take the course.
>
> Stationery is a type of paper.
>
> Bad grammar mars your writing.
>
> You have a very **nice niece.**
>
> There are 3 l's hidden in the word **parallel**
>
> Your school principal is also your **pal.**
>
> A **secretary** can always keep a secret.
>
> **All right** is the same as **all wrong** (vs. alright)
>
> You have to show **courtesy** when you are in **court.**
>
> An airplane is stored in a hangar.
>
> Three **e's** are buried in cemetery.
>
> Dessert or desert: of which would you rather have 2?

FIGURE 10.5

Mnemonic Devices for Spelling Demons

an incentive for students to learn. When employing these activities and techniques, teachers should avoid those that highlight a student's weaknesses. With a little ingenuity, most activities and procedures can be modified to avoid this. Fostering a positive attitude toward spelling can be accomplished by emphasizing student progress, encouraging pride in correctly spelled papers, using a variety of teaching approaches, designing tasks so students can achieve, and showing the student the role of spelling in practical and social situations (Graham, 1985).

Computer-Assisted Instruction

Computer-based approaches represent a relatively new innovation in spelling instruction. Many students find the novelty of computer-based instruction to be a motivating influence. Computer-assisted instruction has the additional advantage of allowing students to practice spelling skills independently, receive immediate feedback and reinforcement, chart their performance, and keep records of progress over time.

As with any material, the quality of software programs for spelling varies. Teachers are advised to evaluate the software in terms of the objectives of the instructional program and the ease with which the student is able to use the program. Teachers should be aware, too, that the computer keyboard may present special problems for students who do not have typing skills. Varnhagen and Gerber (1984) found that the task of locating letters on the keyboard interfered with students' performances on spelling tasks.

Detecting and Correcting Errors

To achieve the long-term goal of competency in spelling, students with mild learning disabilities must be able to detect and correct errors in their written language. Proficiency in spelling requires that students proofread written assignments for errors and learn when a dictionary is needed and how to use the information it contains. Graham and Miller (1980) suggested a variety of activities for teaching proofreading skills. Among them are the following:

1. Provide a short list of words that include misspelled words to be found.
2. Provide a short passage with errors ranging from errors that are apparent to spelling demons.
3. List the total number of words that are purposely misspelled in a written composition, and have the students locate them.
4. Have the student select the correctly spelled words from a series of alternative forms.
5. Provide a passage with words that may be incorrect, and have students use study skills to determine the accuracy of the spellings.

The specific dictionary skills that the student should learn include

- the application of alphabetizing skills to estimate location of a word,
- the use of individual page guide words,
- the use of syllabic markings, and
- the identification of various diacritical markings.

Self-Regulation and Learning Strategy Instruction

For students to learn to become independent problem solvers, they must develop skills that enable them to monitor their own progress. According to Harris and Graham (1998), the key to effective writing and spelling is self-regulation. These authors offered five ways to foster children's self-regulation in spelling:

1. *Goal setting*: Have students find words from their own writing that they want to learn to spell, or have them select the words from high-frequency word lists. With this approach, students develop responsibility for their own learning. Mastering 850 to 1,000 basic words during the elementary years will develop students' spelling vocabulary to 89% of the words commonly used in writing.
2. *Directed spelling/thinking activity*: Conduct activities that help students actively compare and contrast words that fit different but related patterns.
3. *Independent practice*: Have students make an instructional plan and then monitor their own progress and learning. With this approach, students choose the word study activities.

4. *Self-monitoring*: This goes with item 3. By implementing and managing their learning plans, students are able to monitor their progress. At the beginning of the week, they administer a self-test, followed by peer testing at the end of the week.
5. *Arranging the environment, self-instruction, and self-reinforcement*: Have students arrange the conditions they need for learning. In addition, have them reinforce themselves as a natural outcome as they meet their goals.

Consistent with the importance of self-regulation, the learning strategy of cover, copy, and compare has been used effectively to promote student learning of specific skills, including spelling. The strategy offers an approach by which students can engage independently in word study. It is effective, for example, when preparing for a spelling test. McLaughlin and Skinner (1996) suggested the following steps for using the cover, copy, and compare approach:

1. Look at a specific written word.
2. Cover the word.
3. Write the word from memory.
4 Uncover the word for review.
5. Assess the accuracy of the response by comparing the word just written to the original word.

As McLaughlin and Skinner (1996) noted, the cover, copy, and compare strategy requires little instructional time. It can be taught directly by modeling and verbalizing the steps within the strategy and then monitoring the students as they follow the steps. Those authors recommended that a word be dropped from the spelling list and a new word be added after a student has spelled the word correctly for 3 days.

Study Skills

Study skills allow students to acquire, use, and refine knowledge in the absence of direct teacher instruction. Students who have acquired study skills are able to participate more actively in their own learning and thus become more independent learners. Although the literature on teaching study skills to students with mild learning disabilities does not address spelling instruction directly, we believe that the general principles of efficient study techniques apply to all areas of the school curriculum, including spelling. Hoover (1989) developed the following guidelines for teaching study skills:

1. Introduce simple variations of study skills in the early grades.
2. Gradually increase to more complex elements associated with each study still as students progress through the grades.
3. Identify specific goals and objectives for a study skills program prior to program implementation.
4. Let students' individual strengths and weaknesses guide decision making concerning what study skills to emphasize at any particular time.

5. Know what motivates students to use different study skills, and emphasize these motivations in program implementations.
6. Explain and demonstrate proper use of each study skill.
7. Expect students to use different study skills appropriately through guided practice and planned learning experiences.
8. Provide opportunities for practicing study skill usage to assist students in acquiring and maintaining mastery of the skills.
9. Facilitate the use of study skills in natural classroom settings and on a regular basis as the need arises in different subject areas and learning activities.
10. Assist students in generalizing skills acquired through an emphasis on more complex uses of the skills once initial mastery of the basic study skills has been achieved. (pp. 473–474)

▌Summary

Spelling is a complex act that requires the speller to have knowledge of the English orthographic system, the ability to recall or revisualize previously learned words, and the ability to devise, use, or apply strategies for determining the correct spelling of words. Individuals who have difficulty with spelling typically demonstrate isolated deficits in specific spelling skills or a pattern of academic and language-related disabilities.

Spelling develops in individuals in a predictable and hierarchical sequence. Students with mild learning disabilities who have difficulty learning to spell pass through the developmental sequence in the same order but at a slower rate than students who do not experience difficulty in spelling.

Both formal and informal assessment procedures are useful in determining factors related to a student's spelling disability. But informal procedures, particularly curriculum-based measures and error analysis procedures, are more useful in planning an educational program for a student with spelling disabilities.

The most effective of a number of instructional approaches are evidence-based, monitor student progress on a frequent and predictable schedule, teach spelling as an integral part of the literacy and school curriculum, employ a variety of materials and methods to accommodate individual differences, and provide students with direct, explicit instruction, sufficient practice and review, and strategies for locating and correcting spelling errors.

▌References

Allred, R. A. (1977). *Spelling: The application of research findings*. Washington, DC: National Education Association.
Bailet, L. L. (1991). Development of disorders of spelling in the beginning school years. In A. M. Bain, L. L. Bailet, & L. C. Moats (Eds.), *Written language disorders: Theory into practice* (pp. 1–24). Austin, TX: Pro-Ed.

Bear, D. R., Invernizzi, M., Templeton, S., & Johnson, F. (2004). *Words their way: Word study for phonics, vocabulary, and spelling instruction.* Upper Saddle River, NJ: Prentice-Hall.

Bear, D. R., & Templeton, S. (1998). Explorations in developmental spelling: Foundations for learning and teaching phonics, spelling, and vocabulary. *Reading Teacher, 52*(3), 222–42.

Beirne-Smith, M., & Riley, T. F. (2008). Spelling assessment of students with disabilities: Formal and informal procedures. *Assessment for Effective Intervention, 34,* 170–177.

Blachman, B. (1994). Early literacy acquisition: The role of phonological awareness. In G. Wallach & K. Butler (Eds.), *Language learning disabilities in school-age children and adolescents: Some principles and applications* (pp. 253–274). Needham Heights, MA: Allyn & Bacon.

Bruck, M., Treiman, R., Caravolas, M., Genesee, F., & Cassar, M. (1998). Spelling skills of children in whole language and phonics classrooms. *Applied Psycholinguistics, 19,* 669–684.

Brueckner, L. J., & Bond, G. L. (1955). The diagnosis and treatment of learning disabilities. In E. C. Frierson & W. B. Barbe (Eds.), *Educating children with learning disabilities.* New York: Appleton-Century-Crofts.

Butyniec-Thomas, T., & Woloshyn, V. E. (1997). The effects of explicit-strategy and whole language instruction on students' spelling ability. *Journal of Experimental Education, 65,* 293–302.

Cohen, L. (1969). *Evaluating structural analysis methods used in spelling books.* Unpublished doctoral dissertation, Boston University.

Conrad, N. J. (2008). From reading to spelling and spelling to reading: Transfer goes both ways. *Journal of Educational Psychology, 108,* 869–878.

DeMaster, V., Crossland, C., & Hasselbring, T. S. (1986). Consistency of learning disabled students. *Learning Disability Quarterly, 9,* 89–96.

Fitzgerald, J. (1951). *The teaching of spelling.* Milwaukee: Bruce.

Gentry, J. R. (1982). An analysis of developmental spellings in "Gnys at wrk." *Reading Teacher, 36,* 192–200.

Gentry, J. R. (1997). It's midyear! Take stock of kids' spelling progress. *Instructor: Primary, 107*(5), 35.

Gentry, J. R. (2000). A retrospective on invented spelling and a look forward. *Reading Teacher, 54,* 318–333.

Gerber, M. M. (1984). Orthographic problem-solving ability of learning disabled and normally achieving students. *Learning Disability Quarterly, 7,* 157–164.

Gerber, M. M., & Hall, R. J. (1989). Cognitive–behavioral training in spelling for learning handicapped students. *Learning Disability Quarterly, 12,* 159–171.

Gilstrap, R. (1962). Development of independent spelling skills in the intermediate grades. *Elementary English, 39,* 481–483.

Graham, S. (1985). Teaching basic academic skills to learning disabled students: A model of the teaching/learning process. *Journal of Learning Disabilities, 18,* 528–534.

Graham, S. (1999). Handwriting and spelling instruction for students with learning disabilities: A review. *Learning Disability Quarterly, 22,* 78–98.

Graham, S., Harris, K. R., & Fink-Chorzempa, B. (2002). Contribution of spelling instruction to the spelling, writing, and reading of poor spellers. *Journal of Educational Psychology, 94,* 669-686.

Graham, S., Harris, K. R., & Loynachan, C. (1994). The spelling for writing list. *Journal of Learning Disabilities, 27,* 210–214.

Graham, S., & Miller, L. (1979). Spelling research and practice: A unified approach. *Focus on Exceptional Children, 12*(2), 1–16.

Graham, S., & Miller, L. (1980). Handwriting research and practice: A unified approach. *Focus on Exceptional Children, 13*(2), 1–16.

Graham, S., & Voth, V. P. (1990). Spelling instruction: Making modifications for students with learning disabilities. *Academic Therapy, 25,* 447–457.

Hanna, P. R., Hanna, J., Hodges, R. E., & Rudorf, E. H. (1966). *Phoneme–grapheme correspondences as cues to spelling improvement* (USOE Publication No. 0E-32008). Washington, DC: U.S. Government Printing Office.

Harris, K. R., & Graham, S. (1998). Self-regulated learning in spelling: What, how, and why. *Zaner-Bloser spelling* [Online]. Retrieved from http://www.zaner-bloser.com/html/Sp support 2.html

Hasselbring, T. S., & Owens, S. (1981). *A microcomputer-based system for the analysis of student spelling errors.* Nashville, TN: Peabody College of Vanderbilt.

Hodges, R. E. (1966). The case for teaching sound-to-letter correspondences in spelling. *Elementary School Journal, 66,* 327–336.

Hodges, R. (1981*). Learning to spell: Theory and research into practice.* Champaign, IL: National Council of Teachers of English.

Hodson, B. (1994). Helping individuals become intelligible, literate and articulate: The role of phonology. *Topics in Language Disorders, 14*(2), 1–16.

Hoover, J. J. (1989). Implementing a study skills program in the classroom. *Academic Therapy, 24,* 471–478.

Horn, E. (1919). Principles of methods in teaching spelling as derived from scientific investigation. In *Eighteenth Yearbook, National Society for the Study of Education.* Bloomington: Public School Publishing.

Horn, E. (1926). *A basic writing vocabulary: 10,000 words most commonly used in writing* (University of Iowa Monographs in Education, First Series, No. 4). Iowa City: University of Iowa.

Horn, E. (1954). *Teaching spelling.* Washington DC: American Educational Research Association,

Horn, E. (1960). Spelling. In C. W. Harris (Ed.), *Encyclopedia of educational research* (3rd ed., pp. 1337–1354). New York: Macmillan.

Howell, K. W., Fox, S. L., & Morehead, M. K. (1993). *Curriculum-based education for special and remedial education* (2nd ed.). Pacific Grove, CA: Brooks/Cole.

Jennings, M. (1997). Individualize your spelling instruction. *Preventing School Failure, 42,* 44–46.

Kaufman, A. S., & Kaufman, N. L. (2004). *Kaufman Test of Educational Achievement* (2nd ed.). Circle Pines, MN: American Guidance Service.

Kessler, B. (2003). Is English spelling chaotic? Misconceptions concerning its irregularity. *Reading Psychology, 24*(3), 267-289.

Kuska, A., Webster, E. J. D., & Elford, G. (1964). *Spelling in language arts 6.* Ontario, Canada: Nelson & Sons.

Larsen, S. C., Hammill, D. D., & Moats, L. C. (1999). *Test of written spelling* (4th ed.). Austin, TX: Pro-Ed.

Mann, P. H., & Suiter, P. (1974). *Handbook in diagnostic teaching: A learning disabilities approach.* Boston: Allyn & Bacon.

Markwardt, F. C. (1998). *Peabody individual achievement test–Revised.* Circle Pines, MN: American Guidance Service.

McLaughlin,T. F., & Skinner, C. H. (1996). Improving academic performance through self-management: Cover, copy and compare. *Intervention in School and Clinic, 32,* 113–118.

McNaughton, D., Hughes, C. A., & Clark, K. (1994). Spelling instruction for students with learning disabilities: Implications for research and practice. *Learning Disability Quarterly, 17,* 169–185.

Mercer, C. D., & Mercer, A. R. (2005). *Teaching students with learning problems* (7th ed.). Upper Saddle River: Pearson.

Moats, L. C. (1995). *Spelling: Development, disability, and instruction.* Baltimore: York Press.

Moats, L. C. (2006). How spelling supports reading. *Readingrockets*. Retrieved from http://www.readingrockets.org/article8845

Moats, L. C., & Tolman, C. (2008). Why phonological awareness is important for reading and spelling. *Readingrockets*. Retrieved from http://readingrockets.org/article/28655

Morris, D., Blanton, L., Blanton, W. E., Nowacek, J., & Perney, S. (1995). Teaching low-achieving spellers at their "instructional level." *Elementary School Journal, 34,* 163–176.

Norris, J. A. (1989). Facilitating developmental changes in spelling. *Academic Therapy, 25,* 97–107.

Norton, D. E. (1997). *The effective teaching of language arts* (5th ed.). Englewood Cliffs, NJ: Prentice-Hall.

Otto, W., McMenemy, R. A., & Smith, R. J. (1973). *Corrective and remedial teaching* (2nd ed.). Boston: Houghton Mifflin.

Petty, W. T. (1966). Handwriting and spelling: Their current status in the language arts curriculum. In T. D. Horn (Ed.), *Research on handwriting and spelling* (pp. 1–8). Champaign, IL: National Council of Teachers of English.

Roehrig, A. D., Duggar, S. W., Moats, L., Glover, M., & Mincey, B. (2008).When teachers work to use progress monitoring data to inform literacy instruction: Identifying potential supports and challenges. *Remedial and Special Education, 29,* 364–382.

Schlagal, R. C., & Schlagal, J. (1992). The integral character of spelling: Teaching strategies for multiple purposes. *Language Arts, 69,* 418–424.

Smiley, L. R., & Goldstein, P. A. (1998). *Language delays and disorders.* San Diego: Singular.

Spache, D. E. (1940). Characteristic errors of good and poor spellers. *Journal of Educational Research, 34,* 182–189.

Stevens, T. M., Hartman, A. C., & Lucas, V. H. (1982). *Teaching children basic skills: A curriculum handbook* (2nd ed.). Columbus, OH: Merrill.

Stubbs, M. (1980). *Language and literacy: The sociology of reading and writing.* London: Routledge & Kegan Paul.

Templeton, S., & Morris, D. (1999). Questions teachers ask about spelling. *Reading Research Quarterly, 34,* 102–112.

Tompkins, G. E. (1998). *Language arts: Content and teaching strategies* (4th ed.). Upper Saddle River, NJ: Merrill/Prentice-Hall.

Varnhagen, S., & Gerber, M. (1984). Use of microcomputers for spelling assessment: Reasons to be cautious. *Learning Disability Quarterly, 7,* 266–270.

Vaughn, S., & Bos, C. S. (2009). *Strategies for teaching students with learning and behavior problems* (7th ed.). Upper Saddle River, NJ: Pearson.

Westerman, G. (1971). *Spelling and writing.* San Rafael: Dimensions.

Wilkinson, G.W., & Robertson, G. J. (2006). *Wide range achievement test* (4th ed.). Lutz, FL: Psychological Assessment Resources.

Williams, C., Phillips-Birdsong, C., Hufnagel, K., Hungler, D., & Lundstrom, R. P. (2009). Word study instruction in the K–12 classroom. *Reading Teacher, 62,* 570–578.

Willson, V. L., Rupley, W. H., Rodriguez, M., & Mergen, S. (1999). The relationships among orthographic components of word identification and spelling for grades 1–6. *Reading Research and Instruction, 39,* 89–102.

Wong, B. Y. L. (1986). A cognitive approach to teaching spelling. *Exceptional Children, 53,* 169–173.

Woodcock, R. W., McGrew, K. S., & Mather, N. (2001). *Woodcock-Johnson III tests of achievement.* Itasca, IL: Riverside.

Zutell, J. (2000). A student-active learning approach to spelling instruction. *Zaner-Bloser spelling* [Online]. Retrieved from http://www.zaner-bloser.com/html/Spsupport3.html

11

Written Expression

Written communication builds on the language skills of speaking, listening, and reading. Effective written communication requires the application of a wide variety of conceptual and organizational skills. To produce excellence, the writer must make a psychological rather than a mechanical commitment. Though it is considered an honored and respected ability, written communication was often overlooked for many years as an important curricular domain for students with disabilities. This relative lack of attention in the curriculum reflected to some extent the paucity of research in this area. In the last three decades, however, written language has seen significant increases in research and programming, including the development of practical instructional techniques that influenced practice in both general and special education (e.g., De La Paz, 1999a, 1999b; Englert, 2009; Graham & Harris, 2009; Graham, Harris, & Larsen, 2001; Harris & Graham, 1999; McAlister, Nelson, & Bahr, 1999; McMaster & Espin, 2007; Polloway, Patton, & Serna, 2008; Schumaker & Deshler, 2009).

The increased attention to writing instruction corresponds to the parallel increase in the inclusion of students with special needs in general education classrooms. Further, it corresponds to the increased focus on standards-based education with the related requirements that all students be included in school-wide assessments (Gregg, Coleman, Davis, & Chalk, 2007; Isaacson, 2004).

Illustrative of the challenges for all students relative to writing, Troia (2005) reported that fourth-grade students generally indicated they liked to write (66%) and believed they were good writers (67%) although a small minority (27%) performed at or above the proficiency level. Data for eighth graders reflected decreased numbers in each of these three cases in terms of liking to write (52%), believing they were good writers (51%), and proficiency-level achievement (23%). Lienemann, Graham, Leader-Janssen, and Reid (2006) further summarized achievement data in noting that approximately 75% of students at the 4th-, 8th-, and 12th-grade levels achieved only partial mastery of grade-level skills and knowledge. One in 100 students was determined to attain advanced writing skills. These data indicate that a significant majority of high school students write inadequately, do not like the process of writing, and cannot write well enough to ensure that they will always accomplish their purpose for writing.

From the above findings, we can deduce that students with disabilities are likely to face additional challenges that will accentuate these problems. Troia (2005) described the writing patterns of students with disabilities as "shorter, less linguistically sophisticated, more poorly organized, more mechanical errors, poorer in overall quality," and also noted common "difficulties in executing and regulating the cognitive and meta-cognitive processes underlying proficient writing" (p. 251). Further, Lienemann et al. (2006) described the typical writing of students with disabilities as reflecting fewer ideas, being more poorly organized, and having lower overall quality. In the absence of intensive and specialized instruction, adolescents with learning disabilities are likely to write at about a fourth-grade level (Schumaker & Deshler, 2009).

Written expression is a broad instructional area that covers capabilities ranging from writing a simple sentence to organizing research reports and term papers. In their classic work, Johnson and Myklebust (1967) noted that writing has two basic facets: formulation and syntax. **Formulation** refers to the generation of ideas and the creative writing that stem from an intention to communicate. **Syntax** focuses on mechanics and deals with the grammatical structure of written efforts.

Specialized instruction in written communication is essential for all students who have acquired prerequisite skills in reading and oral language. For many children with disabilities, composition is a logical extension of other language skills and relates to prior difficulties they experienced. Other children encounter their first language problems in composition. For a small yet significant group of children with disabilities, disorders in this area may be "pure" in the sense that they do not seem to be related to or consistent with abilities in reading or oral language. Problems in written expression could be attributable to an underlying cognitive processing problem, poor instruction, lack of appropriate experience in manipulating language structures (i.e., difficulty in integrating subject, text, and reader to be able to write coherently), as well as other specific disorders, such as attention deficit and poor self-concept (Gregg, 1991).

When developing a writing instruction program for students with disabilities, the following general considerations should be taken into account (Polloway et al., 2008):

1. Writing draws on previous linguistic experiences. Prior problems, such as in listening, speaking, and reading, may be reflected and perhaps magnified.
2. Writing must be viewed as both process and product. Products have typically been the primary objectives, and educators have had to ensure that students reach that goal. But some students mistakenly believe, for instance, that textbooks are written by scholars who simply transcribed their thoughts directly

to a finished product. These students need to understand the process behind development of the product, such as the concept of the rough draft.

3. Because writing is a form of communication, it requires an identifiable audience to facilitate the setting of purpose. As students learn to write, they need to keep in mind who will read their products.

4. Writing must be an active, cognitive process. Prior to writing, students should be given ample opportunity to discuss what they intend to write so they will be appropriately prepared.

5. Writing provides a unique opportunity for personal expression (see Figure 11.1). In this sense, it is not simply a goal but also a vehicle. Writing can provide opportunities to express feelings, attitudes, and concepts. Writing can and should become both an end and a means.

■Stages of Written Language

The three stages of the writing task are prewriting, writing, and postwriting. Figure 11.2 incorporates the stages within a conceptual model for the written language process.

Prewriting Stage

Prewriting is a planning stage. During this time, the writer develops and elaborates on ideas, organizes ideas in logical fashion, and assesses the reading audience. As indicated in Figure 11.2, for teachers who are helping students develop writing skills, the prewriting stage stems from the three interrelated aspects of input, motivation, and purpose.

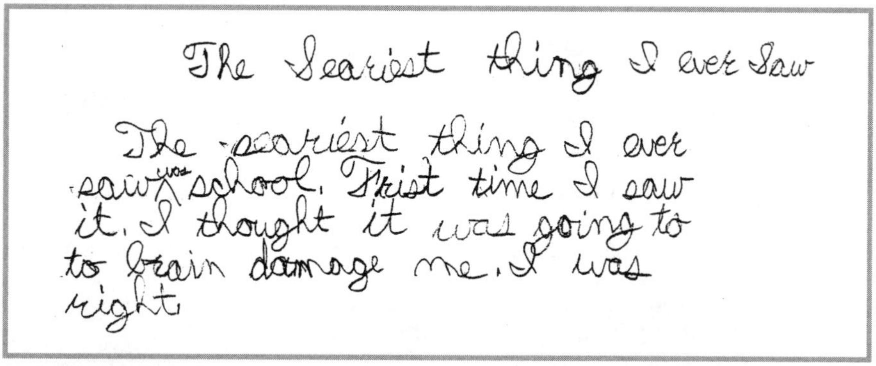

FIGURE 11.1

Writing for Expression

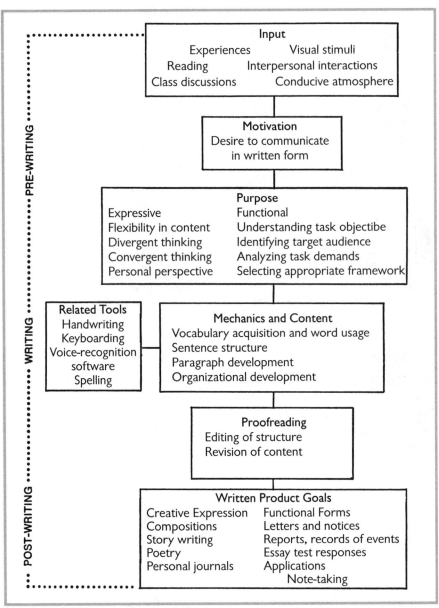

Source: Adapted from "Written Language," by E. A. Polloway, J. R. Patton, and S. A. Cohen, 1993, *Promising Practices for Exceptional Children: Curriculum Implications*, edited by E. L. Meyen, G. A. Vergason, and R. J. Whelan, Denver: Love Publishing, p. 289. Copyright 1993 by Love Publishing. Reprinted with permission.

FIGURE 11.2

Model for Written Language

Input refers to the sources of stimulation to the writer. It reflects the ways in which the educational (and nonschool) environment can be enhanced to influence the would-be writer. Without stimulation, teachers cannot anticipate response. Through the verbalizations of others, opportunities to experience the environment through diverse means (e.g., field trips, athletics, classroom activities), encounters with reading, verbal and nonverbal interpersonal interactions, and continuous and varied auditory/visual stimuli (e.g., multimedia, television, films, photographs) in a conducive environment, the student can develop an interest in a given topic and the familiarity necessary for effective communication.

Motivation relates directly to input. Students must need to communicate, because their attitude toward writing is among the most important instructional considerations. In addition to antecedent events, such as the development of interest in the topic, motivation can be achieved through consequences such as increased personal interaction, positive feedback, and reinforcement for written efforts and products.

As the basis for organizing writing, *purpose* creates an awareness of writing as a natural communication process. Consistent with the National Assessment of Educational Progress (NAEP, 2003), three forms are

1. narrative: stories and personal essays;
2. informative: sharing knowledge and communicating instructions, ideas, and messages; and
3. persuasive: influencing the reader's action and bringing about change.

Typically, narrative writing is considered to be expressive, and informative and persuasive writing are said to be functional. Expressive or creative writing emphasizes the personal communication of experiences and thoughts in an original way. Functional writing conveys information in a more structured form, as with letters and reports.

Despite this oversimplified distinction, the two purposes of writing can be teamed to facilitate the acquisition of abilities. For example, functional writing can become more creative as it becomes more individualistic, novel, and unusual. Thus, although the instructor can initially differentiate the two forms in assisting students with disabilities to set purpose, the relationship between these two forms may ultimately become less disparate.

By helping the writer set and refine purpose, the teacher encourages students to be more attentive to the demands of the topic, to be more reflective of ways to achieve goals, and to become actively involved in each of the three writing stages necessary to produce an acceptable product. These concerns—attention, reflection, and active learning—have traditionally been identified as major deficiencies in the repertoire of students who have high-incidence disabilities.

In **expressive writing**, the specification of purpose entails several critical features. First, the writer must appreciate the inherent flexibility in selecting and developing content for the theme. Next, the writer must be able to use divergent thinking to explore the specific ideas of interest within the parameters of the assignment. Convergent thinking must also be tapped, as it provides the vehicle for organization by narrowing the scope and allowing for the selection of relevant information. Finally, the continuing input of personal perspective ensures a unique and original product.

In **functional writing**, the shift in focus dictates a parallel change in the writer's consideration of purpose. Understanding the task objective is requisite. Further, the writer must identify the target audience, analyze the task demands, and select a format that is matched to the audience's characteristics and the task demands.

Writing Stage

The writing stage includes the drafting, or transcribing, process. This stage encompasses the use of appropriate grammatical conventions, clear expression of ideas, specific word choices, diversity in vocabulary, appropriate forms of varied sentence structures, and appropriate transitions that reflect a logical progression of ideas. It also includes attention to handwriting (or keyboarding) and spelling (as discussed in the previous two respective chapters).

The specific items outlined for the writing stage in Figure 11.2 summarizes the basic mechanics common to semantically, syntactically, and organizationally sound written products. Each of the categories in the figure subsumes subskills related to the development of writing competence.

Vocabulary acquisition and *word usage* are the basic semantic foundations for writing. Two instructional goals related to vocabulary predominate: (a) to encourage students to make use of the variety of words they already possess (in their oral receptive and expressive lexicon) and (b) to help students learn and use new words to aid in the written discussion of a given topic. Word usage is concerned with the appropriate construction of meaningful phrases and sentences based on words chosen from the student's vocabulary. Key instructional objectives include curtailing the redundant use of common words, increasing the use of descriptive words, alternating synonyms for common thoughts, selecting words that most precisely fit meaning, avoiding awkward combinations, and maintaining consistency with the purpose of the writing task and the intended audience.

Sentence structure refers here to the range of major syntactic and morphological concerns within sentences including appropriate verb tense, noun–verb agreement, noun–pronoun agreement, correct forms for other morphological structures, capitalization, and punctuation. Additional emphasis should be placed on variety in the sentence forms and functions used.

Paragraph development reflects the transitional phase in writing from syntactically accurate sentences to well-written compositions or reports. This skill taps the student's ability to organize thoughts in a coherent fashion that conveys a central message to the reader. In a developmental sense, four sequential abilities have to be learned:

1. Paragraphs must express a single concept or main idea.
2. Initial topic sentences should provide a lead-in for the reader.

3. Subsequent sentences should provide further support to the concept being discussed.
4. Final sentences, particularly in longer paragraphs (or stand-alone paragraphs), should serve a summary or transitional function.

Organizational development of a written product derives from how the mechanics and the writing style achieve the identified purposes of the writing task. Students must be alert to the sequence of ideas, consistency between the discussion and the conclusions, clarity of the message communicated, retention of personal style (when appropriate), and relevance of detail to the stated purpose.

Postwriting Stage

Postwriting entails the two key processes of *editing of structure* and *revision of content*. Frequently, the importance of postwriting activities is not apparent to learners who have disabilities because of the emphasis on task completion. In other cases, problem learners may associate editing and revision with failure, as a result of overcorrection of previous writing assignments. For students to understand the importance of postwriting processes and move beyond limited concepts of editing (e.g., capitalization, punctuation), they must be taught specific steps to follow in reviewing their own written work samples.

The three stages of writing have been presented separately here because this distinction directs instruction to the specific tasks facing the would-be writer. In practice, however, the three phases are not discrete. For example, planning continues to take place during the postwriting stage, and some revising certainly takes place during the writing stage. Called recursion (Scarmadalia & Bereiter, 1986), this is a common occurrence. Nevertheless, an initial emphasis on the stages of writing provides a process-type approach for students that can assist them in enhancing their thinking and in developing an "inner voice" to guide their thinking about what they are to do (Thomas, Englert, & Gregg, 1987).

Isaacson (1987) analyzed the writing process as related to skilled and unskilled writers. His findings regarding the unique characteristics of these two groups of writers across the three stages of writing are summarized in Table 11.1. Students with learning disabilities and other struggling writers experience difficulties across all three of these stages (Graham & Harris, 2009).

▌Assessment

The assessment of writing skills is a complex process, with a variety of perspectives on what should be evaluated and how the evaluation should be accomplished. Polloway (2009) noted that

> a key aspect of a commitment (to writing success) must include a careful assessment of students within this domain. With so much of school

TABLE 11.1

The Writing Process of Skilled and Unskilled Writers

Stage	Unskilled Writer	Skilled Writer
Planning (Prewriting)	Does not participate in prewriting discussions. Spends little time thinking about topic before beginning composition. Makes no plans or notes.	Explores and discusses topics. Spends time considering what will be written and how it will be expressed. Jots notes; draws diagrams or pictures.
Transcribing (Writing)	Writes informally in imitation of speech. Is preoccupied with technical matters of spelling and punctuation. Stops only briefly and infrequently.	Writes in style learned from models of composition. Keeps audience in mind while writing. Stops frequently to reread. Takes long thought pauses.
Revising (Postwriting)	Does not review or rewrite. Looks only for surface errors (spelling, punctuation). Rewrites only to make a neat copy in ink.	Reviews frequently. Makes content revisions, as well as spelling and punctuation corrections. Keeps audience in mind while rewriting.

Source: From "Effective Instruction in Written Language," by S. L. Isaacson, 1987, *Focus on Exceptional Children, 19*(6), p. 4. Copyright 1987 by Love Publishing. Reprinted with permission.

success and postsecondary success contingent on the acquisition and use of effective writing skills, it is critical that teachers take advantage of relevant assessment data to provide a basis for designing effective instructional programs. (p. 132)

Similarly, Penner-Williams, Smith, and Gartin (2009) noted that "knowing students' strengths and weaknesses in the writing process will greatly assist educators in knowing how to develop better instructional and intervention programs" (p. 169). Initial and ongoing analyses of writing are necessary components to guide instructional practices for all students (Polloway, 2009).

With regard to the emphases on assessment, Moran (1987) outlined the options available to teachers. Briefly, these include assessment

1. of composition (the creation of written discourse to communicate with the audience) versus assessment of transcription (the mechanics or conventions of writing),

2. by indirect measures (evaluation of contrived samples to determine knowledge of standard English) versus assessment by direct measures (evaluation of actual writing samples),

3. of process (the strategies involved in writing) versus assessment of product (the completed writing samples gathered from students' work), and

4. through holistic rating (overall evaluation of writing based on an established rating scale tied to anchor papers) versus assessment via analytic scoring (evaluation based on specific subskills).

Formal Assessment

In terms of formal assessment, achievement-oriented tests and diagnostic tests are available with subtests related to written language. Whereas achievement tests rarely provide useful information for teaching, diagnostic tests frequently provide instructionally relevant information. Table 11.2 provides a comprehensive listing of formal written language assessment tools.

One diagnostic tool that can provide a comprehensive analysis of written language abilities is the Test of Written Language (TOWL; 3rd ed.; Hammill & Larsen, 1996). The TOWL–3 was developed to assess the adequacy of abilities in handwriting, spelling, and the various other components of written expression. The test includes scales for vocabulary, thematic maturity, word usage, and style. Spontaneous and contrived formats both provide a basis for assessment, with primary emphasis on evaluating an actual writing sample.

Informal Assessment

Various informal writing assessments also have been developed. Table 11.3 describes commonly used informal techniques. The Association for Supervision and Curriculum Development (ASCD, 1997) identified the writing qualities that should be assessed:

- *Ideas and content*—Is the message clear? Does the paper hold the reader's attention?
- *Organization*—Does the paper have an inviting introduction? Are supporting details placed in a logical order? Can the reader move easily through the text?
- *Voice*—Does the writer speak directly to the reader? Is the writer sensitive to the needs of [the intended] audience?
- *Fluency*—Does the writing have a cadence and easy flow? Do sentences vary in length as well as structure?
- *Conventions*—Does the writer demonstrate a good grasp of standard writing conventions, such as grammar, punctuation, and paragraphing? Is punctuation accurate? Is spelling generally correct? (p. 5)

TABLE 11.2

Standardized Assessments for Written Language

Test Title	Normative Group and Publisher Web Site	Spelling	Style and Mechanics	Ages and Group or Individual Administration
Kaufman Test of Educational Achievement–Second Edition	National sample of 3,000 examinees ages 4 years, 6 months, through 25 years, stratified according to educational placement, gender, parent educational level, nationality, and geographic region; http://ags.pearsonassessments,com	Assessed	Assessed	Ages 4 years, 6 months, through 25 years, 0 months, grades K–12; Individual administration
Oral and Written Language Scales	1,373 students at 74 sites nationwide stratified for age, gender, race, geographic region, and socioeconomic status; http://ags.pearsonassessments.com	Assessed	Assessed	Ages 5 years through 21 years, 11 months; Individual or small group administration
Peabody Individual Achievement Test–Revised/Update	Sample of 3,184 students K through 12 with 10 years between the data collection; http://ags.pearsonessessments.com			
Test of Early Written Language–Second Edition	Normative group characteristics correspond to the 1990 U.S. population relative to gender, geographic region, race, ethnicity, and urban rural residence; www.proed.com		Assessed	Ages 3 years, 0 months, through 10 years, 11 months; Individual administration

(continued)

TABLE 11.2 (continued)

Test of Written Expression	1,226 students residing in 21 states representative of the nation in gender, race, and geographic region; www.proedinc.com	Assessed	Assessed	Ages 6 years, 6 months, through 14 years, 11 months; Individual or small group administration
Test of Written Language–3	Total sample: 2,217 over 11 age groups with no less than 105 in any age group; www.proedinc.com	Assessed	Assessed	Ages 7 years through 17 years; Individual administration but has modifiation for group
Test of Written Spelling–Fourth Edition	Norms are a mixture of Edition 2 (3,805 students) and Edition 3 (855), giving a sample total of 4,000+	Assessed		Grades 1 through 12; Individual or group administration
Wide Range Achievement Test–3	A stratified national sampling included nearly 5,000 individuals; www.arinc.com	Assessed	Assessed	Child to adult, ages 5 years to 74 years; Individual or small group administration
Woodcock-Johnson Tests of Achievement III	8,818 individuals representative of the U.S. population; www.riverpub.com	Assessed	Assessed	Ages 2 or 3 through 80; Individual administration
Writing Process Test	5,000 students in Grades 2–12 in class-size groups	Assessed	Assessed	Ages 8 years, 0 months, through 19 years, 9 months; Individual or group administration
Written Expression Scale (part of the Oral and Written Language Scales; see above)	1,795 children and youth stratified for age, gender, race, geographic region, and socioeconomic status http://ags.pearsonassessments.com	Assessed	Assessed	Ages 5 years, 0 months, to 21 years, 11 months; Individual or small group administration

Source: Adapted from "Written Language Expression: Assessment Instruments and Teacher Tools," by J. Penner-Williams, T. E. C. Smith, and B. C. Gartin, 2009, *Assessment for Effective Intervention, 34,* pp. 167–168. Copyright 2009 by Sage Publications, Inc. Journals. Reprinted with permission.

TABLE 11.3

Representative Informal Procedures for Assessing Written Expression

Technique	Description	Methodology	Example	Comment
1. Type–Token Ratio	Measure of the variety of words used (types) in relation to overall number of words used (token)	$\dfrac{\text{Different words used}}{\text{Total words used}}$	type = 28 token = 50 ratio = $\dfrac{28}{50}$ = .56	Greater diversity of usage implies a more mature writing style.
2. Index of Diversification	Measure of diversity of word usage	$\dfrac{\text{Total number of words used}}{\text{Number of occurrences of the most frequently used word}}$	total words = 72 number of times the word appeared = 12 index = 6	An increase in the index value implies a broader vocabulary base.
3. Average Sentence Length	Measure of sentence usage (number of words per sentence)	$\dfrac{\text{Total number of words used}}{\text{Total number of sentences}}$	total words = 54 total sentences = 9 words per sentence = 6	Longer length of sentences implies more mature writing ability.
4. Error Analysis	Measure of word and sentence usage	Compare errors found in a writing sample with list of common errors		Teacher can determine error patterns and can prioritize concerns.
5. T-Unit Length	Measure of writing maturity	1. Determine the number of discrete thought units (T-units) 2. Determine average length of T-unit: $\dfrac{\text{Total words}}{\text{Total number of T-units}}$ 3. Analyze quantitative variables: a. no. of sentences used b. no. of T-units c. no. of words per T-unit Note: Use the following convention for summarizing this information (no. of sentences; no. of T-units; no. of words per T-unit). 4. Analyze qualitative nature of sentences	"The summer was almost over and the children were ready to go back to school." Quantitative: (1; 2; 5 + 10) Qualitative: 1. compound sentence 2. adverbs: of degree—"almost" of place—"back" 3. adjective—"ready" 4. infinitive—"to go" 5. prepositional phrase adverbial of place—"to school"	This technique gives the teacher information in relation to productivity and maturity of writing skills.

Source: From "Written Language," by E. A. Polloway, J. R. Patton, and S. A. Cohen, 1983, *Promising Practices for Exceptional Children: Curriculum Implications*, (pp. 300–301), edited by E. L. Meyen, G. A. Vergason, and R. J. Whelan, Denver: Love Publishing. Copyright 1983 by Love Publishing. Reprinted with permission.

Prewriting Considerations

A foundation for assessing students during the prewriting stage is to consider the experiential background of students regarding writing in general and the specific writing task in particular. Miller (2009) noted this when she indicated that

> many students with disabilities have little experience with writing, have not thought about why people write, and have not considered why writing might be important. Further, they may never have considered how writing might be of use to them, or, if they have, and have concluded that they could probably never learn how to write, that writing is something beyond their capacities. (p. 183)

A consideration of these basic points is important as assessment information is collected to serve as a foundation for instruction.

To evaluate students' *prewriting skills* and *motivation and readiness for writing*, teachers can assess student variables including

- how they spend their free time,
- what books they have read,
- what they talk about when they are at home or with peers,
- their interests as ascertained by interest inventories, and
- their career goals.

Other key areas to consider include whether students can

- set and refine a purpose for their writing,
- brainstorm ideas for content (i.e., use divergent thinking),
- progressively narrow the scope of a topic (i.e., use convergent thinking),
- recognize the major components of their tasks,
- understand the purpose of why they are writing, and
- realize to whom they are writing.

Writing Fluency

Once students begin to write, teachers can assess **fluency,** which refers to the quantity of writing a child produces, and relates to the instructional goal of increasing the length and the complexity of the sentences a child writes. Assessment, for example, could begin by focusing on the number of words used per sentence and later on the variety of sentence styles a child writes.

The words-per-sentence figure is computed by dividing the number of words in a student-written passage by the number of sentences in that passage. In Figure 11.3, the average length of sentences has been computed for a passage written by a 9-year-old child. Naturally, the longer the sentence length, the more mature style the sentence typically represents. For students who show consistent interest in successive writing lessons, this measure can assess positive changes in written fluency that can be tied to

School

People in school are not good friends. They are bad friends. But when they are in school, they are real bad. Sometimes they put fire to the school. But they don't. They will hid you, pick you. People in that school should be good. But they are not!

Determining Words Per Sentence		
No. of sentences	=	8
No. of words	=	48
Words per sentence	=	6

FIGURE 11.3

Assessing Fluency

annual goals or short-term objectives. Although the actual number of words per sentence does not measure the quality of writing, it can indicate increased writing facility.

Teachers should also observe the types of sentences that students use. Basically, sentences can be categorized into four types related to form and four types related to function. Teachers should identify the types of sentences a student uses to determine whether the student's writing shows a variety in style. The four types of sentences *as related to form* are the following:

1. *Fragment:* Wherever the girl wanted to go.
2. *Simple:* The quick brown fox jumped over the lazy dog.
3. *Compound:* The girls were unable to attend the party, and the boys were very disappointed.
4. *Complex:* After the rain had subsided, the game was able to continue.

When assessing sentence form, teachers should be concerned primarily with the frequency of fragments and the varied use of the other three types of sentence. The four types of sentences *as related to function* are as follows:

1. *Declarative:* Bryant has a good jump shot from the corner.
2. *Interrogative:* Does the meteorologist think it will snow tonight?
3. *Imperative:* Line up immediately.
4. *Exclamatory:* What a beautiful day it is!

When assessing sentence function, teachers should look for the varied use of the four sentence types in appropriate situations.

Vocabulary

As a student's writing fluency increases, she needs to develop a broader written vocabulary. With a larger number of words in her repertoire, the writer can avoid redundancy and begin to develop a more specific, descriptive, and fluid style. Two basic approaches to assessing written vocabulary are: (a) determining type–token ratios and (b) documenting the use of unique words.

Type–Token Ratio

A **type–token ratio** is a measure of the variety of words in a writing sample. The ratio is computed by dividing the number of different words the writer uses (types) against the overall number of words used (tokens). A ratio of 1.0 would indicate no redundancy; a ratio of .5 would suggest frequent repetition. Figure 11.4 shows the computation of the type–token ratio for a writing sample by a 12-year-old child.

The ratio can be computed for comparative purposes (as with assessing progress related to IEP goals) as long as the length of the passages analyzed is held constant. Generally, a passage of 50 to 100 words is most valuable for determining the ratio. Based on the use of type–token ratios, an IEP instructional objective might, for example, call for an increase in ratio from .60 to .70. The assumption is that this increase would reflect a significant improvement in the strength of written vocabulary.

Type–Token Ratio		
No. of tokens (total words)	=	60
No. of types (different words)	=	34
Type–token ratio = 34/60	=	58%

FIGURE 11.4

Assessing Vocabulary: Type–Token Ratio

Unique Words

Analysis of the number of unique words in a passage can supplement the type–token ratio. With this technique, the teacher identifies the words in a writing sample that the student did not use in previous efforts. For beginning writers, teachers might look for words that do not appear on high-frequency word lists. For more advanced writers, judgment will tend to be more subjective.

Although this form of assessment is less objective than other measures, it can form the basis for a running list of new words the student is using. Additions to the list then can be tied to reinforcement strategies. Figure 11.5 shows a sample writing passage that a teacher subjectively assessed for unique words. In light of the student's past efforts, the teacher identified the five words listed below the sample as unique for this child. An alternative is to involve students in the process through a self-assessment of their vocabulary.

Syntactical Analysis

The evaluation of structural skills stems directly from the use of error analysis and relates to the prior discussion of sentence forms and functions. The teacher should

I was thinking one day about my future in my bedroom one day. that I was going to be a state police. I alway wanted to drive a police car. the reason why I want to be a state police because they go fast and the other reason is to control the siren and flasher on the roof.

Unique Words/Subjectively Selected	
police	flasher
control	reason
siren	

FIGURE 11.5

Assessing Vocabulary: Unique Words

determine what grammatical components have the most relevance for an individual child and then assess whether those skills are part of the child's writing repertoire. Teachers can record when the skill was first taught and acquired, when evidence showed that the child had applied the skill in compositions, and when subsequent follow-up checks were made. Figure 11.6 presents a sample form that might be used for this purpose.

Based on structural analysis of a child's writing samples, the teacher can look for trends in error patterns, which can then become priorities for remediation. Figure 11.7 presents a writing sample from an 11-year-old boy, along with the teacher's tentative list of priority concerns. Subsequent writing samples would help the teacher clarify the instructional objectives.

Error analysis may focus on a student's weaknesses and thereby produce a failure set toward writing. To overcome this problem and make error analysis a motivator, teachers should involve children in instructional planning aimed at their acquiring new skills instead of correcting mistakes. Teachers can also help children understand the distinction between mistakes that are errors in execution and mistakes that are the result of problems in processing, logical thinking, and expression.

Content Assessment

Content deals with the formation of ideas within a writing sample and thus relies on a more subjective assessment element than does structural assessment. Dual grades can be given for writing so students can be evaluated separately on the aspects of writing represented by content and structure. When assessing content, the teacher can consider the following questions:

1. Is the composition relevant to the topic assigned or selected and consistent with stated objectives?
2. Do the ideas in the composition represent original thinking on the student's part?
3. Does the composition demonstrate expression of personal perspectives on the topic rather than relying on comments by others?
4. Do the ideas expressed show clarity of thought, with the major facets of the topic presented in an appropriate sequence?
5. Does the composition reflect a basic interest in the topic and, thus, a motivation to commit ideas to the written form?

For students who are beginning to write, teachers should judge whether the composition is generally sequential and flows logically and whether it conveys a message consistent with the writer's intent. For students writing at an advanced level, evaluation may assess specific paragraphing skills (e.g., the use of topical sentences, the establishment of one major or central idea, the presence of transitional words within sentences and transitional sentences between paragraphs). Figure 11.8 presents a paragraph written by a 10-year-old student along with an analysis.

Specific Skills	Acquisition	Proficiency	Maintenance
1. Punctuation			
a. period			
1. sentence			
2. abbreviations			
b. question mark			
c. comma			
d. apostrophe			
1. possession			
2. contractions			
e. colon			
f. hyphen			
g. exclamation mark			
h. semicolon			
2. Capitalization			
a. first word in sentence			
b. proper nouns			
c. I			
d. titles			
e. abbreviations			
3. Verb Usage			
a. subject agreement			
b. tense			
c. use of auxiliaries (is, etc.)			
4. Pronoun Usage			
a. subject vs. object			
b. unclear antecedents			
5. Other Word Usage			
a. unneeded words added			
b. omissions			
c. inappropriate plurals			
d. incorrect adjectives			
e. incorrect adverbs			
f. nonstandard English patterns			
6. Sentence Sense			
a. run-on sentences			
b. choppy sentences			
c. overuse of "and"			
d. inappropriate use of fragments			

FIGURE 11.6

Written Structural Analysis: Sample Data Collection Monitoring Form

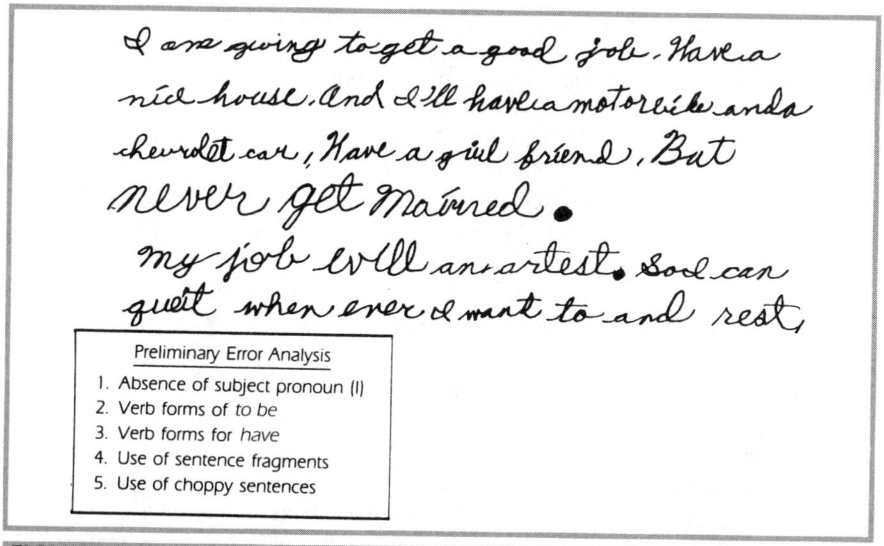

> *I are going to get a good Job. Have a nice house. And I'll have a motorbike and a chevrolet car, Have a girl friend, But never get Married.*
>
> *My job will an artest. So I can quiet when ever I want to and rest,*

Preliminary Error Analysis
1. Absence of subject pronoun (I)
2. Verb forms of *to be*
3. Verb forms for *have*
4. Use of sentence fragments
5. Use of choppy sentences

FIGURE 11.7
Error Analysis of Writing Sample

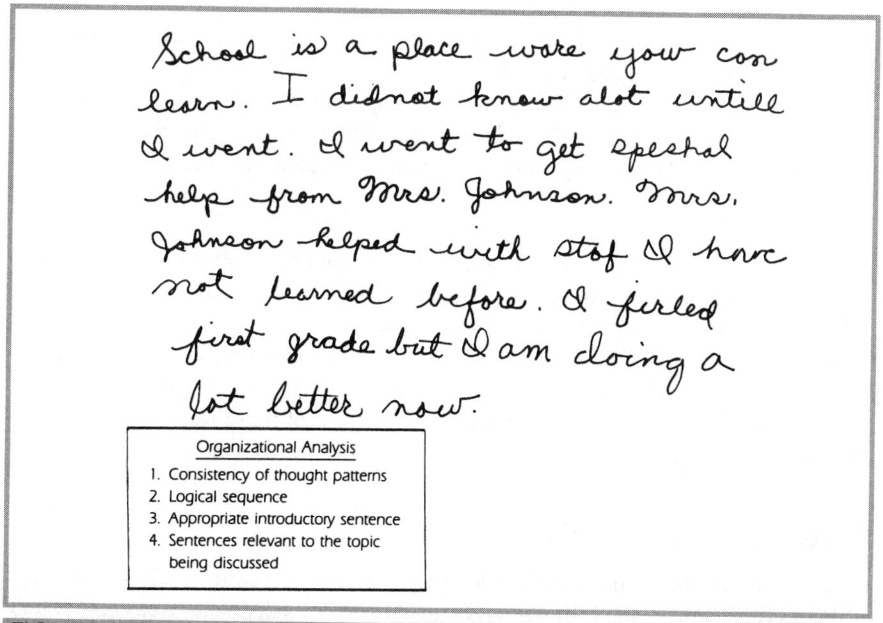

> *School is a place ware you con learn. I didnot know alot untill I went. I went to get speshal help from Mrs. Johnson. Mrs. Johnson helped with stof I have not learned before. I firled first grade but I am doing a lot better now.*

Organizational Analysis
1. Consistency of thought patterns
2. Logical sequence
3. Appropriate introductory sentence
4. Sentences relevant to the topic being discussed

FIGURE 11.8
Assessing Organization Skills

One approach to operationalizing the evaluative process is to develop writing assessment rubrics for evaluating student performance across various dimensions according to predetermined criteria (Schirmer & Bailey, 2000). De La Paz (2009) noted that

> rubrics provide a systematic way for teachers to assess written products.... Many rubrics are based on specific genres or situation-specific criteria, and teachers typically create a scoring guide with a list of the criteria that children are to include in their writing (e.g., writing has a title, a beginning, middle, and end, characters as well as the development and resolution of a problem). Other writing rubrics list more general criteria such as ideas, organization, vocabulary, and mechanics. (p. 134)

It provides a summative way to evaluate both the craft and the content of writing. Table 11.4 presents a more specific rubric intended for compositions focused on comparing and contrasting.

Portfolios are particularly appropriate for a variety of informal assessment purposes. They enable teachers to involve students in evaluating their own writing samples, particularly by allowing students to select samples to be kept and then working with the students to compare their changes in writing over time. Types of portfolios include the following (ASCD, 1997):

- *Sampling of works*: This type is used to compare early writing samples with later writing samples. The portfolios may then be sent on to the student's next teacher.
- *Selected works*: In these portfolios, students save samples of their best writing in response to a teacher prompt.
- *Longitudinal*: These portfolios contain materials showing a student's achievement of curriculum, school, or district goals over an extended time. Review of the materials may yield pretest and posttest measures that can provide accurate assessment.

Another area involves assessing students' skills in using learning-to-learn strategies, particularly as they relate to writing. Given that students with learning disabilities, for example, consistently had difficulty with the use and regulation of strategies necessary for composition writing, teachers have to be sensitive to how students approach the writing task and how they use, or fail to use, specific cognitive strategies. Englert et al. (2009) provided an extensive discussion of these issues with seventh-grade students, which the reader is encouraged to consult.

Postwriting Assessment

To determine whether students are able to use revising and editing skills effectively, evaluation can address the following five questions. For a detailed discussion of how these questions can govern the assessment process during postwriting, the reader is referred to Miller (2009).

TABLE 11.4
Sample Comparison Rubric

		Comparison and Contrast Rubric		
Category	4 - Exemplary	3 - Competent	2 - Emerging	1 - Low
Ideas and Development	The writer selects two topics and creates a complete comparison. Elaboration evenly compares and contrasts specific items within relevant categories.	The writer compares and contrasts two topics. Details and information may be general or only one comparison is supported.	Two topics are compared and contrasted but details are not parallel or supporting information is not relevant.	The paper compares or contrasts but does not include both.
Organization	The chosen organizational structure establishes a point of similarity and a point of difference for each item presented.	Some errors in order or in use of the chosen organizational structure.	Errors in following the chosen organizational structure detract from meaning.	Random organization or extremely difficult to follow.
Sentence Fluency	Sentences clearly connect subjects. There are a variety of sentence structures and appropriate transitions.	Sentences clearly connect ideas. The sentences lack variety or include errors in transitions.	Contains sentences with errors in coherence. Uses simple sentences or minimal transitions.	Sentences are incomplete or incoherent. Transitions are inappropriate or nonexistent.
Mechanics	Correct punctuation, capitalization, spelling, and grammar.	Minor or infrequent errors are noted, but they do not detract from the overall meaning.	Errors are frequent and detract from meaning; however, some aspects of mechanics are adequate.	The writing demonstrates a lack of control; errors interfere substantially with the overall meaning.

Source: From "Rubrics: Heuristics for Developing Writing Strategies," by S. De La Paz, 2009, *Assessment for Effective Intervention, 34,* p. 138. Copyright 2009 by Sage Publications, Inc. Journals. Reprinted with permission.

1. Can students identify specific mechanical errors within a sentence or paragraph?
2. Can they identify organizational and ideational problems within a composition?

3. Can they effectively use strategies for revising and editing (e.g., a sequential list of self-check statements)?
4. Can they evaluate whether the objectives or purposes of the completed written draft have been met?
5. Can they transfer these skills from contrived exercises to actual writing?

The successful analysis of information gathered from informal and formal writing assessment techniques will enable the teacher to develop a profile of an individual students' writing strengths and difficulties, which then can assist the teacher in designing appropriate instructional programs. For a more comprehensive discussion of assessment research and procedures, the reader is referred to the June 2009 special series on written language assessment in *Assessment for Effective Instruction, 34*(3) (see Polloway, 2009).

▐ Instructional Strategies

For instructional programs in writing to be successful, they have to reflect a comprehensive commitment to student success (Polloway et al., 2008). The teacher's task is to begin from a foundation of sound instructional strategies for written communication and then to make modifications that represent effective responses to the individual needs of learners who have disabilities.

Methods of teaching written expression for students with special needs should reflect close ties to, and adaptations of, the general education curriculum. For most students with disabilities, the inclusive classroom is the context for both instruction and evaluation. As a result, students will be taught according to the standards in place for all students. Isaacson (2004) indicated that the increased reliance on writing standards and related testing has resulted in these benefits:

- An increased focus on the importance of writing
- The establishment of more consistent curricular goals, which consequently has led to clearer expectations for students
- Greater emphasis on the need for explicit instruction and for the use of purposeful activities

Isaacson also noted negative consequences including increased anxiety, questions of fairness, an overlooking of individualized goals as grade standards become paramount, and the application of more rigid criteria for assessment.

Prewriting Strategies

During the prewriting stage, teachers have the opportunity to provide rich language experiences that will serve as a foundation for writing to provide assistance in getting ideas and providing structuring ideas and content, setting purpose, determining audience, and building (Scott & Vitale, 2003). The basis for beginning written language instruction is *stimulation*. Students must receive input that fosters the formulation of their own ideas. Teachers should capitalize on the other language domains to enhance this. For example, opportunities to talk about personal experiences and listen to others' encounters can provide a basis for writing purpose and content. Reading interesting stories can develop the student's desire to communicate feelings about the ideas the author expresses. Although stimulation through oral language does not lead to the acquisition of specific writing skills, it does provide the necessary orientation and cognitive basis to begin the writing task.

A preeminent concern for the development of intent to communicate is the desire to share one's thoughts with a given readership. Without teacher and student attention to motivation, an individual's writing will likely reflect only minimal personal perspective and creativity and will fail to realize the basic goals of functional writing tasks. Ideally, motivation should be a function of one's internal needs to communicate and to express feelings, ideas, and needs.

In the case of learners with special needs, motivational problems are often intensified because of the failure set that many of these students have acquired as a result of previous writing experiences In a study of student perceptions about writing, McAlister et al. (1999) described the attitudes of upper elementary and middle school students with language and learning disabilities. The data summarized in Table 11.5 can provide a helpful beginning point for considering student attitudes and hence motivation.

Anchoring a writing program to students' interests is desirable, keeping in mind that what appeals to some students may not appeal to their classmates. For teachers who are concerned about individualizing their students' programs, capitalizing on students' interests makes good pedagogical sense.

First, teachers can help beginning writers set the purpose for their writing and complete instructional exercises designed to emphasize task objectives. Short, specific assignments are valuable for sharply defining the student's task and, therefore, enabling a clear focus on the purpose of the assignment. Exercises with a *creative purpose* could include writing a paragraph on the descriptive properties of an interesting classroom object, on the qualities of friendship, on their favorite time of the day, or on a scene from a favorite movie. Exercises with a *functional purpose* might be to compose an effective email communication; an invitation to a party; an announcement of a school movie; a brief article for the school newspaper; a postcard to be sent to a relative; or text for a personal, class, or school website.

The NAEP (2003) offered these specific strategies for planning:

- Listing ideas, drawing pictures or diagrams
- Making a map or web and connecting various ideas with lines
- The traditional approach of making an outline to highlight both the major points as well as the details

TABLE 11.5

Frequency of Responses to Attitude Questions

Question	Really Don't Like	Sort of Don't Like	Sort of Like	Really Like
Questions about author groups				
How do you feel about				
sharing stories with others?	1		3	3
other kids talking about your story?		1	4	2
listening to other kids' stories in author groups?		1	3	3
talking about other kids' stories?	1		3	3
only the teacher reading your story instead of other kids?	3		2	2
the teacher picking the author groups?	2	1	1	3
Questions about planning and organizing				
How do you feel about				
planning and organizing before your write?	2	1	3	1
thinking up your own ideas?			1	6
getting ideas from other kids?	1	2	3	1
the teacher thinking up ideas for you?	2	1	3	1
making notes or webs on paper before you write your story?	5	1	1	
Questions about writing the story				
How do you feel about				
working on the same story over several sessions?	2		2	3
picking the words for your story?	1		1	5
deciding how long your story should be?		1	6	
figuring out spelling on your own?	2	3	1	
using a computer to help you write?	1			6
other kids helping you write your stories?	2	3		2
the teacher helping you write your stories?	2	2	1	2
Questions about revising and editing				
How do you feel about				
changing things in your stories?	2	2	1	2
having correct punctuation and spelling?			2	5
helping other students revise and edit?		3	1	3
help from the teacher when revising and editing?	1	1	1	4
revising and editing your stories to get them ready for publishing in a book?	1	1	2	3

Source: From "Perceptions of Students with Language and Learning Disabilities about Writing Process Instruction," by K. M. McAlister, N. W. Nelson, and C. M. Bahr, 1999, *Learning Disabilities Research and Practice, 14,* p. 165. Copyright 1999 by Taylor & Francis Informa UK Ltd. Journals. Reprinted with permission.

Setting *purpose* has importance for advanced writers as well. For *expressive writing*, students should consider these questions:

- What interests me most about this topic?
- What information do I already know about this topic?
- What else do I need to learn about it?
- How can I best organize this information?
- What are my personal opinions about the subject?
- How can I convey my personal feelings in my writing?

For *functional writing*, students should consider these questions:

- What is my objective?
- To whom am I writing?
- What do they know about this topic? What do they want to know?
- How can I make sure that I convey the necessary and correct information?
- Do I need to do further research on the topic to be familiar with it?
- How should I arrange and organize my writing to be most effective in meeting my objective?

Writing/Drafting Strategies

Of the three components of the writing model, the writing or drafting stage is the broadest in scope. The two central considerations in writing instruction relate to how skills are learned most effectively and how they are taught most effectively.

General Considerations

Isaacson (1989) distinguished between variant writer responsibilities, discussing two roles that writers take: the author and the secretary. The *author role* revolves around formulating and organizing ideas and selecting words and phrases to express those ideas. The *secretarial role* emphasizes the physical and mechanical concerns of writing, such as legibility, spelling, punctuation, and grammatical rules. Both roles are critical to the writer's success, and balanced orientations toward both are important in an instructional program.

An approach that stresses primarily the secretarial role may emphasize formal grammar instruction, an emphasis on structure, skill exercises, and often a reliance on worksheets and workbook pages. The teach–write approach is common in classrooms; however, its traditional usage does not mean that it has proven effectiveness. After extensively reviewing 50 years of research on this topic, Sherwin (1969) reported little evidence of its success with learners in general and even less reason to expect that the approach would be effective for individuals with disabilities. He concluded that this type of instruction "is an inefficient and ineffective way to help students achieve proficiency in writing" (p. 135) and summarized his review by noting that the most important features of instruction are "motivation, selective criticism, discussion, practical explanation, and revision" (p. 168).

The main concern with such an approach is that instructional activities can be completed without opportunity for true writing. At the same time, the activities may damage motivation, overwhelm students, and lead them to respond with fear and avoidance (Gould, 1991). In addition, the approach requires a major time commitment, something that special education programs, and educational programs in general, may not be able to give for writing instruction.

The alternative is a process orientation to writing that initially stresses the primacy of the author role. It emphasizes content over form, thus primarily honoring ideas and later establishing structure. It also capitalizes on the desire to write and avoids stifling the writing effort. Structure is emphasized later within the context of actual writing opportunities.

Graves (1985) stated the case for such an approach as follows:

> Most teaching of writing is pointed toward the eradication of error, the mastery of minute, meaningless components that make little sense to the child.... Although some growth may be evident on components, rarely does it result in the child's use of writing as a tool for learning and enjoyment. Make no mistake, component skills are important; if children do not learn to spell or use a pencil to get words on paper, they won't use writing for learning any more than the other children drilled on component skills. The writing–processing approach simply stresses meaning first, and then skills in the context of meaning. (p. 43)

Research with students progressing at a typical rate supports the proposition that these students learn to write by writing. Most significant is that, for writing to improve, students need to write regularly. Rankin-Erickson and Pressley (2000) reported that effective teachers had students write from four times a week to several times a day. Further, for instruction to be effective, the amount of time for writing must be increased. Providing opportunities for students to write in a positive, supportive atmosphere is a logical supplement to ongoing classroom instruction. Journal writing, for example, is an approach that has been used effectively for this purpose.

Once the opportunity to write has been established, the challenge is to find strategies that will enhance skill development without interfering with the writing process. Graham (1992) offered these tenets to assist teachers in instructional decision making:

1. Maintain balance between the decontextualized teaching of mechanics (including handwriting and spelling) and the complete deemphasis of skills information to the extent to which acquisition of skills becomes incidental.
2. Focus on skills that are likely to aid the student in terms of generalizable benefits (e.g., learning to spell high-frequency words vs. learning to diagram sentences).
3. Tie skills to instruction on real writing opportunities.

Students should be shown that these skills reflect conventions that are followed to enhance communication.

Rankin-Erickson and Pressley (2000) provided an interesting perspective on the process approach to writing and the attention to mechanics. Based on their survey of teachers nominated by peers as "effective," they wrote:

> This sample of teachers reported . . . their writing instruction consisted of elements of process writing (i.e., planning, drafting, and editing), these being taught in tandem with direct strategies for carrying out the processes as well as instruction in the mechanical aspects of writing such as punctuation and spelling. These writing skills were not taught in isolation, however, but rather as part of an act of purposeful communication. Teachers saw getting ideas down on paper as being different from the editing process. Invented spellings were supported and encouraged when drafting products; accurate spelling was emphasized when revising. These instructional practices are consistent with practices shown to be effective with students with writing and learning difficulties. (p. 219)

To develop writing skills, effective strategies can be based on the implementation of a **supports model** for students with special needs. Strategies that appropriately fit under the concept of a supports model include

- elective checking and feedback,
- focused skills for teacher editing,
- dual grades,
- peer writing groups,
- writing communities,
- sufficient (additional, as needed) time to develop skills,
- use of technology (e.g., word processing, voice recognition software),
- self-monitoring, and
- teacher conferencing.

One of these tools for helping students develop specific skills is to provide **selective feedback** on a limited number of skills. Students will profit most from feedback specific to their own text and specific to the skills of importance to them. Selective feedback is preferred over the extremes of inordinate corrections on papers and generalized, meaningless comments about "good work" or the like.

An effective way to accomplish the feedback goal is through *teacher conferencing*. The teacher proofreads written assignments and provides feedback directly to students, most often in an oral conference. This approach provides opportunities for teachers to introduce and reinforce specific skills and conventions. In addition, the conference approach is consistent with the process orientation to writing, helping to promote writing as a thinking act rather than solely a mechanical act.

Although by no means limited to the beginning writing stage, an option that is increasingly available for students with writing difficulties is voice- or speech-recognition software. This technology is already demonstrating significant potential benefits in helping these students get their words onto paper. By using an oral means, it circumvents the problems that students may otherwise experience with spelling, handwriting, and, to some extent, punctuation (De La Paz, 1999a).

Developing Initial Writing Skills

Most adult writers would probably agree that getting started is the most difficult part of writing. Teachers can help students over this obstacle in several ways.

First, teachers should provide an atmosphere that is conducive to expression by creating a relaxed time period during which students are motivated to view writing as enjoyable rather than punitive. Teachers can foster this atmosphere by stressing the importance of personal expression and playing down the need to adhere rigidly to prescribed forms. This emphasis should be effective in deterring students' feelings of failure with regard to their experiences in writing.

Second, teachers should tie writing to the child's spoken language. Using the **language experience approach (LEA)**, instruction can proceed through the processes outlined in Chapter 8, in terms of the interaction experience, and thus include foci on language, reading, and writing.

A third way to help students get started with writing is to relate functional writing assignments to specific, defined purposes, as discussed earlier. Assignments might be to write letters, notes to friends, invitations, directions, announcements, signs, brief biographies, speeches, news items for school newspapers, or to fill in forms. These assignments can help students see the value and relevance of written communication and increase their intention to write. By keeping the assignments sharply defined, teachers can help students channel their thoughts more easily.

Finally, teachers should keep initial assignments reasonably short. Long assignments or extended writing periods may cause children to link writing with boredom, general disinterest, and perhaps failure. A brief period of 20 minutes should be enough time for beginning writers to formulate and communicate their ideas.

Developing Vocabulary

The goals of vocabulary instruction are to increase students' writing vocabulary and the frequency with which the students use new words (see also the discussion in Chapter 8 on developing a reading vocabulary). The basic aim of instruction is to expose students to varied verbal forms and assist them in incorporating the words into their compositions. Specific objectives should include helping students acquire a store of synonyms for commonly used words, become familiar with a variety of descriptive words, and use unusual words and original phrases as alternatives to more typical lexical options.

Teachers should be aware that many students tend to avoid using words they cannot spell, which reduces the quality of their writing. Only when they can be convinced not to worry about spelling and to concentrate on ideas can a true appreciation of their abilities be obtained (Johnson & Myklebust, 1967). Just as when working with students for whom English is a second language, the concern initially should be with qualitative aspects of expression rather than with correct spelling.

Cohen and Plaskon (1980) stressed that students with disabilities should develop a vocabulary they can use accurately. According to these authors,

> Although the objective is to expand the child's facility with words, it must not be gained at the expense of writing fluency. A functional goal of providing [these students] with word skills which allow them to successfully manipulate a limited core of words is advisable. (p. 295)

Those authors suggested teaching word clusters that could center on topical themes, including words for naming and describing common actions, personal attributes, and time, as well as increasing facility with prefixes, suffixes, synonyms, and common idiomatic expressions.

Various instructional exercises can be developed to assist students in building vocabulary. For individual writing assignments, the entire class could initially generate a list of key words to be written on the board. This would avoid the conceptual break required to select and revisualize specific words, and at the same time students would be provided practice in using these words.

As students mature in their writing, they can benefit from assistance in learning to use words (and phrases) that enable them to accomplish more difficult writing tasks, such as using transitions when adding information or developing contrasts. Table 11.6 provides a list of words and phrases particularly developed for persuasive writing (De La Paz, 2001).

Sentence Development

By stressing well-developed sentences, teachers train students to think clearly and to express themselves in complete thoughts. Many students who have difficulty writing rely on simple, repetitive, safe sentence structures, which results in less fluent writing products. Therefore, the instructional focus must be on teaching students to expand sentences within acceptable structural patterns.

Several approaches to sentence expansion have been developed. An appropriate beginning point is to balance encouragement for "real writing" through the use of patterned sentence guides and structures (Isaacson, 1987). Using guides reduces content demands and structural ambiguities and can help students concentrate on effective communication. In the simplest form of patterned guide, students label a picture using a prescribed sentence pattern. For example, a student might label a picture of a tall boy with the sentence, "This boy is tall."

In teaching sentence extension, teachers ask students questions, and the students respond by writing complete sentences. Emphases can include instruction on nouns (e.g., Who did it?), verbs (e.g., What was done?), descriptors (e.g., What kind?), and objects (e.g., To what? For what?). Some skills can be learned within the context of sentence meaning rather than as specific semi-isolated items in a

TABLE 11.6
Transition Words/Phrases for Persuasive Writing

Introduce Ideas:	I believe that	Granting a Point:	granted that
	I think		even though
	for example		in spite of
	as an illustration		although
	for instance		while this may be true
			despite
		Conclusion or	accordingly
Add an Idea:	in addition	Consequence:	as a result
	furthermore		because
	also		consequently
	moreover		due to
	another reason to		finally
	support this is		hence
	besides		in conclusion
	and		in summary
	secondly		it follows that
	thirdly		as a result
	too		for these reasons
	finally		since
	next		so
	similarly		therefore
			thus
			to sum up
Contrast:	however		
	on the contrary		
	yet		
	but		
	conversely		
	regardless		
	and yet		
	nevertheless		
	on the other hand		
	otherwise		
	still		
	at the same time		
	despite this		
	although		

Source: From "STOP and DARE: A Persuasive Writing Strategy," 2001, by S. De La Paz, *Intervention in School and Clinic*, *36*, p. 238. Copyright by Sage Publications, Inc. Journals. Reprinted with permission.

grammar instructional sequence (Phelps-Terasaki & Phelps, 1980). *Teaching Competence in Written Language* (Phelps-Terasaki & Phelps-Gunn, 2000; see Figure 11.9) is a sentence extension program containing 80 lessons ranging from introduction to the subject of a sentence to persuasive paragraphs. Students work from stimulus pictures to develop and expand descriptive sentences and then develop paragraphs.

A subsequent logical step toward the extension of sentences can come through sentence combining. Sentence combining provides a way to develop more interesting sentences that express ideas in varied ways (Saddler & Preschern, 2007). In sentence-combining activities, students expand simple sentences into more complex ones. Sentence-combining is an effective way to improve the overall quality of writing and can increase syntactic maturity (Graham & Harris, 2009; Isaacson, 1987; Saddler & Preschern, 2007; Scarmadalia & Bereiter, 1986).

In Strong's (1983) original program of sentence combining, students are asked to combine clusters of sentences. Provided with a selection of pairs of sentences, the students are informed that the sentences can be combined in a variety of ways and that no single specific response is indicated. The following is a cluster that appears early in the program; students are instructed to combine the respective pairs of sentences into a single sentence.

CONNECTORS	WHO/WHAT?	DOING WHAT?	DETAILS
And First Second Next Then Last	Which? What kind of? How much? How many?		Why? (because, since, so that) What? When? Where? How?

Source: From *Teaching Competence in Written Language: A Systematic Program for Developing Writing Skills*, p. 6, by D. Phelps-Terasaki and T. Phelps-Gunn, 2000, Austin, TX: Pro-Ed. Copyright 2000 by Pro-Ed, Inc. Reprinted with permission.

FIGURE 11.9

Sentence Guide

2.1 Cowboys swagger around.	2.2 They get their gear together.
3.1 Clowns roll out their barrels.	3.2 The barrels are battered.
4.1 Bulls stand in their pens.	4.2 The bulls are huge.
5.1 The sun beats down.	5.2 The announcer introduces the first entry.
6.1 People lean forward in the bleachers.	6.2 They strain to see the chute.
7.1 A shout goes up.	7.2 The bull comes charging out.
8.1 He is a giant animal.	8.2 He has a tornado's energy.
9.1 His eyes are fierce.	9.2 His horns are wicked.
10.1 The cowboy is tossed to one side.	10.2 He tumbles end over end. (p. 5)

Although Strong's program begins with sentences that are already written, it encourages students to expand and develop their own creations. Following the individual tasks, students are invited to finish the story that they began with the sentence clusters, which requires students to generate their own ideas. A more detailed sequence of steps in teaching sentence combining is provided by Schuster (2001, 2002), which enables students to sequentially acquire further combining skills.

Saddler and Preschern (2007) offered the following suggestions for providing systematic instruction in sentence combining:

- Extensive practice in the manipulation and rewriting of kernel sentences
- Learning how to untangle, tighten, and rewrite sentences
- Increasing the amount and the quality of revisions to create better stories

Paragraph Development

Once children have acquired a working knowledge of sentence structure and grammatical forms, the emphasis can shift to overall organization of paragraphs and short stories. Paragraph instruction should emphasize the following elements:

1. One main idea,
2. A topic sentence that focuses attention on the main idea
3. Supporting sentences that detail information relevant to the topic
4. A summary or transitional sentence (when appropriate)
5. Indentation and a new line for beginning a new paragraph

Specific teaching techniques should help students state their basic premises and expand their thoughts within the context of a well-formed paragraph.

Providing students with brief, functional writing tasks is an excellent way to begin teaching the concept of paragraphs. For instance, students might be instructed to write a letter to purchase an item. The topic sentence would identify the item to be purchased, and additional sentences would provide a description of the item, a discussion of the form of payment, and the address to which the item should be sent. This sort of practice reinforces the concept of expressing only one main idea in a paragraph.

Letter writing is another way to illustrate how paragraphs are related and how they frame an overall successful communication. For example, a friendly letter (prototypically) could include three paragraphs: news about oneself, questions about the friend to whom one is writing, and answers to questions that may have been posed in a previous letter.

A technique that can assist students in building paragraphs and enhance their writing in general is paraphrasing. An example is RAP (Schumaker, Denton, & Deshler, 1984, cited in Ellis & Sabornie, 1986):

Read a paragraph
Ask yourself what the main idea and details in the paragraph are
Put the main idea and details into your own words

See Chapter 8 for further information.

Bruce (2004) developed a useful graphic organizer to construct paragraphs. It is presented in Figure 11.10.

A final suggestion is derived from an initiative to write paragraphs related to IEP goals. Termed *Go For IT...NOW*, Konrad, Trela, and Test (2006) developed this means of promoting self-regulation and self-discrimination, with the following steps:

- Goal
- Objectives
- Identified Timeline (IT)

Indent ⟶	Topic Sentence
Detail sentence	
Detail sentence	
Detail sentence	
Final or Transition sentence	

Visual aid to assist with paragraph organization.

Source: From "Connecting Oral and Written Language through Applied Writing Strategies," by R. C. Bruce, 2004, *Intervention in School and Clinic, 40,* p. 45. Copyright 2004 by Sage Publications, Inc. Journals. Reprinted with permission.

FIGURE 11.10

Sample Paragraph Graphic Organizer

■ NOW: check paragraph to see whether it:
  □ named the topic,
  □ ordered the steps, and
  □ wrapped it up by restating the topic.

Composition Writing Considerations

In their classic work, Johnson and Myklebust (1967) provided an excellent outline of a progression of ideation in developing compositions that can be taught by varying the content of students' writing products. Basically, their sequence follows ideas from the concrete to the abstract. The first stage, concrete–descriptive, involves the use of a simple descriptive sentence or a series of sentences about common things in the child's environment (e.g., The girl is running to the store). In the second stage, concrete–imaginative, students write about inferences drawn from some stimulus or experience. In this stage, students are encouraged to draw generalizations, to imagine what is happening, and then to respond accordingly.

The other two stages in the Johnson and Myklebust progression shift the emphasis to abstractions. The third level, abstract–descriptive, asks students to write their own stories, stressing the concepts of time and sequence, and students are urged to write their stories with logical order, appropriate transitions, and the development of plot and characters. At this final level, abstract–imaginative, students write their perceptions when given open-ended questions or propositions. Stylistic improvements such as figures of speech can be incorporated at this stage.

To instill interest, stimulate thinking, and promote development in expressive writing, teachers should make available a variety of topics that are appropriate for compositions (see Figure 11.11). The following are several methods for introducing a composition assignment that can encourage student expression:

1. Provide a lead-in sentence to serve as the beginning line of a story. This strategy often helps students overcome writer's block and begin to work.
2. Create a hypothetical (What if . . .) situation. This strategy tends to stimulate students' thinking and to encourage speculation on possible occurrences.
3. Use invented circumstances. This strategy can stimulate students' creativity to complete a scenario presented by the teacher.
4. End a short story in the middle of a sentence and prior to a crucial event. This strategy allows students to continue the story with minimal difficulty.

Composition Strategy Training

Implicit in much of the discussion in this chapter is the need for students to be actively involved in the process of writing. Thus, students should be encouraged to develop an "inner voice"—to think about what they are doing as they write (Thomas et al., 1987). Strategy training can help.

Story grammar strategies (that is, the structure of a story revolving around questions such as: Who is the story about? Where does it take place? What is the problem

Who Wants to Be a Millionaire?
My favorite television show is . . .
The most interesting person I know
The day I joined the circus
What TV character would I like to be?
What I plan to do after I graduate from high school
It happened at the junior prom
My favorite movie is . . .
My favorite sports hero is . . .
The secret clubhouse in the woods
The championship Little League game
My discovery of an Egyptian tomb
Who would you like to be for one day if you could be anybody in the
    world?
I wish I could spend my summer vacation in . . .
My best friend is . . .
Why colors remind me of moods
The most disgusting TV commercial I've ever seen
Spending the day with my favorite music group
My favorite song is . . .
My first job
The day I got my license to drive
If you could go anywhere in the world, where would you go and by what
    means?
My dog learns to talk
What if I was a seed
20 years from now
How could I ever explain it to my parents?
"The night was dark and the moon was yellow . . ."
Faster! Faster! I have to get there as soon as I can or else . . .
What if the sun never came up?
You have just invented a special type of chemical potion . . .
My life at age three
The day I became a butterfly
Why I'd like to be on Survivor

FIGURE 11.11

Themes for Written Compositions

in the story? How is the problem solved? How does the main character feel about the solution?) can enhance students' writing and reading skills, especially students who have special needs.

Hagood (1997) outlined strategies to enhance learning for students, including two that use story grammar charts to enhance writing:

1. Teach students to use story grammar to increase their writing skills through explicit instruction. Assist students in organizing their ideas to write for an audience.
2. Teach students to manipulate and analyze the components of story grammar (e.g., rewrite stories by changing the setting and modifying other elements that necessarily change when the setting changes).

The self-regulated strategy development (SRSD) model developed by Harris and Graham (1996, 1999; Graham & Harris, 2009) is based on a number of strategies for enhancing writing, including their story grammar strategy, which derives from this mnemonic:

W-W-W What-2 How-2

Students are to look at a stimulus picture and then use this mnemonic device to develop a story. The mnemonic stands for:

- Who?
- When?
- Where?
- What does main character do?
- What happens when he does it?
- How does it end?
- How does he feel?

Graham and Harris (2009, pp. 63–64) delineate six instructional stages in their SRSD model, as follows:

Stage I: Develop and activate background knowledge necessary to use these strategies.

Stage II: Discuss a strategy that will be learned, and consider its objectives and benefits.

Stage III: Model how to use the strategy.

Stage IV: Memorize the strategy.

Stage V: Support the use of the strategy by students through collaborative writing experiences. Scaffold the strategy used, gradually fading prompts.

Stage VI: Use the strategy independently.

De La Paz (1999b) reported on the successful use of the mnemonics PLAN and WRITE for assisting middle school students through a nine-step writing process (see Table 11.7). The strategy was accompanied by cue cards that assisted students in the writing of five-paragraph essays (see Table 11.8). A full description of each component of the instructional program is provided by De La Paz (1999b).

Successful composition writing requires students to develop appropriate strategies for learning the steps for successful writing and for having a basis for recalling

TABLE 11.7
The Expository Planning Strategy

Planning Strategy: PLAN	Instructions for Each Planning Step
1. Pay attention to the prompt	Read the prompt. Decide (a) what you are being asked to write about and (b) how to develop your essay.
2. List main ideas	Brainstorm possible responses to the prompt. Decide on (a) one topic, then brainstorm at least three main ideas for (b) the development of your essay.
3. Add supporting ideas	Think of details, examples, and elaborations that support your main ideas.
4. Number your ideas	Number major points in the order you will use them.

How to Remember to Keep Planning While Composing Your Essay: WRITE

5. Work from your plan to develop your thesis statement
6. Remember your goals
7. Include transition words for each paragraph
8. Try to use different kinds of sentences
9. Exciting, interesting, $100,000 words

Source: From "Self-Regulated Strategy Instruction in Regular Education Settings: Improving Outcomes for Students With and Without Learning Disabilities," by S. De La Paz, 1999, *Learning Disabilities Research and Practice, 14,* p. 98. Copyright 1999 by Taylor & Francis Informa UK Ltd. Journals. Reprinted with permission.

those steps when completing an assignment. Comprehensive strategies are directed to prewriting, writing, and postwriting. An example is the POWER writing strategy (Ellis, 1997), which provides an orientation to the key steps involved in the writing process (see Table 11.9).

Another example is the DEFENDS strategy (Lenz, Ellis, & Scanlon, 1997) to assist students in learning how to express a point of view in compositions. This strategy can also be used for writing book reports and answers to essay exam questions and for other assignments. The steps are as follows:

1. Decide on the audience, goals, and position.
2. Estimate the main ideas and details.
3. Figure the best order of main ideas and details.
4. Express the position in the opening.

TABLE 11.8
Cue Cards for Writing Five-Paragraph Essays

Introductory Paragraph: Thesis statement first	Introductory Paragraph: Thesis statement last
■ Answer the prompt in your 1st sentence. ■ Write your first main idea in 2nd sentence. ■ Write your second main idea as the 3rd sentence. ■ Write your third main idea as the last sentence.	■ **"Start with an attention getter" and lead up to the thesis statement.** ■ **Answer the prompt in your last sentence. Include your 1st, 2nd, and 3rd main idea in a series.**
(1)	(2)
How to "start with attention getter"	First Body Paragraph: Use transition words to introduce ideas
■ Use a series of questions. ■ Use a series of statements. ■ Use a brief or funny story. ■ Use a mean or angry statement. ■ Start with the opposite opinion from what you believe.	■ First (of all) . . . ■ (The/My) first (reason/example) is . . . ■ One (reason why/example is) . . . ■ To begin with . . . ■ In the first step . . . ■ To explain . . .
(3)	(4)
2nd & 3rd Body Paragraphs: Use transition words to connect or add ideas, or give examples	Concluding Paragraph: Use transition words to summarize ideas
■ Second . . . Third . . . ■ My second (reason/example) is . . . ■ Furthermore . . . ■ Another (reason) to support this is . . . ■ What is more . . . ■ The next step . . .	■ In conclusion/To conclude . . . ■ In summary/To sum up . . . ■ As one can see . . ./As a result ■ In short/All in all . . . ■ It follows that . . . ■ For these reasons . . .
(5)	(6)

Bolded cards were provided for students who wished to attempt more sophisticated introductory paragraphs.

TABLE 11.9
POWER Writing Strategy

Plan
Predict who will read this and what you hope will happen when they do.
List the title, main ideas, and details.

Other
Decide which main idea to write about first, second, etc., and note order on the
     think sheet.
For each main idea, note the best order for presenting the details on the think
     sheet.
Make sure the orders are logical.

Write
Begin with a sentence or two that activates the reader's knowledge about your
     subject.
Introduce the topic and main ideas in the first paragraph. Use cues to signal ideas.
Write about each main idea in the following paragraphs; explain with details.
Tell yourself positive statements about your writing and tell yourself to write more.

Edit
Check to see if the overall paper makes sense. Read it out loud to someone.
Conference with a peer for feedback.
Check to see if each sentence makes sense and if it's complete.
Check for COPS errors
     Capitalization
     Omissions
     Punctuation
     Spelling

Revise
Copy your paper over neatly. Check once again for any errors.

Source: From "Watering Up the Curriculum for Adolescents with Learning Disabilities: Goals of the Knowledge Domain," by E. Ellis, 1997, *Remedial and Special Education, 18,* p. 345. Copyright 1997 by Sage Publications, Inc. Journals. Reprinted with permission.

   5. Note each main idea and supporting points.
   6. Drive home the message in the last sentence.
   7. Search for errors, and correct them.

A particular challenge for writers at the secondary-school level is to respond to writing tasks that require analytical skills. Various strategies can be taught to assist students with this task. One such strategy can include the use of a graphic organizer for a compare-and-contrast essay (see Figure 11.12).

Postwriting Strategies

The quality of a finished product hinges on revising and editing. To expect that most students will revise and edit their work automatically would be naive. Indeed, many students view proofreading as an aversive rather than a positive task. Even those who are willing to revise and edit must be shown how to do this. The teacher's role, therefore, is to model the specific techniques inherent in the revision and editing process and to delineate its advantages to the finished product.

For revision to become acceptable to students, they must be sold on the concept of the working draft. To present this concept, the teacher should discuss the writing stage as the initial effort to put on paper the information to be shared, and the postwriting stage as an alternative to the conceptual breaks that might occur within the task. The postwriting stage must evolve toward a positive association for students; they must move beyond associating rewriting with punitive action.

The instructional goal for students in the postwriting stage is to learn the basic steps necessary to revise their writing and to later apply the steps independently. The following are self-evaluation questions that writers can ask in this stage:

Topic: Racism in 1930s

Germany	Features	United States
	I. Target Group	
Yes	Focus on ethnic groups	Yes
Jews, People w/disabilities	Primary emphasis	African-Americans
	II. Source of Racism	
Nazi Party	Primary source	Local, state governments
Individuals	Other sources	Individuals
	III. Tactics	
Concentration camps, exterminations	Physical	Beatings, lynchings
Property rights/human rights	Legal	Voting rights/Civil rights

Now complete these statements:

1. Racism in the 1930s in Germany and the United States was similar in that....

2. On the other hand, it was different because.....

3. I conclude that....

FIGURE 11.12

Graphic Organizer — Essay Writing, Compare/Contrast

1. Does each sentence make sense?
2. Is every word spelled correctly?
3. Are punctuation marks used correctly? Are any needed marks omitted?
4. Are words capitalized that should be?
5. Have I used descriptive words and phrases?
6. Are any of the points vague and in need of clarification?
7. Can anything be said more clearly?
8. Overall, is the paper organized in a way to make the reader's job an easy one?
9. Have I met the objectives?

The entire postwriting process is too involved for students with writing difficulties to tackle in any one assignment. Therefore, although complete evaluation of a writing sample would require consideration of all of the aspects just stated, teachers should select one or two for given assignments until the students refine both their writing and their editing skills.

Postwriting instructional exercises in the classroom can be organized in a variety of ways. One effective technique to orient students toward revising and editing is to have students practice verbalizing the various steps to the teacher, such as through the teacher conferencing model discussed earlier.

A popular error monitoring strategy, represented by the acronym COPS, has students ask themselves the following questions (Schumaker et al., 1981; Shumaker & Deshler, 2009):

C – Have I Capitalized the first word and proper nouns?

O – What is the Overall appearance? Have I made any handwriting, margin, messy, or spacing errors?

P – Have I used end Punctuation, commas, and semicolons correctly?

S – Do the words look like they are Spelled right? Can I sound them out, or should I use the dictionary?

Once students have learned one of the COPS-related skills, they can be introduced to editing for that skill. After they have been trained to monitor each of the components separately, they can use all four at the same time.

Six steps are involved in the use of the error monitoring strategy (Schumaker & Deshler, 2009):

> Use every other line as you write your rough draft; as you read each sentence, ask yourself the four COPS questions; when you find an error, circle it and put the correct form above the error if you know it; ask for help if you are unsure of the correct form; re-copy the paragraph neatly; and reread the paragraph as a final check. (p. 85)

COPS can subsequently serve as a way to review completed compositions or essays and search for the specific errors indicated. This strategy can be used effectively with students in both general and special education and has proven to be effective with students at or above the upper-elementary or middle-school level (e.g., Shannon & Polloway, 1993).

The postwriting stage, however, involves far more than simply checking for capitalization, overall appearance, punctuation, and spelling. If students acquire these skills, instruction should turn to higher levels of revision, with special attention directed to content and organization. Figure 11.13 provides a guide for content revisions for both fiction and nonfiction writing. The checklist can also be used by peers following a procedure such as the one described next.

One option is to REVISE (Polloway et al., 2008), which includes the following elements:

> R – Reread you paper to make sure your paper says what you want
>   it to say
> E – Edit using the COPS error monitoring strategy

Title _____ Title _____
Author _____ Author _____
Date _____ Date _____
Peer Editor _____ Peer Editor _____

____ Is the beginning interesting?	____ Was there a moral or theme?
____ Does the story make sense?	____ Has the author written for a
____ Are the characters believable?	particular audience?
____ Do they act like real people?	____ Has the author written for a
____ Do the characters use conversation?	specific purpose?
____ Are the character's personalities	____ Does the introduction to the piece
developed?	get the reader involved right away?
____ Does the story have a problem that	____ Are the ideas developed in a logical
needs to be solved?	sequence?
____ Are the descriptions of the scenes	____ Does the author stay on topic?
clear?	____ Are the ideas clear?
____ Does each scene build toward the	____ Are there details to support the
high point (climax) of the story?	main ideas?
____ Is there an exciting or high point	____ Is correct grammar used?
of the story?	____ Are words spelled correctly?
____ Is the conclusion logical? Does it	____ Is there a surprise ending or strong
wrap up all the loose ends?	conclusion?
____ Was the conflict or problem resolved?	

Source: From "The Write Way: Tips for Teaching the Writing Process to Resistant Writers," by M. L. Marchisan and S. R. Alber, 2001, *Intervention in School and Clinic, 36*, p. 158. Copyright 2001 by Sage Publications, Inc. Journals. Reprinted with permission.

FIGURE 11.13

Revision Guide for Fiction and Nonfiction Writing

V – Vocabulary selected to be appropriate for purpose
I – Interesting and lively topic developed
S – Sentences complete and varied
E – Evidence provided to support your points (p. 254)

Peers can make an important contribution to writing through peer review and feedback. In sessions referred to as classroom "writing workshops" or "author groups," students discuss each others' work and suggest revisions (McAlister et al., 1999). Polinko (1985, cited by Levy, 1996) described one such peer mediation strategy:

> "Helpful audience" provides a purpose and an audience for the writing. The teacher first explains the structure of a helpful audience group and, when necessary, models how it works. Groups form as writers are available to discuss their writing.... Each student uses a teacher-prepared questionnaire to guide peer critiquing discussion. In groups of three to four, students read their essays to one another in order to listen to and comment about one another's writings. The physical composition of the student peer groups may vary, depending on which students first complete this stage of writing. Occasionally, the teacher rearranges groups so that a balance is maintained among more and less efficient learners. (p. 99)

■ Summary

Written language represents the highest achievement within the language domains. Because it builds on prerequisite knowledge and abilities in oral language, reading, spelling, and handwriting, individuals not surprisingly can struggle in achieving competency in this domain.

The writing process has three stages. The prewriting, or planning, stage requires consideration of stimulus input, motivation to write, and setting a purpose. It places demands on the writer to become actively involved in thinking about communicative intent and adapting the writing to the audience for whom it is intended.

The writing (or drafting) stage involves both craft and content. The former entails the mechanical skills associated with the secretarial function in writing; the latter involves the author role. Instructional foci in a writing program include vocabulary and sentence development, paragraphing skills, and compositional writing.

The postwriting stage involves the dual processes of revising and editing. Revising typically refers to necessary changes made in content, and editing involves the mechanical aspects of writing.

Comprehensive writing programs direct attention to these three stages of writing and provide students with opportunities to develop a variety of writing products. The programs also include instruction specific to functional and creative writing.

▌References

Association for Supervision and Curriculum Development (ASCD). (1997, Spring). *Teaching young writers* (Curriculum Update). Alexandria, VA: Author.

Bruce, R. C. (2004). Connecting oral and written language through applied writing strategies. *Intervention in School and Clinic, 40,* 38–47.

Cohen, S. B., & Plaskon, S. P. (1980). *Language arts for the mildly handicapped.* Columbus, OH: Merrill.

De La Paz, S. (1999a). Composing via dictation and speech recognition systems: Compensatory technology for students with learning disabilities. *Learning Disability Quarterly, 22,* 173–182.

De La Paz, S. (1999b). Self-regulated strategy instruction in regular education settings: Improving outcomes for students with and without learning disabilities. *Learning Disabilities Research and Practice, 14,* 92–106.

De La Paz, S. (2001). STOP and DARE: A persuasive writing strategy. *Intervention in School and Clinic, 36,* 234–243.

De La Paz, S. (2009). Rubrics: Heuristics for developing writing strategies. *Assessment for Effective Intervention, 34,* 134–146.

Ellis, E. S. (1997). Watering up the curriculum for adolescents with learning disabilities: Goals of the knowledge dimension. *Remedial and Special Education, 18,* 326–346.

Ellis, E. S., & Sabornie, E. J. (1986). *Teaching learning strategies to learning-disabled students in post-secondary settings.* Unpublished manuscript, University of South Carolina, Columbia.

Englert, C. S. (2009). Connecting the dots in a research program to develop, implement, and evaluate strategic literacy interventions for struggling readers and writers. *Learning Disabilities Research & Practice, 24,* 104–120.

Englert, C. S., Mariage, T. V., Okolo, C. M., Shankland, R. K., Moxley, K. D., Courtad, C. A., … & Chen, H. (2009). The learning-to-learn strategies of adolescent students with disabilities: Highlighting, note taking, planning, and writing expository texts. *Assessment for Effective Intervention, 34,* 147–161.

Gould, B. W. (1991). Curricular strategies for written expression. In A. M. Bain, L. L. Bailet, & L. Moats (Eds.), *Written language disorders: Theory into practice* (pp. 129–164). Austin, TX: Pro-Ed.

Graham, S. (1992). Helping students with learning disabilities progress as writers. *Intervention in School and Clinic, 27,* 135–143.

Graham, S., & Harris, K. R. (2009). Almost 30 years of writing research: Making sense of it all with the wrath of Khan. *Learning Disabilities Research & Practice, 24*(2), 58–68.

Graham, S., Harris, K. R., & Larsen, L. (2001). Prevention and intervention of writing difficulties for students with learning disabilities. *Learning Disabilities Research and Practice, 16,* 74–84.

Graves, D. H. (1985). All children can write. *Learning Disabilities Focus, 1*(1), 36–43. Pro-Ed.

Gregg, N., Coleman, C., Davis, M., & Chalk, J. C. (2007). Timed essay writing: Implications for high-stakes tests. *Journal of Learning Disabilities, 40,* 306–318.

Hagood, B. F. (1997). Reading and writing with help from story grammar. *Teaching Exceptional Children, 29*(4), 10–14.

Hammill, D. D., & Larsen, S. C. (1996). *Test of Written Language* (3rd ed.). Austin, TX: Pro-Ed.

Harris, K., & Graham, S. (1996). *Making the writing process work: Strategies for composition and self-regulation.* Cambridge, MA: Brookline.

Harris, K. R., & Graham, S. (1999). Programmatic interventions research: Illustrations from the evaluation of self-regulated strategy development. *Learning Disability Quarterly, 22,* 251–262.

Isaacson, S. L. (1987). Effective instruction in written language. *Focus on Exceptional Children, 19*(6), 1–12.

Isaacson, S. L. (1989). Role of secretary vs. author in resolving the conflict in writing instruction. *Learning Disability Quarterly, 12,* 200–217.

Isaacson, S. L. (2004). Instruction that helps students meet state standards in writing. *Exceptionality, 12,* 39–54.

Johnson, D. I., & Myklebust, H. R. (1967). *Learning disabilities: Educational principles and practices.* New York: Grune & Stratton.

Konrad, M., Trela, K., & Test, D. (2006). Using IEP goals and objectives to teach paragraph writing to high school students with physical and cognitive disabilities. *Education & Training in Developmental Disabilities, 41,* 111–124.

Lenz, B. K., Ellis, E. S., & Scanlon, D. (1997). *Teaching learning strategies to adolescents and adults with learning disabilities.* Austin, TX: Pro-Ed.

Levy, N. R. (1996). Teaching analytical writing: Help for general education middle school teachers. *Intervention in School and Clinic, 32,* 95–103.

Lienemann, T., Graham, S., Leader-Janssen, B., & Reid, R. (2006). Improving the writing performance of struggling writers in second grade. *Journal of Special Education, 40,* 66–78.

Marchisan, M. L., & Alber, S. R. (2001). The write way: Tips for teaching the writing process to resistant writers. *Intervention in School and Clinic, 36,* 154–162.

McAlister, K. M., Nelson, N. W., & Bahr, C. M. (1999). Perceptions of students with language and learning disabilities about writing process and instruction. *Learning Disabilities Research and Practice, 14,* 159–172.

McMaster, K., & Espin, C. (2007). Technical features of curriculum-based measurement in writing: A literature review. *Journal of Special Education, 41,* 68–84.

Miller, L. (2009). Informal and qualitative assessment of writing skills in students with disabilities. *Assessment for Effective Intervention, 34,* 178–191.

Moran, M. R. (1987). Options for written language assessment. *Focus on Exceptional Children, 19*(5), 1–12.

National Assessment of Educational Progress. (NAEP). (2003). Washington, DC: Author.

Penner-Williams, J., Smith, T. E. C., & Gartin, B. C. (2009). Written language expression: Assessment instruments and teacher tools. *Assessment for Effective Intervention, 34,* 162–169.

Phelps-Terasaki, D., & Phelps, T. (1980). *Teaching written expression: The Phelps sentence guide program.* Novato, CA: Academic Therapy.

Phelps-Terasaki, D., & Phelps-Gunn, T. (2000). *Teaching competence in written language: A systematic program for developing writing skills* (2nd ed.). Austin, TX: Pro-Ed.

Polloway, E. A. (2009). Written language assessment: Introduction to the special series. *Assessment for Effective Intervention, 34,* 132–133.

Polloway, E. A., Patton, J. R., & Cohen, S. (1983). Written language. In E. L. Meyen, G. A. Vergason, & R. I. Whelan (Eds.), *Promising practices for exceptional children: Curriculum implications* (pp. 285–320). Denver: Love.

Polloway, E. A., Patton, J. R., & Serna, L. (2008). *Strategies for teaching learners with special needs* (9th ed.). Upper Saddle River, NJ: Pearson.

Rankin-Erickson, J., & Pressley, M. (2000). A survey of instructional practices of special education teachers nominated as effective teachers of literacy. *Learning Disabilities Research and Practice, 15,* 206–225.

Reid, R., & Leinemann, T. O. (2006). *Strategy instruction for students with learning disabilities.* New York: Guilford Press

Saddler, B., & Preschern, J. (2007). Improving sentence writing ability through sentence-combining practice. *Teaching Exceptional Children, 39*(3), 6–11.

Scarmadalia, M., & Bereiter, C. (1986). Research on written composition. In M. C. Wittrock (Ed.), *Handbook of research on teaching* (3rd ed., pp. 778–803). New York: Macmillan.

Schirmer, B., & Bailey, J. (2000). Writing assessment rubric: An instructional approach with struggling writers. *Teaching Exceptional Children, 33*(1), 52–58.

Schuster, E. (2001). *Sentence mastery: A sentence combining approach, Level A*. New York: Phoenix Learning Resources.

Schuster, E. (2002). *Sentence mastery: A sentence combining approach, Level B*. New York: Phoenix Learning Resources.

Schumaker, J. B., & Deshler, D. D. (2009). Adolescents with learning disabilities as writers: Are we selling them short? *Learning Disabilities Research & Practice, 24*(2), 81–92.

Schumaker, J. B., Deshler, D. D., Nolan, S., Clark, F. L., Alley, G. R., & Warner, M. M. (1981). *Error monitoring: A learning strategy for improving academic performance of LD adolescents* (Research Report No. 32). Lawrence: University of Kansas, Institute on Learning Disabilities.

Scott, B., & Vitale, M. (2003). Teaching the writing process to students with LD. *Intervention in School and Clinic, 38,* 220.

Shannon, T., & Polloway, E. A. (1993). Promoting error monitoring in middle school students with learning disabilities. *Intervention in School and Clinic, 28,* 160–164.

Sherwin, J. S. (1969). *Four programs in teaching English: A critique of research.* Scranton, PA: International Textbook (for National Council of Teachers of English).

Strong, W. (1983). *Sentence combining: A composing book* (2nd ed.). New York: Random House.

Thomas, C. C., Englert, C. S., & Gregg, S. (1987). An analysis of errors and strategies in the expository writing of learning disabled students. *Remedial and Special Education, 8*(1), 21–30.

Troia, G. A. (2002). Teaching writing strategies to children with disabilities: Setting generalization as the goal. *Exceptionality, 10,* 249–269.

Troia, G. A. (2005, October). *The writing instructional research we have, the writing instruction research we need.* Paper presented at Literacy Achievement Research Center Symposium on Literacy Achievement, Michigan State University, Lansing.

Vallecorsa, A., Ledford, R. R., Parnell, G. G. (1991). Strategies for teaching composition skills to students with learning disabilities. *Teaching Exceptional Children, 23*(2), 53.

Wong, B. (1997). Research on genre-specific strategies for enhancing writing in adolescents with learning disabilities. *Learning Disability Quarterly, 20,* 140–159.

12

Adolescents with Language Disabilities

In today's world of instant communication, adolescents are expected to use language effectively throughout their school years and beyond (Nippold, Mansfield, Billow, & Tomblin, 2009). Problems with language can have a significant impact on children's social and academic lives. Similar to many other disability issues that children face, language disabilities often do not disappear with adolescence but frequently continue through adolescence into adulthood.

Adolescence is a traumatic time for many students who are struggling to make the transition from childhood to adulthood. How they look, speak, and even listen is important. More than any other developmental group, adolescents want to fit in and to be viewed as acceptable. They want to be like everyone else. They dress alike, listen to the same music, go to the same places, and use similar slang. Language disabilities can have a negative impact. For example, social acceptance is critical during adolescence. Peer approval is vastly more important than parental approval for many adolescents, and language disorders can have a bearing on this approval. Problems with language can result in peer rejection and lowered self-concepts that might have long-lasting effects on the adolescent.

Language problems not only affect adolescents' social status among their peers but also may have a negative impact on their academic success (Polloway, Patton, & Serna, 2008). Language problems can actually be the primary cause of academic failure. Students in secondary school must be able to use and understand spoken and written language (Nippold et al., 2009).

As they matriculate through the grades, being able to acquire information through reading and listening becomes more and more critical. In middle and secondary schools, students are expected to be more independent in their learning. Receptive language skills, including reading and listening, are crucial for completing many high school courses successfully, and deficiencies in these areas make it extremely difficult for students to acquire information. Students have to be able to read for content, listen, and take notes. Without these skills, students in secondary schools are at a significant disadvantage. Unfortunately, many students in secondary schools have deficiencies in language areas (National Assessment of Educational Progress [NAEP], 2007).

In addition to receptive language skills, middle school and high school students must have competence in expressive language. They must be able respond orally to questions, enter into discussions, and express themselves effectively in writing. Problems in these areas make it difficult for them to achieve success. Although some middle school and secondary school teachers are willing to make accommodations for students with oral and written language problems, others are not. Many teachers simply expect students to perform at a certain level, and students who are incapable of performing at that level receive failing grades. Similar to deficiencies in receptive language, many secondary students also have problems with expressive language (NAEP, 2007).

Postsecondary educational success is becoming more important than ever. For individuals with language disorders, achieving academic success in these settings is extremely difficult. Students in high school classes are expected to be able to listen, read, enter into discussions, and write effectively, and these expectations grow in college and university settings. Effective use of language is also important for individuals who enter the labor market after high school. Being able to communicate effectively has an impact on vocational and social success for all adults. Therefore, though it is hoped that children with language disorders will overcome many of these problems prior to secondary school, for those who do not, educators must address the issues and continue their efforts to improve the language skills of all their students.

Many of the language problems of adolescents are similar to those of elementary-aged students, including difficulties with reading, writing, spelling, oral expression, and listening. The purpose of this chapter is to provide an overview of adolescence and the problems facing all children during this often turbulent developmental period. Language problems may compound adolescents' problems, and the nature of adolescence can bear on the importance of language. This chapter provides a basis for understanding adolescents and the effects of language problems on this population.

▌The Nature of Adolescence

Adolescence has been a topic of discussion and research for many years and has been described in many ways. In 1904, G. Stanley Hall wrote:

> Adolescence is a new birth, for the higher and more completely human traits are now born ... [new] qualities to body and soul now emerge ...

suggestive of some ancient period of storm and stress when old moorings were broken and a higher level attained .... Passions and desires spring into vigorous life, but with them normally comes the evolution of higher powers of control and inhibition. (in Dahl & Hariri, 2005, p. 367)

Over the past several years, the literature regarding the uniqueness of adolescence has increased (Fitzgerald, 2005). Adolescence, the period between childhood and adulthood, is a distinct developmental stage in most cultures, a time with a great deal of change related to cognitive control and affective processes (Hardin, Schroth, Pine, & Ernst, 2007). The exact nature of adolescence, however, varies a great deal from culture to culture. In some cultures, where children have to grow up quickly to carry out certain responsibilities, adolescence barely exists. In other cultures, such as in the United States, adolescence continues for many years, often extending well past age 20.

In the United States, approximately 15 million students were enrolled in grades 9–12 in 2006, and this number was expected to increase by more than 600,000 by the year 2017. In addition to students in public schools, another 1.3 million students in grades 9–12 were in private schools (National Center for Education Statistics [NCES], 2009).

Definition of Adolescence

Adolescence is the transitional period between childhood and adulthood. It is a period of rapid changes that impact physical and emotional characteristics. Even though adolescence is marked by rapid changes, children do not simply become adults overnight. Rather, this developmental phase is marked by significant changes in their physical, emotional, and sexual make-up. During this period, children want to be adults, but they often are unprepared for the demands of adulthood. They want to be treated as adults, but they are often unable to conduct themselves as adults.

Adolescence has been referred to as the period when an emotionally immature person reaches the final stages of emotional development. It may be thought of as a time of crisis, when major changes in a person's life cause confusion and turmoil (Woolfolk, 2010). Students who have disabilities must face the typical problems of adolescence with the added burden of their disability. Unfortunately, this makes adolescence more difficult for them than for their nondisabled peers.

The beginning of adolescence is usually marked by puberty, when the body changes and becomes sexually active and capable of reproduction. The ending of adolescence is much less definite, with no physiological marker to indicate that adolescence is complete. Some authorities suggest that adolescence ends when the individual reaches a certain chronological age. Others propose that adolescence ends when the individual achieves economic or emotional independence or both (Shaffer, 2002). When age is used as the upper limit, the question is: What age? Mercer (1997) suggested that adolescence ends after age 22. Others specify age 20 or 21. Still other developmentalists refer to the end of adolescence as "the point at which the individual begins to work and is reasonably independent of parental sanctions" (Shaffer, 2002, p. 4).

Dacey, Kenny, and Margolis (2000) offer a series of questions related to the beginning and ending of adolescence:

- When do their adult hormone levels increase dramatically?
- When do they begin to think about dating?
- When do they begin to develop secondary sex characteristics?
- When do they become moody without reasons?
- When do they become a particular age (e.g., 10, 12, 13)?
- When do they enter a certain school grade?
- When do they engage in certain religious rites?
- When do friendships become more important than family relations?
- When do they begin to question who they are?

Adolescence is marked by major physiological and emotional changes, and teenagers mature in many different ways. Because this developmental period involves such major changes, some professionals divide adolescence into subcategories (Mercer, 1997):

Early adolescence: approximately ages 12 to 15
Middle adolescence: ages 15 to 18
Late adolescence: ages 18 to 22

Regardless of the method of classification, adolescence remains a period of significant transition from childhood to adulthood.

Tasks Associated with Adolescence

The many changes that occur during adolescence result in the need for adolescents to perform a series of significant tasks, including

- developing their sexuality,
- understanding their physical changes,
- becoming self-determinant,
- enhancing their social skills,
- becoming more independent,
- developing peer relationships,
- developing problem-solving abilities and confidence, and
- preparing for their educational and vocational futures.

Everyone going through adolescence must undertake these tasks, but the presence of a disability may affect their accomplishment significantly. For example, students with various disabilities, including language deficits, may have difficulties establishing favorable peer relationships. Table 12.1 summarizes some of the problems that might arise with these tasks as a result of the presence of a disability.

TABLE 12.1
Adolescent Tasks and Problems Resulting from Disabilities

Developmental Tasks	Questions to Consider
1. Creation of a sense of sexuality as part of a personal identity	■ How is this task affected by the presence of a physical disability? ■ Do poor school performance and low social status impact this task?
2. Development of confidence in social interactions	■ Do negative classroom experiences play a role? ■ Do others assume social inadequacy is an automatic result of having a disability?
3. Infusion of social values into a personal code of behavior	■ Do adults protect students with disabilities to such a degree that they do not have experiences that allow them to develop a sense of what social values exist? ■ Does the disability or others' reaction to it prevent experimentation with social behavior?
4. Acceptance of biological changes	■ Are students with disabilities denied accurate information about their own bodies and sexual maturity? ■ Do students with lower intellectual performance sometimes have difficulty gleaning information indirectly or comprehending information?
5. Attainment of a sense of emotional independence	■ Are students with disabilities given the same opportunities as other adolescents to make their own decisions? ■ Do adolescents with disabilities have more difficulty dealing with emotion?
6. Contemplation of vocational interests	■ Are students with disabilities limited in vocational choices because of preconceived notions of their ability? ■ Are vocational training options too tightly tied to labels and not to true individual ability?
7. Identification of personal talents and interests	■ Do students with disabilities have more difficulty identifying positive traits within themselves as a result of the negative events they experience?
8. Awareness of personal weaknesses and strengths	■ Do students focus more on their limitations than strengths? ■ Do students with disabilities have an inaccurate self-concept?
9. Development of sexual interests with nonfamily members	■ If the individual has disabilities, is it more difficult to develop sexual contacts?

(continued)

TABLE 12.1 *(continued)*	
Developmental Tasks	**Questions to Consider**
10. Development of peer relationships	■ Do public prejudices serve as barriers to the development of sexual interests? ■ Do adolescents with disabilities have fewer opportunities to develop peer relationships? ■ Are some students isolated socially by the limitations of their label more than by the actual effects of the condition?
11. Completion of formal educational activities	■ Has PL 94-142 increased the likelihood that formal educational activities will be completed? ■ Should students with disabilities receive special diplomas that identify them as students with disabilities?
12. Preparation for marriage, parenting, and adult relationships	■ Do students with disabilities receive information concerning family responsibilities? ■ Do some community attitudes operate against adolescents so that adult relationships are difficult to achieve?

Source: Adapted from *Mildly Handicapped Children and Adults,* p. 214, by T. E. C Smith, B. J. Price, and G. E. March, 1986, St. Paul: West.

Characteristics of Adolescents

The transition from childhood to adulthood is indeed a complex time (Dahl & Hariri, 2005). Adolescence is characterized by (Lerner & Johns, 2008):

■ conflicts related to freedom and independence versus security and dependence,
■ rapid physical changes,
■ developing sexuality,
■ peer pressure, and
■ self-consciousness.

Although adolescents are an incredible diverse group of individuals, some general characteristics can be associated with most students during this period. The most apparent common characteristic is the physical development into their adult stature and appearance. Usually this physical change is characterized by a rapid growth spurt.

Significant increases in height, strength, and stamina are common during the rapid growth period. In addition, boys develop wider shoulders and girls develop wider hips (Shaffer, 2002). Girls typically begin their growth spurt between the ages of 10 and 11, and it lasts about 3 years. For boys, the rapid growth period begins at about age 12 or 13 and continues for approximately 5 or 6 years (Woolfolk, 2010).

Modern phenomena include the earlier beginning of puberty and the increasing size of people in U.S. society. The average age at which girls experience their first menstrual period dropped from about 14 or 15 at the beginning of the 20th century to 11 or 12 by 1990 (Tanner, 1990). Also, boys and girls are growing bigger and stronger than their parents (Shaffer, 2002). Most adolescents are taller than their parents at the end of their growth period. The earlier onset of puberty and increased growth may be the result of several factors, including better nutrition and medical care.

Sexual maturation of individuals during adolescence is another significant change. Boys and girls become men and women from a sexual perspective. Just as girls' physical growth spurt occurs before boys', girls develop sexually before boys do. The onset of sexual maturity for girls, marked by **menarche**, the beginning of the monthly menstrual cycle, occurs approximately 1–3 years before the onset of sexual maturity for boys. Physical changes in the bodies of girls and boys that accompany sexual maturity include breast development in girls and lowering of the voice in boys.

Physical Development

During adolescence, physical development is one of the most obvious changes. During this time, marked by rapid growth spurts, boys grow up to be men and girls grow up to be women, at least physically. These changes are triggered by significant changes in the levels of hormones produced in the body. Specifically, hormones generated from the thyroid gland, pituitary gland, adrenal cortex, and gonads result in (Sabornie & deBettencourt, 2004):

- rapid changes in height and weight,
- development of secondary sex characteristics and sexual maturity, and
- changes in the skeletal and cardiovascular systems.

Moral Development

In addition, moral development, which begins in childhood, continues through adolescence. The morality of adolescents may be manifested in their attitudes about cheating on schoolwork, aggression toward other persons or property, stealing, and engaging in illegal activities. Adolescents commonly experiment with moral issues during this period. They may shoplift or commit acts of vandalism "just to do it." Adolescents have some inhibitory control issues (Hardin et al., 2007).

Part of the reason that the development of morality is important for adolescents is the increased emphasis on peer approval. Morality as defined by their parents may be replaced by their own thinking along with the thinking of their age peers. This can result in a moral code that is significantly different from that of their parents.

Formal reasoning ability and abstract thinking develop during adolescence. Although intellectual levels remain fairly constant throughout a person's life, specific mental abilities change, as Jean Piaget noted in his research. Adolescents develop the ability to manipulate hypothetical situations and to assimilate information from a variety of sources. These abilities enable them to engage in philosophical and scientific thinking and to plan for their future (Mercer, 1997).

Other characteristics of adolescents may include their

- growing mobility,
- long attention span,
- limited patience for boredom,
- self-motivation, and
- high levels of interaction with their surroundings.

As Mercer (1997) noted, adolescents do not lack motivation, attention, and interaction as long as they are dealing with something in which they are interested. The key—and the challenge for parents and teachers—is to direct these attributes in specific ways.

Challenges Created by Rapid Growth and Sexual Maturation

As a result of rapid physical growth and sexual maturation during this developmental period, adolescents have to get used to their new bodies and physiological changes as well as adjust to these rapid changes. Many adolescents go through a time when they do not like themselves. They do not like the way they look, the way they act, or the way they feel. Normal skin problems in the form of acne may cause an adolescent to withdraw from contact with peers.

In addition to dealing with the physical and sexual changes, adolescents face emotional issues associated with this period. Acceptance of their changing bodies, the importance of peer acceptance, doubts about self-concept, and often growing tensions with parents can create difficulties. Frequently, the end result is a feeling of being "mixed up." Adolescents may cry easily, snap at their parents, and behave in ways that they themselves do not understand.

As noted, a common characteristic of individuals during the adolescent years is the strong influence of peers (Mercer, 1997). For many adolescents, peer group membership and peer approval both take precedence over parental influence. Peers become more important as children move into adolescence, and peer conformity pressures do not peak until mid-adolescence, "when teenagers are highly susceptible to peer-group norms" (Shaffer, 2002, p. 617). The increase in peer pressure is often concomitant with a decrease in parental influence. This in itself can result in problems.

Although the greater influence of peers is difficult for many parents to accept, it is simply a reality that must be considered in parental and adolescent relationships. The influence of teachers over adolescents also lessens during this period. Teachers, like parents, must understand the important role of peer relationships and must work within those relationships. Attempting to sabotage peer relationships will likely backfire, actually making it more difficult for parents and teachers to establish a relationship with the adolescent.

Characteristics of Adolescents with Disabilities

Some characteristics of adolescents seem to be exacerbated by a disability. Adolescents with learning disabilities exhibit more risk-taking behavior than their nondisabled peers (McNamara, Vervaeke, & Willoughby, 2008). This risk-taking behavior is likely the result of developmental changes in cognitive and affective processing during adolescence (Dahl & Hariri, 2005; Hardin et al., 2007). When combined with attention deficit/hyperactivity disorder, adolescents with learning disabilities engaged in even more risk-taking behaviors, including smoking, alcohol use, marijuana use, and sexual activity.

Martinez and Semrud-Clikeman (2004) studied the emotional adjustment of adolescents with single and multiple learning disabilities and compared these groups with nondisabled adolescents. The findings revealed that students with single and multiple learning disabilities, compared to adolescents without disabilities,

- were more socially immature,
- displayed poorer social skills,
- perceived a greater sense of inadequacy, and
- displayed greater signs of maladjustment.

Often, students with learning disabilities are uncertain about their own learning problems. In a qualitative study by Klassen and Lynch (2007), the teachers who were interviewed thought that students with learning disabilities were unaware of their own learning strengths and weaknesses. Added to this, they found that students with learning disabilities did not have the same confidence level as their nondisabled peers.

Adolescents with disabilities are also more prone to dropping out of school than are other students. Daniel et al. (2006) found the school drop-out rate for students with reading problems was six times greater than typical readers. Their findings also indicated that this group of students had significantly more suicide attempts and suicidal ideation as well as more conduct disorders and oppositional defiant disorders.

Academic Deficits

By definition, students identified as having disabilities have academic deficits. That is, the definitions applied to determine the eligibility of students for special education programs include the criterion that the disability must adversely affect the student's educational performance (Smith, Polloway, Patton, & Dowdy, 2008). In reviewing the definitions and characteristics of any of the major disability categories, including mental retardation, learning disabilities, attention deficit disorders (ADD), autism, behavioral disorders, and all others eligible for special education services under IDEA, problems with academics is a consistent issue.

For students with language disorders, the language problem itself could be the primary cause of the academic problem. Difficulties in reading, listening, written expression, and oral language could easily lead directly to academic problems.

Social Skill Deficits

In addition to deficits in academic skills, most adolescents with disabilities have problems with social skills. These students often display inappropriate behaviors and have difficulties with personal relationships (Smith et al., 2008). Problems of this kind will likely affect interrelationships with age peers, parents, and teachers.

Social skills are critically important for students' success academically and later, in postsecondary education and employment settings. Although most students develop social skills naturally, some, especially those with disabilities, have trouble with social skills. Many students with higher functioning disabilities, such as learning disabilities and ADD, have social skills deficits to the extent that that they are actually part of the criteria used to define the disability (Gresham, Sugai, & Horner, 2001). Deficits in social skills influence many different types of disabilities including

- learning disabilities (Hallahan, Kauffman, & Pullen, 2005; Estell, et al., 2008),
- autism (Welton, Vakil, & Carasea, 2004),
- visual and hearing impairments (Smith, et al., 2008),
- emotional problems (Smith, et al., 2008), and
- health and physical impairments (Best, Heller, & Bigge, 2005; Hardman, Drew, & Egan, 2008).

Social skill deficits are not caused directly by most disabilities but, rather, develop because some of these students lack opportunities to develop social skills, are easily distracted, and pay little attention to their environment where they could observe and model appropriate social skills, or have emotional problems that interfere with the development and use of appropriate social skills (Smith, Gartin, & Murdick, in press).

Unfortunately, limited social skills often results in lack of acceptance by peers and others—something that is critically important for adolescents (Boutot, 2007). With adolescents wanting so strongly to be accepted by their peers, peer rejection, resulting from social skills or any other reason, can have a detrimental impact on their self-concept and development.

Motivation Problems

Motivation and learning are often interrelated. Without motivation, students at the secondary level may exert limited effort toward any learning task. Motivation, however, can be enhanced by positive reinforcement (Woolfolk, 2010). This reinforcement can be teacher designed, or it can be the result of a natural reinforcer for the student. For example, in language training, the adolescent may be motivated to improve his oral language skills because of a desire to ask a girl on a date, which would require certain oral language competency. This pending action would be a natural reinforcer and could motivate the student to work on improving his language skills.

Several studies have revealed that students classified as having various disabilities, including mental retardation, learning disabilities, or behavior disorders, have frequent problems with motivation (Smith et al., 2008). By the time students with these disabilities reach adolescence, they may have gone through several years of failure and frustration, which only leads to continued low motivation. As a result, they may have stopped exerting any effort in academic tasks, resulting in continuing academic failure. This lack of motivation can lead to limited efforts in writing and other language skill development, which adds to the lack of academic success (Meyer, Pisha, & Rose, 1991).

Behavior Problems

Behavior problems are fairly common in adolescents with disabilities. For students classified as emotionally disturbed, problem behaviors are widespread (Smith et al., 2008). Even though adolescents with mental retardation and learning disabilities may not exhibit the severity or frequency of behavior problems as students identified as having behavior disorders, they frequently have behavior problems that are likely to result, at least in part, from frustration and low self-esteem.

Deficits in language skills can add to levels of frustration and self-esteem and, thus, more behavior problems. Therefore, direct interventions targeting language disorders could have a positive impact on behavior problems. When working with adolescents, educators should realize that behaviors rarely occur in a vacuum. Rather, they serve a function. By identifying the function of behaviors, educators may be able to impact behaviors positively.

Psychological Problems

Many adolescents with disabilities have a variety of psychological problems, including feelings of anger, incompetence, inadequacy, and frustration; behaviors of impulsivity and boldness; and a lack of motivation, excessive dependency, and shyness (Ness & Price, 1990). These behaviors, which may be the consequence of years of failure, can create many problems for students.

Language disorders, as noted, can lead to academic problems as well as problems associated with social skills, behaviors, and motivation. For example, students who are rejected by their peers because of language disorders or other disabilities may develop psychological difficulties associated with this rejection or failure.

■General Problems Facing Adolescents

Because adolescence is characterized by transition and turbulence, it is not surprising that many problems arise during this developmental period. Indeed, most adolescents face a host of challenges that reflect this developmental period. The most consequential of these are suicidal thoughts and suicide, drug and alcohol abuse, and pregnancy (Shaffer, 2002). Not all adolescents have these problems, of course, but they are prevalent enough to consider here. If students have disabilities, these concerns can become even more problematic.

Suicide and Suicidal Ideation

Suicide has become a leading problem among adolescents in the United States. "For young people ages 15 to 24, the suicide rate has tripled in the past 30 years" (Woolfolk, 2010, p. 106). Suicide now is the third leading cause of death for adolescents aged 15–24. In 2006, the number of deaths from suicide among 15- to 19-year-olds was 8.2 per 100,000 (National Institute of Mental Health [NIMH], 2009). Although this figure is alarming, the number of students who survive suicide attempts or consider suicide is even more unsettling.

> A nationwide survey of youth in grades 9–12 in public and private schools in the United States found that 15% of students reported seriously considering suicide, 11% reported creating a plan, and 7% reported trying to take their own life in the 12 months preceding the survey. (Centers for Disease Control and Prevention [CDC], 2009a)

Students with disabilities are even more at risk for suicide than their peers without disabilities. Adolescents with learning and behavior problems are likely to develop frustration and depression, which can lead to suicidal behaviors. Poor social skills, which are frequent in students with disabilities, have been found to be related to depression (Barr & Parrett, 2001). Esposito-Smythers, Spirito, Uth, and LaChance (2007) found that alcohol-abusive students were more likely to have suicidal ideations than their peers.

Several studies have suggested that students with language disabilities are at greater risk for suicidal behaviors than students without these disorders. Daniel et al. (2006) compared the risk of suicidal ideation and suicide attempts among adolescents with and without reading difficulties. The findings were similar to those from other studies, revealing that students with reading disabilities did have significantly higher rates of suicidal ideation and attempts than did students without reading problems.

Drug and Alcohol Abuse

Because of peer pressure, rapid physical changes, and emotional changes, drug and alcohol abuse among adolescents is common. Unfortunately, drug and alcohol abuse become coping mechanisms for many adolescents who are dealing with the need for recognition and acceptance (Woolfolk, 2010).

Of youth surveyed by the CDC (2009b), 44.7% indicated that they had at least one drink of alcohol on at least one day during the past 30 days. Although this reflects a drop from the 50.8% who indicated the same in 1991, it still reflects that nearly half of all youth consume alcohol. In 2007, 23.9% indicated they had consumed alcohol (other than a few sips) for the first time prior to age 13. More startling, 26% indicated that they had had five or more drinks of alcohol in a row, within a couple of hours, on at least one day during the previous 30 days.

Adolescents commonly use drugs. In 2008, 9.3% of adolescents aged 12–17 were current users of illegal drugs. Marijuana was the most frequently used drug, cited by 6.7% of this age group. These rates were down, slightly, from the previous year and more significantly over the past 5 years. In 2002, for example, 8.2% of youths aged 12–17 indicated marijuana use (U.S. Department of Health and Human Services, 2009). Still, with nearly 10% of school-aged adolescents using illegal drugs, drug abuse among this group of students must be a priority for schools.

Teen Pregnancy and Other Problems

In addition to the previously noted problem areas, adolescents with disabilities have higher rates of teen pregnancy than their peers without disabilities (Barr & Parrett, 2001). These problems often stem from low self-esteem (Smith et al., 2008). Adolescence is truly a difficult period for many students, and for those with disabilities, the problems are exacerbated (Smith et al., 2008).

School Demands on Adolescents

In addition to the demands on adolescents resulting from physical and emotional changes, plus the need to be accepted and peer pressure, schools place demands on this group of students. These include the need to

- attend to lectures and take comprehensive notes,
- develop a high level of competence in written expression,
- complete a comprehensive high school curriculum that requires many different kinds of skills,
- read and comprehend a variety of materials,
- work independently,
- listen and take accurate notes,
- participate in oral discussions, and
- organize large amounts of information from a variety of sources.

These demands tied to academic activities are in addition to the social demands necessary for peer and adult approval. Most students in secondary schools meet these demands without major problems, but for students with language deficits, success in many of these areas is impacted.

Most of the academic demands outlined above require competence in oral and written language. Students have to attend to lectures, understand spoken language, and summarize the content of the information in the form of notes. They have to be able to decode language properly through reading, store and retrieve that information, and participate in oral expressive activities. Students with language disabilities or disorders often cannot accomplish these activities. The end result may be general failure across all subject areas. Language competence, a key element in academic success, is especially critical in secondary schools.

Language Problems and Interventions with Adolescents

If children in elementary schools have difficulty with language, this frequently carries over into adolescence. For example, most students diagnosed with dyslexia as children continued to have these issues through adolescence and into adulthood (Kemp, Parrila, & Kirby, 2008). Problems with receptive and expressive language may create monumental problems for students in secondary school. Therefore, secondary special education teachers and speech–language therapists must be prepared to identify language problems and develop appropriate intervention programs. The discussion that follows complements the previous chapters' attention to instructional programs, focusing specifically on concerns surrounding adolescents.

Receptive Language

Students who have difficulty with receptive language are at a major disadvantage in academic settings. For students who have difficulties in listening or reading, achieving success in secondary classrooms is extremely difficult (Meese, 2001). Although deficits in receptive language present problems for elementary and secondary students alike, the problems are more acute for students in secondary programs because of the emphasis of these programs on competency in content areas. Secondary students are expected to learn about history, science, and literature, and this knowledge must be attained through reading and listening. Deficits in receptive language deter the development of competence in these areas.

Reading

One of the most important skills for adolescents is reading. Students must read if they are to be successful in general education classrooms. Although some accommodations, such as audio recordings of materials, can lessen the impact of reading deficits, secondary students who are unable to read and comprehend written materials efficiently in content courses are at a major disadvantage (Mercer & Mercer, 2001).

Reading involves the ability to decode words and comprehend the content. If secondary students are unable to perform these actions, they will not be able to acquire a great deal of content information. It is extremely limiting to acquire information only from oral presentations and discussions. Without the ability to obtain information through reading, students are at a significant disadvantage.

Teachers in secondary schools, both content teachers and special education teachers, have to provide assistance to students with reading problems. Whereas teaching reading is an assumed task for teachers at the elementary level, confusion often arises concerning reading instruction at the secondary level (Smith et al., 2008). All teachers, however, whether they are secondary special education teachers, biology teachers, or English teachers, must assume the responsibility for helping students learn to read.

Teaching reading is a major concern of all teachers at the secondary level. They are unlikely to have reading groups and use basal reading series, but they nevertheless should engage in improving the reading skills of adolescents. Most secondary schools do not employ teachers to focus on reading instruction, so all teachers should share in this responsibility. Reading is important in all content areas.

Although the bulk of remedial reading programs and strategies are designed for elementary students, several methods target adolescents. Teachers need to carefully plan reading interventions with adolescents to ensure that they are not wasting the students' time. This means that if one strategy is ineffective, teachers should implement different strategies.

Students' reading vocabulary is critical for their overall academic success. When students do not know words they come across in their reading assignments, they likely will not understand the assignment, leading to failure in the subject area. An inadequate vocabulary can also result in such tedious, slow reading that students will quickly get bored with the reading process, with a negative effect on their fluency and comprehension. For these reasons, teaching vocabulary should be a key component of reading instruction for secondary students.

Teachers of content courses can utilize instructional opportunities that facilitate not only learning of the content but also improvement of reading skills (Tompkins, 2002).

In comprehending reading materials in content areas, students must understand certain frequently used terms. Woodward and Peters developed a listing of these terms in 1983 that are still relevant today. Table 12.2 lists words across subject areas that secondary students need to be able to read and understand.

Many adolescents with reading problems can benefit from instruction in how to use strategies for comprehension. An example of a strategy to help students read for content is the SQ3R method. Using this strategy, students

- Survey the material to be read,
- develop Questions about the material while surveying,
- Read the material looking for answers to the questions,
- Recite or ask questions about what was read, and
- Review the material over the next few days.

In addition to SQ3R, numerous strategies might be helpful for students with reading problems. Table 12.3 summarizes some of these strategies.

TABLE 12.2

Important Words for Specific Purposes

Words Used in Cause-and-Effect Patterns

why	as a result of	reasons	so that
if	the effect of	since	hence
so	on account of	therefore	thus
cause	due to	consequently	
because	outcome	this led to that	

Words Used in Sequence Patterns

first	next	later	in 1943	secondly
second	then	still later	in 1958	thirdly
third	finally	later on	after that	eventually
yesterday	tomorrow	last	to begin	to sum up
today	steps	lastly	procedure	
in conclusion		at last	plans	

Words Used in Listing Patterns

several	kind(s)	way(s)	one	number words:
many	type(s)	varieties	another	one, two, three
series	style(s)	in addition	still another	types
few	couple	some	an example	third kind

Words Used in Comparison/Contrast Patterns

different	but	compare
different from	on one hand	both
similar	on the other hand	as well as
same	however	not only
alike	contrast	but also
not alike	although	either . . . so
while	than	unless
yet	equally important	on the contrary
in spite of		

Source: From *The Learning Disabled Adolescent*, pp 47–48, by D. M. Woodward and D. J. Peters, 1983, Austin, TX: Pro-Ed. Copyright 1983 by Aspen Publishers, Inc. Reprinted with permission.

    The key is for students to have a systematic method to increase their comprehension. Teachers must remember that what works with one student may not work with another student. Therefore, they must be prepared to provide a variety of strategies and supports to secondary students with reading difficulties.

TABLE 12.3
Literacy Strategies for Adolescents

DR-TA (Directed Reading–Thinking Activity) (Ruddell, 2008)
- A four-part method
- Helps students develop comprehension and higher-level thinking skills
- Steps include (1) brainstorm what students already know a topic, (2) predict what will happen, (3) read the passage, and (4) discuss what was read
- Helps students read specific content (Allen, 2004)
- Helps develop metacognitive skills (Unrau, 2008)

ReQuest
- Used individually or groups
- Uses text material questioning—student reads text followed by questioning (Ruddell, 2008)
- Step one—students and the teacher **read** materials
- Step two—students generate **questions**
- Step three—teacher adds prepared questions

List-Group-Label (Allen, 2004)
- Uses brainstorming before reading
- Small groups develop a word list based on everyone's input
- Helps students identify and expand their word lists

Cluster Strategies
- Visual arrangements of terms, events, people, or ideas (Unrau, 2008)
- Assist students in understanding relationships between concepts as well as understanding discipline specific vocabulary (Roe, Stoodt-Hill & Burns, 2007)
- May use words or pictures to clarify clusters of concepts and relationships
- *Semantic map* is one example
- May include a theme or concept (*concept mastery maps*)
- Helps students develop meaning to content

Group Mapping Activity (GMA)
- Students develop visual and/or written representation of what has been read
- Present and describe map to the class
- Can evaluate student understanding
- Semantic Feature Analysis (SFA)

Context-Structure-Sound-Reference (CSSR)
- Good readers use to identify unknown word
- Step one—students read unknown word and guess the meaning
- Step two—students analyze the structural features of the unknown word (word root, suffixes or prefixes, plurals, ending, possessives)
- Step three—use phonetic skills to decode word
- Step four—use reference materials

Listening and Attention

In addition to reading for content, adolescents acquire a great deal of information through listening. Listening and taking notes are critical for students in many secondary classrooms because lecturing and classroom discussions are used regularly for providing information (Smith, et al., 2008). This means that students first must be able to attend to the teacher or others who may be providing information. This reveals the criticality of good listening skills for adolescents. Unfortunately, listening has long been neglected as an area for instruction (Tompkins, 2002).

Some students are competent listeners. They "tune in" to the person speaking and are able to comprehend much of the information. Other students, especially those with disabilities, have problems with listening. Teachers must develop programs that will enhance these students' listening and auditory comprehension skills (Smith et al., 2008). Without competence in these areas, students will probably not be able to learn lecture material.

A model presented by Forster and Doyle (1989) provides a way to direct students' attention during listening activities. This model requires students to listen to a simulated newscast and later summarize its contents. Students use an outline to avoid being distracted during the exercise. Outlines, advance organizers, and other means of facilitating attention to auditory input may enable students to attend to a lecture or other verbal discourse long enough to acquire information.

Expressive Language

Just as some adolescents have problems with receptive language, some adolescents have difficulty expressing themselves orally and in writing. The inability to perform in these areas can create major academic problems for students at the secondary level. Not only are students in secondary schools expected to express themselves in writing and orally, but virtually all of the information that teachers receive from these students is either written or oral. Students complete written assignments, take written tests, engage in oral discussions, and respond to oral questions. Obviously, students with difficulties in these areas will have major problems in secondary classes.

Written Expression

Written expression can be described as the expression of thoughts in written format through expressive language. It is a complex cognitive process that is critical for adolescents when expressing what they have learned or what they want others to know. Written expression is composed of three specific stages: prewriting, writing, and postwriting. Writing can be broken into several steps effectively, including the following (*Study Guides and Strategies,* 2009):

■ Develop your topic.
■ Identify your audience.

- Research your topic.
- Organize and prewrite the paper.
- Develop an initial draft, and write a completed paper.
- Revise the paper.
- Proofread for the final version.

Although dividing a writing assignment into these steps will not guarantee success, it does provide students with a structure for completing the task—something that many students, especially those with deficits in written expression, need so they can be successful.

Effective written expression requires a number of skills: Students must be able to put their thoughts together in a coherent manner, physically write the words either manually or electronically, spell appropriately, and use proper punctuation and adhere to other grammar rules. Intervention programs for students who need help with written expression can take an isolated skill approach or a more holistic approach. The isolated skill approach teaches specific skills involved in written expression, such as handwriting, spelling, and syntax.

A drawback to this method is that these skills may not become integrated. After completing a remedial program that takes an isolated skill approach, a student may thoroughly understand of the rules of grammar but may not be able to apply these skills in spontaneous writing, which should be the ultimate goal of any writing program. Another disadvantage is that teachers who use this method tend to criticize discrete errors in student writing rather than to judge the entire writing effort (Gould, 1991).

In taking the more holistic approach to remediation in written expression, students learn writing skills by writing. The overall writing process is taken into account, not just skills related to handwriting, spelling, and syntax. By teaching writing as a collection of different skill rather than as isolated skills, teachers help to prepare students to be spontaneous writers as well as writers who take advantage of planning opportunities that lead to writing.

When writing is taught as a comprehensive set of activities, the following areas are generally included (Tompkins, 2002):

- Prewriting—determining topic and general outline
- Writing—composing a draft
- Responding—reacting to conferences with the teacher
- Revising—making revisions based on content conferences
- Editing—making final changes in content and style
- Publishing—working with the teacher to finalize the product

Students must learn that written expression is not something than can be done successfully without attention to detail. Well-written products are usually the result of numerous drafts and rewrites. If students follow a model similar to the one suggested by Tompkins (2002), they will become accustomed to this process.

Among the numerous strategies for helping students develop written language skills are brainstorming, quick writing, writing prompts, self-talk, and telling personal stories. Figure 12.1 describes a variety of strategies suggested by Tralli, Colombo, Deshler, and Schumaker (1996). Regardless of the specific strategy selected, students must be given opportunities for writing and receive proper reinforcement and feedback during the process.

Sometimes secondary students have difficulty simply choosing what they want to write about. Teachers can provide them with a wide range of topics from which to choose. Some ideas might are

- letters to friends,
- letters of inquiry about a job,
- a biography,
- a short story about something that happened to the student, or
- a summary of things you want to do during the summer.

Spelling

One component of written expression in which many students have problems is spelling. Although spelling, along with the use of proper grammar, may not be emphasized during the beginning of a program to teach written expression, it should be considered after securing initial interest in writing. At the secondary level, spelling instruction should be integrated into the total academic curriculum rather than dealt with in isolation. Spelling should be a component of history, science, English, and all other academic areas in which written products are expected outcomes.

A spelling approach described by Dangel (1987) should appeal to adolescents. The model, which uses the game of football as a basis for the program, is called "The Coach's Spelling Approach." It has three steps: scouting, practicing, and keeping stats. Table 12.4 lists the actions for each step.

Another method for assisting secondary students with spelling is paired proofreading. Pairs of students proofread sample student papers and mark misspelled words, then correct them (Tompkins, 2002).

Handwriting

Handwriting instruction at the secondary level must be integrated into other parts of the curriculum. Just as reading instruction is the responsibility of all teachers, so is handwriting. In the following ways, secondary teachers can implement instruction in handwriting in the context of subject matter:

- Require written work.
- Require written work to be neat and legible.
- Give extra or bonus points for written work that is neat and legible.
- Give students the opportunity to rewrite work that is poorly written.
- Develop activities for students to write letters to various people and groups (such as letters to the editor or letters to U.S. troops overseas) to encourage pride in written work.

Sentence Writing Strategy. Teaches students how to recognize and generate four types of sentences: simple, compound, complex, and compound–complex.

Paragraph Writing Strategy. Teaches students how to write well-organized, complete paragraphs by outlining ideas, selecting a point of view and tense for the paragraph, sequencing ideas, and checking their work.

Error Monitoring Strategy. Teaches students a process for detecting and correcting errors in their writing and for producing a neater written product. Students are taught to locate errors in paragraph organization, sentence structure, capitalization, overall editing and appearance, punctuation, and spelling by asking themselves a series of questions. Students correct their errors and rewrite the passage before submitting it to their teacher.

Theme Writing Strategy. Teaches students to write a five-paragraph theme. They learn how to generate ideas for themes and how to organize those ideas into a logical sequence. Then they learn how to write the paragraphs, monitor errors, and rewrite the theme.

Assignment Completion Strategy. Teaches students to monitor their assignment from the time an assignment is given until it is completed and submitted to the teacher. Students write down assignments; analyze the assignments; schedule various subtasks; complete the subtasks and, ultimately, the entire task; and submit the completed assignment.

Test-Taking Strategy. Aids students during test taking. Students are taught to allocate time and read instructions and questions carefully. A question is either answered or abandoned for later consideration. The obviously wrong answers are eliminated from the abandoned questions and a reasonable guess is made. The last step is to survey the entire test for unanswered questions.

Brainstorming. Sessions are very short and focused (no more than 3 to 5 minutes). Given a general theme or topic, students call out whatever comes to mind related to that topic, and someone records all responses. Brainstorming can be done as a whole group with the teacher recording responses, or most effectively in partners or small cooperative groups. It is very helpful to keep writing tablets or a single whiteboard with dry-erase pen readily available for this purpose. A large-group sharing can follow partner or small-group work.

Writing Prompts. Students are provided with a stimulus such as a poem, story, picture, song, or news items to prompt writing. Teachers keep a file of pictures from magazines, old calendars, postcards, etc., as stimuli for writing activities.

Self-Talk. Teaches students to self-talk through the planning stage of their writing with such questions as, "Who am I writing for? Why am I writing this? What do I know? What does my reader need to know?"

Telling Personal Stories. In cooperative groups, students orally respond to prompts such as, "Can you remember a time you got sick right before something you really wanted to do?" by telling personal stories. After the oral telling and sharing of stories in small, cooperative groups, students write a rough draft or outline of the story they told.

Source: From "The Strategies Intervention Model: A Model for Supported Inclusion at the Secondary Level," by R. Tralli, B. Colombo, D. D. Deshler, and J. B. Schumaker, 1996, in *Remedial and Special Education, 17,* p. 206; and from *How to Reach and Teach All Students in the Inclusive Classroom,* pp. 326–327, by S. F. Rief and J. A. Heimburge, 1996, West Nyack, NY: Center for Applied Research in Education.

FIGURE 12.1

Strategies for Written Expression

TABLE 12.4
Remedial Spelling Approach: The Coach's Spelling Approach

Activities	Description
Scouting the week's spelling words	1. Learn to recognize words 2. Identify tendencies of words 3. Identify difficult words that will require more practice time
Practice words	1. Select a practice approach 2. Practice until mastery
Keep statistics	1. Keep records of success 2. Adjust practice based on performance statistics

Source: From "The Coach's Spelling Approach," by H .L. Dangel, 1987, *Teaching Exceptional Children, 19,* pp. 21–22. Copyright 1987 by Pearson Education, Inc.

Oral Expression

Some adolescents have problems with oral expression. They may have difficulty presenting information orally, responding orally to teachers and peers, or both. Participation in class discussion, a common teaching technique in secondary schools (Masters, Mori, & Mori, 1999), is hampered by students' difficulties with oral expression, and these students often do not want to engage in oral discussion.

Rief and Heimburge suggested Quick-Talks as a way to get students involved in class discussions. Ways to conduct Quick-Talks include the following (1996, pp. 337–338):

■ Each child is asked to speak constantly for 15, 30, or 45 seconds. The students must actively talk for the full amount of time. This is something like a Quick-Write—only this is a Quick-Talk. (One or two "verbally comfortable" students may be asked to model this exercise first. Their doing so usually adds a bit of comic relief, as peers find it funny to watch these students mentally search for things to say nonstop!)

This exercise works well after a vacation period, when the teacher may ask, "What did you do during vacation?" If that question were not part of a Quick-Talk activity, many upper-grade students would typically respond by saying, "Nothing." However, when asked to Quick-Talk their response, they have a very pleasurable experience. After that warm-up, the students seem more eager to share with the rest of the class.

A Quick-Talk exercise might also be the springboard to a writing assignment, for the exercise gives students a foundation on which to build. Teachers should probably mention to the class that most students will use one long run-on sentence connected, of course, with "ands."

- With this Quick-Talk variation, students are told that they may not use the word "and" for the entire time they are talking. This restriction makes the exercise a little more complicated and extends its purpose. Tape-recording several students and letting them listen to the tape can prove very helpful. Teachers may want to videotape themselves doing this activity. Most find it an eye-opening experience!
- To continue with this same idea, students might next be asked to speak for the entire number of seconds without saying "uh" or "um."

Expressive Vocabulary

Students must have a sufficient vocabulary to be able to express themselves effectively. Though many students develop a good vocabulary through reading and exposure to new words in their language environment, some do not have ample opportunities to develop their vocabularies. For these students, teachers must develop and implement vocabulary-building activities. Three such examples follow:

1. The teacher has students choose one new word each day, make up a sentence using the word, and state the sentence to the teacher at a designated time during the day.
2. The teacher divides the class into two teams and has members of the team take turns in properly using words the teacher calls out in a sentence.
3. Students are instructed to listen to the news each evening and make a list of unknown words. The next day, after looking up the meanings of the words, the students are to use each word properly in a sentence.

Developing activities for teaching expressive vocabulary just requires creativity on the teacher's part. The key is to encourage students to use their oral expressive skills and to positively reinforce the use of these skills.

Pragmatics

Pragmatics, the functional use of language, is a primary area of concern for adolescents. Sands, Kosleski, and French (2000) described pragmatics as the ways in which language is used to communicate in different situations. If students are unable to express themselves in a functional manner, making their wishes, needs, feelings, and responses understood, their oral language efforts may be wasted. The importance of pragmatics, especially for adolescents, cannot be overemphasized.

Practicing the functional use of language is the best method for students to learn the proper use of language. Instructional activities emphasizing pragmatics were provided previously in this text. These activities involve modeling, prompting, immediate reinforcement, and self-correction. The following are examples of activities to use in promoting pragmatics with adolescent students (Polloway & Patton, 2008, p. 220):

- Initiate and close conversations appropriately
- Select appropriate topics of conversation

- Make contributions to the conversation truthful
- Make contributions to the conversation relevant
- Matching oral and nonverbal messages
- Detecting and displaying emotion through facial expression
- Maintaining socially acceptable distance
- Maintaining appropriate eye contact

Teaching pragmatics to adolescents requires gaining their confidence and trust and helping them feel good about their ability to use oral language. Structuring the classroom environment to support students in their use of oral language is essential. Teachers have to remember the importance of pragmatics for adolescents with language deficiencies and facilitate appropriate language usage with this population.

General Instructional Considerations with Adolescents

Teaching adolescents who have language problems requires specific intervention techniques. Individual students' strengths and weaknesses, determined through comprehensive assessment, will determine the specific nature of the instructional program. Several general intervention strategies, however, should be considered with any program.

One thing that may be overlooked in secondary schools for adolescents with language disabilities is the importance of the school climate.

> Many school leaders do not appreciate the fact that producing a good school culture, fostering healthy child and adolescent development, and promoting sound academic learning are interactive and mutually facilitating processes. (Comer, 2005, p. 769)

Student Motivation

For students to achieve success with any intervention program, they must be motivated to participate and put forth effort (Shaffer, 2002). A key element in motivating adolescents to participate in a program is to gain their involvement early, because student involvement leads to a sense of ownership in the program. Home influences and peer influences play an important role in this regard. As noted previously, peer influences are extremely important during adolescence. Therefore, school personnel must take this into consideration in motivating students. Regardless of the importance of peers, family members, too, will continue to be instrumental in the motivation of students, especially in the values they place on student achievement (Shaffer, 2002). Esposito-Smythers et al., (2006) found a positive impact when using a cognitive-behavioral treatment approach with students experiencing suicidal ideations.

Curricular Options

The content of the secondary curriculum is a factor in language intervention programs for adolescents. At the secondary level, the curriculum is typically arranged in three areas: college preparatory, general academic, and vocational. Students choose among these curricular areas based on their long-range plans and current abilities. Factors involved in their decisions might include teachers' recommendations, parental desires, their own ambitions, an understanding of capabilities and demands, and peer approval.

Although curriculum choices are important at all grade levels, K through 12, curriculum is most important at the secondary level (Polloway, Patton, Epstein, & Smith, 1989). For students with mild disabilities, three alternative curricular orientations are generally available: (a) remediation, (b) maintenance, and (c) functionality. Remediation covers both academic remediation and social skills remediation. The maintenance option offers students the supports necessary to succeed in general education classroom programs and includes tutoring and instruction in learning strategies. The functionality curriculum deals with the skills necessary for independent living.

For students with and without disabilities, the options of college preparatory, general academic, and vocational are available, but students with disabilities also might need the assistance provided by remediation, maintenance, or functionality. Language intervention for students with disabilities falls within this framework. Because language intervention is most successful when it is implemented in natural settings through spontaneous language exchanges, it may take place in any of the curricular options discussed.

Study Skills

Of particular interest to many secondary students with disabilities is success in integrated, general education classrooms. Study skills intervention can facilitate this success. Even though the development of appropriate study skills should begin during the elementary school years, the application of study skills has particular relevance for adolescents in secondary school programs (Polloway et al., 2008).

Study skills can be defined as those skills that enable a student to acquire, store and retrieve, and express information adequately for success in academic and social environments. Examples of study skills are listening, note-taking and outlining, report writing, time management, and self-management of behavior (Smith et al., 2008). Students with language problems can benefit substantially from study skills intervention. For example, as mentioned, listening is a key to success in secondary classes. If students have a weakness in this area, learning how to listen or how to maximize their listening skills is critical (Tompkins, 2002).

Study skills can be effective in enhancing both receptive and expressive language. For example, providing assistance in listening, note-taking, and reading skills facilitates receptive language abilities, and providing assistance in oral expression and organizing materials for written output improves expressive language (Smith et al., 2008; Tompkins, 2002). Table 12.5 describes some commonly used study skills and their significance for learning.

Accommodations

Accommodations are similar to study skills in that they facilitate the success of students with disabilities in integrated general education classrooms. The difference is that accommodations are efforts by the teacher to modify the environment and curriculum in such a way that students with disabilities can achieve success, whereas study skills are strategies that students can use to facilitate their own success. Teachers can make numerous accommodations to increase the likelihood of success for adolescents with language problems.

TABLE 12.5
Study Skills and Their Significance for Learning

Study Skill	Significance for Learning
Reading Rate	Rates vary with type and length of reading materials; students need to adjust rate of content.
Listening	Ability to listen is critical in most educational tasks and throughout life.
Note-Taking/Outlining	Ability to take notes and develop outlines is critical in content courses and essential for future study.
Report Writing	Written reports are frequently required in content courses.
Oral Presentations	Some teachers require extensive oral reporting.
Graphic Aids	Visual aids can help students who have reading deficits understand complex material.
Test-Taking	Students must be able to do well on tests if they are to succeed in content courses.
Reference Material/ Dictionary Usage	Using reference materials makes learners more independent.
Time Management	Ability to manage and allocate time is critical for success in secondary settings.
Self-Management of Behavior	Self-management assists students in assuming responsibility and leads to independence.

Source: From *Teaching Students with Special Needs in Inclusive Settings* (4th ed., p. 479), by T. E. C. Smith, E. A. Polloway, J. R. Patton, and C. A. Dowdy, 2008, Boston: Allyn & Bacon. Copyright 2008 by Pearson Education, Inc. Reprinted with permission

Many adolescents with language disabilities display poor organizational skills (Smith et al., 2008). Unfortunately, this often leads to problems in a variety of academic areas, including reading, note taking, writing papers, and studying for tests. Helping students organize themselves can enhance their likelihood for success in secondary classes. This often requires only simple procedures such as advanced organizers or post-organizers (Salend, 2008).

Advanced organizers help students prepare for the lesson, and post-organizers can help students organize the information after the lesson. Advanced organizers can be oral, in which the teacher might say,

> Class, for the next 30 minutes we are going to learn how to prepare to dissect a frog. First we will get out our lab kits, then we will inventory and make sure all parts of the lab kit are present, and finally we will organize our work bench to prepare for the dissection.

This oral outline helps students know what will be taking place during the lesson.

After the lesson, post-organizers help students organize the information they have learned. For example, after preparing for the frog dissection, the teacher might say,

> Class, remember how to prepare for the dissection. First we took out our lab kits, inventoried them, and made sure that all components were in working order. Then we organized our work table to be ready to dissect the frog.

This summary helps students remember the things they just learned.

In addition to the organizers, students may use graphic organizers. This form of organizer provides students with a visual organizational tool that teachers can use to help students get the most out of their lessons (Baxendell, 2003). The intent of the numerous types of graphic organizers is to provide a way for students to acquire, store, and retrieve information.

▌General School Survival Skills

When secondary special education teachers attend only to remediating academic deficits, students often fail in general education classes, because they lack certain survival skills (Schaeffer, Zigmond, Kerr, & Heidi, 1990). School survival skills have been defined as "those skills that enable students to meet the demands of the regular curriculum, or regular educators, and of large-group instruction" (Kerr, Nelson, & Lambert, 1987, p. 86). These skills also have been called "teacher-pleasing behaviors" because they can result in positive interactions between student and teacher. These skills greatly enhance the likelihood that students with language disabilities will be successful in the classroom.

For many of these students, including those with language problems, teaching survival skills is an important instructional component. Schaeffer et al. (1990) named six different survival skills that some secondary students need to develop to achieve success:

1. Attending class
2. Arriving promptly
3. Going to class prepared
4. Meeting assignment deadlines
5. Talking to teachers appropriately
6. Reading and following directions

Although these guidelines may seem obvious, many students simply do not adhere to them. Students who do not have disabilities may be able to get by without some of these skills, but for students with disabilities, pleasing teachers may be a critical component for success. Therefore, teaching school survival skills is essential for many students. Table 12.6 suggests some activities that can be used to teach school survival skills.

TABLE 12.6
Activities to Teach School Survival Skills

Survival Skill	Activity
Attending Class and Punctuality	■ Use hall monitors in the school ■ Require written passes; have assigned seats ■ Relate attendance and punctuality to real-life jobs, such as airport security and traffic police officers
Class Preparedness	■ Require students to bring materials to class ■ Establish clear expectations ■ Use peers to ask questions related to class preparedness
Meeting Assignment Deadlines	■ Establish clear assignments and deadlines ■ Develop self-monitoring of assignments ■ Ask questions daily to require self-monitoring ■ Use peers to ask questions related to meeting assignments ■ Require some assignments each day

Source: Adapted from *Helping Adolescents with Learning and Behavior Problems*, pp. 90–104, by M. M. Kerr, C. M. Nelson, and D. L. Lambertt, 1987, Columbus, OH: Charles E. Merrill Publishing.

▐ Summary

Adolescence in U.S. society is a time of transition that is frequently associated with turbulence, including various physical changes and emotional difficulties. Adolescents with disabilities often have academic, social, and emotional problems. Although some difficulties are typical of all adolescents, adolescents with disabilities have a tendency to exhibit them more severely. The unique language problems of adolescents with disabilities include problems with receptive and expressive language.

Methods for providing instruction to adolescents with language problems include strategies to help students with reading and listening problems as well as ways to provide effective intervention for problems in written expression, spelling, handwriting, oral expression, expressive vocabulary, and pragmatics.

Intervention strategies that should be considered with any program for students with disabilities include enhancing student motivation, providing instruction in study skills, making accommodations in materials, and teaching general school survival skills.

▐ References

Barr, R. D., & Parrett, W. H. (2001). *Hope fulfilled for at-risk youth* (2nd ed.). Boston: Allyn & Bacon.

Baxendell, B. W. (2003). Consistent, coherent, creative: The 3Cs of graphic organizers. *Teaching Exceptional Children, 35,* 46–54.

Best, S. J., Heller, K. W., & Bigge, J. L. (2005). *Teaching individuals with physical or multiple disabilities.* (5th ed.). Upper Saddle River, NJ: Pearson.

Boutot, E. A. (2007). Fitting in: Tips for promoting acceptance and friendships for students with autism spectrum disorders in inclusive classrooms. *Intervention in School and Clinic, 42,* 156–161.

Centers for Disease Control and Prevention. (CDC). (2009a). *Suicide prevention.* Retrieved from www.cdc.gov/violenceprevention/pub/youth_suicide.html

Centers for Disease Control and Prevention. (CDC). (2009b). *Healthy Youth.* Retrieved from apps.nccd.cdc.gov/yrbss

Combs, M. (1997). *Developing competent readers and writers for middle grades.* Columbus, OH: Merrill.

Comer, J. P. (2005). Child and adolescent development: The critical missing focus in school reform. *Phi Delta Kappan, 86,* 757–763.

Conti-Ramsden, G. (2009). The field of language impairment is growing up. *Child Language Teaching and Therapy, 25,* 166–168.

Dahl, R. E., & Hariri, A. R. (2005). Lessons from G. Stanley Hall: Connecting new research in biological sciences to the study of adolescent development. *Journal of Research on Adolescence, 15,* 367–382.

Dangel, H. L. (1987). The coach's spelling approach. *Teaching Exceptional Children, 19,* 21–22.

Daniel, S. S., Walsh, A. K., Goldston, D. B., Arnold, E. M., Reboussin, B. A., & Wood, F. B. (2006). Suicidality, school dropout, and reading problems among adolescents. *Journal of Learning Disabilities, 39,* 507–514.

Dacey, J. , Kenny, M., & Margolis, D. (2000). *Adolescent development* (3rd ed.). Carrolltoin, TX: Alliance Press.

Eposito-Smythers, C., Spirito, A., Uth, R., & LaChance, H. (2006). Cognitive behavioral treatment for suicidal alcohol abusing adolescents: Development and pilot testing. *American Journal of Addictions, 15,* 126–130.

Estell, D. B., Jones, M. H., Pearl, R., Acker, V., Farmer, R., Rodkin, T. W., & Phillip, C. (2008). Peer groups, popularity, and social preference. *Journal of Learning Disabilities, 41,* 5–14.

Fitzgerald, B. (2005). An existential view of adolescent development. *Adolescence, 40,* 793–799.

Forster, R., & Doyle, B. A. (1989). Teaching listening skills to students with attention deficit disorders. *Teaching Exceptional Children, 21,* 20–23.

Gould, B. W. (1991). Curricular strategies for written expression. In A. M. Bain, L. L. Bailet, & L. C. Moats (Eds.), *Written language disorders* (pp. 47–59). Austin, TX: Pro-Ed.

Gresham, F. M., Sugai, G., & Horner, R. H. (2001). Interpreting outcomes of social skills training for students with high-incidence disabilities. *Exceptional Children, 67,* 331–345.

Hallahan, D. P., Kauffman, J. M., & Pullen, P. C. (2005). *Exceptional Learners.* (10th ed.). Boston: Allyn & Bacon.

Hardin, M. G., Schroth, E., Pine, D. S., & Ernst, M. (2007). *Journal of Child Psychology and Psychiatry, 48*(5), 446–454.

Hardman, M. L., Drew, C. J., & Egan, M. W. (2008). *Human exceptionality.* (9th ed.). Boston: Houghton-Mifflin.

Kemp, N., Parrila, R. K., & Kirby, J. R. (2008). Phonological and orthographic spelling in high-functioning adult dyslexics. *Dyslexia, 15,* 105–128.

Kerr, M. M., Nelson, C. M., & Lambert, D. L. (1987). *Helping adolescents with learning and behavior problems.* Columbus, OH: Merrill.

Klassen, R. M., & Lynch, S. L. (2007). Self-efficacy from the perspective of adolescents with LD and their specialist teachers. *Journal of Learning Disabilities, 40,* 494–505.

Lerner, R. M. & Johns, L. (2009). The scientific study of adolescent development. In R. M. Lerner & L. Steinberg (Eds.), *Handbook of Adolescent Psychology* (3rd ed.). Hoboken, NJ: Wiley.

McNamara, J., Vervaeke, S., & Willoughby, T. (2008). Learning disabilities and risk-taking behavior in adolescents. *Journal of Learning Disabilities, 41,* 561–574.

Martinez, R. S., & Semrud-Clikeman, M. (2004). Emotional adjustment and school functioning of young adolescents with multiple versus single learning disabilities. *Journal of Learning Disabilities, 37,* 411–429.

Masters, L. W., Mori, B. A., & Mori, A. A. (1999). *Teaching secondary students with mild learning and behavior problems.* Austin, TX: Pro-Ed.

Meese, R. L. (2001). *Teaching learners with mild disabilities* (2nd ed.). Belmont, CA: Wadsworth.

Mercer, C. D. (1997). *Students with learning disabilities* (5th ed.). Upper Saddle River, NJ: Merrill/Prentice Hall.

Mercer, C., & Mercer, A. (2001). *Teaching students with learning problems* (6th ed.). Columbus, OH: Merrill.

Meyer, A., Pisha, B., & Rose, D. (1991). Process and product in writing: Computer as enabler. In A. M. Bain, L. L. Bailet, & L. C. Moats (Eds.), *Written language disorders* (pp. 101–129). Austin, TX: Pro-Ed.

National Assessment for Educational Progress. (NAEP). (2007). *Nation's report card.* Washington, D.C.: National Center for Education Statistics.

National Center for Education Statistics. (2009). *The condition of education, 2008.* Washington, D.C.: U.S. Department of Education.

National Institute of Mental Health. (NIMH). (2009). *Suicide in the U.S.: Statistics and prevention.* Washington, DC: Author.

Ness, J., & Price, L. A. (1990). Meeting the psychosocial needs of adolescents and adults with LD. *Intervention, 26,* 16–21.

Nippold, M. A., Mansfield, T. C., Billow, J. L., & Tomblin, J. B. (2009). Syntactic development in adolescents with a history of language impairments: A follow-up investigation. *American Journal of Speech-Language Pathology, 18,* 241–251.

Polloway, E. A., & Patton, J. R. (2008). *Strategies for teaching learners with special needs* (6th ed.). Columbus, OH: Merrill.

Polloway, E. A., Patton, J. R., Epstein, M. H., & Smith, T. E. C. (1989). Comprehensive curriculum for students with mild handicaps. *Focus on Exceptional Children, 21,* 1–12.

Polloway, E. A., Patton, J. R., & Serna, L. (2008). *Strategies for teaching learners with special needs* (9th ed.). Columbus, OH: Merrill.

Rief, S. F., & Heimburge, J. A. (1996). *How to reach and teach all students in the inclusive classroom.* West Nyack, NY: Center for Applied Research in Education.

Sabornie, E. J., & deBettencourt, L. U. (2004). *Teaching students with mild and high-incidence disabilities at the secondary level.* (2nd ed.). Upper Saddle River, NJ: Pearson.

Salend, S. J. (2008). *Creating inclusive classrooms: Effective and reflective practices.* (6th ed.). Upper Saddle River, NJ: Prentice-Hall.

Sands, D. J., Kozleski, E. B., & French, N. K. (2000). *Inclusive education for the 21st century.* Belmont, CA: Wadsworth.

Schaeffer, A. L., Zigmond, N., Kerr, M. M., & Heidi, E. F. (1990). Helping teenagers develop school survival skills. *Teaching Exceptional Children, 23,* 6–9.

Shaffer, D. R. (2002). *Developmental psychology* (6th ed.). Belmont, CA: Wadsworth.

Smith, T. E. C., Gartin, B. G., & Murdick, N. (in press). *Teaching secondary students in inclusive settings.* Upper Saddle River, NJ: Pearson.

Smith, T. E. C., Polloway, E. A., Patton, J. R., & Dowdy, C. A. (2008). *Teaching students with special needs in inclusive settings.* (5th ed.). Boston: Allyn & Bacon.

Smith, T. E. C., Price, B. J., & Marsh, G. E. (1986). *Mildly handicapped children and adults.* St. Paul, MN: West.

Study guides and strategies (2009). Seven stages of writing assignments. Retrieved from www.studygs.net/ writing/index/htm

Tanner, J. M. (1990). *Foetus into man.* Cambridge, MA: Harvard University Press.

Tompkins, G. E. (2002). *Language arts: Content and teaching strategies.* Columbus, OH: Merrill.

Tralli, R., Colombo, B., Deshler, D. D., & Schumaker, J. B. (1996). The strategies intervention model: A model for supported inclusion at the secondary level. *Remedial and Special Education, 17,* 204–216.

U.S. Department of Health and Human Services. (2009). *Results from the 2008 national survey on drug use and health: National findings.* Washington, DC: Substance Abuse and Mental Health Services Administration.

Welton, E., Vakil, S., Carasea, C. (2004). Strategies for increasing positive social interactions in children with autism: A case study. *Teaching Exceptional Children, 37,* 40–46.

Woodward, D. M., & Peters, D. J. (1983). *The learning disabled adolescent.* Austin, TX: Pro-Ed.

Woolfolk, A. E. (2010). *Educational psychology* (10th ed.). Boston: Allyn & Bacon.

Glossary

AAC devices range from low tech (including directed eye gaze, head pointing, finger pointing, and using a headstick or laser light to point) to high-tech computer-assisted speaking

Abstract nouns – names of ideas, concepts, thoughts

Accounts almost always begin with, "You know what?" and are initiated by children to tell others about their experiences, thoughts, or feelings

Adages – popular sayings thought to be wise renderings of truth, usually containing relatively unusual syntax, unfamiliar words, or words used in an unfamiliar way

Adverb forms create common adjectives by adding the bound morpheme *-ly* to an adjective

Agentive verb forms identify the person performing the actions of the verb by adding the bound morpheme *-er*, as in *sing > singer*

Anticipatory set – what one already knows about a topic in anticipation of learning something new about it when processing new information

Aristotelian definitions are composed of a superordinate term and a description with one or more characteristics

Attempts – a story episode that contains the actions the protagonist takes in response to the initiating event

Augmentative communication (AAC) – strategies and devices used to facilitate communication for people with disabilities; can range from low to high tech

Automaticity – the immediate recognition of written words

Auxiliary verb – a verb which accompanies another verb to convey tense, mood, number, or person

Basic episode – a simple narrative that includes an initiating event, an attempt, and a consequence

Bilingualism – the ability to communicate in two languages

Bitransitive – verbs which have both a direct and an indirect object (*take* the book to the teacher)

Bound morpheme – a set of morphemes that cannot stand alone as a word; a grammatical tag or marker, such as the plural *-s*, past tense *-ed*, or negative *un-*

Chain narrative shows some notion of cause–effect, but the plot is still weak; it may include some information about the character's feelings or intentions and a basic episode

Chronemics – the timing factors that influence how we interpret our conversational partners' utterances

Chunking – the process of categorizing and subcategorizing words based on their semantic relationships

Classroom discourse, or school talk, is rules of communication specific to the educational environment: teachers control what is said, when people talk, and what they say; these rules vary in different educational contexts

Clause density – the average number of main and subordinate clauses in the sample; also called the **subordination index**

Cloze procedure – a contextual analysis skill–building activity where approximately every fifth word is removed from reading passages at the student's instructional level and students are required to complete the sentences by filling in the blanks

Code mixing – indiscriminate use of more than one language system within a single communication

Code switching – the intentional use of two languages within a single communication

Cohesive markers – parts of speech that indicate that the meaning of an utterance lies in a previous utterance; these include pronouns, conjunctions, conjunctive adverbs (e.g., *on the other hand, moreover*), ellipses (e.g., eliminating redundancies through omission), and the definite article *the*

Collective nouns – names of groups of things

Common nouns – general classes of things, people, places, events, processes

Communication temptations – structuring a situation in which the child is strongly motivated to communicate to the adult, followed by a quick and positive response from the adult

Communicative intentions – the reasons why children are communicating: to get things done, to make things happen, and to get what they want

Complete episode includes the components of a basic episode plus an internal response, a plan, and a reaction or ending

Complex sentence contains a dependent and an independent clause

Compound sentence consists of two or more independent clauses connected by a conjunction

Comprehension – the process of constructing meaning from written texts

Comprehension monitoring – the ability to recognize when one does and does not understand something

Concrete nouns – names of real things

Configuration – outlining the shapes of words to help a student to learn difficult-to-spell words

Conjunctions link propositions within sentences; they include both coordinating conjunctions (e.g., *and, or, neither, nor*) and subordinating conjunctions (e.g., *for, so, because, while, whether, what, as, until*).

Conjuncts link propositions across sentences and include both concordant (e.g., *similarly, therefore, furthermore, moreover*) and discordant (*yet, instead, nevertheless, rather, conversely*) forms

Connectives – a form of high-level syntax that includes both conjunctions and conjuncts

Consequence – a story episode that contains the result of the protagonist's actions

Construct bias – a failure of tests to assess what they purport to assess

Content bias – an evaluation that includes items representing values different from those to which students of minority cultures are often familiar

Contextual analysis – the use of syntactic and semantic cues to anticipate words that are likely to appear in a given phrase, sentence, or story

Contractions – shortened forms of words or pairs of words

Conversational competence – skill in negotiating, persuading, making appropriate assumptions about conversational partners, and using the appropriate tone and style of speaking in different social contexts

Conversational repair – the skill of providing information that assists the listener who requests clarification

Coordinating conjunctions (*see* **conjunctions**)

Copula – linking verb; present tense of the verb *to be*

Count nouns – names of things that can be counted

Criterion-referenced tests (CRTs) are designed to compare the student's performance to a specified level of mastery or achievement rather than to the abilities of age mates

Culture – a group of individuals who share similar values, norms, and traditions

Decoding – includes skills-oriented approaches characterized by attention to reading letters, then words, sentences, and paragraphs

Developmental scales – instruments that list developmental milestones in order, usually arranged according to area of development such as: Communication, Cognition, Gross Motor, Fine Motor, Personal-Social, Receptive Language, Expressive Language, etc.

Difference position – the view that regional or cultural dialects or competence in a language other than English are differences rather than an absence of language functionality

Direct instruction – a systematic, intensive, and explicit approach to teaching that begins by gaining students' attention, followed by precise sequencing of content, monitoring of students' responses, and corrective feedback.

Direct request – states explicitly what the requester desires

Discourse functions – more advanced communicative intentions that refer to previous speech acts, including requests for information, acknowledgements, and answers

Discourse genres – forms of discourse, with each carrying its own set of stated and unstated usage rules

Disproportionality – overrepresentation or underrepresentation of a group with respect to expectations for that group or the representation of other groups

Dynamic assessment – observation of the child's ability to change a communicative or language behavior with structured help; focus is on the relevance of the behavior

Dyslexia – a deficit in single-word decoding, based on a problem in the phonological domain of oral language

Ebonics – a rule-based language system used predominantly by African Americans for communication purposes

Education of the Handicapped Act Amendments of 1986 (Part H) – Public Law 99-457, the federal legislation enacted to help states establish early identification and intervention services for infants, toddlers, and their families, reauthorized in its most recent form as Individuals with Disabilities Education Act (IDEA, PL 108-446)

Embedding – the placement of phrases within clauses or combination of two or more clauses into one

Emergent literacy – the gradual emergence of language learning about what stories are and how they work, what print is and what it looks like, what books are and how to interact with them, how sounds relate to letters and what letters look like, and what makes up reading and writing

Empiricism – the belief that the mind is a blank slate, or *tabula rasa*, on which experience is impressed; experience and the environment play crucial roles in learning everything, including language

Ending – a story episode that resolves or presents a moral to the story

English orthography – a fundamentally alphabetic system in which speech sounds (phonemic units) are represented by letters or letter combinations (graphemes)

Episode elements include an initiating event, an attempt to achieve a goal in response to the initiating event, a consequence, an internal response, a plan and a reaction or ending

Episodes – events within a story, including initiating event, attempts, consequence, internal response, a plan, reactions, and an ending

Error analysis – a technique where the teacher analyzes a representative sample of the student's spelling performance to discern trends in errors and to determine the reasons for the problem

Eventcasts – imagined events listed to manipulate others' behavior and bring about the desired events

Expository discourse – includes descriptive, explanatory, persuasive/argumentative, letter, and biographical forms of communication

Factitives – verbs that presuppose the truth of what follows (e.g., "We *acknowledge* receipt of your letter")

Fictionalized narratives are used by children to describe events or processes that are based in reality, using a story form for the telling

Figurative language – nonliteral language that expresses the quality of one thing by comparing it to another, either implicitly or explicitly, as in metaphor, simile, idioms, proverbs, adages, maxims, and humor

Fluency – the ability to read smoothly, accurately and with expression

Formulation – the generation of ideas and the creative writing that stem from an intention to communicate

Free morpheme – a set of morphemes that can stand alone as a word (*see* **bound morpheme**)

Generalization – the transfer of skills and concepts to other situations

Gerunds – a verb that functions as a noun ending in -*ing*

Grapheme – letters or letter combinations that represent a sound

Graphic organizers (GO) – a variety of strategies that provide a visual model for students to understand text and concepts and see relationships

Graphophoneme awareness – the ability to associate letters of the alphabet and the sounds these letters most often represent

Handwriting – the complex motor act of transcribing words on paper by hand

Heap story consists of labels and descriptions with no central theme or organization from sentence to sentence, which are most often simple declaratives

Heaps – loosely related utterances that comprise early attempts at protonarrative

Holistic – an approach to reading that emphasizes the meaning of what is read and thus focuses on the way the reader comprehends the printed word

Iconicity – the extent to which symbols resemble what they refer to

Idioms – unique figurative expressions specific to a cultural group

Indirect request – implies what is desired indirectly; for example, requesting a drink by observing, "I'm thirsty"

Individual Family Service Plan (IFSP) – the document required by IDEA that specifies the child's disability and the services that will be provided to support the child from ages 0–3

Individualized Education Plan (IEP) – the document required by IDEA that specifies the child's disability and the accommodations that will allow the child access to the general education curriculum in the least restrictive environment from the ages 3–21

Individuals with Disabilities Education Act (IDEA, PL 108-446) – the federal law which regulates the provision of education to individuals with disabilities, guaranteeing a free appropriate public education in the least restrictive environment to meet the student's needs

Inferential set (*see* **anticipatory set**)

Infinitive – a verb that usually appears after "to" (e.g., to run) that functions in a sentence both like a verb and a noun

Inflections – the addition of a grammatical morpheme to modify a word's meaning, including possessive and tense markers

Initiating event – a story episode that motivates the protagonist to act

Initiation-Response-Evaluation (IRE) – a format for teaching where the teacher Initiates a topic, a student Responds, and then the teacher Evaluates the student's response

Internal response – a story episode that represents how the protagonist feels about the initiating event

International Phonetic Alphabet – a notational system for representing phonemes

Interrogative forms – the expression of inquiry, formed early in development by rising intonation, as in "Doggie?" or "Juice?"

Invented spellings – spellings in which consonant or vowel sounds closest to the letter name they represent serve as the written word, which occur in children in a pre-phonetic stage or in the phonetic stage

Irregular verb forms deviate from the standard conjugation pattern

Joint attention is the process of a parent drawing a baby's attention to an object by establishing eye contact and then drawing the baby's gaze to an object while using motherese to talk about it

Kinesics – the set of body and facial gestures, movements, and expressions used in communicating

Language – a code or set of conventions for representing experiences, ideas, feelings, thoughts, and so on; an arbitrary set of abstract symbols and the rules that govern them that we use to communicate; encompasses oral, printed, electronic, or gestural codes

Language – a formal system of communication

Language content – the rules governing how meaning is derived from words and sentences, or our knowledge of vocabulary, objects, processes, ideas, events, and so on

Language experience approach (LEA) – using the child's own oral language, which the student and the teacher develop into stories for reading and writing

Language form – the structures of language that govern sounds, meanings, words, and sentences.

Language use – the rules governing the social functions of language, or how language is used in various communicative contexts

Language-learning disability (LLD) – a variety of problems in learning to read, write, or spell, marked by weaknesses in oral language development during the prelinguistic, emerging, and/or developing stages of development

Literacy – the set of competencies children develop with both oral and printed language (including electronic forms): listening, speaking, reading, and writing, regardless of the medium; the set of linguistic competencies that children must acquire to succeed in school, as well as in their lives outside school

Literate lexicon includes six types of literate vocabulary: advanced adverbial conjuncts (*similarly, moreover, consequently, in contrast, rather, nonetheless*), adverbs of likelihood (*definitely, possibly*) and magnitude (*extremely, considerably*), verbs with components related to presupposition (*regret*), metalinguistic reference (*imply, predict, infer*) and metacognitive reference (*observe, hypothesize*), technical and precise terms (*pollination, demagoguery, cosine, ordinate*), multiple-function words (*sweet juice, sweet thought, sweet paint job*), and multiple-meaning words (*harbor a fugitive, boat harbor; boat tender, tender finger*)

Macrostructure – overall text structure that serves to organize content

Maintenance – the ability to retain what has been learned over time

Manner of articulation – how consonants are produced (plosive, fricative, affricate, nasal, lateral, glide, semivowel)

Mass nouns – names of things that are conglomerates and cannot be counted

Matthew effect – the tendency of achievement gaps to increase over time; originates from the biblical verse Matthew 25:29, "For everyone who has will be given more and he will have abundance. Whoever does not have, that what he has will be taken from him."

Maxims – popular sayings thought to be wise renderings of truth, usually containing relatively unusual syntax, unfamiliar words, or words used in an unfamiliar way

Mean length of utterance is computed by counting the total number of free morphemes and the total number of bound morphemes in each utterance of a language sample collected from the child; that total is then divided by the total number of utterances in the sample to yield the MLU

Mediated teaching – a social constructivist teaching method that helps the student understand the goal of the session(s), why the language structure or function being worked on is important, how it is related to what the student already knows, and how to remember to use it in other settings

Menarche – the beginning of the monthly menstrual cycle, which occurs approximately 1–3 years before the onset of sexual maturity for boys

Metacognition – the ability to reflect on and assess one's own cognitive processes, composed of **comprehension monitoring** and **organizational and learning strategies**

Metacognitive ability – the capacity to reflect on and talk about one's own thinking and reasoning skills

Metalinguistic ability – proficiency with figurative language and the ability to reflect on and talk about language

Metalinguistic awareness – recognition that language is an object of knowledge whose structures can be learned and understood

Metaphor – a figure of speech involving an implied comparison between two dissimilar things

Metapragmatic ability – competence in reflecting on and talking about how language is used

Metapragmatic requirements – the purpose of one's communication; the composition of one's audience; a discourse genre that matches audience need as well as the goal, or purpose, of communication; appropriate construction of one's sentences to match discourse type and audience need

Metapragmatic strategies – navigation of the different rules governing conversations, which include assessment of varying social contexts, who has more authority in any given conversation, the degree of formality surrounding any given conversation, the relative ages of the conversational participants, the role of cultural differences among participants, one's own and others' conversational breakdowns, initiating and maintaining conversational turns, when and how to interrupt, and how to manage others' interruptions

Modifiability – a combination of the child's responsiveness during instruction (how the child responds to and uses new information); how much examiner effort is required to teach the child the new language form, content, and/or function (both the quantity and the quality of the effort necessary to help the child change); and how well the child can transfer or generalize new language skills to new contexts

Morpheme – the smallest grammatical unit that carries meaning

Morphology – the set of rules governing how phonemes are combined into syllables and words to convey meaning

Morphosyntactic markers – the combination of morphological and syntactic forms that result in changes to the structure of words; for example, markers of tense, number, gender, mood, and case

Multicultural education meets the needs of and recognizes the strengths and values of all cultures within that population; uses all students' cultural backgrounds to develop effective classroom instruction and school environments; supports and extends the concepts of culture, diversity, equality, social justice, and democracy in the school setting

Multiple intelligences (MI) – the idea proposed by Gardner (2006) that people are smart in several different ways; MI includes linguistic, spatial, quantitative, logical, musical, intrapersonal, interpersonal, physical, and naturalist categories of intelligence

Mutual attending – parent and baby attending solely to each other, not to something else, as in **joint attention**

Narrative – a sequence of events tied together in a story; the rules governing how conversations and stories are structured in terms of sequence, cause–effect relationships, and character motivations

Narrative ability – acquiring knowledge about and the ability to produce narratives; at the secondary level, this includes the ability to understand characters' motivations, plans, and feelings; the inferences that can be drawn to summarize the story; and the ability to provide listeners and readers with sufficient cohesive marking in stories so that they understand how the various elements and components are tied together

Narrative discourse – rules governing how books and stories work, what print is, and how letters represent sounds

Narrative genres – distinct forms of narrative; those which children are likely to encounter include structured play, wordless books, comic books, books on video or DVD, folk tales, and trade books

Nature–Nurture Continuum – the range of language acquisition theories between the extreme positions of **rationalism** and **empiricism**

Negation – the expression of rejection (*no*), nonexistence or disappearance (*allgone*), or cessation or prohibition of action

Nonfactitives – verbs that presuppose uncertainty about what follows (e.g., "I *imagine* that's true")

Nonreversible passives – sentences in which meaning dictates that only one order of subject and object is possible

Nonverbal communication – meanings conveyed outside of written or spoken words through gestures, facial expressions, glances, postures, movements, tone of voice, and body language

Norm-referenced – standardized instruments whose results are compared to others of the same chronological age

Norms – statistical groupings of age mates against which individual children are compared on standardized tests

Object complement clauses – a clause in which a complement (word or words used to complete the predicate and identified with the object) is coupled to an object (typically the receiver of the action of the predicate)

Organizational and learning strategies – the methods children use to organize themselves for learning

Paralinguistics – the aspects of language carried by the pitch and range of the voice

Participle – a verb functioning as an adjective

Phonemes – the smallest linguistic units to carry meaning; pronounceable sounds in a given language

Phonemic awareness – the awareness and manipulation of the speech sounds in words

Phonetic analysis – the use of sound–symbol correspondences to decode unknown words; **phonics**

Phonetically consistent forms – word forms used by children that differ from the adult version but that the child's conversational partners recognize as having a particular meaning

Phonics – *see* **phonetic analysis**

Phonological awareness – knowledge of the sound–letter correspondences and phonological syntheses that comprise decoding

Phonological processes – simplifications of adult forms of words, including deletion of unaccented syllables, deletion of final consonants, and velar fronting

Phonology – the rules governing how we use sounds to make syllables and words

Place of articulation – the location of articulatory contact or movement in the mouth (lips, teeth, alveolar ridge, hard and soft palate)

Plan – a story episode that contains the characters' thoughts about what actions they can take

Planning – a process of identifying the goal or purpose of the writing

Portfolio assessment – samples of the student's writing collected by the teacher over a period of time; it may include written samples (notes, drafts at various stages of completion, teacher feedback), as well as various non-print materials (photos, illustrations, tape recordings, reference materials, computer disks); students may be actively involved in selecting the material as a self-evaluation strategy

Pragmatics – the functions of language, especially as related to social contexts; how linguistic utterances are used to perform "speech acts"

Prepositional phrases – a preposition and its object

Presupposition – an assumption the speaker makes about what the listener already knows in order to say just the right thing to make the communication work

Primitive narrative – a story with a core person, object, or event containing a **basic episode**

Principle of minimal distance – a general rule governing which noun in a sentence serves as subject or subordinate clause, in which the preceding noun closest to the verb serves as the subject

Pronouns stand in for particular nouns and convey gender (female, male, or neutral), position in the sentence (subjective, possessive, or objective), and number

Proper nouns – specific members of any given class

Protagonist – the main character of a story

Protonarratives – developmentally early attempts at narrative which take the form of loosely related utterances called **heaps**

Proverbs – popular sayings thought to be wise renderings of truth, usually containing relatively unusual syntax, unfamiliar words, or words used in an unfamiliar way

Proxemics – the conventions for establishing physical distance in our communications with various people over a diverse set of social contexts

Rapid automatic naming (RAN) – a teaching method in which students are asked to name, as rapidly as they can, common objects that are presented to them in rapid sequence; teachers can modify the RAN naming task by asking students to recite "overlearned" lists (e.g., months of the year, days of the week) as rapidly as possible

Rationalism – the belief that the mind directs sensory experience through separating and organizing the information that reaches us through our sensory apparatus; the capacity for acquiring language, or protogrammar, is innate in humans and unfolds in relatively universal ways; the child's mind is ready to learn language given the opportunity and is seen as an active constructor of reality, including language

Reactions – a story episode that represents the characters' thoughts and feelings about the consequences of their actions

Recounts – a list of events experienced by the child, always in response to adult initiation

Regular verb forms follow the standard conjugation pattern

Relational words – non-nouns that express the relationships between objects (i.e., prepositions)

Relative clause refers to an antecedent in the sentence

Reversible passives – sentences in which subject and object can be reversed without rendering the sentence meaningless, though the meaning changes considerably

Revision – reviewing and critiquing what has been written to refine or reorganize the piece, perhaps through several drafts

Rubrics – sets of benchmarks differentiating levels of performance

Scaffolding – the process by which adults mediate specific experiences, such as using particular language forms or functions, to help students become more competent with those forms or functions

Selective feedback – teacher response to a limited number of skills specific to their own text and specific to the skills of importance to them

Semantic mapping – developing a diagram of what is to be read using prior knowledge of a topic

Semantics – the meaning level of language; the relations of words to reality

Sentence generation – selecting syntactic structures and vocabulary to match the selected discourse genre and target audience

Sequence story – a story in which events are labeled around a central theme, character, or setting without discernible or temporal or causational progression

Setting – where and when a story takes place

Sight vocabulary – words that are often phonetically irregular that children must memorize in order to read fluently

Simile – an explicit comparison of two dissimilar things

Social interactionist model – the view of language development that takes into account the interaction of genetic and biological abilities with environmental—particularly social—influences

Speech – the conventionally established combining of speech sounds into meaningful units of language; the oral sounds of the language code; oral language

Speech recognition software – computer programs that translate the spoken word to computer commands or electronic text

Spelling by analogy – spelling attempts where the speller spontaneously categorizes, compares, and contrasts words at a preconscious level of perception and applies knowledge of the redundancies in words to learning to spell new words

Story components include setting information, character information, temporal order, and causal information

Story grammar – the structural elements of narrative, including setting and episodes

Structural analysis – a word analysis tool that focuses on word form, requiring students to learn the parts of a word that serve as meaning or pronunciation units

Subordinating conjunctions (See **conjunctions**)

Subordination index (See **clause density**)

Substantive words are nouns and are used to name people, pets, and toys, and objects the child operates on directly, such as preferred foods, labels for objects, and for social games and routines

Syllabication – breaking down multisyllabic words into their component syllables

Syntax – the study of the linguistic conventions for generating meaningful phrases and sentences

True babbling – the use of consonant–vowel (CV) syllables, such as "mamam" or "nanana"

True narrative – a story that contains a central theme, character, and plot; the character is motivated to act, events are sequenced logically, and it contains a **complete episode**

T-unit length – the number of different main clauses (main clause + attending subordinate clauses) and coordinate clauses in a sample

Turntaking – the skill of alternating receptive and expressive roles in conversation

Type–token ratio – a measure of the variety of words in a writing sample where the ratio is computed by dividing the number of different words the writer uses (types) against the overall number of words used (tokens)

Vocal play includes grunts, squeals, growls, screams, and "raspberries"

Wh- question clauses – interrogative clauses that begin with who, what, when, where, how, or why

Whole language approach – teaching handwriting skills in context with other language skills, which fosters language arts skills by having students write their own compositions

Whole language uses children's literature to introduce students to reading and emphasizes the communicative functions served by written language, integrates oral and written language across the curriculum, and often occurs in the context of theme-based units

Word analysis skills – the reader's ability to analyze words not easily identified on sight

Zone of Proximal Development (ZPD) – the difference between what a learner can do with help and what she or he can do without help

Name Index

Z

Subject Index

A